The Fourth
Louisiana Battalion
in the Civil War

The Fourth Louisiana Battalion in the Civil War

A History and Roster

TERRY G. SCRIBER and
THERESA ARNOLD-SCRIBER

McFarland & Company, Inc., Publishers
Jefferson, North Carolina, and London

The present work is a reprint of the library bound edition of The Fourth Louisiana Battalion in the Civil War: A History and Roster, *first published in 2008 by McFarland.*

LIBRARY OF CONGRESS CATALOGUING-IN-PUBLICATION DATA

Scriber, Terry G.
The Fourth Louisiana Battalion in the Civil War:
a history and roster / Terry G. Scriber
and Theresa Arnold-Scriber.
p.   cm.
Includes bibliographical references and index.

ISBN 978-0-7864-7520-9
softcover : acid free paper ∞

1. Confederate States of America. Army. Louisiana Infantry Battalion, 4th.
2. Louisiana — History — Civil War, 1861–1865 — Regimental histories.
3. United States — History — Civil War, 1861–1865 — Regimental histories.
4. United States — History — Civil War, 1861–1865 — Campaigns.
5. Confederate States of America. Army. Louisiana Infantry Battalion, 4th — Registers.
I. Arnold-Scriber, Theresa, 1961–
II. Title.

E565.54th .S37   2013   973.7'63 — dc22   2007023822

BRITISH LIBRARY CATALOGUING DATA ARE AVAILABLE

© 2008 Terry G. Scriber and Theresa Arnold-Scriber. All rights reserved

No part of this book may be reproduced or transmitted in any form or by any means, electronic or mechanical, including photocopying or recording, or by any information storage and retrieval system, without permission in writing from the publisher.

On the cover: *Battle of Atlanta, 1864*. Lithograph
1888 by Kurz & Allison, (Library of Congress)

Manufactured in the United States of America

McFarland & Company, Inc., Publishers
Box 611, Jefferson, North Carolina 28640
www.mcfarlandpub.com

To those whose love for us is, and was,
always unconditional,

Elaine T. Benevides Arnold and Helen Mae Scriber,
our much loved mothers, and

Kenneth Francis Arnold, Sr.,
our beloved father and father-in-law.

Your love and support for us will be cherished
and returned eternally.

Table of Contents

Preface and Acknowledgments — 1

The History

1 — Clouds of Conflict: Louisiana Exits the Union — 5
2 — Sweet Sunlight of Victory: Covered in Glory — 16
3 — Cold Mist of Defeat: The Vicksburg Campaign — 43
4 — Hard Rain of War: The Battle of Chickamauga — 76
5 — Downpour of Disaster: The Battles for Chattanooga — 112
6 — Blizzard of Bad Tidings: The Atlanta Campaign — 156
7 — The Storm Breaks: The Close of the War — 227

The Biographical Register

A Guide to Using the Register — 249
Term Definitions — 249

Commanding Generals — 251

Department	251	*Corps*	259
District	255	*Division*	265
Army	257	*Brigade*	266

Field and Staff — 270

Lieutenant Colonel	270	*Commissary*	273
Major	271	*Ordnance*	273
Adjutant	271	*Hospital Steward*	273
Surgeon	271	*Battalion Druggist*	273
Sergeant Major	272	*Musician*	274
Quartermaster	272	*Chaplain*	275

Color Bearers/Guard — 275

Ensign	275	*Color Bearer*	276
Color Sergeant	275	*General Guides*	276
Color Corporal	275		

Company A: "Madison Infantry," Madison Parish — 276

Captain	276	*Corporal*	278
Lieutenant	276	*Private*	279
Sergeant	277		

Company B: "Ouachita Blues," Ouachita Parish — 287

Captain	287	*Corporal*	289
Lieutenant	287	*Private*	290
Sergeant	288		

Company C: "Franklin Life Guard," Franklin Parish — 298

Captain	298	*Corporal*	300
Lieutenant	298	*Private*	300
Sergeant	299		

Company D: "Carroll Rebels," Carroll Parish — 308

Captain	308	*Corporal*	310
Lieutenant	308	*Private*	311
Sergeant	309		

Company E: "Natchez Rifles," Adams County, Mississippi — 315

Captain	315	*Corporal*	317
Lieutenant	315	*Private*	318
Sergeant	316		

Company F: "Ouachita Rebels," Ouachita Parish — 327

Captain	327	*Corporal*	329
Lieutenant	327	*Private*	330
Sergeant	328		

Chapter Notes — 335
Biographical Register Notes — 346
Bibliography — 347
Index — 349

Preface and Acknowledgments

Louisiana. The name can conjure up many varied images to different people. The multicultural diversity, bayous, alligators, plantation homes, moss-covered oak trees, Mardi Gras, and the French Quarter are just a few of the iconic images that immediately come to mind.

Unfortunately, while we were in the process of composing this work, a catastrophe unequaled in devastation since the days of the mighty Civil War struck Terry's beloved home state. This destruction occurred not at the hands and weapons of man, but of nature, a massive hurricane named Katrina, leaving the great Queen City of the South, New Orleans, and her metropolitan areas in ruins. The images associated with Louisiana as of this writing are of flooding, evacuation, homelessness, destruction, fire, and death. As happened during the aftermath of the most destructive war in American history, it is hoped that these images, too, will pass, and be replaced with the far more pleasant ones of pre–Katrina laissez-faire and "les bon temps rouler."

The spirit of the people of the Pelican State is unequaled in overcoming adversity. At the beginning of the War between the States in 1861, Louisiana was the richest state in the South. At the end of the war in 1865, she was the poorest in the newly united nation. Yet her people managed to rise from the ashes of the war and rebuild, without slave labor, into an agricultural powerhouse. In modern times, Louisiana has become a tourist destination unequaled in the country, boasting the finest cuisine in the world, attractions without rival, and home to the world's largest celebration of life, Mardi Gras. In addition, the abundance of outdoor activities, such as fishing, hunting, and boating, serves to justify Louisiana's claim as the most unique state in the country. Yet, it is her *People*, that gumbo of cultures, races, and heritages, that are truly her greatest asset. If any group can bounce back and rebuild from the greatest natural disaster in United States history, it is Louisianans. As of this writing, it is a Louisiana son who is directing the hurricane relief efforts in New Orleans and on the Mississippi Gulf Coast on behalf of the federal government: Lieutenant-General Russel Honore, a native of Pointe Coupee Parish, Louisiana.

We have been fortunate enough to be co-authors of this work. It was Theresa who kept Terry's mind focused on the project at hand during these trying times, once the initial shock of the devastation of Katrina had dulled somewhat for us both. As a native Rhode Islander with a deep admiration for the old Confederacy and her citizen-soldiers, Theresa's participation in and enthusiasm for this project has never waned. Though short of becoming a "galvanized Confederate," Theresa and her knowledge of the war and research expertise have been an invaluable addition to this work.

The idea for a book on the Fourth Louisiana Battalion Infantry sprouted from the knowledge that Terry's great-great-uncle, Duncan Buie, served as the major of the battalion. Upon researching the actions and engagements that this gallant unit was involved in during the war, and the discovery that no literary work existed to preserve their heroic deeds and many sacrifices for future generations, compelled us to correct this injustice to this brave body of men. The battalion suffered frightful casualties during the conflict as a result of being involved in some of the most bloodiest battles of the war: Chickamauga, New Hope Church, Missionary Ridge, Secessionville, and Ezra Church, to name a few. All were appalling in the number of casualties suffered on both sides, Blue as well as Gray. The men who were lucky, or unlucky, enough to escape the icy grip of death on the field of battle and be taken as prisoners of war were shipped to some of the most brutal Northern prisons to exist in the annals of humanity: Rock Island, Illinois; Camp Chase, Ohio; Camp Morton, Indiana; Ship Island, Mississippi. These were the names of a private hell on earth for the Southern inhabitants, many of whom would never tread the soil of the South again after once entering these gates of human cruelty. These prisons were the epitome of man's inhumanity toward man.

And yet, the soldiers that did survive the war and imprisonment would become the leaders and citizens of the South that emerged in the aftermath. They would become government officials, farmers, and tradesmen, putting behind them the nightmares of a war that claimed more American lives, North and South, than any other in United States history. Major Duncan Buie would survive the trauma of being wounded, and the brutality of combat command, to become sheriff of Franklin Parish, Louisiana, before becoming a judge of the same. Private Henry J. Lea would not permit his hardships as a soldier for the Lost Cause to become an obstacle in reaching the elected office of clerk of court of Franklin Parish, as well as a recorder of the wartime exploits of the Fourth Louisiana Battalion for *Confederate Veteran* magazine. Such were, and are, the spirit and determination of the people of Louisiana, which define the words *faith*, *hope*, and *perseverance*.

This book is divided into two sections. The first section is a history of the battalion, beginning with the events in Louisiana that led to her withdrawal from the Union. Subsequent chapters chronicle the activities of the unit as they deployed into the theaters of war at Richmond, Virginia, in 1861, their initial assignment to the seacoast defenses of South Carolina and on detached duty to General Joseph E. Johnston during the Vicksburg Campaign, followed by their participation in the various campaigns and battles of the Army of Tennessee. Their activities off the battlefield, their diaries and letters, as well as losses and triumphs under fire are covered, ending with the final heartbreaking Confederate surrender at Gainesville, Alabama, on May 4, 1865.

The second section consists of a detailed biographical register of these heroic men, a combination military record, civilian history, pension information, and burial location register. This section is discussed in more detail in the section entitled "Guide to Using the Biographical Register." It is hoped that this register will be a useful research and genealogical tool for current and future generations to come. Many weeks and months went into its compilation and verification by the authors and, though exhausting at times, recreating the lives of these brave soldiers was an immensely rewarding experience.

A work of this magnitude could not have been accomplished without the assistance of a great number of people and institutions. Terry's mother, Helen M. Scriber, deserves accolades for the many Louisiana meals she prepared while we were hard at work on this project. Northeast Louisiana historian, and Fourth Louisiana Battalion descendant, Robert "Bob" Archibald, as always, deserves more thanks than mere words on paper can ever provide. Thanks go out also to family member Debra Arnold Clark for her cheerful assistance with the maps included in this work, and our precious granddaughter Hailei Metz, who helped us relax after working on this project with many games of Candy Land. Many thanks to Theresa's son, Michael Metz,

Jr., for his encouragement and interest. We would also like to thank Warren Grabau, James Knechtmann, Jim Hancock, Tim Conner, Robert J. Vejnar, Sara Pollastrini, Major-General Patrick Stevens IV (Ret.), Mary Lynn Felsberg, Amy Hedrick, Dave Richardson, Virginia Crilley, Carol Van Cleef, and David Marshall, in addition to Arnott T. Wilson and Irene Ferguson of the University of Edinburgh, Scotland; Ervin L. Jordan, Jr., and Byrson Clevenger of the University of Virginia; Elizabeth West of the University of South Carolina; Allen Tuten of the Central of Georgia Railway Historical Society; Albert Castel and Laura Stull of the University of Kansas; Judy Bolton of Louisiana State University; and Retha Stevens of Kennesaw Mountain National Battlefield Park. Last, but not least, we thank the many descendants of the men of the battalion, foremost of whom were Timothy D. Hudson and Shawn Choat Martin, for providing information and photographs of the individual soldiers that were otherwise unattainable.

From the Confederacy and the Union, we sincerely hope that you find our efforts to be a worthwhile addition to the volumes regarding Louisiana Confederate history, as well as to the memory of the Fourth Louisiana Battalion Infantry.

May God bless, and long live, Louisiana — and her people.

The History

Chapter 1

Clouds of Conflict: Louisiana Exits the Union

As long as the abolitionists and the Republicans seem to threaten the safety of slave property so long will this excitement last, and no one can foresee its result; but all here talk as if a dissolution of the Union were not only a possibility but a probability of easy execution.
— Louisiana State Seminary of Learning Superintendent William Tecumseh Sherman, New Orleans, December 12, 1859

Times were good in Louisiana in the year 1860. The population of the state had increased to 708,002 and was steadily rising, largely due to the abundance of fertile land that promised unheard-of prosperity in the form of the cotton and sugar trade.[1] New Orleans alone boasted a population of 168,675, primarily attributable to her commercial and banking activities. A March 26, 1860, report from the U.S. treasury secretary ranked Louisiana first among the slave holding states in the amount of specie, capital stock, and deposits in her thirteen banking facilities. Total capital was an astonishing $24,496,866, with the amount of specie pegged at $12,115,431 and deposits at $19,777,812.[2] The Louisiana state auditor had assessed taxable property in the state at a staggering $400,450,757.[3] The financial future and prospect of prosperity had never looked brighter for the residents of the Pelican State.

The political future, however, was far from being as rosy a picture as the financial one. The Northern states' fury regarding the Fugitive Slave Law, the hostilities in Kansas, as well as the debate in Congress over the Kansas/Nebraska Bill, coupled with the rapid growth of the Republican Party and its abolitionist factions, had created great apprehension among many Louisianans regarding Northern intentions. Throwing fuel on the fire was the October 1859 raid of abolitionist fanatic John Brown at Harpers Ferry, Virginia, and the subsequent sympathy which it seemed to garner among the Northern populace. It was small wonder that when the Louisiana Legislature convened at Baton Rouge on January 17, 1860, outgoing Governor Robert Charles Wickliffe devoted one-fourth of his farewell message to the inflammatory topic of Louisiana's "Federal Relations."

Governor Wickliffe warmed to the subject by addressing these comments to the legislative body:

> I had hoped to retire from the exalted position with which the people of the Commonwealth have honored me without extended reference to national affairs or national politics. I had fondly wished that I might bring my administration to a close with a simple, yet favorable allusion to

those subjects. It is, however, with profound regret that I feel constrained to announce to you my hopes in this respect have been blighted, and that I deem it my solemn duty, as your Chief Magistrate and representative of the people, to enlarge upon a disagreeable topic. Its importance demands my best attention and commands your closest consideration.[4]

The governor then launched into a fiery oratory regarding the "quarter-century sectional warfare waged by the North against the South." He proclaimed that the Northern "fanatics" had become a malevolent and powerful organization; "once a mere speck upon the horizon," that organization had attained such dimensions that it blackens the skies of the majority section of the Confederacy." He further effused that Northern intentions must be "confronted and beaten back. The state should provide for the equipment of her own men, in all respects, within herself, so as to be independent should the hour of trial come, of all outside assistance." He concluded with the following recommendation regarding the Harpers Ferry affair:

> To assure her [Virginia], as well as the other border slave States of the active cooperation of Louisiana; to show them that we recognize their cause as our cause, I recommend the immediate appropriation by the Legislature of $25,000, as Louisiana's quota toward these expenses, accompanied by a solemn pledge that our State will stand by our sister Southern States to the utmost extent of the men and means she can command, in any course they may see proper to adopt to secure our Constitutional rights.

The chairman of the House Committee on Federal Relations, one Henry Watkins Allen of West Baton Rouge Parish, wasted no time in answering the retiring governor's call for action. He sponsored a resolution that stated that Northern sympathy regarding the John Brown raid was proof of an open hostility in the North toward Southern rights and was regarded as an attack upon the same, that Louisiana would stand by Virginia in the event of another such episode, and should the unthinkable happen — the election of a "Black Republican" president in the November elections — that Louisiana would consider this grounds for a dissolution of the Union. Should the ascension of such a person to the presidency occur, the resolution specified that the "Governor shall order an election of delegates to represent Louisiana in a Southern Convention, and to cooperate with other states in taking such steps as the circumstances of the case and honor of the country may require."[5]

The flames of animosity toward the North were further kindled on January 23, 1860, with the inauguration of incoming Louisiana Governor Thomas Overton Moore. Moore, a slaveholding sugar planter from Rapides Parish, would serve as governor for most of the coming war. Moore devoted a large portion of his inaugural address to the growing crisis with the North. Louisiana, he stated, was more than just another state of the Union. It was a Southern slaveholding state whose duties to itself and its fellow slaveholding states might possibly be brought into tortured conflict with its devotion to the Union. He expounded on the theme that a powerful political party had been assembled in the North with malicious intentions in regard to the institutions of the slaveholding states. He summarized that unless each state was able to determine its own social institutions and observe them in peace, and there was abandonment of the demand that there be no more slave states admitted to the Union, that the Union would not, and could not, stand. This speech was given more than ten months before Abraham Lincoln's election to the presidency.[6]

The Democratic Party in Louisiana was also in considerable turmoil, with the "New Liners" faction of the party openly supporting Stephen Arnold Douglas for the presidency, while the Southern rights faction, known as the "Old Liners," and led by U.S. senator John Slidell, was determined to elect a candidate that would keep the current status quo regarding Southern institutions. When the state Democratic convention met on March 5 at Baton Rouge to select delegates for the national convention at Charleston, South Carolina, Senator Slidell's followers held a marked majority. The *New Orleans Daily-Picayune* offered this observation on the first day of the convention:

> Squatter sovereignty and the popular sovereignty doctrines of Mr. Douglas will receive their final quietus at the hands of the convention, as far as Louisiana is concerned. The Douglas men, who come principally from Lafourche, Assumption, Ascension, and that section of the State will be found in a sad minority, and it is thought they will not attempt to bring Douglas forward. So far as I can learn, Mr. Breckinridge is the favorite of the convention; but, as I telegraphed this morning, no expression of opinion will be made in his favor, over any other man who favors the Administration — at least that is the expectation at the moment.[7]

Amid the divisiveness, the convention adopted a series of resolutions in line with the Old Liners' philosophy. Regarding the current Buchanan Administration, it expressed "undiminished confidence," and regarded Slidell as eminently qualified to assume the office of U.S. president due to his abilities and statesmanship.[8] A motion offered by the New Liners to strike the resolution praising Slidell was soundly defeated by a vote of 206 to 34. A motion to instruct the Charleston convention delegates to cast their votes for candidate, and former U.S. vice president, John Cabell Breckinridge was also struck down, 233 to 29.[9] Another resolution expressed support for the opinion that, should the unthinkable happen and a Republican Party candidate be elected president, Louisiana should "meet in council her sister slaveholding States to consult as to the means of future protection." And, alas, regarding the heated issue of slavery, the following resolution was adopted:

> That the territories of the United States belong to the several States as their common property, and not to the individuals thereof. That the federal constitution recognized property in slaves, and, as such, the owner thereof is entitled to carry his slaves into any of the Territories of the United States, and hold them there as property; and in case the people of the Territories, by inaction, unfriendly legislation, or otherwise should endanger the tenure of such property, or discriminate against it, by withholding that protection given to other species of property in the Territories, it is the duty of the General Government to interpose by active exertion of its constitutional powers to secure the rights of slaveholders.[10]

The delegates chosen to represent Louisiana in Charleston were comprised of large landholders and slaveholders, with one politician and one attorney rounding out the group. Representing a net worth of several million dollars in sugar and cotton plantation property, the group consisted of future Confederate Lieutenant-General Richard Taylor, James A. McHatton, F. H. Hatch, Charles Jones, Robert Alexander Hunter, Emile La Sere, Augustus G. Talbot, D. D. Withers, Alexander Mouton, Effingham Lawrence, John Tarleton, and future Confederate Louisiana Lieutenant-Governor Benjamin Wiley Pearce.[11] Firmly opposed to the Douglas platform and representing the Old Liners, the group was to cast its votes as one at the Charleston convention upon its assembly on March 21.[12] A reporter for the *New Orleans Daily-Crescent* assigned to cover the convention gave the following account of the Charleston activities on March 26:

> Senator Slidell keeps himself in the background. He is rarely seen in the streets and never in the Convention Hall. He is quietly engaged in endeavoring to stack the cards as that Douglas will be defeated and some one nominated whom he can be intimately associated with, politically, of course, as well as personally.... The Louisiana delegation, as a body, compares favorably with that from any other State in point of solid attainments, make whatever use of the word you may choose. They are firm and decided in their expression of views, and are not generally regarded as being of the ultra stripe, though two or three of them are as much so as Yancey himself.[13]

Though the delegates of Louisiana, Maryland, Virginia, Georgia, and North Carolina were viewed as holding moderate opinions on the fiery issues that were bubbling beneath the surface of the convention, Arkansas, Mississippi, Florida, Texas, and Alabama were viewed as sparks in a powder keg. South Carolina, as host to the convention, played the part of gracious host, though the true feelings behind that conciliatory mask would all too soon be exposed. Add the spark of William Lowndes Yancey of Alabama to the combustible atmosphere, and one can see why a sectional explosion soon ensued in Charleston.

Louisiana delegate Mouton, a former governor of, and U.S. senator from, the Pelican State offered the resolution endorsing congressional protection of slaveholders in the Territories, and the platform committee gave a majority report endorsing the resolution, only to see the convention adopt the minority report which endorsed the philosophy of Stephen Douglas.[14] On Monday, April 30, the delegations of Louisiana, Mississippi and Alabama withdrew from the convention, though delegates McHatton and Fetters did so under protest.[15] The Louisiana delegates did send a communication to the convention president, Caleb Cushing of Massachusetts, stating that their withdrawal was due to their fellow delegates' refusal to "recognize the fundamental principles of the Democracy of the State we have the honor to represent."[16]

Opinion back home was somewhat more divided, with the Bayou State's newspapers offering varying editorials on the decision of the Louisiana conventioneers. The May 2 *New Orleans Daily-Delta* defended the action in Charleston as the "natural and justifiable consequences of the arrogant pretensions set up by the Northern delegations to govern the Convention in its choice of a nominee, and to impose upon it a platform of principles which would be rejected by every Southern State." The *New Orleans Daily-Crescent*, edited by James Oscar Nixon, a native of New Jersey who would rise to the rank of lieutenant-colonel of the First Louisiana Cavalry (Confederate) in the approaching conflict, countered with an announcement on May 7 that included the names of 107 Douglas supporters that stated, "All citizens opposed to the secession movements of the Louisiana and other State delegations at the Charleston Convention, and who approve the course pursued by Stephen A. Douglas, are invited to meet in Lafayette Square, at 7 o'clock, to take counsel together, and to protest against any action of any citizens of this State, which, at Charleston or elsewhere, would commit the people of Louisiana to any measure or scheme destructive of the Union." The May 17, 1860, *Alexandria–American*, the May 25, 1860, *Bossier-Banner*, and the May 15, 1860, *New Orleans Daily–Picayune* also weighed in on the subject, all which succeeded in increasing the already high tensions of the Louisiana populace.

The warring factions of the state Democratic Party each held their own separate meetings to determine the course of the state in the wake of the Charleston withdrawal. Consequently, two separate state conventions were scheduled to meet in June, the Douglas supporters on June 6 at Donaldsonville, and the state Democratic convention, which was to reconvene at Baton Rouge on June 4. At the Baton Rouge convention, the withdrawal of the Charleston delegates was sustained and their right to seats at the Baltimore, Maryland, Democratic convention was affirmed, though they were instructed to withdraw from that body also if they saw fit, and to join the Richmond, Virginia, Democratic convention in nominating candidates.[17] The Donaldsonville, or "pro–Douglas," convention met as scheduled with 141 delegates from twenty-one of the forty-eight parishes. This convention, in contrast to its counterpart in Baton Rouge, declared that the Charleston delegates had by their actions "severed themselves from the great National Democratic family." Regarding the issue of protection from Congress on the slavery issue in the Territories, the Donaldsonville delegates had these words for their brethren in Baton Rouge: "The attempt to call for the interference of Congress in questions concerning slavery in the Territories can only be productive of a conflict between the North and the South, which must inevitably end in the disruption of this great confederacy of ours." They then elected their own delegates to the Baltimore convention, endorsing Douglas but instructing the delegates to throw their support to whomever was chosen as the Democratic nominee in Baltimore.[18]

Hence, two sets of delegates with widely varying agendas arrived at the Baltimore convention on June 19. The Charleston delegates were refused admission to the convention, and on June 21 the Donaldsonville delegates were seated in their place. The Charleston delegates were seated at the Southern Constitutional Democratic Convention that was also being held in Baltimore, with representatives from twenty-one states in attendance. John C. Breckinridge was nominated as the presidential candidate of this convention, with Louisiana's own Richard Taylor serving as one of the convention vice presidents.[19] At least now the actual campaigning could begin in earnest among the presidential candidates.

The months of July through November were a whirlwind of political activity throughout Louisiana as the campaign heated up, with cannon, parades, fireworks, and banners employed to sway the voters of the state. Breckinridge and John Bell were the clear front-runners, with the Douglas base of support centered in New Orleans. The popular vote on Election Day was tallied as follows: Breckinridge with 22,681 had carried sixteen of twenty parishes in central and northern Louisiana; Bell with 20,204 had carried the parishes of East and West Baton Rouge, Jefferson, Orleans, Madison, Saint Tammany, Ouachita, Saint James, and Saint John the Baptist; and Douglas with 7,625 had carried Lafourche, Assumption and Ascension. The winner of the national elections, one Abraham Lincoln of Illinois, a dreaded "Black Republican," was not even on the ballot in Louisiana.[20] It was now that the secession spark ignited into an all-consuming wildfire.

A minority of the state's leaders pleaded for delaying any radical actions that could tear the Union asunder until after Lincoln's inauguration, in the hopes that a compromise could be reached with the North.[21] The majority were equally vehement in their belief that the time for vigorous action had arrived, and the only decision to be made was whether Louisiana should secede as an independent state or wait to act in concert with the other slaveholding states. The *New Orleans-Bee* on December 14 asserted that "The Union is broken in two" and that one might as well "breathe life into a corpse ... as imagine that the Union may yet be preserved." The editorial made the conclusion that "We are doomed if we proclaim not our political independence." The gloomy prospect of Union preservation was dimmed even further by the non-conciliatory speeches of Republican U.S. senators John Parker Hale, William Henry Seward and Benjamin Franklin Wade.[22]

Governor Moore took the step of calling the legislature into special session to address the stormy issues confronting the state. Meeting on December 10, the governor explained to the assembled body that the purpose of their meeting was nothing less than to decide the course of future relations between Louisiana and the federal government "before the control of that Government is lodged in the hands of a party whose avowed principles are in antagonism to the interests, the dignity, and the well being of Louisiana."[23] The governor stated that the secession issue had been thrust upon the South by the fanatical opposition of the Republican Party to slavery and the nullification of the Fugitive Slave Law in the North. According to Moore, the proverbial straw that had broken the bonds with the Union was the election of Lincoln, who had stated that the Union could not remain part free and part slave. Moore concluded his opening address with these chosen words:

> I have earnestly desired that a Conference or Convention of the slavehoding States should be held in order that they might counsel together, and act unitedly in this grave crisis. I still desire that such a conference shall be had, if practicable in point of time. Louisiana ought not to refuse to meet her sister slaveholding States in council, and there unitedly determine upon a firm demand to be made of the Northern States for the repeal of their obnoxious legislation, and the guarantee and security of those rights, which have so long been persistently refused. Still, although such a course has seemed to my mind desirable, and I had hoped that a practical and practicable plan might ere this have been suggested to accomplish this object, I do not think the action of Louisiana should be unreasonably postponed under the mere hope or expectation that such a Body would be at some distant time convened. It should meet at once, and determine at once, before the day arrives for the inauguration of a Black Republican President.[24]

The legislature wasted no time in approving the governor's recommendation for the creation of a military board comprised of Moore and four others to be chosen by him, whose chief purpose was to procure arms and ammunition to be distributed to volunteer cavalry or infantry companies in each parish in the state. The monetary sum of $500,000 was appropriated to secure the formation of the companies and acquire weaponry, which was to be held at both the state seminary in Rapides Parish and in New Orleans.[25] Moore chose future Confederate General Braxton Bragg, former Governor Paul Octave Hebert, Isaac Garret, and future Confederate Brigadier-General Daniel Weisiger Adams to comprise the military board.[26] In addition, the governing body also passed a measure requiring the governor to call an election to be held on January 7, 1861, for the purpose of electing delegates to a state convention that would convene on January 23 to decide the issue of secession. Another resolution was passed requesting Moore to communicate the actions taken by this session of the Louisiana Legislature to his fellow Southern state governors and to ask that they "communicate to him the action and views of their respective states in regard to the present critical condition of the country."[27]

An all-out political campaign was waged throughout Louisiana concerning the delegate election, with speeches both for and against dissolution of the ties with the Union.[28] On December 21, news of South Carolina's secession reached the Crescent City and was met with joyous outbursts of approval. The *New Orleans Daily-Picayune* of that day offered this description of the scene in the streets:

> At 12 o'clock today a salute of 800 guns, 200 per district, was fired in honor of South Carolina. As the first gun was heard, the flag of Louisiana was hoisted from the third story window of the rooms of the Southern Rights Association, No. 72 Camp Street, amid the cheers of the assembled multitude. A brass band placed beneath the windows struck up the Marsellaise, which was encored. The flag is, like the original flag of Louisiana, of spotless white, with the addition in the centre of a red star, containing in its centre the emblematic pelican. On the second story window could be seen a fine bust of John C. Calhoun, with a blue badge passed around the neck. After the flag had unfolded itself to the breeze, Gen. Miles, in response to loud calls, addressed the crowd which had blocked up Camp Street from side to side. He alluded to the importance of the event made the occasion for the hoisting of the flag of Louisiana, and appealed to Louisiana, having common wrongs with South Carolina, to range themselves under the banner of the revolution. He was frequently interrupted by cheers.... While we write the crowd is still in the street, and loud acclaims greet the remarks which are made by the speakers called and by the excited crowd. It is a stormy event in the history of the Southern movement.

On January 10, the governor decided the time had come for action on his part to strengthen the defensive posture of the state with an eye toward Northern aggression. Upon receiving a secret communiqué from Senator Slidell and Senator Judah Philip Benjamin warning of a plot in Washington to garrison the ports of the South, the following communication from Governor Moore was addressed to Brevet Major Joseph Able Haskin, the commanding officer of the United States Arsenal and Barracks at Baton Rouge:

> Sir: The safety of the State of Louisiana demands that I take possession of all Government property within her limits. You are, therefore, summoned hereby to deliver up the barracks, arsenal, and public property now under your command. With the large force at my disposal this demand will be enforced. Any attempt at defense on your part will be a rash sacrifice of life. The highest consideration will be extended to yourself and command.[29]

Haskin wisely surrendered the requested facilities and items to Moore at 5 P.M. the same day, with Fort St. Philip and Fort Jackson, both located on the Mississippi River, seized as well. Fort Pike, located on the Rigolets, would soon be seized by the governor also. Among the items confiscated from the Baton Rouge arsenal were 29,222 percussion muskets, 8,283 flintlock muskets, 2,287 Hall rifles, and enough gunpowder to supply ten artillery batteries of six guns each.[30] A large number of these arms were shipped to the state seminary, where seminary superintendent William Tecumseh Sherman was required to receive and account for the weapons. Sherman later recalled his feelings of that day:

> Thus I was made the receiver of stolen goods, and these goods the property of the United States! This grated on my feelings as an ex-army officer, and on counting the arms I noticed that they were packed in the old familiar boxes, with the "U.S." simply scratched off.[31]

Mississippi Governor John Jones Pettus, upon hearing of the seizure of the arsenal, promptly requested from Governor Moore that any arms that could be spared from the weapons windfall be shipped to Mississippi to provide for the defense of Louisiana's eastern neighbor. Moore responded by shipping 5,000 flintlock muskets, 1,000 Hall rifles, 3,000 percussion muskets, 1,000 pounds of rifle powder, 200,000 cartridges, six 24-pounder cannons with carriages, 1,000 pounds of cannon powder, and five hundred 24-pounder shot. Though concern for a Southern neighbor was surely a factor in his decision, the approaches from above, open to Union troops via Mississippi, were very much on the mind of the Louisiana governor in fulfilling this request.[32]

When the campaigning dust settled over the election of delegates, the makeup of the convention was to be comprised of the following delegates: 80 avowed secessionists, 44 cooperationists, and 6 undecided. The returns of the popular vote were 20,448 for pro-secession delegates versus 17,296 for cooperationist delegates, with a minimal nineteen of the forty-eight parishes voting cooperationist.[33]

Thus was the composition of the convention upon assembling in Baton Rouge on January 23 with 127 delegates in attendance. Alexander Mouton was elected to serve as president of the assembly. Governor Moore submitted a copy of his annual address to the legislature that he had made the previous day to the convention delegates, in addition to these ominous words for the convention to mull over:

> The vote of the people has since confirmed the faith of their Representatives, in legislative and executive station, that the undivided sentiment of the State is for immediate and effective resistance, and that there is not found within her limits any difference of sentiment, except as to minor points of expediency in regard to the manner and time of making such resistance, so as to give it the most imposing form for dignity and success. Our enemies, who have driven on their conflict with the slaveholding States to this extremity, will have found that throughout the borders of Louisiana we are one people — a people with one heart and one mind — who will not be cajoled into an abandonment of their rights, and who cannot be subdued. The common cry throughout the North is for coercion into submission, by force of arms, if need be, of every State, and of all the States of the South, which claim the right of separation, for cause, from a Government which they deem fatal to their safety. There can no longer be doubt of the wisdom of that policy which demands that the conflict shall come, and shall be settled now![34]

A "Committee of Fifteen" was named to report to the convention on an ordinance of secession for Louisiana. Former South Carolina Governor John Laurence Manning, accompanied by former Alabama Governor John Anthony Winston, were in attendance at the convention in their roles as commissioners representing their respective states.[35] On January 25, the body received a communication from Louisiana's representatives in the U.S. Congress, Judah P. Benjamin and John Slidell in the Senate, and Thomas Green Davidson and John Morgan Landrum in the House, giving their endorsements for immediate secession from the Union.[36] The "Committee of Fifteen" returned with an ordinance of secession and the matter was put to the vote of the convention on January 26. The Ordinance of Secession was adopted by a vote of 113 to 17, destroying "the Union now subsisting between Louisiana and other States, under the name of The United States of America," and declaring her now a "free, sovereign, and independent power."[37] In the Crescent City, the following description of the scene on the street following news of the convention's actions was reported by the January 27, 1861, *Daily-Picayune*:

> When the news that the secession ordinance had been passed by the State Convention reached us by telegraph yesterday the effect, as might have been expected, was such as to suspend all thoughts of other matters, to concentrate the public mind on the one solemn event which changed the destinies of Louisiana. The church bells proclaimed the fact in vibrating tones, whilst the deep

voice of the cannon announced it even more loudly. From public edifices, hotels and private buildings, the Pelican flag was hoisted and displayed its ample folds to the breeze. In the streets people met in groups, inquiring about the news and exchanging congratulations or comments upon the important step taken by the people of Louisiana.

A more somber and sentimental tone was displayed in an editorial in the *Shreveport-Southwestern* on February 6:

> As Louisiana is no longer a member of the Federal government, we this day, as orderly citizens, lower the stars and stripes from our masthead. It is with heart-felt emotions, better imagined than portrayed, that we fold the saucey looking star spangled banner that we have always loved, and place the precious memento under our pillow.

The business of the convention was far from complete with the adoption of the secession ordinance, though due to the convening of the regular session of the legislature, the convention was moved to New Orleans on January 26, where it reconvened on January 29 after procuring a meeting hall. Delegate John J. Perkins, a member of the Committee on Confederation, reported an ordinance to elect, via the convention body, a group of six delegates to the convention of seceding states that was scheduled to meet in Montgomery, Alabama, on February 4. These delegates to the Montgomery convention were to assist in the construction of a provisional central government based on the fundamentals of the United States Constitution. The delegates elected were Henry Marshall, John Perkins Jr., Charles Magill Conrad, Alexander DeClouet, Duncan Farrar Kenner, and Edward Sparrow, all known to be of high character and committed to the best interest of the Bayou State.[38] The next order of business for the New Orleans convention was to adopt an ordinance pertaining to federal employees still performing duties in the state. This ordinance provided that:

1. All Federal Officers in the civil service of the United States, and all laws of the United States relating to such officers, not incompatible with state laws, should be continued in force as officers and laws of the state, except the officers of the judiciary, postal, and land departments of the United States.
2. The Revenue, collection, and navigation laws of the United States should continue as laws of Louisiana, except that no duties were to be collected on imports from the states forming the late Federal Union known as the United States of America.
3. The president of the convention or the Governor of Louisiana should require all Federal officers in Orleans Parish to recognize the sole and exclusive authority of Louisiana and should administer to them the oath of office, and should they refuse to take the oath, the convention president or Governor should declare the office vacant and take possession of all effects, property, and money held by the officer in his official capacity.
4. The State of Louisiana does guarantee and indemnify all Federal officers aforesaid within the State who comply with the Ordinances of the convention, against all claims and demands of the United States arising out of compliance.[39]

Copies of the Ordinance of Secession were forwarded to Senator Slidell and Senator Benjamin in Washington, who had them read to the full U.S. Senate. After the reading, the two senators made dramatic resignation speeches to the assembled body, in which Slidell prophesied that all Northern factories would be boycotted, Southern ships would ply the world's oceans with impunity, and that foreign intervention would prevent a blockade of Southern harbors. Slidell, fired with passion, then added these threatening words before taking his leave:

> This will be war ... and we shall meet it with ... efficient weapons![40]

A convention committee that was created to inventory the public property in the hands of officers of the United States Government in New Orleans reported a total of $483,984.98 in silver and gold located in the vault of the U.S. Mint in the French Quarter. The precious minerals were now in the custody of Antoine Joseph Guirot, a representative of the independent state of Louisiana's monetary repository.[41] The next order of business was the creation of a flag for the state, and a committee of three members was appointed to oversee this task. On the morning of February 12, a few minutes before 11 A.M., the delegates, headed by convention president Mouton and Lieutenant-Governor Henry Michael Hyams, a cousin of Senator Judah Benjamin and the first person of the Jewish faith to be elected to the office of lieutenant-governor in the former United States, marched with a military escort in double file to Lafayette Square to observe the unfurling of Louisiana's new colors. As the bells sounded 11 o'clock, the flag was run up the City Hall staff, where it received a twenty-one-gun salute from New Orleans's own, and soon to be much vaunted, Washington Artillery. The flag was described as being of thirteen horizontal stripes with the first stripe blue, the second stripe white, the third stripe red, the fourth stripe white, the fifth stripe blue, the sixth stripe white, the seventh stripe red, the eighth stripe white, the ninth stripe blue, the tenth stripe white, the eleventh stripe red, the twelfth stripe white, and the thirteenth stripe blue. The canton of the flag was a red square equal to the width of seven stripes, with a five-point pale yellow star in the middle.[42] The February 12, 1861, *New Orleans Daily-Picayune* reported the festivities in Lafayette Square during the unveiling of the flag for its readers:

> After the firing of the salute, three hearty cheers were given in honor of the flag, when the members again marched in front of the military, which saluted them as they passed. The balconies of the private and public buildings, which surrounded the square, were densely crowded with the fair ladies of our city, and as the breeze unfurled the heaven-born hues of Louisiana's flag against the sky, displaying the beauteous harmony of its combined colors, a thrill of joy and admiration filled the spectators.

On February 18 at Baton Rouge, the Louisiana Legislature passed the following resolution concerning the right of secession by Southern States:

> Be it resolved.... That the right of a sovereign State to secede or withdraw from the Government of the Federal Union, and resume her original sovereignty when in her judgment such an act becomes necessary, is not prohibited by the Federal Constitution, but is reserved thereby to the several states, or people thereof, to be exercised, each for itself, without molestation. That any attempt to coerce or force a sovereign State to remain within the Federal Union, come from what quarter and under whatever pretence it may, will be viewed by the people of Louisiana, as well on her own account as of her sister Southern states, as a hostile invasion, and resisted to the utmost extent.[43]

On March 7, the legislature passed an act abolishing the state military board, replacing it instead with a "board" composed of Governor Moore and the Louisiana Adjutant General, empowering the two with distribution powers of arms, ammunition, and accouterments to the various volunteer military companies being formed throughout the state.

Oddly enough, the convention adjourned for a recess on February 12, the U.S. president-elect's birthday, and reconvened on March 4, the day of his Washington inauguration, a day in which he declared the Southern states' ordinances of secession to be null and void and ominously vowed to use his powers as United States president to "hold, occupy, and possess the property and places belonging to the government." The Confederate States of America Constitution was adopted by the Montgomery delegates on March 11 and sent to the member states for ratification. The constitution was received by the New Orleans convention on March 19 and taken up for consideration on March 21. Despite several attempts to delay acceptance of the document by several members of the assembled body, it was ratified on March 21 by the convention and declared binding upon all Louisianans by a vote of 101 to 7.[44] Louisiana was now a full-fledged member of the long dreamed and touted great Southern nation, the Confederate States of America.

On March 25, the convention passed an ordinance that set up six Confederate congressional districts within Louisiana, with the election for representatives to the Confederate States of America Congress scheduled to be held on the first Monday in November.[45] An additional ordinance provided that all property formerly used by the United States Government, such as arsenals, forts, lighthouses, and mints, could now be used by the Confederate Government in the same manner.[46] On March 26, the final day of the convention, the last action taken was to repeal and amend previous ordinances to accommodate Louisiana's new status as a state of the new Southern nation, instead of its status after secession as an independent state.[47] With the drastic measures associated with secession from the United States now behind them, both the convention and the legislature adjourned on March 26, 1861. Though history would prove these decisions to have tragic, and long-lasting, consequences for Louisiana over the course of the next four years, the delegates and legislators adjourned confident that they had set the state and her citizens on the path to future glory and prosperity.

With the political aspects regarding secession now behind the state, attention now turned full force to the military situation. The Provisional Congress of the Confederate States of America, in session February 4 through March 16, had passed acts on February 28 and March 6 that created the Provisional Army of the Confederate States. President Jefferson Davis was empowered to receive into the Confederate military forces all state militias of its members, as well as the arms and munitions acquired from the seizures of former U.S. installations. On March 9, Confederate Secretary of War Leroy Pope Walker made an urgent appeal to Governor Moore for 1,700 Louisiana sons to bear arms for the Confederacy in her coming struggles.[48] On April 8, the ante was raised to 3,000 men, and, on April 12, after Fort Sumter at Charleston, South Carolina, was fired on by Confederate batteries under the command of Louisiana native Pierre Gustave Toutant Beauregard and the Lincoln Administration refused to receive the Confederate government "peace commissioners," the call was made for 5,000 armed and equipped Bayou State troops, ready to move at a moment's notice.[49]

Moore speedily issued appeals to the male populace for volunteers for Confederate military service that were answered proudly throughout all sections of Louisiana, with New Orleans named as the rendezvous point for the new recruits. Camp Walker, situated on the grounds of the Metairie Race Course on what today comprises the New Orleans Country Club and the Metairie Cemetery, was established and placed under the command of Brigadier-General Elisha Leffingwell Tracy of the state militia. This was a poor choice of location for a camp of instruction for military recruits due to the lack of effective drainage and lure of the vices of the French Quarter, and it would later be moved north to the pine woods of Tangipahoa Station on the New Orleans, Jackson and Great Northern Railroad in what is now modern-day Tangipahoa Parish, and renamed Camp Moore, in honor of the governor.[50] Moore would later also issue strict guidelines pertaining to the formation and discipline of volunteer companies throughout the state, with no companies to be formed without the commission of Louisiana's chief executive to be officially recognized. In addition, any member of a company that was duly recognized by the governor and who refused to attend drills, parades, or musters would be labeled as "suspicious" in the eyes of the state and subject to a fine of between $5 and $200 dollars for officers, depending upon rank, and $1 for non-commissioned officers and privates, per occurrence.[51] Banks and insurance companies were strongly recommended to close at 2:00 P.M. each day, and builders, merchants, and manufacturers at 3:00 P.M., in order to provide their employees ample time to "obey the orders for the performance of a duty they owe to their country."[52] Declared exempt from the perfunctory attendance were employees, clerks, and officers of the State of Louisiana and Confederate Government, as well as of dockyards, foundries, telegraphs, and factories that were "actually engaged on works for the state and Confederate governments."[53] The October 5, 1861, *New Orleans Price-Current* newspaper reported on the compliance to the governor's order in the Confederacy's largest city:

> The prompt and voluntary action of our citizens in organizing military companies, either specifically for the defense of the city or for the war, has occupied the attention of our mercantile classes to such an extent as to leave but a few hours for business pursuits. Our Banks and public offices now close their doors at 2 o'clock P.M. A large number of our merchants shut up at 3 P.M. The afternoons are devoted to drilling and every man in the community is preparing to meet and repulse the enemy should he dare attack us.

On March 20, the Louisiana Legislature had voted to reallocate $500,000 of the tax-filled Levee Fund toward defensive measures for the state. Most parishes responded by appropriating money from police jury funds to arm and equip their respective troops for Confederate service.[54] Planters and merchants also contributed generously to supply companies that they aspired to command. In Franklin Parish, local planter and school teacher Duncan Buie formed and equipped the Franklin Life Guard, which would later become Company C of the Fourth Louisiana Battalion Infantry, and was made the company's captain. Louisiana had almost 16,000 sons bearing arms by June 1, 1861, with 5,000 in New Orleans; 1,700 on seacoast and harbor defenses; 2,100 at Pensacola, Florida; 1,000 in Arkansas; 2,300 in Virginia; and 4,000 drilling for service at Camp Moore.[55] The entire state was one continuous scene of war preparation, with parades, flag presentations, drills, and departures for war as commonplace as everyday commerce, with departures often facilitating fireworks and fiery speeches of a patriotic nature. River banks were crowded with family, friends, and sweethearts giving fond farewells and assurances of a quick and safe return for the new soldiers from their mission to quell the aggressions of the Lincoln-led Northern hordes.[56] It was reported that in July of 1861, military companies were daily passing through Monroe, Louisiana, on their way to the active theaters of the war.[57]

On May 25, 1861, at the small northeast Louisiana town of Richmond in Madison Parish, a meeting was held at the courthouse for the purpose of forming a company of volunteers for Confederate military service. The meeting was called to order at 11:00 A.M. by W. J. Powell and, after some oratory concerning the rapidly deteriorating state of affairs between the North and South, a call was made for volunteers. Eighty citizens promptly signed their names to form the company that would come to be known as the "Madison Infantry," and later become Company A of the battle-scarred Fourth Louisiana Battalion Infantry. While organizing and electing officers, a dispatch was received from the other Richmond, in far-off Virginia, stating that they would be received into the Confederate military upon arriving there. The meeting ended after electing George C. Waddill as captain, S. W. Hamilton as first lieutenant, F. M. Couch as second lieutenant, and W. B. Brockett as third lieutenant, and the men promptly went into camp. While in camp, the future soldiers drilled and procured uniforms, as well as the necessary military equipage, minus arms, before preparing to depart for Richmond on June 9th.[58]

One of the citizens in attendance at the May 25th meeting was an immigrant homeopathic physician from Zurich, Switzerland, who had settled at Milliken's Bend, Louisiana, with his new wife and her two young daughters in 1856, and had quietly and purposefully enlisted in the Madison Infantry to serve the Confederate cause. Described as "well read," and fluent in the languages of English, French, and German, the immigrant doctor was known in his adopted Madison Parish as Doctor Hartmann Heinrich Wirz, a man of caring and compassion to the sick and needy.[59] Enlisting for Confederate service as a private, as thousands of other Louisiana citizens did in 1861, Wirz's Americanized name in Northern society, besides sending shivers through many blue-clad spines, would become synonymous with cruelty, atrocity, and barbarity, and in the former Confederacy with martyrdom. By the close of the war in 1865, he would be the only person tried, and executed, for war crimes allegedly committed during the Civil War. Meeting death on a Union gallows in the shadow of the Capitol Building in Washington as Captain Henry Wirz, his last assignment was as commandant of the infamous Confederate prisoner of war camp, and epitome of hell on earth, known as Andersonville.

Chapter 2

Sweet Sunlight of Victory: Covered in Glory

We feel that our cause is just and holy; we protest solemnly in the face of mankind that we desire peace at any sacrifice save that of honor and independence; we ask no conquest, no aggrandizement, no concession of any kind from the States with which we were lately confederated; all we ask is to be let alone
—*Confederate States of America President Jefferson Davis,*
Montgomery, April 29, 1861

By late 1861, Richmond, Virginia, was home to four seats of government. The city of Richmond, the county of Henrico, the state of Virginia, and the Confederate States of America capitol, relocated from Montgomery, Alabama, as a concession to Virginia for siding with the South in the conflict, were all located in Richmond. A bustling, vibrant city, alive with martial airs, she would see the individual north Louisiana military companies bearing the militaristic names of Madison Infantry, Ouachita Blues, Franklin Life Guard, Carroll Rebels, and, from Adams County, Mississippi, the Natchez Rifles, alive with patriotic fervor, report for Confederate service and be formed into the Fourth Louisiana Battalion Infantry.

The journey for the Natchez Rifles, who began organizing in May of 1861, involved the election of officers on the eastern side of the great river at Natchez, and then a march to the western side of the Mississippi to Lake Concordia, Louisiana, where it encamped on the Tecona Plantation, owned by the newly elected company captain, Alfred Vidal Davis. The future Company E of the Fourth Louisiana Battalion would remain on the fertile land of Tecona, drilling and mastering the age-old art of war, before moving back to Natchez in June and traveling via the steamer *Mary E. Keene* to Memphis, Tennessee, and then on to Richmond. Upon their arrival in Richmond, the Natchez Rifles would encamp on Libby Hill, and on this spot would be mustered into the Fourth Louisiana Battalion, under the command of Madison Parish, Louisiana, native, and newly minted major, George C. Waddill.[1]

Upon being formed into a battalion on July 10, 1861, their early service would consist of the prestigious assignment of being a bodyguard detail for the new president of the Confederacy, Jefferson Davis. The soldiers would also see service as guards at Richmond's many makeshift prisoner of war facilities located near the site of the future Libby Prison, standing guard over the captured Union soldiers from the Battle of First Manassas. The soldiers assigned as keepers of the prisoner "barns" were housed in tents on nearby vacant lots on Cary Street and Twentieth Street.[2]

Before enlisting to serve the Confederacy, 29-year-old Private John W. McNeil of Company A, a New York–born carpenter residing in Warsaw, Madison Parish, Louisiana, recorded the events surrounding the Madison Infantry's journey to, and arrival in, the Confederate capitol:

Monday, May 27, 1861

Commenced Drilling. We were kept pretty busy getting Uniforms and Equipment and Drilling until June the 9th, when we started for Virginia, well equipped in everything but Arms. We stopped in Lynchburg, Va. and went into camp at Howard's Grove. Stayed there about a week and then moved to the new Fair Ground. We were now furnished with old flint muskets to learn the Manual of Arms. We Drilled with them for some time, then we got the Percussion Musket and drilled with them awhile when we were Detailed to guard the Prisoners taken in the Battle of Manassas. We now moved Camp to Libby's Hill to be near the prisons at the foot of Main Street, and commenced guarding Prisoners. While we were here, we were formed in a Batt. with four other Company's. Capt. Waddill was appointed Major and John Green was Adjt. (When our Batt. was first formed there was six company's and Capt. Jones ran against Capt. Waddill for Colonel and was elected. Waddill, becoming rather disappointed, raised a dispute about it. Jones then drew his Company out of the Batt., then Waddill was appointed Major of the remaining five Company's called the Fourth La. Batt.) We guarded Prisoners a month. We were now relieved from our Guard Duty and moved Camp to Crigan Hill. We elected W. S. Parsin Capt. and sent word home to him to that effect, our third Lieut. was appointed Quarter Master of the Batt. and Sergeant Amis was elected to his place.[3]

Shortly after arriving in Richmond, Private D. Wansley Elliott of Company C walked into the bookstore and stationers shop at 53 Main Street, owned by George T. Baldwin, and purchased stationary in order to write his beloved sister back home in Archibald, Franklin Parish, Louisiana. The stationery, carrying the design of a 12-star First National Confederate flag confidently waving above a discharging cannon, also had a decidedly patriotic poem pre-printed at the top. Below is a transcription of the early-war letter from Private Elliott and the stationary poem:

> Stand firmly by your cannon,
> Let ball and grape-shot fly,
> And trust in God and Davis,
> But keep your powder dry.
> —Confederate States of America

Richmond, Va. Aug. 19th, 1861

Dear Sister,

We did not go to Camp Moore, we kept through to Richmond where we are at this time. Head left Delhi sick, he remained sick until he got to Lynchburg, Va. He is well at this time, for myself I stood the trip very well until now, I am not well today. I have the Diarrhea this morning but nothing serious. I am better this evening. We was mustered in service this morning. We will belong to the brigade from La. I do not know how long we will remain here, probably some two months. I have seen the prisoners that we captured at Manassas, some 2010 of them. They are fine looking men. We keep guard over them day and night. We have not had our guard yet but I see them every day in the prisoner barns. Telegraph says that we had a fight in Missouri last week. We lost some 10 to 15 hundred killed and wounded. The other side lost 25 hundred killed and wounded, so says the telegraph.

I am at least 1500 miles from home, but yet expect to return after the wars end. Some say it will not be long but I don't believe it. As for myself, I think it will last some twelve months, I expect to return when the wars over and not before. Our camp is in a beautiful place situated on a high hill at the East End of Main St. I go out in town every day. You and Jack must write as soon as you get this. If you want me to get your letters, direct your letters to Richmond, Va in care of Capt. Buie of Louisiana Battalion. This is the way you must direct your letters. If Mother has not gone to Ala., tell her Head and myself are tolerably well at this time. Tell Bill the same, and I will write to Mother at Gainesville, Ala. Write to me if you hear from Jack. Soldiers life is hard but I think I can bear it for five years. I will write to Mr. Baskin as soon as I get time in relation to my horse. I want him to have him if he wants him, as I would rather he wanted him. Write as soon as you get this, I want to hear from home. My love to you and Jack and children. So farewell for the present, if not always. My love to all friends and relations.

Your Brother,
Wansley Elliott[4]

The Fourth Louisiana Battalion would undergo the reorganization mentioned by Private McNeil on September 19, after which they were ordered to western Virginia's Kanawha Valley on September 25, located in modern-day West Virginia.[5] The strongly pro–Union populace, bound more to Pennsylvania and Ohio than eastern Virginia, had strongly opposed secession and were looked upon sympathetically by the Lincoln Administration. Since the early part of May, both sides had eyed the valley as a way of invasion into the eastern section of the state, prompting the Confederates to burn several bridges on the Baltimore and Ohio Railroad. Most notable of these were the bridges located west of Grafton and the crossing over the Monongahela River, where the rail lines from Wheeling and Parkersburg united. This effectively cut the line of communications from Washington to the west, hence Union General George Brinton McClellan received extreme pressure from Lincoln to reopen communications and drive the Confederates from western Virginia.[6]

In September, General Robert Edward Lee instructed Brigadier-General William Wing Loring to test the strength of Union outposts that were located at Cheat Mountain and Elkwater, the results of which were lively skirmishes on the 12th and 14th. Union Brigadier-General Joseph Jones Reynolds responded on October 3 with a counterattack on the Confederate position located at Greenbrier River, which was handily repulsed. Both forces now remained idle while warily watching each other through October.[7] But Lee had other destructive plans in mind for the Union army. During October, he had ordered Brigadier-General John Buchanan Floyd, with 4,000 troops that included the Fourth Louisiana Battalion Infantry, to move up the south side of New River for the purpose of making a demonstration against Union forces located on Gauley Bridge under the command of Brigadier-General William Starke Rosecrans. Upon crossing New River on October 16, Floyd proceeded to the small village of Fayette and, upon occupying it, established his camp on Cotton Hill, a rocky mass located in the angle of the junction of the New and Kanawha rivers. Floyd then began to move his artillery over the precipitous hills by hand, with the Gauley Bridge outpost as his intended target.[8]

Private McNeil of Company A, now keeping a war-time journal of his experiences as a soldier, recorded the events of the journey relating to the Fourth Louisiana Battalion:

> Here on the 25th day of Sept. that we received Orders to go to Western Va. under General Floyd. We got a few Uniforms and things that was needed when on Wednesday, Oct. 2nd at 11 o'clock, received orders to be at the Depot at 3 o'clock. All things being ready, we struck tents and was at the Depot at the time appointed. We had to wait here until about nine o'clock, then we got into box cars and started for Western Va. About 3 this morning when daylight broke over the horizon, it brought to our review the giant forms of the Allegheny's towering high on every side of us, but the steel horse in bold defiance kept its onward course under mountains and over the Valley, with its wheels spoke the Mountaineers, receiving us with waving of Handkerchiefs and biding us God's Speed. We arrived at Jackson River, the end of the Rail Road.
>
> *Friday, Oct. 4th, 1 o'clock P.M.*
> Here we have to wait for transportation. Pitch tents and went into camp. Nothing happening worth notice tonight. Tuesday, the 8th when we got orders to march. It has been raining the last twenty four hours, our tents all wet. We have to build fire inside them to dry them before striking them, and the sun coming out at five this morning, our tents soon got dry. We struck them, left four of our Company here sick and two whole Company's sick. The remaining three took up the line of march, our Company acquired a wagon to carry our knapsacks, which relieved us a great deal. Made Hickman about dark, Dist. 15 miles. Cooked and eat supper and lay down to sleep under a tree.

Camp, White Sulphur Springs, Oct. 9th

Feel low and tired this morning. Got breakfast and started about Eight o'clock. We had a pretty good road today and arrived here about three o'clock, Dist. about 11 miles. Felt pretty tired. We draw provisions every evening and cook them for the next day. Done our cooking and laid asleep under a tree.

Camp, Five miles west of Lewisburg, Oct. 10th

Left White Sulphur Springs about Eight o'clock, climbed a mountain and came through a pretty country. Came through Lewisburg, here Lieutenant Hamilton, now acting Capt., drew us up in front of a Hostel and treated us to the whiskey. This is a fine little Mountain City. Came on and arrived here about Five o'clock. Pitch tents, will stay here for further orders.

Camp, Five Miles west of Lewisburg, Oct. 12th

Felt alright this morning. Shook out a few bullets, made some slugs and went a-hunting Pheasants, but have not found any. In coming home, killed a Groundhog, thought to Barbecue and have a good supper. Fixed him up nicely, but when came to eat him it was a hard job, so tough and rank had to let him pass by.

Camp, Two miles west, Sunday, Oct. 13th

Received marching orders this morning. Struck tents, loaded wagons and left about Nine o'clock. Came on to Meadow Bluff. We learned that Floyd was at Jackson Ferry near river, and arrived here about Three o'clock P.M. Done our cooking and went to sleep under the stars.

Oct. 14th, 10 miles south

Came a short cut through the woods and arrived here about noon. The wagons, having to go around, did not get here until evening. We are now 10 miles from Floyd. Our Adjut. is gone on to report. I am getting so that I can march all day and not feel tired at night. Tomorrow we expect to be with Floyd. All of our cooking and eating done and a good fire burning. I will lay down by it and go to sleep.

New River, Oct. 15th

Started this morning about Eight o'clock, ran down hill nearly all the way over a rough rocky road and arrived here about noon, one mile from the Ferry. We just had orders to be at the Ferry to cross at midnight, but they were countermanded and we are ordered to be there at daybreak in the morning. As it was raining, we pitched tents and rested for the night.

Camp, west side New River, Oct. 16th

Up early, struck tents and was at the Ferry in time. Crossed the river in two flatboats, took us about three hours. Went up about a mile this side the river and pitched tents. We are now up with Floyd's main army and will wait his orders. While we were here, have formed in a Brigade with the Twentieth Miss. Reg. under Col. Dan Russell of Miss.

Oct. 17th

Went a-fly fishing awhile today but did not catch any. This has a beautiful river, running as it does between high mountains on each side. It is a very romantic scenery. The current is so strong that boats cannot come up this far! Received orders to march tomorrow.

Camp, Six miles west of New River, Oct. 18th

Left New River about Eight o'clock, climbed a mountain four miles long and arrived here about Three o'clock. Commenced raining this evening, pitched tents and will stop for the night. Our Batt. and the Miss. Regt. are together in Camp.

Camp, 10 miles west of New River, Oct. 19th

Got up this morning about daylight, still a-raining. Everything is wet and the roads are very bad, full of rocks and mud holes. Received some letters last night, Major Waddell received one from W. S. Parsin saying that on account of business, he could not come to take the Captaincy of our Company. The letter was read to us this morning. We now had another Captain to elect, and as it was raining, and we waiting for it clear up, we went to work to elect a Capt. Three were now nominated, First Lt. Hamilton, W. B. Brockett, who was our Third Lt. but had been appointed Quartermaster of the Batt., and W. J. Powell, a Private. The vote was cast, and Powell was elected by a large majority over the other two and was made Captain. The weather clearing up about noon, orders were given to strike tents and prepare to march. Everything was soon got ready and we started again, but the roads being so bad and rocky, we only made four miles. Commenced raining again, pitched tents for the night. We are now the advance of Floyd's army.

Raleigh Court House, Oct. 21st

Left camp yesterday as usual, came to Pinch Gut Creek two miles and while we were stopped here making a road, a dispatch came for us to leave our baggage behind and hasten to this place. We have had to carry our knapsacks the last two or three days on account of our wagon breaking down. We now unsling knapsacks. Got our two ammunition wagons and a few cooking tricks. Left the baggage wagons and a small Guard here to come on as fast as they could. Forty rounds of cartridges was given us. Took our overcoats and started, we now had Pinch Gut Mountain to climb, about three miles long and about the same height. It took us two hours pulling ourselves up by the bushes, the two wagons going around a kind of a road. At last we got to the top at about Three o'clock P.M. We were now drawn up in a line, and Col. Russell told us that we had to make roughly tonight a Dist. 17 miles. The Brigade Band struck off and with a loud "Hurra" we started for this place in fine spirits. We marched about five miles more over the mountain, and then struck the turnpike. Here we stopped a few minutes and eat up what little grub we had in our haversacks for a supper. Our Batt., having gained the reputation of being the best travelers, we was ordered to take the lead. The band struck off and we started again. We happened to come in to a good piece of the turnpike, and we all thought to make our trip easy. We had not gone over a mile before we were doomed to disappointment. About dark, it commenced raining and the roads full of mudholes we would have to go through about knee deep a quarter of a mile out at a time. The little mountain streams that are nearly dry in fine weather, now came rushing down the mountain and crossed the road two or three feet deep with such a sweeping current, that it was dangerous to wade through.

Past Shady Springs — 9 o'clock P.M.

Very dark and still a-raining. We thought we had come about nine miles and inquired the distance here, and found out to our great disappointment that we have nine miles further to go. Was told that the Yankees were there, and that they had driven in our pickets this evening. But the roads were now better, we kept our course. Our overcoats were getting very heavy from the rain, and by trying to get around the mudholes on the side of the bank would often step up and find yourself in them on all fours. This would raise a laugh at first, but it soon became so common that it was not noticed. We got within five miles of Raleigh and found out that, about the Yankees being there, was all false. I suppose it was told us to encourage us on here, the Regt. behind us commenced to drop off, could not go any further. Some lay down by the side of the road and some in old houses, so that when we got to Raleigh at this A.M., a very few was with us. Our Batt. all came in but one or two, and when we got in we, our Company, had to march back nearly a mile to get a little old house to stay in, and then not more than half of us could get into it. The rest built a large fire and laid down outside. We were a pretty pitiful looking crowd and tired, Oh Lordy!, every nerve seemed to be strained to its utmost. We all laid down in our wet clothes the best we could, and was soon fast asleep. Soon after daylight this morning, I got up. Felt very stiff and sore and have caught a very bad cold. We got a larger house to stay in, in town today. Got nothing to eat since last night until two o'clock today. The Brig. has been coming in all day, will stay here tonight and tomorrow start for Fayette Court House. Feel some better tonight, but have got a bad cough. It has been a fine day, and we have cleaned and laid ourselves pretty well.

Camp McCoy, Oct. 22nd

Left Raleigh about Nine o'clock this morning. The roads are drying up fair. Arrived here about two o'clock, felt pretty well used up. My cough is very bad. Will stay here tonight. Dist. 12 miles.

Fayette Court House, Oct. 23rd

Left McCoy's about Eight o'clock, arrived here about Three o'clock. The Yankees was here two or three days ago and ransacked the town. The[y] burned down one store, broke the windows and doors of several others and took everything of value they could carry. We are now about 14 miles from their camps on the Kanawha River. I felt very bad tonight. I expect we will stay here until our wagons come up with our baggage.

Fayette, Oct. 24th

Felt sick all day, scarcely able to get around. My cough is no better. Will leave tomorrow for Cotton Hill.

Camp, Foot of Cotton Hill, Oct. 25th

Left Fayette about Ten o'clock. Arrived here about Five o'clock. Our baggage had now caught up with us, so we pitched our tents. Will wait here for further orders. This is as far as we can take our baggage. We are about six miles from the enemy. Floyd's Headquarters is about a mile behind us. There are about 5,000 of Floyd's Brigade here now, or not far from here, but not more than one-half are fit for duty on account of sickness. They have been here all Summer, and most of them look as though they are completely used up.

Camp, Oct. 27th

Nothing unusual happening since the 25th. I have improved a great deal and my cough is not so bad. Received orders this evening to be ready to advance by daylight in the morning.

Cotton Hill, Sunday, Oct. 28th

Our brigade left camp about daylight this morning to advance to the Kanawha, and supposing some of the enemy to be on this side of the river, everything was prepared for a fight. We started in our Shirt Sleeves and got on top of the mountain. Here we was ordered to load. We followed the turnpike carefully until we were within a quarter of a mile of the river. The Regt. was left here to guard the road, and our Batt. was here detailed to scout the mountain. We now left the road and commenced to climb the mountain. This was a hard job, we had to pull ourselves up by the underbrush and rocks. Two men were accidentally shot by their own men, a-slipping and falling. We got on top at last and passed in fine view of two of the Enemy's camps on the other side of the river, and found out that the Enemy had no force on this side of the river but a few Pickets. We made the trip and got back to the Regt. about dark. Our Major, finding out that we had to stay here, had sent for our overcoats, which came about the time we got back. We were now stationed about half way up the mountain at a place selected to place some cannon. Sent out some Pickets and laid down for the night.

Cotton Hill, Oct. 31st

We have been here ever since the 28th guarding Capt. Jackson's Arty. Company, getting up two or three pieces which they had to carry most of the way on their shoulders. It has been raining the last twenty-four hours and very cold. Our Company is on duty at a time. We have to lay down here the best we can to sleep, we have to lay against a log, or astride a sapling, to keep from sliding down the hill. With no covering but the canopy of Heaven we wake up in the morning, wet, stiff and almost freezing. Not permitted to light a fire, speak above a whisper or even smoke a pipe until eleven o'clock today, when we open fire on the Enemy. They return the fire, but it took them a long time to get our range. We were so much higher than they, that they could not elevate their pieces to reach us for some time. Our first two or three shots killed or wounded several of the Enemy. We could see them carrying some off and knock two or three tents down.[9]

Rosecrans was given the surprise of his life by the opening salvo of artillery fire on the Union outpost, followed by the crack of sharpshooter musketry that resulted in the sinking of a ferryboat that was serving as a makeshift replacement for a burned-out bridge. With the Federal post much harassed by the relentless Confederate fire, on November 10 Rosecrans ordered the Second Kentucky Infantry (U.S.) ferried across the Kanawha at the mouth of the Gauley, where they engaged in a brisk skirmish with Floyd's forces before being repulsed. After being heavily reinforced on the following day, the Union force renewed the attack and after several "hot" skirmishes, forced Floyd to abandon the front of the mountain and move his camp to the rear. Rosecrans, now somewhat recovered from the initial shock of Floyd's bombardment of the 10th, laid plans to capture the Confederate general by turning his position from below by sending the brigade of Brigadier-General Robert Cumming Schenk to occupy Cotton Hill, while the brigade of Brigadier-General Henry Washington Benham moved from Loop Creek to attack Floyd from the rear. Floyd, anticipating the trap that was being laid for him by Rosecrans, evaded capture by falling back upon Loop Mountain and, after another skirmish on the 14th, proceeded to the Holston Valley Railroad, taking up position on Piney Creek. Rosecrans angrily contributed the failure of his plan to bag Floyd to General Benham's failure to follow orders, the results of which, Rosecrans contended, were several avoidable delays.[10]

Private McNeil's diary once again gives a glimpse into the events that transpired following the initial bombardment of the Union outpost and the subsequent retreat:

Cotton Hill, Nov. 3rd

Been cannonading since Oct. 31st, most of the time not doing much damage. The Enemy's shot and shell has been coming around us pretty thick the last day or two, but no one hurt. A small scouting party of Yankees fired at two of our Pickets down on the road. Our Pickets returned the fire and the Enemy left, no one hurt on our side. We have had a great deal of rain and nothing to shelter us. We will be relieved to fight and go back to our camp. Being exposed so much the last week my cough is worse and sick, besides that I was put on the Sick List. The Batt. stayed in camp a day or two and started again for Cotton Hill, taking their knapsacks and blankets with them. I stayed in camp two or three days longer, got a little better, and went to them, and had to do Picket Duty. We were now stationed in a large house, pretty comfortable. Major Waddill and our First Lieut. Hamilton left me here, I think on the 6th, and went home at Jonesborough. Our house was on the turnpike about a mile and a quarter from the river. We had to then Picket two and three miles from the house. All things went on as well as we could expect until the night of the Eleventh. About Ten o'clock, a dispatch came up from our Battery, which is a mile further down the road, that the Yankees were crossing the river in large force, and was expected to come up the road. Our Batt. went down there to meet them. They had not gone long before a scout coming down from above to our house, where there was about twenty-five left sick, and reported that the Yankees were coming in behind us. A dispatch was sent down to the Batt. The Adjt. came up, and with twenty of us that was sick, here determined to make a stand here and if possible, to hold them in check until reinforced. About this time two or three volleys were heard in the direction of our Battery. Supposing the Enemy was advancing up the road, and about two-thousand coming down behind us, we was in a tight place, and only about 700 of us from our Batt. returned to our assistance. A Miss. Regt. coming down another road over the mountain met some of our Va. Pickets, and through some mistake fired into each other, wounding four or five on each side. That was the firing we heard. About Two o'clock at night, orders came to retreat. Our Batt. went down to protect the Battery while they were taking it off the mountain. About daylight, everything was ready and the retreat commenced. We got back to our tents, took every thing with us, and retreated four miles further and pitched tents. We had not left quarters this morning more than two hours before a large force of Yankees came down the road. We was expecting them and burned down the house we was quartered in, and then they pursued us. About Four o'clock, they had got as far as where our tents was. Floyd sent back two Regt.'s to meet them. They had a small fight, drove the Yankees off, and returned.

Fayette Court House, Nov. 13th

Left our camp this evening and got here about Nine o'clock, expected to stay here tonight, our sick was all here. Eleven o'clock, orders came for us to keep on the retreat. The Yankees could cut us off as far back as Raleigh. We had to load our sick on four wagonloads. Everything was soon got ready and the whole of Floyd's army commenced retreating. Went two miles and tents, cooking tricks, and almost everything was thrown away, the road being so bad they could not be carried. Our Batt. was stopped here until the Army had passed by.

> Camp McCoy, Nov. 14th
> As soon as the army had passed by us last night we came on, bringing up the rear. We marched all night and arrived here about Ten o'clock P.M. The Yankees were following us pretty close. Here we have made a stand to meet them, but they do not appear to want to fight, as they keep a respectable distance off. Colonel Charrone was sent back with a Company of Cavalry to see what they was doing. About a half-mile back, he met with the Enemy laying in ambush. They opened a fire on our men, killing Col. Charrone, when our men came back in disorder.
>
> Raleigh Court House, Nov. 15th
> Finding out that the Enemy would not attack us, but following along behind picking up stragglers and watching us, we left McCoys about midnight and came on through a wretched road. Some of our horses gave out, got stuck in the mud, and could not get them out. Had to cut their throats and let them lay. We arrived here about Ten o'clock in a miserable condition, mud all over, nothing to eat for a long time. We stopped here, got some provisions, and started again. About noon, came on about four miles farther.
>
> Camp Saw Mill, Nov. 15th
> We have now got so far back that the Yankees could not get behind us. Here we rested a day or two, we have had very cold weather on the retreat, and here we have a slight fall of snow. We have orders to fall back as far as Petersville. We now commenced retreating at our leisure, being out of danger. Nothing happening unusual, we in due time arrived at Petersville, we stayed here about a week and then received orders to go to Richmond. Left Petersville first of December, we now started for Newburn, the nearby Rail Road Depot, Distance about 35 miles.
>
> Newburn Depot, Dec. 3rd, 1861
> We left Petersville, and after two days march, we got out of the mountains and today had a good road to Tenn. on, and arrived here about Four o'clock. We have orders to be on the cars at Twelve o'clock tonight.
>
> Richmond, Va. December 5, 1861
> We arrived here off the cars today, feeling well worn out and glad to get back. We met with the other two Company's of the Batt. that we left at Jackson River, and went into camp at Camp Chimborazo.[11]

With the passing of November, General Floyd was ordered to report for duty at Dublin Depot in western Virginia and abandon the Kanawha Valley, and the Fourth Louisiana Battalion was ordered back to Richmond, where they would remain for a short time.[12] The battalion major, George C. Waddill, would resign in December and be replaced by John McEnery of Monroe, Louisiana.[13] The men of the battalion had performed well upon receiving their initial baptism by fire into the war, small though it was, but the true initiation into warfare would come on their next military assignment to the cradle of Southern secession, the State of South Carolina.

Traveling by train, the battalion was assigned to occupy Skidway Island, located off the Georgia coast, approximately twenty miles south of Savannah. The battalion would close out the first year of the war on the island. Then, on March 17, 1862, they were ordered to move to the Isle of Hope. They would remain there for only a short time before being transferred nearer to Savannah to a military encampment named Camp Mercer, in honor of Confederate Brigadier-General Hugh Wheedon Mercer. While stationed at Camp Mercer, the battalion, five companies strong, would gain another company raised from northeast Louisiana. The company, named the "Ouachita Rebels" and led by Captain James H. Walker, was formed on March 2, 1862, from citizens of the city of Monroe and the outlying areas of Ouachita Parish. The company was designated Company F of the battalion, and shipped out from Monroe to Camp Mercer in mid–March, arriving there on the 24th.[14] Private McNeil relates the events of this time period from the perspective of the common soldier:

Camp Chimborazo, Dec. 15th

Today we received orders to go to Charleston, South Carolina. We had to get ready to leave again.

Charleston, Dec. 21, 1861

We left Richmond on the 18th and arrived here alright today, and will wait here for further orders. Before we left Richmond, we had tents and cooking tricks furnished us. Found things that was necessary for another Campaign.

Charleston, 23rd

Received orders to go to Savannah, Georgia, and will leave tomorrow.

Savannah, Dec. 24th

Left Charleston early this morning on open flat cars, very cold all day until arrived here. Arrived here about dark this evening. Was marched uptown and stayed in a large Hall for the night. Next morning, went out on a Parade Ground back of the Public Square and pitched tents, waiting for orders.

Savannah, Dec. 26th

Received orders to go down on Skidway Island. We struck tents and got everything on board a boat and came down by water about twenty miles, and landed on Skidway Island, sixteen miles from Savannah by land and twenty by water.

Camp Adams, Dec. 27th

Left the landing this morning and came across the island about eight miles to this place called Adams Point. We pitched tents here, this being our Post of Duty. We have five points on the Romney Marsh to Picket from there to fifteen men at a point. The Enemy have possession of Warsaw Island, which is across the marsh from us. The Blockade Fleet lays at the head of Warsaw Island. There is any amount of oysters here.

Camp Adams, Dec. 28th

I was on Picket last night, came off this morning and detailed for a scouting expedition tomorrow, Dec. 29th. Last night, Nine o'clock, one of our Pickets came in and reported that they had found a boat floating that belonged to the Yankees and suppose that they were landing somewhere. Our scouting party had to leave at once. We got back to camp this morning but found no Yankees, another party has been out today, but found nothing.

Camp Adams, Jan. 15th

Nothing of importance transpiring, more than ordinary camp life. Eating a great many oysters. We have been eating this Marshland Beef which is very bad and smells bad but we are getting beef from the city, which is a great deal better. There is a Negro boy who comes down every morning from the city with a wagon, so that if you have money, you can get things from the city. Received news today that Major Waddill had resigned. Senior Capt. McEnery has been in command since Waddill left us in Western Va., and I expect he will be our next Major, although not very popular.

Camp Adams, Feb. 5, 1862

The night of the Nineteenth of Jan., a party of the Enemy, eight or nine in number, came through Romney Marsh in a boat and landed in front of one of our Picket Post. Our Picket fired into them, they returned the fire and then left. Owing to dense fog at the time, no harm was done more than aroused us out of our beds. After we found out the Yankees had left, we went back to bed again. Fifteen or twenty Yankee ships have arrived here the last week or two and have been reconnoitering the inlets and posts, as here apparently, for to attack Savannah. People are leaving the city and cannon are being planted up and down the river, and in different parts of town. Heavy firing is heard around here now every day, and we are expecting a fight every day. It is evident the Enemy knows the waters well, by pulling up some obstructions. They are about to get into the

Savannah River without passing Fort Pulaski. The other day our little fleet went to Fort Pulaski with a lot of provisions and ammunition, as they were liable to be cut off, and had a lively engagement for a while, but they landed the provisions safe and returned in good order with but little damage.

Camp Adams, February 13, 1862

We have been expecting a fight day and night for some time, as yet nothing has been done but preparing for the Enemy. Gunboats come in pretty near our Batteries sometimes, apparently wanting our guns to open on them to find out their range, but unless they come too close, they are not molested. Two pieces of Art. came down here this morning, and I believe will stay with us a while. The Inspector-General was down here last Tuesday, and we had a general inspection of equipment, and with a few exceptions, passed off satisfactory. We have just commenced building a breastwork across the island from one marsh to the other, about one-half a mile back of our camp. Three Company's worked on it one day and two the next, and with forty detailed for Guard and Picket Duty, it keeps us busy all the time.

Camp Adams, February 22nd

No fight yet, the Yankees appear to be very busy in front of us. It is reported that they have had a Sawmill on Warsaw Island running for some time, and building Gunboats. Three of the Enemy's Gunboats is in Walls Cut, near Savannah River above Fort Pulaski, but it is thought they cannot get into the river, as they have been in the Cut for some time. Some fear is entertained about Fort Pulaski, in having no guns mounted on the side towards the city, except that the city is strongly fortified. The Enemy will get a warm reception if they ever attempt to take Savannah. No doubt but the Yankees took victory over a handful of our men at Roanoke Island, which encourages them greatly. It has been reported in the Northern Papers that Savannah has fallen and gives some particulars how it was taken, but the Stars and Bars still wave over the city, and bids defiance to the Enemy. There is from twenty to thirty Yankee ships besides Gunboats laying in the Sound, but they appear to dread what they have undertaken to do.

Camp Adams, March 6th

We have just heard of terrible losses in Tennessee, after three days of terrible fighting. The 12th, 13th, and 14th of Feb. our forces drove the Enemy back at every front, damaging their Gunboat so that they had to fall back out of range. On the morning of the 15th, Enemy was reinforced with a great number of fresh troops, making its whole force to fifty thousand, against about fifteen thousand of our forces that have been fighting for three days. Our Officers, Pillow, Floyd and Buckner, held a council of war. It was agreed to surrender the Fort, which was completely surrounded by an overwhelming force. About ten thousand prisoners were taken, the rest cut their way out. The slaughter was terrible on both sides. Nashville was surrendered without a fight soon after Fort Donelson. It has caused a sad gloom over the Country, but has caused a greater energy everywhere, and everybody must be a Soldier. The Yankees appear to be leaving us at this point. Some of their ships have gone and some are getting to think there will be no fight here after all. Fifteen of us out of our Batt., with a lot more from other Regt.'s, have been at work about six miles from here blockading Skidway River with us. We have to load the ties on a flatboat and a steamboat, taking us down to the places to throw them out on our way down, which is about three miles. We have a place, by the very appropriate name of, Isle of Hope. It is situated around a bend of Skidway River, a beautiful, secluded and romantic spot, seems selected by nature. A fitting place for the retired men of the city to come here and live the rest of their days in ease and comfort. It is about eight miles from Savannah, it is about a mile below this place that the river is blockaded. We are relieved from this work every third day by another squad. We have finished our breastwork on the island and will move our camp in back of it tomorrow. We have a Company, Capt. Dawson's Company, with four pieces of cannon with us now. Dr. B. Powell, from Richmond, La., arrived here on Tuesday the 4th, as Surgeon of our Batt. Our former Surgeon resigned some time ago.

Camp Hope, March 18th, 1862

We evacuated Skidway Island yesterday. All the guns and everything was taken off. Nothing was lost but the work we done there. The Enemy appeared to be leaving us there. Being only two or three Yankee vessels seen in the Sound, they have been planting Batteries on some points up the river, cut off communication with Fort Pulaski. Received bad news from the West this morning, New Madrid evacuated by our forces and lost all our artillery, and now hear North Carolina has fallen. I was in town last Saturday. The weather is very warm now, we are now on the mainland.

Camp, Isle of Hope, March 28th

We are very busy building breastworks and roads across the marshes. We are either on guard or at work every day. Last Tuesday night, hearing that some Yankees had landed on Skidway Island, an expedition was got up to go down there about Twelve o'clock at night. About four hundred of us started across the bridge and scouted the island, but found no Yankees. They had landed here the day before, burned down a large house and some logs we had put up to represent cannon, and went back on their ship again. The Yankees have made an attempt to land between this and Charleston, but they have not made a stop anywhere yet. We are held in readiness to march at any moment. We do not expect any attack here now, Savannah is almost impregnable at this point.

Camp, Isle of Hope, Sunday, April 6th

Nothing has happened of much importance since the 28th. About sixty of us went down on Skidway a week ago but found nothing. I have had a very bad cold for some time, but I am getting better now. The weather is very warm here now. The Batt. is very bad, nothing but smoke will drive them off.

April 10th, 1862, Thursday

The enemy commenced shelling Fort Pulaski this morning and continued throughout the day. We can hear the guns very plain from our camp. It is thought the Fort can not hold out long against such terrible bombardment.

April 11th

The Enemy kept firing at intervals all last night. At daybreak this morning, they commenced again in good earnest, firing from four to five times a minute until Two o'clock this afternoon. We hear the Fort surrendered sooner than it was expected, the Fort was almost falling down. The shots of the Enemy's Parrott guns going straight through and laying the magazine open.

Camp, Isle of Hope, April 12th

Quartermaster Brockett was court-martialed last Thursday for striking and cursing Private Phillips. I was a witness against him. He was found guilty, but reprieved by General Mercer and again returned to duty.

Camp Mercer, April 19th

We have had a bloody battle at Shiloh. Gen. A. S. Johnston killed, have losses on both sides. Confederates victorious. We are expecting an attack on the city everyday. Major McEnery came back last evening and brought a new Company with him to join our Batt., which will make six Companies. We moved camp today about five miles nearer town, about a mile from Thunderbolt Battery.

Camp Mercer, April 25th

We send a large Picket down on the Isle of Hope everyday. The enemy has not attacked us yet. The troops around here are in good spirits and ready to meet the Enemy any time. Our Company has been drilling in the Bayonet and Skirmish Drill under Adjutant Sthreshley for some time. We are getting pretty perfect in it.

Camp Mercer, May 6, 1862

We had a General Review last Saturday, all passed off well. Received a new gray uniform last Saturday, coat and pants cost $18.75, and a cap $3. Our Batt., with our Art., is formed into a Brigade under General Mercer. We are a-waiting on the Yankees to do something next. We have not heard from them since they took Fort Pulaski. What they are doing, I do not know. New Orleans has fallen and we are expecting to hear of a great battle at Corinth. They may be fighting while I write. Our forces are falling back from Yorktown. Our troops are getting desperate on account of our late disasters and terrible fighting is expected to our north.

Savannah, May 9th

Detailed today with two others to work on the Floating Battery that is building here. Johnston has had some fighting, and is falling back from Yorktown and Norfolk. He drove the Enemy back and kept his men in good order. The Yankees are probing towards Richmond. Drew a pair of single shoes, Amt. $2.50.

Savannah, May 18th

Still working on the Battery, expect to launch it tomorrow. All below water line is covered with steel, ⅜ of an inch thick. The top to be covered with Rail Road Iron, it will draw from six to eight feet of water when finished. The Yankee General McClellan, with a large army, is marching slowly on Richmond. Their Gunboats are in the James River, everybody is in good spirits and confident of our ability to whip them on land, if we can not on water. The Yankees have not come far up the river from New Orleans yet. We are expecting an attack here daily. I do not think we can hold the city against them, as they can come up in their boats and we have nothing to oppose them until the Battery is finished.

Sunday, May 25th, 1862

One year ago today we entered the Confederate service. We have gone through all the hardships of a Soldiers life, except on the battlefield, although our Batt. has been in the advance most all the time. We have been in active service, but a very few has ever had a shot at a Yankee. We have marched day and night through mud and water knee deep. We have laid on our arms and slept on the Rocky Mountains of Western Virginia in the sleet and rain of a cold November night without any covering, expecting to be attacked every minute. We have had the Enemy's shot and shell whistling around our heads, and we have gone through the horrors of a retreat by night with the Enemy close after us, where provisions and camp equipage is burned up by wholesale, where horses got stuck fast in mudholes and have their throats cut and wagons set on fire, where the poor exhausted Soldier falls down by the road side, and impossible to go any further, and would as soon lay in a mudhole as a feather bed. We have been crowded together, sleeping one on top the other, traveling in old box cars. We have gone through all this cheerfully and almost without a murmur. It is wonderful to see how danger and excitement raises the spirit of a Soldier. There is often serious quarrels, strife, and discontent in a camp of illness, but when there is a prospect of meeting the hated Yankee, it is all forgotten and all join hands in the one great cause. Each one feels dependent on the fellow near him in rank, each one feels the responsibility that is resting on him, and the duty he owes to his Country. Each one strives to be worthy, his name written among the heroes in the history of his Country. In fact, each one feels that he is a man, and that he is in a man's place. We have been around near Savannah since the 25th of December, doing Guard and Picket Duty, and building breastworks. We built a large breastwork across Skidway Island. The Yankees were then expected to land at Adam's Point, where we was on Picket. About the time we had it done, orders came to evacuate the island, breastworks and all, which caused us boys to be down on building breastworks. But we have had to build breastworks and bridges since then. We have never seen any fruits of our labor, which makes it tiresome and laborious, and a good deal of discontent reigns in camp sometimes. Rumors come into camp that the Yankees are conducting landings somewhere, and we are sent to drive them off. The boys then appear more lively and cheerful, and want to fight the Enemy yet, but it has all turned out to be nothing, and time would pass on as tiresome as ever. There is some talk about our being ordered away from here soon, but it is uncertain. I am still working on the Battery, but we launched it last Monday. Although I believe we have done our duty, as near as any other troops, I hope our next years service will be of more importance, and interesting, than our last. The Yankees have been pressing us hard the last two months, and causing the destruction of a great deal of property. The destruction of Norfolk is a great loss, but the loss of the Virginia, perhaps the strongest War Vessel in the world, is the most regretted, besides hundreds of thousands of bales of cotton burned on the Mississippi since the Yankees got in to New Orleans. The further the Enemy gets into our Country, the more his forces is scattered, and no one doubts the ability of the South to gain her independence now, than did at the Battle of Manassas. The South is more active and determined now than she ever was before. We have two large Army's now, face to face with the Enemy, one at Corinth under Beauregard, and one near Richmond under Johnston. A great battle is expected from either, every day they may be fighting while I write. The Company I belong to is now entitled to Fifty Dollars Bounty. I suppose we shall get it in a few days, as we have always been paid up every two months and have no right to complain on that score. We have also had clothing and provisions aplenty so far.[15]

On June 4, the battalion was ordered to vacate Camp Mercer and move to Charleston, South Carolina. A detachment of the Fourth Louisiana Battalion was in the process of constructing a floating battery near Fort Jackson on the Savannah River when the order arrived for the battalion to hastily pack for the trip north. Many of the soldiers were under the impression that they were stopping briefly in Charleston en route to Richmond to counter McLellan's push against the Confederate capitol, and thus left their camp equipage under a skeleton guard at Savannah. Arriving in Charleston, they were assigned to the largest island off the Charleston coast, James Island, by the Confederate military commander of the area, Major-General John Clifford Pemberton, commanding the Department of South Carolina and Georgia.[16] Pemberton, a native of Pennsylvania married to a Virginian, was a former U.S. Army officer who had offered his sword to the Confederacy, at the urging of his wife, upon the outbreak of hostilities. Somewhat distrusted by Southerners because of his Northern blood, he would later the following year be labeled an outright traitor by Southern citizenry, after his transfer to command of the Vicksburg, Mississippi defenses, and the city's subsequent surrender, along with its 29,500 troop garrison, on July 4, 1863, to Union Major-General Ulysses Simpson Grant.[17]

The Fourth Louisiana Battalion had been ordered to James Island in anticipation of hostilities to be initiated by Union Major-General David Hunter. In November 1861, Union forces had made a rather easy capture of Port Royal, located some seventy miles from Charleston, and had fortified the port towns of Hilton Head and Beaufort, which made for easy resupply of Union warships operating in the Charleston vicinity. Adding to the Confederate apprehension was the May 13, 1862, abduction of the fast, light-draught steamer *Planter*, used in the transportation of ordnance and stores to the harbors and forts of the Charleston area, by her eight black crew members. The day before her abduction, the *Planter* had been loaded with heavy ordnance bound for the Middle Ground Battery in Charleston Harbor, consisting of a banded, rifled 42-pounder, an 8-inch howitzer, an 8-inch Columbiad, and a 32-pounder, as well as a 32-pounder and a 24-pounder howitzer for her own defense.[18] Disobeying written orders to stay with the ship until the artillery was delivered, the white captain, Charles J. Relyea, and his white mate and engineer disembarked the *Planter* for a sojourn into Charleston, leaving the all-black crew, consisting of Jacob Small, Robert Small, Alfred Gradine, Abraham Jackson, and David Jones, under the leadership of Jacob Small, the pilot of the *Planter*, to gather steam before daylight and make a dash out of the harbor. Taken by the forts as a guard boat and allowed to pass without interference, the *Planter* and the crew members' information regarding the removal of Confederate guns from the Georgetown and Cole Island defenses were turned over to the Union Navy, which was operating in the area. The U.S. Government awarded the crew of the *Planter* $5,000 dollars for the captured ship, of which Small kept $1,500.[19] Ironically, he would later use his treacherous prize money to buy his former master's home in Beaufort at a U.S. Government tax sale of confiscated Confederate property. During the Reconstruction era, Small would be appointed a U.S. congressman by the Johnson Administration to represent the Beaufort district, where he would pass a bill appropriating money to construct a small naval coaling station on an island located south of Beaufort. The coaling station is now a training facility for the United States Marine Corps, better known as Parris Island.

Private McNeil recorded these entries in his diary relating to the Fourth Louisiana Battalion's departure:

> Savannah, June 7th, 1862
> Our Batt. was ordered off to Charleston last Wednesday, the 4th. Expecting to be attacked there, they left all their tents behind and a Guard, to go on when called for. I am still at work on the Battery and can not get away until it is finished, which will take about two weeks more. We get a Dollar a day extra for working on it. I have been sick since last Tuesday, and have not been able to work. I am getting better now and expect to go to work in two or three days. Our tents and the Guard that was left with them went on to Charleston today, and the Batt. has been ordered on to Richmond. Stonewall Jackson and his Victorious Army are in Maryland. He must be doing things up about right there, it is causing great excitement at the North. It is reported that McClellan is falling back from Richmond. Corinth has been evacuated by our forces, this movement will cause our forces to fall back for Fort Pillow and Memphis, and give the Yankees the entire Mississippi River. But it is considered a good move.[20]

Pemberton had set up his James Island defenses in a line that ran from Fort Johnson on the northeast corner of the island to Fort Pemberton on the northwest corner, with no road running between the two due to the marsh land that ran on either side of James Island Creek, making direct travel between the two forts virtually impossible. The largest town on the island, Grimball, lay considerably south of Fort Pemberton on the road to Charleston, with another road from the town running to Fort Johnson, whose artillery covered the south channel of Charleston Harbor. In the center of the island was another small town, bestowed with the very patriotic sounding name of Secessionville, though the town had received its name years before the beginning of the latest sectional strife. Populated by summer homes that were isolated from the rest of the activities and residents of James Island, the residents had jokingly bestowed their small hamlet, lying on the very edge of inhabitable land, with the name Secessionville. Located directly east of Grimball, it was bordered on three sides by swamp land and a body of water that lay in the center of the island. Soon after the fall of Port Royal, Pemberton had constructed an observation tower at Secessionville, estimated to be two to three hundred feet high by Private Henry J. Lea of Company F of the Fourth Louisiana Battalion, that was protected by earthworks. This was done in response to the ever probing Union gunboats that patrolled the Stono River since the capture of Port Royal.[21] On the night of June 2, General Hunter landed a corps consisting of two divisions of Union troops, totaling 11,000 muskets, at Grimball on the island side of the Stono River. These troops were under the command, coincidentally, of Brigadier-General Henry W. Benham, who had been reassigned to South Carolina since falling from favor with Rosecrans.

Benham had graduated first in the 1837 class of West Point. Though highly intelligent, his demeanor was one of contempt and isolation, obviously not endearing him to his subordinates, or, for that matter, his superiors. He had been assigned to the U.S. Army Engineers Corps upon graduation from West Point, but in turning down a commission in the infantry after the Mexican War, he had missed his chance to gain an infantryman's instincts for fighting terrain, or when to launch an attack and when to demur.[22] His superior, General Hunter, was a fellow West Pointer from the class of 1822 whose assignment before the war was in the Paymaster Department. A friendship with the U.S. president-elect in 1861 had won him a seat on the train carrying Lincoln to Washington, as well as a generalship in the volunteer army. Thus was the composition of the Union Army command around the South Carolina coast, two ambitious men that knew the path to glory might run through Richmond but that the Northern public's desire for revenge against South Carolina for causing the late troubles by firing on Sumter, and the adoration that would follow upon whetting that desire, ran through Charleston.

Benham had learned from the crew of the *Planter* and Confederate deserters that the Secessionville fortifications consisted of a common earthwork with six cannon, protected in the front by abatis, and that it would soon be considerably strengthened by the addition of another seven guns. Meeting with Hunter on June 9, Benham pleaded with his commander to allow him to make a quick assault on the Secessionville fortifications before they could be completed, stating that it was important to "have and hold those points for the security of our camps, and even for the occupation of the Stono." Arguing that the capture would place the Union forces squarely in the center of James Island and poised for a push on Charleston, Benham also produced a map showing Hunter how the observation tower and earthwork were a threat to his encampment.[23] Though agreeing that the fortifications posed a possible threat, Hunter was of the opinion that no action should be made until the Confederate strength was ascertained. Perhaps sensing the blind ambition of his subordinate, before departing the island for his headquarters at Hilton Head on June 10, Hunter left the following written orders for Benham regarding the Confederate position:

> In any arrangements that you may make for the disposition of your forces now in this vicinity, you will make no attempt to advance on Charleston or to attack Fort Johnson until largely reinforced or until you receive specific instructions from these headquarters to that effect. You will however provide for a secure entrenched encampment, where your front can be covered by the fire of our gunboats from the Stono on your left and the creek from Folly River on the right.[24]

The window of opportunity left by the vague orders to provide a "secure encampment" was too much to endure for the ambitious Benham. Coupled with a skirmish that same day in front of Grimball that was initiated by the Forty-Seventh Georgia Infantry, the Fourth Louisiana Battalion Infantry, and the Thirty-Second Georgia Infantry, his plans to attack Secessionville, as well as expedite his own advancement, were already cemented in his head before the day closed. After being convinced by his subordinates that the Union troops needed rest after landing on the island and building their camps, he set the date for attack as Sunday, June 15. Unable to contain his zeal for the undertaking, he had a battery of three rifled guns initiate and continue a steady, but ineffectual fire on the Confederate works at Secessionville.

The June 10 skirmish involving the Fourth Louisiana Battalion was brought on by the Federals landing a force on the southeast side of James Island. The Confederate units involved consisted of the First South Carolina Infantry, the Twenty-Fourth South Carolina Infantry, the Eutaw Battalion, and the Fourth Louisiana Battalion, and these troops pushed the Union forces through the thick swamp back to their landing vessels. At the fall of darkness, the Fourth Louisiana Battalion was ordered to fall back to the open ground and remain silent to prevent the Union forces from gaining their location, as well as the range, for artillery fire. They remained there for the duration of the night, subjected to a constant bombardment of unnerving mortar fire. Private Henry J. Lea of Company F would reflect years after the war that, "Needless to say that no one there was sleepy that night." Upon discovering that no further Union attempts would be made to advance from the safety of the gunboats, the Fourth Louisiana Battalion retired to the rear of the fortified line east of King's Highway, where they would remain until the morning of June 16, though two pickets from the battalion would be captured on June 14 by a roving Federal patrol.[25]

General Pemberton had not been idle in preparing for the much anticipated Union assault. By June 15, he had assembled a force that was about evenly matched with his Federal antagonist, General Benham. Pemberton had positioned his forces behind the batteries, as well as the defensive lines from Fort Pemberton on the Stono River, at Elliot's Cut, all the way to Secessionville on the extreme east, and placed them under the chief command of Brigadier-General Nathan George "Shank" Evans, supported by Brigadier-General States Rights Gist and Brigadier-General William Duncan Smith. The Advance Guard, under the overall command of Colonel Johnson Hagood, was comprised of the Fourth Louisiana Battalion, the First South Carolina

Infantry under the command of Colonel Hagood, the Twenty-Fourth South Carolina Infantry commanded by Colonel Clement Hoffman Stevens, and the Eutaw Battalion, commanded by Lieutenant-Colonel Charles Henry Simonton. This force was encamped outside of the line of defense and charged with guarding the front of the defensive line. Excluded from the advance guard's line of protection was the front of Secessionville, which was protected by its own outposts.

On the evening of the 15th, Benham called a pre-attack meeting with his senior officers, consisting of Brigadier-General Horatio Gouverneur Wright, commander of the First Division; Brigadier-General Isaac Ingalls Stevens, commander of the Second Division; and Colonel Robert Williams, commander of the Third Brigade. Also in attendance was the U.S. Navy senior commander in the Charleston region, Captain Percival Drayton. It was at this meeting that Benham revealed his true plans regarding the works at Secessionville, stating to the attendees that they would be called upon to take the works by force. They later recalled that everyone in attendance, with the exception of Benham, was mortified at the proposition. General Stevens pointedly remarked that Federal artillery fire had been virtually useless in reducing the defenses, and that with each lull in firing, the Confederates had returned to man the guns with more determination than ever. He further stated that volunteer troops had never successfully assaulted works as strong as the Secessionville defenses, and this attempt would be no different. Benham retorted that this was to be a reconnaissance, "made in force, with the object, if it were successful and the fort not too strong, of capturing and holding the same." General Wright shot back that his orders as spoken were not for a reconnaissance, they were to fight a battle. General Stevens urged that, at the least, an assault in daylight be made to provide for better targets. Captain Drayton, whose ships would provide covering fire for the assault, was visibly disturbed by his observance of the lack of enthusiasm for Benham's scheme from the army officers in attendance.[26]

Benham could not have cared less about his subordinates' apprehensions regarding his plans for glory and self-advancement. Overriding their objections with his characteristic cold contempt, he outlined his battle plans that he fully expected to be carried out at daybreak the following day, June 16. General Wright recalled this account of Benham's plans:

> The division of General Stevens was to form the assaulting column against the enemy's works at Secessionville, and, being formed in the utmost silence at its outer pickets, was to move forward at the first break of day upon the enemy's batteries, while the remainder of the troops, comprising Williams' brigade and a part of my division, moving together from the camp at Grimball's, were to act as a support to General Stevens, protecting his left and rear from an attack of the enemy's forces from that direction.[27]

With daybreak at this time of the year at Secessionville coming at 4:53 A.M., Benham stressed that he wanted the soldiers of Stevens's division charging at the fort, with bayonets leveled and ready, by 3:00 A.M., "before good aiming light, and with guns loaded."[28] A gravely sullen General Stevens returned to his headquarters from the meeting later that night, when Captain Alfred P. Rockwell of the First Connecticut Light Artillery apprehensively approached and inquired, "General, may I ask what is the plan of battle?" Stevens erupted with, "Damn it, sir, there isn't any plan! You will fire when you get a chance, and be careful not to hit any of our own men!"[29]

While Benham's military conference was in progress on the 15th, Colonel Thomas Gresham Lamar of the First South Carolina Artillery, commanding the fort at Secessionville known as the Tower Battery but that would later bear his name, was observing unusual activities in the Union encampment. Becoming convinced that an attack was fast becoming imminent, Lamar notified General Evans of his convictions that an assault on the fort would probably be made that night or the following day.[30] At this time, the garrison of the Tower Battery consisted of Companies B and I of Lamar's own regiment, under the command of Captain George Daniel

Keitt and Captain Samuel J. Reid, as well as infantry support consisting of the Charleston Battalion under Lieutenant-Colonel Peter Charles Gaillard, and the Pee Dee Battalion under Lieutenant-Colonel Alexander D. Smith. The artillery at the fort was comprised of an 8-inch Columbiad, two 24-pounder rifles, several 18-pounders, and a mortar, but with the dismounting of the floating battery anchored at Big Folly Creek that was commanded by Captain F. N. Bonneau, the fort was scheduled to mount these additional guns on the 16th.[31] Upon receiving Colonel Lamar's alarming message regarding his anticipation of an assault, at 1:00 A.M. General Evans sent 100 chosen men from the Twenty-Second South Carolina Infantry, commanded by Captain Joshua Jamison, to the Tower Battery to assist in mounting the extra artillery. This detail arrived at the fort shortly before daybreak. The Secessionville picket guard, on duty at River's Place, was located one mile in front of the Tower Battery, with the Twenty-Fourth South Carolina Infantry, six companies of the First South Carolina Infantry, and one company of the Forty-Seventh Georgia Infantry, all under the command of Colonel C. H. Stevens, covering the front of the eastern lines.[32] Inside the Tower Battery, a gun detachment was on watch, with the rest of the garrison sound asleep — but not for long.

Precisely at daybreak, the first Union troops of the assaulting force, Companies C and H of the Eighth Michigan Infantry, accompanied by Company E of the First New York Engineers and armed with picks, axes, and shovels to clear the Confederate abatis, attacked the Confederate picket line, capturing four soldiers whom they promptly sent to the rear.[33] The main picket force, after firing a volley, broke into a dead run for the Tower Battery to sound the alarm. Companies C and H formed into open skirmish order in the open field, halted, and knelt, awaiting the arrival of the remainder of the Eighth Michigan. Once the rest of the regiment broke through the hedges, they deployed into full line of battle behind the skirmishers. Brigade commander Colonel William Matthew Fenton of the Eighth Michigan, who had pulled himself from a sick bed in order to be present at the battle, pulled out his field glasses to survey the Confederate position before him. General Stevens would later describe the scene laid out before Fenton on that fateful summer morn:

> The front on which the attack was made was narrow, not over 200 yards in extent, stretching from the marsh on the one side to the marsh on the other. It was at the saddle of the peninsula, the ground narrowing very suddenly at this point from our advance. On either hand were bushes on the edge of the marsh for some little distance. The whole space at the saddle was occupied by the enemy's work, impracticable abatis on either hand, with carefully prepared "trous de loup" on our left and in front a ditch 7 feet deep, with a parapet of hard-packed earth, having a relief of some 9 feet above the general surface of the ground. On the fort were mounted six guns, covering the field of our approach. The whole interior of the work was swept by fire from the rifle pits and defenses in the rear, and the flanks of the work itself and the bushes lining the marsh on either hand were under the fire of riflemen and sharpshooters stationed in the woods and defenses lying between the work and the village of Secessionville.[34]

Fenton wisely ascertained that to attack the position directly in his front was suicidal. He made the decision to march his men forward at an oblique angle in order to reach the high ground to his right, deciding this location would enable his men to fire into the Confederate position. He then dispatched couriers to the rear to advise the regiments following him of his intentions so that they could follow his lead. These regiments, in addition to the Eighth Michigan and First New York Engineers, consisted of the Seventh Connecticut Infantry, the Seventy-Ninth New York Infantry, the Twenty-Eighth Massachusetts Infantry, the One-Hundredth Pennsylvania Infantry, the Forty-Sixth New York Infantry, and the light batteries of Rockwell and Strahan.

As the Eighth Michigan began to move, the alert Colonel Lamar, acting as gun commander of the Columbiad located in the center of the fort, opened fire with the massive gun, which had been loaded with broken glass, horseshoes, spikes, and scrap iron. The blast tore gaping holes in the Union line. Lamar, who personally sighted the massive weapon before each discharge, stated that, "My reason for pointing the Columbiad myself was to fire at the center of the line and thereby break it, in order to cause confusion and delay, so that I might get my infantry into position previous to their reaching my lines."[35] His tactic had worked beyond even his expectations. Colonel Fenton would later describe the scene of destruction wrought by the Columbiad on his forces:

> During this advance, the enemy opened on our lines an exceedingly destructive fire of grape, canister, and musketry, and yet the regiment pushed on as veterans, divided only to the right and left by a sweeping torrent from the enemy's main gun in front. This brought a portion of the regiment to the left near the tower, or lookout, and a brisk fire of musketry was soon opened on both sides. The enemy's fire proved so galling and destructive that our troops on the parapet were compelled to retire under its cover, and that of the ditch and slope on our right at the marsh, slope and trees on our left.[36]

Twenty-three-year-old Lieutenant Benjamin Lyons, assigned to General Stevens's staff, led the attack on the Tower Battery. Screaming at the top of his lungs, "Come on, boys!" he ran pell-mell into the ditch fronting the fort and up the other side before being struck down with a mortal wound. As he turned to make his way to a field hospital in the rear, he was passed by a mass of blue surging forward.[37] The company of New York Engineers, deciding that picks and shovels were about as useful as petticoats for this affair, had wisely dropped their tools and unshouldered their weapons, sprinting forward with the first wave of attackers. The Confederate artillery played havoc in their ranks, and several had to be shoved forward by Corporal George Hughes so the momentum of the attack was not broken. The Eighth Michigan, who initiated the assault, had somehow managed to cross the ditch in front of the Tower Battery and reach the top of the parapet, but with no support from the halting regiments behind them. Met with the murderous fire of the infantry inside the fort, they were either killed, captured, or forced to run for their lives. The survivors of the Eighth Michigan had gathered around their colors, which miraculously had been brought off the field of battle. Of the 509 that had initiated the assault, 182 were killed, missing, or wounded, and the Michiganders gave no further participation for the remainder of the battle.[38]

Colonel Lamar, capitalizing on the stalled Union assault, rushed 250 infantry from the First South Carolina Battalion and the Ninth South Carolina Battalion into position behind the fort. The First South Carolina was posted on the left where the Eighth Michigan attack had failed, and the Ninth South Carolina along the right and center. Though the numerical disparity was mostly nullified by the narrow causeway that limited the Union front, Lamar was now holding at bay a force of 6,600 with a total force of 500 determined Southerners.[39]

The Seventh Connecticut had formed into line as the Eighth Michigan was making their forlorn dash to overrun the earthworks. Though under orders to rely on the bayonet, the Seventh had stopped some 130 yards from Fort Lamar and opened fire, supported by the 500-yard range howitzer fire of spherical and canister shot of the First Connecticut Light Battery, supported by a James rifle from the battery's right section. The predominately Irish Twenty-Eighth Massachusetts fell in behind the Seventh Connecticut, but lost all form of organization due to the Confederate abatis that the embattled Company of New York Engineers had failed to clear. The Seventh Connecticut halted behind the hedge, with many of their number going on the battle side to add their musket fire to the artillery battery. General Stevens finally ordered the Eighth, Seventh and Twenty-Eighth to return to camp, and the rest of his men to fall back 1,200 yards away from the fort in an attempt to reform and have his fresh troops that had seen no action thus far to have a crack at the Confederate fort.[40]

The Second Brigade, led by the Seventy-Ninth New York Infantry and the One-Hundredth

Pennsylvania Infantry, was sent to the Union line as support, as the pleading of Fenton for reinforcements was reaching the hysteria level. This line was sent forward by General Stevens on the double-quick and upon reaching the First Connecticut Light Battery, Stevens called to the battery commander, "Connecticut boys, go in and the day is ours!"[41] The battery, pumped with adrenaline, limbered up and fell in behind the Second Division for support. Private Edward Griswold, a gunner with the battery, recalled the following scene:

> We had to cross a cotton field, some 800 yards, and the enemy was raking that field with cannonades, and the seacoast howitzer that had been taken from the Government. The cannoneers were not mounted.... Corporal Scannton mounted one of the limbers and sitting astride, managed to hold on. I grasped the muzzle of the gun, with my thumb over the sight pin. How those horses went![42]

The First Connecticut stopped not far from the outside of the Tower Battery, and under heavy fire from the Confederate artillery, ran their guns on to the line. Griswold remembered that "We worked the guns lively, and most of the time in a stooping position." The artillery fire from the Tower Battery played deadly havoc on the next attacking wave from the Second Brigade.[43] The brigade commander, Colonel David Leasure, recalled the deadly barrage:

> We entered the range of a perfect storm of grape, canister, nails, broken glass, and pieces of chains fired from three very large pieces on the fort, which completely swept every foot of ground within the range, and either cut the men down or drove them to the shelter of the ravine on the left. I now turned to look after and lead up the One-Hundredth Pennsylvania Regiment, and found its center just entering the fatal line of fire, which completely cut it in two, and the right, under Major Leakey, obliqued to the right, and advanced to support the right of the Seventy-Ninth New York, and many of the men reached the foot of the embankment, and some succeeded in mounting it, with a few brave men of the Seventy-Ninth, who were there with a portion of the Eighth Michigan.[44]

Private John C. Wilson of Company C of the One-Hundredth Pennsylvania, with a bit of after-battle bravado, described the scene that was in his midst:

> We ran up close to the fort, and the rebels were raining showers of grape, canister, chains, and musketballs, but I did not care for them a bit more than if it had been a shower of rain. Henry Guy has three holes through his blouse, but he is not hurt. There was one ball struck my bayonet. I was the only one standing for several rods around for a while. The rest laid down to avoid the grape, but I wanted to see where it was coming from. Several that laid down never got up again, but there was not one of the balls touched me. We could not get in the fort when we got to it. We stayed for over an hour and then we got the order to retreat.[45]

Some of the assaulting force did manage to evade the storm of artillery fire and reach the exterior walls of the Tower Battery, where they began a mad dash to reach the top. Lieutenant-Colonel David Morrison of the Seventy-Ninth New York did reach the top, stopping to stare in admiration at the strength of the fortification before being toppled by a shot to the head.[46] Captain Richard N. Doyle of the Eighth Michigan managed to fire a few rounds from his service revolver before succumbing to Confederate fire, soon to be followed by Captain Benjamin B. Church, also of the Eighth Michigan, who had energetically been waving his men on with his sword before falling dead inside of the fort, the victim of a well placed minié ball.[47]

The fighting was so intense that Lieutenant James Campbell of the Ninth South Carolina Infantry grabbed an artillery handspike, the club-like apparatus used to move gun-tails, and began swinging at the blue-clad masses wildly before finding a dropped musket to use instead. The Confederates' steel-like resistance caused this Union assault to stall also. For twenty minutes, many of the Federal soldiers lay on the outside of the walls of the fort, rising periodically to fire at the gray-clad defenders, before giving up hope and returning under fire to the safety of their lines. Leasure pleaded with an officer of the First Division, who was silently watching the Second Division get cut to doll rags, "For God's sake, come up to the front and support me in a charge!"[48] The officer remained motionless, recalling orders not to support a failed attack, but finally responded by saying that his division could not be ordered into battle by anyone from the Second Division. Leasure did the only thing he could do under those circumstances, and ordered his brigade to retire from the field, with the Seventy-Ninth New York leaving some 40 of their dead there, but managing to escape with 6 corpses and 60 wounded back to the Union lines. Benham, perhaps knowing his fate if the "reconnaissance" was not turned in his favor, refused to concede defeat. He ordered the First Brigade to fall back and re-form for another strike at the fort, while simultaneously ordering Colonel Williams and his 1,500-strong Third Brigade to move out in open order to provide covering fire for the retreating First Brigade.

When the first Union shots of the attack were fired at daybreak, in the camp of the Fourth Louisiana Battalion the alarm was sounded and the long roll beat by the drummers. The line, 260 strong, was quickly formed and the order given to Lieutenant-Colonel McEnery by Colonel Hagood to march immediately to aid the beleagured garrison at the fort, some two and one-half miles away. Marching west at the double-quick down King's Highway, the battalion was held up for a brief period at the first crossroad, unsure of the correct road to take to come up in support of the fort. After being assured of the correct route, the men were once again off at the double-quick for a date with what would soon be wartime glory. Taking the road that ran south across the front of the Confederate defensive line and crossing single-file the 200-yard-long Secessionville Causeway, under fire from overshot Federal artillery, the battalion then turned to the east, bringing them within 400 yards of the Tower Battery, when Union musket fire opened on them from the opposite side of Lighthouse Creek at a range of 100 yards. Lieutenant-Colonel McEnery gave the order to halt, wheel to the right, advance to the outer edge of the marsh line, and then fire at will at the ambushing party. This was kept up only a short time when, seeing the Union troops massing for the next assault in front of the now depleted 500-effectives Tower Battery, the order was given to face to the left and double-quick to the fort to meet the attackers, where they were placed on the right of the defenders position.[49]

The Fourth Louisiana Battalion had received letters from family back home in Louisiana, as well as read newspaper accounts, of the fall of New Orleans to Union naval forces and its occupation by the Union Army under the supervision of Major-General Benjamin Franklin "Beast" Butler. Stories of Butler's harsh treatment of civilians in the Crescent City had inflamed the passions of many Louisiana citizens, and with this on their minds, a chance was within reach to avenge the wrongs the "Beast" had committed on their undefended citizenry. With a loud cheer, and screaming at the top of their lungs, "Remember Butler!" they poured a galling fire into the mass of onrushing blue uniforms.[50] Lieutenant-Colonel McEnery stated that "at this point ... the fire on both sides was indeed terrific."[51] Private Henry J. Lea of Company F thought that "It seemed that every man there in defense of the fort felt as though the whole responsibility of holding the fort rested on him."[52] For a full fifteen minutes, the Fourth Louisiana Battalion and the assaulting Northerners conducted a brutal knock-down slug fest with minié balls across a mere 100 hundred yards of marshland. According to the Fourth Louisiana Battalion's adjutant, William H. Sthreshley, "We poured into the ranks of the vandals volley after volley."[53]

Colonel Williams had sent forth the Third New Hampshire Infantry and the Ninety-Seventh Pennsylvania Infantry, who scrambled straight ahead before stopping in a deep ditch almost 200 yards away from the Confederate works, where they lay ducking under a brutal fire. Williams then ordered the Ninety-Seventh Pennsylvania, led by Colonel Henry R. Guss, to a point on the left, putting a swamp between the two positions which the men had to traverse before reaching another ditch, which they unceremoniously dove into. Colonel Guss then sent a reconnaissance party to attempt to locate another avenue of attacking the Confederate position. The Third Rhode Island Heavy Artillery, under the command of Lieutenant-Colonel Edwin Met-

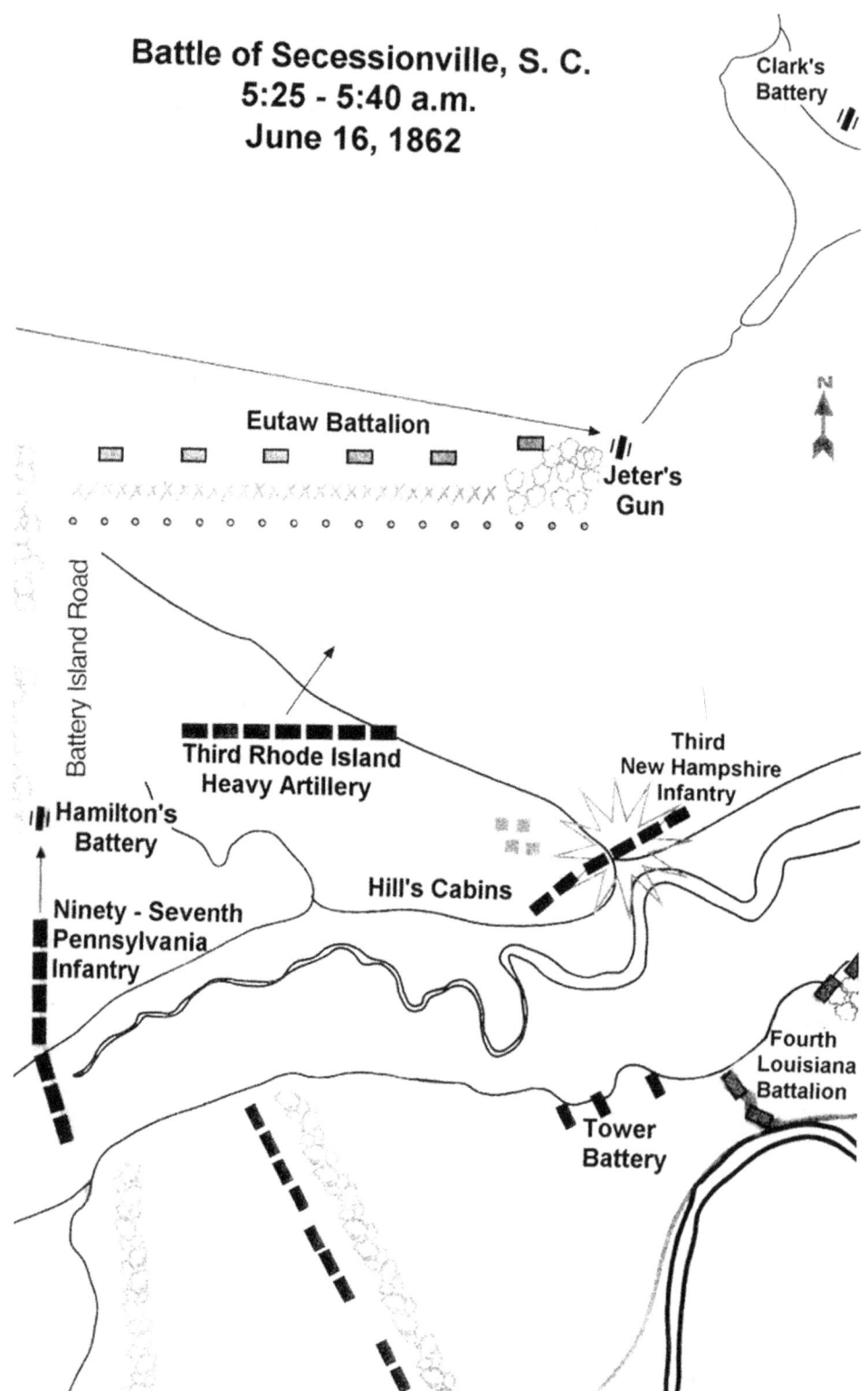

First map of Secessionville, South Carolina (by Terry G. Scriber).

calf, was ordered out to support the Third New Hampshire and the Ninety-Seventh Pennsylvania, and upon reaching their position, spotted a Confederate battery partially concealed in a thicket alongside the fort that was wreaking havoc on the Third New Hampshire line. Assuming the role of infantry, he had his gunners make their way through the heavy woods to a point where they could actually see the Confederate guns and count the number of infantry supporting the three-gun battery. The Rhode Island men, under fire for the first time and unsure of their ability to take the battery, wisely returned to their starting position without making an effort to silence the guns. General Wright had sent the Forty-Seventh New York Infantry to the left of the line to attempt to silence heavy fire coming from a row of bushes behind a marshy ravine. Assuming a position some 400 yards from the Tower Battery, they spent almost 15 minutes there firing volleys at an unseen foe while canister was poured into their position.[54]

After getting his forces in line for another assault, Benham ordered his men forward again, only to be stopped 500 yards from the fort by the mixture of musket fire and the lethal array of scrap fired from the Confederate guns. The survivors of this onslaught ran for the rear and the relative safety of the hedge line. It was now 8:00 A.M., and Stevens gathered his survivors around the colors to attempt another try at storming the Tower Battery. As he was waiting for the officers to form their companies, he saw Williams's brigade falling back, as he would learn from a staff officer, under Benham's orders. A messenger then arrived informing him that Wright's division was also withdrawing from the field. At 9:00 A.M., Stevens finally received orders from Benham to wait until all of Wright's division except the Ninety-Seventh Pennsylvania were past, then begin his own division's retreat.[55]

Inside the fort, Union musket fire had struck Colonel Lamar in the head during the second assault, forcing him to relinquish command to the commander of the Ninth South Carolina Infantry, Lieutenant-Colonel P. C. Gaillard. Gaillard's tenure as commander was also cut short by Federal fire, compelling him to turn over command to Lieutenant-Colonel Thomas M. Wagner of the First South Carolina Artillery. Members of the Fourth Louisiana Battalion were ordered to take the place of the Tower Battery's decimated gun-crews, when Lieutenant-Colonel McEnery, as the senior officer present, assumed command and, as stated in his after-action report, "caused an incessant volley of grape and canister to be poured into the broken and retreating columns of the enemy until they passed beyond view."[56]

Indeed, the victorious Confederate forces kept up an unrelenting fire on the retreating Federals. The captain of Company F of the Ninety-Seventh Pennsylvania, DeWitt Clinton Lewis, witnessed one of his men struck down in the swamp and then sink below the murky waters, sucked down by the heavy wool uniform and accouterments he was wearing. Lewis braved the galling fire being poured forth from the defenders and ran back, pulling the drowning Pennsylvanian from what was to be his watery grave and carrying him to the safety of his own lines. For this extraordinary display of gallant bravery, Lewis would become the recipient of the U.S. Medal of Honor.[57]

The Union losses were staggering for Benham's "reconnaissance." Stevens's division suffered 133 killed, 365 wounded, and 31 missing, with the Eighth Michigan losing 13 of the 22 officers it had begun the attack with at daybreak. General Wright reported an aggregate loss of 129. The Confederates reported the capture of 65 wounded and 42 unwounded Union prisoners, as well as burying 168 Northern sons on the battlefield.[58]

Lieutenant-Colonel McEnery reported the following abandoned Federal equipment, which he estimated at one-third of the total found, brought off the battlefield by the Fourth Louisiana Battalion alone: 27 Enfield Rifles (working), 4 Enfield Rifles (damaged), 83 Rifled Muskets (working), 62 Springfield Muskets (working), 6 Springfield Muskets (damaged), 78 Cartridge Boxes, and 2 Saddles.[59] One member of the battalion recalled that in combing the battlefield, the soldiers recovered "Federal canteens, haversacks, oil clothes, a few watches, and some Fed-

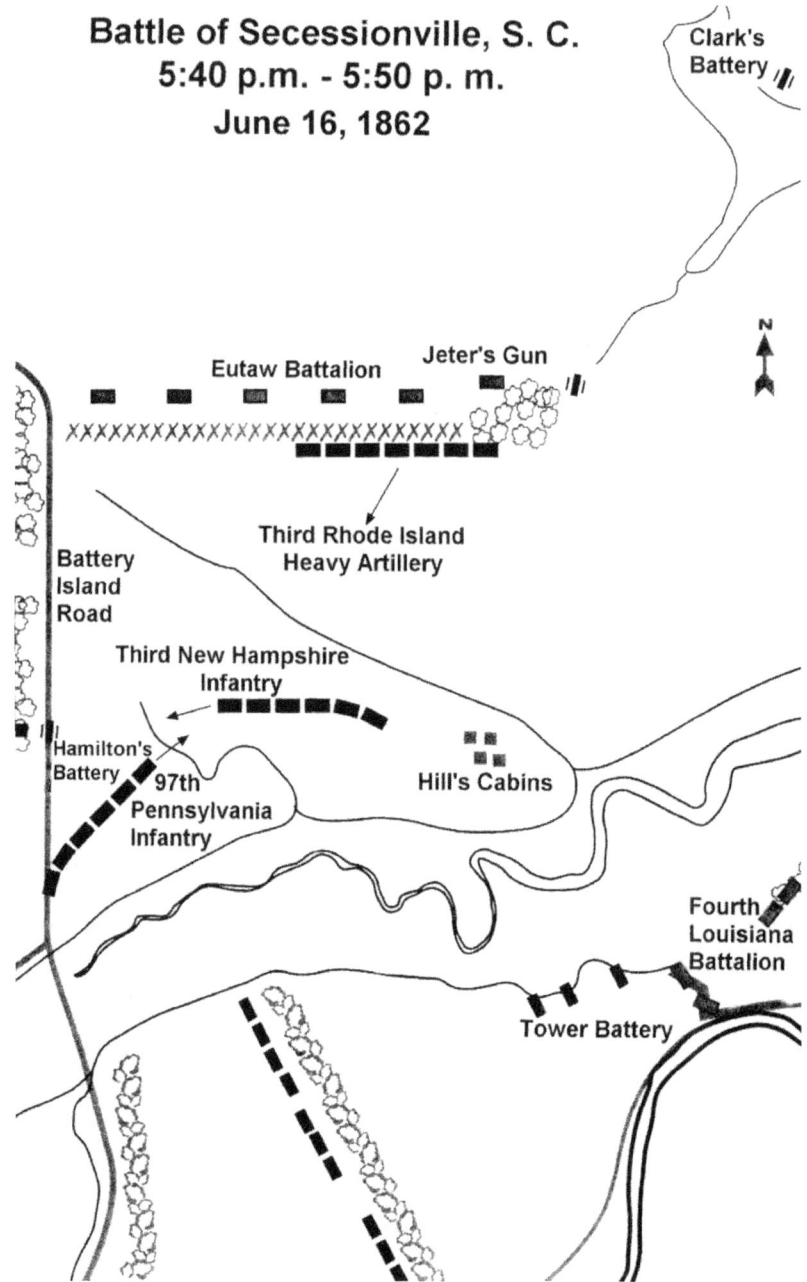

Second map of Secessionville, South Carolina (by Terry G. Scriber).

eral money."[60] Casualties for the Louisianans were reported at 6 killed and 22 wounded. Among the wounded was Captain James H. Walker of Company F, who was pierced through the torso by a rifle ball.

Benham's fight did not end with the battle on James Island. Condemned by everyone in the Union ranks who participated in the affair, Captain William Thompson Lusk of the Seventy-Ninth New York summed up the feelings of the survivors of the ill-fated assault: "Let there be no mercy shown to one who shows no mercy. He must be crushed at once or we are all lost. I

The Fourth Louisiana Battalion Flag (author's collection).

will not enumerate half the examples of imbecility he has shown, or the wickedness of which he has been guilty. The last act is too real."[61] An outraged General Hunter would have Benham arrested and sent back North, where Union Army General-in-Chief Henry Wager Halleck revoked the brigadier-general commission of Benham. Benham defended his actions by contending that the attack was indeed a "reconnaissance" made with the intention of "ascertaining the nature of the fort and the position in front on our rear, as also the character of the ground in advance of our left as far as may be necessary to secure our camps here," and ended by declaring the "reconnaissance" was accomplished.[62] Benham also blamed the failure of the attack on Stevens for not attacking sooner, which, of course, brought Stevens into the fray, stating that Benham had attacked the Tower Battery in spite of the misgivings of all his subordinate commanders. But Benham managed to persuade the governors of five New England states to petition Lincoln for his reinstatement to the army, to which Lincoln asked Joseph Holt, a non-military man assigned as the U.S. Judge Advocate General, to investigate the merits of Benham's appeal. Holt found that the way Hunter's orders were worded, Benham could have reasonably understood them as calling for an attack. Restored to brigade command by Lincoln, Halleck made sure that Benham would not again be able to launch foolhardy battles and waste lives, assigning him to command the two regiment Army of the Potomac Engineer Brigade, much of whose time was spent designing plans for bridges.[63]

Private McNeil, who missed the Battle of Secessionville due to being on detached service, recorded these observations in his journal:

> Oglethorpe Hospital, Savannah, June 21st, 1862
>
> Through imprudence I was taken sick again and came into the hospital last Thursday. I am better and will be alright in a day or two. Our Batt. was in the fight on James Island on Monday, the 16th of June. There was five killed and about twenty wounded. There was none killed and only two wounded in my Company. J. Williams and R. Vaughn, they drove the Yankees back and captured several prisoners. The papers say it was very severe fighting and the 4th La. done their duty in gallant style. I said in my last the Batt. was gone to Richmond, but I was mistaken, they are

still near Charleston. The Floating Battery will be done in a few days, and then I hope I shall be able to go and join the boys. But I learned it is uncertain, as they want to keep building Gunboats as long as they can. There is sixteen or seventeen of our Batt. here to work, and whether they will let us go when the Battery is done or not, I do not know. It is thought the Yankees will not attack this place for a while, perhaps they intend to take Charleston first. I expect they will have a hard time of getting it if it is rumored that France is recognizing the Confederate States, and for some reason, is not allowed to be published. But whether it is so or not, I do not know. It is rather doubtful.

Oglethorpe Hospital, Savannah, June 23, 1862

Everything appears to be at a standstill on all sides just now. Beauregard, falling back from Corinth, has broken into the Yankees arrangement up there. They have built immense breastworks there and roads in all directions with heavy siege guns, and is now of no use, and they have a great horror in coming any farther south. Since our Army fell back, General Bragg has taken command and Beauregard has been called off to some other point, but where, it is not known yet, and the two days fighting, the thirty-first of May and the 1 of June in front of Richmond, has stopped them there and cooled the Yankees spirits up considerable there. It is hard to tell where the next great Battle will be. General Stuart, with about fifteen-hundred men, has made a successful dash around the whole Yankee army in front of Richmond, burning a large lot of Yankee stores, and three transports, and capturing a large number of horses and mules which he brought into our lines loaded with plunder, and nearly two-hundred prisoners. It is considered the greatest exploit of the war. All eyes are now turned toward Stone Hill. Jackson, he has been largely reinforced since his last fight, and is said to be advancing, but to what point he is marching to or what his orders are is kept in the dark, yet it is expected we shall hear from him before long. England and France are talking about intervention and the blockade a great deal, but the South is taking but little notice of it. I have not heard from the Batt. since the fight, only what I have read in the News Papers. I am getting better and will be out in a few days. There is a great deal of sickness among the Soldiers, but not of a very dangerous character. If we should get the Yellow Fever among us here now, it would be a serious case.

Secessionville, July 2, 1862

I arrived here with three more of our Company's today from Savannah, and I am now with the Batt. again. I visited the Battleground of the 16th. It appears to have been well peppered with shot and shell from the Enemy's Batteries and Gunboats. Houses were riddled, trees cut to pieces and the ground tore up in all directions. The Yankees made three desperate charges, advancing close up to our breastworks and some climbing on top, and a mere boy had got on top and sung out, "Here's your little Scotchman, ain't I brave," but the next minute he fell back over the breastwork a corpse, and the Enemy was repulsed the third time. By this time, a Regt. of Sharp Shooters had flanked our Battery and drove our Gunners from the guns. Our little force of Infantry was almost out of ammunition and worn out, and stopped firing. The Enemy was preparing for another charge. This was the critical moment, the Enemy Sharp Shooters kept our gunners from the guns, our Battery was therefore silenced. The Enemy had only to come up and take possession, which they was preparing to do about this time. Our Batt. came on the field at a double-quick, threw themselves in front of the Enemy Sharp Shooters, and after a fight of about twenty minutes, drove them from the field. They now had to go to the Battery to repulse the Enemy's charge. Some of our men had taken charge of some of the guns in the Battery and were using them with effect. The charge was repulsed, the Enemy was routed and the day was won. The Enemy's loss is about one thousand, ours about two hundred. Our boys got Yankee canteens, haversacks, oil clothes, a few watches and some Yankee money. Five of our Batt. has since died of their wounds. The Battery has been strengthening and eight or ten more guns planted there. It is about a quarter of a mile from this place. We are stationed here in the houses on hard crackers, kipper, pork, and cold water.

Secessionville, July 4, 1862

The Yankees fired a salute of several guns this morning. The Confederates fired a salute this noon from all the Batteries and finishing with the big guns of Fort Sumter, all in honor to the glorious Fourth of '76, when the North and South stood as one. It is far different now. A dispatch was read to us this evening on Drill Parade of our victory at Richmond and the capture of large numbers of prisoners. It has been raining nearly all day and cold. The Yankees are leaving the Island.[64]

The victory at Secessionville was heralded throughout all portions of the Confederacy, and the Fourth Louisiana Battalion was praised for its determined resistance and coolness under fire. The men had "seen the monkey show" and performed honorably in their first taste of heated combat in the face of a numerically superior and determined enemy. With the withdrawal of Union forces from James Island at the end of June to Hilton Head, Beaufort, and north Edisto, the soldiers of the battalion would depart James Island a few days after the Battle of Secessionville by boarding a steamer at the point of the peninsula, a short cruise that would take them past Fort Sumter, before disembarking at Charleston. The battalion would depart Charleston for Savannah, arriving there on July 7 and encamping at Camp Van Dorn, where they would remain until December 14, performing guard and picket duty, as well as detached assignments to garrison Fort Jackson. With the sighting off Wilmington, North Carolina, of Union warships that were assumed to be the lead elements of an invasion force, the Fourth Louisiana Battalion, as well as the remainder of Colonel George Paul Harrison's Brigade, were transferred to Wilmington, remaining at Camp Beauregard until February 1863, when they were again assigned to duty at Savannah, this time encamping at Camp City Lines while detachments were assigned to garrison duty at Fort Boggs.[65] It was during this time that an act of appreciation was bestowed upon Lieutenant-Colonel McEnery by the soldiers in his command. The February 21, 1863, edition of the *Savannah-Republican* recorded the event:

> Sword Presentation—On Wednesday evening last the officers and men of the Fourth Battalion Louisiana Volunteers presented Lieut. Col. McEnery with a magnificent sword. The presentation was made on dress parade, by Sgt. J. K. Penny, of Co. E, in a brief and appropriate address, and was a complete surprise to the Colonel. On accepting the compliment, Col. McEnery replied in a feeling manner. Altogether, the affair passed off most happily.

The Fourth Louisiana Battalion would remain at Camp City Lines until early May 1863, when they would receive an assignment that would bring them closer to their much beloved homes in north Louisiana and Natchez.[66] This assignment would see them arrive in Jackson, Mississippi, and be placed under the overall command of General Joseph Eggleston Johnston, culminating in what would be a slow death blow for the Confederacy known as the Vicksburg Campaign.

SECESSIONVILLE, S.C., ORDER OF BATTLE
June 16, 1862

Union Forces: Department of the South
Major-General David Hunter

Northern District Commander
Brigadier-General Henry Washington Benham

Left Column
Williams's Brigade
Colonel Robert Williams (1st Massachusetts Cavalry)
3rd Rhode Island Heavy Artillery (5 Cos.): Major Edwin Metcalf
3rd New Hampshire Infantry: Lt. Colonel John Jackson
97th Pennsylvania Infantry (Detached from Chatfield's Brigade): Colonel Henry Guss
3rd U.S. Artillery (1 section—Detached from Welsh's Brigade): Captain Ransom

First Division
Brigadier-General Horatio Gouverneur Wright

First Brigade
Colonel John Chatfield
6th Connecticut Infantry (2 Cos.): Colonel John Chatfield
47th New York Infantry: Major P. C. Kane

Second Brigade
Colonel Thomas Welsh
45th Pennsylvania Infantry (6 Cos.): Colonel Thomas Welsh
76th Pennsylvania Infantry (8 cos., Detached as Camp Guard): Colonel J. M. Power
1st New York Engineers (5 Cos.): Major Butts
3rd U.S. Artillery (2 Sections)
1st Massachusetts Cavalry (2 Squadrons)

Right Column-Second Division
Brigadier-General Isaac Ingalls Stevens

First Brigade
Colonel William Fenton
8th Michigan Infantry: Lt. Colonel Frank Graves
7th Connecticut Infantry: Lt. Colonel Joseph Roswell Hawley
28th Massachusetts Infantry: Lt. Colonel McClelland Moore
1st Connecticut Light Artillery (4 Guns): Captain Alfred Rockwell

Second Brigade
Colonel Daniel Leasure
79th New York Infantry: Lt. Colonel David Morrison
100th Pennsylvania Infantry: Major David Leckey
46th New York Infantry: Colonel Rudolph Rosa
1st New York Engineers (1 Co.): Captain Alfred Sears
1st Massachusetts Cavalry (1 Co.): Captain Lucius Sargent

CONFEDERATE FORCES: DEPARTMENT OF SOUTH CAROLINA AND GEORGIA
Major-General John Clifford Pemberton

First Military District of South Carolina Commander
Brigadier-General Nathan George "Shanks" Evans

James Island
Brigadier-General William Duncan Smith
Brigadier-General States Rights Gist

Tower Battery
Colonel Thomas G. Lamar
1st South Carolina Artillery (2 Cos.): Colonel Thomas G. Lamar
22nd South Carolina Infantry (100 Soldier Detachment): Captain Joshua Jamison
9th South Carolina Battalion Infantry (Pee Dee): Lt. Colonel Alexander D. Smith
1st South Carolina Battalion Infantry (Charleston): Lt. Colonel Peter Gaillard
4th Battalion Louisiana Infantry: Lt. Colonel John McEnery

Advanced Forces
Colonel Johnson Hagood
24th South Carolina Infantry (Detachments from 4 Cos.): Colonel Clement Stevens
1st South Carolina Infantry (Detachments from 4 Cos.): Colonel Johnson Hagood
Eutaw Battalion: Lt. Colonel Charles Simonton
Boyce's Light Battery (Macbeth Light Artillery) 1 Gun: Lieutenant B. A. Jeter
47th Georgia Infantry: Colonel Gilbert Williams
51st Georgia Infantry: Colonel William Slaughter

Clark's Point Battery
24th South Carolina Infantry: Lt. Colonel Ellison Capers
1st South Carolina Artillery (1 Co.): Lieutenant J. B. Kitching

Chapter 3

Cold Mist of Defeat: The Vicksburg Campaign

> *HO! FOR JOHNSTON!— The most agreeable news nowadays is to hear from Gen. Johnston. But we have nothing to record of his movements, except that we may look forward at any time to his approach. We may repose the utmost confidence in his appearance within a very few days. We have to say to our friends and the noble army here that relief is close at hand. Hold out a few days longer, and our lines will be opened, the enemy driven away, the siege raised, and Vicksburg again in communication with the balance of the Confederacy.*
>   Vicksburg Daily-Citizen Editorial by editor
>   James M. Swords, Vicksburg, June 18, 1863

While the Fourth Louisiana Battalion was still on active service in the east, events were unfolding in other theaters of the war that would soon have a direct impact on the battalion. In the early days of 1861, leaders on both sides in the coming hostilities realized that control of the Mississippi River was vital to any plan for winning the looming conflict. Stretching 2,348 miles from its headwaters in northern Minnesota to the point where it empties into the Gulf of Mexico, it served as drainage for a basin covering 1,244,000 square miles. Bordering on its western bank the states of Arkansas, Louisiana, Minnesota, Iowa, and Missouri, and on the eastern bank Mississippi, Wisconsin, Illinois, Tennessee, and Kentucky, its tributaries touched virtually every state and territory between the Rockies and the Appalachians.[1] Considered the backbone of the American economy with the dawn of the steam age, it was no wonder that shortly after his inauguration, President Lincoln called on then general-in-chief of the U.S. Army, Winfield Scott, to devise a plan to quickly subdue the uprising and gain control of the mighty Mississippi. Scott's two-pronged response, dubbed the "Anaconda Plan," was extremely simple, on paper. First, conduct a massive saltwater blockade around the states in rebellion, extending from the Chesapeake Bay all the way to the extreme tip of Florida, then west across the Gulf Coast to the Rio Grande, effectively sealing Southern ports from foreign supplies of war and trade. This phase of the plan would be done in conjunction with a massive ship-building project in the North that the South, due to a severe shortage of adequate shipyards and materials, would be unable to counter. Second, gain control of the Mississippi River, and with two coordinated military forces moving to a juncture simultaneously, one upriver from New Orleans, and the second downriver from Cairo, Illinois, seizing control as they went, effectively split the Confederacy in half and deny the eastern half supplies brought in from Texas and the neutral country of Mexico. In Scott's own words, "to clear out and keep open this great line of communication" would bring the South "to terms with less bloodshed than by any other means."[2]

Lincoln liked the plan. In his youth he had often plied the river, working his way downstream from the Ohio, past the mouths of the Big Black and Yazoo, all the way to the Queen City of New Orleans. Intimately familiar with the mighty Mississippi, Lincoln, more than anyone, had an appreciation of what control, or loss of, could mean for either side.[3] And at that time, cities such as New Orleans, St. Louis, Memphis, and Vicksburg controlled the Father of Waters.

While blockading the Southwest Pass of the river in the Gulf, a career U.S. Navy man, Commander David Dixon Porter, had actually devised a plan to capture New Orleans. Traveling to Washington in November 1861 for a meeting with U.S. Navy Secretary Gideon Welles, Porter outlined his plan to the secretary, who was so impressed he took him to the White House for an audience with Lincoln. Porter, in his own words, described his plan:

> To fit out a fleet of vessels-of-war with which to attack the city, fast steamers drawing not more than 18 feet of water, and carrying about 250 heavy guns; also a flotilla of mortar-vessels, to be used in case it should be necessary to bombard Forts Jackson and St. Philip before the fleet should attempt to pass them. I also proposed that a body of troops should be sent along in transports to take possession of the city after it had been surrendered.[4]

Lincoln's reply was enthusiastic. "This should have been done sooner. The Mississippi is the backbone of the Rebellion; it is the key to the whole situation. While the Confederates hold it, they can obtain supplies of all kinds, and it is a barrier against our forces."[5] Lincoln then summoned Secretary of State William H. Seward and Major-General George B. McClellan to join the meeting. Once getting the newcomers briefed on Porter's plan, Lincoln stressed what he considered the primary target of the expedition: Vicksburg, Mississippi. He offered these thoughts regarding the Hill City:

> This is a most important expedition. It is not only necessary to have troops enough to hold New Orleans, but we must be able to proceed at once toward Vicksburg, which is the key to all that country watered by the Mississippi and its tributaries. If the Confederates once fortify the neighboring hills, they will be able to hold that point for an indefinite time, and it will require a large force to dislodge them. See what a lot of land those fellows hold, of which Vicksburg is the key.... The war can never be brought to a close until that key is in our pocket. I am acquainted with that region and know what I am talking about. We may take all the northern ports of the Confederacy and they can still defy us from Vicksburg![6]

McClellan agreed to send 20,000 troops under the command of Major-General Benjamin Butler, and at Porter's recommendation it was decided that the naval portion of the plan should fall under the command of Porter's adopted brother, Captain David Glasgow Farragut, a naval veteran with over fifty years of experience. The plans were pushed forward in extreme secrecy, and in early December, an advance contingent of Butler's troops landed at and occupied Ship Island, located in Mississippi Sound, some sixty-five miles east of New Orleans. But the Confederacy was also aware of the importance of Vicksburg to the war effort, and that at some point the Union was bound to make an attempt to capture the city, and hence, the river. In the Confederate capitol, the publisher of the *Richmond Daily-Examiner*, Edward Alfred Pollard, offered this editorial regarding the importance of the City of a Hundred Hills:

> Vickburg ... the most important point in the Valley of the Mississippi. Thousands of men, supplies, and material were continually crossing the river — much of our provisions for the armies in the East and West being derived from Texas, parts of Louisiana, and Arkansas. Could the Federals obtain possession of Vicksburg, all the agricultural products of the Northern and Western States would pass down unmolested to the Gulf; the enemy would gain free access to the whole river front, supply themselves abundantly with cotton, sugar, molasses, and other products, dis-

join the east and west Mississippi States, and, having the Confederacy fairly on its flanks, could operate with impunity upon numberless points, divide our forces, and open a new prospect of subjugation.[7]

On the morning of April 18, 1862, the attempt at subjugation was launched with the firing on of Fort Jackson and Fort St. Philip by the mortar boats under the command of Porter, with 18,000 of Butler's infantry crowded aboard transports to assume control of the soon to be conquered Southern cities. But what had been predicted by Porter to take forty-eight hours saw the Confederate forts still standing defiantly some five days later. An exasperated Farragut, at the urging of an equally exasperated Butler, then decided to gamble on the unthinkable; he would make a run past the forts and capture New Orleans on his way to Vicksburg. He issued his "General Orders to the Fleet" on April 23, and the order was simple and to the point: Prepare to weigh anchor at 2:00 A.M. on April 24. The activity aboard the seventeen Union ships reached a feverish pace, with hulls painted a muddy brown to obscure visibility, sand strewn on decks to prevent slipping in the blood of the wounded and killed, and chain hung over the ship sides to protect the engine rooms. At precisely the scheduled time, Farragut, aboard his flagship *Hartford*, along with the rest of the conquering flotilla, cast off.

Despite the precautions taken, the ships were spotted immediately by the ragtag Confederate Defense Fleet, consisting of twelve vessels of various design that had been converted to warships from river steamers, tugs, and double-ended ferries. Of the two most formidable ships in the fleet, the ram *Manassas* was hampered by insufficient power and the iron-clad *Louisiana* was no more than a floating battery due to the incomplete installation of her machinery. On board the *Governor Moore*, a converted paddle-wheeler, the Union ships were spotted by Lieutenant Beverly Kennon, who summoned the crew to battle stations and gave the order to open fire. Upon hearing the firing from the *Governor Moore* and correctly deducing that Farragut's ships had been spotted, Porter ordered the mortar fleet to open up with all they had. Farragut, realizing that stealth was now out of the question, gave the order for his vessels to return fire. Porter later described the scene of more than thirty warships doing battle in an area of a half-mile wide and not much more in length:

> From almost perfect silence — the steamers moving slowly through the water like phantom ships — one incessant roar of heavy cannon commenced, the Confederate forts and gunboats opening together on the head of our line as it came within range. The Union vessels returned the fire as they came up, and soon the guns of our fleet joined in the thunder which seemed to shake the very earth. A lurid glare was thrown over the scene by the burning rafts, and, as the bomb-shells crossed each other and exploded in the air, it seemed as if a battle was taking place in the heavens as well as on the earth.[8]

In one hour and ten minutes, it was all over. Farragut had passed the forts and destroyed or chased away the Southern fleet, with a Union loss of two hundred killed and wounded, one ship lost, and two others seriously damaged. With the river now open to New Orleans, the decks were cleaned, the dead buried, and the fleet hurried upriver to challenge the Crescent City. After encountering token resistance from Confederate batteries mounted at Chalmette, Farragut anchored in front of the city, with his guns pointing ominously down Canal Street. Fort Jackson and Fort St. Philip surrendered to Porter on April 28, and on May 1, Butler marched his occupying force through the streets of New Orleans. The Queen City of the South had fallen, and the first obstacle to Union control of the great river had been overcome.

Farragut departed New Orleans with 1,400 of Butler's infantry, under the command of Brigadier-General Thomas Williams, for his ascent up the river en route to his primary target of Vicksburg. After first securing the easy surrender of an undefended Baton Rouge, Louisiana, it was followed by an even easier taking of Natchez, Mississippi. The Union fleet descending the river from Cairo was now almost at Memphis, and the Gibraltar of the West seemed destined to follow in the path of the other river towns. But Vicksburg would prove to be the toughest nut yet for Farragut to crack. On May 18, an advance contingent of Farragut's fleet, under the command of Samuel Phillips Lee, arrived in front of Vicksburg and sent the following message to the Vicksburg authorities:

> The undersigned, with orders from Flag Officer Farragut and Major-General Benjamin Butler, respectively, demand the surrender of Vicksburg and its defenses to the lawful authority of the United States, under which private property and personal rights will be respected.[9]

The message was signed, "S. Phillips Lee, Commanding Advance Naval Division," and stated that a reply was expected in three hours. In five hours, Lee received not one but three replies to his surrender demand. The first, from Vicksburg Mayor Lazarus Lindsay, declared that "neither the municipal authorities nor the citizens will ever consent to a surrender of the city."[10] This was followed by the defiant response of Colonel James Lockhart Autry, military governor of the post, stating, "Mississippians don't know, and refuse to learn, how to surrender. If Commodore [sic] Farragut or Brigadier-General [sic] Butler can teach them, let them come and try."[11] Last was the response of Major-General Martin Luther Smith, commander of Confederate forces at Vicksburg, "Having been ordered to hold these defenses, it is my intention to do so."[12] Lee was at a loss. With all of the other river towns surrendering so easily, he could not understand why Vicksburg was so confident in their defiance. As he surveyed the fortress-like bluffs through his field glasses, he began to get a clearer picture of the Hill City's confidence, or more specifically, a clearer picture of the artillery batteries that were emplaced in the hills to protect the city. Lee wisely decided to await the arrival of Farragut before bringing on an engagement with the rapidly multiplying Confederate reinforcements arriving daily in Vicksburg.

With Farragut's arrival on the river below Vicksburg, May 26, a Monday, marked the beginning of the ineffectual Federal bombardment of the city, with Confederate gunners barely bothering to return fire. Farragut, in calling a conference with General Williams, readily admitted that Vicksburg could not be forced to surrender by naval firepower alone, with the Confederate bluff batteries too high for his guns to reach. Inquiring if Williams could storm the city with his 1,500 infantry, Williams incredulously responded that to do so in the face of an estimated 8,000 rebel infantry would be suicidal. With the Western Flotilla that was descending the river still above Fort Pillow, Farragut decided to call the operation a "reconnaissance in force" and return to New Orleans. When Secretary Welles heard of his abandonment of the plan to take Vicksburg, he and Assistant Secretary of the Navy Gustavus Vasa Fox ordered Farragut to return at once to the Hill City and proceed as ordered. Fox sent the following message to Farragut reiterating the wishes of President Lincoln:

> The President requires you to use your utmost exertions (without a moment's delay, and before any other naval operations are permitted to interfere) to open the Mississippi and effect a junction with Flag Officer Davis.[13]

Reluctantly, Farragut started back up river, this time accompanied by Porter and his mortar flotilla, as well as an infantry force of 3,200 and several batteries of light artillery on loan from Butler to General Williams. Arriving before Vicksburg on June 25, less than four weeks after he had left, Vicksburg was now stronger than ever, with more reinforcements still en route. Flag Officer Davis had managed to communicate with Farragut across DeSoto Peninsula that lead elements of his flotilla were now twenty miles upriver from Vicksburg, after viciously fighting their way down from Cairo. With the Welles, Fox, and Lincoln admonishments fresh on his mind, Farragut knew he must attempt to make a junction with the Western Flotilla. Unfortunately, this required running past the Vicksburg batteries. Setting the date and time for the hazardous mission as Saturday, June 28 at 2:00 A.M., he ordered Porter to open a continuous, around-the-clock mortar bombardment. Taking all of the precautions he previously had taken on passing Forts Jackson and St. Phillip, when the smoke had cleared on the violent passage, it had taken Farragut three hours to run the Vicksburg gauntlet, with a loss of three ships disabled and forty-five casualties among the crew. But he had fulfilled his orders and made his junction with Davis, adding four ironclads and six additional mortar scows to the armada arrayed against Vicksburg. But General Williams's infantry was still below the city, and the transports were far too slow to attempt a run past the batteries, and, even if successful, there were still too few Union troops to confront the swelling ranks of the defenders of Vicksburg. Now what?

For lack of a better plan, Farragut and Williams decided upon attempting an "experiment." The infantry, supplemented with impressed slaves from the countryside, would dig a canal across the base of the peninsula that would bypass Vicksburg altogether, creating a channel that the Union ships could use to avoid the batteries surrounding the city. The plan was executed on June 27, with Porter continuing his incessant, and still ineffectual, shelling, which was returned sporadically by the Confederate batteries. Porter recalled just how little effect this did have on the Confederates:

> The whole power of the Confederacy had been set to work to save this Gibraltar of the Mississippi, the railroads poured in troops and guns without stint, enabling it to bid defiance to Farragut's ships and the mortar flotilla.... Our combined fleet lay there and gazed in wonder at the new forts that were constantly springing up on the hill tops ... while water batteries seemed to grow on every salient point. It was evident enough that Vicksburg could only be taken after a long siege by the combined operations of a large military and naval force.[14]

On July 10, Porter was summoned for service on the James River in Norfolk, Virginia, along with half of his mortar flotilla and a number of gunboats to tow them. To add to Farragut's worries, the canal digging "experiment" was a complete failure due to the falling waters of the river, succeeding only in causing most of the infantry to be felled by sickness from unaccustomed exposure to the hot and humid Mississippi climate. But the icing on Farragut's cake of woe was the appearance of a Confederate ironclad named the *Arkansas*, who, after being constructed in secrecy at Greenwood, Mississippi, on the Yazoo River, had made a complete mockery of the Union fleet by her deadly appearance. Captained by Lieutenant Isaac Newton Brown, and constructed from basically scrap, she had made a run through the combined ships of two Union fleets on July 15, inflicting heavy damage, and anchored defiantly beneath the guns of Vicksburg. An irate Farragut, barely able to speak, decided on immediate action to neutralize the new Confederate threat. He would take his fleet past the Vicksburg batteries again, before sundown, and with their combined massive firepower sink the *Arkansas* in the process. Flag Officer Davis, though opposed to the action, did agree to keep the water battery north of the city occupied while Farragut made his run.

But Farragut's luck did not improve with this attempt. After the run was made, the ugly duckling of the Confederate Navy still sat nestled under the protective wings of the Vicksburg batteries. At the urging of Secretary Welles, who stated in a wire to Farragut that the fleet must redeem itself by "the destruction of the *Arkansas*," Farragut managed to coerce Davis into agreeing to send the ram *Queen of the West* and the *Essex* to destroy the *Arkansas* in her protective berth.[15] The strategy was simplistic in design: send the two warships with their iron beaks into the side of the naval pride of the Confederacy. On July 22, the plan was put into action, and Farragut notched another failure on his masthead. Once the smoke had cleared, the *Arkansas* was still floating proudly. Days later, Farragut threw in the towel. With the rapidly falling river and the increasing sickness among the infantry, as well as the sailors, Farragut wired Welles as to whether he should "go down or remain up the rest of the year." Welles's terse reply belied his disgust, "Go down river at discretion."[16] On July 24, Farragut and his fleet weighed anchor and headed south with the troop transports, minus one ram and one ironclad left behind to patrol the river below Vicksburg and "blockade" the *Arkansas*. Davis followed suit on July 28, heading upstream three hundred miles to Helena, Arkansas. The Union's Vicksburg operation of 1862 had been a complete failure, to which Secretary Welles gave vent:

> The most disreputable naval affair of the war was the descent of the steam ram Arkansas through both squadrons, until she hauled into the batteries of Vicksburg, and there the two Flag Officers abandoned the place and the iron-clad ram, Farragut and his force going down to New Orleans, and Davis proceeding with his flotilla up the river.[17]

With the immediate Union threat to Vicksburg over for the time being, President Davis enacted plans to strengthen the Vicksburg defenses, as well as effect a makeover of the command structure in the Confederacy. After Secessionville, the leaders and citizens in Charleston had raised their cries for the removal in command of John C. Pemberton, and the return of the more refined General P. G. T. Beauregard, to a pitched wail. Relenting to the uproar in Charleston, Davis had sent Beauregard back to command the seacoast defenses there, while elevating Pemberton to the rank of lieutenant-general and placing him in command of the newly created Department of Mississippi and East Louisiana, with an emphasis on defending Vicksburg. Arriving at Jackson, Mississippi, on October 14, 1862, Pemberton remained there long enough to establish his headquarters before moving on to inspect the Confederacy's "sacred ground" he had been entrusted by Davis to defend.

While this excitement was transpiring in and around Vicksburg, Private McNeil was still faithfully recording the events surrounding the battalion on the east coast, as well as the Confederacy in general. He made these interesting entries in his journal:

> Savannah, July 7, 1862
> Received orders last night to go to Savannah today. Some got up at Twelve o'clock and cooked their food, others that could not eat it when it was cooked laid still until daybreak, when we got on a Steamboat, which took us to the Depot. We left there about Ten o'clock and arrived here about Eight P.M. all safe, but very hungry. Some of us ran the Blockade and got something to eat, which helped us considerable. Will sleep in the Depot Ground tonight.

> Tuesday, Camp Van Dorn, July 15, 1862
> We left the Depot on the morning of the 8th about Ten o'clock, and marched out of here about five miles from town on the Shell Road towards White Bluff. We have a pretty shady place here to camp. I received my Bounty last Friday, and my two months pay yesterday. Got lots of money now. The boys are running the Blockade all the time, and will as long as the money last. The Papers are of accounts of the great Battles in front of Richmond, both sides fought with great determination, but the Yankees had to give way. The Yankee Generals have to tell all sorts of lies about it, some say it was a __ that gave __ to fall back to __ the Rebels on but the fact of it is, they were badly whipped and nothing but their Gunboats saved them.

> Camp Van Dorn, July 26th
> Our Major went off to Richmond last Monday, I believe to try to get orders to go North. On July 7th, when we left Charleston, General Smith placed four of our Company under arrest for getting drunk and getting into a fight with some of the 46 Georgia Regt. Three of them have been Discharged and came to Savannah last night. There is a great deal of sickness here, but our Batt. stands it better than any, we have but very few sick compared with others. The Yankees appear to have left the coast, except the Blockaders. Our Dashing Colonels Morgan and Forrest are in Kentucky, the Yankees are flying before them. A dispatch in this mornings Papers states that they have captured eleven cities and towns, with a large amount of provisions, horses, and mules. Our cause looks brighter up there. A large Force is reported to be marching on Nashville. Lincoln has called for three hundred thousand more troops, it is thought he will have to draft them to get them. In the meantime, our Army's on the move, but nobody appears to know where. We expect to have stirring times soon. No Country ever stood together with a more determined spirit for their rights than the South, as so far great confidence is placed in our Leaders.

Camp Van Dorn, August 1, 1862

I have just shook hands with five of our Company and our Capt., who are going home on a thirty day furlough in compliance with orders read at Dress Parade two or three evenings ago, that six Privates and one commissioned Officer from a Company at a time could get a ten day furlough. And as they are all Georgia troops here, but our Batt., ten days is long enough for them to go home, and to give our Batt. an equal chance, our Brig. General Mercer has given our Batt. thirty days to go home. The Yankees are not pressing us here now. It will give them that wish to go home a chance to do so, and be back again in the Fall when the Yankees will probably visit us again. The boys have been in the habit of running the blockade and going to town too much to suit the General, and orders were read to us last evening that no Private could not go to town with or without a pass, and the commissioned Officers would have to get a pass from the Commander of the camp. I do not believe it will stop it much. I was in town the other day and bought two undershirts and four pair of cotton socks for Eleven dollars, and that is cheap now. I bought a half a bushel of Irish potatoes about a week ago for Three dollars and twenty cents, and flour at Thirty dollars a barrel, and everything is up out of all reason. There has been some complaints among the Planters of Georgia on account of General Mercer calling for One-Thousand Negroes to work on the fortifications around Savannah. He did not get as many as was wanted, and had to issue orders for all Planters to furnish one Negro man for every five he had, and if he was not willing, to take him anyhow. I think they ought not to complain unless they want the Soldiers to do it all. Our Major received a letter from Col. Breasley a day or two ago stating that orders have been sent out to General Mercer, that if he could spare us, to send us to Richmond to form a Brig. with Major Wheat's Batt., but it is reported that he has refused to send us and I expect it is true. I believe all of us would like to form a Brigade, but I expect we have better times here than we would at Richmond. Our Guerrilla parties are alarming the Yankees in Tennessee and Kentucky. Bragg is suppose to be moving in that direction. I am on Guard today.

Camp Van Dorn, August 5, 1862

The following little piece of poetry made its appearance in Camp today, a little explanation will be necessary to understand it right. It is got up on Lieut. Doyle of the Franklin Life Guards, who did not stand firm at the James Island fight on the 16th of June, and has gained some notoriety for putting the boys in the Guardhouse for not walking their post on Guard. When he is Officer of the Guard, he puts on a great many airs and is disliked by the boys generally. He used to cause a good deal of amusement when he was a-drilling his Company, with his hand grasped around the hilt of his sword and the blade parallel with the ground. He would command them to left wheel, with all the customary remarks such as, Steady.... Steady.... On the pivot.... Come around like a gate now.... Hepp.... Hepp.... Hepp. The Fort Doyle that I am speaking of is, the boys that he had put in the Guardhouse, they gathered up some old camp kettles and mounted them in front of the Guardhouse, calling the Fort after him.

Latest From The War
The Last Fight at Secessionville!

We went to Secessionville — a disturbance to quell
Where the Yankees were storming our Batteries — In fact causing Hell
The boys all pitched in — as all who were brave
Not one of them flinching — and none of them caved
Except one Mr. Doyle — who stopped when he saw
Shot falling so fast — for want of sand in his craw
He turned on his pivot — swung around like a gate
And made strides from the field — from six foot to eight
He left in a hurry — and we all really suppose
His time is the fastest on record — yet nobody knows
He went to the Surgeon — and struck for a job
To act as Assistant — or be placed in a squad
The Surgeon was busy — and made no reply
So Doyle left the tent — another place to try
He left swift footed — and we saw him no more

Until the day was far spent — and the Battle was o'er
When he again turned on his pivot — swung around like a gate
Walked in to supper — sat down and ate
So in honor of him — we've erected Fort Doyle
Costing large sums of money — besides great toil
A gun shall be fired — at the raising of each can
In honor of Doyle — who at Secessionville ran
Now listen to me — take the advice of a friend
Be true to the Country — you've taken arms to defend
Let your motto be answered — and go straight ahead
Though you marched through blood — and stood on the dead
To onward it is — don't flinch nary time
Glory, honor, and victory — shall surely be thine
Be kind to the boys — and treat them all well
Or they'll blow up the Fort — and send you to Hell

PATRIOTIC

Camp Van Dorn, August 7th, Thursday

Colonel McEnery came back last Tuesday from Richmond, there is no prospect of our leaving here that I know of. Our living is worse now than it has been before for a long time. Together our allowance is, for one man per week: Four lbs. of flour, Two lbs. corn meal, Four lbs. fresh beef, One lb. of pork, Six pounds of sugar, Three ounces of coffee, One pint of molasses, and we can help our self to rice, but rice is not very good by itself and is used as the last resort. It is not quite half allowance. Our Officers started a Brass Band about a month ago, raised money enough by subscriptions to buy us the music instruments, and as many of the boys have been a-practicing and are learning fast. They say they will play in Dress Parade next Saturday evening. A teacher comes out from the city once or twice a day to teach them. There is about a hundred Negroes at work now throwing up very strong fortifications close to our camp.

Brigadier-General Hugh W. Mercer (courtesy of the Library Congress).

Camp Van Dorn, Wednesday, August 13th

A sad accident has happened to Mr. L. M. Young of our Company this morning. He was at a house just outside of our camp lines where a German family lives, and he being a German, was in the habit of going over there often. It appears that someone had fetched a Yankee twelve-pound conical shell that had not exploded to the family to see it. Young prepared to open it and clean it out, he had got about half the powder out, working at it near a fire in the yard, when the powder left in the shell ignited when holding it in his hand. The butt-end of the shell struck him in the groin. He lived about two hours in great pain. A wagon is just sent after a coffin. A Recruit arrived today from home to join our Company. Colonel McEnery is going home on a furlough tomorrow. A fine Negro Brass Band belonging to the 47th Georgia Regt., which is in camp about a quarter of a mile below us, gave us a serenade last Monday night. The weather is very hot here now, from seventy to a hundred degrees in the shade.

Camp Van Dorn, Wednesday, Aug. 20, 1862

There is a considerable of trouble in camp this morning between the boys and Major Buie. The Major, who the boys has no respect for and openly talk of him with a great deal of contempt on account of his behavior in the Battle of James Island, and since Col. McEnery went home, he has made his threats of what he is going to do, and boasted that he is going to make this a good Batt. by the time the Col. comes back again, and that we shall have to toe the mark. Now such talk as this is not received very well by men who fought and won the Battle at Secessionville, from one who should have led them on, instead of forming up excuses to stay behind. A day or two ago, he gave orders for Company Drill in the morning and Batt. Drill in the evening through the burning hot sun. The boys, not liking it very well, have not turned out to suit the Major. Last evening we fell in for Battn. Drill. We were drawn up on the Shell Road in front of our camp and counted off, and orders given to the Quartermaster to issue provisions only to those that are on drill or on duty, and about one-half of the Batt. has drawn no rations today. Some of the messes that drew seven or eight lbs. of fresh beef for fifteen or sixteen men, has took it back and gave it to the Major. Some refused to go on Guard today on account of having nothing to eat, so that the Guardhouse is full. There is about four hundred and fifty men in the Batt., but only about two hundred and fifty fit for duty. The rest are sick, but not any way dangerous. Pete White came into camp from the hospital last night. We have had some very cold weather the last two or three days, it rained last night and is cloudy this morning.

Thursday, 21st

Eight of our Company has been taken to the barracks this evening. There is from thirty to forty of our Battn. there now, charged with disobedience of orders.

Camp Van Dorn, Monday, August 25th

Two more of our Co. was taken to the barracks last Saturday morning, but the Commander there would not receive them, and sending a note to Buie telling him that he must take care of his own men.

Camp Van Dorn, Monday, Sept. 1st, 1862

The boys that has been home on furlough came back yesterday. Our Capt. has not come yet, expecting him today. Four new recruits came on with them. Our new Brass Band played on Dress Parade last Saturday evening for the first time. We had a Review and Muster yesterday. The weather is cool and pleasant today. I had a fever Saturday all day, all well again now. Capt. Powell has now arrived in camp, another lot is getting ready to go.

Camp Van Dorn, Saturday, Sept. 6

Five more of our Company, and with Lieut. Couch, started home on furlough last Thursday. Two of our Company were caught trying to steal whiskey last Wednesday morning about Three o'clock from the assistant Surgeon. They have been arrested and will, I suppose, wait trial. We was paid up to the first of the month last Thursday. We have good news from the West. The Yankees are flying before our Victorious Army, Washington is in great danger, terrible excitement in the North. They are beginning to think that Southern Soldiers, with such Officers as Lee, old Stonewall, and others at their head are not to be trifled with, although they are poor, naked, half-starved Rebels. Some of our tents have been condemned, and today have been furnished with some new ones.

Camp Walker, Tuesday, 9th, 1862

Our Company came here yesterday to guard a Battery of two guns. The Ouachita Blues have been here for some two or three weeks and we have come to relieve them. This is about a mile from our old camps. I believe we are now going to learn the Artillery Drill. The news continues to be good from the West.

Camp Walker, Monday, Sept. 15th, 1862

We have an easy time of it here, nothing to do but to stand guard. In one or two weeks we shall commence drilling, in a day or two. The worst of it is we don't get quite provisions enough to eat. We draw a half allowance only, we do not suffer much but feel as though we could eat a little more if we had it. It is expected that General Lee, at the head of a large army, crossed the Potomac and entered Maryland last Friday week.

Camp Walker, Tuesday 23rd, 1862

General Beauregard arrived in town last Saturday. I went to see him yesterday, but he had gone back to Charleston in the morning before I got in. There has been a terrible fight in Maryland, neither party got much the advantage. The Papers say this morning that Lee has recrossed the Potomac, but reports from there are so conflicting that it is hard to tell anything about it. One of our Battn. Company's, the Ouachita Blues, have been ordered to Fort Jackson, and will go tomorrow. What to do, I do not know. It has been raining the last two or three days, but it is clearing up a little today.

Camp Walker, Sunday, Sept. 28, 1862

General Beauregard took command of this department last Friday. The health of the troops is improving, very few of our Batt. now on the sick list. Capt. Powell drew a lot of over thirty pair of drawers for us yesterday. The prisoners captured at Fort Pulaski have been exchanged and arrived home a few days ago. They complain of bad treatment by the Yankees.

Camp Walker, Friday, Oct. 3, 1862

We are measured for a new pair of pants last Monday, Cost $12 per pair. Our coats are not here yet, the drawers and the shirts were give out to us last Tuesday. We had to pay 75 cents for a shirt and a Dollar for a pair of drawers. Our Capt. was put under arrest for our misbehavior in the city the same day. The Batt. has rather a bad name in Savannah. There is some in the Batt. that are of a wild, reckless character, and some of them are often in town on a spree and raising the Devil. A Court-Martial is now going on in town a-trying several of our boys for one thing and another. Two of our Company, the first time that either has been in trouble, were arrested last Tuesday for raising a fuss in the Pulaski House and breaking things generally. General Mercer was there at the time and has preferred charges against them. Those that were off on furlough returned yesterday. The other two, being detailed on detached service at home, they brought five new recruits. Colonel McEnery also came back the same day. Our overcoats and surplus blankets that were sent to Augusta last Spring has been sent for and are now in town. The overcoats will be in camp today, the blankets we will not want for a week or two. We have good tents to stay in, they are about seven feet square. They are intended for four to stay in and we have not got much room to spare. Three more of our Company started home on furlough this morning.

Savannah, Sunday, Oct. 12th

Nearly all the Carpenters in our Brigade has been detailed to build platforms and mount guns in the fortifications around the city. The details was made from our Company last Monday, but I, being sick with the Chills, did not go to work until Thursday morning. We get Two Dollars and a half per day and board ourselves in the city. It has been raining all the last week and we have not done much.

Savannah, Sunday, Oct. 19th

We are still a-working on the fortifications. We was a-paid Twenty Dollars apiece last night. Our Batt. has been under marching orders the last two or three days, I believe the order was countermanded yesterday. I think prospects look favorable for a peace this Winter. General Beauregard and a part of his Staff came here this evening.

Savannah, Sunday, Oct. 26th

Our Batt. serenaded Beauregard last Monday night. He came out and said a few words. He said he was not much of a speaker, but when he did speak, it was from the mouth of his cannon. He is still here. The Yankees are stirring us up again around the coast. They made an attack on the Charleston and Savannah Railroad last Monday. They got up to the road, but our troops were on them and drove them back before they done much damage. Our Batt. was sent to Coffy Bluff last Tuesday. It was thought the Yankees were going to land there, but they did not do it. Again I had an attack of the Chills, and of which lasted four or five days. I went to work last Thursday all right again. We are expecting an attack here at Charleston every day. We are preparing for it as much as possible, the city is considered safe by most of the people, but we can add a great deal to its strength in a few weeks more. Our Army's appear to be at a standstill in the North now. Bragg's Kentucky Campaign is considered a bad failure, and he has to stand the blame. [18]

Upon Pemberton's arrival in Vicksburg and subsequent inspection of the fortifications, he immediately realized that much work was yet to be done to strengthen the city to withstand the Union offensive that was sure to come. Pemberton also realized that on their encore visit, they would make sure to bring the required army support and not rely solely on the navy. The following four weeks were a whirlwind of activity as earthworks, batteries, and forts began to ring the Hill City as every soldier, slave, and able-bodied man able to use a pick and shovel was put to toil for defensive purposes. To the north of Vicksburg and overlooking the Yazoo, Snyder's Bluff was strongly fortified, while six miles below, batteries and earthworks stared menacingly from the bluffs at Warrenton. A strong line of rifle pits, earthworks, and redoubts ran through the hills in the rear of the city to impede a drive from the east, and houses were dismantled that happened to be in the line of fire of the batteries. Pemberton was taking no chances.

Back in Washington, Lincoln had received a visit from an old friend from Illinois in September named John Alexander McClernand, now a major-general in the volunteer Union army, courtesy of his friendship with Lincoln. Though he had no formal military training and was a "political general," the purpose of McClernand's visit was a topic dear to the president's heart: a plan to capture Vicksburg. The plan was simple enough: with Lincoln's permission, he would recruit an army in the midwest and after drilling them into tip-top fighting shape, he would lead that army in a decisive battle at Vicksburg, conquer the city, and free the Mississippi River from Rebel control. His would be an independent command, independent, that is, of the commander in whose military department he would be operating, one Major-General Ulysses Simpson Grant.

McClernand had served under Grant as a brigadier-general at Cairo, and Grant had found fault with his performance at Fort Donelson and Shiloh. To say that personal animosity existed between the two is an understatement, as they detested every inch of each other. Nevertheless, on October 20, 1862, Lincoln gave McClernand the green light to proceed with the plan.

But Grant was not sitting idle either, and was formulating his own plan to capture Vicksburg. Establishing his base on the river at Columbus, Kentucky, he had started a movement south on November 2 by gathering his 30,000-man force around the railway at Grand Junction, Tennessee, with the intention of pushing on to Holly Springs on the line of the Mississippi Central Railroad, which would also furnish his supplies and communications. If all went as planned, he would arrive in Jackson, Mississippi, a short forty-five miles to the east of Vicksburg. But Grant had several surprises in store for him.

Upon his arrival at Holly Springs, Grant realized that a two-hundred-mile-long supply line stretching back to Columbus would extend an invitation for Confederate cavalry to wreak havoc. Establishing his new base at Holly Springs, he immediately began to stockpile supplies there. Pemberton, hearing word of Grant's movements, had shifted his forces from Vicksburg and Jackson up to the Tallahatchie River in an attempt to impede any further progress. Finding his flank threatened by Union troops that had crossed the Mississippi River from Arkansas, Pemberton fell back sixty miles below the Tallahatchie to Grenada, Mississippi, located on the Yalobusha River. It was at this time that Grant received, courtesy of the Northern newspapers, reports of McClernand's expedition to capture Vicksburg. With great indignation, Grant telegraphed General-in-Chief Henry W. Halleck for an explanation, asking, "Am I to understand that I lie still here while an expedition is fitted out from Memphis, or do you want me to push south as far as possible?"[19] Halleck, also in the dark regarding McClernand's plan, and very much angered by the plot that was hatched behind his back, wired back to Grant, "You have command of all troops sent to your department, and have permission to fight the enemy where you please."[20] That was all the leeway the chain-smoking Union general needed to derail his nemesis McClernand's grab for glory.

Newly promoted Admiral David Porter now confirmed to Grant that the troops of

McClernand's command were daily streaming through Cairo, Illinois, on their way to Memphis, the base of the operation, while McClernand was in Illinois preparing to marry his former sister-in-law on December 23. At this point, Grant contacted his most trusted lieutenant, Major-General William T. Sherman, instructing him to proceed to Memphis, and with the assistance of Porter's fleet, commandeer the expedition and troops from under McClernand, and proceed down the Mississippi River. With the assistance of Porter's gunboats, Sherman could land below Snyder's Bluff on the Yazoo River and assault the city from the north, while Grant kept Pemberton and the bulk of his Confederate forces occupied at Grenada, leaving Vicksburg defended by the lone division of Major-General Martin L. Smith.

The evening of McClernand's wedding found Sherman on the Mississippi River a few miles below Helena with his "hijacked" army, preparing to execute his portion of Grant's master plan. But Sherman was unaware that the plan had gone terribly awry, and that fate had hoisted the banner of the Confederacy, aided by two of the South's most able cavalry leaders, Earl Van Dorn and Nathan Bedford Forrest.

Pemberton had instructed Van Dorn, his chief of cavalry, to proceed to Holly Springs and play smash with Grant's supply depot. Arriving in the early morning hours of December 20 with his 3,500 horsemen, Van Dorn found the depot garrisoned by 1,500 Wisconsin and Illinois troops under the command of Colonel Robert C. Murphy of the Eighth Wisconsin Infantry. Storming into the town from multiple directions and bagging the sleepy garrison, Van Dorn applied the torch to the provisions, ammunition, trains, wagons, and storage sheds that were to supply Grant in his foray against Vicksburg. In Van Dorn's estimate, some $1,500,000 worth of Union supplies went up in smoke, along with Grant's ability to wage a campaign in Mississippi. But this was only half of Grant's supply problem. Pemberton had requested from General Braxton Bragg in Tennessee that an auxiliary cavalry raid be made on Grant's supply line running from Columbus. Bragg sent none other than Nathan Bedford Forrest to see what he could do to aid Pemberton. Leading his force of 2,500 hardened cavalry through middle Tennessee in mid–December, Forrest routed Union forces near Lexington before striking the railroad between Jackson, Tennessee, and Columbus. Forrest incinerated depots, trestles, and bridges, in addition to tearing up sixty miles of track and destroying the telegraph line on the route. In short, it would be a long time before the Union army received supplies down the rail line from Columbus.

Grant, with no supplies courtesy of Van Dorn, and no way to replace them courtesy of Forrest, had no choice but to fall back from Grenada to Grand Junction, a move that would free Pemberton and his forces to return to Vicksburg. Cut off from communication with Sherman, Grant was unable to order Sherman to abort the assault on the Vicksburg bluffs, an assault that he now knew was doomed to disaster. Sherman would not find the lone division of Martin L. Smith to contend with, but the whole of Pemberton's army.

As the armada carrying Sherman's fleet steamed up the Yazoo, Pemberton was alerted to their presence and had his men under arms and manning the fortifications. The day after Christmas 1862, Sherman landed 30,000 blue-clad soldiers, composing four divisions, at the Johnston Plantation at the mouth of Chickasaw Bayou and began making his way inland from the Yazoo to the bluffs. Dividing his forces, Sherman sent the two divisions of Brigadier-General Morgan Lewis Smith and Brigadier-General Andrew Jackson Smith to the right toward Vicksburg as a feint to draw off the gray-clad defenders in the center of the Confederate line, opposite the triangular fork of Chickasaw Bayou, where the main assault would take place. The assault in the center would be led by Brigadier-General George Washington Morgan's division, supported by the division of Major-General Frederick Steele. On December 28, the assault was launched as Morgan's troops reached the fork in Chickasaw Bayou. For seven hours they pounded the Confederate rifle pits to no avail. Darkness mercifully brought an end to the attack, but it resumed the next day, with the same frightful results for the Federals. By the time Sherman threw in the towel, the Union army had suffered a dreadful 1,779 casualties, compared to 187 for the Confederates. Sherman's simplistic after-action report summed up the futility of what would become known as the Battle of Chickasaw Bayou:

> I reached Vicksburg at the time appointed, landed, assaulted and failed, reembarked my command unopposed and turned it over to my successor.[21]

His "successor" was none other than McClernand, who upon discovering his army missing upon his arrival at Memphis, had hurried down the river in pursuit, catching up with Sherman after the Chickasaw Bayou debacle at the mouth of the Yazoo. Sherman, being McClernand's junior in rank, had no choice but to relinquish command of the troops to the newlywed general, at least until his benefactor, General Grant, could arrive to assume command.

While these events were transpiring in Mississippi, Private McNeil was still dutifully recording the events of the war in his journal:

> Coffee Bluff, Sunday, Nov. 16, 1862
> We worked on the breastworks up to last Thursday night. Then twelve, all from our Batt., was sent out to help build a bridge, we are now getting out the timber. We get two days time for working Sunday. Our Batt. is formed into a Brigade with other Regt.'s under Colonel Harrison, acting Brigadier. Yesterday, they all moved camp to the Brigade camp near the jail. Mr. Butler, our Paymaster, gave us Ten Dollars a piece last Thursday.

> Coffee Bluff, Sunday, Nov. 23, 1862
> We are still at work a-getting out the timber. We will have it out, I expect, by Tuesday. We have to get all our provisions from Savannah, which causes us some trouble.

> Coffee Bluff, Sunday, Nov. 30th, 1862
> We have finished getting timber, and have got it near formed. We fixed the foundation for the bridge, which was done at low tide by building cribs on each side and filling it in with Oyster Shells. It is about seventy feet long and runs from the Mainland across to Rosedew Island. They are building a Battery on the island to command the Ogechee River. The Yankees are in the habit of running up this river, shelling the country for two or three miles around. On Friday, the 21st, they came up and threw shells at Genesis Point nearly all day, but only wounded three men. Our guns did not reply, they being too short-range. This Battery, if the Yankees do not shell us out before it is done, is expected to stop their fun and not to let them have it long their own way.

> Coffee Bluff, Monday, Dec. 8th
> We have nearly finished the bridge. Two of our men are in the woods sawing with a lot of men detailed from two Company's stationed here as Pickets, a-scaring timber for the Magazine to be built on the island. We have not received any money since we have been down here, and we have some trouble in getting provisions, but we have been promised some this week. There is no news from any part for some time. The great Yankee Army and Arty. that is to take all our seaport cities has not yet made its appearance, and the news from our Army's in the West is pretty good, and they have been greatly reinforced since our last Battles, and being commanded by the gallant Lee, we are assured the results.

> Coffee Bluff, Dec. 14th, 1862
> We finished the bridge today, all except putting up a handrail and spiking a few planks. We shall commence on the Magazine, I expect next Tuesday. Mr. Butler was down here last Friday and paid us up to the first of the month, except our Sunday work that we have to get through the Engineers.

> Coffee Bluff, Wednesday, Dec. 17th, 1862
> Our Batt. left with Harrison's Brig. last Sunday evening. I am not certain where they are going, but it is expected they are gone to Goldsboro, North Carolina. I was in town last Monday and bought a pair of common shoes for Eighteen Dollars. Commenced on the Magazine today.

> Coffee Bluff, Sunday, Dec. 21st
>
> We have gained a great Victory at Fredericksburg, it is expected that we killed twenty thousand Yankees. We have had to quit the Magazine to build two cribs, twenty-five feet square, to make one end of the road that sinks on to the bridge, the tide keeps washing the dirt away. The tide is very high this morning. We have not worked any this forenoon, but I believe will work this afternoon. The wind is blowing hard and very cold.
>
> Coffee Bluff, Saturday, Dec. 27th
>
> I cut my leg last Tuesday with the edge, but it was not bad. I only lost one day by it, it is healing up fast. We had some fine Eggnog at Christmas Day. Four of our squad went to town to spend Christmas and have not got back yet. I have had a fever today and have not been able to work. Our Batt. is at Wilmington, North Carolina.
>
> Coffee Bluff, Sunday, January 4, 1863
>
> Four of our squad was ordered to town last Thursday to work around the city somewhere. It leaves eight of us here now. We are now getting Three Dollars a day since the first of January, and Four Dollars for Sunday, but our work is over with the first work, and it is not necessary to work Sundays, so we are not to work today.
>
> Coffee Bluff, Sunday, Jan. 11th, 1863
>
> We have our large Magazine done, and a small one all done but the roof. We finished a covered passway this forenoon, thirty-five feet long, which runs from the Magazine to the Gun. Two Yankee steamers came up the river last Friday at noon within about a mile of our work. We all quit work and hid our tools in the woods. Expected that the Yankees had found us out, but they went back again without firing a gun. We shall have some guns up next week if all goes well.
>
> Coffee Bluff, Sunday, Jan. 18th, 1863
>
> We have got everything ready for four guns. One gun, a sixty-inch rifled, came out today and will be mounted tomorrow.
>
> Coffee Bluff, Sunday, January 25th
>
> We mounted the rifled guns last Monday, some ammunition came out here last Thursday. We have been in the woods getting out timber for another Battery on another point of the island. We expect another gun down here tomorrow. I received Twenty Dollars from Butler last Friday. We have had beautiful weather ever since we came here.
>
> Coffee Bluff, Tuesday, Jan. 27th
>
> A Yankee Gunboat and four vessels came up the big Ogechee and opened a vigorous fire on Fort McAllister at Genesis Point at daylight this morning, which continued until about Two o'clock, when the vessels went back. We had a fine view of the firing from our Battery. It was sharp work for a while, the Gunboat running up within good range. Another rifled gun for our Battery came out this evening. We was paid up to the third of January yesterday, except our Sunday work. We have not got paid for that yet.
>
> Coffee Bluff, Sunday, Feb. 1st, 1863
>
> The Yankees attacked Fort McAllister again this morning. The firing was very rapid until about One o'clock. One of their Monitors, being about a mile from the Battery and four wooden boats laying off at long-range, throwing shells. At about One o'clock, the Monitor came back to the other boats, all falling out of range. There was no one hurt on our side last Tuesday and the Battery not much damaged. We are done getting out timber and will commence hauling tomorrow.[22]

Upon assuming command of the army from Sherman, McClernand had no plans as to what to do with it. Sherman, however, eager to redeem himself after the humiliating repulse at Chickasaw Bayou, did have a plan. Twenty miles up the Arkansas River lay a Confederate outpost known as the Post of Arkansas, which was garrisoned by some 5,000 troops under the command of Brigadier-General Thomas James Churchill. Sherman's plan called for attacking the fort with 10,000 Union troops and the aid of Porter's gunboats. McClernand liked the plan so well he took it over for himself. On January 10, Porter's gunboats began shelling the fort, and on the following day after an assault by the corps of Sherman and Morgan, the fort surrendered, though the price tag was high. Confederate losses were pegged at 150 killed and wounded, compared to a ghastly 1,060 for the Federal forces.[23]

In his after-action report, McClernand totally ignored the role of Porter and his fleet in reducing the fort. Outraged, Porter and Sherman sent a communication to Grant, with whom contact was now restored, demanding that, according to Grant, he "come and take command in person, and expressing distrust of McClernand's ability and fitness." As Grant concluded, "Nothing was left, therefore, but to assume the command myself."[24] On January 30, 1863, Grant arrived at Young's Point on the Mississippi River and assumed command. McClernand undertook a wild letter-writing campaign accusing Grant of "creating confusion," Stanton of betrayal, and Halleck of "willful contempt and utter incompetency." It got him nowhere. McClernand was made a corps commander under Grant and instructed by Lincoln to "confine his attention to the common goal of Union harmony and victory."[25]

Grant still believed the key to taking Vicksburg was to get his troops below the city, but Mother Nature had enlisted in Confederate service. The heavy rains during the winter of 1862–1863 had risen the Mississippi and its tributaries to flood stage, compelling Grant's army to camp along the levees within Milliken's Bend. Grant then attempted what can only be described as a series of engineering "experiments." The first was a continuation of the canal digging operation that General Williams and his forces had started upon their arrival with Farragut's fleet in 1862. Thousands of Sherman's troops began to resume the excavation at the abandoned canal project to bypass Vicksburg, before throwing in the towel in March. At the same time, Union troops began a canal project at Duckport, Louisiana, in an effort to connect with a winding channel through the myriad of Louisiana bayous before reentering the Mississippi River some twenty miles below the Hill City. A sudden drop in the water level in mid–April would see towel number two thrown in. The next scheme would see the troops of Union Major-General James Birdseye McPherson put to task to clear a 350 mile channel from Lake Providence, Louisiana, into a maze of bayous that ran to the Red River. The idea was that once the channel was complete, they could steam down the Red River aboard transports, cross the Mississippi, and land south of Vicksburg. Though Grant let work continue on this project, it was more to keep his troops busy, thus allowing less time for introspection on how they were getting nowhere fast.

Even Porter got in on the act, hoping to find a passable route eastward from the Mississippi to the Yazoo River, with the idea that transports could steam south and deliver the army behind Vicksburg. At a point 325 miles upriver from Vicksburg, the Mississippi and Coldwater rivers were separated by a mere 10 miles, and Union scouts had reported that light-draught ships could navigate the Coldwater and proceed south to the Tallahatchie River before entering the Yazoo and landing on the dry land above Vicksburg. Engineers opened a cut in the eighteen-foot-thick levee to clear an old channel called the Yazoo Pass to the Mississippi. The reasoning was that if the Yazoo Pass could be cleared, the Union Army would have a route open to take Vicksburg. Pemberton then begun a bit of counter-engineering to foil the latest of Grant's experiments, instructing his men to begin obstructing the channel. Grant still managed to advance a few miles each day until they neared the Yazoo, only to find a Confederate outpost manning thirteen guns placed on a narrow 500-yard spit of land, aptly named Fort Pemberton, under the command of Major-General William W. Loring. Though several attempts were made to reduce the fort by naval firepower, all ended in failure, compelling Grant to reach into his rapidly dwindling supply of towels once more and throw in another.

Last, but not least, of the Union experiments was the ill-fated Steele's Bayou Expedition that was concocted jointly by Grant and Porter. A twisting, turning route of two hundred miles through Steele's Bayou led to the Yazoo above the Haynes Bluff Confederate fortifications. Porter committed a considerable portion of his fleet to the expedition, before becoming entangled on March 19 in the log- and willow-filled bayou, encountering Confederate sharpshooters who drove his crews inside the vessels to escape a certain death. But the welcoming party the Confederates had planned for Porter was just beginning. Rebel axe-men began felling trees ahead of, and behind, the trapped fleet in an effort to further entrap the Union gunboats. Finding a bayou-savvy slave, Porter paid the man to carry a message to Sherman, who arrived just in time to save the Navy vessels from certain destruction or capture. Sherman later recalled with a certain wicked humor that "I doubt if he [Porter] was ever more glad to meet a friend than he was to see me."[26] Thus concluded the great Union engineering experiments of 1863, with Vicksburg still standing as defiant as ever in the face of Lincoln's military might.

While the experiments were being conducted in Louisiana and Mississippi, Private McNeil recorded the events unfolding on the Atlantic Coast:

Coffee Bluff, Sunday, Feb. 15th, 1863

We have got through here and are going to another job tomorrow somewhere about six miles from Savannah. We have built a Battery of four guns and a Mortar Battery. There is but two guns mounted yet, and the dirt work of the Mortar Battery is not finished, nor will not be for a month. Our Batt. came back from North Carolina last Tuesday the 10th.

ThunderBolt, Sunday, Feb. 22nd

Came down here last Friday, we have a large bomb-proof to build. We are expecting an attack here any day. There was a General Review in the city last Friday. General Beauregard and Staff were there. We have a Battery here of nine heavy guns, it commands the Thunderbolt River, which runs into Warsaw Sound. Beauregard has ordered the women and children to leave the city.

ThunderBolt, Sunday, March 1st, 1863

This is the day the Yankees were to make the attack, but it is now about Eleven o'clock and no firing is heard yet. It is reported this morning that a small force of the Yankees landed on Wilmington Island last night. The Nashville, trying to run out of the Ogechee yesterday, ran aground and was burned to keep from falling into the hands of the Enemy. We are getting out timber for the Bombproof. It takes a little over three-thousand feet line measure. We have built ourselves a log shanty, we are pretty comfortable. I drew a pair of shoes from the Company on Friday.

ThunderBolt, Sunday, March 8th, 1863

The Yankees attacked Fort McAllister with three Ironclads last Tuesday, and continued until Eleven this morning when the Yankees left, and have not been heard from since. Very little damage done to the Fort, all is quiet here now. I have nine Negroes getting out timber in the woods, the rest are framing the Bombproof. One of our squad is going to town to try to get money or provisions. We have not been paid off for so long that we are out of money and can not get provisions, and unless some arrangement be made, we shall go back to our Company tomorrow.

Sunday, March 15th, 1863

We are now drawing rations from the Government, no money has came yet. All is quiet here now, expecting an attack at Charleston this week. Commenced to draw rations on Monday, March 9th. General Taliaferro is in command of our Brigade, he has been in command of Stonewall Jackson's old Brig.

Tuesday, March 24th, 1863

The Gunboat Atlanta, joined by the Fingal, came down the river last Friday. The Charleston, a small steamer, ran out through the blockade last Saturday night. Our squad was paid up to the 1st of March last Saturday. I received One-Hundred and Sixty One Dollars. F. Vollman, one of our squad, went home on furlough yesterday. Our Batt. drew a new uniform last Sunday, furnished by the Government. It is over time whether we shall get one or not. A small schooner came in through the blockade this morning. General Taliaferro is in command of our Brigade.

Thunder Bolt, Sunday, March 29th

The Negroes that were to work here were all discharged last week, we expect a new lot here within a week or two. I was on board the Fingal, which is still laying off our Battery this morning. Our scouts captured eight Yankees last Monday night.

Sunday, April 5th

The detailed squad cannot draw a uniform from the Government. We shall commence to raise the Bombproof tomorrow. The Fingal left here last week. All is quiet here now, no firing being heard for several days. Our Batt. is ordered to Charleston, they will leave tonight.

Sunday, April 12th

The Yankees attacked Charleston last Tuesday afternoon about Three o'clock. We sunk one of their strongest Gunboats, the Keokuk, she having two turrets, and caught these Devils and a nondescript they had for removing torpedoes, when all the fleet fell back out of range, more or less damaged, and have not come up since.

Thursday, April 23rd, 1863

The Yankees have not come up to fire at Charleston yet, and it is doubtful whether to try it again or not. I was in town last Saturday and bought a common hat for Ten Dollars. We have finished all we can do to the Bombproof today until we get help to put on the covering logs. The State has failed to furnish Negroes to finish the work. Our Batt. came back from Charleston last Sunday. We was paid up last Saturday to the 28 of March, $70.50.[27]

Grant's string of failures had not discouraged him in his determination to capture Vicksburg, and with this determination came a radical new strategy that would again require the assistance of Porter and his fleet. Ordering McClernand to march with his corps on the western bank of the Mississippi through Louisiana to the town of New Carthage, some twenty miles below Vicksburg, Grant envisioned that the force could be moved across the river to overrun the Warrenton batteries, or even the fortifications at Grand Gulf, before returning to assault Vicksburg. The catch was that the troops would be useless at New Carthage without a naval force to ferry them across the river, and the only way to get a naval force there was to run by the fire of the Vicksburg batteries.

Porter agreed to make the attempt but laid bare one fact, that this was an all-or-nothing proposition due to the river itself. Once below the city, if they made it, his fleet would be unable to return past the batteries due to the fact his ships would only make two knots against the current, and would be subjected to a certain death from the Vicksburg artillery. In short, this was the point of no return. But Grant was out of options, and the end of March saw McClernand and an advance contingent of his corps at Milliken's Bend, ready to make the march to New Carthage.

On the night of April 16, Porter was ready to run the Vicksburg gauntlet with eight warships and three transports. As they approached the frowning bluffs of Vicksburg at 11:16 P.M., musket fire rang out and illumination fires were lit on the banks of the river. The fleet had been spotted by Confederate pickets. Next came the ear-splitting roar of cannon fire as the first of Vicksburg's thirty-four heavy artillery pieces roared to life. When the smoke had cleared at midnight, the fleet, minus one transport and three barges, had successfully ran the gauntlet. By daybreak of April 17, Porter and his ships had reached New Carthage, and a jubilant Grant, unable to restrain himself, had his horse brought to him and rode the forty circuitous miles to offer his congratulations to Porter in person on overcoming the first obstacle to wresting control of the Rebel citadel from the clutches of Jeff Davis.[28]

On April 20, Grant issued Special Order Number 110, outlining his plan for gaining a foothold on the east bank of the Mississippi River. The march through Louisiana would proceed with McClernand's corps in the lead position, McPherson in the middle, and Sherman in the rear. Confederate Brigadier-General John Stevens Bowen, at the Grand Gulf fortifications with his Missouri brigade, notified Pemberton on April 27 that "all the movements of the enemy during the last twenty-four hours seem to indicate an intention on their part to march their army still lower down in Louisiana ... then to run their steamers by me and across."[29] Arriving at New Carthage on April 23, Grant found the area mostly underwater and correctly deduced that to attempt to use this area as a staging ground for his invasion would be folly. After a reconnaissance of the surrounding areas, Grant decided the jumping-off point for his invasion would be a small community aptly named Hard Times, located around the bend in the river from Grand Gulf. The plan agreed upon by Grant and Porter was for the navy to silence the Grand Gulf batteries while the army made its assault crossing. The date for the joint operation was set for April 29.

At 7:00 A.M., Porter and his fleet engaged the Grand Gulf batteries in a scorching artillery duel that lasted until 1:00 P.M. with no clear-cut victor. Conferring with Grant aboard the *Benton*, it was decided that Grant would march his men farther downstream where they could reembark on the transports, cross the river, and storm the batteries from the rear. At dusk, Porter reengaged the Grand Gulf batteries in an attempt to screen the transports while they slipped downstream to ferry the army across the river. Whether due to weariness on the part of Confederate gunners or a newfound respect for the navy guns, the transports passed Grand Gulf unhurt. Grant now changed his plans once more and decided to cross the river at the town of Bruinsburg, where a good road ran twelve miles to Port Gibson. On April 30 at 8:00 A.M., the invasion fleet cast off, and by noon most of the 17,000 troops of McClernand's corps had landed unopposed, followed by the corps of McPherson, with Sherman on the way. The greatest amphibious crossing in American history to date was right on schedule.[30]

General Bowen realized that to impede the Federal army in its march toward Vicksburg, he would have to redeploy his available troops to Grand Gulf to supplant the forces of Brigadier-General Martin Edwin Green, who commanded the forces there. Both generals were in agreement to place their troops, in addition to the 5,000 reinforcements Pemberton had sent from Vicksburg, to defend the two roads leading to Grand Gulf, the Bruinsburg and Rodney roads, along which Grant's army would march, and await the arrival of the invaders. They did not wait long, for shortly after midnight on May 1 the brigade of Iowans under the command of Colonel William M. Stone fired the first volley of what would be known as the Battle of Port Gibson.

Stone, joined by McClernand at 2:00 A.M., broke off the engagement until he could apprise the situation by the light of day. A short time after 6:30 A.M., the battle began in earnest with an artillery duel involving the Botetourt Artillery of Virginia with their twelve-pounder Napoleons and the Seventh Michigan Battery with ten-pounder Rodman rifles. For the next twelve hours, fewer than 7,000 determined Confederates held their own against a Union force that eventually totaled 24,000. But the overwhelming Union numbers eventually carried the day, and Bowen and his forces were forced to retreat behind Bayou Pierre, burning the bridge behind them. Grant's bridgehead over the Mississippi River was now secure.

On May 1, Pemberton had notified President Davis of Grant's crossing of the river and the defeat of General Bowen in the subsequent battle at Port Gibson. The following day, Confederate Secretary of War James Alexander Seddon wired General Beauregard in Charleston that "Advices show the enemy abandoning their attacks on the eastern coasts and concentrating great forces on the Mississippi. Send with utmost dispatch 8,000 or 10,000 men, including those ordered heretofore to Tullahoma, to General Pemberton's relief."[31] Beauregard responded on

May 4 by assembling a brigade at Charleston consisting of the Forty-Sixth Georgia Infantry under Colonel Peyton H. Colquitt, Sixteenth South Carolina Infantry under Colonel James McCullough, Twenty-Fourth South Carolina Infantry under Colonel Clement H. Stevens, Eighth Georgia Battalion under Captain Z. L. Watters, and Ferguson's South Carolina Battery under Captain Thomas B. Ferguson. This brigade was placed under the command of Brigadier-General States Rights Gist. In addition, Beauregard called on the Savannah brigade of Brigadier-General William Henry Talbot Walker, consisting of the Twenty-Fifth Georgia Infantry, Twenty-Ninth Georgia Infantry, Thirtieth Georgia Infantry, First Georgia Sharpshooter Battalion, Martin's Georgia Battery, and the Fourth Louisiana Battalion, detached from Harrison's Brigade and assigned to Walker's Brigade. Beauregard wired Pemberton on May 6 that the 5,000-strong detachment, men he considered his best troops, were on the way.[32]

The two brigades began departing for central Mississippi on May 5, 1863, via the dilapidated, and fragmentary, rail lines. As the rundown cars made their way through Georgia and into Alabama, the first snag on the journey for the Fourth Louisiana Battalion was encountered at Montgomery. With no direct rail connection between there and Selma, the only rail route to Meridian, Mississippi, was by taking an immense detour by way of the Alabama and Florida Railroad to Mobile, Alabama, and then connecting with the Mobile and Ohio Railroad to Meridian. Gist's Brigade detrained at Montgomery and boarded steamers for the trip to Selma, while Walker's Brigade, the first to arrive at Montgomery, clenched their teeth and endured the harrowing, and roundabout, journey aboard the cars.[33] From Meridian westward, progress was further slowed by a lack of locomotives and cars due to their being impressed by the Confederate and state authorities in an attempt to remove the war materials and public property from Jackson, Mississippi, to points of greater safety.[34] The bright spots of the journey for the troops crowded into the wooden boxcars and flatcars was the frequent stops of the trains, where they were greeted by the civilian populace waving handkerchiefs and flags and patriotically cheering them on in their journey to do battle with the Lincoln vandals. The soldiers responded energetically, waving their hats and cheering heartily, before the bone-jarring and death-defying journey of travel on a Confederate railroad resumed.[35]

In Savannah, Private McNeil, still detached on engineering duty at Battery Thunderbolt, recorded the events leading up to the Fourth Louisiana Battallion's departure for the approaching showdown in Mississippi:

Sunday, May 3rd
We are now to work on a Magazine. We were paid up to last night, 88 Dollars and 50 cents. We are expecting stirring news from all quarters every day.

Thunder Bolt, Tuesday, May 5th
Our Batt. received orders to go to Jackson, Miss. yesterday, they left this afternoon. We have been up to see them off and have just got back. General Lee has gained another Victory over the Yankees at Fredericksburg and captured ten thousand prisoners.

Sunday, May 10
F. Vollman got back last Thursday. It is reported that we captured fifty-three pieces of cannon at Fredericksburg. General Stonewall Jackson died today from wounds received at Fredericksburg by his own men through a mistake. It has caused a sad gloom over the Country. General Van Dorn was killed at Tullahoma through intimacy with another man's wife.[36]

Pemberton had other help on the way as well, in the form of a man who was considered the second best general in all the Confederacy, General Joseph Eggleston Johnston, a career military man. Although weakened by a month long illness at the headquarters of Braxton Bragg's Army of Tennessee in Tullahoma, upon receiving an order from Secretary of War Seddon on May 9 to report to Mississippi and assume "chief command of the forces, giving to those in the field, as far as practicable, the encouragement and benefit of your personal direction," Johnston dutifully boarded a train the following day and begun the arduous journey to Jackson.[37] May 13 saw Johnston at Lake Station, some fifty miles from Jackson, where he received a telegram from Pemberton dated May 12 outlining the rapidly deteriorating situation in his department.[38]

After beginning his advance on May 7, Grant had sent his forces forward with McClernand paralleling the Big Black River, Sherman in the middle, and McPherson on the eastern flank moving toward the crossroads at the town of Raymond. Here on May 12, elements of McPherson's corps would fight the Battle of Raymond against the Confederate brigade of Brigadier-General John Gregg, a native of Texas. Though a hard-fought and vicious battle, Confederate casualties were 515 versus 442 for McPherson, once again sheer numbers carried the day, and Gregg's battered brigade retired through Raymond toward Jackson.[39] Grant had won another victory in his march toward the Confederate Gibraltar.

Joseph E. Johnston (courtesy of the Library of Congress).

Upon Johnston's arrival in Jackson, he established his headquarters at the Bowman House and conferred with General Gregg regarding the situation in Mississippi. Gregg advised Johnston that ten miles to the west, four of Sherman's divisions now occupied Clinton. To oppose them, Johnston had 6,000 men composed of Mississippi militia, Gregg's own brigade, and the advance elements of Walker's and Gist's brigades, though when, on May 14, the entire force that Beauregard had sent arrived, as well as a brigade from Port Hudson commanded by Brigadier-General Samuel Bell Maxey, he would then have a force totaling 12,000. Johnston immediately wired Richmond of his assessment of the events transpiring in the president's home state: "I arrived this evening, finding the enemy's force between this place and General Pemberton, cutting off the communication. I am too late."[40] Johnston then ordered the capital city of Mississippi evacuated to the northeast toward Canton, and ordered Gregg to cover the evacuation. Johnston also sent three copies of a dispatch to Pemberton by the same amount of couriers that stated the news of his arrival and the occupation of Clinton by the Federals. Johnston pointed out the necessity of establishing communications between Vicksburg and Jackson, and advised Pemberton to, if practicable, strike the four divisions at Clinton. Johnston was unaware that one of his couriers was a Union spy who would deliver his message into the hands of General McPherson.[41]

At 3:00 A.M. on the morning of May 14, Gregg instructed Colonel Peyton H. Colquitt, commanding the advance units of Gist's Brigade, to march his command out of Jackson on the Clinton Road to impede the Union advance on Mississippi's capital city. Stopping three miles northwest of the center of Jackson, Gregg instructed Colquitt to post his men on the O. P. Wright farm astride the Jackson-Clinton Road. Five companies of the Forty-Sixth Georgia Infantry and a battalion of the Fourteenth Mississippi Infantry were posted on the right of the road which was covered by a thick growth of oak, with the Twenty-Fourth South Carolina Infantry and the four rifled guns of the Brookhaven Light Artillery posted on the left along a prolongation of a ridge.[42] The Fourteenth Mississippi and Brookhaven Artillery were on loan from Brigadier-General John Adams's Fourth Military District and had been summoned to augment Johnston's forces. General Walker's command, now consisting of the Thirtieth Georgia Infantry, First Georgia Sharpshooter Battalion, Martin's Georgia Battery, Third Kentucky Mounted Infantry, and the Fourth Louisiana Battalion Infantry, were marched out of Jackson behind Colquitt's troops. Stopping two miles outside of the city but within easy supporting distance of Colquitt's force, Gregg instructed Walker to remain at this position in preparedness to move to Colquitt's assistance should reinforcements be needed.[43] All the while, a torrential downpour was drenching the gray-clad soldiers.

Gregg notified his own brigade, under the temporary command of Colonel Robert Farquharson, to stay prepared to march at a moment's notice where needed. Gregg completed his arrangements by moving the troops belonging to the First Battalion of Mississippi State Troops into the partially finished earthworks covering the approaches to the city. They were assisted by civilian volunteers who would also help man the seventeen pieces of artillery mounted in the ill-prepared fortifications.[44]

On the night of May 13, Grant had established his headquarters near Raymond at the residence of John B. Peyton, where he energetically planned his moves for the next day, sending his orders to Sherman, McClernand, and McPherson. McClernand was instructed to have his troops on the march by 4:00 A.M. and to "Move one division of your corps through to Clinton, charging it with destroying the railroad as far as possible. Move another division three or four miles beyond Mississippi Springs ... and a third to Raymond, ready to support either of the others."[45] Sherman and McPherson were ordered to begin advances on Jackson at dawn. Upon receipt of their orders from Grant, McPherson and Sherman made arrangements to coordinate their marches so as to arrive at Jackson simultaneously. McPherson also alerted Sherman of the arrival of Joe Johnston, a soldier held in respect even in the blue-clad ranks, and warned, "They have fortified on the different roads on this side, and are forming abatis."[46]

McPherson's corps made the move toward Jackson at 5:00 A.M. in a heavy rain that caused the infantry to be called upon numerous times to push caissons, wagons and ambulances through the bottomless pit of mud that formerly was known as a road. Upon crossing the right of way of the Southern Railroad two miles east of Clinton, Lieutenant-Colonel Leonidas Horney of the Tenth Missouri shook out an advanced guard consisting of Company C, under the command of Captain Charles A. Gilchrist, with Companies I and D in support.[47] At 9:00 A.M., they eyed Colquitt's force positioned on a ridge approximately 1¼ miles in the distance, and the brigade of Colonel Samuel A. Holmes was deployed with the Seventeenth Iowa Infantry, under the command of Colonel David B. Hillis, anchored with its left on the railroad and its right on the Clinton-Jackson Road; the Eightieth Ohio Infantry, under the command of Colonel Matthias H. Bartilson, positioned to the right of the road; and the Tenth Missouri, in line of battle, to the right of the Eightieth Ohio.[48] The deployment of Holmes brigade was conducted under a heavy shelling, courtesy of the Brookhaven Artillery, which had opened fire upon the realization that they had been spotted by the Union advance guard. The Federals responded by bringing up the four 10-pounder Parrott rifles of Company M of the First Missouri Light Artillery and placing three of the guns on a ridge between the W. T. Mann home on the left and an old cotton gin to the right, before placing the remaining piece between the Clinton-Jackson Road and the Mann home.[49] The remaining two brigades of Brigadier-General Marcellus Monroe Crocker's division were brought up in support of Holmes. McPherson, upon receiving the intelligence that the Confederates were in his front, ordered Brigadier-General John Alexander Logan to press forward to Crocker's assistance as quickly as the roads would allow.[50]

The lead elements of Sherman's corps had departed Mississippi Springs promptly at 5:00 A.M. as well, before being overtaken by Grant and his staff, who made their headquarters with the Fifteenth Corps for the rest of the day, while scouts of the Fourth Iowa Cavalry screened the line of march to Jackson. Brigadier-General James Madison Tuttle's division, in the van of the column, had Brigadier-General Joseph Anthony Mower's brigade in the lead, followed by the two light artillery batteries of the Second Iowa Battery and Company E of the First Illinois Light Artillery, and then the brigades of Brigadier-General Charles "Karl" Leopold Matthies and Brigadier-General Ralph Pomeroy Buckland.[51] As the corps closed in on Jackson, the thunder of the artillery duel on the Clinton-Jackson Road began to roll through the ranks of Sherman's men. Five miles from Mississippi Springs, three companies of the Fifth Minnesota Infantry, composing the advance guard of Sherman's corps, were brought up short while attempting to make their way down a slope to the Lynch Creek Bridge. On the other side of the rain-swollen, unfordable creek, a large force consisting of the Third Kentucky Mounted Infantry, the First Georgia Sharpshooter Battalion, and four guns of Martin's Georgia Battery had been ordered out to the position to delay Sherman's approach by a surprised General Gregg, who was unaware of Sherman's march on the capital until apprised of the movement by alert scouts. The Confederate force was barely in position when the Minnesota infantry had made their approach toward the bridge, resulting in Captain Robert Martin ordering the Georgia cannoneers to hammer the advancing blue column with artillery fire.[52]

Sherman immediately rode up and made a hasty reconnaissance, ordering General Tuttle to mass his division in preparation for an attack. To cover the infantry deployment, Captain Nelson T. Spoor, General Tuttle's chief-of-artillery, placed the Second Iowa Battery to the right of the road and Company E of the First Illinois Light Artillery to the left, in all twelve guns, before ordering them to drive the Georgians from the field. In a mere twenty minutes the uneven artillery fight was over. The overwhelmed Confederates were forced to fall back from Lynch Creek into a skirt of woods that fronted the rifle pits lining the southwestern approaches to Jackson.[53] Due to the downpour of rain that had fallen that morning, the retreating force was unable to burn the bridge over the creek, allowing Sherman's forces a dry route to cross, though it quickly became a bottle-neck that slowed any attempt at pursuit. This gave the Confederates time to re-form in line of battle at the edge of the woods.

Once the crossing was complete, Tuttle redeployed his division in the open field fronting the woods in which the Rebel forces were formed. Mower's brigade was placed to the left of the road, Matthies's brigade to the right, the two artillery units were placed in the center, and Buckland's brigade formed in the rear of Matthies.[54] As the brigades of Mower and Matthies formed into line of battle and started forward to charge the outnumbered Confederate line, the Rebels wisely retreated into the protection of the Jackson earthworks and its 10 guns, where, aided by the Mississippi State Troops and civilian volunteers, they again unleashed a murderous artillery fire that halted the Union advance.[55] Captain Spoor moved his two batteries forward on the double quick and fiercely engaged the Rebel guns, though now he was outnumbered 14 to 12 due to the quick emplacement of Martin's Georgia Battery upon entering the fortifications. Tuttle committed to calling up his reserve of Buckland's brigade, which pushed forward in regimental columns to the position on the right of Matthies. Upon advancing from the woods, Buckland's men were met with a perfect storm of canister from six guns emplaced in a redoubt, causing them to retire to the shelter of the woods from which they had just emerged. It was now 1:30 in the afternoon, and Sherman's attack had ground to a halt.

After a conference with Grant, Sherman sent his acting chief engineer, Captain Julius Pitzman, accompanied by the Ninety-Fifth Ohio Infantry under the command of Colonel William L. McMillen, to reconnoiter to the right of the Jackson fortifications and exploit any flaws that he observed in the earthworks.[56] With Captain Pitzman acting as a guide and one company of the Ohioans deployed as skirmishers, the group entered the woods to the right before a circuitous trek brought them out onto the New Orleans, Jackson and Great Northern Railroad near an abandoned Rebel encampment. Pushing forward on the rail line toward Jackson, the group anxiously approached the rifle-pits, anticipating an ambush, only to find the pits deserted. Once the nerves of everyone had settled, the Ohioans planted their flags on the entrenchments. Moments later, an elderly black man approached the group, advising them that the Confederates had evacuated the city and the cannonading that was impeding their advance was the work of a relatively small number of artillerymen left behind to man the guns.[57]

At this point, General Steele arrived with the lead elements of his division after being ordered by Sherman to pursue any successes gained by the Ninety-Fifth Ohio. With reinforcements now on hand, McMillen resolved to capture the cannoneers that were impeding the Union advance. Using the black informant as a guide, the men assumed a position in the rear of the unsupported artillerists before surging forward to capture at this location six guns and fifty-two Rebel prisoners.[58] Not to be outdone, the brigades of Mower and Mathies raced forward and seized another four guns and ninety-eight prisoners. With the mission now accomplished, Sherman ordered the divisions of General Tuttle and General Steele to halt and set up camp in the open fields southwest of Jackson.[59] But the other half of the Union pincer movement, McPherson, was having a great deal of trouble in fulfilling his end of the attack on Jackson.

After sending Colonel Albert P. Thompson on the mission to delay Sherman's advance, General Gregg ordered Colonel Farquharson to move his brigade out of Jackson some two and one-half miles on the Clinton Road and march by the right flank through an open field before crossing a bridge spanning Town Creek, then turn northwest and deploy his brigade in assault formation upon an open ridge that ran parallel to the creek. The colonel's intentions were to make a feint upon McPherson's left flank in hopes of delaying the Union general until more troops could be brought up.[60] Unfortunately for Farquharson, more troops were already at hand in the form of Logan's division, which had just arrived from Clinton. Logan deployed them in support of General Crocker, with Brigadier-General John Eugene Smith's brigade in the woods some 400 yards in the rear of Colonel George B. Boomer's brigade, Brigadier-General John Dunlap Stevenson's brigade across a ravine on Boomer's left, and the brigade of Brigadier-General Elias Smith Dennis in the rear to serve as guard of the corps' baggage train. When the rain stopped falling at 11:00 A.M., McPherson ordered Crocker's division to advance and attack.[61]

As the men of Crocker's division ran forward, the Brookhaven Light Artillery opened a galling fire that tore huge gaps in their ranks, supplemented by the supporting fire of Confederate sharpshooters. The survivors reached the shelter of a ravine almost 500 yards in front of the Confederate position near the Wright home, halting to reform their ranks for the final charge. Sending out skirmishers to probe the defenses, the men closed on the position held by the Twenty-Fourth South Carolina skirmish line, located behind a fence in the ravine that fronted the main Confederate defensive line.[62] After determining that only a small force was nearby, Crocker ordered his men to "Fix bayonets and charge through the ravine and all the way to the batteries."[63] Unfurling their flags, the men let loose a cheer before driving the South Carolinians from the ravine in front of the Wright home, stopping only to catch their breath before continuing their advance under a blistering fire of Rebel artillery and musketry. Reaching the main Confederate defensive line, a savage hand-to-hand struggle ensued along the Wright farm, with the Twenty-Fourth South Carolina and the Tenth Missouri engaged in a bayonet contest for control of the ridge, before the South Carolinians fell back in the face of superior numbers. Vastly outnumbered, Colquitt had no alternative left but to fall back to the safety of the Jackson earthworks. General W. H. T. Walker, observing the retreat of the Confederate forces from his position in support, and correctly deducing the futility of attempting to staunch the tide of blue surging forward, also fell back with his forces into the entrenchments.[64]

Upon gaining possession of the former Confederate position along the Clinton-Jackson Road, the Federals stopped to regroup before resuming their advance, but wisely brought up the six-gun Sixth Wisconsin Battery to ensure that the retreating Confederates did not stop to

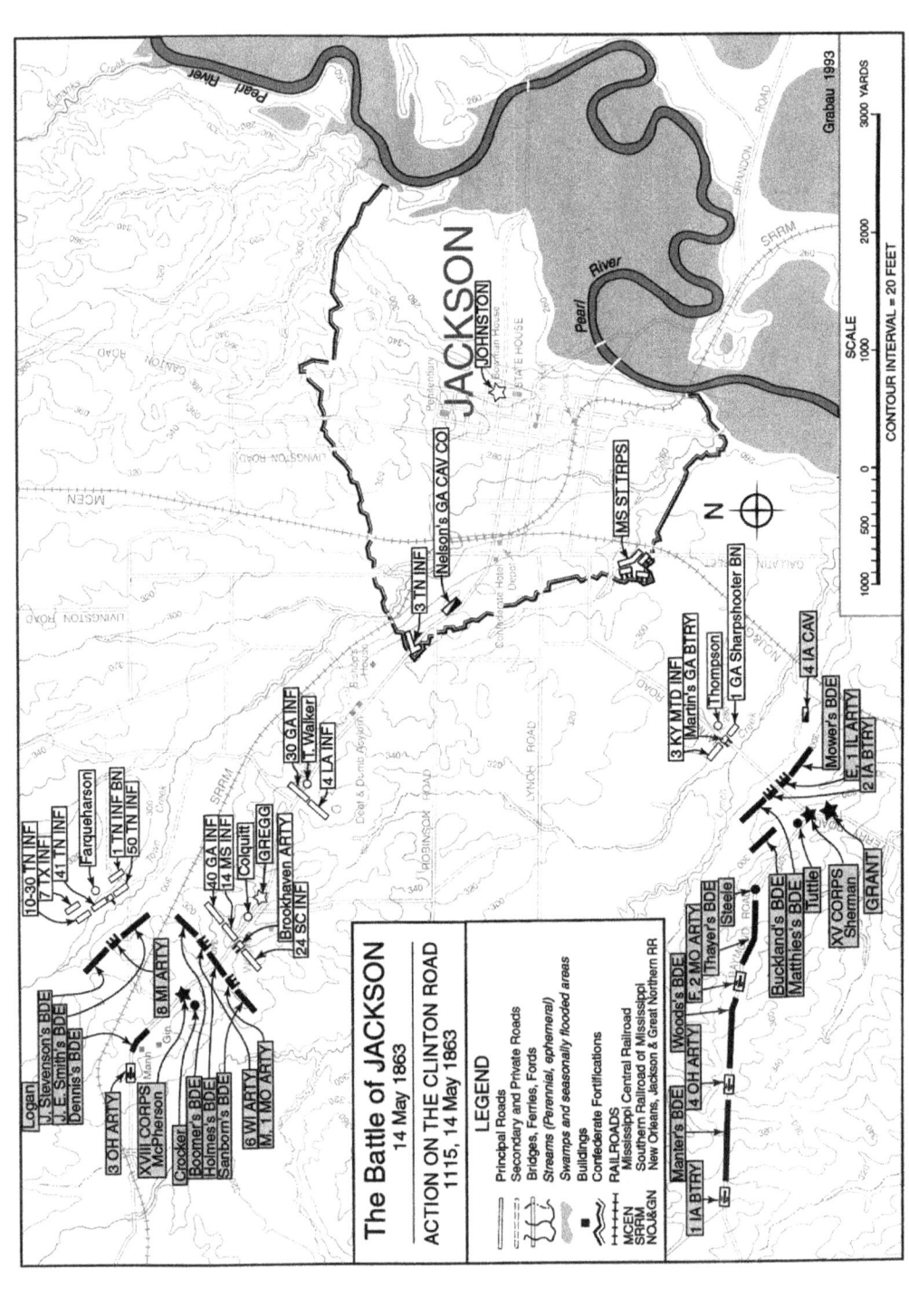

regroup also. Resuming their march toward Jackson on the road, the men again came under fire from Confederate gunners upon reaching the earthworks that protected the northwest approach to the city. The Sixth Wisconsin and Company M of the First Missouri Light Artillery were swiftly wheeled into position and began a bombardment of the earthworks to cover the infantry deployment. Colonel Holmes ordered Colonel Horney and Colonel David B. Hillis to advance skirmishers to test the strength of the fortifications. Captain David A. Craig, commanding a group of skirmishers from the Seventeenth Iowa, entered one of the redoubts and, much to their surprise, found the works abandoned, subsequently capturing four guns.[65]

The Confederate evacuation of Jackson was complete. At 2:00 P.M., General Gregg arrived within the earthworks with Colquitt's force, where he was handed a message from General John Adams alerting him that the army supply wagons were then en route to Canton. Gregg, having accomplished his mission to delay the Union forces as long as possible, ordered Colonel Thompson to disengage from Sherman's troops on the Raymond-Jackson Road but to conceal the movement for as long as possible. The First Georgia Sharpshooter Battalion and Martin's Georgia Battery fell back immediately, while the Third Kentucky Mounted Infantry and Nelson's Georgia Cavalry Company covered their retreat, leaving the skeleton force to man the guns in the works facing Sherman, which were later captured by the Ninety-Fifth Ohio.[66] The forces of Colquitt and Walker, including the Fourth Louisiana Battalion, were also withdrawn toward Canton. At 3:00 P.M., McPherson received the news that Jackson had been abandoned, and ordered General Crocker's division to occupy the city. Captain Lucien B. Sanborn, accompanied by Fred Grant, the young son of General Grant, raised the national colors of the Fifty-Ninth Indiana over the Mississippi State Capital building.[67] Jackson was once again in the hands of the Union.

Total casualties for the capture of Jackson were relatively light for the Union at 41 killed, 251 wounded and 7 missing for an aggregate of 299, compared to the Confederate total of 845 casualties and the loss of 17 cannon.[68] But the battle for Mississippi's capital can more be judged in its loss for the Confederacy. By turning his forces east and stealing a march on Pemberton, Grant scattered what within 24 hours would have been a significant force of troops. With those troops, under the command of Johnston, in a railroad hub like Jackson that could have provided even more reinforcements, would have been a serious threat to Grant, whose lifeline for troops and military equipage at that time consisted of a dirt road running to Grand Gulf. General Johnston, traveling with the troops of General Gregg, which were retreating northeast on the line of the New Orleans, Jackson and Great Northern Railroad, sent word to General Maxey at Hazelhurst, Mississippi, to return to Brookhaven with his brigade. The command of General Gist, approaching from the east on the Southern Railroad, was ordered to turn back and disembark at Forest, Mississippi, while the two Army of Tennessee brigades of Brigadier-General Matthew Duncan Ector and Brigadier-General Evander McNair that were en route from Tullahoma were instead halted at Meridian. One can only wonder at the outcome of the Vicksburg Campaign had the earthworks been defended a while longer to swell the ranks of Johnston's army with the in-transit reinforcements.

As news of the events surrounding Vicksburg and Jackson spread throughout the Confederacy, Private McNeill expressed his thirst for news regarding his comrades while still on detached duty at Savannah:

> Sunday, May 17th
> A gun was fired every half hour yesterday from sunrise to sunset by order of General Beauregard in honor of General Jackson, whose death is a very serious loss to our cause. He has fought

Opposite: First map of Jackson, MS. (courtesy of Warren Grabau, *Ninety-Eight Days: A Geographer's View of the Vicksburg Campaign*, University of Tennessee Press, 2000.

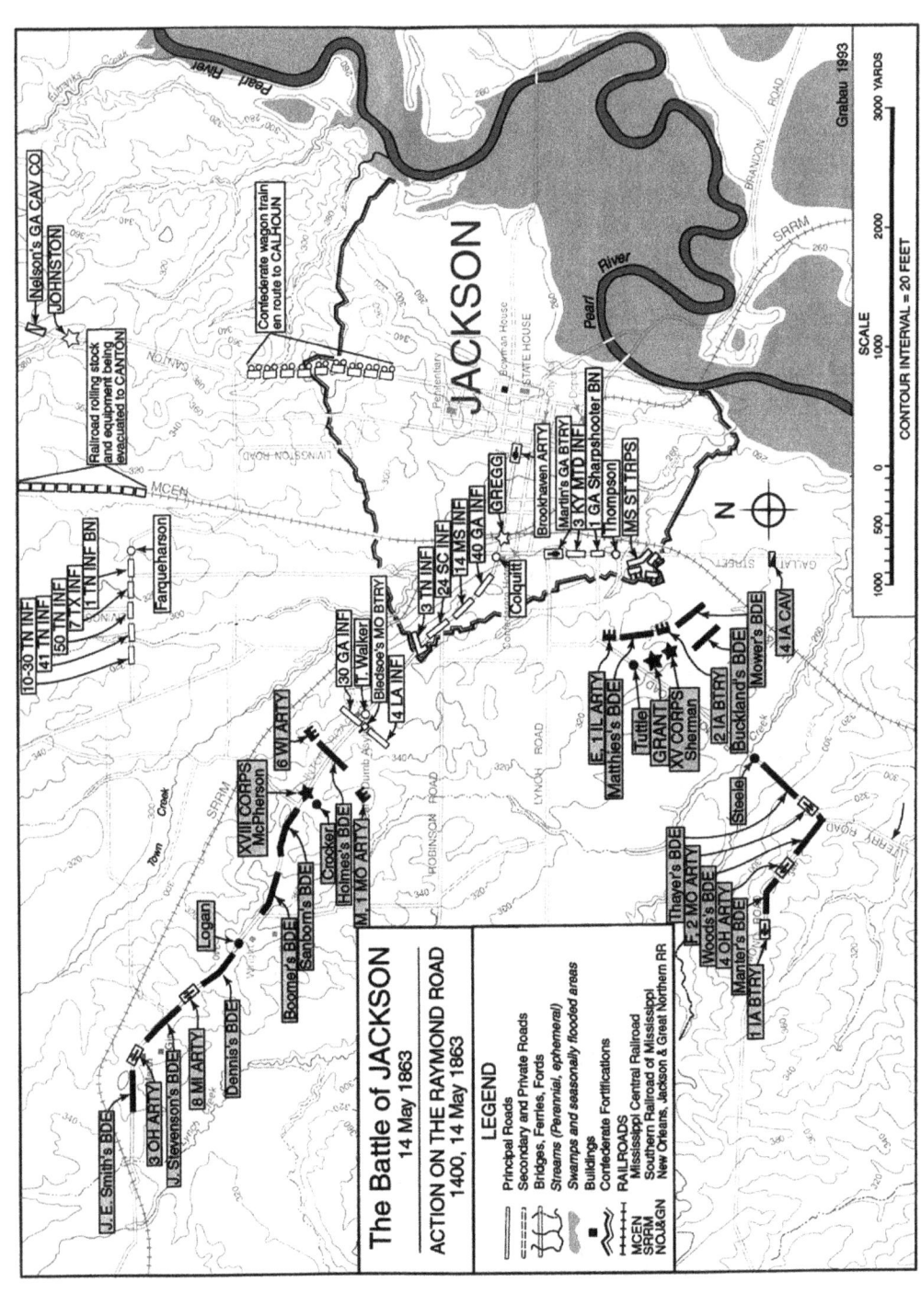

more battles than any other General in the field, and victory in all. We are expecting news from Jackson, Miss. every day. The last news from there says they were fighting, that was three days ago. Great fare is expected for the result.[69]

The night of the battle, Grant had ordered McPherson to march the next morning on Bolton, Mississippi, to prevent Johnston from getting to the Southern Railroad to effect a junction with the forces of Pemberton. Grant also sent a courier to McClernand with word of the fall of Jackson and instructing him to march on Bolton Station with all possible speed. Sherman was ordered to perform the handywork of which his name would become synonymous with later in the war, that is, the destruction of a city. He was ordered to effectively eliminate Jackson's usefulness to the Confederate war effort by destroying the railroad and any other establishments that could be of benefit, though some of his men took wide discretion in determining the term "useful." A textile factory, carriage factory, stables, foundry, paint shop, hotel, carpenter shop, the state penitentiary, two railroad depots, two hospitals, banks, and a Catholic church were among the victims of Sherman's torch.[70] The railroad was destroyed to the point it was not completely repaired until well after the war. In short, it was a warm-up for the "March to the Sea" that would make Sherman a pariah in the South for years after the war ended, and to some extent, still today.

Grant departed from Jackson on the afternoon of May 15 on his way to Clinton, where that night he would send a message to Sherman advising him that Pemberton was advancing eastward from Edwards Station and instructing Sherman to march one of his divisions towards Bolton, and follow personally with the other as soon as Jackson's "Welcome Back to the Union" party was complete. Steele's division left immediately upon receipt of the message on the morning of May 16, followed at 12:00 noon by Tuttle's. Sherman ordered all of the Confederates captured at Jackson paroled, in order to free as many of his men as possible from guard duty for the showdown with Pemberton.[71]

The showdown would occur on the plantation of Sid and Matilda Champion, and the ensuing battle, thought by many to be the "Gettysburg of the West" due to its importance and ferocity, would become known as the Battle of Champion Hill. Fought on May 16, Pemberton would suffer a disastrous defeat at the hands of Grant, and be forced to retreat to the east bank of the Big Black River, where he would suffer another humiliating defeat known as the Battle of Big Black River Bridge on May 17. The forces of the Pennsylvania-born Confederate general would retire in disorder to the safety of the Vicksburg fortifications while being pursued by Grant and his victorious army. But the disasters that had befallen Pemberton would be avenged on May 19 and May 22, when Pemberton would see his troops, now ensconced behind breastworks, slaughter many of Grant's army in two desperate Federal assaults upon the Vicksburg fortifications in an effort to storm the Confederate citadel. Appalled at the loss of life, Grant's forces would now resign themselves to receiving reinforcements and placing Vicksburg under a siege that would last for the next 47 days, effectually starving the city and its 29,500 defenders into surrender on the Fourth of July after a constant bombardment. All the while, Pemberton and his troops held out hope that the vaunted General Joseph E. Johnston was on the way with an army to lift the siege.

A member of the First Georgia Sharpshooters Battalion, formerly of Walker's Brigade, wrote the following communication to the *Savannah-Republican* newspaper on June 24, 1863, regarding the brigade's experiences in Mississippi:

Batt. Ga. S. S., Wilson's Brigade, Walker's Division,
Camp near Vernon, Miss., June 24, '63.
    Our battalion is attached to Col. Wilson's brigade; (Col. W. is now acting Brigadier General;)

Opposite: Second map of Jackson, MS (courtesy of Warren Grabau).

the forces under him are the 29th, 30th and 25th regiments Ga. Vols. and the 4th Louisiana Battalion ... I don't believe there is a tent in the army, and I don't know that there is any more sickness than when we had our full share of them-to be sure it is by no means as comfortable or as pleasant, but then we are not troubled with lugging them about. I have been wet to the skin I suppose twenty times since I have been here, but feel none the worse; I think it does one good.

At Yazoo City our baggage was cut down to the limited supply of what we could pack on our backs, and not being particularly fond of that kind of work, having had a benefit, my wardrobe is exceedingly short — I will give you a list: 2 pair of socks, 2 shirts, 2 pair drawers, 1 pair pants. I left everything else I had, which did not consist of a great deal, in care of Col. White, who kindly offered to take care of them for me at Yazoo City.

B.

Johnston was being bombarded during the siege of Vicksburg with communications from Seddon urging him to attempt an attack to relieve Pemberton. Still, Johnston methodically gathered reinforcements and dawdled while the Vicksburg garrison starved in the oppressive Mississippi summer heat. By June 3, Johnston's forces had swelled to thirty-one thousand soldiers and seventy-eight cannon, and he still deemed it inadequate. Of course, Grant was receiving reinforcements as well, to the tune of a total force in mid–June of 77,000 soldiers, 34,000 of which he assigned to Sherman with the intention of making sure that Johnston did not interfere with his stranglehold on Vicksburg.

After the fall of Vicksburg, Grant issued orders to Sherman stating, "I want you to drive Johnston from the Mississippi Central Railroad; destroy bridges as far as Grenada with your cavalry, and do the enemy all the harm possible."[72] Sherman immediately issued orders to his commanders and replied to Grant, "Already my orders are out to give one big huzza and sling the knapsack for new fields."[73] Faced with a desperate shortage of water and the scorching heat, the advance of Sherman's forces were still able to arrive in front of Jackson on July 9, where Johnston had been desperately trying to improve the fortifications in anticipation of the Union movement against his small army.

Johnston had fallen back to Jackson on July 7, placing his lines in a semicircle that enclosed what remained of the city. Johnston placed Major-General Loring's Division on the right, crossing the Canton Road. General Walker's Division, including the Fourth Louisiana Battalion, occupied the position between Loring's left flank and the Clinton Road. The division of Brigadier-General Samuel Gibbs French held the line between Walker and the division of Major-General John C. Breckenridge on the south flank of the Confederate defensive line, with the cavalry of Brigadier-General William Hicks "Red" Jackson guarding the fords on the Pearl River above and below the city. Johnston's plan was that thirst would force Sherman into directing an immediate assault upon the entrenchments that the Confederates could easily repel. On July 8, Sherman had the bulk of his army in the vicinity of Clinton, 10 miles west of Jackson, where he issued orders for the investment of the city, rejecting outright any idea for an immediate assault. Sherman placed the Fifteenth Corps under Steele in the center position between the Clinton and Raymond roads, while Major-General Edward Otho Cresap Ord's Thirteenth Corps moved to the right of Steele, and the Ninth Corps under Major-General John Grubb Parke took position on the left of the Union line. Spotting some low hills that would make excellent artillery sites, Sherman ordered guns placed there as quickly as possible. Sherman's arrangements hinged on the assumption that Johnston could not withstand a lengthy siege, and that once the Rebel forces left their fortifications, he would launch an assault on more equal footing. In the meantime, Sherman ordered his troops to begin pulling up the railroad to the north and south, while extending his own lines to reach the Pearl River beyond the Jackson fortifications, surmising that a successful crossing of his forces would hasten a Confederate withdrawal.[74]

With his artillery in place on July 11, Sherman called for an hour-long intensive bombardment to commence at 7:00 A.M. the following morning to damage the city and demoralize the defenders. This was to be followed up with a slower harassing fire directed at specific targets throughout the days and nights. Sherman used a flag of truce on July 14 to send Johnston copies of newspapers reporting on the twin catastrophes of Vicksburg and Gettysburg, gleefully assuming, "that, with our cannon tonight, will disturb his slumbers."[75] Active skirmishing was ongoing but accomplished little for either side. Johnston did send his cavalry in an attempt to cut Sherman's communications near Clinton and to intercept a train carrying ammunition, but the raiders were driven off by the division of Brigadier-General John McArthur before causing much damage.

On the morning of July 12, Union Brigadier-General Jacob Gartner Lauman, disobeying General Ord's orders regarding a reconnaissance in force, moved the brigade of brevet Brigadier-General Isaac C. Pugh and a supporting regiment against the front of Breckinridge without bothering to conduct reconnaissance or arrange for support from other forces. The Federals received a hellish fire from two Rebel batteries and elements of several supporting regiments before being either cut down or forced to surrender. Losses for Pugh were placed at 465 of the 800 men who made the assault, as well as several regimental colors. Not learning of the fiasco for an hour, Ord immediately removed Lauman from command, charging that he did not even know how to reorganize his decimated command. Decomposing rapidly in the blistering sun, a truce was arranged on July 14 so that the Union dead could be properly buried.[76]

Sherman continued to extend his lines, and Johnston came to the realization that to remain in Jackson would be to invite disaster. Wiring President Davis on July 15 to advise him that the enemy would not assault, his forces could not withstand a siege, and that to attack Sherman's lines would be sheer madness, the following day saw Johnston issue orders to ensure a safe abandonment of Jackson once more. Skirmishers and pickets were to carry on with their activities, while work on the fortifications was to be continued in an effort to convince Sherman that no evacuation was imminent. However, beginning at 9:00 P.M., the mobile guns were to be wheeled by hand, with a dozen men on each wheel, at a minimum a half-mile to the rear before the horses were hitched up. The infantry was to move out as fast and as quietly as possible by brigades beginning at 10:00 P.M., with detailed routes planned for each division by staff officers who had been ordered to familiarize themselves with the roads during the day. Johnston, who would gain quite a reputation for retreating later in the war, saw his plan work perfectly, with Union forces not confirming the withdrawal until the following morning.[77] The Siege of Jackson was over.

With a commanding lead over any pursuing force, and Sherman mindful of the rigors his forces had been subjected to during the long summer campaign for Vicksburg, Sherman wrote to John Aaron Rawlins, Grant's assistant adjutant-general, on July 14: "If he moves across Pearl River and makes good speed, I will let him go."[78] Grant replied for Sherman to make pursuit as he deemed necessary without straining the Northern-bred infantry too much in the unaccustomed heat of July in Mississippi. Johnston was pursued as far as a dozen miles east of Jackson to Brandon Station, where his losses consisted mostly of stragglers picked up by the Federals. Returning to Jackson to complete what he had begun in May, Sherman ordered the assault upon the railroads of Jackson renewed with a vengeance, gloating that "The good folks of Jackson will not soon again hear their favorite locomotive whistle."[79] Though officially ordering the troops not to engage in wanton pillaging, Sherman confided to Admiral Porter that "our men, in spite of guards, have widened the circle of fire, so that Jackson, once the pride and boast of Mississippi, is now a ruined town."[80] With the destruction now complete, Sherman and his troops returned to encampments along the Big Black River to reflect on their handiwork.

Private McNeil, like the rest of the Confederacy, was eagerly awaiting news from the Mississippi campaign while still on detached service in Savannah. He recorded these entries in his diary:

Thunder Bolt, June 7th, 1863

The Enemy has made several assaults on Vicksburg, but have been driven back with terrible slaughter. Johnston is moving in his rear with a large force and a great battle is expected every day. It will be one of the most important battles of the war. We are still working on the Bombproof. I was in town yesterday and bought cloth to make two shirts, paid $3.40 for it, and two pair of socks, Five Dollars. We was paid up last night until the first of June, received Sixty-Two Dollars and Ten Cents.

Sunday, June 14th

We have been to Fort Jackson the last two days to drive pilings, but we have not been able to get the pile driver yet, so we done nothing. We have no news from Vicksburg yet, other than the garrison still holds out. No news from the Batt. I was in town yesterday and bought a shirt for Five Dollars. There is no news from any part just now.

Sunday, June 21

The ironclad Gunboat Atlanta went out to fight the Blockaders last Tuesday morning, and was captured by the Enemy, and all the crew, it is supposed. There was treachery on board, but not one escaped to tell the tale. I bought a pair of shoes last Wednesday, paid Thirty-Five Dollars, a pair of jean pants, Nineteen Dollars.

Thursday, Charleston, July 14, 63

Three of our squad received orders last night to go to Charleston and report to Capt. Eckells, Chief of Engineers. Today we arrived here about One o'clock and reported. We are to go to James Island to build a Battery somewhere named Fort Johnston tomorrow. Vicksburg fell on the Fourth of July, Port Hudson on the ninth. Bragg has had to fall back. It has caused a sad gloom over the Country. The Yankees have gained a foothold on Morris Island here, and it will require all we can do to keep them back. This is the darkest hours of the Confederacy. I believe our fighting nerves are nearly all out.

Fort Johnston, July 19th, 63

We are having a lively time of it here. The Yankees made a desperate assault on Fort Wagner yesterday, and were repulsed with large loss, it was a grand sight. Heavy cannonading is going on all the time. We mounted two ten-inch guns on our Battery yesterday, but on account of some bolt heads, they would not trail, so we could not open on the Enemy. We shall be ready tomorrow or the next day.

Sunday, Fort Johnson, July 26th

Our Battery opened on the Enemy yesterday at daybreak with two ten-inch Columbiads, one six-inch rifle and three ten-inch mortars. The six-inch rifle bursted this morning, killing one man and wounding two. The firing is still going on. A Flag of Truce boat went out last Friday with some prisoners. The Yanks threw a great many shells around here yesterday, they are not firing much today. We are fortifying all around here. Last Friday morning the Yanks commenced a terrible bombardment of Fort Wagner, but it only lasted two hours. It was a gross neglect to let the Yanks get a footing on Morris Island. Our fortifications was very fast there, no one can tell now what the results will be. Lee has had to fall back into Virginia again. Our Cause looks rather gloomy now, more so than at any other time.

Fort Johnson, Sunday, August 2

We finished Battery Simkins, I believe it is called, last Wednesday and commenced another eight-gun battery about a mile and a half from here called Battery Cheves. Battery Simkins keeps up a continual shelling all the time, the Yankees have not fired much lately. A small scouting party started out on Morris Island last night and captured nine Yanks. I have caught a very bad cold in the last day or two.

Fort Johnson, Monday, 11th

Things remain about the same here, slow firing a-going on all the time, but not doing much damage. We finished up everything complete belonging to the two Batterys yesterday, and we expected to go back to Savannah today, but orders came last night to build a Bombproof at Battery Cheves and we have to do that now. We are very tired, and staying here, we live very hard. Nothing to eat but oysters and stinking beef that would turn the stomach of a dog, and no chance to better it.

Thunder Bolt, Sunday, August 23rd, 1863

No news of importance here. The Yankees attacked Fort Sumter last Monday and have continued nearly all the week. Sumter is badly damaged, they threw shells for five hours, and brought to the city from there a hundred-pound Parrott Gun. A steamer has run the blockade at Wilmington and brought in valuable cargo and Government property, among the rest is two very heavy guns, one of them has been sent to Charleston and I expect it is mounted by this time. Reports say they will throw a shot weighing eight-hundred pounds seven miles. We have got about done here and we are now ordered to report to Savannah tomorrow.

Savannah, Sunday, Sept. 12th

J. T. Shaffer died yesterday morning at half past Five o'clock, he had a very severe spell of sickness for twenty days and died very hard. He was very decently buried last evening at Five o'clock. We still hold Fort Sumter with the bayonet. It is all in ruins but some Bombproofs. The Yankee commander is pushing down into the North part of the State. A big fight is expected there in a few days, great confidence is felt of the result. I have not heard from our Batt. by letter for some time. It is expected they are in Atlanta, Ga., and I expect it is so. I shall write to them today to acquaint them of Shaffers Death.[81]

Union losses for the second campaign for Jackson were listed as 129 killed, 762 wounded, and 231 captured or missing. Confederate losses were pegged at 71 killed, 504 wounded, and 25 missing, though Sherman announced the capture of 764 prisoners, most of whom were the stragglers previously mentioned, making the Confederate loss in excess of 1,300.[82]

The Vicksburg Campaign was now over, and the Confederate citadel was in the hands of the Union, where it would remain for the duration of the war. The campaigns for Jackson, though not large in scope, did destroy a vital rail hub and manufacturing center of the Confederacy, which could ill afford to lose any of its meager resources. In addition, it drove the Rebel forces out of that portion of Mississippi and considerably weakened civilian resolve to prosecute the war further.

The Fourth Louisiana Battalion would encamp near Morton, Mississippi, following the evacuation of Jackson until late August of 1863, when General Braxton Bragg's calls for reinforcements near Chattanooga would see them report for duty in the Army of Tennessee as part of Walker's Division in Colonel Claudius Charles Wilson's Brigade. Though the men had no way of foreseeing what the fortunes of war held in store for them at this point, their previous battles would pale in comparison to the bloodbaths that lay ahead of them while assigned to Bragg's army, beginning with a battle at a site in north Georgia whose name in the Cherokee Indian language meant "River of Death," but better known in the English language, and annals of warfare, as the killing field of Chickamauga.

JACKSON, MISS., ORDER OF BATTLE
May 14, 1863

Union Forces: Army of the Tennessee
Major-General Ulysses Simpson Grant

Fifteenth Corps Commander
Major-General William Tecumseh Sherman

Cavalry
4th Iowa Cavalry: Lt. Colonel Simeon D. Swan

Third Division
Brigadier-General James Madison Tuttle

Artillery
2nd Iowa Battery: Lieutenant J. R. Reed (6 Guns)
1st Illinois Light Artillery — Co. E: Captain A. C. Waterhouse (6 Guns)

First Brigade
Brigadier-General Ralph Pomeroy Buckland
114th Illinois Infantry: Colonel J. W. Judy
93rd Indiana Infantry: Colonel D. C. Thomas
72nd Ohio Infantry: Lt. Colonel L. Crockett
95th Ohio Infantry: Colonel William L. McMillen

Second Brigade
Brigadier-General Joseph Anthony Mower
47th Illinois Infantry: Colonel J. N. Cromwell
5th Minnesota Infantry: Colonel L. F. Hubbard
11th Missouri Infantry: Colonel A. J. Webber
8th Wisconsin Infantry: Colonel G. W. Robbins

Third Brigade
Brigadier-General Charles "Karl" Leopold Matthies
8th Iowa Infantry: Major F. S. Palmer
12th Iowa Infantry: Lt. Colonel S. R. Edington
25th Iowa Infantry: Major H. O'Connor
Seventeenth Corps Commander: Major-General James Birdseye McPherson

Cavalry
6th Missouri Cavalry: Colonel C. Wright
Provisional Cavalry Battalion: Captain J. S. Foster
2nd Illinois Cavalry — Cos. A & E: Lieutenant W. B. Cummins
4th Missouri Cavalry — Co. F: Lieutenant A. Mueller
4th Independent Co. — Ohio Cavalry: Captain J. S. Foster

Seventh Division
Brigadier-General Marcellus Monroe Crocker

Artillery
Captain F. C. Sands
1st Missouri Light Artillery — Co. M: Lieutenant J. W. McMurray (4 Guns)
6th Wisconsin Light Artillery: Captain H. Dillon (6 Guns)

First Brigade
Colonel John Benjamin Sanborn
48th Indiana Infantry: Colonel N. Eddy
59th Indiana Infantry: Colonel J. I. Alexander
4th Minnesota Infantry: Lt. Colonel J. E. Tourtellotte
18th Wisconsin Infantry: Colonel G. Bouck

Second Brigade
Colonel Samuel A. Holmes
17th Iowa Infantry: Colonel D. B. Hillis
10th Missouri Infantry: Lt. Colonel L. Horney
24th Missouri Infantry — Co. E: Lieutenant D. Driscoll
80th Ohio Infantry: Colonel M. H. Bartilson

Third Brigade
Colonel George B. Boomer
93rd Illinois Infantry: Colonel H. Putnam
5th Iowa Infantry: Lt. Colonel E. S. Sampson

Chapter 3 — Cold Mist of Defeat

10th Iowa Infantry: Colonel W. E. Small
26th Missouri Infantry: Major C. F. Brown

CONFEDERATE FORCES: DEPARTMENTS OF TENNESSEE AND MISSISSIPPI

General Joseph Eggleston Johnston

Jackson, MS Confederate Commander
Brigadier-General John Gregg

Gregg's Brigade
Colonel Robert Farquharson
3rd Tennessee Infantry: Colonel C. H. Walker
10th and 30th Consolidated Tennessee Infantry: Lt. Colonel J. J. Turner
41st Tennessee Infantry: Lt. Colonel J. D. Tillman
50th Tennessee Infantry: Lt. Colonel T. W. Beaumont
1st Tennessee Infantry Battalion: Major S. H. Colms
7th Texas Infantry: Colonel H. B. Granbury
Bledsoe's Missouri Battery: Captain H. M. Bledsoe (2 Guns)

Gist's Brigade
Colonel Peyton H. Colquitt
46th Georgia Infantry: Captain T. B. Hancock
14th Mississippi Infantry: Lt. Colonel W. L. Doss
24th South Carolina Infantry: Lt. Colonel E. Capers/Major M. T. Appleby
Brookhaven Light Artillery: Captain J. A. Hoskins (4 Guns)

Walker's Brigade
Brigadier-General William Henry Talbot Walker
30th Georgia Infantry: Colonel T. W. Mangham
1st Georgia Sharpshooter Battalion: Major A. Shaaff
4th Louisiana Battalion Infantry: Lt. Colonel John McEnery
Martin's Georgia Battery: Captain R. Martin (4 Guns)

Unattached Commands
3rd Kentucky Mounted Infantry: Colonel A. P. Thompson
Independent Company — Georgia Cavalry: Captain T. M. Nelson
1st Battalion — Mississippi State Troops
Civilian Volunteers of Jackson

Chapter Four

Hard Rain of War: The Battle of Chickamauga

> *An American battle that surpassed in its ratio of carnage the bloodiest conflicts in history outside of this country ought to be better understood by the American people. Sharpsburg, or Antietam, I believe, had a larger proportion of killed and wounded than any other single day's battle of our war, and that means larger than any of the world's wars. Chickamauga, however, in its two days of heavy fighting, brought the ratio of losses to the high-water mark. Judged by percentage of killed and wounded, Chickamauga nearly doubled the sanguinary records of Marengo and Austerlitz; was two and one-half times heavier than the loss sustained by the Duke of Marlborough at Malplaquet; More than double that suffered by the army under Henry of Navarre in the terrific battle at Coutras; nearly three times as heavy as the percentage of loss at Solferino and Magenta; five times greater than that of Napoleon at Wagram; and about ten times as heavy as that of Marshal Saxe at bloody Racoux. Or, if we take the average percentage of loss in a number of the world's great battles— Waterloo, Wagram, Valmy, Magenta, Solferino, Zurich, and Lodi— we shall find by comparison that Chickamauga's record of blood surpassed them nearly three to one.*
> — Confederate Major-General John Brown Gordon, reflecting on the Battle of Chickamauga, *Confederate Veteran* magazine, November 1913

Though the Vicksburg Campaign was now over and the Confederacy effectively split in half, events were still unfolding in other theaters of the war at a rapid pace. General Braxton Bragg, commander of the Confederate Army of Tennessee, was now asking for reinforcements in northern Georgia so as to once again confront his old nemesis, the Union Army of the Cumberland, under the command of Major-General William S. Rosecrans. The brigade of General William H. T. Walker, who had been promoted to major-general and assigned to command of a division, was now under the leadership of Colonel Claudius Charles Wilson in Walker's Division, and included the Fourth Louisiana Battalion. Walker's Division left Mississippi by train on August 23 to join Bragg's army for the coming campaign.[1]

And an important campaign it was. With the twin disasters of Vicksburg and Gettysburg still fresh on the minds of the Confederacy's populace, President Davis desperately wanted a victory to bolster Southern morale. Just as desperate to keep the momentum of victory rolling forward was President Lincoln, who was impatient to free east Tennessee and her decidedly pro–Union citizenry from Confederate governance. All that was needed by both presidents was to get their generals, who were facing each other across thirty miles of the rugged Cumberland Plateau in southeastern Tennessee, to move. Finally, on August 16, Rosecrans was ready to open the ball by advancing on the gateway to the deep South, the city of Chattanooga, Tennessee. A simultaneous movement by the Union Army of the Ohio, under the command of Major-General Ambrose Everett Burnside, was made from Kentucky by marching on the city of Knoxville, Tennessee, the other entrance to east Tennessee. This movement threatened to sever Bragg's rail link with Virginia, as well as presenting him with a nightmare scenario if the two armies were to form a juncture and overwhelm the Rebels with sheer numbers. To add to Bragg's headaches were the Cumberland Mountains, which screened Rosecrans's movements and afforded him the opportunity to emerge at more places than Bragg could possibly cover. Bragg decided to gamble that Rosecrans and Burnside would attempt to form a juncture and, accordingly, heavily deployed his forces to the northeast of Chattanooga.

General Braxton Bragg (courtesy of the Library of Congress).

Bragg lost this wager, as Rosecrans correctly surmised that Bragg would believe that to be his objective. Instead, Rosecrans moved one of his three corps, the Twenty-First, under the command of Major-General Thomas Leonidas Crittenden, to threaten Chattanooga and fake an upstream crossing to the northeast while the other two corps, the Twentieth under Major-General Alexander McDowell McCook and the Fourteenth under Major-General George Henry Thomas, marched wide to the southwest to cross the Tennessee River far below the city. With the obstacle of the Tennessee behind him, Rosecrans faced the numerous mountain ranges in his front. But he now had a plan in mind to use the mountains to trap Bragg inside the confines of Chattanooga, much as Grant had trapped Pemberton inside the Vicksburg defenses earlier that summer.[2]

After crossing the barren Sand Mountain, Rosecrans was then confronted with the towering behemoth of Lookout Mountain, which ran the length from the Tennessee River at Chattanooga southwestward through northwest Georgia and into the state of Alabama. With its slopes covered with trees and massive rocks, wagon travel was impossible except through the three natural gaps that ran through the escarpment. The first was the gorge of the river that passed around the north end of the mountain into Chattanooga itself, the second was Stevens Gap, which was located eighteen miles to the southwest, and the third was Winston Gap in Alabama, located over forty miles from Chattanooga. Rosecrans decided on a risky course of action that would pay huge dividends if successful in the form of catching the flank of the Army of Tennessee as they retreated from Chattanooga, then either routing the Rebels or sending them reeling back into the Chattanooga trap. The plan called for sending his three corps on separate routes, with Crittenden continuing on his present course to threaten Chattanooga directly, while the corps of Thomas marched through Stevens Gap and McCook proceeded to Winston Gap. The plan contained substantial risk for the Union Army, as each corps would be out of supporting distance of the other and highly susceptible to being attacked and destroyed in detail if discovered by Bragg. Nevertheless, Rosecrans decided the potential for destroying Bragg once and for all outweighed the risks, and the plan was put into motion.[3]

Traveling with the troops of General Thomas on September 8, Rosecrans received a message from General Crittenden stating that Bragg had abruptly evacuated Chattanooga and was retreating toward Atlanta, Georgia. Confederate "deserters," sent by Bragg to spread misinformation among the Army of the Cumberland high command, reported to Rosecrans that the forces of Bragg were in full retreat and in a state of demoralization bordering on disintegration. Though Rosecrans fell for the ruse, nothing could have been further from the truth, as Bragg was receiving heavy reinforcements from different points within the Confederacy. The corps of Major-General Simon Bolivar Buckner, unable to stop the advance of General Burnside in east Tennessee, was transferred to Bragg, as well as the division of Major-General John C. Breckinridge from Mississippi. To further supplement the Army of Tennessee, Richmond was tapping into what was considered its heavy-hitters by sending two divisions under the command of Lieutenant-General James Longstreet from the Army of Northern Virginia, though they would take ten days in arriving due to a circuitous rail route down the eastern seaboard and then back up through Atlanta.[4]

Bragg concentrated his army facing west to block Rosecrans from advancing on his supply line once his troops cleared the mountains, with his left at La Fayette, Georgia, and his right at Lee and Gordon's Mill, located where the La Fayette Road crossed Chickamauga Creek on its way to Chattanooga. This deployment placed him directly in front of the center column of Rosecrans' stretched-out army, and for good measure, Bragg ordered his cavalry to delay any advance of the outside Union columns while he prepared to give Rosecrans's army a proper Southern welcome as soon as it appeared from the mountains.

On September 9, the opportunity presented itself in the form of Thomas's lead division, under the command of Major-General James Scott Negley, as it descended Lookout Mountain and encamped along the upper reaches of Chickamauga Creek. The Union camp was located some six miles west of La Fayette but separated from the town by a spur of Lookout named Pigeon Mountain, which angled northeastward from the main ridge of Lookout some twelve miles to the south. Inside this angle were the headwaters of Chickamauga Creek, in a cul-de-sac of a valley known as Mclemore's Cove, and it was here that Bragg planned to push the Union corps belonging to Thomas, leaving it with no options except surrender or annihilation.[5]

But he also knew he had to move quickly, before the Federal flanking columns began to close in. He ordered Major-General Daniel Harvey Hill to send from his corps at La Fayette the tough-as-leather division of Major-General Patrick Ronayne Cleburne, over Pigeon Mountain via Dug Gap, to pounce on the unsuspecting Yankees, while also ordering Major-General Thomas Carmichael Hindman to sweep south from his position at Lee and Gordon's Mill and up the Chickamauga to assist in destroying Negley. As an insurance policy, Bragg had the rest of his army in place to support the assault. The plan looked foolproof, and in effect it was, except destiny had determined that nothing was foolproof in the Army of Tennessee, at least while Bragg was at the helm. Though Hindman made his night march and got into position for his flank attack, suddenly he got cold feet, imagining that all sorts of dangers hid beyond Lookout Mountain, and consequently refused to move, even at the frantic urging of Bragg. Hill made no movement at all, choosing instead to inundate Bragg with a steady barrage of imagined fears and excuses that served to demonstrate why General Robert E. Lee had banished him from the Army of Northern Virginia. By the time Bragg finally got his army in motion on the afternoon of September 11, Negley had become aware of the threat and pulled back onto Lookout Mountain, neutralizing the Confederate threat to his command.[6] Golden opportunity for victory number one was now lost for Bragg.

But just as quickly, opportunity number two now presented itself to the luckless Confederate commander, with even more promise of success than the first. Crittenden and his corps had occupied Chattanooga on September 9, the day after the Confederate withdrawal, and had been moving south along the La Fayette Road while driving in the Rebel outposts on his right flank, forcing the Confederates to abandon Lee and Gordon's Mill while pulling back to the east bank of Chickamauga Creek. This had been a stroke of misfortune for Bragg while he was attempting to get his insubordinate generals to move on Negley, but it now placed Crittenden in an extremely precarious and vulnerable position, with Negley recoiling to the west and McCook still well to the south out of supporting distance. Again planning well, on September 12 at 3:00 A.M., Bragg ordered his top-ranking subordinate, and chief underminer, Lieutenant-General Leonidas Polk, to proceed with his corps and the newly created Reserve Corps of General W. H. T. Walker,

Lieutenant-General Leonidas Polk (courtesy of the Library of Congress).

thirteen brigades total, and strike the nine brigades of Crittenden in front and flank.[7] Walker's Reserve Corps contained the Fourth Louisiana Battalion, still assigned to Wilson's Brigade, though Walker's Division was now commanded by Brigadier-General States Rights Gist. Wilson's Brigade consisted of the Fourth Louisiana Battalion Infantry; the Twenty-Fifth Georgia Infantry, commanded by Lieutenant Colonel A. J. Williams; the Twenty-Ninth Georgia Infantry, commanded by Lieutenant-Colonel George R. McRae; the Thirtieth Georgia Infantry, commanded by Lieutenant-Colonel James S. Boynton; and the First Georgia Battalion Sharpshooters, commanded by Major Arthur Shaaff.

Again the cruel hand of fate would deny Bragg his opportunity for victory, once more in the form of an insubordinate general. Polk began his movement, got into position, and then stalled, complaining that he did not have enough troops for a successful attack. Bragg complied by ordering Buckner's Corps to join Polk with his seven brigades. But Polk, the former Bishop of the Episcopal Church in Louisiana, was about to get a taste of what it was like to deal with an insubordinate general himself. After calling Walker and Brigadier-General St. John Richardson Liddell to a council of war to explain his plans and the part that he expected the Reserve Corps to play in the planned attack, Polk had to defend his proposals to Walker, who found nothing but fault in the Bishop's plans. Moreover, when Polk made changes to accommodate Walker, he raised new objections regarding the accommodations. Nevertheless, at 3:00 A.M. Polk ordered Walker into line on the right of Major-General Benjamin Franklin Cheatham, where

Polk's whole command did nothing but lie immobile.[8] Refusing to attack unless attacked first, Crittenden simply slipped away, and another grand opportunity for the Army of Tennessee to destroy the Army of the Cumberland cheaply, easily, and piecemeal had slipped through Bragg's fingers due to a failure to carry out orders by his lieutenants.

At this point, Rosecrans was beginning to ascertain that his picture of a demoralized Confederate army in full retreat might be a little off the mark. Intelligence reports that indicated Bragg was concentrated and ready for a battle near La Fayette, and that Negley's encounter with the Rebels in McLemore's Cove was no brush with the rear guard of the Army of Tennessee, prompted the Union commander to order the flanking columns of McCook and Crittenden to close in on the Union center in preparation for a possible attack by Bragg. Even more unnerving for Rosecrans, who had not had proper rest or nourishment for the past several days, was the troublesome report that Longstreet was on his way from Virginia to aid in his destruction. A high-strung, nervous individual in the best of circumstances, these components were beginning to tell on Rosecrans, resulting in the general issuing vague and confusing orders.[9]

By the evening of September 17, Rosecrans had his three corps within supporting distance of one another and arranged his line facing east toward Chickamauga Creek, with his left flank at Lee and Gordon's Mill. He had also located his headquarters at the handsome Lee-Gordon Mansion, barely a half-mile from the mill. With the arrival of the lead elements of the Army of Northern Virginia troops, Bragg was now ready to let his failures of recent days fade to memory. Bragg prepared to turn the left of the Army of the Cumberland, placing his army between Rosecrans and Chattanooga with an eye to pushing the Federals southward into McLemore's Cove, where they could be efficiently destroyed. The first step for Bragg was to seize the crossings of the Chickamauga so as to put the Confederates on the west side and in position to sweep down on Rosecrans's flank at Lee and Gordon's Mill. With this in mind, at midnight on September 17, Bragg first instructed Walker to cross his corps at either Alexander's Bridge or Lambert's Ford at 6:30 A.M., while Buckner would wade across at Thedford's Ford on his left, and Polk kept Crittenden distracted at the mill. In the early morning hours of September 18, it dawned on Bragg that he had the two corps crossing the creek too near Crittenden's left. His amended orders were as follows:

1. Johnson's column [Hood's], on crossing at or near Reed's Bridge, will turn to the left by the most practicable route and sweep up the Chickamauga, toward Lee and Gordon's Mills.

2. Walker, crossing at Alexander's Bridge, will unite in this move and push vigorously on the enemy's flank and rear in the same direction.

3. Buckner, crossing at Thedford's Ford, will join in the movement to the left, and press the enemy up the stream from Polk's front at Lee and Gordon's Mills.

4. Polk will press his forces to the front of Lee and Gordon's Mills, and if met by too much resistance to cross, will bear to the right and cross at Dalton's Ford, or at Thedford's, as may be necessary, and join in the attack wherever the enemy may be.

5. Hill will cover our left flank from an advance of the enemy from the cove, and by pressing the cavalry in his front ascertain if the enemy is re-enforcing at Lee and Gordon's Mills, in which event he will attack them in flank.

6. Wheeler's cavalry will hold the gaps in Pigeon Mountain and cover our rear and left and bring up stragglers.[10]

One oversight in Bragg's plan had Walker and Buckner using the same road to reach their individual crossing locations, and an inevitable and time-consuming entanglement occurred, resulting in the two corps approaching the creek in the early afternoon of September 18.

Rosecrans, alarmed at the reports of a buildup of Rebel forces, placed the mounted infantry brigade of Colonel John T. Wilder, armed with seven-shot Spencer repeating rifles, at Alexander's Bridge on September 17 with instructions to prevent any crossing there or at the other four fords between the bridge and Lee and Gordon's Mill. Wilder's men, known as the Lightning Brigade, went to work throwing up crude breastworks on the west bank of the creek and soon felt ready to meet any advance by the Rebels. The opportunity to prove their readiness would soon present itself the following day at 1:00 P.M., in the form of General Liddell's Division of Walker's Reserve Corps.

Less than one-half mile from Alexander's Bridge, Liddell ordered Brigadier-General Edward Cary Walthall to deploy his Mississippi brigade in line of battle, with his left on the Alexander's Bridge road, and advance guiding steadily to the left. Walthall formed his five regiments with the Thirty-Fourth Mississippi Infantry on the left, the Twenty-Fourth Mississippi on the right, and the Thirtieth Mississippi, Twenty-Ninth Mississippi, and Twenty-Seventh Mississippi in the middle. As the skirmishers sprinted forward some 200 yards, Walthall's Brigade stepped off into a dense thicket, where the tangled undergrowth and thick vegetation wreaked havoc on the regimental line. Entering a cornfield 300 yards southeast of the creek, the skirmishers ran head-on into the Lightning Brigade's skirmishers.

Wilder's men leaped into action. Running to the bridge, they ripped up the flooring to fashion a crude lunette astride the road, where they opened on the Mississippians with their repeaters. Due to a sharp turn in the creek, there was no room to maneuver Colonel Daniel Govan's Brigade on Walthall's left, where the Spencers were spitting carnage as fast as the men could reload. Instead of searching for a ford farther north, for four hours Walker and Liddell let Walthall pound away at the bridge, with frightful results, leaving 105 bodies on the field. With the bridge now on fire, the Mississippians withdrew and joined the rest of the reserve corps in a march north to Lambert's Ford, where the corps spent the night crossing the icy waters of Chickamauga Creek.[11] The Fourth Louisiana Battalion, after crossing at 1:00 A.M., spent the night guarding the division ordnance train that had made the crossing of the creek, while the Thirtieth Georgia protected the part of the train that had yet to cross the Chickamauga.[12] Buckner, who had seized Thedford's Ford at 2:00 P.M. on the 18th, spent an inactive day waiting for Walker to appear on the far bank.

One and a half miles to the north of Alexander's Bridge lay Reed's Bridge, where Rosecrans had placed the cavalry brigade of Colonel Robert H. G. Minty to obstruct any attempt at a crossing by Bragg's forces. The windings of the creek at this point worked against the defenders, making the west bank a potential trap, though Minty bravely held the position most of September 18 in the face of Major-General John Bell Hood's Division, under the temporary command of Brigadier-General Bushrod Rust Johnson. Due to a lack of cavalry to screen his movements, Johnson was exhibiting an abundance of caution in pressing forward. After receiving reports from his skirmishers that he had allowed 973 Union cavalry to impede his crossing of the creek for some four hours, Johnson shook out a brigade in line of battle and forced his way across the creek, while the brigade of Brigadier-General John Gregg outflanked Minty. Minty and his men made a wild dash for the bridge, trailed closely by the screaming Rebels. At 3:00 P.M., the lead elements of Johnson's Division stepped off on the west bank of Chickamauga Creek, where they proceeded to flank Wilder and his Lightning Brigade from their position at Alexander's Bridge.[13] Darkness brought an end to the skirmishes of September 18, and by the next morning, Bragg had the bulk of his army on the west bank of the creek, ready to put his plan into motion.

For Rosecrans, it had been a troublesome day of confusing reports that were coming in from the field regarding Confederate dispositions. With his gut telling him that Bragg was feeling for his left, the Union commander's response was a complex set of maneuvers that involved ordering Crittenden, on the left, to send his two right divisions over to the left, while pulling three of the four divisions in Thomas's corps that were in the center of the Federal line and having them pass behind Crittenden, before making a night march up the Dry Valley Road and entering the La Fayette Road, so as to be in position to block any attempt by Bragg to get between the army and Chattanooga. As the sun rose on the morning of September 19, the first division of Thomas's men, commanded by Brigadier-General John Milton Brannan, arrived at their objective, a field belonging to a farmer named Elijah Kelly, where they promptly fell out of ranks for a much-needed rest after the exhausting night march. But rest was not in the cards for the weary blue-clad soldiers.[14]

Bragg's intelligence reports still placed Rosecrans exactly where he wanted the Yankee general to be, with his left at Lee and Gordon's Mill and the rest of his army strung out southward into McLemore's Cove. Having no idea of Thomas's night march, Bragg concentrated on opening the battle of September 19 on what he assumed to be the Union left flank. As an afterthought on the morning of the 19th, Bragg instructed his cavalry commander, Brigadier-General Nathan Bedford Forrest, to make a reconnaissance up the Jay's Mill Road and see what was going on west of the mill, on what was Bragg's own right flank. This offhand order would shape the course of the bloody day of fighting that lay ahead on this cold September day.

As Thomas was arriving near the Kelly Field, he was approached by an excited Colonel Daniel McCook, Jr., who told Thomas that a single Confederate brigade, lost and alone, lay ripe for the picking in the forest to his front if only Thomas would amend earlier orders from Rosecrans and let him attack. Thomas reluctantly refused, but could not get the idea of easily capturing a thousand or more Rebels out of his head, and with this in mind, he sent the night march—weary brigade of Colonel John Thomas Croxton of Brannan's division forward to "develop" the enemy. The call to arms came while the men were boiling their morning coffee, and subsequently, many of the men proceeded with their hands full of hardtack and coffee. Moving the brigade down a farmer's lane that he mistook for the Reed's Bridge Road, but that was in essence a parallel trail between it and the Brotherton Road, Croxton formed a line of battle in an undergrowth-choked pine forest with the Seventy-Fourth Indiana Infantry on the right, the Fourth Kentucky Infantry on the left, the Tenth Indiana Infantry in the center, and the Fourteenth Ohio Infantry and Tenth Kentucky Infantry in reserve. Skirmishers from the Tenth Indiana were thrown forward to protect the brigade front. With none of the brigade officers doubting McCook's story of a lost and isolated Confederate brigade, confidence was high.[15]

Upon being ordered by Bragg to make his early morning cavalry reconnaissance, Forrest had dispatched the brigade of Brigadier-General Henry Brevard Davidson, accompanied by division commander Brigadier-General John Pegram, to Jay's Mill. Davidson dismounted his troopers in a hollow behind the mill so they could cook their breakfast, and deployed a detachment from the Sixth Georgia Cavalry into the woods to form a skirmish line at the edge of a cornfield. Less than 200 yards away, a Union detachment from McCook's command was quietly dipping their canteens into the mill spring, when they were discovered by the Georgians. Rifle shots split the still morning air, and Pegram quickly rushed the First Georgia Cavalry and one gun from the battery of Gustave Huwald toward the sounds of engagement. In hot pursuit of the Union soldiers that were at the mill spring, the Confederate cavalry stampeded McCook's unsuspecting command. The First Georgia began a leisurely pursuit up the Reed's Bridge Road before being recalled by Pegram, who sent the Tenth Confederate Cavalry out to reconnoiter the ground between the Reed's Bridge and Brotherton roads, before riding up the Reed's Bridge Road himself to survey the situation, though now accompanied by none other than General Forrest in person. The remainder of the brigade was resting 200 yards west of the mill on a wooded ridge, awaiting instructions.[16]

As Croxton's brigade entered the woods, the crunching of the dead foliage on the forest floor and the swishing of vines as the men advanced made an eerie sound in the morning stillness. Suddenly, the reports of rifle fire from the advance skirmishers and the sickening thud as miniés struck the front line jolted the brigade from their fatigue of the previous night's march. Over a rise and in their rear thundered the Tenth Confederate Cavalry, hell-bent on destroying the Yankee brigade that had now formed in a line of battle. When the horsemen closed the range to within 150 yards, the three frontline regiments of infantry opened fire on the approximately 250 cavalry, emptying saddles and sending the few remaining survivors into a mad dash along the route over which they had just come. The front line of the Union brigade then redeployed the skirmishers, fixed bayonets, and resumed the advance.[17]

As the survivors of the Tenth Confederate Cavalry raced to the ridge where the remaining men of Davidson's Brigade were leisurely preparing breakfast, their wild appearance threw the men of the Sixth Georgia and the First Tennessee Legion into confusion. Forrest and Pegram had returned from the Reed's Bridge Road and were frantically trying, with the help of Colonel Hart of the Sixth Georgia and Colonel C. T. Goode of the Tenth, to restore some semblance of order to the brigade's left when Croxton struck that portion of the Confederate line. Managing in the chaos to form a scratch line along the ridge to which Rebels were added as they rallied, the Union advance gradually ground to a halt in a thick fringe of black oak saplings located at the base of a second ridge opposite the cavalrymen.[18] Croxton sent word of his engagement to his commander, to which Brannan responded by ordering the brigade of Colonel Ferdinand Van Derveer to move out down the Reed's Bridge Road in an effort to turn the right flank of the Confederates. Van Derveer marched his men up the La Fayette Road to the farm of John McDonald, where they turned onto a wagon path that led to the Reed's Bridge Road, though without a guide Van Derveer had no inkling as to where he was going. Deciding to advance on the side of caution, he deployed his brigade into two lines of battle, effectively reducing his march to a crawl, but lessening the risk of being taken by a surprise attack. It also let the opportunity to envelop Davidson's right slip away.

Although his cavalry was making a respectable showing, Forrest realized that his men could not hold out much longer in the face of one of the largest infantry brigades in the Union army. Dispatching a courier to Polk's headquarters requesting that the cavalry division of Brigadier-General Frank Crawford Armstrong be sent to him, Forrest then rode down the Jay's Mill Road in search of infantry support. At 8:00 A.M. near the house of the Alexander family, he ran into Colonel Claudius Wilson, who had just gotten the last of his brigade across the creek and was allowing them a few minutes to prepare their breakfast before moving into position behind the corps of Major-General John Bell Hood. Forrest's pleas for Wilson to aid him were to no avail, as Wilson insisted on authorization from Walker before becoming engaged. Walker, instead of turning Wilson over to Forrest, insisted on obtaining approval from Bragg before doing so. Upon being notified, Bragg immediately ordered Walker to release Wilson to Forrest to aid the beleaguered cavalry, though the news of fighting in an area he considered devoid of Federals unnerved him.[19]

Riding part of the way to Jay's Mill with Wilson and his command, Forrest ordered Wilson to choose a position near Davidson, then sped off to encourage his troopers to hold out until the infantry could get into position. He found a slight improvement in the situation, though overall it was still desperate. Polk had sent only the Tennessee cavalry brigade of Colonel George Gibbs Dibrell instead of Armstrong's entire division, though Dibrell wasted no time in dismounting his men and placing them into position on Davidson's right, all before 9:00 A.M. The Tennessee brigade extended north far beyond the left flank of Croxton, who was already having his line strained by the added Rebel firepower, compelling him to call on the Tenth Kentucky Infantry to move up from the second line to the left of the Fourth Kentucky Infantry to counter the threat, thus giving away any chance of continuing his advance.

Colonel Dibrell pushed his dismounted cavalry up the Reed's Bridge Road in an effort to probe for the rear of Croxton, and ran headlong into the brigade of Van Derveer. The opposing skirmish lines met 400 yards to the left and rear of Croxton, when Van Derveer edged his men down the slope of a slight hill and ordered them to lie down at its base to escape the rain of rifle fire from the still unseen Confederates. The Second Minnesota Infantry took cover on the left front, while the Thirty-Fifth Ohio Infantry hugged the ground on its right, leaving the Eighty-Seventh Indiana, held in reserve, with nowhere to lie but the crest of the ridge, subjecting them to a severe fusillade from the fire that was passing over the front line. Calling up a section of Battery I of the Fourth U.S. Artillery, Van Derveer crammed it in between his frontline regiments and waited for events to unfold. After fifteen minutes of listening to the fire of his skirmishers draw steadily nearer, at last the skirmishers ran for the Union line, pursued by a solid line of gray screaming the blood-curdling Rebel yell. At 125 yards the Union line let fly their first volley, melting Dibrell's front line, though it was soon replaced by the second line, which stepped up to return the compliment. When the fire finally slackened at 9:30 A.M., the two sides were blanketed in smoke, though Dibrell was slowly backing away from the engagement.[20]

As the first sounds of skirmishing reached Brannan, he ordered his remaining brigade into the woods east of the Kelly farm, while on the ridge near Jay's Mill, Davidson's cavalrymen were still having a hard go of it. The inadvertent run-in between Dibrell and Van Derveer had permitted Croxton to turn his full attention toward Davidson. Three times Forrest's men fell off the ridge, only to be put back in line by Pegram, though a third of the brigade was wounded or dead and Huwald's Battery had lost most of its horses and was nearly out of ammunition. Forrest was everywhere, attempting to reassure the men by his very presence and words: "Hold on, boys, the infantry is coming; they'll soon be here to relieve you." As he neared the guns of Huwald, his admonishments became more emphatic: "Stay by the battery, men; support the battery. General Walker will be here in five minutes to help us."[21]

The infantry was on the way. A few minutes past 9:00 A.M., the Fourth Louisiana Battalion, along with the rest of Wilson's Brigade, swept north across the Brotherton Road toward the right of Croxton, where they were spotted by Colonel Charles Chapman of the Seventy-Fourth Indiana. With his skirmish line melting before him, Chapman struggled to retire his right flank to meet Wilson's men, when his orders were misunderstood in the din and the Indiana soldiers began to withdraw. Chapman was saved by Croxton, who sent the Tenth Kentucky at the double-quick from the brigade left to shore up the disintegrating right, where they lined up in time to deliver a volley that momentarily halted Wilson, while Chapman reformed his men on the right of the Kentuckians. Croxton disengaged his men from the fight with Davidson and filed them by the right to meet Wilson, where he formed them in a single line in the thickets north of the weed-choked Winfrey cornfield, facing south to meet Wilson head on. But after two hours of continuous fighting with the Rebel cavalry, Croxton slowly but inevitably began to fall back.[22] Croxton then sent a courier to General Thomas, who was taking his breakfast, wryly asking which of the four or five enemy brigades in his front was the one he was supposed to capture.[23]

Thomas rode forward to apprise the situation for himself. Correctly deducing that he was committed to the contest, Thomas sent orders to Brigadier-General Absalom Baird, whose division was resting in line of battle south of the Kelly house, to move rapidly to Croxton's relief. The plan was that once Wilson was defeated, Baird could wheel to the right and sweep south, though he would need someone to apply pressure to the Confederates to prevent them from reinforcing Jay's Mill.[24]

Forrest was taking a more direct approach to gaining additional infantry support, this one ignoring Walker altogether. With Brigadier-General Matthew Duncan Ector's Brigade of the Reserve Corps a half-mile away in the Youngblood field, Forrest called up Ector himself when

Dibrell made contact with Van Derveer, in an effort to search out his opponents flanks. Reporting in at 9:30 A.M. to find Wilson smoothly driving Croxton on the left, Ector was sent in on the right by Forrest to shore up Dibrell's attack. Emerging from the smoke, they were greeted by a scorching fire from Van Derveer's frontline regiments and the Union artillery. Ector halted his men and began returning the Federal fire, though he had no battery of his own with which to reply to the Federal artillery. This lasted for approximately thirty minutes before Ector was forced to withdraw with great loss.[25]

Croxton, in the meantime, had received support in the form of the Thirty-First Ohio Infantry from the brigade of Colonel John M. Connell. Inserting the Ohioans into the left of his line moments before Wilson attacked, the result was negligible, and only the arrival of the U.S. Regular Brigade commanded by Brigadier-General John Haskell King in their rear seemed to cheer Croxton's beleaguered soldiers. Making a difficult battlefield maneuver of a passage of lines while under fire, the retreat of Ector's Brigade had distracted the battalions of the Regular Brigade, causing them to incline too far to the east. This left only the First Battalion of the Eighteenth U.S. Infantry, commanded by Captain George Smith, which had moved by the right flank and filed rapidly through the left of Croxton's line, to alone confront Wilson's entire brigade.[26]

Smith received a break by the orders of General Forrest for Wilson to break off the pursuit of his withdrawing opponent, in the fear Wilson would overextend himself. Before he could comply, the brigade of Colonel Benjamin Franklin Scribner sprung into action on Wilson's left flank, causing it to fold. In the dark as to the fact that Ector had gone into action an hour earlier, Wilson sent a staff officer to the Youngblood farm to urge him to reinforce his left. Upon hearing the disconcerting news that only dead cornstalks remained in the Youngblood field, Wilson attempted to retire his left, which consisted of the Fourth Louisiana Battalion and First Georgia Battalion Sharpshooters, only to find they had disintegrated under the murderous fire. Moments later, the Thirtieth Georgia in the center gave way. Only the Twenty-Fifth Georgia and the Twenty-Ninth Georgia on the right remained, and they too began to waver. Wilson steadied the remaining Georgians and then galloped down his line to rally the Thirtieth Georgia, while Scribner continued to march around his left. As Union skirmishers entered the field through which Wilson had charged less than a half-hour before, Wilson withdrew the remnants of his brigade to the woods south of the Brotherton Road, leaving almost half of his troops either dead or dying in the woods north of the road. Nightfall would see fewer than 450 of Wilson's 1,200 men answer the brigade muster.[27]

Captain A. B. Clay, the inspector-general of Pegram's Division, described the scene as Wilson was forced to withdraw: "Wilson seemed to have only about One-Hundred left in formation, and I was told he had lost two guns and his battery was cut to pieces."[28] The battery attached to Wilson's Brigade was Martin's Georgia Battery, commanded by Lieutenant Evan P. Howell, and it would later bear his name. The battery boasted two 6-pounder bronze guns and four 12-pounder howitzers. After-action reports of the two days fighting at Chickamauga showed that the battery had three guns disabled, two whose poles were broken and one with a shattered wheel. Casualties were recorded at three men killed and four wounded, with three horses killed and three wounded, and 112 rounds of ammunition expended.[29]

But the first day of fighting in what would become known as the Battle of Chickamauga was far from over, as both sides pushed fresh troops into the fray. Before Walker could complain to Bragg regarding Forrest's commandeering of Ector, Bragg ordered him to send his other division, under the command of Brigadier-General Liddell, into the rapidly escalating contest. Liddell's two brigades smashed into Baird's flank and routed his three-brigade division before being thrown back by the now composed division of Brannan, led by the all–German Ninth Ohio. Bragg, realizing that Walker was in desperate need of help, sent in the five-brigade division of Major-General Benjamin F. Cheatham shortly after noon. The effect was offset by the fact that at about the same time, Rosecrans committed two more of his divisions to the struggle, those of Major-General John McCauley Palmer and Brigadier-General Richard Johnson. Marching side by side eastward from the La Fayette Road, the two divisions extended the battle lines farther south, while Cheatham's brigades were moving in the opposite direction. As the two lines crashed into one another, the fighting reached new heights, with Johnson seeing great success as the brigade of Brigadier-General August von Willich steamrolled Cheatham's right flank brigade before pushing eastward over the ground Cheatham had just recovered.[30]

On the right, Palmer faced the bulk of Cheatham's men. As he was forming his line along the La Fayette Road before advancing, he received a dispatch from Rosecrans suggesting he move en echelon, with his left brigade leading, his center brigade a few hundred yards to the right and rear, and the right brigade still farther to the right and rear. The suggestion was a sound one, as Palmer met Cheatham advancing south of, but basically along the same axis as, Walker's troops had previously. Palmer's echeloned line met Cheatham squarely and stopped him cold in his tracks. On the left of Johnson's division, the brigade of Brigadier-General William Babcock Hazen struck the Confederates in a cornfield belonging to John Brock, whose two sons, John Jr. and Roland, were in the fighting that day on behalf of the Confederacy.[31] A close-range fight ensued that at the end of the day had resulted in nothing more than a bloody stalemate.

The other two brigades of Palmer's division met the Rebels in the dense woods by the Brotherton Road, where they formed a line facing southeast with their right within a few hundred yards of the La Fayette Road, though visibility in the growth was under 50 yards. The heavy undergrowth worked to the Union advantage, however, as Cheatham's left flank brigade became confused and nearly fell apart before blundering into the Federal line with its left flank. The results, of course, were disastrous. Rosecrans then sent in the two-brigade division of Major-General Joseph Jones Reynolds, which was just arriving after making a night march also, forming a buttress for the Brotherton Road line. The division of Major-General Horatio Phillips Van Cleve extended the Union line even further south of the positions held by Reynolds and Palmer. Deploying his men, Van Cleve had formed his line at an angle with Palmer that faced due east and ran along a slight ridge through the woods some 300 yards east of the La Fayette Road, giving his troops an excellent position from which to fire into the flank of the troops of Cheatham's Division that were attacking Palmer. With that end of Cheatham's Division now completely wrecked, and a gap threatening to open between Cheatham and Hood's Corps to the south, Bragg pulled the three-brigade division of Major-General Alexander Peter Stewart from its reserve position and ordered it in on Cheatham's left, though it was no small task to achieve this through the shell-splintered, dense forest. In the resulting confusion, only one of Stewart's brigades, consisting of the Eighteenth Alabama Infantry, Thirty-Sixth Alabama Infantry, and the Thirty-Eighth Alabama Infantry, under the command of Brigadier-General Henry DeLamar Clayton, actually struck Van Cleve's line head-on. The other two brigades came up behind Cheatham, were they were warned that their position put them at risk of being enfiladed. With Van Cleve's frontline brigades overlapping Clayton on both flanks, and Palmer's division now relieved of any threat from Cheatham, the Alabamians never stood a chance in the contest as Clayton's line fell back in disorder.[32]

Stewart then sent the Tennessee brigade of Brigadier-General John Calvin Brown into the fight, with the same results in the beginning, before the fortunes of war shifted in favor of the Confederates. The cause of this shift was that in all the chaos of battle and shuffling of divisions from various Union corps up the La Fayette Road, the Federal army had become entangled within itself, creating a half-mile gap in the Federal line south of Van Cleve that had gone unnoticed in the woods and thickets. Van Cleve realized that he was not in touch with anyone on his right, and attempted to resolve the situation by moving up his reserve brigade to extend his line in that direction. The reserve brigade had doggedly attempted to make contact with the Union forces on the right and, in the process, had opened up a gap between themselves and the rest of Van Cleve's division on their left. As Confederates began to pour through the breach, an even worse disaster for the Federals occurred on the right. Another Tennessee brigade, this one under the command of Colonel John S. Fulton, drove through the 600-yard gap that remained on Van Cleve's right where, after encountering no resistance, the truth struck them like a ton of bricks. Fulton wasted no time in wheeling his brigade to the north and crashing down on the flank of Van Cleve, crushing his division and sending the Yankees fleeing back across the La Fayette Road to safety. With the troops they could rally and their existing reserves, Van Cleve and Reynolds managed to throw together a line just west of the La Fayette Road in the Brotherton cornfield, where most of the reserve artillery, 20 guns in all, was posted along a ridge in the middle of the field. It was now 4:00 P.M.[33]

Rosecrans, from his new headquarters at the home of a widow named Eliza Glenn, had been moving his forces from their old position at Lee and Gordon's Mill all day, and when the division of Brigadier-General Jefferson Columbus Davis arrived early in the afternoon, Rosecrans could only issue a vague directive to take his command toward the sound of the fighting and attempt to turn the Rebel southern flank, wherever it lay.[34] Davis boldly moved his division forward across the La Fayette Road and attempted to gain his bearings from the sounds of battle emanating from the woods, which was an enormously difficult task. Davis advanced far to the south of Van Cleve, thus creating the half-mile gap that Fulton had the good fortune to discover. Davis also became involved in a vicious fight with the Tennesseans of General Bushrod Johnson's Division just east of the La Fayette Road and north of a field owned by a farmer named Viniard. Davis had unfortunately left one of his three brigades behind to guard the division wagons, and thus entered the fray with only two, though his lead brigade was commanded by the capable Colonel Hans Christian Heg of the Fifteenth Wisconsin Infantry, and was rounded out with the Eighth Kansas Infantry, Twenty-Fifth Illinois Infantry, and Thirty-Fifth Illinois Infantry. After crossing the La Fayette Road a few minutes after 2:00 P.M., Heg entered the woods and advanced only a few hundred yards before running into Johnson's surprised men formed in line of battle, where both sides unleashed a close-range volley almost into each others' faces. Recovering quickly from the unexpected appearance of the blue-clad soldiers, Johnson soon had his divisional artillery in play as frightful casualties began to mount on both sides, before Heg's men began to fall back at 2:15 P.M.[35]

At 2:30 P.M., Bragg ordered Hood to locate and destroy the Federal southern flank so as to relieve the pressure on Cheatham and Stewart to the north. Hood ordered Johnson to wheel to his right, a movement that yielded less than the anticipated results due to Johnson's heavy fighting with Heg. One and one-half of Johnson's brigades made the wheel and helped to break Van Cleve's line, while the remaining troops continued to press Heg after finding it impossible to disengage from the fight. Heg, finding the pressure eased, dug in and halted the Confederate advance. General Crittenden, back on the La Fayette Road, had taken matters into his own hands in an effort to take control of the fighting in the Viniard Field sector that was unfolding largely unnoticed by Rosecrans. Crittenden ordered the brigade of Brigadier-General William Passmore Carlin of Davis's division to advance across the Viniard Field and fall in on Heg's right, while sending Wilder's Lightning Brigade with their Spencers in on the left.[36] With these reinforcements, the Federal line moved forward again.

As part of his plan to turn the Union right, Hood had followed up Johnson's Division with the division of Brigadier-General Evander McIvor Law. This division included Hood's own Texas brigade, which had achieved glory on the fields of Antietam and Gaines Mill, though they were now led by Brigadier-General Jerome Bonaparte Robertson. With Johnson's Tennesseans loading and firing from a prone position, the Texans rushed forward, calling out, "Rise up, Tennessee, and see Texas go in!"[37] Things went well initially for Law until a move was made to threaten one of the Federal batteries supporting Carlin. Seeing the threat from his supporting position, which he had reentered, Wilder unleashed two regiments to counter the threat with the rapid-fire Spencers, driving the Texans back in disorder. Encountering Johnson's line as they fell back, a Tennessean cried out, "Rise up, Tennessee, and see Texas come out!"[38] But the fighting around the Viniard Field was far from winding down.

Hood regrouped his two divisions and sent them forward again to press Davis, as well as requesting reinforcements from Bragg that arrived in the form of Colonel Robert C. Trigg's Brigade from the division of Brigadier-General William Preston. This brigade consisted of the Fifty-Fourth Virginia Infantry, First Florida Cavalry (Dismounted), First Florida Infantry, and the Seventh Florida Infantry. Crittenden countered by acquiring a detached brigade from Van Cleve's division that had not been engaged, as well as the division of Brigadier-General Thomas John Wood. Even with these reinforcements and the help of Wilder's repeaters, used to break up attacks that threatened to flank Crittenden or split his line, the Union position became desperate. Carlin was pushed back on a slight rise just east of the La Fayette Road, while Heg grimly held on in the woods that lined the east side of the road to the north of Carlin, and a handful of the Fifteenth Wisconsin made a determined stand in a log schoolhouse. With the pressure building, the surviving members of Davis's division crumbled and fled across the La Fayette Road before stopping to seek succor in a dry streambed located 100 yards west of the road. Heg, in an attempt to rally the fugitives, was mortally wounded for his efforts, falling among the heaps of blue that were being slaughtered as the Confederates poured a galling fire into their ranks. To the left of their position, the Southerners streamed across the road and into the Widow Glenn's field, where Rosecrans was forced to flee from his new headquarters after coming under fire.[39]

Though Carlin, Crittenden, and Davis had hoped to make a stand in the dry streambed, their attempts were futile, as the demoralized Union troops stampeded toward Wilder's position at the far west edge of the field when pressed by the advancing Rebels. As the approaching men of Robertson's command neared his position, Wilder let loose with a rapid fire from the Spencers, accompanied by the artillery fire of four batteries that devastated the advancing grayclads, leaving the survivors fleeing for the safety of the dry streambed themselves to escape the barrage. In an effort to dislodge them, Wilder attempted to get his attached artillery battery in position on his left front where, supported by the repeaters, he could fire triple loads of canister down the length of the streambed that was now crammed full of Confederates. The slaughter was so great that even Wilder was appalled by the butchery he had ordered, compelling him to reflect later: "It actually seemed a pity to kill men so. They fell in heaps; and I had it in my heart to order the firing to cease, to end the awful sight."[40] The survivors, in retreat, fled back across the La Fayette Road. The arrival of Sheridan's division, which had come up from Lee and Gordon's Mill, now made Federal control of the Viniard Farm a certainty as the fighting in this sector of battle sputtered out. It was now almost sundown.

At the Brotherton Field, the temporary calm that had prevailed was suddenly shattered at 4:00 P.M. as Stewart threw his regrouped division at the angle of the Union line where the La Fayette and Brotherton roads intersected. Though some three separate attacks had met with failure at this point, this attempt was destined to have a different outcome. The ridge in the Brotherton Field along which the exhausted Federal soldiers were esconced was a deceptively weak defensive position, providing the defenders with little cover save for broken corn stalks. To add to their troubles, the men of Johnson's Division with whom they had clashed earlier were now gaining a position in the wooded ravine on the southern edge of the field, from which they were leisurely picking off the artillerymen manning the guns emplaced on the ridge.

The brigade Stewart chose to lead the assault was fresh, and also led by a hard fighter named Brigadier-General William Brimage Bate, a native of Tennessee. Bate's Brigade consisted of the

Fifty-Eighth Alabama Infantry, Thirty-Seventh Georgia Infantry, Fourth Georgia Battalion Sharpshooters, Fifteenth and Thirty-Seventh Tennessee Infantry (Consolidated), and the Twentieth Tennessee Infantry. Delivering a pep talk to his regimental commanders before they advanced, Bate singled out Colonel Thomas Smith of the Twentieth Tennessee for this pre-battle admonishment: "Now Smith, I want you to sail on those fellows like you were a wildcat!"[41] His words had their intended effect, as Bate and his entire brigade advanced and sailed on the Union line like a whole pack of wildcats, shattering Van Cleve's entire line before sending it fleeing across the Brotherton Field, through the woods on the other side, and out into the Dyer Field, before making a dash toward the Dry Valley Road with the brigades of Brown and Clayton in hot pursuit. The pursuit sputtered out as they met the reserve division of Major-General James Scott Negley that Rosecrans had ordered up earlier, which arrived in the nick of time to halt the pursuers.[42]

Bate had angled his "wildcat" brigade more to the right and bearing northward up the La Fayette Road, where due to hard fighting they were threatening to roll up the whole Federal line north of the Brotherton Road before the danger was realized by Reynolds and Hazen. Once realized however, both took quick action to blunt the threat. Both Union generals moved to the Poe Field, a clearing up the La Fayette Road some 300 yards away, where Reynolds desperately attempted to throw together a scratch line from the debris of several assorted brigades and regiments. Hazen, meanwhile, devoted his energies into assembling some twenty artillery pieces from four different batteries, getting them in line just in time to meet the screaming wildcats of Bate's Brigade as they charged unsupported out of the woods some 350 yards away at the south end of the field. As they burst into the open field, they were met with the deafening roar of the Federal artillery as the guns spewed forth their missiles of death in the form of canister. By some miracle, Bate and over two-thirds of his brigade managed to escape the carnage and return to the Confederate line.[43] With the sun sitting low in the sky, Stewart's assault was over, but one more battle was still destined to be fought before nightfall would bring a merciful close to the day. Bragg had ordered up the three-brigade division of one of the best generals in the Army of Tennessee, Major-General Patrick Ronayne Cleburne, the "Stonewall of the West," in support of Cheatham's worn-out right-flank brigades. Attacking the divisions of Baird and Johnson as they were about to fall back to a superior defensive position, the men engaged in a short, vicious, and inconclusive encounter lit by the setting sun, before breaking off the fight due to nightfall. The one certainty that the day's fighting had produced is that the following day, Sunday, September 20, would see more devastating carnage for both armies.

Now shrouded in darkness, the sounds of battle were replaced with the far more haunting sounds of the suffering of the wounded that were left strewn on the fields of battle. As the temperature plummeted, a cold north wind blew through the trees as frost formed on the ground, turning sweat soaked uniforms into sheets of ice. The Confederates suffered the most, lightly clothed in the cotton homespun sent from home. With no rainfall in over a month, streams that normally supplied clear, cool water were bone dry. Though the Rebels had Chickamauga Creek from which to draw water, the Federals were left with a small cattle pond located near the Widow Glenn's house. So many wounded had crawled to the pond hoping to get a small sip to relieve their suffering that the pond was now putrid with blood, and the soldiers aptly renamed it the "Bloody Pond."[44] More heart-rending for the soldiers of both sides were the wails of the wounded. Lieutenant R. M. Collins of the Fifteenth Texas Cavalry (Dismounted) recorded the scene in his journal: "All night we could hear the wounded between ours and the Federal lines calling some of their comrades by name and begging for water."[45] Private William Heartsill of the same regiment also recorded the macabre night: "We have literally walked on dead men all night, and now while campfires are casting their flickering rays over the battlefield, the scene looks horrible, hundreds of ghastly corpses mangled and torn are scattered around us. I can sit here by my little glimmering light and count a score of Federals, dead and dying.... It is now nearly daylight and I have not had a particle of sleep; nor do I want any while this bloody work is going on."[46] The sounds were also heard in the Union lines, prompting a sergeant of the Seventy-Second Indiana Infantry to write in his journal: "The roar of the battle's bloody storm has ceased, and all is still save the waves that sob upon the shore — those waves are the shrieks of the wounded and dying — and these are more horrible and trying to our hearts than was the storm of battle. In that storm manly courage bore us up; in this storm of groans and cries for help that come on the black night air, manly sympathy for comrades and enemy makes our hearts bleed."[47] Also tormented by the sounds of agony that permeated the night was Private Alva Griest of Company B of the same regiment, who also recorded his anguished thoughts that grim night: "The thunder of battle has ceased ... but, oh, a worse, more heartrending sound breaks upon the night air. The groans from thousands of wounded in our front crying in anguish and pain, some for death to relieve them, others for water. Oh, if I could only drown this terrible sound, and yet I may also lie thus ere tomorrow's sun crosses the heavens. Who can tell?"[48]

Amid the suffering and agony of the night, the leadership of both armies was engrossed in finalizing plans for the next day's fighting. Holding a council of war with his generals, Rosecrans made the decision to stay and fight it out with Bragg the next day, while keeping his left flank strong at all costs. Holding the La Fayette Road was deemed imperative to prevent Bragg from getting between the Army of the Cumberland and Chattanooga. General Thomas, with his three divisions and a division each from the corps of Palmer and Johnson, would hold a position in the woods east of the Kelly Field, while the rest of the army would close up on his right, gradually easing back and to the north. The position at Lee and Gordon's Mills would be abandoned altogether. With the issue settled, the Union high command settled into a friendly camaraderie for the remainder of the night.[49]

Things were not so friendly among the Confederate hierarchy across the lines in the Army of Tennessee as the remainder of the reinforcements from the Army of Northern Virginia arrived, accompanied by Lieutenant-General James "Old Pete" Longstreet. Upon arriving at Catoosa Station outside of Ringgold, Georgia, at 2:00 P.M. via rail, Longstreet was angered that no one from Bragg's staff was on hand to greet such a distinguished person as himself. Killing time until the 4:00 P.M. train arrived with his horse and the horses of staff members Lieutenant-Colonel Moxley Sorrel and Lieutenant-Colonel P. T. Manning, the three saddled up and headed for Bragg's headquarters. Inadvertently riding into the Union lines before bluffing their way out of capture, the trio arrived at Bragg's headquarters in a decidedly cross frame of mind.[50] Nevertheless, Bragg made the decision to restructure the command of the Army of Tennessee to accommodate Old Pete, dividing the army into two wings, of which the left was to be commanded by Longstreet. The right wing would fall under the command of the next highest ranking general in the army who, unfortunately, was none other than Leonidas Polk. The left wing would consist of the corps of Hood and Buckner, with Hindman's Division thrown in for good measure. The right wing would contain the corps of Walker and Hill, as well as Cheatham's oversized division.[51] The battle plan for the next day would remain the same as for the 19th, except now that the Union position had been located, the army would face west instead of south. The goal was the same: Shove Rosecrans away from Chattanooga and into McLemore's Cove where his force could be annihilated once and for all. Bragg's plan called for the attack to begin at daybreak on the right, sweeping southward along the line while bending back the Union left flank. The wings were to be formed in depth with an abundance of reinforcements to exploit any successes. Hill's Corps of Polk's wing would open the battle by striking the Federals around the Kelly Field.[52]

In what had become a pattern for Bragg's plans, something went terribly wrong. This time, as usual, that something was insubordinate generals. Polk made only a lackadaisical attempt to contact Hill concerning his role in opening the battle the following morning, and promptly went to bed without ensuring that Hill received and understood his role in Bragg's battle strategy.[53] The result was as could only be expected: Polk awoke to discover that no attack was being launched, and, compounding his problems, no one could tell him where Hill could be located. Polk then dictated orders to a staff officer to carry to Hill's divisional commanders, Cleburne and Breckinridge, instructing them to attack as soon as they could get into position. Polk then decided it was time for his breakfast, which is where a member of Bragg's staff, who had been sent to find out why all was quiet in the sector where an assault should be in progress, found him. A now enraged Bragg mounted his horse to see Polk personally, only to find that the well-fed Polk had ridden to the front. Attempting to overtake the bishop-general, Bragg arrived at the location of Cleburne's Division to find Hill there with Cleburne, whereupon he personally reiterated his order for Hill to attack at once.[54] Precious time slipped away while Bragg and Hill made the preparations for an assault that Polk should have seen to the previous night. Hill at least had the good sense to see the vulnerability of Cleburne and Breckinridge as they advanced to the attack, and sent a staff officer with a note to Polk reminding him that the corps was in single line without reserves, and if broken at one point, was broken at all. Polk was then with General Walker, who was moving his Reserve Corps into position behind Cleburne when handed Hill's reminder. Polk then ordered Walker to continue on north until within supporting distance of Breckinridge. Cavalry was brought up to provide cover for the right flank, but Cheatham's Division was overlapping Stewart's to the point where Bragg had no choice but to order Cheatham to pull his troops back into reserve. While this tangle of humanity was being straightened out and positioned, ever since daylight from the woods to the west they could hear the sounds of Federal axes striking trees, as the Federals worked to erect breastworks that would ensure that any Confederate assault would come at a high price. The attack that was supposed to be launched at daybreak (which occurred at 5:45 A.M. on this day) at last got under way at 9:30 A.M.[55]

Besides having his men constructing breastworks that morning, Thomas was also working on his own troop dispositions, hindered by the fact that a large portion of the units that were to be used as a reserve to counter any Rebel breakthroughs did not begin arriving in the Kelly Field until several hours after daybreak. Thomas also decided that he needed to control the intersection of the Reed's Bridge and La Fayette roads, a half-mile to the north of his current left flank, and sent in a request to Rosecrans for his remaining corps' division, that of Negley. Rosecrans ordered Negley to pull out of his position in the line to the south and march to Thomas, and thus one brigade arrived in time for Thomas to place it in the gap from the intersection of the two roads to his left flank.[56] All he needed now was for the rest of Negley's division to arrive, and he could breathe easier. Unfortunately for Thomas, the time was now 9:30 A.M.

Breckinridge's Division, the rightmost division in Bragg's army and in position on Hill's flank, advanced westward with his left flank on the Reed's Bridge Road and completely missed Thomas's main line as it passed north of the waiting Federals. Continuing forward, they ran head-on into Negley's lone brigade, tearing the hapless blue-clads to shreds. Upon reaching the La Fayette Road with the brigades of Brigadier-General Daniel Weisiger Adams and Brigadier-General Marcellus Augustus Stovall, Breckinridge realized that he had obtained the position for which the Army of Tennessee had been reaching all week, beyond the Federal left flank. Breckinridge quickly deployed a brigade on either side of the La Fayette Road and moved south toward the flank and rear of Thomas's position around the Kelly Field.[57] But Breckinridge's third brigade, known as the Orphan Brigade, Kentuckians commanded by none other than Brigadier-General Benjamin Hardin Helm, brother-in-law of President Lincoln, was faced with a much more daunting task. Located on the left of Breckinridge's line, and too far south to clear the Yankee breastworks, Helm immediately came under fire when he drew near to the fortifications that curved back to the west in a semi-circle. In the woods amid the confusion of battle, half of Helm's Brigade broke apart from the other half and slid off to the right, while on the left, where Cleburne's Division was supposed to be adding its muscle to the assault, only trees stood. Helm repeatedly charged the Union line in a futile attempt to break it, only to see his casualties climb to a frightful number in the face of the Federal muskets and artillery.[58] The assaults on this portion of Thomas's line would claim the life of Lincoln's favorite brother-in-law, and it was reported that Lincoln wept upon learning of the death of Helm.[59]

By the time Polk and Walker arrived to meet with Hill at 11:00 A.M., Hill was obsessed with filling the gap in his lines created by the repulse of Helm. Upon being advised that the brigade belonging to Brigadier-General Gist of Walker's Reserve Corps had crossed the Chickamauga earlier that morning after a grueling night march, Hill had sent a staff officer to instruct him to bring his brigade forward to take the place of Helm. Gist had not yet arrived when Polk and Walker showed up with the four brigades of Walker's Corps, prompting Hill to complain that he had only requested a brigade, not two divisions. Walker responded that there was a brigade coming up behind him as they spoke, but Hill wanted the brigade of Gist, of which he had heard glowing reports. For some unexplainable reason, Polk and Walker consented to Hill's bizarre request, and the three generals sat down to wait for Gist's arrival, which occurred at 11:30 A.M.[60] After Gist protested that his men were in no condition to launch an attack after the torturous night march, Walker intervened, suggesting that he take his entire corps and attack toward the La Fayette Road.[61] Things turned ugly between Walker and Hill, and harsh words were exchanged between the two generals. Polk, tired of the dispute, rode away. Walker finally consented to assign Gist to command of the division containing his own brigade and those of General Ector and Colonel Wilson.[62] Gist turned his brigade over to the senior colonel, Peyton Colquitt of the Forty-Sixth Georgia, who placed the Twenty-Fourth South Carolina on the left, the Eighth Georgia Battalion in the center, and the four companies present from the Forty-Sixth Georgia on the right. Several minutes before noon, he stepped off into the same thick woods that Helm had traversed two hours earlier. Almost as an afterthought, Hill ordered Gist to send Ector and Wilson in behind Colquitt as support. The now fuming Walker recalled, "My command being thus disposed of, my only occupation was to help form the detached portions of my command as they came out from a position I felt certain they would have to leave when they were sent in."[63]

Colquitt struck the now reinforced (since the attack of Helm) Federal breastworks at 11:45 A.M. In maneuvering through the thick woods, his brigade had inclined too far to the right, so that only the Twenty-Fourth South Carolina on the left actually fronted the works. The remainder of the brigade drifted beyond an angle held by the Regulars of General King, where they were raked by an enfilading fire from an opponent they could not see. Colquitt wheeled the Forty-Sixth Georgia and Eighth Georgia Battalion to the left so they could at least return fire on King's men.[64] Meanwhile, the Twenty-Fourth South Carolina was being slaughtered like sheep in a pen. Colquitt left the Forty-Sixth Georgia and ran down the line toward the Twenty-Fourth, where he was killed instantly upon reaching their position. After 25 minutes of the one-sided contest, the South Carolinians broke and fled, leaving half of their regiment dead or dying in the woods, including their colonel, Clement Stevens, and the regimental major. The remainder of the brigade fell back five minutes later, their withdrawal covered by the muskets of Wilson's and Ector's brigades, which maintained a harassing fire from the timber for another ten minutes to prevent any pursuit attempt by the Federals.[65]

Due to a lack of preparation that must be blamed on the negligence of Polk, Cleburne's poorly aligned brigades veered off their intended course and became entangled with Stewart's Division of Longstreet's wing of the army. Stumbling into the Union line unsupported and at an oblique angle, the carnage was terrific, resulting in heavy casualties for Cleburne and reaping no gains for the Rebels.[66] Thomas could have breathed a sigh of relief at this point except for the fact that Breckinridge appeared in the Kelly Field in the rear of his battle line at 10:30 A.M. Though the Federal reserves managed to halt one of Breckinridge's brigades that was advancing west of the La Fayette Road, the other brigade, which was moving on the east side of the road, advanced to the edge of the woods on the north side of the field, where it opened a blistering fire on everything in blue. Van Derveer's brigade, ordered to support Thomas in any way possible, emerged from the woods on the west side of the road and immediately saw his left-flank regiments fall under a flanking fire from the Confederates in the woods just 200 yards distant. Adding to Van Derveer's confusion was the fire that was roaring from the Kelly family home and barn near his right flank. Hearing the sounds of Thomas desperately fighting off Cleburne's assault, Van Derveer, determining the greatest threat was in that sector, ordered his brigade to wheel across the field, where the left flank was forced to endure the fire of the Southerners in the trees. Upon coming parallel to the Confederates, Van Derveer's men poured forth a volley into Breckinridge's advancing brigade that sent them staggering back into the woods. For almost ten minutes, the opposing forces blazed away at each other over 200 yards of open field, though the Federals got the worst of it from their exposed position, while the Confederates were content to fire from the protection of the trees.[67] This soon changed as Colonel August Gustave Kammerling of the Ninth Ohio Infantry, an all–German regiment, ordered his men to fix bayonets and advance through the lines of the Second Minnesota Infantry. With his front now clear, he ordered his men to level bayonets and advance at quick time. An awe-struck sergeant of the Second Minnesota jumped forward and shouted to his men, "Don't let the Ninth Ohio charge alone!"[68] The brigade surged forward screaming like banshees, disintegrating the Confederate line and chasing Breckinridge's fleeing men a half-mile to the Reed's Bridge Road. It was now 11:30 A.M.

As Breckinridge's Division was making its unsupported advance against the Union flank, Bragg had given the order for every division in his army to advance immediately, without waiting for the division on its right. This was in response to the hopeless confusion when the divisions of Cleburne and Stewart, of different wings, had become entangled in each other. Stepping off shortly after 11:00 A.M., Stewart marched across the Poe Field from east to west, where he was met with a deadly fire from the Federal lines that fronted it on two sides, the first from behind the La Fayette Road on the west, and the second from the woods at the northern end where the Union line curved eastward to form Thomas's salient around the Kelly Field. The result was that Stewart's men were caught in a scorching crossfire that stacked up the Rebels like cordwood and sent the few survivors running for the woods, from whence their attack had originated.[69]

To the south of Stewart, Longstreet had arranged the main body of his wing for the assault in a powerful attacking column, with Stewart as its right flank, Major-General Thomas Carmichael Hindman as the column left, and in the center, the entire corps of Hood. Leading Hood's Corps would be the three-brigade division of Bushrod Johnson, with two brigades in front and one following in reserve. Behind Johnson was the division of Law, in the same formation, followed by the two-brigade division of Brigadier-General Joseph Brevard Kershaw.[70] By 11:00 A.M., it was poised like a knife aimed at the Union center, and the determined Rebels were about to get some unexpected help from the sleep-deprived, and very apprehensive, commanding general of the Army of the Cumberland.

Rosecrans, still determined to reinforce Thomas, began another complicated shuffling of divisions, beginning with sending Van Derveer north and pulling two brigades of the division of Major-General Phillip Henry Sheridan, located on the far right of the line, and sending them marching toward Thomas, with the third brigade to get underway as soon as practicable. Wilder's brigade, now holding the extreme Union right flank, was positioned at Glenn Hill. Rosecrans had also moved his headquarters to the open north end of a knoll that gave him a bird's-eye view of the farm and home of John Dyer, located several hundred yards west of the Brotherton Field. Thomas, meanwhile, had sent another urgent appeal for reinforcements, as well as instructing his staff officer, and nephew, Captain Sanford C. Kellogg, to relay orders to Brigadier-General John Milton Brannan to bring up his division that was supposedly being held in reserve for just such an emergency. Unknown to Thomas, Brannan had moved from his reserve position earlier that morning to fill a gap existing between the divisions of Brigadier-General Thomas John Wood and Reynolds. Kellogg nonetheless delivered the order to Brannan at his current position, and a reluctant Brannan ordered his brigade commanders to prepare to pull out of line, while Kellogg rode off to report the movement to Rosecrans. Initially approving the action, Rosecrans's muddled brain began to realize that the movement of Brannan from the line would reopen the gap he had filled, and subsequently ordered Wood to close up on Reynolds to plug the gap.[71]

Upon reflection, Brannan was having second thoughts regarding opening up a hole in the Federal line, and thus orders went out to his brigade commanders canceling the previous order to pull out until replacement troops arrived. Wood, still smarting from a dressing-down Rosecrans had given him a few days earlier in front of his staff regarding his failure to follow a vague and confusing order, received the order to close up on Reynolds at 11:00 A.M. Confused, but determined not to endure humiliation at the hands of Rosecrans again, Wood ordered his brigade commanders to pull out of the line at once. With his skirmishers engaged heavily in the Brotherton Field, and despite the objections of his brigadiers, Wood pulled his division out of line.[72] Davis, located further south and realizing the hole this would leave between himself and Brannan, attempted to make a sideways maneuver to fill the gap with the decimated brigade of Heg, just as the hair-raising sound of the Rebel yell arose from the far side of the Brotherton Ridge. Longstreet had just launched Hood's column straight at the gap created by Wood's blind obedience to orders. Johnson's Division poured over the ridge and caught Davis's troops completely out of position, before delivering a volley and then charging forward with bayonets leveled, sweeping the Federal division from the field, and doing the same to the rear brigade of Wood's division. Johnson's men chased the fleeing Federals through the Brotherton woods before entering the open field, which provided an unobstructed view of almost 500 yards. In the middle of the field on the open knoll sat Rosecrans's headquarters, where, after hastily making the sign of the cross, the Union commander expeditiously mounted up and, with his staff in tow, rode hard for the back of the hill and its shelter from the avalanche of gray.[73]

Rosecrans's only hope of containing the Rebel penetration of his lines was in the form of units that were positioned on the hills on either side of the Dyer Field. Located on the top of the ridge to the right of Rosecrans's former headquarters was a line of rapidly increasing artillery pieces that would soon grow to twenty-nine guns, while on the open hill on the other side was the infantry brigade of Colonel Bernard Laiboldt of Sheridan's division, drawn up in four regimental battle lines, one behind the other. This formation allowed them to deliver a massive amount of firepower as each regiment fired over the heads of the one in front further down the slope. In addition, Sheridan's other two brigades were en route from the Widow Glenn's to assist them. The strong position was negated, however, by the appearance of Major-General Alexander McDowell McCook, who ordered Laiboldt to fix bayonets, charge down the slope, and drive the Confederates back to the Brotherton woods. Charging into a tanyard with a hodgepodge of shacks, vats, and other equipage of the trade, Laiboldt was met by several times his number in screaming Confederates, who mowed down more than 400 of his men before sending the remainder off in a dash for cover. Caught in the maelstrom also were the two brigades belonging to Sheridan, one of which was commanded by the renowned poet, and brigadier-general, William Haines Lytle, who had taken up position on the slope of the hill vacated by Laiboldt, just as the Rebels were surging up the slope in pursuit of the remainder of the wrecked brigade. A short but vicious fight ensued that saw Lytle killed, as his brigade was destroyed in the Confederate juggernaut. Also mauled was Sheridan's third brigade in their position between Lytle's men and the Widow Glenn's. Sheridan's division was routed, and the surviving members mournfully joined the procession of blue that was frantically making its way toward Chattanooga by the Dry Valley Road. Included in the demoralized jumble of soldiers, wagons, and caissons were McCook, Crittenden, and Rosecrans.[74]

Out in the Dyer Field, the Union guns posted on the ridge were raining missiles on the advancing members of Longstreet's wing. Realizing that until this threat to his right flank was neutralized he could not possibly undertake a pursuit of the demoralized Federals, he ordered his attacking column to wheel to the north and clear the ridge of the guns. Hood ordered Johnson to "Go ahead, and keep ahead of everything."[75] With Law's Division advancing straight across the open field, Johnson reached the ridge south of the artillery and closed in on their flank, sending the infantry support of the guns in flight to escape, while the artillerists attempted to remove their pieces to prevent capture. It was all for naught, as 17 guns became prizes of war for the Confederates. As Hood moved his corps further north through the Dyer Field and approached a rail fence, a sheet of flame erupted from the fence line courtesy of Colonel Charles Garrison Harker's brigade of Wood's division. As Hood was attempting to rally his men, who had broken under the fire, a ball slammed into his right leg just below the hip, forcing him to be carried from the field, just as the brigades of Brigadier-General Benjamin Grubb Humphreys and Kershaw were advancing through the field toward Harker's line, with their Army of Northern Virginia battle flags waving in the breeze.[76]

Miraculously, the fire from Harker's line, running from a high hill at the northwest corner of the field and along the far edge to the low land at the field's northeast corner, stopped. Even more peculiar to the advancing Rebels was the sight of the Union color-bearers, standing at full height and proudly waving the national colors over their heads. Used to seeing the more rugged style of uniforms and flags of the Army of Tennessee, Harker and Wood were not sure if the neatly attired men approaching with their unusual flags were friend or foe, and thus ordered the deadly fire of their men halted until the identity of the approaching troops could be ascertained. As the rifle range between the two bodies of troops shortened, Kershaw's Brigade gave the Union commanders their answer as they unleashed a volley that initiated another vicious confrontation, before the two brigades were able to overlap Harker's flanks, breaking his brigade. Kershaw's men swarmed over the hilltop at the northwest corner of the Dyer Field before running down the farther slope in pursuit of the retreating Federals. Harker's troops reformed on the next open ridge toward the north where a small group of Federal soldiers with fight still in them were forming to make a final stand near the home of a farmer named George Washington Snodgrass.[77]

General Thomas, in charge of the motley assortment of refugees gathered on Snodgrass Hill, dipped into the reserves he had been holding in the Kelly Field to provide a few fresh units around which to rally the troops of the Federal right. As Kershaw's exultant men came forward expecting to drive the Yankees as they had in the Dyer Field, the Union line erupted in repeated volleys of musket fire, driving back two separate charges of Kershaw's South Carolinians.[78] More gray-clad troops attempted to break the Snodgrass Hill and the adjoining Horseshoe Ridge line, but the Federals under Thomas were hanging on for their lives, and with each failed Confederate attack, their confidence was returning. A major portion of the cause of the repulses of the Southerners in their assaults lay in coordination. Longstreet was counting on Hood to handle the up-close and personal coordination of the attacks, and Hood was now on his way to having his leg amputated at a field hospital. Strangely, Longstreet did not see his way to appoint anyone to fill the void caused by the wounding of Hood.

Whether anyone had appointed him or not, Bushrod Johnson was determined that if the

Federals could not be driven from their position, he would at least attempt to flank them out of it. Bringing up his division and swinging it in on the Confederate left, he advanced toward a point further up Horseshoe Ridge, from whence the previous assaults had occurred. Standing squarely in his way was the Twenty-First Ohio Infantry, of which seven of the ten companies were armed with the five-shot Colt Revolving Rifle, a repeater that was designed like a revolver pistol on a rifle frame. Turning back the first several assaults with the firepower of their Colts, the sheer numbers of the Confederates were taking a toll on the Ohioans as Johnson's men finally reached the ridge on the Twenty-First Ohio's flank and began to apply a steady pressure to sweep them off the ridge and get on with rolling up the last Union defensive line. Both sides were startled when a cheer arose from the back slope of the ridge beyond the Union flank and a blue-clad line of battle consisting of Brigadier-General James Blair Steedman's division of the Reserve Corps crested the ridge and knocked the dazed Confederates right back down the slope to their starting point. Commanded by Major-General Gordon Granger, the Reserve Corps had been stationed north of the battlefield at Rossville, where it was assigned to cover a gap in Missionary Ridge. As Granger had heard the second day's fighting to the south swell to a roar, he correctly assumed that all help was needed in the fight and marched two of his brigades to the sounds of battle, where a jubilant General Thomas rushed him into place on the right flank beyond the Twenty-First Ohio.[79]

As casualties on both sides continued to climb to sickening numbers, a message reached Thomas in the late afternoon from Rosecrans, who was en route to Chattanooga, ordering him to withdraw his forces and retreat. This was easier said than done with the unrelenting Confederate pressure being applied to Thomas's Snodgrass Hill front. Longstreet had reported to Bragg in person of his accomplishments of the day, and urged Bragg to renew the assault by Polk's right wing. Bragg, refusing to accept that a portion of his army had achieved great results, retorted sarcastically, "There is not a man in the right wing who has any fight in him."[80] In other words, Longstreet was on his own to gain further successes. Nevertheless, at 5:00 P.M., Longstreet had reformed his left wing and was ready to grab for further glory. As the Rebels advanced once more toward the Union breastworks, the troops that had been so vigilantly holding that position were in the process of pulling back into, and across, the Kelly Field, made necessary by the fact that the Snodgrass Hill line covered Dry Valley Road, the only Union line of retreat, thus the Kelly Field troops must pull out first. When caught in the process by the advancing Rebels, all hell broke loose as the Southerners poured over the breastworks and into the Kelly Field, aided by a battery of guns that swung into line and began blasting loads of canister into the fleeing Union soldiers. As the elated Confederate soldiers met in the field, they assumed they had destroyed a major portion of the Federal army, and the fearsome Rebel yell rang out through the evening air. James Cooper of the Twentieth Tennessee Infantry recalled: "At sunset ... everyone seemed wild with joy, from generals down to privates, all joined in the exultant cheer that rang over that blood-stained field, telling in tones as loud as Heavens artillery, that we were victorious. Wild shouts ran from one end of our lines to the other and even the poor wounded fellows lying about through the woods joined in."[81]

Most of the Federal units had managed to get away in some semblance of order, and some still had a spark of fight left in them. As Reynolds's division was ordered to throw back a Confederate division that was threatening to move down the La Fayette Road and block the route of retreat from the Kelly Field before the other Union units could begin their withdrawal, in the confusion, Reynolds misunderstood his orders. Under the impression that he was to open a route for the entire army to follow, he proceeded up the La Fayette Road where he handily brushed aside a gray-clad division, then proceeded on to Chattanooga unmolested on a route that was presumed closed to the Federal forces. The remainder of the Union soldiers retreated through the Snodgrass Field and along Horseshoe Ridge, before proceeding down onto the Dry

Valley Road in the fast approaching darkness, as the soldiers on the open Snodgrass Hill pulled back to Horseshoe Ridge from the position they had so gallantly defended all afternoon. The retreat was a nightmare for those involved, as they were forced to withdraw with a fragmentary chain-of-command over rugged terrain, in the face of an aggressive pursuer flushed with success. Fragmentary fighting flared up as Rebel detachments, cautiously probing through the darkening woods, ran into Federal soldiers covering the retreat. Among the Union prisoners taken that evening was almost the entire Twenty-First Ohio, the heroes of Horseshoe Ridge, who had not received word to withdraw from their position. As darkness enveloped the two opposing armies, the two-day Battle of Chickamauga was mercifully brought to a close.[82]

Six members of the Fourth Louisiana Battalion Infantry would have their names added to the Confederate Roll of Honor on August 10, 1864, for gallantry at the Battle of Chickamauga, though three of the men would receive the honor posthumously. The six men whose names were added per General Order Number 64 of the Adjutant and Inspector General's Office in Richmond were Private Daniel W. Frisbey of Company A, Private M. Rearden of Company D, and Private Robert L. Walker of Company F. The remaining three who gave the ultimate sacrifice on the battlefield in north Georgia were Private William Shively of Company B, Private Peter Orr of Company C, and Private Girard Ballance of Company E.[83]

On Monday, September 22, the Army of the Cumberland began establishing its headquarters in Chattanooga, followed by Thomas, who had kept his force at Rossville, on the following day. Bragg held the field of battle, though it would prove to be a hollow victory for the Confederacy. A gut-wrenching total of 34,633 men of the South and North had fallen, with the Army of Tennessee's losses tallied at a staggering 18,454 out of a force of 68,000, slightly larger than the Army of the Cumberland's 16,179 from a force of 57,840.[84] Each army, through the loss of officers, horses, and equipment, was seriously hampered from undertaking any immediate offensive movements, though both armies were still intact, if badly cut up. Bragg's failure to turn the Federal north flank and cut it off from its base had allowed the Army of the Cumberland to survive its brush with disaster in north Georgia. If accomplished, this movement could have yielded truly decisive results for the Army of Tennessee. Though much blame for this failure must be placed on Bragg's fractious and insubordinate generals, those very underlings were quick to blame their commanding general for the failure to destroy Rosecrans. Credit must also be given to Rosecrans and Thomas for their alertness in sidling the Federal army quickly northward toward Chattanooga, and in keeping their northern flank strong in the face of Bragg's repeated attempts to break it. In the aftermath of the battle, Bragg opted for the only course left available to his army in its considerably weakened state: Lay siege to Chattanooga and attempt to starve Rosecrans into submission, as the Union had so effectively done to the Rebel garrison at Vicksburg almost three months previous. But Lincoln was not about to let the momentum that the Union had established slip away in the waning months of 1863. Bragg, and his army, were soon to face the Federal army's heavy-hitter. General Grant was coming to Chattanooga.

CHICKAMAUGA, GA., ORDER OF BATTLE
September 19–20, 1863

Union Forces: Army of the Cumberland
Major-General William Starke Rosecrans

Army Headquarters
1st Battalion Ohio Sharpshooters: Captain Greshom M. Barber
10th Ohio Infantry (Provost Guard): Lt. Colonel William Murray Ward
15th Pennsylvania Cavalry (Escort): Colonel William J. Palmer

Fourteenth Corps
Major-General George Henry Thomas

14th Corps Headquarters
9th Michigan Infantry (Provost Guard): Colonel John G. Parkhurst
1st Ohio Cavalry — Co. L (Escort): Captain John D. Barker

First Division
Brigadier-General Absalom Baird

First Brigade
Colonel Benjamin Franklin Scribner
38th Indiana Infantry: Lt. Colonel Daniel F. Griffin
2nd Ohio Infantry: Lt. Colonel Obadiah C. Maxwell
33rd Ohio Infantry: Colonel Oscar F. Moore
94th Ohio Infantry: Major Rue P. Hutchins
10th Wisconsin Infantry: Lt. Colonel John H. Ely

Second Brigade
Brigadier-General John Converse Starkweather
24th Illinois Infantry: Colonel Geza Mihalotzy
79th Pennsylvania Infantry: Colonel Henry A. Hambright
1st Wisconsin: Lt. Colonel George B. Bingham
21st Wisconsin: Lt. Colonel Harrison C. Hobart

Third Brigade
Brigadier-General John Haskell King
15th U.S. Regulars — 1st Battalion: Captain Albert B. Dod
16th U.S. Regulars — 1st Battalion: Major Sidney Coolidge
18th U.S. Regulars — 1st Battalion: Captain George W. Smith
18th U.S. Regulars — 2nd Battalion: Captain Henry Haymond
19th U.S. Regulars — 1st Battalion: Major Samuel K. Dawson

Artillery
Indiana Light Artillery — Fourth Battery: Lieutenant David Flansburg
1st Michigan Light Artillery — Battery A: Lieutenant George W. Van Pelt
5th U.S. Artillery — Battery H: Lieutenant Howard M. Burnham

Second Division
Major-General James Scott Negley

First Brigade
Brigadier-General John Beatty
104th Illinois Infantry: Lt. Colonel Douglas Hapeman
42nd Indiana Infantry: Lt. Colonel William T. B. McIntire
88th Indiana Infantry: Colonel George Humphrey
15th Kentucky Infantry: Colonel Marion C. Taylor

Second Brigade
Colonel Timothy R. Stanley
19th Illinois Infantry: Lt. Colonel Alexander W. Raffen
11th Michigan Infantry: Colonel William L. Stoughton
18th Ohio Infantry: Lt. Colonel Charles H. Grosvenor

Third Brigade
Colonel William Sirwell
37th Indiana Infantry: Lt. Colonel William D. Ward
21st Ohio Infantry: Lt. Colonel Dwella M. Stoughton
74th Ohio Infantry: Captain Joseph Fisher
78th Pennsylvania Infantry: Lt. Colonel Archibald Blakeley

Artillery
Illinois Light Artillery — Bridges Battery: Captain Lyman Bridges

1st Ohio Light Artillery — Battery G: Captain Alexander Marshall
1st Ohio Light Artillery — Battery M: Captain Frederick Schultz

Third Division
Brigadier-General John Milton Brannan

First Brigade
Colonel John M. Connell
82nd Indiana Infantry: Colonel Morton C. Hunter
17th Ohio Infantry: Lt. Colonel Durbin Ward
31st Ohio Infantry: Lt. Colonel Frederick W. Lister
38th Ohio Infantry: Colonel Edward H. Phelps

Second Brigade
Colonel John Thomas Croxton
10th Indiana Infantry: Colonel William B. Carroll
74th Indiana Infantry: Colonel Charles W. Chapman
4th Kentucky Infantry: Lt. Colonel P. Burgess Hunt
10th Kentucky Infantry: Colonel William H. Hays
14th Ohio Infantry: Lt. Colonel Henry D. Kingsbury

Third Brigade
Colonel Ferdinand Van Derveer
87th Indiana Infantry: Colonel Newell Gleason
2nd Minnesota Infantry: Colonel James George
9th Ohio Infantry: Colonel Gustave Kammerling
35th Ohio Infantry: Lt. Colonel Henry V. N. Boynton

Artillery
1st Michigan Light Artillery — Battery D: Captain Josiah W. Church
1st Ohio Light Artillery — Battery C: Lieutenant Marco B. Gary
4th U.S. Artillery — Battery I: Lieutenant Frank G. Smith

Fourth Division
Major-General Joseph Jones Reynolds

First Brigade
Colonel John T. Wilder
92nd Illinois Infantry: Colonel Smith D. Atkins
98th Illinois Infantry: Colonel John J. Funkhouser
123rd Illinois Infantry: Colonel James Monroe
17th Indiana Infantry: Major William T. Jones
72nd Indiana Infantry: Colonel Abram O. Miller

Second Brigade
Colonel Edward A. King
68th Indiana Infantry: Captain Harvey J. Espy
75th Indiana Infantry: Colonel Milton S. Robinson
101st Indiana Infantry: Lt. Colonel Thomas Doan
105th Ohio Infantry: Major George T. Perkins

Third Brigade
Brigadier-General John Basil Turchin
18th Kentucky Infantry: Lt. Colonel Hubbard K. Milward
11th Ohio Infantry: Colonel Philander P. Lane
36th Ohio Infantry: Colonel William G. Jones
92nd Ohio Infantry: Colonel Benjamin D. Fearing

Artillery
Indiana Light Artillery — 18th Battery: Captain Eli Lilly
Indiana Light Artillery — 19th Battery: Captain Samuel J. Harris
Indiana Light Artillery — 21st Battery: Captain William W. Andrew

Twentieth Corps
Major-General Alexander McDowell McCook

20th Corps Headquarters
81st Indiana Infantry — Co. H (Provost Guard): Captain William J. Richards
2nd Kentucky Cavalry — Co. I (Escort): Lieutenant George W. L. Batman

First Division
Brigadier-General Jefferson Columbus Davis

First Brigade
Colonel Sidney Post
59th Illinois Infantry: Lt. Colonel Joshua C. Winters
74th Illinois Infantry: Colonel Jason Marsh
75th Illinois Infantry: Colonel John E. Bennett
22nd Indiana Infantry: Colonel Michael Gooding
Wisconsin Light Artillery — 5th Battery: Captain George Q. Gardner

Second Brigade
Brigadier-General William Passmore Carlin
21st Illinois Infantry: Colonel John W. S. Alexander
38th Illinois Infantry: Lt. Colonel Daniel H. Gilmer
81st Indiana Infantry: Captain Nevil B. Boone
101st Ohio Infantry: Lt. Colonel John Messer
Minnesota Light Artillery — 2nd Battery: Lieutenant Albert Woodbury

Third Brigade
Colonel Hans Christian Heg
25th Illinois Infantry: Major Samuel D. Wall
35th Illinois Infantry: Lt. Colonel William P. Chandler
8th Kansas Infantry: Colonel John A. Martin
15th Wisconsin Infantry: Lt. Colonel Ole C. Johnson
Wisconsin Light Artillery — 8th Battery: Lieutenant John D. McLean

Second Division
Brigadier-General Richard W. Johnson

First Brigade
Brigadier-General August Willich
89th Illinois Infantry: Lt. Colonel Duncan J. Hall
32nd Indiana Infantry: Lt. Colonel Frank Erdelmeyer
39th Indiana Infantry: Colonel Thomas J. Harrison
15th Ohio Infantry: Lt. Colonel Frank Askew
49th Ohio Infantry: Major Samuel F. Gray
1st Ohio Light Artillery — Battery A: Captain Wilbur F. Goodspeed

Second Brigade
Colonel Joseph B. Dodge
79th Illinois Infantry: Colonel Allen Buckner
29th Indiana Infantry: Lt. Colonel David M. Dunn
30th Indiana Infantry: Lt. Colonel Orrin D. Hurd
77th Pennsylvania Infantry: Colonel Thomas E. Rose
Ohio Light Artillery — 20th Battery: Captain Edward Grosskopff

Third Brigade
Colonel Philemon P. Baldwin
6th Indiana Infantry: Lt. Colonel Hagerman Tripp
5th Kentucky Infantry: Colonel William W. Berry
1st Ohio Infantry: Lt. Colonel Bassett Langdon
93rd Ohio Infantry: Colonel Hiram Strong
Indiana Light Artillery — 5th Battery: Captain Peter Simonson

Third Division
Major-General Philip Henry Sheridan

First Brigade
Brigadier-General William Haines Lytle
36th Illinois Infantry: Colonel Silas Miller
88th Illinois Infantry: Lt. Colonel Alexander S. Chadbourne
21st Michigan Infantry: Colonel William B. McCreery
24th Wisconsin Infantry: Lt. Colonel Theodore S. West
Indiana Light Artillery—11th Battery: Captain Arnold Sutermeister

Second Brigade
Colonel Bernard Laiboldt
44th Illinois Infantry: Colonel Wallace W. Barrett
73rd Illinois Infantry: Colonel James F. Jaquess
2nd Missouri Infantry: Major Arnold Beck
15th Missouri Infantry: Colonel Joseph Conrad
1st Missouri Light Artillery—Battery G: Lieutenant Gustavus Schueler

Third Brigade
Colonel Luther P. Bradley
22nd Illinois Infantry: Lt. Colonel Francis Swanwick
27th Illinois Infantry: Colonel Jonathan R. Miles
42nd Illinois Infantry: Colonel Nathan H. Walworth
51st Illinois Infantry: Lt. Colonel Samuel B. Raymond
1st Illinois Light Artillery—Battery C: Captain Mark H. Prescott

Twenty-First Corps
Major-General Thomas Leonidas Crittenden

21st Corps Headquarters
15th Illinois Cavalry—Company K (Escort): Captain Samuel B. Sherer

First Division
Brigadier-General Thomas John Wood

First Brigade
Colonel George P. Buell
100th Illinois Infantry: Colonel Frederick A. Bartleson
58th Indiana Infantry: Lt. Colonel James T. Embree
13th Michigan Infantry: Colonel Joshua B. Culver
26th Ohio Infantry: Lt. Colonel William H. Young

Second Brigade
Brigadier-General George Day Wagner
15th Indiana Infantry: Colonel Gustavus A. Wood
40th Indiana Infantry: Colonel John W. Blake
57th Indiana Infantry: Lt. Colonel George W. Lennard
97th Ohio Infantry: Lt. Colonel Milton Barnes

Third Brigade
Colonel Charles G. Harker
3rd Kentucky Infantry: Colonel Henry C. Dunlap
64th Ohio Infantry: Colonel Alexander McIlvain
65th Ohio Infantry: Lt. Colonel Horatio N. Whitbeck
125th Ohio Infantry: Colonel Emerson Opdycke

Artillery
Indiana Light Artillery—8th Battery: Captain George Estep
Indiana Light Artillery—10th Battery: Lieutenant William A. Naylor
Ohio Light Artillery—6th Battery: Captain Cullen Bradley

Second Division
Major-General John McCauley Palmer

First Brigade
Brigadier-General Charles Cruft
31st Indiana Infantry: Colonel John T. Smith
1st Kentucky Infantry: Lt. Colonel Alva R. Hadlock
2nd Kentucky Infantry: Colonel Thomas D. Sedgewick
90th Ohio Infantry: Colonel Charles H. Rippey

Second Brigade
Brigadier-General William Babcock Hazen
9th Indiana Infantry: Colonel Isaac C. B. Suman
6th Kentucky Infantry: Colonel George T. Shackelford
41st Ohio Infantry: Colonel Aquila Wiley
124th Ohio Infantry: Colonel Oliver H. Payne

Third Brigade
Colonel William Grose
84th Illinois Infantry: Colonel Louis H. Waters
36th Indiana Infantry: Lt. Colonel Oliver H. P. Carey
23rd Kentucky Infantry: Lt. Colonel James C. Foy
6th Ohio Infantry: Colonel Nicholas L. Anderson
24th Ohio Infantry: Colonel David J. Higgins

Artillery
1st Ohio Light Artillery — Battery B: Lieutenant Norman A. Baldwin
1st Ohio Light Artillery — Battery F: Lieutenant Giles J. Cockerill
4th U.S. Artillery — Battery H: Lieutenant Harry C. Cushing
4th U.S. Artillery — Battery M: Lieutenant Francis L. D. Russell

Unattached
110th Illinois Battalion Infantry: Captain E. Hibbard Topping

Third Division
Brigadier-General Horatio Phillips Van Cleve

First Brigade
Brigadier-General Samuel Beatty
79th Indiana Infantry: Colonel Frederick Knefler
9th Kentucky Infantry: Colonel George H. Cram
17th Kentucky Infantry: Colonel Alexander M. Stout
19th Ohio Infantry: Lt. Colonel Henry D. Stratton

Second Brigade
Colonel George F. Dick
44th Indiana Infantry: Lt. Colonel Simeon C. Aldrich
86th Indiana Infantry: Major Jacob C. Dick
13th Ohio Infantry: Lt. Colonel Elhannon M. Mast
59th Ohio Infantry: Lt. Colonel Granville A. Frambes

Third Brigade
Colonel Sidney M. Barnes
35th Indiana Infantry: Major John P. Dufficy
8th Kentucky Infantry: Lt. Colonel James D. Mayhew
21st Kentucky Infantry: Colonel S. Woodson Price
51st Ohio Infantry: Colonel Richard W. McClain
99th Ohio Infantry: Colonel Peter T. Swaine

Artillery
Indiana Light Artillery — 7th Battery: Captain George R. Swallow
Pennsylvania Light Artillery — 26th Battery: Captain Alanson J. Stevens
Wisconsin Light Artillery — 3rd Battery: Lieutenant Cortland Livingston

Reserve Corps
Major-General Gordon Granger

First Division
Brigadier-General James Blair Steedman

First Brigade
Brigadier-General Walter Chiles Whitaker
96th Illinois Infantry: Colonel Thomas E. Champion
115th Illinois Infantry: Colonel Jesse H. Moore
84th Indiana Infantry: Colonel Nelson Trusler
22nd Michigan Infantry: Colonel Heber Le Favour
40th Ohio Infantry: Lt. Colonel William Jones
89th Ohio Infantry: Colonel Caleb H. Carlton
Ohio Light Artillery—18th Battery: Captain Charles C. Aleshire

Second Brigade
Colonel John G. Mitchell
78th Illinois Infantry: Lt. Colonel Carter Van Vleck
98th Ohio Infantry: Captain Moses J. Urquhart
113th Ohio Infantry: Lt. Colonel Darius B. Warner
121st Ohio Infantry: Lt. Colonel Henry B. Banning
1st Illinois Light Artillery—Battery M: Lieutenant Thomas Burton

Second Division

Second Brigade
Colonel Daniel McCook
85th Illinois Infantry: Colonel Caleb J. Dilworth
86th Illinois Infantry: Lt. Colonel David W. Magee
125th Illinois Infantry: Colonel Oscar F. Harmon
52nd Ohio Infantry: Major James T. Holmes
69th Ohio Infantry: Lt. Colonel Joseph H. Brigham
2nd Illinois Light Artillery—Battery I: Captain Charles M. Barnett

Cavalry Corps
Brigadier-General Robert B. Mitchell

First Division
Colonel Edward M. McCook

First Brigade
Colonel Archibald P. Campbell
2nd Michigan Cavalry: Major Leonidas S. Scranton
9th Pennsylvania Cavalry: Lt. Colonel Roswell M. Russell
1st Tennessee Cavalry: Lt. Colonel James P. Brownlow

Second Brigade
Colonel Daniel M. Ray
2nd Indiana Cavalry: Major Joseph B. Presdee
4th Indiana Cavalry: Lt. Colonel John T. Deweese
2nd Tennessee Cavalry: Lt. Colonel William R. Cook
1st Wisconsin Cavalry: Colonel Oscar H. LaGrange
1st Ohio Light Artillery—Battery D (Section): Lieutenant Nathaniel M. Newell

Third Brigade
Colonel Louis D. Watkins
4th Kentucky Cavalry: Colonel Wickliffe Cooper
5th Kentucky Cavalry: Lt. Colonel William T. Hoblitzell
6th Kentucky Cavalry: Major Louis A. Gratz

Second Division
Brigadier-General George Crook

First Brigade
Colonel Robert H. G. Minty

3rd Indiana Battalion Cavalry: Lt. Colonel Robert Klein
4th Michigan Cavalry: Major Horace Gray
7th Pennsylvania Cavalry: Lt. Colonel James J. Seibert
4th U.S. Cavalry: Captain James B. McIntyre

Second Brigade
Colonel Eli Long
2nd Kentucky Cavalry: Colonel Thomas P. Nicholas
1st Ohio Cavalry: Lt. Colonel Valentine Cupp
3rd Ohio Cavalry: Lt. Colonel Charles B. Seidel
4th Ohio Cavalry: Lt. Colonel Oliver P. Robie

Artillery
Chicago Board of Trade Battery: Captain James H. Stokes

CONFEDERATE FORCES: ARMY OF TENNESSEE

General Braxton Bragg

Army Headquarters
Dreux's Company Louisiana Cavalry (Escort): Lieutenant O. DeBuis
Holloway's Company Alabama Cavalry (Escort): Captain E. M. Holloway

Right Wing
Lieutenant-General Leonidas Polk

Right Wing Headquarters
Greenleaf's Company Louisiana Cavalry (Escort): Captain Leeds Greenleaf

Cheatham's Division
Major-General Benjamin Franklin Cheatham

Division Headquarters
2nd Georgia Cavalry — Co. G (Escort): Captain Thomas M. Merritt

Jackson's Brigade
Brigadier-General John King Jackson
1st Georgia Infantry — 2nd Battalion: Major James Clarke Gordon
5th Georgia Infantry: Colonel Charles P. Daniel
2nd Georgia Battalion Sharpshooters: Major Richard H. Whitely
5th Mississippi Infantry: Lt. Colonel W. L. Sykes
8th Mississippi Infantry: Colonel John C. Wilkinson

Smith's Brigade
Brigadier-General Preston Smith
11th Tennessee Infantry: Colonel George W. Gordon
12th and 47th Tennessee Infantry (Consolidated): Colonel William M. Watkins
13th and 154th Tennessee Infantry (Consolidated): Colonel A. J. Vaughan, Jr.
29th Tennessee Infantry: Colonel Horace Rice
Dawson's Battalion Sharpshooters: Major J. W. Dawson

Maney's Brigade
Brigadier-General George Earl Maney
1st and 27th Tennessee Infantry (Consolidated): Colonel Hume R. Field
4th Tennessee Infantry: Colonel James A. McMurry
6th and 9th Tennessee Infantry (Consolidated): Colonel George C. Porter
24th Tennessee Battalion Sharpshooters: Major Frank Maney

Wright's Brigade
Brigadier-General Marcus Joseph Wright
8th Tennessee Infantry: Colonel John H. Anderson
16th Tennessee Infantry: Colonel D. M. Donnell
28th Tennessee Infantry: Colonel Sidney S. Stanton
38th Tennessee Infantry and Murray's Tennessee Battalion (Cons.): Colonel John C. Carter
51st and 52nd Tennessee Infantry (Consolidated): Lt. Colonel John G. Hall

Strahl's Brigade
Brigadier-General Otho French Strahl
4th and 5th Tennessee Infantry (Consolidated): Colonel Jonathan J. Lamb
19th Tennessee Infantry: Colonel Francis M. Walker
24th Tennessee Infantry: Colonel John A. Wilson
31st Tennessee Infantry: Colonel Egbert E. Tansil
33rd Tennessee Infantry: Colonel Warner P. Jones

Artillery
Major Melancthon Smith
Carnes Tennessee Battery: Captain William W. Carnes
Scogin's Georgia Battery: Captain John Scogin
Scott's Tennessee Battery: Lieutenant John H. Marsh
Smith's Mississippi Battery: Lieutenant William B. Turner
Stanford's Mississippi Battery: Captain Thomas J. Stanford

Hill's Corps
Lieutenant-General Daniel Harvey Hill

Cleburne's Division
Major-General Patrick Ronayne Cleburne

Division Headquarters
Sanders' Company Tennessee Cavalry (Escort): Captain C. F. Sanders

Wood's Brigade
Brigadier-General Sterling Alexander Martin Wood
16th Alabama Infantry: Major John H. McGaughy
33rd Alabama Infantry: Colonel Samuel Ashford
45th Alabama Infantry: Colonel E. B. Breedlove
18th Alabama Battalion Infantry: Major John H. Gibson
32nd and 45th Mississippi Infantry (Consolidated): Colonel M. P. Lowrey
15th Mississippi Battalion Sharpshooters: Major A. T. Hawkins

Polk's Brigade
Brigadier-General Lucius Eugene Polk
1st Arkansas Infantry: Colonel John W. Colquitt
3rd and 5th Confederate Infantry (Consolidated): Colonel J. A. Smith
2nd Tennessee Infantry: Colonel William D. Robison
35th Tennessee Infantry: Colonel Benjamin J. Hill
48th Tennessee Infantry: Colonel George H. Nixon

Deshler's Brigade
Brigadier-General James Deshler
9th and 24th Arkansas Infantry (Consolidated): Lt. Colonel A. S. Hutchison
6th and 10th Texas Infantry and 15th Texas Cavalry (Dismounted): Colonel Roger Q. Mills
17th, 18th, 24th and 25th Texas Cavalry (Dismounted and Cons.): Colonel F. C. Wilkes

Artillery
Major T. R. Hotchkiss
Calvert's Arkansas Battery: Lieutenant Thomas J. Key
Douglas' Texas Battery: Captain James P. Douglas
Semple's Alabama Battery: Captain Henry C. Semple

Breckinridge's Division
Major-General John Cabell Breckinridge

Division Headquarters
Foules' Company Mississippi Cavalry: Captain H. L. Foules

Helm's Brigade
Brigadier-General Benjamin Hardin Helm
41st Alabama Infantry: Colonel Martin L. Stanset

2nd Kentucky Infantry: Lt. Colonel James W. Hewitt
4th Kentucky Infantry: Colonel Joseph P. Nuckols
6th Kentucky Infantry: Colonel Joseph H. Lewis
9th Kentucky Infantry: Colonel John W. Caldwell

Adams's Brigade
Brigadier-General Daniel Weisiger Adams
32nd Alabama Infantry: Major John C. Kimbell
13th and 20th Louisiana Infantry (Consolidated): Colonel Randall Lee Gibson
16th and 25th Louisiana Infantry (Consolidated): Colonel Daniel Gober
19th Louisiana Infantry: Lt. Colonel Richard W. Turner
14th Louisiana Battalion Infantry: Major J. E. Austin

Stovall's Brigade
Brigadier-General Marcellus Augustus Stovall
1st and 3rd Florida Infantry (Consolidated): Colonel William S. Dilworth
4th Florida Infantry: Colonel W. L. L. Bowen
47th Georgia Infantry: Captain William S. Phillips
60th North Carolina Infantry: Lt. Colonel James M. Ray

Artillery
Major Rice E. Graves
Cobb's Kentucky Battery: Captain Robert Cobb
Graves' Kentucky Battery: Lieutenant S. M. Spencer
Mebane's Tennessee Battery: Captain John W. Mebane
Slocomb's Louisiana Battery: Captain C. H. Slocomb

Reserve Corps
Major-General William Henry Talbot Walker

Walker's Division
Brigadier-General States Rights Gist

Gist's Brigade
Colonel Peyton H. Colquitt
46th Georgia Infantry: Major A. M. Speer
8th Georgia Battalion Infantry: Lt. Colonel Leroy Napier
16th South Carolina Infantry: Colonel James McCullough
24th South Carolina Infantry: Colonel Clement H. Stevens

Ector's Brigade
Brigadier-General Matthew Duncan Ector
Stone's Alabama Battalion Sharpshooters: Major T. O. Stone
Pound's Mississippi Battalion Sharpshooters: Captain M. Pound
29th North Carolina Infantry: Colonel William B. Creasman
9th Texas Infantry: Colonel William H. Young
10th Texas Cavalry (Dismounted): Lt. Colonel C. R. Earp
14th Texas Cavalry (Dismounted): Colonel J. L. Camp
32nd Texas Cavalry (Dismounted): Colonel Julius A. Andrews

Wilson's Brigade
Colonel Claudius Charles Wilson
25th Georgia Infantry: Lt. Colonel A. J. Williams
29th Georgia Infantry: Lieutenant George R. McRae
30th Georgia Infantry: Lt. Colonel James S. Boynton
1st Georgia Battalion Sharpshooters: Major Arthur Schaaff
4th Louisiana Battalion Infantry: Lt. Colonel John McEnery

Artillery
Ferguson's South Carolina Battery: Lieutenant R. T. Beauregard
Howell's Georgia Battery: Captain Evan P. Howell

Liddell's Division
Brigadier-General Saint John Richardson Liddell

Liddell's Brigade
Colonel Daniel Chevilette Govan
2nd and 15th Arkansas Infantry (Consolidated): Lt. Colonel Reuben F. Harvey
5th and 13th Arkansas Infantry (Consolidated): Colonel L. Featherston
6th and 7th Arkansas Infantry (Consolidated): Colonel D. A. Gillespie
8th Arkansas Infantry: Lt. Colonel George F. Baucum
1st Louisiana Infantry: Major A. Watkins

Walthall's Brigade
Brigadier-General Edward Cary Walthall
24th Mississippi Infantry: Lt. Colonel R. P. McKelvaine
27th Mississippi Infantry: Colonel James A. Campbell
29th Mississippi Infantry: Colonel William F. Brantly
30th Mississippi Infantry: Colonel Junius I. Scales
34th Mississippi Infantry: Major William G. Pegram

Artillery
Captain Charles Swett
Fowler's Alabama Battery: Captain William H. Fowler
Warren Light Artillery (Mississippi Battery): Lieutenant H. Shannon

Left Wing
Lieutenant-General James Longstreet

Hindman's Division
Major-General Thomas Carmichael Hindman

Division Headquarters
Lenoir's Company Alabama Cavalry (Escort): Captain T. M. Lenoir

Anderson's Brigade
Brigadier-General James Patton Anderson
7th Mississippi Infantry: Colonel W. H. Bishop
9th Mississippi Infantry: Major T. H. Lynam
10th Mississippi Infantry: Lt. Colonel James Barr
41st Mississippi Infantry: Colonel W. F. Tucker
44th Mississippi Infantry: Colonel J. H. Sharp
9th Mississippi Battalion Sharpshooters: Major W. C. Richards
Garrity's Alabama Battery: Captain James Garrity

Dea's Brigade
Brigadier-General Zachariah Cantey Deas
19th Alabama Infantry: Colonel Samuel K. McSpadden
22nd Alabama Infantry: Lt. Colonel John Weeden
25th Alabama Infantry: Colonel George D. Johnston
39th Alabama Infantry: Colonel Whitfield Clark
50th Alabama Infantry: Colonel J. G. Coltart
17th Alabama Battalion Sharpshooters: Captain James F. Nabers
Dent's Alabama Battery: Captain S. H. Dent

Manigault's Brigade
Brigadier-General Arthur Middleton Manigault
24th Alabama Infantry: Colonel N. N. Davis
28th Alabama Infantry: Colonel John C. Reid
34th Alabama Infantry: Major John N. Slaughter
10th and 19th South Carolina Infantry (Consolidated): Colonel James F. Pressley
Water's Alabama Battery: Lieutenant Charles W. Watkins

Buckner's Corps
Major-General Simon Bolivar Buckner

Corps Headquarters
Clark's Company Tennessee Cavalry (Escort): Captain J. W. Clark

Stewart's Division
Major-General Alexander Peter Stewart

Bate's Brigade
Brigadier-General William Brimage Bate
58th Alabama Infantry: Colonel Bushrod Jones
37th Georgia Infantry: Colonel A. F. Rudler
4th Georgia Battalion Sharpshooters: Major T. D. Caswell
15th and 37th Tennessee Infantry (Consolidated): Colonel R. C. Tyler
20th Tennessee Infantry: Colonel Thomas B. Smith

Brown's Brigade
Brigadier-General John Calvin Brown
18th Tennessee Infantry: Colonel Joseph Benjamin Palmer
26th Tennessee Infantry: Colonel John M. Lillard
32nd Tennessee Infantry: Colonel Edmund C. Cook
45th Tennessee Infantry: Colonel Anderson Searcy
23rd Tennessee Battalion Infantry: Major Tazewell W. Newman

Clayton's Brigade
Brigadier-General Henry DeLamar Clayton
18th Alabama Infantry: Colonel J. T. Holtzclaw
36th Alabama Infantry: Colonel Lewis T. Woodruff
38th Alabama Infantry: Lt. Colonel A. R. Lankford

Artillery
Major Wesley Eldrige
1st Arkansas Battery: Captain John T. Humphreys
Dawson's Georgia Battery: Lieutenant R. W. Anderson
Eufaula, Alabama Battery: Captain McDonald Oliver
9th Georgia Artillery Battalion — Company E: Lieutenant William S. Everett

Preston's Division
Brigadier-General William Preston

Gracie's Brigade
Brigadier-General Archibald Gracie, Jr.
43rd Alabama Infantry: Colonel Young M. Moody
1st Alabama Battalion Infantry — Hilliard's Legion: Lt. Colonel John H. Holt
2nd Alabama Battalion Infantry — Hilliard's Legion: Lt. Colonel Bolling Hall, Jr.
3rd Alabama Battalion Infantry — Hilliard's Legion: Lt. Colonel John W. A. Sanford
4th Alabama Battalion Infantry — Hilliard's Legion: Major John D. McLennan
63rd Tennessee Infantry: Lt. Colonel Abraham Fulkerson

Trigg's Brigade
Colonel Robert C. Trigg
1st Florida Cavalry (Dismounted): Colonel G. Troup Maxwell
6th Florida Infantry: Colonel J. J. Finley
7th Florida Infantry: Colonel Robert Bullock
54th Virginia Infantry: Lt. Colonel John J. Wade

Third Brigade
Colonel John H. Kelly
65th Georgia Infantry: Colonel R. H. Moore
5th Kentucky Infantry: Colonel Hiram Hawkins
58th North Carolina Infantry: Colonel John B. Palmer
63rd Virginia Infantry: Major James M. French

Artillery
Major A. Leyden

Jeffress' Virginia Battery: Captain William C. Jeffress
Peeples' Georgia Battery: Captain Tyler M. Peeples
Wolihins' Georgia Battery: Captain Andrew M. Wolihin

Longstreet's Corps
Major-General John Bell Hood

McLaw's Division
Major-General Lafayette McLaws
Brigadier-General Joseph Brevard Kershaw

Kershaw's Brigade
Brigadier-General Joseph Brevard Kershaw
2nd South Carolina Infantry: Lt. Colonel Franklin Gaillard
3rd South Carolina Infantry: Colonel James D. Nance
7th South Carolina Infantry: Lt. Colonel Elbert Bland
8th South Carolina Infantry: Colonel John W. Henagan
15th South Carolina Infantry: Colonel Joseph F. Gist
3rd South Carolina Battalion Infantry: Captain Joshua M. Townsend

Humphreys' Brigade
Brigadier-General Benjamin Grubb Humphreys
13th Mississippi Infantry: Lt. Colonel Kennon McElroy
17th Mississippi Infantry: Lt. Colonel John C. Fiser
18th Mississippi Infantry: Captain W. F. Hubbard
21st Mississippi Infantry: Lt. Colonel D. N. Moody

Hood's Division
Brigadier-General Evander McIvor Law

Law's Brigade
Colonel James L. Sheffield
4th Alabama Infantry: Colonel Pinckney D. Bowles
15th Alabama Infantry: Colonel W. C. Oates
44th Alabama Infantry: Colonel William F. Perry
47th Alabama Infantry: Major James M. Campbell
48th Alabama Infantry: Lt. Colonel William M. Hardwick

Robertson's Brigade
Brigadier-General Jerome Bonaparte Robertson
3rd Arkansas Infantry: Colonel Van H. Manning
1st Texas Infantry: Captain R. J. Harding
4th Texas Infantry: Lt. Colonel John P. Bane
5th Texas Infantry: Major J. C. Rogers

Anderson's Brigade
Brigadier-General George Thomas Anderson
7th Georgia Infantry
8th Georgia Infantry
9th Georgia Infantry
11th Georgia Infantry
59th Georgia Infantry

Benning's Brigade
Brigadier-General Henry Lewis Benning
2nd Georgia Infantry: Lt. Colonel William S. Shepherd
15th Georgia Infantry: Colonel Dudley M. DuBose
17th Georgia Infantry: Lt. Colonel Charles W. Matthews
20th Georgia Infantry: Colonel J. D. Waddell

Reserve Artillery
Major Felix H. Robertson
Barret's Missouri Battery: Captain Overton W. Barret

LeGardeur's Louisiana Battery: Captain G. LeGardeur, Jr.
Havis' Georgia Battery: Captain M. W. Havis
Lumsden's Alabama Battery: Captain Charles L. Lumsden
Massenburg's Georgia Battery: Captain T. L. Massenburg

Wheeler's Cavalry Corps
Major-General Joseph Wheeler

Wharton's Division
Brigadier-General John Austin Wharton

First Brigade
Colonel C. C. Crews
Malone's Alabama Cavalry: Colonel J. C. Malone, Jr.
2nd Georgia Cavalry: Lt. Colonel F. M. Ison
3rd Georgia Cavalry: Colonel R. Thompson
4th Georgia Cavalry: Colonel Isaac W. Avery

Second Brigade
Colonel Thomas Harrison
3rd Confederate Cavalry: Colonel W. N. Estes
3rd Kentucky Cavalry: Lt. Colonel J. W. Griffin
4th Tennessee Cavalry: Lt. Colonel Paul F. Anderson
8th Texas Cavalry: Lt. Colonel Gustave Cook
11th Texas Cavalry: Colonel G. R. Reeves
White's Tennessee Battery: Captain B. F. White, Jr.

Martin's Division
Brigadier-General William Thompson Martin

First Brigade
Colonel John T. Morgan
1st Alabama Cavalry: Lt. Colonel D. T. Blakey
3rd Alabama Cavalry: Lt. Colonel T. H. Mauldin
51st Alabama Cavalry: Lt. Colonel M. L. Kirkpatrick
8th Confederate Cavalry: Lt. Colonel John S. Prather

Second Brigade
Colonel A. A. Russell
4th Alabama Cavalry: Lt. Colonel J. M. Hambrick
1st Confederate Cavalry: Captain C. H. Conner
Wiggins' Arkansas Battery: Lieutenant J. P. Bryant

Forrest's Cavalry Corps
Brigadier-General Nathan Bedford Forrest

Corps Headquarters
Jackson's Company Tennessee Cavalry (Escort): Captain J. C. Jackson

Armstrong's Division
Brigadier-General Frank Crawford Armstrong

Armstrong's Brigade
Colonel James T. Wheeler
3rd Arkansas Cavalry: Colonel A. W. Hobson
2nd Kentucky Cavalry: Lt. Colonel Thomas G. Woodward
6th Tennessee Cavalry: Lt. Colonel James H. Lewis
18th Tennessee Battalion Cavalry: Major Charles McDonald

Forrest's Brigade
Colonel George Gibbs Dibrell
4th Tennessee Cavalry: Colonel William S. McLemore
8th Tennessee Cavalry: Captain Hamilton McGinnis
9th Tennessee Cavalry: Colonel Jacob B. Biffle

10th Tennessee Cavalry: Colonel Nicholas Nickleby Cox
11th Tennessee Cavalry: Colonel Daniel Wilson Holman
Shaw's and Hamilton's Battalions, and Allison's Squadron Cavalry: Major Joseph Shaw
Huggins' Tennessee Battery: Captain A. L. Huggins
Morton's Tennessee Battery: Captain John W. Morton, Jr.

Pegram's Division
Brigadier-General John Pegram

Davidson's Brigade
Brigadier-General Henry Brevard Davidson
1st Georgia Cavalry: Colonel J. J. Morrison
6th Georgia Cavalry: Colonel John R. Hart
6th North Carolina Cavalry: Colonel George N. Folk
Rucker's 1st Tennessee Legion: Colonel E. W. Rucker
Huwald's Tennessee Battery: Captain Gustave A. Huwald

Scott's Brigade
Colonel John S. Scott
10th Confederate Cavalry: Colonel C. T. Goode
1st Louisiana Cavalry: Lt. Colonel James O. Nixon
2nd Tennessee Cavalry: Colonel H. M. Ashby
5th Tennessee Cavalry: Colonel George W. McKenzie
Detachment from John H. Morgan's Cavalry: Lt. Colonel R. M. Martin
N. T. N. Robinson's Louisiana Battery—1 Section: Lieutenant Winslow Robinson

Chapter 5

Downpour of Disaster: The Battles for Chattanooga

> *I am not here to pass civilities or compliments with you, but on other business. You commenced your cowardly and contemptible persecution of me soon after the battle of Shiloh, and you have kept it up ever since. You robbed me of my command in Kentucky, and gave it to one of your favorites, in a spirit of revenge and spite, because I would not fawn upon you as others did. Now this second brigade, in order to humiliate me, you have taken from me. You did it because I reported to Richmond facts, while you reported damned lies. I have stood your meanness as long as I intend to. You have played the part of a damned scoundrel, and are a coward, and if you were any part of a man I would slap your jaws and force you to resent it. You may as well not issue any more orders to me, for I will not obey them, and I will hold you personally responsible for any further indignities you endeavor to inflict upon me. You have threatened to arrest me for not obeying your orders promptly. I dare you to do it, and I say to you that if you ever again try to interfere with me or cross my path, it will be at the peril of your life!*
> — Brigadier-General Nathan Bedford Forrest, confronting General Braxton Bragg during the Chattanooga Campaign, October 7, 1863

In Washington, events were soon put in motion to remove Rosecrans from command of the Army of the Cumberland, even as he lay besieged in Chattanooga. After receiving word of the Union disaster on the afternoon of September 20, Secretary of War Stanton met with Lincoln, who promptly called a cabinet meeting to discuss options in the wake of the debacle. Stanton persuaded Lincoln to transfer from the Army of the Potomac the two corps of Major-General Oliver Otis Howard and Major-General Henry Warner Slocum to the Chattanooga area to attempt to succor the beleaguered Federals. Overall command of the two corps was given to Major-General Joseph "Fighting Joe" Hooker.[1] Lincoln had come to believe also that the three Union military departments of the Cumberland, the Ohio, and the Tennessee should be combined, with one military commander in charge to coordinate operations in a newly created Military Division of the Mississippi. His choice was none other than the hero of Vicksburg, General U.S. Grant, upon whom also would be thrust the decision as to whether or not Rosecrans should be replaced with the administration's choice, General Thomas.[2] For Grant, the decision was easy. Though he had no love for Thomas, he held Rosecrans in low esteem for his performance in north Mississippi in 1862. Grant had the order removing Rosecrans from command telegraphed to Chattanooga on October 19. General W. T. Sherman was placed in charge of the Department of the Tennessee, and instructed by Grant to move with elements of two corps toward Chattanooga from his headquarters in Mississippi.³

In Savannah, Private McNeil was making preparations to, at last, rejoin the Fourth Louisiana Battalion, and made these entries in his journal of his journey to, and reunion with, his Louisiana comrades:

Major General Ulysses S Grant (courtesy of the Library of Congress).

> Savannah, Thursday, Oct. 1st
> We were all discharged yesterday. Six of our Batt. has joined the Engineer Troops, but none of our Company. We shall start for our command next week. They are near Chattanooga. We were all paid up yesterday except for my extra time I made in Charleston, which I will have to wait a day or two for. It lacks six days of having been on duty since we were detailed.

> In Front, Tuesday, Oct. 11, 1863
> I left Savannah last Sunday at 4 o'clock P.M., passed Millen at 9:30, took supper at wayside home. Arrived in Macon at 5:30 A.M. on the 5th, took breakfast at leisure, though left for Atlanta at 9 A.M. Arrived in Atlanta at 4 o'clock P.M. There I found some of our Company that was wounded in the fight at Chickamauga. Among the rest our Orderly Sergeant, wounded through the lung and out of his head. Poor fellow was pitiable sight to be seen, as good an Orderly and as fine a Soldier as there is in the service. The nurse tells me that he calls the rolls of his Company two or three times a day, I fear that he can not live long. The rest are doing pretty well. This city is crowded with men of all kinds. I shall stay here until tomorrow evening, I leave for Chickamauga at 6 that evening.

> Chickamauga, 17th
> Arrived here this morning at daybreak. Raining this morning. Went with the Ordnance Wagon of our Batt. and will ride from here to our Brigade, which is about eight miles.

> This Afternoon, Chattanooga Valley, Oct. 18th
> I am now with the Batt., what is left of it, about one-hundred in camp. We lost twenty-seven of our Company, four was killed on the field and four died of their wounds since. Our Orderly Sergeant today. The highest Officer in our Company is Third Sergeant. Our Capt. was wounded at Jackson, Miss., our two Lieut.'s was killed here and one Lieut. went home on furlough a long time ago and has not returned yet. We are expecting our Capt. here everyday. We relieved General Gregg's Brig. that has been on Picket Duty today. Our Brig. is now about a mile from Chattanooga and our Picket Line within ½ mile and about two-hundred yards from the Yankee Picket Line. I was on Picket today, one of our boys changed Papers with the Yankees just now.⁴

Though the beleaguered army esconced in Chattanooga was on the verge of starvation, ironically, things were no better in the camps of the besiegers, as the Army of Tennessee was faced with supply shortages also. As the standoff drew on through the month of October, both sides suffered horribly from the effects of malnourishment, sickness, and the inclement weather. The *Savannah-Republican* newspaper recorded the events transpiring in, and concerning, the situation around Chattanooga through the month of October:

October 12, 1863

A Liberal Donation.— The Roswell Manufacturing Company of Roswell, Cobb county, have generously contributed $5,000 for the relief of the wounded soldiers of Bragg's army.

October 11, 1863

Gen. Hood was doing well yesterday, and his physician considers that he has passed the crisis. The wounded here are receiving every care and attention. I return to the front as soon as I can complete my outfit for the winter. A suit of winter clothes at $500 — think of that! P.W.A.

October 16, 1863

Enquiry at the Quartermaster's Department, in Richmond, and personal observation in the armies of Gen. Lee and Gen. Bragg, leave no doubt that the greatest want of the troops this winter will be for blankets. It is not probable that there will be an adequate supply of either clothing, shoes, or hats, or even of provisions, unless we recover East Tennessee; but the chief want, as already stated, will be blankets. Arrangements were made sometime since to procure supplies of clothing and shoes, and if our adventures are attended by auspicious gales, the army will be able to get through the winter, with such help as the people at home can, and doubtless will, render. Their response to the call made upon them last winter was the sublimest incident of the war, and will be recorded in history, as it has already been in "the books" which are kept beyond the sun, and in which all our accounts, whether for good or evil, are entered with an unerring hand.

As in the past, so at this time, I would address my appeal chiefly to the women of the Confederacy. The men have always done their duty in this respect, but the women have done more than their duty — they have helped their husbands, fathers, and brothers to do theirs. True, they do not enter the field, nor brave the blast of battle, nor use cannon, minnie rifles and swords; and yet the vast army of heroic women who have given their hands and hearts to the cause, have done their parts as well as their brave brothers in the field. The weapons they employ are the Needle, the Spinning Wheel and the Loom, Words of Encouragement to the weary and faint-hearted, and kind and generous Deeds in the hospital and by the wayside. With these arms they have done as much to defeat our wicked enemies as an army of resolute men. If they have not met these enemies in battle, they have met them at the loom and around the couch of the wounded and sick. If they have not gone to the field in person they have ever been there in spirit. In every blanket they have given to the soldier, in every pair of socks they have put upon his bleeding feet, in every garment they have woven for his manly limbs, they have been present in the hour of battle, and have given blows for the freedom of their race. It is to these heroines of the needle, the loom and the spinning wheel that brave veterans who have for three years stood between them and danger, now turn for relief. Shall their appeal be made in vain? Not as long as there is a blanket, a yard of carpeting or of cloth, or a sheep skin, that can be spared.... P.W.A.[5]

Within the Army of Tennessee, Bragg, instead of attempting to boost the morale of his soldiers and officers in the wake of the Confederate victory at Chickamauga, was waging a vendetta against his detractors. First to feel the wrath of the army's commander was his old antagonist, Lieutenant-General Leonidas Polk, who was charged with incompetence and delay during the Battle of Chickamauga for not issuing orders to his subordinates to attack as planned. Bragg charged that Polk's delay cost the Army of Tennessee six hours that enabled the Federals to fortify their positions, resulting in unnecessary casualties. Deciding to fight fire with fire, on September 26 Polk and fellow anti–Bragg faction members General Longstreet, General Daniel H. Hill, and General Simon Buckner held a secret meeting to weigh their options in disposing of Bragg once and for all. Thereafter, Polk and Longstreet dispatched letters to Richmond seeking Bragg's removal as commander of the Army of Tennessee. On September 29, Bragg formally suspended Polk and General Thomas C. Hindman from command and sent the two generals to Atlanta, Georgia, to await orders from Richmond as to their future roles in the Confederate war effort.[6]

On September 30, Jefferson Davis was briefed on the troubles within his victorious Western army, a matter which he saw as a "public calamity." Davis responded on October 1 by sending his aide-de-camp, Colonel James Chesnut Jr., to investigate the matter. After meeting with Polk in Atlanta and conferring with Longstreet soon thereafter, Chesnut reported to Davis that his presence was in dire need to resolve the open hostility toward Bragg.[7] Davis acted by leaving Richmond the following day, and by October 8, he was in Atlanta meeting with his old friend General Polk, who was telling the president that he would resign his commission before serving under Bragg again. The next day, Davis was wearily on his way to Bragg's headquarters where, after meeting with the North Carolinian, he summarily called a meeting on the night of October 10 with the Army of Tennessee's disaffected generals. One by one Davis listened to the convictions of General's Cleburne, Longstreet, Hill, Cheatham, and Buckner, as they all conveyed their lack of faith in the abilities of Bragg, who was also present at the conference. The entire meeting was a farce, as Davis had no intention of removing Bragg from command. In fact, Bragg had offered to resign, to which Davis emphatically said no, even going so far as to confide in Secretary of War Seddon that he had no inclination of removing his old friend from command. The only alternatives among the full generals who were available to replace Bragg, Johnston and Beauregard, were considered personal enemies by the Confederate president. Longstreet's ambitions were clearly perceived by Davis, and he was discounted as a possible replacement due to the political ramifications of promoting a junior general to command of an army.[8]

Davis admonished all in attendance at the October 10 meeting, and firmly stated that Bragg would be retained as commander. The generals were told to support, rather than criticize, Bragg, and were told that "shafts of malice" would bear no injury to him in the eyes of Richmond, as he was "worthy of all confidence." In a none too veiled jab at Longstreet, Davis stated that "selfish aspiration" would not prevail over the common good of the war effort. In a letter to the Army of Tennessee several days later, Davis warned that "He who sows the seeds of discontent and distrust prepares for the harvest of slaughter and defeat."[9] For Jefferson Davis, the matter was settled, and for better or worse, the Army of Tennessee was stuck with Bragg at the helm.

Bragg now saw the opportunity to further shake up the command structure of his army, and deal his enemies a further blow. General D. H. Hill, accused by Bragg of delaying the attack at Chickamauga, was removed from command duties on October 15 and sent to Richmond for further disposition. General Simon B. Buckner was removed from his independent department command and reassigned as a mere division commander. Brigadier-General William Preston, a close ally of Buckner, was reduced from command of a division to brigade command.[10] Among the other organizational changes made in the month of October was the transfer of the Fourth Louisiana Battalion from Wilson's Brigade in Walker's Division to the brigade of Brigadier-General Daniel Weisiger Adams in Major-General Alexander Peter Stewart's Division on the 31st. This left only the "Old Warhorse" of General Robert E. Lee to be dealt with, and Bragg decided to bide his time regarding the politically connected Longstreet.

Private McNeil made these entries in his journal regarding the visit of the Confederate president to the Army of Tennessee. These would be the final words recorded by McNeil in his journal in reference to his wartime experiences. Private McNeil, who was so filled with patriotic fervor early in the war, would commit desertion from the Confederate Army in 1864.

> Nov. 10th
> Was roused two hours before day this morning and put behind the breastworks. President Davis, with a large mention of Officers, reviewed us today, among the rest were Generals Longstreet, McLaws, and Jenkins. The President looks in good health but about ten years older than when we first went to Richmond. Everything is quiet here now and no prospect of a fight just now.

> One Mile from Chattanooga, Sunday, 18th, 1863
> Last Tuesday was on Picket, raining all day.

Thursday

On working squad, still raining.

Friday

Cleared up a little last night, not raining today. I felt sick all day. All quiet.

Saturday

Detailed to go back to the ammunition wagons after ammunition. Weather fine and pleasant today, rained a little this morning but cleared up towards evening.[11]

On October 20, Grant departed Louisville, Kentucky, by train, bound for Nashville, Tennessee. Upon his arrival that afternoon, Grant spent the night at the St. Cloud Hotel, before arising the next morning to board the cars to Stevenson, Alabama. Traveling by boat to Bridgeport, Grant planned to make the final fifty-five miles of his journey to Chattanooga by horseback, despite a leg injury suffered in New Orleans on September 4 when his mount slipped on a rain-slickened street and fell on his leg.[12] Riding over the nearly impassable Walden's Ridge in a deluge of rain on October 22 and 23, Grant arrived at Thomas's headquarters on the night of the latter, where he listened to the appraisals of the situation from the senior generals of the Army of the Cumberland. After many pointed questions from the commanding general, Grant made it clear that he expected them to reopen the new supply lines that Bragg had effectively sealed off, as well as seizing the initiative and taking the offensive. Thomas presented the plan of Brigadier-General William Farrar "Baldy" Smith for opening the crucial supply lines for Grant's consideration. Smith had visited a small earthwork located on the neck of land north of Moccasin Point, where an artillery unit was positioned so as to prevent a Rebel crossing at Brown's Ferry and a road from Lookout Valley led down to the river. Making a mental note that the sharp range of hills on the opposite shore of the river was broken at Brown's Ferry by a narrow gap, Smith surmised that by occupying that location, the Union army could control the road through the valley to Kelley's Ferry, as well as possibly disrupting the Confederate operations within Lookout Valley. This would be done in conjunction with troop movements from Bridgeport to open the river and a bridge-building operation at the Brown's Ferry site once the location had been seized from Bragg's control. Though unsure of the soundness of the plan, Grant agreed to make a personal reconnaissance of the location the following morning, before limping off to bed at 11:00 P.M.[13]

As planned, at 10:00 A.M. Grant was up in the saddle and off to see the Brown's Ferry location for himself. Grant was able to walk up to the river's edge in full view of the Confederate skirmishers on the opposite shore, due to an informal agreement between the opposing pickets not to fire on one another. After a careful examination of the site, he returned to the headquarters of Thomas and gave his nod to the plan. Soon thereafter, Grant received an intelligence report from Henry Halleck stating that Bragg was soon to be reinforced with more Army of Northern Virginia troops, prompting Grant to make additional operational changes. In a dispatch to Sherman, who was then on his way to Chattanooga from the Mississippi Valley, Grant stated, "drop everything ... and move with your entire force towards Stevenson until you receive further orders." Grant wanted Sherman in position to attack Bragg should he "break through our lines and move on Nashville." Hooker, who Thomas had ordered prior to Grant's arrival to concentrate at Bridgeport or Stevenson and prepare to make a forced march along the south river bank to Rankin's Ferry in an effort to reopen the wagon road and facilitate the repair of the railroad from Bridgeport to Chattanooga, was instructed to leave a division to guard the rail line from Murfreesboro to Stevenson.[14]

Adding to Grant's woes in Tennessee was the realization of just how sadly depleted the resources of the Army of the Cumberland actually were. The chief ordnance officer of the army reported that there was only enough ammunition on hand to fight a single day's battle. A lack of forage for the artillery horses had forced all except one hundred per division to be sent to Stevenson in an effort to keep them alive.[15] With the rapidly deteriorating supply situation weighing heavy on Grant's mind, on October 25 Baldy Smith was placed in charge of the Brown's Ferry expedition and Hooker was ordered to march from Bridgeport into Lookout Valley. The time for decisive action had arrived.

Ironically, Bragg was at this point being drawn into events that would see him substantially weaken his army, by allowing his personal vendetta against Longstreet to cloud his military judgment. Major-General Samuel Jones, the Confederate commander for east Tennessee, had been sent to the eastern Tennessee-southwestern Virginia border in early September to oversee the protection of the lead and salt mines in the region. Jones was astounded on September 6 to learn that Buckner's Division that was based at Knoxville had been sent to reinforce Bragg at Chattanooga, causing Knoxville to fall with but token resistance on September 2 to the approaching columns commanded by Union General Ambrose Burnside. Adding to his plight was the surrender of the sizable garrison at Cumberland Gap by the timid Brigadier-General John Wesley Frazer, despite Jones's orders to hold the position until reinforcements could go forward.[16] With many of Burnside's 15,000 troops pushing northward up the Holston River Valley toward Virginia, Jones had repeatedly asked Richmond for reinforcements for his 2,800 soldiers. Realizing what the loss of the salt and lead mines would mean to the Confederate war effort, Richmond had quickly sent several cavalry units, as well as the brigade of Brigadier-General Montgomery Dent Corse from Major-General George Edward Pickett's Division of the Army of Northern Virginia, to reinforce Jones. In a case of bad judgment, Jones had returned Corse's Brigade to Lee when Burnside halted his northern advance due to the disaster at Chickamauga, which Jones wrongly assumed was a withdrawal to Knoxville before an assumed Federal march to Chattanooga to relieve the besieged Rosecrans. Pushing many of his troops forward into east Tennessee and garrisoning Greeneville in early October, Jones had wrongly anticipated the easy reoccupation of the north end of the Holston River Valley.[17]

But the unpredictable Burnside had decided to leave Rosecrans to his own devices, and instead attempt to reconquer the northern Holston River Valley. With the arrival of 6,000 men of his Ninth Corps that had been on detached service at Vicksburg, Burnside had undertaken an offensive in the direction of Greeneville, and a little more than a week later, was back in Knoxville declaring the defeat of Jones's forces, stating that they had been driven from the state of Tennessee.[18] A shaken Jones once more contacted Richmond for assistance in defending the salt works "to the last extremity." The War Department responded by returning Corse's Brigade to Jones, as well as forwarding a copy of his frantic telegram to Bragg on October 15. Bragg responded by sending the division of Carter Littlepage Stevenson up the valley road on October 17 with instructions "to threaten the enemy's rear ...

Major-General Carter L. Stevenson (courtesy of the Library of Congress).

driving him back as far as possible." A confounded Jones learned later that same day that Burnside had halted and withdrawn many of his troops south into the valley, finally realizing that maybe it was not the Union general's intention to threaten the mines in Virginia after all. With troops on the way to confront Burnside, Jones suddenly hatched a plan to take the offensive "to drive Burnside from east Tennessee." Jones wired Bragg on October 22 advising that he would "move on the enemy as soon as practicable, which will be in two or three days." With a stalemate transpiring in Chattanooga, Bragg was receptive to action on some front, and embraced Jones's plan for offensive operations. In fact, that same night he sent the division of Brigadier-General John King Jackson to reinforce Stevenson for operations against Burnside, as well as ordering the main body of Major-General Joseph Wheeler's cavalry corps to Cleveland, Tennessee, to assist in the operation.[19]

Like most of Bragg's poorly thought-out plans, in less than a week the offensive against Burnside ground to a halt, with Stevenson blocked at Loudon, Tennessee, by elements of the Federal Ninth and Twenty-Third corps, and Jones failing to advance beyond Kingsport, Tennessee, due to what he termed as insufficient forces. Burnside, intimidated by the flurry of Confederate troop movements, had decided to go on the defensive, withdrawing all garrisons and outposts from the south side of the Tennessee River and attempting to hold only that portion of east Tennessee that he currently occupied.[20] Upon receiving Jones's plea for additional troops on October 30, Bragg now saw the opportunity to rid himself of Longstreet. Wiring Jefferson Davis upon receipt of Jones's request, Bragg outlined for Davis the "disobedience of orders and slowness of movements" of Lee's warhorse, as well as his receiving correspondence that was "disrespectful and insubordinate."[21] Administering the coup de grace, Bragg closed his telegram by stating that if he sent Longstreet to east Tennessee, it would be a "great relief to me."[22]

On November 3, Longstreet was called to Bragg's headquarters and the plan of his east Tennessee expedition outlined for him. On November 4, the 12,000 troops of Longstreet's command were preparing to depart from the Army of Tennessee, and Bragg was finally about to be rid of the antagonistic presence of James Longstreet, though the folly of weakening his army in the presence of a Federal buildup would return to haunt him several weeks later.[23]

In the Federal camps, Baldy Smith had diligently prepared for the Brown's Ferry operation, with the actual assault scheduled to be launched at daybreak on October 27. The operation had two distinct parts. The first called for 1,600 handpicked men of Brigadier-General William B. Hazen's brigade to silently float down the Tennessee River from Chattanooga in pontoon boats in the middle of the night, so as to prevent detection by the Confederate pickets along the shoreline. Upon arriving at Brown's Ferry, these troops would disembark and make an assault upon the detachment of Rebel soldiers found there, while the rest of Hazen's brigade and the brigade of Brigadier-General John B. Turchin marched overland to the point opposite Brown's Ferry, where they would wait to be ferried across the river by the boats that had carried Hazen's assault party. Once combined, this force would consist of almost 5,000 blue-clads, who would then solidify the crossing before pushing up the road toward Lookout Valley. Meanwhile, the boats would serve as the pontoon base for a floating bridge to be constructed across the river by the First Michigan Engineers and Mechanics. This would be done in conjunction with a movement by Hooker with 11,000 men that would leave Bridgeport and follow the Nashville and Chattanooga Railroad south of Raccoon Mountain to Wauhatchie, where he would wheel east to sweep away any Rebel forces in Lookout Valley, before joining up with the forces at Brown's Ferry. If all went as planned, the siege of Chattanooga would be lifted, and the "cracker line," as the supply route was known, would be open.[24]

At 2:00 A.M. on the morning of October 27, Hazen's assault force marched to the river and climbed into Smith's boats, silently skimming the waters surface undetected all the way to Brown's Ferry. At 5:00 A.M., the men of the Twenty-Third Kentucky Infantry hit the shore and headed for the Confederate picket camp, sending the Rebels fleeing after firing several ineffective rounds. Lieutenant-Colonel James C. Foy instructed his troops to gain control of the ferryman's house, and as more Federal troops streamed ashore, Foy had them push up the road to within 500 yards of Lookout Valley, where they were ordered to begin entrenching. In less than one hour, the 5,000 Union soldiers involved in the expedition were across the river and united.[25]

In response to the wild firing of the pickets earlier, Brigadier-General Micah Jenkins had ordered 150 men of the Fifteenth Alabama Infantry through the gorge between the two hills just beyond Brown's Ferry, where they succeeded in driving back the lead elements of the Twenty-Third Kentucky almost to the waters edge. Unable to carry the Federal position, Jenkins's troops retreated to the entrance of Lookout Valley where they threw up a defensive line that included artillery. Foy's call for reinforcements was answered by Lieutenant-Colonel E. Bassett Langdon, who ordered the Sixth Indiana Infantry to form across the road and move to the assistance of the Kentuckians. Jenkins reacted by advancing to the high ground to the right of the gorge, where he began to shell the advancing Union troops, in addition to offering a spirited resistance before being forced to retreat in the face of elements of five Federal regiments. By 4:30 A.M., the bridge was completed and Union forces held both banks of the Tennessee River at Brown's Ferry. The cost of the expedition was 5 killed, 21 wounded and 9 missing for the Federals, opposed to 6 killed and 14 wounded for the Confederates.[26]

Hooker, who had been less than enthusiastic regarding his role in the operation, began moving his troops on October 27, a full day behind schedule. Leaving one division under Brigadier-General John White Geary at Wauhatchie Station to guard his line of communications, Hooker moved with his remaining soldiers into Lookout Valley, all the while under the watchful eyes of the Rebels atop Lookout Mountain. Before receiving his assignment to depart for east Tennessee, Longstreet ordered a night attack on Geary's division at Wauhatchie Station on October 28, only to have the sounds of the engagement heard by Hooker shortly after midnight, who promptly dispatched two divisions under Major-General Oliver Otis Howard to aid Geary. After two hours of heavy fighting, the Confederates fell back to Lookout Mountain. Casualties were assessed at 408 Confederate versus 420 Union troops. At 4:00 P.M. on October 28, Hooker's forces united with Hazen's troops. On the morning of October 30, the steamers *Chattanooga* and *Paint Rock* landed at Kelly's Ford with 40,000 rations and several tons of forage. The "cracker line" was now open.[27]

The November 1, 1863, edition of the *Richmond Press* summed up the Confederacy's reaction to the Brown's Ferry operation: "The admirably conceived and perfectly executed coup at Brown's Ferry, on the night of the 27th and 28th of October, has robbed the Confederacy of all its dearly earned advantages gained at Chickamauga."

With his supply line now open, Grant was able to turn his full attention to offensive operations. Upon Sherman's arrival at Bridgeport on the evening of November 13, Grant eagerly wired his most trusted lieutenant to "Leave directions for your command and come up here yourself. Get ready for moving as soon as possible."[28] Late in the afternoon of the following day, Sherman boarded a steamer for Kelley's Ferry, where he disembarked and rode horseback the remainder of the way to Grant's headquarters in Chattanooga. After meeting at length with Sherman on the 14th, the following day saw Sherman, Grant, Thomas, Baldy Smith and David Hunter, accompanied by various staff officers, reconnoiter opposite the mouth of South Chickamauga Creek. Grant's plan, proposed by Smith, was to attempt to turn the right flank of Bragg's army by utilizing Sherman's troops, once Sherman had an opportunity to examine the site of the proposed maneuver. After eyeing the location for some time through his telescope, Sherman snapped shut the device and, turning to Smith, said simply, "I can do it."[29]

Later that afternoon, the plan was agreed upon. Sherman would bring his forces from Bridgeport through Lookout Valley while threatening Lookout Mountain near Trenton, Georgia, to divert the attention of Bragg. The following afternoon, Sherman returned downriver to begin operations, though he would encounter several delays in getting his army to their intended destination. Then on the morning of November 23, Grant received the shocking, but false, news from a Confederate deserter that Bragg and his army were retreating.[30] The deserter had reported that Rebel troops were moving over Missionary Ridge to the Chickamauga Station railroad depot during the previous day. This corroborated reports from several sources that Rebel troops were seen on the march during the same day, as well as a report from Union General Jefferson C. Davis that the Confederate camps on his right appeared deserted. What Grant was mistaking for a retreat was actually a movement by Patrick Cleburne with two divisions sent by Bragg to protect his line of communications with Longstreet in response to Sherman's threatening columns that had been detected in the vicinity of Brown's Ferry. Grant, deceived into thinking that Bragg might escape before being brought to a conclusive battle, urgently sent the following dispatch to General Thomas: "The truth or falsity of the deserters who came in last night, stating that Bragg had fallen back, should be ascertained at once. If he is really falling back, Sherman can commence at once laying his pontoon trains, and we can save a day."[31] Grant simply wanted a probing reconnaissance made by Thomas to determine if Bragg was still in his front in large strength. If Thomas discovered that Bragg was on the retreat, Sherman would be ordered to immediately recross the Tennessee River so as to shave a day off the pursuit. Grant was not willing to let Bragg, and his army, escape "in good order."[32]

General Thomas, the careful, methodical "Rock of Chickamauga," was not about to advance against prepared enemy fortifications without overwhelming numbers. Ordering a "reconnaissance in force" with four full divisions (about 20,000 troops), with another two divisions totaling 6,000 men in reserve, was still somewhat of an overreaction, to say the least.[33] Nevertheless, at 11:00 A.M. Major-General Gordon Granger was instructed to "Throw one division of the Fourth Corps forward in the area of Orchard Knob and hold a second division in supporting distance to disclose the position of the enemy, if he still remain in the vicinity of his old camp. Howard's and Baird's commands will be ready to cooperate if needed."[34] In turn, Granger had instructed his key subordinates to carry out these instructions, with Brigadier-General Thomas J. Wood's division assigned as the main offensive unit and Brigadier-General Sheridan's division in support. Wood's column would advance and drive the Rebel skirmish line in on their reserves, forcing them to deploy what troops were available. Nothing more was discussed at the corps level, as all believed Bragg to be retreating and a significant collision with the enemy a virtual impossibility. Only Bragg was not retreating.[35]

At 1:00 P.M., the afternoon calm in the Federal camps was broken by the shrill notes of the bugle, followed by the drums sounding assembly. As the long lines of blue began to form along the plain outside of the Chattanooga fortifications, an observer recorded the martial spectacle:

> Flags were flying, the quick earnest steps of thousands beat equal time. The sharp commands of hundreds of company officers, the sound of the drums, the ringing notes of the bugle, companies wheeling and countermarching, and regiments getting into line, the bright sun lighting up ten thousand polished bayonets till they glistened and flashed like a ... shower of electric spirits—all looked like preparations for a peaceful pageant, rather than for the bloody work of death.[36]

Even General Wood seemed awe-struck by the scene unfolding before him, Grant, Thomas, Hunter, and Granger, recording: "It scarcely ever falls to the lot of man to witness so grand a military display."[37] Even the Confederate pickets seemed to enjoy the spectacle of what they assumed to be a Union military review.

Directly in front of the Union formations were open fields through which the Atlantic and Western Railroad passed. Beyond the railroad lay a dense stand of timber that ran from between one-quarter to three-quarters of a mile in width. To the east of the stand of timber and 2,100 yards from the Union fortification named Fort Wood stood Orchard Knob, a rugged hill rising almost 100 feet above Chattanooga Valley and its adjacent spur ridge. The rock-strewn ridge, running to the southwest, was not quite as tall as Orchard Knob, though it was covered with timber and had an abrupt slope on its western side. It was this slope that was the target for Thomas's reconnaissance, though at the last minute Brigadier-General Willich was instructed to take Orchard Knob with his brigade and hold it until further orders. With the lines formed and orders issued, Granger called for the bugler to sound the order to advance, causing the brigades of Hazen and Willich to lunge forward with flags flying and rifles poised at 1:50 P.M.[38]

The Twenty-Fourth Alabama Infantry, along with the Twenty-Eighth Alabama, had been enjoying a leisurely day on picket duty in front of Orchard Knob. Colonel Newton N. Davis of the Twenty-Fourth was in his tent writing a letter home when a messenger arrived from the picket line advising that the Federals were forming in large numbers. Running to the top of a small knoll, Davis was astonished to see the Union line of battle, formed in two ranks with a third column behind, only several hundred yards distant. Davis, who initially had thought that they were preparing for a grand review, had this illusion shattered when he heard the order given, "Load at will!" Ordering his reserves to deploy along the line of breastworks on the ridge south of Orchard Knob, Davis then sent a messenger to alert his brigade commander, Brigadier-General Arthur Middleton Manigault, on Missionary Ridge. Within minutes of receiving the dispatch from Davis, Manigault was peering through his field glasses at the massed Union forces from atop his perch on the ridge. Manigault wasted no time in ordering his brigade formed and artillery brought into position, before the appearance of acting division commander Brigadier-General James Patton Anderson provoked a lively debate as to the enemy's true intentions. The discussion soon ended when both men observed the enemy deploy a second line of skirmishers to reinforce those already in front, and the order of "Forward!" resulted in the entire Federal center division advancing toward the position of the two isolated Alabama regiments in front of Orchard Knob.[39]

Once the approaching Union line had advanced 50 yards, a firefight erupted between the opposing skirmishers, while the heavy artillery at Fort Wood began to shell the Rebel camps located along Missionary Ridge. The men of the Twenty-Fourth Alabama had abandoned their line and ran the 1,200 yards to the fortified line at the base of Missionary Ridge, while the commander of the 300-man-strong Twenty-Eighth Alabama, Lieutenant-Colonel William L. Butler, received word to hold his line in the face of the oncoming blue wave of 2,256 Yankees. Fortunately for the Alabamans, there was a 100-yard open space between their line and the timber through which the Federals were advancing. Screened by a battalion of skirmishers in front, Hazen's brigade was deployed in two lines when the skirmishers were halted abruptly by a volley from Butler's line. With the Forty-First and Ninety-Third Ohio closing fast on the skirmishers, Colonel Aquila Wiley of the Forty-First ordered a charge that brought them to within 50 yards of the breastworks before being met by a sheet of flame that dropped nearly one-fourth of his men in seconds. Doggedly continuing on, the Ohioans were unaware that the Rebel breastworks ran in an irregular manner until being met by a storm of lead that came from their front and right flank. Of the 447 men in Wiley's line, 117 were mowed down, bringing the charge to a standstill. Suddenly a rush began on the left of Wiley's line, led by the Fifth and Sixth Kentucky, that fell upon the open flank of the Twenty-Eighth Alabama. Covered in an avalanche of blue uniforms, 146 of the Alabamans surrendered while the remainder sped for the safety of Missionary Ridge, leaving behind their regimental colors.[40]

It had taken a mere five minutes since the first sporadic firing along the ridge, but the action was now over. Butler and Davis had suffered 186 casualties from a force of 634, while the casualties of Hazen's brigade were totaled at 167, 14 of whom were officers. On Hazen's northern flank, Willich's brigade had dashed up the slope of Orchard Knob and now occupied the crest, encountering minimal opposition from the few Confederate skirmishers there. This "reconnaissance" had resulted in the seizure of important terrain that commanded the surrounding valley to half of its width.[41] Wood, mindful of his orders to retire once the reconnaissance was completed, signaled Thomas at Fort Wood: "I have carried the first line of the enemy's intrenchments."[42] Signal flags sent Wood the reply of his commander: "Hold on, don't come back; you have got too much, intrench your position."[43] Thomas then ordered Sheridan's division to close up and entrench adjacent to Wood's right flank to serve as an extension, while Howard's corps was instructed to advance from their position in reserve and occupy the ground along Citico Creek on Wood's left. Later that afternoon, artillery was ordered up and by the morning of November 24, Grant considered the captured area safe from a Confederate counterassault.[44] It was now time to plan for further offensive operations.

On the ridge where his headquarters lay, Bragg had been greatly shaken by the sight of massed Federal ranks advancing in his direction, prompting his repeated messages to Cleburne at Chickamauga Station to abort his departure for east Tennessee. Ordering Lieutenant-General William Joseph Hardee to take his nearest division and "press forward" to the army's right flank from his position guarding the Lookout Mountain flank, Bragg's new priority was to confront the massive Union buildup in front of Missionary Ridge. Upon Cleburne reporting to Bragg's headquarters that night, he was instructed to place his men immediately behind Missionary Ridge to act as a reserve for the entire Army of Tennessee, and to report directly to Bragg. Orders also went out that night for the construction of a line of defenses on the crest of Missionary Ridge, while the artillery that was located at the foot of the slope would be wheeled to the crest. The lower rifle pit line at the base of the ridge would be abandoned as the primary defensive position. Stewart's Division, including the Fourth Louisiana Battalion, had been in position in the soggy fields of Chattanooga Valley from the east bank of Chattanooga Creek to the base of Missionary Ridge since November 12. Breckinridge ordered Stewart to stretch his already attenuated line, now stretching some two miles, a bit further to the right so as to rest at the foot of Missionary Ridge, or about one-half mile south of Bragg's headquarters. Stewart was also ordered to begin work on trenches on the crest of the ridge, which rose a mile to his rear.[45] But, as usual with Bragg's attempts to define the enemy's intentions, he had guessed wrong.

Lieutenant-General William Joseph Hardee (courtesy of the Library of Congress).

Grant had not the slightest intention of attacking the formidable center of the Confederate Missionary Ridge line, not while he could avoid the strength of Bragg's middle line and attack his exposed flank along the northern end of the ridge, where Sherman could envelop the Rebel right flank and cut off Longstreet from the Army of Tennessee. Grant's master plan for victory called for Sherman's four divisions to cross the pontoon bridge at Brown's Ferry to the north bank, then by using the large hills of Moccasin Point to screen his troops from Rebel eyes, they would pass along northern roads to a point west of the mouth of South Chickamauga Creek and remain hidden in heavy timber until all units were up and the attack coordinated. Using Baldy Smith's pontoon boats, Sherman's men would then be ferried during predawn hours across the Tennessee River just south of the mouth of the creek to establish a beachhead, where, under cover of artillery support from the north bank, a pontoon bridge would be laid across the river to bring up his remaining troops. Sheridan would then launch an aggressive assault on the north end of Missionary Ridge before Bragg could concentrate forces to oppose him, while Thomas sent one detached division to support Sherman's right flank. The remainder of the Army of the Cumberland would remain in a threatening but inactive posture deployed along the center of the Confederate Missionary Ridge line. Cruft's division from the Twelfth Corps would hold Lookout Valley, while Howard's Eleventh Corps would keep itself in readiness to support either Sherman or Thomas from their location on the north bank opposite Chattanooga. To cut off Bragg's communications with Longstreet, a brigade of cavalry would be rushed across South Chickamauga Creek to tear up the railroad between Chickamauga Station and east Tennessee following Sherman's lodgment on the south bank.[46]

A week later, Grant was becoming painfully aware that modifications would have to be made to his plans, as the afternoon of November 23 saw Sherman still struggling to get his four divisions in place. Three were in place opposite the mouth of South Chickamauga Creek, but the fourth, belonging to Brigadier-General Peter Joseph Osterhaus, was stranded on the south bank of the Tennessee River due to a broken pontoon bridge at Brown's Ferry. Osterhaus was ordered to report to Hooker on the 24th since Sherman was assured of strong support on his right flank by the emergence of Howard's Eleventh Corps into Chattanooga, giving Sherman a total of 25,000 troops for his part of the operation.[47]

On November 22, Sherman outlined his plan to his subordinate generals, assigning the key roles to Morgan L. Smith and John E. Smith. M. L. Smith's men would begin the operation by crossing the river before daylight in pontoons floated down from North Chickamauga Creek by the brigade of Giles Smith. After entrenching the beachhead, they would provide cover while the remainder of Sherman's forces were crossing on the pontoons. Once ample numbers of soldiers were safely on the south bank, Sherman would begin his offensive against the north end of Missionary Ridge. In the early morning hours of November 24, the operation was launched and succeeded beyond even Sherman's wildest dreams. With Confederate resistance virtually nonexistent besides a slow artillery fire, at 1:00 P.M. that afternoon Sherman was ready to begin his advance. Again, the red-haired Ohioan could not believe his good luck as his men advanced to what was thought to be the north end of Missionary Ridge, encountering only slight opposition.[48]

Daylight the next morning revealed a major mistake on the part of William Tecumseh Sherman. He had not taken the north end of Missionary Ridge at all, but a separate height detached from the ridge known as Billy Goat Hill, appearing from the western banks of the river as a continuation of the actual ridge itself. Instead of occupying a dominating position on the northern terminus of Missionary Ridge, Sherman had seized a detached height and was therefore unable to apply maximum pressure on the exposed end of Bragg's line. To make matters worse, at 12:24 A.M. that night a lunar eclipse occurred that some of Sherman's men foresaw as an evil omen.[49]

Bragg was concerned more about the Union occupation of Orchard Knob and the threat to Missionary Ridge on that immediate front, thus his troop dispositions did not extend along the northern portion of the ridge, reaching only as far north as three-quarters of a mile south of the railroad tunnel through the ridge. Deployed along his extreme right flank was the cavalry brigade of Colonel J. Warren Grigsby, who had reported the Federals threatening to cross the river at that location. Due to the fog and darkness, Grigsby had been unable to ascertain whether the enemy was across in force or had merely sent a reconnaissance team. The only new troop dispositions Bragg made on the morning of November 24 was ordering Brigadier-General Marcus J. Wright to proceed to the mouth of the Chickamauga to develop the strength of the Federals, while instructing Major-General Carter Stevenson to be prepared to move in any direction from his position on Lookout Mountain. Stevenson had sent a message to Hardee's headquarters on the 23rd advising that he had witnessed what he interpreted to be an enemy deception to threaten the Rebel far-right flank before attacking the left. Signaling his deduction at 5:00 P.M. to Hardee, it was summarily ignored and discounted as improbable.[50]

Thomas, whose signal officers had broken the Confederate signal code several weeks earlier, read Stevenson's message almost as soon as its intended recipient. As a result of the interception, Thomas instructed Hooker to "endeavor to take the point of Lookout Mountain" the following morning, in an attempt to further confuse the Confederates as to the danger to the Lookout Mountain flank. Though later modified by Grant to be a mere "demonstration" that could be turned into an effort to take Lookout Point if circumstances permitted, Hooker was instructed to use Wood's division of Sherman's command, which was still stranded on the south bank by the broken pontoon bridge. To Hooker, who had been looking for an opportunity to redeem himself in battle after the thrashing he had suffered at Chancellorsville, this was the chance he had been waiting for. Giving specific instructions for an advance on the point, Hooker announced to one of his leading divisional commanders: "I am ordered to take Lookout Mountain. Have your command in readiness to move at the earliest dawn of day."[51]

Hooker had concocted a grand plan to serve as his redemption for the Chancellorsville debacle. Fully aware of the assorted natural and Rebel-emplaced obstacles that loomed from the slopes of Lookout Mountain, Hooker had decided to attack from south to north along the side of the mountain instead of frontally up the slopes. By sending a large body of troops, commanded by Brigadier-General John White Geary, down Lookout Valley to a location some two and a half miles below the nose of the mountain, they could cross Lookout Creek and establish a lodgment on the side of the mountain without encountering heavy opposition. This would be followed by a sweeping movement north along the slopes from the base of the mountain to the face of the palisades midway up the slopes, allowing the attackers to take the Confederate troops facing down the mountainside in flank. This would be done in conjunction with the majority of Hooker's troops, who would skirmish with the enemy below Lookout Point to occupy their attention until the flanking column appeared, at which time Hooker's entire command would advance and trap the Confederates in a deadly pincer movement. By 8:30 A.M., Geary's troops were filing up the mountainside unopposed, and in little less than an hour his line stretched from Lookout Creek to the steep wall forming the palisades, though the lack of resistance was due to the thick fog that had blanketed the mountain overnight.[52]

Carter Stevenson had spent the night of the 23rd attempting to ascertain where all of his troops were located, now that responsibility for defending a twenty-mile stretch of Lookout Mountain had been thrust upon him by the transfer of Hardee to Missionary Ridge. Stevenson was convinced that the northwest slopes of the mountain, defended by Edward Walthall's Brigade, was no place to fight an approaching force due to the exposure of the slopes to a raking artillery fire from the high hills across Lookout Creek and the batteries on Moccasin Point. To make matters worse, he had only the brigade of Brigadier-General John Creed Moore stationed midway up the slopes on the plateau at the house of Robert Cravens. Stevenson rightly assumed that, at best, he could delay an attack on the mountain only before they reached the plateau, where there lay a strong defensive position. With Walthall's troops as the first line of defense, Stevenson would rely on them to provide notice of any threatening movements.[53]

At 9:00 A.M., the dense fog in Lookout Valley began to lift, exposing in Walthall's immediate front a brigade of Federal troops that were maneuvering as if to force a crossing of Lookout Creek. This was soon followed by the sounds of skirmishing, prompting Walthall to form his brigade behind a series of makeshift breastworks fronting Lookout Creek. While writing a dispatch to General Moore for artillery support, word arrived from a number of scouts that Yankee troops had crossed the creek in force and now occupied the slopes above Walthall's picket line. Amending his dispatch to request heavy reinforcements, a worried Walthall hunkered down to await developments. His wait would be of short duration.[54]

The skirmishing that had alarmed Walthall was the result of Geary's troops running into the Confederate picket line. In pursuit of the fleeing pickets, Geary's men soon found themselves confronted by the breastworks belonging to Walthall's Mississippians, hastily constructed to defend from an attack in front, but not from one originating from the sides of the mountain. With orders to "Fix Bayonets, Double Quick! Forward March!" the blue-clad soldiers soon had swept their front clean of the Rebels, who were hastily attempting to ascend the mountain to a point of safety. Walthall's Brigade lost four flags and suffered 845 casualties in less than fifteen minutes of fighting.[55]

Daylight had found Carter Stevenson beginning to breathe a little easier regarding his situation as caretaker of the Lookout Mountain defenses. After establishing his headquarters at the Cravens house, he had then ridden to the top of the summit to examine his two-brigade line located there. Stevenson believed he had done all within his power to provide a strong defensive line, with two brigades posted along the foot of the mountain at Chattanooga Creek, two brigades midway up the northwestern face slopes, and two brigades guarding the crest and southern ridges. His comfort level was shattered at 10:00 A.M. when he was alerted by a messenger from Brigadier-General John K. Jackson that Walthall had spotted Federal troops moving along Lookout Creek in the direction of Wauhatchie. Stevenson sent a messenger to Jackson ordering him to place his troops in line of battle along the Cravens house plateau. At the Cravens house, General John Moore, somewhat puzzled by the fact that more was not being done to defend the northern slopes, had also formed his brigade in line of battle before sending a courier to Jackson for orders. It was almost noon when one of Jackson's staff officers arrived to inform Moore that he was to place his brigade behind the breastworks along the plateau to the north of the Cravens house. His men had just begun to push forward when the whole plateau suddenly became a scene of madness.[56]

Geary's troops were still in pursuit of Walthall's men when they reached the Cravens house plateau, eliciting cheers from the observant Army of the Cumberland down in Chattanooga Valley. Rushing toward the white clapboard house, the Federals were met by sharpshooter fire from the palisades above, though onward they swept toward the two abandoned six-pounder brass guns positioned in the Cravens house garden. Two regiments of Colonel David Ireland's brigade, the Sixtieth New York and One-Hundred-Thirty-Seventh New York, raced wildly through the peach orchard onward toward the stone wall located along the edge of the house, before being met by a withering musketry fire from two directions. Now beyond the Rebel rear and in danger of being isolated, the colonel of the Sixtieth ordered his troops to halt and cease firing, prompting the New Yorkers to fling themselves to the ground in an attempt to escape the hail of small arms fire. On their right, the Fortieth Ohio had joined in the impetuous charge along the narrow plateau, making their way forward even farther than the New York troops. Now the Ohioans found themselves with a strong Confederate force in their front, and their left flank threatened by a strong column of troops in position to overwhelm them. In desperation, the commander of the Ohioans gave the order to fall back.[57]

Confederate Brigadier-General John C. Moore had been stunned to find Union forces in possession of a portion of the stone wall when his brigade had sped forward to occupy the trenches below the Cravens house, all the while under a heavy fire from Geary's New Yorkers that were near the house. Moore's advance had scattered a few members of the One Hundred Forty-Ninth New York from the trench line, but this position he quickly discovered was untenable. With Ireland's other regiments past his left flank and firing from above into his rear, Moore ordered his men to fall back to the line near the Summertown Road. But before withdrawing a mere 100 yards, the Rebels found the isolated Fortieth Ohio beyond their left flank, attempting to flee. Impulsively, the colonel of the Fortieth Alabama ordered his men to charge, only to be met by a hailstorm of lead from the Ninety-Sixth Illinois of Whitaker's second line of troops.

Colonel Champion of the Ninety-Sixth now ordered his men to left-wheel and charge the Alabamians, causing the Southerners to halt before running pell-mell to the rear. The Illinois troops ran to a crude rail fence and delivered volley after volley into the backs of the fleeing enemy. At 12:30 P.M., Geary began to consolidate his position by ordering Cobham's brigade to proceed over the cliffs on the right so as to reach over Lookout Point and enfilade any attacking Rebel troops. Anticipating another advance with the arrival of Hooker's units from the mouth of Lookout Creek at 1:15 P.M., Geary was dismayed when he received the order to halt and strengthen his position issued by Hooker, who also advised Geary that he had gone well beyond the intended target of the point of Lookout Mountain.[58]

In response to what had seemed like a disaster for Carter Stevenson's forces on Lookout Mountain, the Confederate general had ordered the all–Alabama brigade of Brigadier-General Edmund Winston Pettus into the position formerly occupied by Walthall's troops, who had been sent to the rear. It was apparent to Pettus that the Yankees were in force in his front and, noting Moore's weak line on his right, he was hopeful for strong reinforcements. Upon receiving reports that the Federals were moving around the northern face of Lookout Mountain to cut off the Summertown Road below, Pettus sent for instructions from the missing division commander, "Mudwall" Jackson. Unsure as to how to proceed, Jackson had sought out Stevenson for guidance. Earlier that morning, Stevenson had been instructed by Bragg's headquarters to call on the adjacent corps of Breckinridge for reinforcements as needed. Stevenson had sent the request earlier and was dutifully waiting the arrival of the reinforcements so as to seize the initiative. His plan called for utilizing his sharpshooters to keep the enemy pinned down, then descend a trail over the palisades to the western slopes, taking the Federals in the rear and driving them from the mountain. Instead of the expected reinforcements, Stevenson received a message from Bragg at 4:00 P.M. that nearly floored the defender of Lookout Mountain.[59]

Earlier that morning, Bragg had sent a dispatch to Stevenson outlining contingency plans in the event he was attacked in overwhelming numbers. Stevenson's main mission would be to defend the Chattanooga Creek line in the valley, reflecting Bragg's concern for the protection of his precarious left flank along Missionary Ridge. If the Federals were to penetrate along the valley in the direction of Rossville Gap, his entire Missionary Ridge line would become outflanked and untenable. Stevenson was instructed to prevent his forces from becoming isolated from the bulk of the Army of Tennessee on Missionary Ridge. Therefore, at 2:30 P.M., Bragg sent the fateful message to Stevenson that no reinforcements would be sent, and that he was to withdraw from Lookout Mountain "as best he could." Sometime later, Bragg's chief-of-staff sent a written confirmation to Stevenson of Bragg's earlier verbal order, stating, "you will withdraw your command from the mountain to this side of Chattanooga Creek, destroying the bridges behind. Fight the enemy as you retire. The thickness of the fog will enable you to retire, it is hoped, without much difficulty."[60] Lookout Mountain was considered by Bragg to be an expendable piece of real estate, and as such, the Battle of Lookout Mountain was now over, along with the 63-day Confederate occupation of the summit. By 3:00 A.M. on the morning of November 25, the Confederate withdrawal was completed, and by midmorning, the Stars and Stripes floated from the top of the mountain.[61]

Bragg's retreat from Lookout Mountain had come as no surprise to Ulysses S. Grant on the night of the 24th. Fully expecting the Confederate commander to evacuate the mountain, Grant had issued orders that night for a pursuit the following day. Sherman, in his primary role, was to move along Missionary Ridge from north to south, while Thomas's troops were to pin the Confederates down by occupying a threatening position in the front of Bragg's center. Hooker would advance from Lookout Mountain across the Chattanooga Valley to carry the pass at Rossville in an effort to turn Bragg's southern flank on Missionary Ridge. With any luck, the Army of Tennessee would be trapped between the two attacks and destroyed.[62]

Bragg was at a loss as to what avenue to pursue on the night of November 24, thus he did the worst possible thing, consult with two of his many enemies within the Army of Tennessee, Hardee and Breckinridge. Hardee was firm in his belief that the army should cut its losses and retreat across South Chickamauga Creek. Just as firm was Breckinridge, who vehemently argued that the army should remain and fight it out from the strong position on Missionary Ridge. Though Bragg would later claim that Breckinridge was drunk, it was his advice that he accepted. Assuming that the real threat would come from Sherman against the right flank, Bragg sent Cheatham and Stevenson to reinforce the right held by Hardee. Breckinridge immediately ordered Stewart's Division from its position in Chattanooga Valley onto the ridge, upon whom the responsibility of guarding the extreme left at Rossville Gap would rest.[63]

The morning of November 25 found Sherman wallowing in uncertainty regarding the strength and dispositions of the Confederate troops in his front, allowing Patrick Cleburne additional time to prepare for the defense of the north end of Missionary Ridge. Cleburne, arguably the best fighter in the Army of Tennessee, was defending a naturally strong position with about 4,000 troops, against what he would later discover was 30,000 hardened Union soldiers under the command of Grant's favorite general. Cleburne was relying upon several primary defensive sites to defend the northern part of Missionary Ridge. The northern apex and adjacent western perimeter of the main ridges of Tunnel Hill was defended by the all–Texas brigade of Brigadier-General James Argyle Smith, who would face the brunt of any attack from Union-occupied Billy Goat Hill. Four Napoleon guns of Swett's Battery were posted in Smith's support along the highest elevation of the crest, while south of Swett's guns and directly over the tunnel, Calvert's Battery was unlimbered facing west. Infantry support, consisting of three regiments of Brown's Brigade of Stevenson's Division, were placed just north of the guns to defend the western slopes of Tunnel Hill. To prevent being outflanked and his line of retreat across South Chickamauga Creek cut off, Cleburne retained Govan's Brigade in its position along a spur of the main ridge east of Smith's line. Here they could overlook a small valley formed by the gap between Billy Goat Hill and the main ridge, and were supported by Douglas's Battery, who were in position to enfilade an enemy attack toward Smith's right flank. The two remaining regiments of Lowrey's Brigade were sent forward to the next detached hill north of Govan's line to join with the two regiments already positioned there. At this point, Lowrey would be able to support Smith or Govan as needed and block any Federal assault following the south bank of South Chickamauga Creek. The small brigade of Brigadier-General Lucius Polk was moved to a hill on the opposite side of, and overlooking, the creek. At the last minute, Cleburne ordered Smith's troops to fall back and to the right, placing them higher up toward the crest of Tunnel Hill along its northern apex. Smith's new line ran almost at right angles to the former perimeter, and his men had energetically begun erecting breastworks.[64]

Sherman began his attack against Cleburne's position with a laconic remark to his brother-in-law, Brigadier-General Hugh Ewing: "I guess, Ewing, if you're ready you might as well go ahead."[65] It was to set the stage for what would be a long day for the Union forces under Sherman's command. After several desperate assaults that were repulsed by Cleburne, late afternoon of November 25 found Sherman despondent and angry. Corse's attack on the north face of Tunnel Hill had met with defeat, as well as the primary assaults on the western face by Ewing and John E. Smith. The soldiers of Howard and of Morgan L. Smith were confronted along South Chickamauga Creek with unfavorable topography and massed Confederate troops. Despite having overwhelming numbers in his favor, though he had made the tactical error of using them in piecemeal attacks, it was apparent to Sherman that his offensive was stalled and defeated. To add to the Federal woes, Hooker had failed to get underway when scheduled and now was in the process of building a bridge across Chattanooga Creek so as to cross his troops, though it was apparent to Grant that relying on Hooker to roll up Bragg's southern flank was a long prospect indeed. Thus at 3:00 P.M., Grant exercised his only remaining option to aid Sherman: Thomas and the Army of the Cumberland.[66]

Approaching Brigadier-General Thomas J. Wood, Grant remarked, "General Sherman seems to be having a hard time. I think we ought to try to do something to help him." Wood agreed, stating, "I think so, too, General, and whatever you order we will try to do."[67] Grant now outlined his plan: "I think that if you and Sheridan were to advance your divisions and carry the rifle pits at the base of the ridge, it would so threaten Bragg's center that he would draw enough troops from the right to secure his center, and insure the success of General Sherman's attack."[68]

Wood was once again in agreement: "Perhaps it might work that way. If you order it we will try it, and I think we can carry the entrenchments at the base of the ridge."[69]

Unaware of Sherman's inability to resume his attack, what Grant had put in motion to aid his protégé seemed to be a recipe for disaster to the frontline commanders. By advancing to take the rifle pits at the foot of Missionary Ridge, Thomas's troops would be trapped immediately under the cannon atop the ridge and subject to such a bombardment as to make it impossible to remain there. Thus, the four divisions involved in this "demonstration" would have to keep advancing or face certain destruction from Rebel artillery.[70]

The Rebel fortifications opposite Thomas's troops certainly seemed invincible; arrayed along a front slightly less than three miles long were the better part of four Confederate divisions and nine artillery batteries. Contributing to the menacing appearance of the seemingly impregnable heights defended by almost 16,000 gray-clad troops was nearly a mile of open ground that the attackers would have to cross to reach the rifle pits.[71]

Opposite Baird's division and running nearly a half a mile beyond its left front were the Rebel brigades of Walthall, Moore, and Jackson of Cheatham's Division, followed in line by Hindman's Division, under the command of Patton Anderson. Holding the right of the division was the small Tennessee brigade of Alfred Vaughan. Next came Zachariah Deas's Brigade, followed by Arthur Manigault's. On the division left lay Anderson's own brigade, under the temporary command of Colonel William F. Tucker, whose left flank rested along the Bird's Mill Road. To the left of Anderson's Division was that of Breckinridge, under the command of the reckless William Bate. A gap of almost 400 yards had been opened between the left of Anderson and Bate's right the previous night, after Bragg had ordered Lewis's Brigade out of the line to reinforce Cleburne. That left Bate with just his own brigade, led by Colonel R. C. Tyler, and the Florida brigade of Jesse Finley. The right two brigades of Stewart's Division, Otho Strahl's and the all-Louisiana brigade of Randall L. Gibson, which included the Fourth Louisiana Battalion, were the southern-most units of the Confederate center and stood almost opposite the Federal division of Richard Johnson. To their left, stretching nearly two miles, were the brigades of Marcellus Stovall and Henry Clayton, though Clayton's was under the command of Colonel J. T. Holtzclaw.[72]

But for all its appearance of invincibility to the Federals, the Confederate defenses were actually a paper tiger, riddled with flaws all too apparent to the soldiers manning the lines. Their neglected state was due chiefly to the misguided assumptions of Bragg and Breckinridge that any serious assault would be launched only against their flanks. A multitude of problems plagued the center of the Rebel defenses, some inherent to the formation of the ridge itself, while others were created by the commanders themselves. Neither Bragg nor Breckinridge had ordered that the ridge itself be fortified until the last possible moment, contenting themselves with the line of rifle pits along the base. Firm in their belief that an assault could be repulsed there, both had neglected to have fallback positions laid out on top of the ridge. Not until the night of November 23 had Breckinridge ordered that work be started on entrenchments on the crest of Missionary Ridge.[73] It was an oversight that would have disastrous consequences.

For the artillery of Stewart's Division, the ascent from Chattanooga Valley had not begun until early evening of the 24th, with Dawson's Georgia Battery coming into line at 3:45 P.M. the following day, long after Thomas's troops were already on the move. Once Stewart's four batteries were up, scant attention was paid to their placement. They remained tightly packed in the exact location where they had been hauled to the crest, which happened to be just to the left of Bragg's headquarters. Responsibility fell upon Stewart to defend the two miles of ridge between there and Rossville Gap with his four small brigades of infantry. Realizing by noon on the 25th that a demonstration might be made against his center, atop the ridge, Breckinridge ordered Bate and Stewart to move to the right to connect with the general line of battle on the ridge. Bate, finding that Gibson's Brigade stood in the way of his closing on Anderson's left, notified Breckinridge of the impediment. Breckinridge ordered Gibson to withdraw, face about, march behind the ridge and then come back up on Bate's left. Thus, the troop movements of the Confederate commanding generals on this day had all the elements of a classic Greek tragedy.[74]

As Thomas's army maneuvered into line of battle and anxiously awaited the order to advance, confused and misunderstood verbal instructions were issued to the commanders. Gordon Granger had instructed Thomas Wood to "advance your division and carry the entrenchments at the base of the ridge, if you can, and if you succeed, halt there."[75] The signal for the advance would be the rapid firing of six cannon on Orchard Knob, and Wood was to notify headquarters when he was ready to advance. Yet the other key Union commander, Phil Sheridan, was not at Orchard Knob to receive instructions directly from Granger. Sheridan was given his instructions by a staff officer, and he, in turn, issued verbal orders to the brigade and regimental commanders. Inevitably, the communications became garbled and confused. Brigadier-General George Day Wagner claimed he was told to carry the enemy's works at the foot of the ridge and "possibly storm the heights." Some of Wagner's regimental commanders understood their orders to "take all before us." Colonel Gustavus A. Wood of the Fifteenth Indiana Infantry thought the orders were to storm the ridge itself. Sheridan's other brigades received instructions to carry the first line of Confederate works and conform to the movements of Wagner's brigade on the extreme left. In the other two divisions designated to participate in the demonstration, the miscommunication was even worse. Brigadier-General Absalom Baird, whose division was located on Thomas's extreme left, received

Brigadier-General Randall L. Gibson (courtesy of the Library of Congress).

verbal instructions at about 3:30 P.M. from Baldy Smith to move forward at the signal firing of the guns and take the rifle pits in front.[76] When the confused Baird inquired, "And when I have captured the rifle pits, what then?" Smith could only repeat the instructions.[77] On the far right flank, Brigadier-General Richard W. Johnson had so little notice of the pending operation that his troops were told only to prepare for an advance and conform to the movements of Sheridan's troops. Sheridan, confused as to whether he was to carry the first line of rifle pits or the ridge, sent a staff officer to Granger for clarification. Before the staff officer could return, six successive booms were heard from Orchard Knob, signaling for the advance to begin.[78]

A force of 24,500 Union soldiers lurched forward toward the imposing height before them. Once in the open onto the level plain, almost fifty Rebel cannon opened fire on the blue lines with shell and spherical case shot, prompting return fire from the batteries at Fort Wood, Fort Negley, and Orchard Knob. Sheridan's line reactively began to trot under the fire, and when they came within sight of the rifle pits a half-mile distant, they began to run. The advanced Confederate skirmishers that had opened fire upon the first barrage of artillery were now running for their lives up the slope of the ridge, closely pursued by a screaming wave of blue. Some of the soldiers in the rifle pits had not received the orders from Hardee to fire a volley and retire up the slopes, thus many fought to the last breath, even while others raced past them. Soon, the stampede from the lower breastworks was on, with many Rebels falling exhausted before reaching the crest, or struck down by the artillery fire from Orchard Knob. Those that did make it to the summit were thoroughly demoralized and broken down. For the troops positioned on the crest there was an even larger problem. Those at the top could not fire down the slope for fear of hitting their own comrades, while the artillery could not be depressed enough to fire effectively at the breastworks below. It had all of the markings of another Bragg-led debacle.[79]

Unaware that the Confederate infantry had been ordered to withdraw upon their approach, Brigadier-General August Willich's brigade believed that the enemy were beaten, as most of the Rebel parapets were abandoned upon the arrival of Willich's skirmishers. Their elation was short-lived as the minié balls and blasts of canister began to rain down uncomfortably close from the ridgeline, causing Willich and his commanders to conclude that their stay in the entrenchments would be a short one. As Willich's aide and another officer were moving along the line to get the men moving up the slopes, Lieutenant-Colonel William P. Chandler of the Thirty-Fifth Illinois suddenly jumped from the trenches and yelled "Forward!" Willich's troops immediately sprang from the trenches and began scrambling upward toward the ridgeline some 400 hundred yards distant. The slopes, covered with downed timber and loose rock, made the ascent to the crest even more challenging than the sheets of flame and smoke emanating from the Confederate troops.[80]

On Willich's right flank, the troops of Hazen's command had reached the breastworks soon after Willich, only to make the same discovery as to their ability to remain there for any period of time. Hazen signaled to Lieutenant-Colonel Robert L. Kimberly to move forward, and soon Hazen's men were also advancing up the slopes. Likewise, the troops of Brigadier-General Samuel Beatty's brigade, followed by the entire division of Thomas J. Wood, sprung forward within minutes of one another to also begin the ascent. They would have plenty of company on their journey in the form of Sheridan's and Baird's divisions, who had also made the assumption that to remain in the abandoned entrenchments would be suicidal. For Thomas's army, it was no longer a matter of tactics, but a matter of survival, with a tinge of pride thrown in for good measure.[81]

Back on Orchard Knob, U.S. Grant was mortified at the sight of the blue-clad soldiers fighting their way up the slopes of Missionary Ridge in direct disobedience of his orders to simply carry the rifle pits at the base. Turning to Thomas, Grant angrily demanded "Thomas, who ordered those men up the ridge?"[82]

"I don't know. I did not," Thomas answered in a quiet, measured tone that masked his fear that the Army of the Cumberland was about to be obliterated in front of his very eyes.[83]

Turning to Granger, Grant barked, "Did you order them up, Granger?" Nervously, Granger replied, "No, they started without orders. When those fellows get started all hell can't stop them." Grant was not amused by Granger's remark, announcing, "Well, somebody will suffer if they stay there." Grant then bit down on his cigar and uneasily watched the events unfold on the slopes of the ridge through his field glasses.[84]

On top of the ridge, the defenders were also beset by problems that struck many as fatal. Rebel troops were continuing to disrupt fields of fire as they were chased by the Federals up the slopes, and the smoke was blanketing the front of the crest and settling in the ravines to which

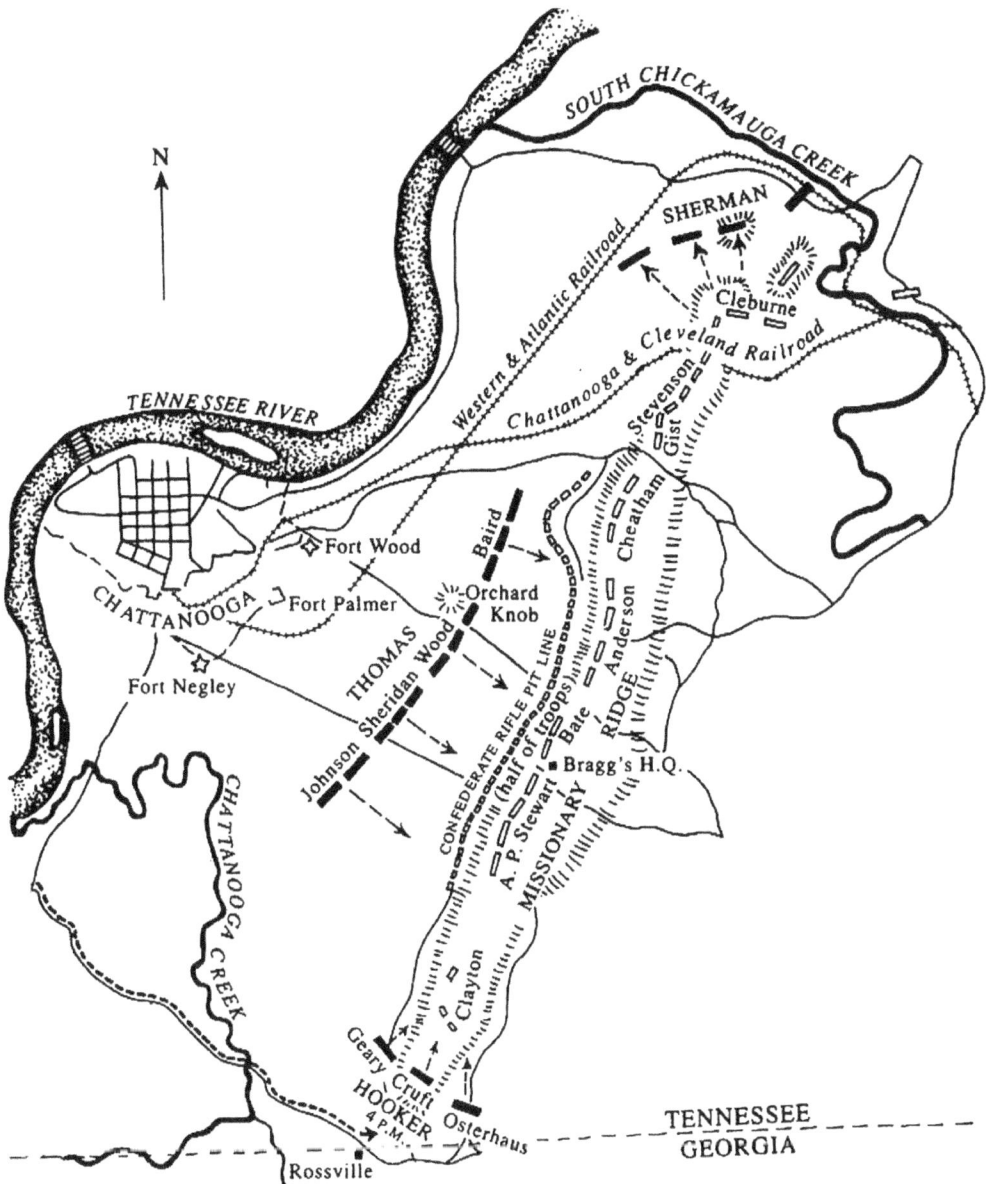

First map of Missionary Ridge (map modified by Terry G. Scriber).

the Yankees were heading. In addition, the Confederates were badly overshooting their intended targets due to the above-mentioned impediments and a reluctance to expose themselves above the trenches. Finally, most of the artillerists could no longer depress their cannon tubes to engage the attacking force, and had resorted to flinging lighted shells down the slope. Hazen's troops, now within pistol range of the cannoneers, began to pick off their tormentors gathered around the guns. Along the line below Sharp's Spur, the command "Fix Bayonets!" was once more heard in the advancing Union ranks, as the men readied themselves for the final push to the crest.[85]

The Thirty-Second Indiana and the Sixth Ohio were the first to reach the crest of Missionary Ridge, though they were intermixed, as the Ohioans were from Hazen's brigade and the Indianans from Willich's. Within seconds, the combined Union regiments cleared the breastworks and leaped in among the Rebels. As Willich's other units began swarming over the crest and reached a point within a dozen yards of the entrenchments, the Confederate line broke in wild confusion and began a dash for the reverse slopes on the east. Amid the smoke and confusion, Rebel officers were attempting to rally their troops; Garrity's Battery had already limbered up, and everywhere clusters of gray-clad soldiers were running in all directions. The Union breakthrough was like a rapid and out-of-control wildfire being fanned by the wind.[86]

Manigault was watching the approach of the Federal line toward his right flank when he was advised by a staff officer that "the enemy had broken the Mississippi brigade on the left, and were in possession of a great part of the line."[87] An incredulous Manigault could not see the position of Colonel William F. Tucker due to a rise in the ridge, but he quickly rode in that direction. Manigault was shocked to discover Tucker's position abandoned by Confederate troops, though two Federal flags were flying amid large numbers of soldiers in blue. With Tucker's line gone, his entire left flank was "now swinging in the air." Though knowing that something must be done, the shock caused him to hesitate before sending a staff officer to apprise Patton Anderson of the crisis. As the agonizing minutes ticked away, Manigault witnessed a captured gun spray his line with canister from the flank. Finally, the aide dashed up with orders from Anderson to pull a regiment from the front, form a line parallel to the enemy's along the ridge, and drive the invaders off. Turning to the commander of a battery of six 12-pounder Napoleons that supported the brigade front, Manigault ordered him to turn two of his guns on the enemy that were atop the ridge. He then sent staff officers scurrying to withdraw the Confederates and form a new line.[88]

Suddenly, along the center of Manigault's line, his men broke under the fire of the captured gun along the ridge. Mortified, Manigault looked to his right, where Deas's Brigade was in full flight in the face of the avalanche of blue now pouring over the crest of the ridge. Looking back to his center, several Stars and Stripes now floated where his men had been posted only seconds before. Looking up, Manigault saw the Yankees were within 50 yards and advancing rapidly. Ramming his spurs into his horse while miniés whizzed around him, Manigault headed for the rear. The Army of Tennessee was on the brink of disaster.[89]

Brigadier-General Zachariah Deas's brigade had held the position that had seemed the most threatened by the advance of Absalom Baird's division on Thomas's extreme left flank. At the time Tucker's line had broken well to the south, Deas was engaged in a firefight with a heavy column of Van Derveer's troops. Providing a huge advantage for Van Derveer was the massing of three regiments from the brigade of Brigadier-General John Turchin on the rim of the ridge immediately to the south, the position formerly held by Manigault's right flank troops. Turchin's exultant soldiers were madmen, overrunning the narrow ridge crest from south to north, even as his two separated regiments on the left flank joined with a few of Van Derveer's regiments to apply pressure to Deas's soldiers from the front. Two regiments of Turchin's brigade had used the cover of a ravine to swing far to the left before rushing over the southern crest of Polk's Spur to capture two guns of Deas's artillery. Meanwhile, more of Van Derveer's men began pouring over the crest of the ridge, as the captured guns were turned on Deas's Brigade.[90] As Deas would later state, "Resistance now had ceased to be a virtue."[91] Ordering his brigade back from the crown of the ridge, he led the retreat down the eastern slopes, leaving behind three guns of Waters' Alabama Battery to the jubilant Federals. Deas would later join with fragments of other brigades from his division along the Shallow Ford Road, where they would withdraw across Chickamauga Creek.[92]

Deas's withdrawal left only the brigade of Brigadier-General Alfred Vaughan along the line of Anderson's Division at the far right. Vaughan had skirmished with the Federals earlier while posted in the rifle pits below the ridge, and by the time of his reunion with the remainder of his troops along the crest north of Deas's position, he was both tired and apprehensive. Although the Union brigade of Colonel Edward H. Phelps was advancing in their front, Vaughan's Tennessee troops had but little trouble with these Yankees. The real threat to Vaughan was on his left flank, where the lines of Manigault, Deas, and Tucker had broken. Vaughan attempted to form a second line in that direction so as to recover Deas's old position. The Tennesseans came surging forward along the crest, driving back some of Van Derveer's men before being stopped cold by a mass of Federal troops gathering for a renewed assault. The Eleventh Tennessee reeled backwards just at the moment Vaughan was attempting to bring forward two additional regiments for support. Following a brief hand-to-hand struggle, Vaughan's line gave way, forcing him to order his brigade to fall back north along the ridge. There was now no organized Confederate battle line along Anderson's northern perimeter, and only Hardee's and Cleburne's troops along the north of Missionary Ridge stood in the way of a complete Union sweep of the northern ridge.[93]

Only a single brigade attached to Anderson's Division was still fighting, that of Brigadier-General Alexander W. Reynolds, positioned along the division's extreme southern position. Soon, they gave way also as the adrenaline-filled Yankees overran their position. A gap of a mile and a half now existed in the center of the Confederate line where Anderson's Division had been posted, in what was considered by Bragg to be the strongest portion of "impregnable" Missionary Ridge.[94]

Although Bragg was preoccupied with the fighting along the ridge adjacent to his headquarters, the Confederates in this sector were fighting well. Bate held the ground from Anderson's left flank along the Bird's Mill Road south to the Crutchfield Road, where Bragg's headquarters was established at the Thurman family home. Beyond Bate's position, the division of Major-General Alexander P. Stewart extended south along the ridge beyond the Crutchfield Road. The Fourth Louisiana Battalion, in position with the rest of Gibson's Louisiana Brigade of Stewart's Division, was supported by Lieutenant Frank P. Gracey's Kentucky Battery, while Strahl's Brigade had the artillery support of Lieutenant R. W. Anderson's Georgia Battery. The famed Fifth Company of the Washington Artillery of New Orleans, commanded by Captain Cuthbert H. Slocomb, was positioned along two prominent eminences on the far right of Bate's line. Because the New Orleanians two James rifles and four 12-pounder Napoleons were in a position to enfilade the Federal lines attacking Sharp's Spur, Slocomb's pieces had attracted the attention of Hazen's troops as they advanced on the far right flank up the ridge. Slocomb had placed three of his guns on the spur south of the Bird's Mill Road under the command of Lieutenant J. A. Chalaron, with the remaining three under Lieutenant W. C. D. Vaught on a similar eminence farther to the south and near the Crutchfield Road. With Hazen's troops reforming along the ridge at Tucker's former position, Chalaron swung his guns to the right and began to fire at the jubilant Federals, though he had no infantry support.[95]

At this point of the battle, fate donned a blue uniform. Slocomb, running low on ammunition for his guns, had sent a caisson to Chalaron to secure additional ammunition. Slocomb watched in horror as a well placed artillery shot from Orchard Knob exploded two of Chalaron's ammunition-filled caissons, resulting in a towering ball of flame. When the smoke cleared, Slocomb saw the effects of the explosion: floundering horses, dead and wounded gunners, and the shattered debris of half his battery. Hazen's men looked on in disbelief. They had been exposed to a brutal fire from the adjacent ridge after Slocomb's repositioned guns opened on them. Now they witnessed scattering Rebel troops in the wake of the blast. Suddenly, the Yankees rushed forward toward the menacing muzzles of Slocomb's battery, whose guns were loaded with canister but no friction primers were available. When the charging blue line closed to within 30 yards, the gunners turned and fled, leaving all but one gun to be claimed as prizes. To their right, Hazen's troops saw Sheridan's left regiment advancing about halfway up the ridge. Immediately, one of Chalaron's captured guns was spun around in the direction of Bragg's headquarters, where a quick-thinking soldier of the Forty-First Ohio dumped a musket cartridge into the vent and fired his musket over the opening. Suddenly the artillery piece roared to life, showering canister into the nearby ridge among the fleeing gray ranks.[96]

Bate had seen scattered troops several hundred yards to his right making their way to the top of the ridge without resistance. Wrongly believing them to be Confederates, Bate had forbade his men from firing on them. It would prove to be a costly mistake, as he discovered too late the presence of Hazen's brigade along the adjacent crest where Anderson's Division had been posted. Bate suddenly realized that he was witnessing the unfolding of a Southern disaster. Not only were Hazen's troops threatening his now exposed right flank, but a long line of Sheridan's division was swarming up the ridge immediately in his front. Ahead of them, Rebels were still trying to reach the supposed safety of the crest. Seeing Braxton Bragg riding along the line nearby, Bate immediately sent to the commanding general for orders. Bragg's response was immediate. He ordered Bate to stop the flanking attack along the ridge, though he did advise

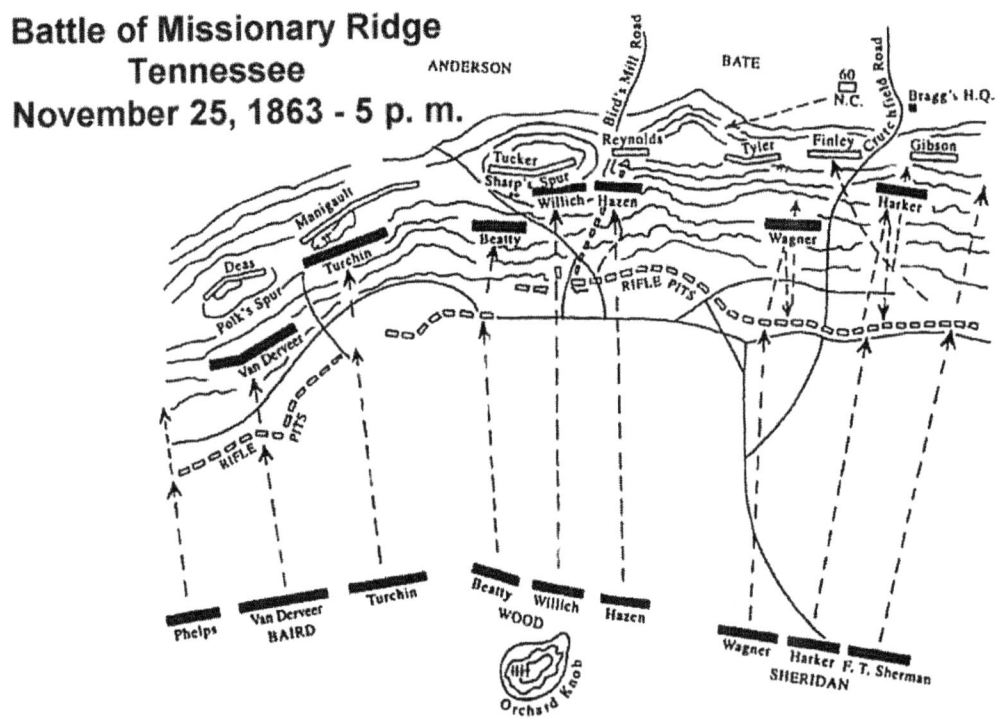

Second map of Missionary Ridge (map modified by Terry G. Scriber).

him to pull back what soldiers could be spared. Thinking fast, Bate led a portion of the Sixtieth North Carolina in a charge against Hazen's men, only to be stopped cold by Slocomb's captured guns. Leaving the North Carolinians to at least keep the enemy in check, Bate then returned to his main line, where he discovered that Sheridan's advanced troops were now dangerously close to the crest of the ridge.[97]

Francis T. Sherman's men were almost at the crest. On Sherman's left flank, the eighteen-year-old adjutant of the Twenty-Fourth Wisconsin Infantry saw the regimental color-bearer fall and immediately grabbed the colors. Behind Sherman's line, Sheridan was excitedly urging on the Seventy-Third Illinois. The final push to the top occurred almost simultaneously in some units, with the adjutant of the Twenty-Fourth Wisconsin dashing forward to plant his flag on the ridge in front of Bragg's headquarters. The adjutant, Lieutenant Arthur MacArthur, Jr., would receive the Medal of Honor for this action. MacArthur would later become a celebrated turn-of-the-century general in the American army. His fame would be eclipsed during World War II by that of his son, General of the Army Douglas MacArthur.[98]

With the Confederate line now being attacked from three separate directions, a collapse was all but inevitable. Hazen's advance along the crest from the north had scattered the Sixtieth North Carolina, throwing Bate's right flank into disorder. On Sherman's left flank, Harker's brigade and portions of Wagner's brigade began pouring over the crest. Bragg's entire mid-ridge line was now in complete chaos, and word had just reached him that Stewart's Division was being rolled up on the far left flank by Hooker's troops, who had suddenly appeared from Chattanooga Valley. In fear that his position on the ridge was almost surrounded, a visibly shaken Bragg issued urgent orders to retreat. The order was unnecessary, as most of the Confederates were now retreating without orders. Bate's and A. P. Stewart's men dashed for the safety of the ridge's eastern slopes amid a hailstorm of lead.[99]

Mid-Missionary Ridge now belonged to the Union, as it was all over along the crest near Bragg's headquarters. It was now almost sundown, and the whole affair had taken only about one and a half hours.

Hooker's progress from Chattanooga Creek had been plodding, at best. Confronted by the burned bridge at the creek, the pioneers had to work until 3:00 P.M. to rebuild enough of the structure to get Osterhaus's leading troops across. The Twenty-Seventh Missouri Infantry had been sent across on a makeshift bridge constructed of driftwood in order to scout ahead. While the rebuilding of the bridge continued, the Missourians advanced and encountered Rebels in Rossville Gap about one and a half miles southeast along the same road. The Confederates had four guns with infantry support on both sides of the gap, and the Twenty-Seventh Missouri opened a skirmish fire as it waited for Hooker's column to arrive. It was almost 4:00 P.M. when Osterhaus's leading brigade, led by Brigadier-General Charles R. Woods, emerged along the Rossville Road. Waiting until portions of his second brigade came up, Osterhaus sent Woods to the right and Colonel James A. Williamson with the trailing regiments to the left to seize the ridge. The maneuver had hardly begun when the Rebels, consisting of two regiments of Clayton's Brigade, withdrew from their position. The Missourians then moved up and occupied the gap, discovering ammunition, equipment, and a house full of commissary stores that had been abandoned by the Confederates.[100]

Fighting Joe Hooker, finding no opposition from which to sweep from his front, then ordered Osterhaus to turn left and march northward along the eastern valley bordering Missionary Ridge. The two brigades commanded by Brigadier-General Charles R. Cruft, marching in rear of Osterhaus, would ascend to the crest of the ridge and follow it northward. The trailing division of Brigadier-General John W. Geary would march in tandem with Cruft in the valley along the western base of the ridge. This would enable Hooker's three main columns to advance northward while remaining able to mutually support one another, while sweeping any

Confederates encountered from their fronts. With the heaviest responsibility resting on Cruft, he had ridden ahead with his staff and a small cavalry escort to scout the crest of the ridge. Reaching the top, he ran head-on into a skirmish line of Confederate infantry which fired a volley that nearly cost Cruft his life. Racing backward on their mounts, Cruft immediately deployed the Ninth Indiana Infantry into line of battle. The colonel of the Ninth, Isaac C. B. Suman, ordered his men to fix bayonets and charge the Rebel line. The Confederates scattered before Suman's troops had a chance to reach the breastworks, though the Indianans did fire a volley into the backs of the retreating gray-clad ranks. Spotting the main line of Confederate breastworks some 300 yards ahead, Suman ordered another charge. Again the Rebels scattered, though the Ninth did claim almost 200 prisoners.[101]

The all–Alabama brigade that had scattered before Suman's troops was not a happy one, even before the appearance of the Federals. Clayton's Brigade had retreated from Lookout Mountain early that morning, and after marching all night the Alabamans were exhausted. To add to their pile of woes, as the day had progressed the men had been shifted from their position near Bragg's headquarters to the far left flank, from which they had marched at daylight. Arriving near the gap, the Eighteenth Alabama had taken position as skirmishers in a section of the breastworks that Rosecrans had abandoned after Chickamauga. The remainder of the brigade had then split into several units for deployment along the ridge and at Rossville Gap, where after about forty minutes, the Federals had appeared on the ridge. When the Eighteenth Alabama had given way at the skirmish line, the brigade had attempted to form a line of battle. The line was broken when the Thirty-Sixth Alabama and Thirty-Eighth Alabama broke and ran through the brigade line. The commander of the Fifty-Eighth Alabama, John W. Inzer, had attempted to defend the second line of breastworks when some of Cruft's men passed beyond his left flank. Someone yelled "Retreat!" and the race was on.[102]

The brigade had fallen apart in the face of Cruft's assault, only to run straight into Osterhaus's men along the eastern base of the ridge. Yelling to his troops, "We've got them in a pen!" the exuberant Osterhaus had watched as his men claimed almost 2,000 prisoners and a brass 6-pounder field gun.[103] Clayton's Alabama Brigade, all but destroyed, had been the only troops protecting the extreme Confederate left flank. As Cruft advanced for more than a mile along the crest, his men encountered virtually no enemy opposition. The Thirteenth Illinois Infantry had captured the flag of the Eighteenth Alabama, and was now in pursuit of the regiment. Beyond Hooker's front, the 4,000 man division of Brigadier-General Richard W. Johnson, posted on the extreme right flank of Thomas's line, was now doing battle with A. P. Stewart's Division. Stewart's Division extended southward from Bate's line along the Bragg headquarters front and was composed of the three small brigades of Stovall, Strahl, and Randall L. Gibson. Two brigades of Johnson's division, those of Brigadier-General William P. Carlin and Colonel William L. Stoughton, were experiencing difficulty after linking up on the southern flank with Sheridan's division. Carlin's brigade had discovered upon approaching the base of the ridge that it was overlapped on the right by the greater length of Stewart's line. Brought to a halt along the line of the lower rifle pits, Carlin's troops had attempted to advance to escape from the murderous fire, only to be driven back. Though counterattacked by Marcellus A. Stovall's Georgians, Johnson's two brigades were able to rally, and by sheer numbers, repulse the assault. Led by Stoughton's brigade on the left flank, Johnson's division pushed on toward the crest, scattering the detachments of Stovall's, Gibson's, and Strahl's brigades in its front.[104]

Most of the detachments of the three Confederate brigades never made it to the top of the ridge. The thin Rebel line at the crest never stood much of a chance as Johnson's two brigades washed over the crest like an unstoppable wave. Following the word of Clayton's rout and the advance of Cruft's soldiers along their southern flank, Bragg's line had all but dissolved in panic when Johnson's division made their final push forward. It was now almost sunset, and as Cruft's men neared the vicinity of Breckinridge's headquarters at mid-ridge, they saw the jubilant soldiers of Johnson's division in their front. Hooker's troops had at long last joined those of Thomas, and Missionary Ridge was secured for the Union for almost four and a half miles.[105]

Bragg, attempting to rally the remnants of his broken command, had jumped off his horse, imploring: "I am here! Stop, don't disgrace yourselves, fight for your country!"[106] The men surrounding him kept on running. Occasionally, a shout would be heard directed at Bragg from the fleeing Confederates. "Here's your mule!" "Bully for Bragg, he's hell on retreat!"[107] With these taunts ringing in his ears, Bragg had no choice but to join his chaotic army in their retreat down the Crutchfield Road toward Chickamauga Station.

Along the Crutchfield Road, Bragg and General Bate had managed to rally some of the troops of Bate's and Stewart's commands in the hopes of holding back the pursuit of Sheridan's forces until the shattered army could cross the pontoon bridge over Bird's Mill. These men were placed along a ridge and high knoll almost two-thirds of a mile beyond the captured main ridge. Bate placed his eight field pieces from the reserve battalion under the command of Captain Slocomb. Bate's orders were to hold as long as possible, then fall back across Chickamauga Creek to Chickamauga Station, the location in which Bragg hoped to reunite his army. Though a brisk fight did erupt before the Confederates could cross the creek, at 3:00 A.M. Sheridan found the bridge burned at the Bird's Mill site and called off his pursuit for the night.[108]

At 7:00 P.M., Bragg wired the following message to Jefferson Davis in Richmond: "After several unsuccessful assaults on our lines today, the enemy carried the left center about 4 o'clock. The whole left soon gave way in considerable disorder. The right maintained its ground, repelling every attack. I am withdrawing all to this point."[109] Soon thereafter, Bragg sent the following orders to his troops: "Corps commanders will immediately put their commands in motion toward Ringgold, [Georgia] keeping their trains in front."[110] Due to the disorganized condition of the soldiers, the order was later amended to commence at 2:00 A.M. Bragg's planning was now reduced to its most basic element: survival.

The Confederate disaster at Missionary Ridge was the result of a very explainable phenomenon: poor planning and decisions. Bragg had planned for a siege, to either starve his enemy into submission or force their retreat. He had wrongly concluded that his strong natural position precluded a frontal assault by the besieged. As a result of this assumption, cleared fields of fire, breastworks, and placement of artillery were all lacking or neglected until the last moment. The in-fighting among Bragg and Longstreet resulted in almost one-third of his force being sent to east Tennessee and absent from the decisive battle. The cost of this negligence to the Confederates was high: 38 pieces of artillery, as well as two 24-pounder rifled siege guns captured by the enemy. Moreover, 6,175 Enfield muskets were lost, and casualties were listed as 361 killed, 2,180 wounded, and 4,146 missing for a total of 6,687. Federal casualties were listed at 753 killed, 4,722 wounded, and 349 missing for a total of 5,824.[111]

Upon reaching Chickamauga Station, the extent of the disaster was apparent to all in the gray-clad ranks. Vast stores of quartermaster's goods and provisions were piled everywhere, causing much bitterness among the dejected, starving Confederates who had been on short rations for months. Piles of sacks containing crackers, bacon, corn, sugar, coffee, onions, peas, potatoes, and rice were all on mocking display for the Southerners. As one soldier recorded, "Who do you think was to blame?"[112] All blamed the commander of the Army of Tennessee for allowing their starvation while he accumulated huge stockpiles.

Bragg decided to retreat to Dalton, Georgia, to escape the pursuing Grant. Once again, Patrick Cleburne was asked to save the army by fighting a delaying action in the gorge at Ringgold Gap to check the Federal pursuit until Bragg's trains and soldiers were well on their way. Once more, Cleburne performed the impossible by holding in check three Union divisions of 8,868 effectives under Hooker with his lone division of 4,157 troops and two field guns. At a cost of 20 killed, 190 wounded, and 11 missing, Cleburne inflicted 507 casualties on Hooker before withdrawing from the Ringgold Gap battlefield to follow the rest of Bragg's army on November 27.[113] Grant was forced to call off the pursuit the same day due to a lack of supplies. As Charles A. Dana, the War Department observer, recorded: "The condition of the roads, and the impossibility of getting supplies even as far as Chattanooga ... render a movement upon Rome [Georgia] and Atlanta impracticable for the present. Such a movement cannot safely be undertaken until six months' supply for both troops and animals is accumulated here [Chattanooga], so that we shall no longer be under the necessity of employing a great part of our force to guard railroads in our rear."[114] Even Grant admitted that "I had not rations to take nor the means of taking them, and this mountain country will not support an army."[115] In other words, Bragg would be allowed to escape to the safety of Dalton, Georgia, to lick his wounds for the winter, at least until the Union Army was capable of taking the offensive in to Georgia in the spring of 1864.

November 30, 1863, saw the Army of Tennessee finally rid itself of General Braxton Bragg once and for all. In a telegram to the Davis Administration on November 29, a melancholy Bragg had wired: "My first estimate of our disaster was not too large, and time only can restore order and morale. I deem it due to the cause and to myself to ask for relief from my command and an investigation into the causes of the defeat."[116] Though Bragg fully expected Davis to decline his offer of resignation, the political pressure in Richmond was more than even the president could withstand. The next day Bragg received the official reply from Richmond that he was "relieved from command." Two days later, Bragg departed for home, though three months later he would be appointed as a "special military advisor" to his old friend Jefferson Davis. Temporary command of the army would be given to Lieutenant-General William Hardee, who declined appointment to permanent command. A Richmond newspaper, in an editorial on Bragg's departure, concluded that it was far better to have "an army of asses led by a lion, than an army of lions led by an ass."[117]

On December 27, 1863, General Joseph Johnston, the man who had failed to rescue Vicksburg, assumed command of the Army of Tennessee.[118] It was he who would lead the army into the spring campaign, which would once more pit him against his old nemesis, William T. Sherman. The following year's campaign would culminate in a series of battles in the heart of Georgia that would decide the fate of the dream of Southern independence. The men of the Fourth Louisiana Battalion would enter their third year of a war that seemed to have no end, and see their ranks decimated even further in a military action known as the Atlanta Campaign.

CHATTANOOGA, TENN., ORDER OF BATTLE
November 22–24, 1863

UNION FORCES: MILITARY DIVISION OF THE MISSISSIPPI

Major-General Ulysses Simpson Grant

ARMY OF THE CUMBERLAND

Major-General George Henry Thomas

Army Headquarters
1st Battalion Ohio Sharpshooters: Captain Greshom M. Barber
10th Ohio Infantry (Provost Guard): Lt. Colonel William Murray Ward

Fourth Corps
Major-General Gordon Granger

First Division
Brigadier-General Charles Cruft

First Division Headquarters
92nd Illinois Cavalry—Co. E (Escort): Captain Mathew Van Buskirk

Second Brigade
Brigadier-General Walter Chiles Whitaker
96th Illinois Infantry: Colonel Thomas E. Champion
35th Indiana Infantry: Colonel Bernard F. Mullen
8th Kentucky Infantry: Colonel Sidney M. Barnes
40th Ohio Infantry: Colonel Jacob E. Taylor
51st Ohio Infantry: Lt. Colonel Charles H. Wood
99th Ohio Infantry: Lt. Colonel John E. Cummins

Third Brigade
Colonel William Grose
59th Illinois Infantry: Major Clayton Hale
75th Illinois Infantry: Colonel John E. Bennett
84th Illinois Infantry: Colonel Louis H. Waters
9th Indiana Infantry: Colonel Isaac C. B. Suman
36th Indiana Infantry: Major Gilbert Trusler
24th Ohio Infantry: Captain George M. Bacon

Second Division
Major-General Philip Henry Sheridan

First Brigade
Colonel Francis Trowbridge Sherman
36th Illinois Infantry: Colonel Silas Miller
44th Illinois Infantry: Colonel Wallace W. Barrett
73rd Illinois Infantry: Colonel James F. Jaquess
74th Illinois Infantry: Colonel Jason Marsh
88th Illinois Infantry: Lt. Colonel George W. Chandler
22nd Indiana Infantry: Colonel Michael Gooding
2nd Missouri Infantry: Colonel Bernard Laiboldt
15th Missouri Infantry: Colonel Joseph Conrad
24th Wisconsin Infantry: Major Carl von Baumbach

Second Brigade
Brigadier-General George Day Wagner
100th Illinois Infantry: Major Charles M. Hammond
15th Indiana Infantry: Colonel Gustavus A. Wood
40th Indiana Infantry: Lt. Colonel Elias Neff
51st Indiana Infantry: Lt. Colonel John M. Comparet
57th Indiana Infantry: Lt. Colonel George W. Lennard
58th Indiana Infantry: Lt. Colonel Joseph Moore
26th Ohio Infantry: Lt. Colonel William H. Young
97th Ohio Infantry: Lt. Colonel Milton Barnes

Third Brigade
Colonel Charles Garrison Harker
22nd Illinois Infantry: Lt. Colonel Francis Swanwick
27th Illinois Infantry: Colonel Jonathan R. Miles
42nd Illinois Infantry: Colonel Nathan H. Walworth
51st Illinois Infantry: Major Charles W. Davis
79th Illinois Infantry: Colonel Allen Buckner
3rd Kentucky Infantry: Colonel Henry C. Dunlap
64th Ohio Infantry: Colonel Alexander McIlvain
65th Ohio Infantry: Lt. Colonel William A. Bullitt
125th Ohio Infantry: Colonel Emerson Opdycke

Artillery
Captain Warren P. Edgarton
1st Illinois Light Artillery—Battery M: Captain George W. Spencer
10th Indiana Battery: Captain William A. Naylor
1st Missouri Light Artillery—Battery I: Lieutenant Gustavus Schueler
1st Ohio Light Artillery—Battery G: Captain Hubert Dilger
4th United States Artillery—Battery G: Lieutenant Christopher F. Merkle
5th United States Artillery—Battery H: Captain Francis L. Guenther

Third Division
Brigadier-General Thomas John Wood

First Brigade
Brigadier-General August Willich
25th Illinois Infantry: Colonel Richard H. Nodine
35th Illinois Infantry: Lt. Colonel William P. Chandler
89th Illinois Infantry: Lt. Colonel William D. Williams
32nd Indiana Infantry: Lt. Colonel Frank Erdelmeyer
68th Indiana Infantry: Lt. Colonel Harvey J. Espy
8th Kansas Infantry: Colonel John A. Martin
15th Ohio Infantry: Lt. Colonel Frank Askew
49th Ohio Infantry: Major Samuel F. Gray
15th Wisconsin Infantry: Captain John A. Gordon

Second Brigade
Brigadier-General William Babcock Hazen
6th Indiana Infantry: Major Calvin D. Campbell
5th Kentucky Infantry: Colonel William W. Berry
6th Kentucky Infantry: Major Richard T. Whitaker
23rd Kentucky Infantry: Lt. Colonel James C. Foy
1st Ohio Infantry: Lt. Colonel Bassett Langdon
6th Ohio Infantry: Lt. Colonel Alexander C. Christopher
41st Ohio Infantry: Colonel Aquila Wiley
93rd Ohio Infantry: Major William Birch
124th Ohio Infantry: Lt. Colonel James Pickands

Third Brigade
Brigadier-General Samuel Beatty
79th Indiana Infantry: Colonel Frederick Knefler
86th Indiana Infantry: Colonel George F. Dick
9th Kentucky Infantry: Colonel George H. Cram
17th Kentucky Infantry: Colonel Alexander M. Stout
13th Ohio Infantry: Colonel Dwight Jarvis, Jr.
19th Ohio Infantry: Colonel Charles F. Manderson
59th Ohio Infantry: Major Robert J. Vanosdol

Artillery
Captain Cullen Bradley
Illinois Light Battery (Bridges's): Captain Lyman Bridges
6th Ohio Battery: Lieutenant Oliver H. P. Hayes
20th Ohio Battery: Captain Edward Grosskopff
Pennsylvania Light Artillery—Battery B: Lieutenant Samuel M. McDowell

Eleventh and Twelfth Corps (Combined Field Command)
Major-General Joseph Hooker

Eleventh and Twelfth Corps Headquarters
15th Illinois Cavalry—Co. K (Escort):

Eleventh Corps
Major-General Oliver Otis Howard

Eleventh Corps Headquarters
8th New York Cavalry — Independent Co. (Escort): Captain Anton Bruhn

Second Division
Brigadier-General Adolph von Steinwehr

First Brigade
Colonel Adolphus Bushbeck
33rd New Jersey Infantry: Colonel George W. Mindil
134th New York Infantry: Lt. Colonel Allan H. Jackson
154th New York Infantry: Colonel Patrick H. Jones
27th Pennsylvania Infantry: Major Peter A. McAloon
73rd Pennsylvania Infantry: Lt. Colonel Joseph B. Taft

Second Brigade
Colonel Orland Smith
33rd Massachusetts Infantry: Lt. Colonel Godfrey Rider, Jr.
136th New York Infantry: Colonel James Wood, Jr.
55th Ohio Infantry: Colonel Charles B. Gambee
73rd Ohio Infantry: Major Samuel H. Hurst

Third Division
Major-General Karl Schurz

First Brigade
Brigadier-General George Hector Tyndale
101st Illinois Infantry: Colonel Charles H. Fox
45th New York Infantry: Major Charles Koch
143rd New York Infantry: Colonel Horace Boughton
61st Ohio Infantry: Colonel Stephen J. McGroarty
82nd Ohio Infantry: Lt. Colonel David Thomson

Second Brigade
Colonel Vladimir Krzyzanowski
58th New York Infantry: Captain Michael Esembaux
119th New York Infantry: Colonel John T. Lockman
141st New York Infantry: Colonel William K. Logie
26th Wisconsin Infantry: Captain Frederick C. Winkler

Third Brigade
Colonel Frederick Hecker
80th Illinois Infantry: Captain James Neville
82nd Illinois Infantry: Lt. Colonel Edward S. Salomon
68th New York Infantry: Lt. Colonel Albert von Steinhausen
75th Pennsylvania Infantry: Major Auhust Ledig

Artillery
Major Thomas W. Osborn
1st New York Light Artillery — Battery I: Captain Michael Weidrich
13th Battery New York Light Artillery: Captain William Wheeler
1st Ohio Light Artillery — Battery I: Captain Hubert Dilger
1st Ohio Light Artillery — Battery K: Lieutenant Nicholas Sahm
4th United States Artillery — Battery G: Lieutenant Christopher F. Merkle

Twelfth Corps
Major-General Henry Warner Slocum

Second Division
Brigadier-General John White Geary

First Brigade
Colonel Charles Candy
Colonel William R. Creighton

5th Ohio Infantry: Colonel John H. Patrick
7th Ohio Infantry: Colonel William R. Creighton
29th Ohio Infantry: Colonel William T. Fitch
66th Ohio Infantry: Lt. Colonel Eugene Powell
28th Pennsylvania Infantry: Colonel Thomas J. Ahl
147th Pennsylvania Infantry: Lt. Colonel Ario Pardee, Jr.

Second Brigade
Colonel George A. Cobham, Jr.
29th Pennsylvania Infantry: Colonel William Rickards, Jr.
109th Pennsylvania Infantry: Captain Frederick L. Gimber
111th Pennsylvania Infantry: Colonel Thomas M. Walker

Third Brigade
Colonel David Ireland
60th New York Infantry: Colonel Abel Godard
78th New York Infantry: Lt. Colonel Herbert von Hammerstein
102nd New York Infantry: Colonel James C. Lane
137th New York Infantry: Captain Milo B. Eldredge
149th New York Infantry: Colonel Henry A. Barnum

Artillery
Major John A. Reynolds
Pennsylvania Light Artillery — Battery E: Lieutenant James D. McGill
5th United States Artillery — Battery K: Captain Edmund C. Bainbridge

Fourteenth Corps
Major-General John McCauley Palmer
Fourteenth Corps Headquarters
1st Ohio Cavalry — Co. I (Escort): Captain John D. Barker

First Division
Brigadier-General Richard W. Johnson

First Brigade
Brigadier-General William Passmore Carlin
104th Illinois Infantry: Lt. Colonel Douglas Hapeman
38th Indiana Infantry: Lt. Colonel Daniel F. Griffin
42nd Indiana Infantry: Lt. Colonel William T. B. McIntire
88th Indiana Infantry: Colonel Cyrus E. Briant
2nd Ohio Infantry: Colonel Anson G. McCook
33rd Ohio Infantry: Captain James H. M. Montgomery
94th Ohio Infantry: Major Rue P. Hutchins
10th Wisconsin Infantry: Captain Jacob W. Roby

Second Brigade
Colonel Marshall F. Moore
Colonel William L. Stoughton
19th Illinois Infantry: Lt. Colonel Alexander W. Raffen
11th Michigan Infantry: Captain Patrick H. Keegan
69th Ohio Infantry: Major James J. Hanna
15th United States Infantry — 1st Battalion: Captain Henry Keteltas
15th United States Infantry — 2nd Battalion: Captain William S. McManus
16th United States Infantry — 1st Battalion: Major Robert E. A. Crofton
18th United States Infantry — 1st Battalion: Captain George W. Smith
18th United States Infantry — 2nd Battalion: Captain Henry Haymond
19th United States Infantry — 1st Battalion: Captain Henry S. Welton

Third Brigade
Brigadier-General John Converse Starkweather
24th Illinois Infantry: Colonel Geza Mihalotzy

Chapter 5 — Downpour of Disaster

37th Indiana Infantry: Colonel James S. Hull
21st Ohio Infantry: Captain Charles H. Vantine
74th Ohio Infantry: Major Joseph Fisher
78th Pennsylvania Infantry: Major Augustus B. Bonnaffon
79th Pennsylvania Infantry: Major Michael H. Locher
1st Wisconsin Infantry: Lt. Colonel George B. Bingham
21st Wisconsin Infantry: Captain Charles H. Walker

Artillery
1st Illinois Light Artillery — Battery C: Captain Mark H. Prescott
1st Michigan Light Artillery — Battery A: Captain Francis E. Hale
5th United States Artillery — Battery H: Captain Frances L. Guenther

Second Division
Brigadier-General Jefferson Columbus Davis

First Brigade
Brigadier-General James Dada Morgan
10th Illinois Infantry: Colonel John Tillson
16th Illinois Infantry: Lt. Colonel James B. Cahill
60th Illinois Infantry: Colonel William B. Anderson
21st Kentucky Infantry: Colonel Samuel W. Price
10th Michigan Infantry: Lt. Colonel Christopher J. Dickerson
14th Michigan Infantry: Colonel Henry R. Mizner

Second Brigade
Brigadier-General John Beatty
34th Illinois Infantry: Lt. Colonel Oscar Van Tassell
78th Illinois Infantry: Lt. Colonel Carter Van Vleck
3rd Ohio Infantry: Captain Leroy S. Bell
98th Ohio Infantry: Major James M. Shane
108th Ohio Infantry: Lt. Colonel Carlo Piepho
113th Ohio Infantry: Major Lyne S. Sullivant
121st Ohio Infantry: Major John Yager

Third Brigade
Colonel Daniel McCook, Jr.
85th Illinois Infantry: Colonel Caleb J. Dilworth
86th Illinois Infantry: Lt. Colonel David W. Magee
110th Illinois Infantry: Lt. Colonel E. Hibbard Topping
125th Illinois Infantry: Colonel Oscar F. Harmon
52nd Ohio Infantry: Major James T. Holmes

Artillery
Captain William A. Hotchkiss
2nd Illinois Light Artillery — Battery I: Lieutenant Henry B. Plant
Minnesota Light Artillery — 2nd Battery: Lieutenant Richard L. Dawley
Wisconsin Light Artillery — 5th Battery: Captain George Q. Gardner

Third Division
Brigadier-General Absalom Baird

First Brigade
Brigadier-General John Basil Turchin
82nd Indiana Infantry: Colonel Morton C. Hunter
11th Ohio Infantry: Lt. Colonel Ogden Street
17th Ohio Infantry: Major Benjamin F. Butterfield
31st Ohio Infantry: Lt. Colonel Frederick W. Lister
36th Ohio Infantry: Lt. Colonel Hiram F. Devol
89th Ohio Infantry: Captain John H. Jolly
92nd Ohio Infantry: Lt. Colonel Douglas Putnam, Jr.

Second Brigade
Colonel Ferdinand Van Derveer
75th Indiana Infantry: Colonel Milton S. Robinson
87th Indiana Infantry: Colonel Newell Gleason
101st Indiana Infantry: Lt. Colonel Thomas Doan
2nd Minnesota Infantry: Lt. Colonel Judson W. Bishop
9th Ohio Infantry: Colonel Gustave Kammerling
35th Ohio Infantry: Lt. Colonel Henry V. N. Boynton
105th Ohio Infantry: Lt. Colonel William R. Tolles

Third Brigade
Colonel Edward H. Phelps
Colonel William H. Hays
10th Indiana Infantry: Lt. Colonel Marsh B. Taylor
74th Indiana Infantry: Lt. Colonel Myron Baker
4th Kentucky Infantry: Major Robert M. Kelly
10th Kentucky Infantry: Colonel William H. Hays
18th Kentucky Infantry: Lt. Colonel Hubbard K. Milward
14th Ohio Infantry: Lt. Colonel Henry D. Kingsbury
38th Ohio Infantry: Major Charles Greenwood

Artillery
Captain George A. Swallow
Indiana Light Artillery — 7th Battery: Lieutenant Otho H. Morgan
Indiana Light Artillery — 19th Battery: Lieutenant Robert G. Lackey
4th United States Artillery — Battery I: Lieutenant Frank G. Smith

Engineers
Brigadier-General William Farrar "Baldy" Smith
1st Michigan Engineers and Mechanics (Detachment): Captain Perrin V. Fox
13th Michigan Infantry: Major Willard G. Eaton
21st Michigan Infantry: Captain Loomis K. Bishop
22nd Michigan Infantry: Major Henry S. Dean
18th Ohio Infantry: Colonel Timothy R. Stanley

Pioneer Brigade
Colonel George P. Buell
1st Battalion: Captain Charles J. Stewart
2nd Battalion: Captain Correll Smith
3rd Battalion: Captain William Clark

Army Artillery Reserve
Brigadier-General John Milton Brannan

First Division
Colonel James Barnett

First Brigade
Major Charles S. Cotter
1st Ohio Light Artillery — Battery B: Lieutenant Norman A. Baldwin
1st Ohio Light Artillery — Battery C: Captain Marco B. Gary
1st Ohio Light Artillery — Battery E: Lieutenant Albert G. Ransom
1st Ohio Light Artillery — Battery F: Lieutenant Giles J. Cockerill

Second Brigade
1st Ohio Light Artillery — Battery G: Captain Alexander Marshall
1st Ohio Light Artillery — Battery M: Captain Frederick Schultz
Ohio Light Artillery — 18th Battery: Lieutenant Joseph McCafferty
Ohio Light Artillery — 20th Battery: Captain Edward Grosskopff

Second Division
First Brigade
Captain Josiah W. Church

1st Michigan Light Artillery — Battery D: Captain Josiah W. Church
1st Tennessee Light Artillery — Battery A: Lieutenant Albert F. Beach
3rd Wisconsin Artillery Battery: Lieutenant Hiram F. Hubbard
8th Wisconsin Artillery Battery: Lieutenant Obadiah German
10th Wisconsin Artillery Battery: Captain Yates V. Beebe

Second Brigade
Captain Arnold Sutermeister
4th Indiana Light Artillery Battery: Lieutenant Henry J. Willits
8th Indiana Light Artillery Battery: Lieutenant George Estep
11th Indiana Light Artillery Battery: Captain Arnold Sutermeister
21st Indiana Light Artillery Battery: Lieutenant William E. Chess
1st Wisconsin Heavy Artillery — Co. C: Captain John R. Davies

Second Division-Second Brigade Cavalry
Colonel Eli Long
98th Illinois Mounted Infantry: Lt. Colonel Edward Kitchell
17th Indiana Mounted Infantry: Lt. Colonel Henry Jordan
2nd Kentucky Cavalry: Colonel Thomas P. Nicholas
4th Michigan Cavalry: Major Horace Gray
1st Ohio Cavalry: Major Thomas J. Patten
3rd Ohio Cavalry: Lt. Colonel Charles B. Seidel
4th Ohio Battalion Cavalry: Major George W. Dobb
10th Ohio Cavalry: Colonel Charles C. Smith

Post of Chattanooga, TN
Colonel John G. Parkhurst
44th Indiana Infantry: Lt. Colonel Simeon C. Aldrich
15th Kentucky Infantry: Major William G. Halpin
9th Michigan Infantry: Lt. Colonel William Wilkinson

ARMY OF THE TENNESSEE
Major-General William Tecumseh Sherman

Fifteenth Corps
Major-General Francis Preston Blair, Jr.

First Division
Brigadier-General Peter Joseph Osterhaus

First Brigade
Brigadier-General Charles Robert Woods
13th Illinois Infantry: Lt. Colonel Frederick W. Partridge
3rd Missouri Infantry: Lt. Colonel Theodore Meumann
12th Missouri Infantry: Colonel Hugo Wangelin
17th Missouri Infantry: Colonel John F. Kramer
27th Missouri Infantry: Colonel Thomas Curly
29th Missouri Infantry: Colonel James Peckham
31st Missouri Infantry: Lt. Colonel Samuel P. Simpson
32nd Missouri Infantry: Lt. Colonel Henry C. Warmoth
76th Ohio Infantry: Major Willard Warner

Second Brigade
Colonel James Alexander Williamson
4th Iowa Infantry: Lt. Colonel George Burton
9th Iowa Infantry: Colonel David Carskaddon
25th Iowa Infantry: Colonel George A. Stone
26th Iowa Infantry: Colonel Milo Smith
30th Iowa Infantry: Lt. Colonel Aurelius Roberts
31st Iowa Infantry: Lt. Colonel Jeremiah W. Jenkins

Artillery
Captain Henry H. Griffiths
1st Iowa Light Artillery Battery: Lieutenant James M. Williams
2nd Missouri Light Artillery — Battery F: Captain Clemens Landgraeber
4th Ohio Light Artillery Battery: Captain George Froehlich

Second Division
Brigadier-General Morgan Lewis Smith

First Brigade
Brigadier-General Giles Alexander Smith
55th Illinois Infantry: Colonel Oscar Malmborg
116th Illinois Infantry: Colonel Nathan W. Tupper
127th Illinois Infantry: Lt. Colonel Frank S. Curtiss
6th Missouri Infantry: Lt. Colonel Ira Boutell
8th Missouri Infantry: Lt. Colonel David C. Coleman
57th Ohio Infantry: Lt. Colonel Samuel R. Mott
13th United States Infantry-1st Battalion: Captain Charles C. Smith

Second Brigade
Brigadier-General Joseph Andrew Jackson Lightburn
83rd Indiana Infantry: Colonel Benjamin J. Spooner
30th Ohio Infantry: Colonel Theodore Jones
37th Ohio Infantry: Lt. Colonel Louis von Blessingh
47th Ohio Infantry: Colonel Augustus C. Parry
54th Ohio Infantry: Major Robert Williams, Jr.
4th West Virginia Infantry: Colonel James H. Dayton

Artillery
1st Illinois Light Artillery — Battery A: Captain Peter P. Wood
1st Illinois Light Artillery — Battery B: Captain Israel P. Rumsey
1st Illinois Light Artillery — Battery H: Lieutenant Francis DeGress

Fourth Division
Brigadier-General Hugh Boyle Ewing

First Brigade
Colonel John M. Loomis
26th Illinois Infantry: Lt. Colonel Robert A. Gillmore
90th Illinois Infantry: Colonel Timothy O'Meara
12th Indiana Infantry: Colonel Reuben Williams
100th Indiana Infantry: Lt. Colonel Albert Heath

Second Brigade
Brigadier-General John Murray Corse
40th Illinois Infantry: Major Hiram W. Hall
103rd Illinois Infantry: Colonel Willard A. Dickerman
6th Iowa Infantry: Lt. Colonel Alexander J. Miller
15th Michigan Infantry: Lt. Colonel Austin E. Jaquith
46th Ohio Infantry: Colonel Charles C. Walcutt

Third Brigade
Colonel Joseph R. Cockerill
48th Illinois Infantry: Lt. Colonel Lucien Greathouse
97th Indiana Infantry: Colonel Robert F. Catterson
99th Indiana Infantry: Colonel Alexander Fowler
53rd Ohio Infantry: Colonel Wells S. Jones
70th Ohio Infantry: Major William B. Brown

Artillery
Captain Henry Richardson
1st Illinois Light Artillery — Battery F: Captain John T. Cheney

Chapter 5 — Downpour of Disaster

1st Illinois Light Artillery — Battery I: Lieutenant Josiah H. Burton
1st Missouri Light Artillery — Battery D: Lieutenant Byron M. Callender

Seventeenth Corps
Second Division
Brigadier-General John Eugene Smith

First Brigade
Colonel Jesse I. Alexander
63rd Illinois Infantry: Colonel Joseph B. McCown
48th Indiana Infantry: Lt. Colonel Edward J. Wood
59th Indiana Infantry: Captain Wilford H. Welman
4th Minnesota Infantry: Lt. Colonel John E. Tourtellotte
18th Wisconsin Infantry: Colonel Gabriel Bouck

Second Brigade
Colonel Green B. Raum
Colonel Francis C. Deimling
Colonel Clark R. Wever
56th Illinois Infantry: Major Pinckney J. Welsh
17th Iowa Infantry: Colonel Clark R. Wever
10th Missouri Infantry: Colonel Francis C. Deimling
24th Missouri Infantry: Captain William W. McCammon
80th Ohio Infantry: Lt. Colonel Pren Metham

Third Brigade
Brigadier-General Charles "Karl" Leopold Matthies
93rd Illinois Infantry: Colonel Holden Putnam
5th Iowa Infantry: Colonel Jabez Banbury
10th Iowa Infantry: Lt. Colonel Paris P. Henderson
26th Missouri Infantry: Colonel Benjamin D. Dean

Artillery
Captain Henry Dillon
Illinois Artillery Battery (Cogswell's): Captain William Cogswell
6th Wisconsin Light Artillery Battery: Lieutenant Samuel F. Clark
12th Wisconsin Light Artillery Battery: Captain William Zickerick

CONFEDERATE FORCES: ARMY OF TENNESSEE
General Braxton Bragg

Army Headquarters
1st Louisiana Infantry (Regulars): Colonel James Strawbridge
1st Louisiana Cavalry: Major J. M. Taylor

Longstreet's Corps
Lieutenant-General James Longstreet

McLaws' Division
Major-General Lafayette McLaws

Kershaw's Brigade
Brigadier-General Joseph Brevard Kershaw
2nd South Carolina Infantry: Colonel John D. Kennedy
3rd South Carolina Infantry: Colonel James D. Nance
7th South Carolina Infantry: Colonel D. Wyatt Aiken
8th South Carolina Infantry: Colonel John W. Henagan
15th South Carolina Infantry: Colonel Joseph F. Gist
3rd South Carolina Battalion Infantry: Lt. Colonel William G. Rice

Humphreys's Brigade
Brigadier-General Benjamin Grubb Humphreys
13th Mississippi Infantry: Colonel Kennon McElroy

17th Mississippi Infantry: Colonel William D. Holder
18th Mississippi Infantry: Colonel Thomas M. Griffin
21st Mississippi Infantry: Colonel William L. Brandon

Wofford's Brigade
Colonel S. Z. Ruff
16th Georgia Infantry: Colonel Henry P. Thomas
18th Georgia Infantry: Colonel S. Z. Ruff
24th Georgia Infantry: Colonel Robert McMillan
Cobb's Legion: Lt. Colonel Luther J. Glenn
Phillips' Legion: Lt. Colonel E. S. Barclay
3rd Georgia Battalion Sharpshooters: Lt. Colonel N. L. Hutchins

Bryan's Brigade
Brigadier-General Goode Bryan
10th Georgia Infantry: Colonel John B. Weems
50th Georgia Infantry: Colonel Peter McGlashan
51st Georgia Infantry: Colonel Edward Ball
53rd Georgia Infantry: Colonel James P. Simms

Artillery Battalion
Major Austin Layden
Georgia Battery: Captain Tyler M. Peeples
Georgia Battery: Captain Andrew M. Wolihin
Georgia Battery: Captain Billington W. York

Hood's Division
Brigadier-General Micah Jenkins

Jenkins's Brigade
Colonel John Bratton
1st South Carolina Infantry: Colonel Franklin W. Kilpatrick
2nd South Carolina Rifles: Colonel Thomas Thomson
5th South Carolina Infantry: Colonel A. Coward
6th South Carolina Infantry: Colonel John Bratton
Hampton South Carolina Legion: Colonel Martin W. Gary
Palmetto South Carolina Sharpshooters: Colonel Joseph Walker

Robertson's Brigade
Brigadier-General Jerome Bonaparte Robertson
3rd Arkansas Infantry: Colonel Van H. Manning
1st Texas Infantry: Colonel A. T. Rainey
4th Texas Infantry: Colonel J. C. G. Key
5th Texas Infantry: Colonel R. M. Powell

Law's Brigade
Brigadier-General Evander McIvor Law
4th Alabama Infantry: Colonel Pinckney D. Bowles
15th Alabama Infantry: Colonel William C. Oates
44th Alabama Infantry: Colonel William F. Perry
47th Alabama Infantry: Colonel Michael J. Bulger
48th Alabama Infantry: Colonel James L. Sheffield

Anderson's Brigade
Brigadier-General George Thomas "Tige" Anderson
7th Georgia Infantry: Colonel W. W. White
8th Georgia Infantry: Colonel John R. Towers
9th Georgia Infantry: Colonel Benjamin Beck
11th Georgia Infantry: Colonel F. H. Little
59th Georgia Infantry: Colonel Jack Brown

Benning's Brigade
Brigadier-General Henry Lewis Benning
2nd Georgia Infantry: Colonel Edgar M. Butt
15th Georgia Infantry: Colonel Dudley M. DuBose
17th Georgia Infantry: Colonel Wesley C. Hodges
20th Georgia Infantry: Colonel J. D. Waddell

Artillery Battalion
Colonel Edward Porter Alexander
South Carolina Battery: Captain William W. Fickling
Virginia Battery: Captain Tyler C. Jordan
Louisiana Battery: Captain George V. Moody
Virginia Battery: Captain William W. Parker
Virginia Battery: Captain Osmond B. Taylor
Virginia Battery: Captain Pichegru Woolfolk, Jr.

Hardee's Corps
Lieutenant-General William Joseph Hardee

Cheatham's Division
Major-General Benjamin Franklin Cheatham

Jackson's Brigade
Brigadier-General John King "Mudwall" Jackson
1st Georgia Infantry (Confederate): Major James C. Gordon
5th Georgia Infantry: Colonel Charles P. Daniel
47th Georgia Infantry: Captain J. J. Harper
65th Georgia Infantry: Lt. Colonel Jacob W. Pearcy
2nd Georgia Battalion Sharpshooters: Lt. Colonel Richard H. Whitely
5th Mississippi Infantry: Major John B. Herring
8th Mississippi Infantry: Major John F. Smith

Moore's Brigade
Brigadier-General John Creed Moore
37th Alabama Infantry: Colonel James F. Dowdell
40th Alabama Infantry: Colonel John H. Higley
42nd Alabama Infantry: Lt. Colonel Thomas C. Lanier

Walthall's Brigade
Brigadier-General Edward Cary Walthall
24th and 27th Mississippi Infantry (Consolidated): Colonel William F. Dowd
29th and 30th Mississippi Infantry (Consolidated): Captain W. G. Reynolds
34th Mississippi Infantry: Colonel Samuel Benton

Wright's Brigade
Brigadier-General Marcus Joseph Wright
8th Tennessee Infantry: Colonel John H. Anderson
16th Tennessee Infantry: Colonel D. M. Donnell
28th Tennessee Infantry: Colonel Sidney S. Stanton
38th Tennessee Infantry: Lt. Colonel Andrew D. Gwynne
51st and 52nd Tennessee Infantry (Consolidated): Lt. Colonel John G. Hall
Murray's Tennessee Battalion: Lt. Colonel Andrew D. Gwynne

Artillery Battalion
Major Melanchthon Smith
Alabama Battery: Captain William H. Fowler
Florida Battery: Captain Robert P. McCants
Georgia Battery: Captain John Scogin
Mississippi Battery (Smith's): Lieutenant William B. Turner

Hindman's Division
Brigadier-General James Patton Anderson

Anderson's Brigade
Colonel William F. Tucker
7th Mississippi Infantry: Colonel William H. Bishop
9th Mississippi Infantry: Major Thomas H. Lynam
10th Mississippi Infantry: Captain Robert A. Bell
41st Mississippi Infantry: Colonel W. F. Tucker
44th Mississippi Infantry: Lt. Colonel R. G. Kelsey
9th Mississippi Battalion Sharpshooters: Captain W. W. Tucker

Manigault's Brigade
Brigadier-General Arthur Middleton Manigault
24th Alabama Infantry: Colonel N. N. Davis
28th Alabama Infantry: Major W. L. Butler
34th Alabama Infantry: Major John N. Slaughter
10th and 19th South Carolina Infantry (Consolidated): Major James L. White

Deas's Brigade
Brigadier-General Zachariah Cantey Deas
19th Alabama Infantry: Colonel Samuel K. McSpadden
22nd Alabama Infantry: Captain Harry T. Toulmin
25th Alabama Infantry: Colonel George D. Johnston
39th Alabama Infantry: Colonel Whitfield Clark
50th Alabama Infantry: Colonel J. G. Coltart
17th Alabama Battalion Sharpshooters: Captain James F. Nabers

Vaughan's Brigade
Brigadier-General Alfred Jefferson Vaughan, Jr.
11th Tennessee Infantry: Colonel George W. Gordon
12th and 47th Tennessee Infantry (Consolidated): Colonel William M. Watkins
13th and 154th Tennessee Infantry (Consolidated): Lt. Colonel R. W. Pitman
29th Tennessee Infantry: Colonel Horace Rice

Artillery Battalion
Major Alfred R. Courtney
Alabama Battery: Captain S. H. Dent
Alabama Battery: Captain James Garrity
Tennessee Battery (Scott's): Lieutenant John Doscher
Alabama Battery (Water's): Lieutenant William P. Hamilton

Buckner's Division
Brigadier-General Bushrod Rust Johnson

Johnson's Brigade
Colonel John S. Fulton
17th and 23rd Tennessee Infantry (Consolidated): Lt. Colonel Watt W. Floyd
25th and 44th Tennessee Infantry (Consolidated): Lt. Colonel John L. McEwen, Jr.
63rd Tennessee Infantry: Major John A. Aiken

Gracie's Brigade
Brigadier-General Archibald Gracie, Jr.
41st Alabama Infantry: Lt. Colonel Theodore G. Trimmier
43rd Alabama Infantry: Colonel Young M. Moody
1st Battalion — Alabama Legion (Hilliard's): Major Daniel S. Troy
2nd Battalion — Alabama Legion (Hilliard's): Captain John H. Dillard
3rd Battalion — Alabama Legion (Hilliard's): Lt. Colonel John W. A. Sanford
4th Battalion — Alabama Legion (Hilliard's): Major John D. McLennan

Reynolds's Brigade
Brigadier-General Alexander Welch Reynolds
58th North Carolina Infantry: Colonel John B. Palmer
60th North Carolina Infantry: Captain James T. Weaver

Chapter 5 — Downpour of Disaster 151

54th Virginia Infantry: Lt. Colonel John J. Wade
63rd Virginia Infantry: Major James M. French

Artillery Battalion
Major Samuel C. Williams
Mississippi Battery (Darden's): Lieutenant H. W. Bullen
Virginia Battery: Captain William C. Jeffress
Alabama Battery: Captain R. F. Kolb

Walker's Division
Brigadier-General States Rights Gist

Maney's Brigade
Brigadier-General George Earl Maney
1st and 27th Tennessee Infantry (Consolidated): Colonel Hume R. Field
4th Tennessee Infantry: Captain Joseph Bostick
6th and 9th Tennessee Infantry (Consolidated): Lt. Colonel J. W. Buford
41st Tennessee Infantry: Colonel Robert Farquharson
50th Tennessee Infantry: Colonel Cyrus A. Sugg
24th Tennessee Battalion Sharpshooters: Major Frank Maney

Gist's Brigade
Colonel James McCullough
46th Georgia Infantry: Lt. Colonel William A. Daniel
8th Georgia Battalion: Lt. Colonel Leroy Napier
16th South Carolina Infantry: Colonel James McCullough
24th South Carolina Infantry: Colonel Clement H. Stevens

Wilson's Brigade
Colonel Claudius Charles Wilson
25th Georgia Infantry: Colonel Claudius Charles Wilson
29th Georgia Infantry: Colonel William J. Young
30th Georgia Infantry: Colonel Thomas W. Mangham
26th Georgia Battalion Infantry: Major John W. Nisbet
1st Georgia Battalion Sharpshooters: Major Arthur Schaff

Artillery Battalion
Major Robert Martin
Missouri Battery: Captain Hiram M. Bledsoe
South Carolina Battery: Captain T. B. Ferguson
Georgia Battery: Captain Evan P. Howell

Breckinridge's Corps
Major-General John Cabell Breckinridge

Cleburne's Division
Major-General Patrick Ronayne Cleburne

Liddell's Brigade
Colonel Daniel Chevilette Govan
2nd and 15th Arkansas Infantry (Consolidated): Major E. Warfield
5th and 13th Arkansas Infantry (Consolidated): Colonel John E. Murray
6th and 7th Arkansas Infantry (Consolidated: Lt. Colonel Peter Snyder
8th Arkansas Infantry: Major Anderson Watkins
19th and 24th Arkansas Infantry: Lt. Colonel A. S. Hutchison

Smith's Brigade
Colonel Hiram Bronson Granbury
6th and 10th Texas Infantry and 15th Texas Cavalry (Dismounted): Colonel Roger Q. Mills
7th Texas Infantry: Colonel Hiram B. Granbury
17th, 18th, 24th and 25th Texas Cavalry (Dismounted): Major William A. Taylor

Polk's Brigade
Brigadier-General Lucius Eugene Polk

1st Arkansas Infantry: Colonel John W. Colquitt
3rd and 5th Confederate Infantry: Lt. Colonel J. C. Cole
2nd Tennessee Infantry: Colonel William D. Robison
35th and 48th Tennessee Infantry (Consolidated): Colonel Benjamin J. Hill

Lowrey's Brigade
Brigadier-General Mark Perrin Lowrey
16th Alabama Infantry: Major Frederick A. Ashford
33rd Alabama Infantry: Colonel Samuel Adams
45th Alabama Infantry: Lt. Colonel H. D. Lampley
32nd and 45th Mississippi Infantry (Consolidated): Lt. Colonel R. Charlton
15th Mississippi Battalion Sharpshooters: Captain Daniel Coleman

Artillery Battalion
Major T. R. Hotchkiss
Arkansas Battery (Calvert's): Lieutenant Thomas J. Key
Texas Battery: Captain James P. Douglas
Alabama Battery (Semple's): Lieutenant Richard W. Goldthwaite
Mississippi Battery (Swett's): Lieutenant H. Shannon

Stewart's Division
Major-General Alexander Peter Stewart

Adam's Brigade
Colonel Randall Lee Gibson
13th and 20th Louisiana Infantry (Consolidated): Colonel Leon von Zinken
16th and 25th Louisiana Infantry (Consolidated): Colonel Daniel Gober
19th Louisiana Infantry: Colonel W. P. Winans
4th Louisiana Battalion Infantry: Lt. Colonel John McEnery
14th Louisiana Battalion Sharpshooters: Major J. E. Austin

Strahl's Brigade
Brigadier-General Otho French Strahl
4th and 5th Tennessee Infantry (Consolidated): Colonel Jonathan J. Lamb
19th Tennessee Infantry: Colonel Francis M. Walker
24th Tennessee Infantry: Colonel John A. Wilson
31st Tennessee Infantry: Colonel Egbert E. Tansil
33rd Tennessee Infantry: Lt. Colonel Henry C. McNeill

Clayton's Brigade
Colonel James Thadeus Holtzclaw
18th Alabama Infantry: Major Shep. Ruffin
32nd Alabama Infantry: Captain John W. Bell
36th Alabama Infantry: Colonel Lewis T. Woodruff
38th Alabama Infantry: Colonel Charles T. Ketchum
58th Alabama Infantry: Lt. Colonel John W. Inzer

Stovall's Brigade
Brigadier-General Marcellus Augustus Stovall
40th Georgia Infantry: Colonel Abda Johnson
41st Georgia Infantry: Colonel William E. Curtiss
42nd Georgia Infantry: Colonel R. J. Henderson
43rd Georgia Infantry: Colonel Hiram P. Bell
52nd Georgia Infantry: Major John J. Moore

Artillery Battalion
Captain Henry C. Semple
Georgia Battery (Dawson): Lieutenant R. W. Anderson
Arkansas Battery (Humphrey's): Lieutenant John W. Rivers
Alabama Battery: Captain McDonald Oliver
Mississippi Battery: Captain Thomas J. Stanford

Chapter 5 — Downpour of Disaster

Breckinridge's Division
Major-General William Brimage Bate

Lewis's Brigade
Brigadier-General Joseph Horace Lewis
2nd Kentucky Infantry: Lt. Colonel James W. Moss
4th Kentucky Infantry: Major Thomas W. Thompson
5th Kentucky Infantry: Colonel H. Hawkins
6th Kentucky Infantry: Lt. Colonel W. L. Clarke
9th Kentucky Infantry: Lt. Colonel John C. Wickliffe
John Hunt Morgan's Dismounted Cavalry (Detachments)

Bate's Brigade
Colonel Robert Charles Tyler
37th Georgia Infantry: Colonel A. F. Rudler
4th Georgia Battalion Sharpshooters: Lieutenant Joel Towers
10th Tennessee Infantry: Colonel William Grace
15th and 37th Tennessee Infantry (Consolidated): Lt. Colonel R. Dudley Frayzer
20th Tennessee Infantry: Major W. M. Shy
30th Tennessee Infantry: Lt. Colonel James J. Turner
1st Tennessee Battalion Infantry: Major Stephen H. Colms

Florida Brigade
Brigadier-General Jesse Johnson Finley
1st and 3rd Florida Infantry (Consolidated): Captain W. T. Saxon
4th Florida Infantry: Lt. Colonel E. Badger
6th Florida Infantry: Colonel Jesse Johnson Finley
7th Florida Infantry: Lt. Colonel Tillman Ingram
1st Florida Cavalry (Dismounted): Colonel G. Troup Maxwell

Artillery Battalion
Captain Cuthbert H. Slocomb
Kentucky Battery (Cobb's): Lieutenant Frank P. Gracey
Tennessee Battery: Captain John W. Mebane
Louisiana Battery (Slocomb's): Lieutenant W. C. D. Vaught

Stevenson's Division
Major-General Carter Littlepage Stevenson

Brown's Brigade
Brigadier-General John Calvin Brown
3rd Tennessee Infantry: Colonel Calvin H. Walker
18th and 26th Tennessee Infantry (Consolidated): Lt. Colonel William R. Butler
32nd Tennessee Infantry: Captain Thomas D. Deavenport
45th and 23rd Tennessee Battalion (Consolidated): Colonel Anderson Searcy

Cumming's Brigade
Brigadier-General Alfred Cumming
34th Georgia Infantry: Colonel J. A. W. Johnson
36th Georgia Infantry: Lt. Colonel Alexander M. Wallace
39th Georgia Infantry: Colonel J. T. McConnell
56th Georgia Infantry: Lt. Colonel J. T. Slaughter

Pettus's Brigade
Brigadier-General Edmund Winston Pettus
20th Alabama Infantry: Captain John W. Davis
23rd Alabama Infantry: Lt. Colonel J. B. Bibb
30th Alabama Infantry: Colonel D. R. Hundley
46th Alabama Infantry: Captain George E. Brewer

Vaughn's Brigade
Brigadier-General John Crawford Vaughn
3rd Tennessee Infantry (Provisional Army)

39th Tennessee Infantry
43rd Tennessee Infantry
59th Tennessee Infantry

Artillery Battalion
Captain Robert Cobb
Tennessee Battery: Captain Edmund D. Baxter
Tennessee Battery: Captain William W. Carnes
Georgia Battery: Captain Max Van Den Corput
Georgia Battery: Captain John B. Rowan

Wheeler's Cavalry Corps
Major-General Joseph Wheeler

Wharton's Division
Major-General John Austin Wharton

First Brigade
Colonel Thomas Harrison
3rd Arkansas Cavalry: Lt. Colonel M. J. Henderson
65th North Carolina Cavalry: Colonel George N. Folk
8th Texas Cavalry: Lt. Colonel Gustave Cook
11th Texas Cavalry: Lt. Colonel J. M. Bounds

Second Brigade
Brigadier-General Henry Brevard Davidson
1st Tennessee Cavalry: Colonel James E. Carter
2nd Tennessee Cavalry: Colonel Henry M. Ashby
4th Tennessee Cavalry: Colonel William S. McLemore
6th Tennessee Cavalry: Colonel James T. Wheeler
11th Tennessee Cavalry: Colonel Daniel W. Holman

Martin's Division
Major-General William Thompson Martin

First Brigade
Brigadier-General John Tyler Morgan
1st Alabama Cavalry: Lt. Colonel D. T. Blakey
3rd Alabama Cavalry: Lt. Colonel T. H. Mauldin
4th Alabama Cavalry (Russell's): Lt. Colonel J. M. Hambrick
Malone's Alabama Cavalry: Colonel James C. Malone
51st Alabama Cavalry: Captain M. L. Kirkpatrick

Second Brigade
Colonel J. J. Morrison
1st Georgia Cavalry: Lt. Colonel S. W. Davitte
2nd Georgia Cavalry: Lt. Colonel F. M. Ison
3rd Georgia Cavalry: Lt. Colonel R. Thompson
4th Georgia Cavalry: Colonel Isaac W. Avery
6th Georgia Cavalry: Colonel John R. Hart

Armstrong's Division
Brigadier-General Frank Crawford Armstrong

First Brigade
Brigadier-General William Young Conn Humes
4th Tennessee Cavalry (Baxter Smith's): Lt. Colonel Paul F. Anderson
5th Tennessee Cavalry: Colonel George W. McKenzie
8th Tennessee Cavalry (Dibrell's)
9th Tennessee Cavalry: Colonel Jacob B. Biffle
10th Tennessee Cavalry: Colonel Nicholas N. Cox

Second Brigade
Colonel C. H. Tyler

Kentucky Battalion Cavalry (Clay's): Lt. Colonel Ezekiel F. Clay
Virginia Battalion Cavalry (Edmundson's): Major S. P. McConnell
Kentucky Battalion Cavalry (Jessee's): Major A. L. McAfee
Kentucky Battalion Cavalry (Johnson's): Major O. S. Tenney

Kelly's Division
Brigadier-General John Herbert Kelly

First Brigade
Colonel William B. Wade
1st Confederate Cavalry: Captain C. H. Conner
3rd Confederate Cavalry: Colonel W. N. Estes
8th Confederate Cavalry: Lt. Colonel John S. Prather
10th Confederate Cavalry: Colonel Charles T. Goode

Second Brigade
Colonel J. Warren Grigsby
2nd Kentucky Cavalry: Colonel Thomas G. Woodward
3rd Kentucky Cavalry: Colonel J. R. Butler
9th Kentucky Cavalry: Colonel W. C. P. Breckinridge
Tennessee Squadron Cavalry (Allison's): Captain R. D. Allison
Tennessee Battalion Cavalry (Hamilton's): Lt. Colonel O. P. Hamilton
Legion Cavalry (Rucker's): Colonel E. W. Rucker

Cavalry Corps Artillery
Tennessee Battery: Captain A. L. Huggins
Tennessee Battery: Captain Gustave A. Huwald
Tennessee Battery: Captain B. F. White, Jr.
Arkansas Battery: Captain J. H. Wiggins

Army Reserve Artillery
Major Felix H. Robertson
Missouri Battery: Captain Overton W. Barret
Georgia Battery (Havis's): Lieutenant James R. Duncan
Alabama Battery (Lumsden's): Lieutenant Harvey H. Cribbs
Georgia Battery: Captain Thomas L. Massenburg

Chapter Six

Blizzard of Bad Tidings: The Atlanta Campaign

There's many a boy here today who looks on war as all glory ... but, boys, it is all HELL!
— Major-General William Tecumseh Sherman,
conversing with his subordinate generals during
The Atlanta Campaign, 1864

Prior to General Johnston's arrival at Dalton, Georgia, to assume command of the Army of Tennessee, he received a letter from President Davis outlining his hopes for the Confederacy's western army. In this communication, Davis painted an optimistic picture regarding the army's condition after the disasters surrounding Chattanooga. Davis's assessment came from a distorted report submitted on December 11 by temporary commander William J. Hardee, in which he stated that "the army is in good spirits ... and we are ready to fight."[1] Davis wrote that the army had a sufficient supply of artillery, wagons, ammunition, horses, and clothing, and that there was a thirty-day supply of rations on hand. Hence, Davis concluded his letter by stating his desire that Johnston would "soon be able to commence active operations against the enemy."[2]

What Johnston discovered upon his arrival in Dalton on December 27 was anything but reassuring. In contrast to the president's letter, Johnston discovered an army in tatters. With 40,000 troops present for duty, only two-thirds were "effectives," or, capable of battle. Instead of a well-supplied military force, Johnston discovered that many of the men were without shoes, blankets, or overcoats. There were not enough horses to pull all of the artillery, nor enough mules to haul the supply wagons. Rations were poor and inadequate, prompting a large percentage of the men, or those not sick with scurvy, to roam the countryside in search of food. To add to the desperation, at least thirty men a day were deserting to the Federals at Chattanooga.[3] Writing to Davis on January 2, Johnston attempted to set the record straight regarding the condition of the Army of Tennessee, as well as quell the expectations of Davis regarding a Confederate offensive. After outlining his assessment of the army's condition, Johnston concluded his letter by writing, "I can see no other mode of taking the offensive here than to beat the enemy when he advances, and then to move forward."[4]

Johnston spent the better part of January inspecting the army, becoming acquainted with its generals, and taking steps to improve conditions. Johnston first secured the addition of more rolling stock to the rail lines in order to procure more rations. He then implemented his General Orders No. 5, a forty-four-paragraph document that dealt with the discipline problem of the army. In it, Johnston outlined the time for reveille, meals, sick call, drills, and dress parade. It also dictated the methods to be used for roll call, inspections, and guard details, among other things. Though the Army of Tennessee had been in the field for two years, it was receiving a basic training refresher course. The improved rations and stricter discipline caused the army's morale to soar, though nothing compared to another of Johnston's orders. Through a system of furloughs, one out of every thirty enlisted men, and one company officer of every three, were allowed a thirty-day leave. For many of the troops, it was their first chance to return home since the war began. Upon their return to the army, they were refreshed, and brought new clothing and news from home to share with the less fortunate. Many also left future mementos of their visit home in the form of yet to be born children. As January 1864 drew to a close, the Army of Tennessee was on the mend.[5]

Major-General William T. Sherman (courtesy of the Library of Congress).

On February 3, Major-General William T. Sherman rode out from Vicksburg with four divisions of infantry, a cavalry brigade, and nine batteries of artillery. His objective was Meridian, Mississippi, an important Confederate city with warehouses that were crammed full of stores. With two rail lines that bisected the city, it was able to ship supplies, and troops to the Rebel supply bases of Mobile and Selma. Sherman's plans called for destroying the railroad to prevent Confederate troops from being rushed to west Tennessee or the Mississippi River. This would free the bulk of his army for offensive operations in the spring. A more sinister aspect of Sherman's plan called for taking the war to the civilian Southern population by destroying crops, slaughtering livestock, and demonstrating to the inhabitants that the only way to avoid such misery was by submitting to Union rule. To prevent Lieutenant-General Leonidas Polk, stationed in Mississippi with 10,000 troops, from being reinforced, a joint army-navy force would move up the Yazoo River to threaten Grenada. This would be done in conjunction with Rear Admiral David Farragut threatening Mobile, and General Thomas demonstrating against Johnston at Dalton. Brigadier-General William Sooy Smith, head of cavalry for the Military Division of the Mississippi, would ride out of Memphis with 7,000 horsemen and link up with Sherman.[6]

Sherman's plan worked well in confusing Polk as to his true intentions, resulting in the bishop's forces remaining scattered while Sherman moved at a fast pace through the interior of Mississippi. Reaching Hillsburgh, Mississippi, on February 10, upon the Federal departure it was destroyed by fire. At last ascertaining that Sherman's objective was Meridian, Polk ordered Major-General Samuel Gibbs French and his two infantry brigades to Meridian in order to evacuate all military supplies to Demopolis, Alabama. The last trainload of supplies and troops departed minutes before Sherman's arrival on February 14. More frustrating to Sherman than the empty warehouses he found at Meridian was the absence of Smith's cavalry, which were nowhere to be seen. Sherman was puzzled, as according to his calculations, Smith should have arrived before he did. Nevertheless, Sherman spent five days in and around Meridian completing his destruction of the city. In addition, his troops fanned out over the countryside plundering farms, villages, and plantations, and also burning thousands of bushels of corn and bales of cotton. They killed livestock and poultry in uncountable numbers, torched houses, shops, and farm buildings, and took thousands of slaves. His work of destruction now completed, Sherman marched his troops back to Vicksburg. But where was Smith?[7]

On the very day that Sherman was returning victorious to Vicksburg, Smith was returning to Memphis in utter disarray, courtesy of the "Wizard of the Saddle," Nathan Bedford Forrest. With only 2,500 troops to oppose Smith's 7,000, Forrest had so manhandled the Union general that he was barely capable of retreating. On February 26, Smith and his defeated command began straggling back into Memphis, demoralized, bedraggled, and some without horses. Smith had learned a lesson that many Federal commanders had learned since the beginning of the war: Never underestimate Forrest, regardless of his disparity in numbers.[8]

Thomas's demonstration on February 24 through the 26th against Johnston had developed some interesting intelligence. For three days he had skirmished with the Confederates along Rocky Face Ridge, an almost solid range of steep hills to the south, north, and west of Dalton. On the afternoon of February 25, the Thirty-Ninth Indiana Mounted Infantry entered Dug Gap and almost succeeded in cutting Johnston off from Atlanta via the railroad south of Dalton. Though Thomas was smart enough to realize that Johnston would not be caught off guard again at Dug Gap, he began to examine his maps for other passes through the southward extension of Rocky Face Ridge. One such pass that caught his eye ran almost twelve miles south of Dalton, and had the sinister sounding name of Snake Creek Gap. It lead to a village on the north bank of the Oostanaula River, and from there on to the Western and Atlantic Railroad. This unassuming little village was named Resaca.[9]

During the month of February, the men of the Fourth Louisiana Battalion wrote letters to loved ones back home. The following letter was written by Sergeant-Major Robert W. Wells to his sister in Natchez, Mississippi. Though parts of the letter are indecipherable, it does outline the high expectations of the troops for the coming campaign.

Head Quarters 4th Batt. La. Vols.
Near Dalton, Ga. February 14th 1864

My Dear Sister May,

I am just in receipt of your letter of the 23rd January and you cannot imagine how delighted I am to hear from you all once more, and to know that you are all well and doing as well as these war times will admit of. I have been sadly disappointed in not being able to pay you a visit during the winter. I could have gotten a leave of absence at anytime but I did not think it would be safe for me to visit that portion of country whilst yankee raids are so frequent. Benton and George CW did it, they ____ but ____ most afraid to venture, had they have gone I, too, would have gone with them. I know that we would have had a gay time. I frequently see the boys and find them very kind and agreeable. Benton has been absent for several weeks with Gen. Hardee down in AL, but has returned. George has written to me longer and sent me letters from cousin Mary Simpson to read, that I might hear from my friends at home. She spoke of having seen Ross and Mack and said was all very well at home. I have written to her and also to ____, and hope they have received the letters.

We are still quietly resting in our winter quarters, waiting for the spring campaign to open with its qualifying marches and honorable battles. We anticipate a very active campaign in the department next summer, which the Generals are making great preparations to me. The ball will open as soon as he may choose to advance. We were glad to see that you have heard from Will once more and that he has been promoted to a Lieut. Col. of Cavalry. I think he will make a good Officer. I intend writing to him soon and I will also write to the other boys also. I am glad you have sent me their addresses. Why don't they write to me? I am surprised at Mack, he used to write to me frequently and now he has been owing me a letter ever since last Spring! What do you think ought to be done with him! But I will return ____ ____ over any wrote to him some of these days. ____ ____ not have an opportunity of seeing my friend Mr. Charles Babbitt. He is now at Dublin Depot in western Virginia, having been sent there several weeks since.

I have just received a long letter from my friend Mrs. Vaughan, she is quite well and sends much love to all of you. She and her sister Mrs. Baynard sent me a large lot of clothing and commissaries. The latter consists in a magnificent ham of bacon, a large middling, a jar of splendid lard, a quantity of fresh back bone, and a supply of sausage, sugar, coffee, black pepper, soda, pepper sauce, tomatoe catsup, sardines, mackerel, and a box of raisins and a number of other little articles such as blacking, knives, forks, pocket knives, etc., and among other things, they sent me a beautiful hat with conf. and tassle to match, shirt and collars of the very latest of aristocracy. Many of these articles were smuggled out of Natchez by my friends in the ____ ____ ____ ____, though such friends are worth having. I tell you, May, they never allow me to want for anything if it can be had by them.

Poor Mrs. Vaughan, it seems that her troubles will never cease. She has just lost her Mother, and is distressed nearly to death. She was quite an old lady, and had been failing for a long time. The war had a great effect upon her exit. I think it hurried her off. She was a good Christian and a kind Mother and valuable member of society.

My friend, William _laway, has gone off on furlough to visit our Mississippi. John was going, I fear he will have a good deal of trouble dodging from the Yankees. I miss him a great deal, and was almost selfish enough to try to persuade him not to go. He is my bosom friend, and a most valuable companion he is to me. I have not heard one word from Er. since I wrote to you the last time. She has left from Augusta, but where she has gone I know not. I think she might have written to me, as she had such a fine opportunity. Some of the boys from my Company saw her and Mr. Harris at Augusta. They say Mr. H is a very nice fellow. I hope for E's sake he may prove to be such. I am somewhat surprised at her for marrying a stranger soldier. For it is hard to tell what they were at home. I profess to know something about soldiers and believe but little they tell me about certain things.

How sorry I am that William and John McLeod have acted so badly. Both of them right now ____ ____ ____ ____ and not how they can content ____ ____ ____ ____ ____ ____ ____ much trouble without agony____ a ____. I could not ____ ____ any ____ ____ quit ____ ____ army this day. I would not do ____ ____ when my Country needs every available man for defense. I will not desert her in this "The Darkest Hours of Her Trials." I thank God that none of my brothers are deserting their duty to the Country. I had the offer of a discharge from the army last Spring whilst I was at home sick, but I informed the army and as soon as I was able I joined my command and have shared with them all of the hardships of army life. I also shared their fortunes in terrible battles, many of which nearly half have fallen. ____ ____ ____ to say that my command has never been in an engagement, but when I was of service with them I did share all of the dangers.

I have given up my music and quit the band in consequence of my health. The Surgeon advised me to do so. I have not played any with them scarcely since I was so sick last Spring. I have been appointed Sergeant-Major of our Battn. and am now acting in that capacity. I do nearly all of the Adjt.'s business and it keeps me quite busy. My health is better at present than it has been since the war commenced. I hope now I am through with sickness for some time to come.

I shall go to Dalton tomorrow to see Benton and George and will get George to forward this letter to you, as he has kindly offered to do for me. He forwards them through a friend in Orange County. I believe I have given you all of the news I have in our Department. Make Bess write to me. How I would love to see all of you. Take good care of yourselves and write to me every chance you have. Give my love to all of my friends at Front Royal and to Aunt Kate. Address me "4th La. Battalion, Gibsons Brigade, Stewarts Division, Hindmans Corps," Dalton, Georgia. Tell me all of the news and everything else. And believe me, Dear May, as ever your Loving and devoted Brother.

Rob

I will write to Bess in a few days! Take good care of yourselves.[10]

Private J. J. Prewitt, also of the Fourth Louisiana Battalion, wrote the following brief correspondence to his wife at Archibald, Franklin Parish, Louisiana:

Camp 2 Que Vie
Feb. 21, 1864

Dear Wife and Children,

As I have an opportunity of sending you a few lines, I will endeavor to do so. I received your letter last Saturday and was glad to hear from you, but was sorry to hear about so many of you having the chills. I would try and get some one to get willow root and try that. It is likely we will draw four months pay today, which is ninety-six dollars, and if I can get any quinine, I will send you some at the first opportunity. Your letter found me in tolerable health. Send me an answer to this if possible.

We are now in the command of Gen. Gibson. I expect we will remain here until run by the Yankees. Ted Birds father is dead. Lou was well the last account. John Fife and Elbert is here in the Guardhouse. Elbert is well. Orren is well at present but has the chills occasionally. Now, other news. From the Baskins, tell Dock and Bob to look out, the government is pressing all the horses and mules they find and stealing all the hogs and cows they can find. I want you to try and hire Godfrey from Dock to make some corn. Dear Wife, as Mr. Luster is waiting, I must close.

Your affectionate husband until death.

J. J. Prewitt[11]

As February drew to a close, the United States Congress passed a bill that revived the rank of lieutenant-general, a rank that was last held by none other than the father of the U.S., George Washington. On February 29, Lincoln affixed his signature to the bill, making it law. The bill was passed in response to the dazzling successes of Ulysses S. Grant in 1863, and Lincoln planned to appoint Grant to the rank. More importantly, Grant would be responsible for directing the actions of the entire Union army to ensure maximum effectiveness and for bringing the war to a close. On March 3, Grant received the following telegram from General-in-Chief Henry Halleck:

Major-General Grant
Nashville, Tenn.:

The Secretary of War directs that you will report in person to the War Department as early as practicable, considering the condition of your command. If necessary you will keep in telegraphic communication with your command while en route to Washington.

H. W. Halleck
General-in-Chief[12]

Grant was aware that he was being called to Washington to be given command of all the Union armies in the field. March 4 was spent preparing for his trip and sending messages regarding his absence to generals Sherman, Schofield, and McPherson, the commanders of the armies comprising the Military Division of the Mississippi. The following day, Grant departed on the trains for Washington in the company of his 13-year-old son, Frederick, and his chief of staff, John A. Rawlins. At 1:00 P.M. on March 9, Grant was presented with his lieutenant-general commission by Lincoln. Among the dignitaries present for the ceremony were members of the Lincoln cabinet, Halleck, Rawlins, and Frederick. Upon asking Lincoln what special service was demanded of him, Lincoln simply stated, "Take Richmond. Our generals have not been fortunate in that direction."[13] After leaving the White House, Grant boarded a train to Brandy Station, Virginia. There lay the first step in taking Richmond: The headquarters of the commander of the Army of the Potomac, Major-General George Gordon Meade. Grant spent the evening talking to Meade and his generals regarding the situation in the east, and ended up spending the night at Meade's headquarters. By the time Grant departed for Washington the following morning, he had made two decisions. The first was that Meade would be retained as the head of the Army of the Potomac. The second was to make his headquarters in the east, where he could join Meade's army in the field. The Army of the Potomac was lacking in aggressiveness, and that is something that Grant could supply in abundance. Meade would conduct the army's tactical operations, but it was Grant that would develop strategy for dealing with the Confederacy's heavy-hitter, Robert E. Lee.[14]

The following evening, Grant was on his way back to Nashville. On March 12, the War Department announced Grant's promotion, as well as Halleck's new role as chief-of-staff under Grant and Stanton. The promotion of Sherman to replace Grant as commander of the Military

Division of the Mississippi, as well as James McPherson's promotion to command of the Army of the Tennessee, were also announced. On March 18, Sherman met with Grant to discuss plans for the coming campaigns. The following day, they finalized a master plan for Union victory over the Southern armies. Grant, directing the Army of the Potomac, would endeavor to destroy the Army of Northern Virginia as part of his plan to capture Richmond, while Sherman would attempt to do the same to the Army of Tennessee and Atlanta. Both men agreed to keep the pressure on the Confederacy in the east and west, until somewhere the Southerners cracked from the pressure.[15]

Atlanta, with four rail lines running from the city, was the center of a rail network that bound together almost all that remained of the Confederacy east of the Mississippi River. Because of the rail lines emanating from the city, the government in Richmond had made Atlanta its main administrative, industrial, and logistical base in the lower South. Inside the city were two foundries, a pistol manufacturer, and an arsenal that produced shells, cartridges, gun carriages, friction primers, knapsacks, and saddles. Also located within the confines of Atlanta were flour mills, packing plants, warehouses, and six military hospitals. To capture Atlanta would deal the Confederate government a huge blow, and Sherman was keenly aware of this.[16]

On the morning of March 22, the soldiers of the Army of Tennessee awoke to discover that a heavy snowstorm during the night had deposited five inches of the powdery substance in their camps. Consequently, snow ball fights quickly became the order of the day. Friendly rivalries between regiments quickly escalated into challenges among states, brigades, and divisions. In Bate's Division, the brigade of Brigadier-General Robert Charles Tyler quickly provoked a fight with the Florida brigade of Brigadier-General Jesse Johnson Finley. After a two-hour contest, the Florida troops were forced to surrender to the men of Tyler's Brigade. As anxious couriers reported the approach of the brigades of Stovall and Clayton of Alexander P. Stewart's Division, a new alliance was formed between the former antagonists. Also, Lewis's Brigade arrived to bring Bate's Division to full strength. As Stewart's men advanced into the line of battle, Finley took command of the troops in his sector and placed his brigade on the left, Tyler's in the center, and Lewis's on the right. As Finley sent out skirmishers, Stewart's men came into view, advancing over the hill in perfect order. The rival skirmishers engaged each other with random lobs, then Finley's men withdrew to the main line. Stewart's troops approached to a point out of range, dressed their lines for the final advance, and charged upon the signal. The attack first struck the Floridians, then enmeshed the whole line. Finley's troops withstood the shock and repulsed the charge after a wild melee, then reorganized for a quick counterattack. The resulting assault bagged a number of prisoners, among whom were two of Stewart's brigadiers, Stovall and Clayton.

Though both sides incurred a number of casualties—black eyes, bruised limbs, and sore jaws—the major result of the contest was the wounded pride of Stewart's men. They were not quite ready to concede the contest, especially with only half of the division engaged. So Stovall and Clayton, now returned to the ranks as paroled prisoners of war, called on the Louisiana and Alabama brigades of Randall Lee Gibson and Alpheus Baker of Stewart's Division. Stewart's Division now advanced again with grim determination. This time the onslaught simply overpowered Finley's line. One soldier of Tyler's brigade lamented, "They moved down upon us like an avalanche and literally swept us ... out of our shanties, down to the spring branch, and there rubbed our faces in the snow. This last proved another Missionary Ridge affair, only on a smaller scale."[17]

These scenes were repeated throughout the camps of the Army of Tennessee as the brigades of Daniel C. Govan and Lucius E. Polk of Cleburne's Division did battle with one another. Also seeing action that day were the Tennesseans of Major-General Benjamin F. Cheatham's Brigade, who engaged the Georgians of Major-General William H. T. Walker in what must be classified as the worlds largest snowball battle at 5,000 participants.

Despite the determined nature of the day's fighting, no long-term resentment lingered after the Great Confederate Snow Ball Battle of 1864. But if the men harbored no grudges, they did for the short-term carry more visible evidence of the severity of the battles. Black eyes, knots on the head, bruises, and a variety of aches and pains were the chief injuries of the contestants due to some of the participants loading their snowballs with rocks and lead. A Louisiana artilleryman recorded the casualties in his company: "All the privates had bruises, one lieutenant had a black eye, and the captain had two front teeth missing."[18] The Fourth Louisiana Battalion of Gibson's Brigade neglected to report their casualties, though one must assume they were severe.

On March 25, Sherman and McPherson caught a train from Nashville to confer with the other leaders of the Union's western armies that Sherman now commanded. Stopping first at Athens, Georgia, they met first with Major-General Grenville Mellen Dodge, commander of the left wing of the Sixteenth Corps of the Army of the Tennessee. Sherman wanted to know if there were practicable routes through which a large force could march through northeastern Alabama into the Coosa River Valley near Rome, Georgia. Dodge answered in the affirmative, and two days later he sent McPherson a detailed report on the various river crossings and roads. After a brief stop at the headquarters of the Army of the Tennessee in Huntsville, Alabama, Sherman and McPherson inspected the bridges over the Tennessee River and other facilities in north Alabama. On the morning of March 28, the two generals arrived in Chattanooga at the headquarters of George H. Thomas, where they discussed the upcoming plans for the conquest of Atlanta. From there, McPherson returned to Huntsville, while Sherman journeyed on to Knoxville, Tennessee, the headquarters of the Army of the Ohio and its commander, Major-General John McAllister Schofield. Sherman advised Schofield that his army would constitute the left wing of the Union forces invading Georgia, and that he was to make preparations to move to the Chattanooga area within the month. The following day, March 31, Sherman headed back to Chattanooga to finalize plans for the coming campaign with Thomas. On April 2, he was enroute to Nashville, his tour of inspection of his new command, and plans, completed.[19]

After studying his maps, Sherman was convinced that the grand battle for Atlanta would probably take place somewhere in the vicinity north of Rome, Georgia. Though equally sure that the two armies would make initial contact near the Confederate camp at Dalton, Sherman knew that the high ridge named Rocky Face and the gorge through it called Mill Creek Gap precluded Dalton as the battle site. Several weeks earlier, Thomas had proposed a plan to Sherman where he would lead the Army of the Cumberland through the gap to reach the railroad at Resaca, Georgia, thereby turning Johnston's position. Simultaneously, Schofield and McPherson would occupy Johnston's attention at Dalton. Sherman liked the plan, though he did modify it to reverse the roles of McPherson and Thomas. The Army of the Tennessee, whose movements would be screened by the high ridges west of Dalton, would strike quickly near Resaca, while the Army of the Cumberland would demonstrate against Johnston at Dalton. To bring the Confederates to battle on terrain favorable to the Federals, McPherson would have to entrench across the Western and Atlantic Railroad somewhere north of Calhoun, Georgia. Johnston's communications with Atlanta would then be cut, compelling him to either attack or retreat toward Atlanta itself. The Army of the Tennessee was to leave their camp near Rossville, Georgia, on May 5, and rapidly march to sweep around the Rebel left through Villanow and Ship's Gap. They were then to seize the pass at Snake Creek by May 7, and from this position to attack the rail line in the vicinity of Resaca. All that was required was speed and boldness to ensure success. In the event the Rebels fell back along the railroad, Sherman gave McPherson specific instructions to make the most of the opportunity by the most vigorous attack possible.[20]

The hilly farmland around Resaca was studded with thick underbrush. Cutting through the landscape was the Western and Atlantic Railroad, crossing the Oostanaula River at Resaca on its path north from Atlanta to Chattanooga. The village had been named in the 1850s by the workers constructing the rail line, many of whom were veterans of the Battle of Resaca de la Palma in the Mexican War. By 1864, Resaca had grown to only several dozen buildings clustered around the freight station, with small farms dotting the surrounding countryside. To the west of the village lay a narrow valley through which flowed Camp Creek and its tributaries, while to the southwest the creek emptied into the Oostanaula. A mile north of Resaca, the railroad swept sharply off to the east where it paralleled for a short distance the Conasauga River, a broad body that joined the Coosawattee River just east of the village. The Coosawattee and Conasauga formed the Oostanaula. Almost three miles east of the Resaca station, the railroad again resumed its northerly route to Tilton, Dalton, and beyond. It was within this rectangle formed by the creek and rivers, and dissected by the railroad, that the first battle of the Atlanta Campaign would be fought.[21]

The battle began to develop on the evening of May 7, when Johnston received reports from cavalry at Ship's Gap of the presence of at least a division of Federals at a small town west of their picket post named Lafayette. Deducing that Sherman intended to attack the Confederate rear at Rome, Georgia, Johnston ordered the cavalry to protect the rail line from Rome northward to Calhoun. To assist the cavalry in this assignment, Johnston ordered the division of Major-General William W. Loring, the vanguard of reinforcements from the Army of Mississippi under Lieutenant-General Leonidas Polk, to support the two regiments of Cantey's Brigade previously ordered to Resaca on May 5. Still, by May 9, Johnston had only Cantey's two regiments of untried troops and Colonel J. Warren Grigsby's small cavalry brigade in place to defend the railroad. They were soon greeted by the appearance of the advance of Grenville Dodge's Sixteenth Corps as it marched down the Resaca road.[22]

Ferociously attacked by Grigsby's troopers, Dodge deployed the leading units of his corps before resuming his advance on Resaca. His mission, as he understood it, was to press upon the village while Union troops farther to the north cut the Western and Atlantic. In actuality, there were no Union troops in position to cut the rail line between Resaca and Dalton. The closest troops to Resaca other than those of Dodge were Major-General John Logan's Fifteenth Corps, assigned to follow Dodge in a support capacity. Dodge's confusion as to his role was the result of a misinterpretation of orders by McPherson, who understood Sherman's orders to be to cut the railroad if possible, then fall back and take a strong defensive position in Snake Creek Gap. Sherman actually had intended that McPherson make a determined effort to break the rail line and entrench across it, and only to retreat to the gap if in danger of being overwhelmed by superior numbers.[23]

As Dodge's advance closed in on Resaca, the Thirty-Seventh Mississippi Infantry of Cantey's Brigade prepared to give the Yankees a warm reception from their post on top of Bald Hill. The Mississippians were quickly put to flight when Dodge reinforced his skirmish line with four regiments, supported by artillery, and charged the hill. The Rebel lines were quickly overwhelmed by the charge, which sent the Southerners not captured or killed fleeing back into the fortifications at Resaca. McPherson now held a commanding position on the west side of Camp Creek that was within musket range of the village itself. Dodge then ordered all of his available cavalry to scout the country to the north and east to ascertain the most feasible route to the railroad. Traveling along the main wagon road north of the village toward Dalton, the horsemen reached the rail line just north of Resaca about two miles south of Tilton. They quickly set to work burning a wood station, cutting the telegraph wire, and destroying a short section of track before returning to Dodge shortly after sunset. In their absence, McPherson had instructed Dodge to defend Bald Hill at the creek with one division, while a second division felt eastward for the railroad. The second division, led by Brigadier-General James Clifford Veatch, crossed

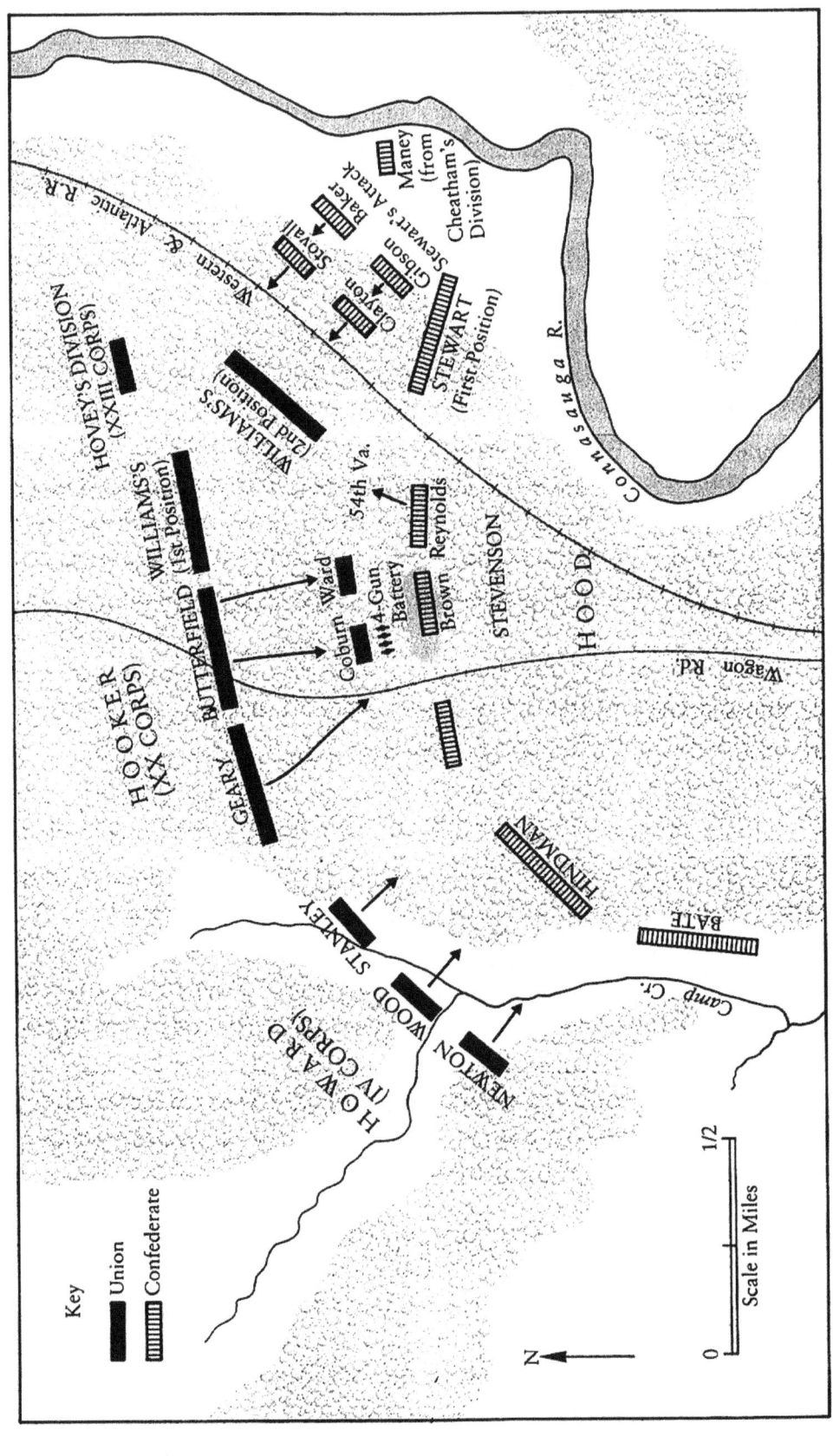

the forks of Camp Creek and entered the open fields to the east. They were greeted by a regiment of Cantey's infantry, with artillery support, who promptly opened fire on their densely packed column. Upon receiving a report that Veatch's skirmishers had spotted the railroad, Dodge ordered one of the two brigades to charge the Confederate position, while the other brigade swung farther to the north and pressed forward on the railroad. Before these orders could be executed, Dodge received instructions from McPherson to recross the creek and fall back to the vicinity of Bald Hill. At nightfall, McPherson ordered the Army of the Tennessee to abandon the attempt to cut the Western and Atlantic and return to Snake Creek Gap, where they began throwing up defensive works. Unknown to McPherson at this time, he had just let a golden opportunity to sever Johnston's communications slip through his fingers.[24]

Johnston responded to the reports of Union activity by sending Stewart's Division from Hood's Corps and Bate's Division of Hardee's Corps into Buzzard Roost Gap. He also posted Cheatham's Division on the northern end of Rocky Face, and deployed Stevenson's and Hindman's Divisions of Hood's Corps in Crow Valley astride the Cleveland Road. Cleburne's and Walker's Divisions were held in reserve at Dalton so as to be prepared to move where needed. On Sunday, May 8, Thomas completed his assignment to keep Johnston occupied at Dalton by having Harker's brigade of Newton's division seize the northern end of Rocky Face Ridge. Thomas then completed the second part of his diversion by having his troops threaten Buzzard Roost Pass, where they were forced to halt due to a man-made lake the Rebels had created by damming Mill Creek to impede any Union attack. When Johnston finally began to ascertain that the immediate threat was at Resaca, he abandoned Dalton, the headquarters of the Army of Tennessee for the past six months. He then issued orders to Hardee, Hood, and Wheeler to converge upon Resaca with their commands.[25]

Upon the arrival of his forces at Resaca, Johnston placed Polk's Army of Mississippi, just arriving from the Magnolia State, on the left and in front of Resaca. Hardee's Corps was then placed in the center, while Hood's Corps was placed on the right, giving Johnston almost 50,000 troops on hand with which to confront Sherman.[26]

Sherman, much frustrated at McPherson's failure to cut the railroad at Resaca, attempted to salvage what he could of his derailed plans. On May 11, he ordered all of his scattered forces to converge on Resaca via Villanow and Snake Creek Gap beginning the following morning. Howard's Fourth Corps was instructed to follow Johnston's army on the direct route from Dalton on the rail line to Resaca. By the afternoon of May 13, the arriving Yankee units began to assume their positions near Resaca along the range of wooded hills lining the western side of the valley skirting Camp Creek and its tributaries. McPherson's army reoccupied Bald Hill, extending their right flank to the Oostanaula River and covering the direct road from Snake Creek Gap. Thomas and the Army of the Cumberland were placed on McPherson's left. Upon their arrival on May 14, Schofield's Army of the Ohio was ordered to extend the line northward along the creek bank. By 10:00 A.M., Sherman was ready to advance against the Confederate positions east of the creek and valley.[27]

Learning that Howard's corps was approaching Resaca from the north along the railroad, Sherman ordered the divisions of Brigadier-General Henry Moses Judah and Brigadier-General Jacob Dolson Cox of the Army of the Ohio, and the divisions of Baird and Johnson of the Army of the Cumberland, to advance and strike what he assumed to be the Rebel right. As soon as the advance was underway, the lines became disorganized from the thick underbrush in the gulleys and ravines that the men traversed. After advancing almost one-half mile, Baird's division reached the crest of a ridge from which he spied the Confederate defensive works. Attempting

Opposite: Map of Battle of Resaca, GA (courtesy of Albert Castel, ***Decision in the West: The Atlanta Campaign of 1864***, University Press of Kansas, 1992).

to halt to re-form his lines, Judah's division suddenly lunged forward through Baird's division, causing even more disruption. Seeing some of his regiments carried along by Judah's troops, Baird ordered his division to charge the works also. Unable to catch up to Judah's sprinting men, who were also far ahead of Cox's division on their left, Judah's lines attacked alone and unsupported. They were met by a withering barrage of musket and artillery fire that forced them to seek refuge in Camp Creek. Baird's division suffered the same fate, and joined Judah's troops on the muddy banks of the creek. They remained there until a slackening of the Rebel fire enabled the Federals to make their way back up the ridge and to the rear. The slackening of the defensive fire was the result of Cox's division approaching the Confederate position from the north. After four desperate assaults to dislodge the Rebels defending the west branch of Camp Creek, Cox ordered his men to convert the rifle pits they had just seized into trenches for themselves. His troops were relieved an hour later by three brigades from the Fourth Corps, and Sherman's attempt to push back Johnston's right ended at 3:00 P.M. in total futility. Sherman then ordered up artillery to bombard the Confederate works, placing the guns on the hills to the west and north of the upper reaches of Camp Creek.[28]

On the extreme left of Sherman's line, the division of Major-General David Sloane Stanley of the Fourth Corps was deployed just beyond the Tilton-Resaca Road facing southeast. They were "in the air," or, vulnerable to a flank attack by Johnston, whose right wing under Hood reached almost to the Conasauga. Aware of Stanley's predicament, at 4:00 P.M. Johnston ordered Hood to attack the Federal left flank, destroy it, and then sweep forward until he reached the road running between Snake Creek Gap and Resaca. If successful, Sherman would then be cut off from the gap, and would either have to surrender or face annihilation. Hood ordered the division's of Stewart and Stevenson to move out of their works and form a double line of battle. As they were executing this order, two of Walker's brigades moved up from the south side of the Oostanaula River to reinforce Stewart, while another of Walker's brigades and one of Loring's moved into reserve behind Stewart and Stevenson. Upon receiving word from his scouts that the Rebels were massing in large numbers on his front and flank, Stanley sent word to Howard of the impending assault. He also ordered his chief-of-artillery to post the six Napoleons and Rodman cannons of the Fifth Indiana Battery to cover the rear of Cruft's brigade on the extreme left.[29]

After Howard received Stanley's message, he rode off to inform Thomas of the coming attack. Thomas immediately ordered Hooker to send one of his divisions to Stanley's assistance. Hooker chose William's division, personally escorting the troops to the endangered Union position. Stanley had strung out his division in a single rank to present as broad a front as possible, resulting in huge gaps between each pair of regiments. At 5:00 P.M., Hood's battle lines began advancing, charging forward with the chilling Rebel yell. The Rebels swept through, over, and around Cruft's and Whitaker's brigades, causing the Federals to flee in panic. Three brigades of Stevenson's Division then occupied the shallow trenches previously held by the panic-stricken Union soldiers, but just long enough to catch their breath and re-form. They then surged forward down the side of a thickly wooded hill toward the open field lying just beyond. The six guns of the Indianans belched forth shot and shrapnel from the hill at the opposite end of the field that staggered the Southerners. At 400 yards the gunners switched to canister, causing scores of Stevenson's men to collapse in a heap of mangled bodies. Those who remained unhurt swerved to the right and took shelter in the woods to the north of the battery. The Indianan artillerists then turned their guns in that direction, while Cruft and Whitaker managed to rally a few hundred of their fleeing troops to support the battery.

As Stevenson's men emerged from the woods, they were quickly driven back by double-shotted canister fire from the guns. As they began to advance again, Hooker arrived on the field with William's division and repulsed the attack of the Southerners. As darkness fell, Stevenson's

Division retired to the railroad, leaving behind a mass of corpses in front of Simonson's Indiana Battery. They were followed by Stewart's Division, which had advanced almost two miles without encountering any serious opposition. This was due to the fact that Stewart had swung so far to the right that he had become separated from Stevenson and had found no Federals to attack.[30]

At the time Hood's attack got underway on the Union left, the Union brigades of brigadier-generals Giles Smith and Charles Woods waded across Camp Creek and attempted to capture the Confederate-held hill beyond the creek. Once across the body, they re-formed their lines and advanced toward the hill, where they were met by a storm of lead and iron. The men refused to stop, and in a few minutes were swarming across the piled-up logs that had sheltered two of Cantey's regiments. Johnston had weakened his line at this point to support Hood's attack, and now the time had come to pay the piper. Ahead 400 yards lay the main Confederate fortifications separating McPherson from Resaca. If a breakthrough could be made at this point, Johnston's direct line of communications and retreat would be cut. Polk immediately ordered Cantey, who had been reinforced by Vaughan's Brigade, to recapture the hill. Beginning at 7:30 P.M., Vaughan's Tennesseans made three separate assaults that were repulsed by the Federals with the aid of the six-gun "German Battery." Polk finally called off the attack, and the Rebels withdrew to the main Confederate line.[31]

That night, Johnston received reports that two divisions of the Union army had crossed the river at Lay's Ferry on a pontoon bridge, and of Polk's loss of the hill. He immediately issued orders for Walker to hasten with his entire division to the road between Lay's Ferry and Calhoun, issued orders for his engineers to lay a pontoon bridge across the Oostanaula River east of the railroad bridge, and sent Wheeler to the south side of the Oostanaula to protect the railroad bridge and adjoining wagon bridge. His plans had shifted from attempting to cut Sherman off from Snake Creek Gap to striving to prevent Sherman from cutting the Army of Tennessee off from Atlanta. Sherman's plans were to basically attempt to do tomorrow what he had attempted to do on this day. He ordered Howard and Hooker to "attack in the morning directly south down upon Resaca." McPherson was ordered to mass his army west of Resaca in anticipation of a Confederate attack to regain the hill taken by Smith and Woods. Palmer's corps would extend its front to the right so as to cover the gap in the line made by McPherson's massing of forces. Last, he ordered Schofield to move his forces to the extreme left.[32]

At daybreak on May 15, the artillerists, sharpshooters, and skirmishers of both sides began their deadly work. While Johnston spent the morning inspecting his lines, Howard and Hooker spent theirs preparing for the attack Sherman had ordered. At 1:00 P.M., the attack got underway, with Howard covering the main assault that was to be conducted by Hooker. Three of Howard's brigades jumped over their works and advanced toward a hill just beyond the road that was held by Hindman's Division. In Hazen's brigade, 120 men fell in thirty seconds alone, prompting Hazen to order the remainder to return to their fortifications. They were quickly followed by the two remaining brigades. Hooker deployed across the Dalton-Resaca Road with Geary's division on the right, Butterfield's in the center, and Williams's on the left. His objective was the hill that anchored the Confederate line at the point where it bent away from the road toward the Conasauga River, with the actual assault to be made by Butterfield's and Geary's divisions.[33]

The assault was launched at 1:30 P.M., with Geary and Butterfield advancing through ravines, up and down hills, and through the dense underbrush. Of course, their lines were soon disorganized and broken, with the inevitable outcome being a series of disjointed charges that were easily repulsed by the defenders. The exception was the brigade of Brigadier-General William Thomas Ward of Butterfield's division, which observed the four guns of Captain Max Van Den Corput's Cherokee Battery almost 80 yards in front of their objective. Ward immediately ordered his troops to charge and take the battery, where they were greeted by salvos of canister from the battery and a hail storm of lead from the infantry on the hill. Ward's men kept going and swarmed over the battery, bayoneting most of the cannoneers. They were quickly driven back by the infantry of Brown's Brigade of Stevenson's Division, which poured volley after volley into the Federals, prompting them to flee for their lives. Later, another of Butterfield's brigades, that of Colonel John Coburn, captured the battery but was forced to abandon it also. Colonel David Ireland's brigade of Geary's division then lay down 15 yards away and opened fire on the Rebel works to prevent them from attempting to retrieve the guns. As the cannon lay in a "no man's land," Brown's Tennesseans taunted the Federals with "Come on, take those guns!" The Union troops retorted with "Come and take them yourselves!" Regardless of who had actual possession of the guns, Hooker's assault was a bloody failure. His casualties were pegged at 1,200, almost as many soldiers as Brown had in his whole brigade.[34]

Arriving at Hood's headquarters at 3:00 P.M., Johnston ordered Hood to instruct Stewart to wheel his division to the west and launch an assault on Sherman's left flank. He also ordered Stevenson and Hindman to assault the enemy in their front, and detached a brigade each from Polk's and Hardee's corps to add muscle to Stewart's attack. Stewart immediately formed his division into a double line of battle with Clayton's Alabama Brigade and Gibson's Louisiana Brigade on the left, and Stovall's Georgia Brigade and Baker's Alabama Brigade on the right. Stewart also ordered Maney's Tennessee Brigade, on loan from Hardee, and a small cavalry detachment into position on his extreme right to cover that flank. Shortly before 4:00 P.M., Stewart received information that a heavy movement of the enemy was occurring in his front, and relayed the intelligence to Hood. Receiving no response, at 4:00 P.M. he ordered all of his brigades to make a half-wheel to the left, then advance straight ahead. Stewart's attack was under way.

At this time, Johnston received a communication from Walker stating that Sherman's right had crossed the Oostanaula. Johnston immediately ordered Hood to cancel the attack by Stewart, as they must now concern themselves with their own left and rear, not Sherman's. Hood sent Lieutenant-Colonel Edward Cunningham to notify Stewart of the cancelation order, but by the time he located Stewart, his troops were already heavily engaged. Instead of encountering the exposed flank of the Union army, they had run head-on into William's division, whose troops occupied a row of hills that paralleled the railroad. Geary's division anchored their right, and two batteries of rifled artillery add their muscle to the position. Waiting until Stewart's lines emerged from the woods on the other side of the railroad, they unleashed rapid volleys that drove Clayton's Brigade back into the woods. Next to advance from the woods were Stovall's troops, which did not advance as far as Clayton before fleeing back into the woods to escape the blasts of canister. Following in Stovall's wake, Baker's Brigade advanced to within 30 yards of the Federal line before being driven from the field also. Stewart, who had had three horses shot from under him, realized that the assault was a dismal failure and called back Maney's and Gibson's brigades before they became seriously engaged. He then ordered all his forces back to their original line.

Stewart's losses for an attack that had virtually no chance for success, and would have been meaningless should it have succeeded, were high. Casualties were tallied at approximately 1,000 killed, captured, and wounded. Almost half of this number came from Clayton's Brigade. Union losses were 48 killed and 366 wounded.[35] Severely wounded in the charge was the commander of the Fourth Louisiana Battalion, Lieutenant-Colonel John McEnery of Gibson's Brigade. Shortly after nightfall, Major Duncan Buie assumed command of the battalion.[36]

Soon after sunset, Johnston met with Hood and Hardee in a field behind Stewart's Division to advise them that the army would withdraw to the south bank of the Oostanaula that night. Johnston then gave orders as to the timing and manner of the withdrawal, which was no easy task in the face of a powerful enemy. The wagon train, most of which was already on the south bank of the river, would cross on the pontoon bridge; the troops would use the wagon and railroad bridges. Skirmishers would be left behind in the fortifications to cover the withdrawal, then they would follow once the main force had crossed. As soon as everyone was over the river, the engineers would take up the pontoon bridge and burn the remaining bridges.[37]

Beginning at midnight, Hardee's Corps crossed the river on the wagon bridge while Hindman's and Stevenson's divisions crossed on the railroad bridge. Polk's troops followed Stevenson's Division, and Stewart's Division, formed in line of battle, served as rear guard. By 3:30 A.M., all the wagons, infantry, and artillery were across, prompting the engineers to torch the remaining bridges. Soon after, Union skirmishers discovered that the Confederate fortifications were empty, and pushed on toward Resaca. Seeing the flames from the bridges, they rushed forward and were able to partially save the wagon bridge. After a few repairs, Sherman would be able to use it to cross the Oostanaula in pursuit of the Army of Tennessee. The Battle of Resaca, the first of the Atlanta Campaign, was now officially over.[38]

Brigadier-General Randall Lee Gibson, commanding the Louisiana brigade that included the Fourth Louisiana Battalion, wrote this after-action report concerning the engagements of his brigade since first coming in contact with Union forces at Dalton:

> I have the honor to report that my command has been engaged with the enemy in a way to speak of at three points during the recent operations. While in position on the left in Mill Creek Gap, my right resting at Redoubt Fisk, very near the railroad, and my left in Redoubt Winans, in which was posted Fenner's battery, and which position was assigned to me on the 7th of May, the enemy attacked us with strong lines of skirmishers, and shelled the line three or four times, but accomplished nothing.
>
> The day before quitting Dalton my command was moved to the right of Stewart's division upon Rocky Face Ridge, from which elevated point we soon discovered the enemy moving from our front to the left. After taking position at Resaca my command, with the balance of the division, charged the enemy's left flank. In the first charge I could not get up with the enemy, who was at a considerable distance from us when we started, and retired hastily before us as we advanced, shelling the woods through which we were approaching. In the second charge mine was the supporting line, and just as we discovered that the first line had already retired through the thick chaparral, and as we were about to charge the enemy-whose fire we were receiving but not returning, as I had been instructed that Clayton's brigade was ahead of me-I received orders to retire to the ravine from which we had moved.
>
> On the movement from Resaca my own and Stovall's brigade (Colonel Johnson commanding) were assigned the duty of protecting the rear of our army. I had not yet formed my own line of battle when the enemy attacked our pickets and began to throw shot at our position. I was ordered to take command of both brigades, and throwing forward a very heavy line of skirmishers, was soon prepared to drive back the enemy should he attempt to make a night attack. This disposition continued until long after midnight, when Major-General Stewart directed me to cross the bridge and move with the army, holding the command in readiness to repel any attack. The steadiness of both commands on this occasion I was especially pleased with. There was a confident tone pervading both officers and men that was in earnest of their resolution to perform the responsible duty devolving upon them to the fullest extent. The shelling had no effect, and every man seemed determined to drive back any line that might show itself.[39]

Sherman did pursue Johnston, forcing him to withdraw from two other positions at Adairsville and Cassville that he determined were indefensible. Upon the Confederate pull-out from Cassville, the Union and Confederate armies were now less than 50 miles from Atlanta. Johnston encamped his army around Allatoona, Georgia, while Sherman established his headquarters at Kingston. For the next several days, each army would regroup and rest their troops before the campaign resumed on May 23. On that day, Sherman placed his forces in motion with an eye towards the crossroads village of Dallas and on to Marietta. Upon learning of the movements of Federal troops, Johnston ordered Hardee and Polk to march for Dallas, while sending Wheeler with 800 cavalry to cross over to the north side of the Etowah River and scout the Cartersville area. While he was awaiting developments, Johnston stayed at Allatoona with Hood's Corps. After receiving a report from his cavalry that Union troops were spotted heading southward from Milam's and Gillem's bridges, Johnston assumed that Sherman was moving to the west in an attempt to outflank him. Consequently, Johnston ordered Hood's Corps to follow Polk and Hardee to the Dallas area, where he joined them later that evening.[40]

On the morning of May 25, Johnston had placed Hardee's Corps astride the Atlanta-Marietta Road directly east of Dallas, with Polk's Corps deployed along Hardee's right. Hood's Corps was ordered to a crossroads northeast of Dallas where a log Methodist chapel had been established. The name of the peaceful place of worship was New Hope Church.

Hood formed his lines in their customary deployment, with Hindman on the left, Stevenson on the right, and Stewart in the center around New Hope Church. Stewart's men began digging rifle-pits and erecting barricades of logs and rocks. Stovall's Georgians were spared the task of fortifying their position, as they were provided cover behind the tombstones in the church cemetery.[41]

When the Army of the Cumberland resumed its march on the morning of May 25, Thomas sent Hooker's corps on three separate roads leading from Burnt Hickory toward Dallas. Butterfield's division was on the corps' left, Williams's division on the right, and Geary's in the center. After advancing three or four miles, Geary's division reached a bridge that spanned Pumpkinvine Creek at Owen's Mill. After driving away a small body of Rebels that had attempted to torch the bridge, the men encountered a fork in the road on the south side of the creek. One branch led south to Dallas, while the other led to New Hope Church. Since McPherson was approaching Dallas from the west, Hooker was ordered to take the fork leading southeast. Around 10:00 A.M., Geary crossed the creek and resumed the march.[42]

While the Federals were crossing Pumpkinvine Creek, Stewart was preparing his position at the church. His front line consisted of Stovall's Brigade on the left, Clayton's Brigade in the center, and Baker's Brigade on the right. Stewart posted Gibson's Brigade in reserve, along with

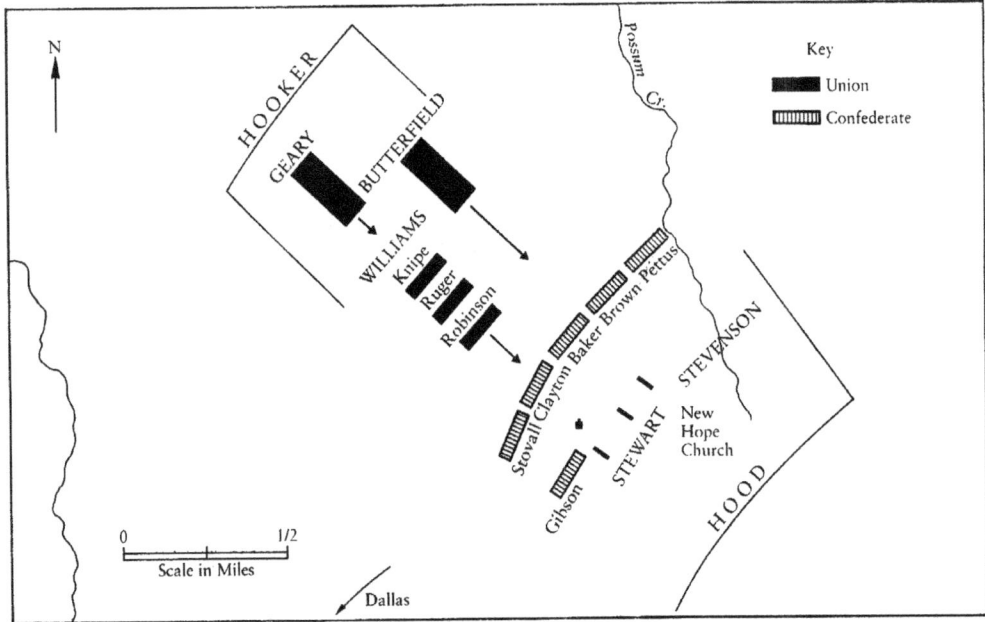

Map of Battle of New Hope Church (courtesy of Albert Castel, *Decision in the West: The Atlanta Campaign of 1864*, University Press of Kansas, 1992).

Brown's Brigade, on loan to him from Stevenson's Division. In support along this section of the line were sixteen artillery pieces massed together. Hood also threw out the Fourteenth Louisiana Battalion Sharpshooters and two Alabama regiments to act as skirmishers to delay Hooker's advance.[43]

After making their way for a mile and a half after crossing the creek, Geary's lead brigade was attacked by Hood's advanced detachments. The short but intense fight continued until Geary deployed three brigades and slowly pushed the Rebels back. From prisoners, the Yankees learned that Hood's Corps, supported by other elements of the Confederate army, were in their front. Geary immediately put his men to work erecting fortifications, while Hooker sent couriers to bring up Butterfield and Williams. Thomas issued orders for the other corps of his army to hasten to Hooker's support. Sherman, who rode up to Hooker's position at this time, believed that Hooker and Thomas were mistaken about a large body of the enemy being in their front. The crimson-haired Federal commander wanted to push forward and occupy the crossroads before a large body of Rebels could be gotten into position there. He finally yielded to the remonstrances of his subordinates and agreed to wait until the arrival of reinforcements.[44]

At 4:00 P.M., as the sky darkened and thunder boomed across the heavens, the Northern advance was resumed. With Geary in the center, Butterfield on the left, and Williams on the right, the men forced their way through the tangled landscape toward Hood's position at New Hope Church. William's troops were the first to encounter the Confederates, and unfortunately for the Northerners, they were deployed in columns of brigades that narrowed the front of divisions to the width of a brigade. Hooker's line was therefore about the same width as Stewart's Division, a fact that enabled Stewart's troops to concentrate their fire along the narrow front of the Union advance. As Williams's division reached the foot of a slope, they were met by a hurricane of canister, shrapnel, and bullets that forced them to seek shelter behind boulders, trees, logs, or anything that looked like it might afford some protection. To Williams it seemed as if the fire were coming from "all directions except the rear." Up ahead, the crouching Federals saw piles of logs and red dirt spewing forth clouds of blue smoke. In Robinson's brigade, forming the first line of Williams's division, the soldiers fired off their sixty rounds of ammunition in a half an hour. The brigade of Brigadier-General Thomas Ruger took their place, and before long they were pilfering cartridges from the dead and wounded.[45]

Facing Hooker's three divisions were all of Stovall's and Clayton's brigades, and elements of Gibson's and Baker's brigades: 4,000 Confederates against 16,000 Federals. Johnston had joined Hood at his headquarters earlier that afternoon, and sent a messenger to Stewart asking if he needed reinforcements. Stewart, who was riding along behind his firing line as his men handily repulsed the attack, declined the offer, stating, "My own troops will hold the position." At 7:30 P.M. a drenching downpour began falling that, along with darkness, mercifully brought an end to the Union slaughter. Stewart's troops raised a "prolonged cheer of victory" while Hooker's fell back sullenly and in defeat. In Williams's division, over 800 men had fallen in their attack against Stewart's position. Geary's loss was pegged at 376, and Butterfield's at 418. Stewart's losses were placed at "between 300 or 400," with a tenth of these being in Eldridge's Artillery Battalion. Two brothers were among the casualties in Fenner's Louisiana Battery, who fell as they manned the dangerous position of rammer at the muzzle of their gun. A third brother was serving as rammer when the battle ended. Both Hood and Johnston praised Stewart for his division's unflinching defense of their position, and placed him in line for promotion to lieutenant-general should a vacancy occur.[46]

Elsewhere along the lines, McPherson moved into position close to Hooker's right flank, though still separated from it by a mile. Howard's corps came up in supporting distance of Hooker later that evening, but Palmer's corps was farther to the rear and had not been able to follow until the battle at New Hope Church was over. The Army of the Ohio stayed near Burnt

Hickory until 5:00 P.M., when Schofield received orders to move forward to support Hooker. Brigadier-General Jefferson C. Davis's division was in place on Hooker's right and rear. Schofield's march was along the roads traveled by the wagon trains of Hooker's corps, and were so few and crowded that his forces were still west of Pumpkinvine Creek at midnight. Schofield halted the column there and rode forward to obtain instructions from Sherman. On his return, his horse slipped in the mud and fell on the general, forcing him to relinquish command of his army to Brigadier-General Jacob Cox for several days.[47]

Dawn of May 26 found the Union army scattered through the woods to the north and west of Dallas. The efforts to pull his forces together occupied Sherman for most of the day. McPherson, whose advance reached Dallas, was placed on the right of the line, while Logan's corps occupied the right and Dodge's corps the left. To the right of Logan, Brigadier-General Kenner Garrard and his cavalry were posted. Davis's division was moved up on McPherson's left, though a gap remained between it and the rest of the Army of the Cumberland that was facing Hood at New Hope Church. Hooker remained in the position he had occupied on the previous evening, and Howard's corps extended the line on Hooker's left. The Army of the Ohio was placed on Howard's left, with its left reaching as far as the Allatoona–New Hope Church–Dallas Road line. Cavalry was posted to protect the left flank. Due to the scarcity and poor conditions of the roads, these troop dispositions were not completed until it was too late for further operations.[48]

Throughout the day, constant skirmishing occurred along the line but no major fighting took place. Johnston, realizing that the majority of the Union forces were now in place near New Hope Church, began shifting troops to that sector. Hood moved Hindman's Division to his right, and then placed Cleburne's Division, on loan from Hardee's Corps, to the right of Hindman. Polk moved up toward Hood's left, and Hardee was placed on the left of Polk. Walker's Division was held in reserve, while Bate's Division remained on the far left to hold the Dallas-Atlanta Road. A span of one and a half miles separated Bate from the remainder of Hardee's Corps. Wheeler was posted so as to cover the Confederate right, with Brigadier-General William Hicks "Red" Jackson's cavalry division on the left.[49]

Sherman had decided that, in lieu of a costly frontal assault, he would attempt to turn the right of Johnston's position and assault it from the flank or rear. Sherman ordered Howard to take Brigadier-General Thomas J. Wood's division of the Fourth Corps and with the support of other units, march to the left until he was past the Confederate line, then launch an attack. On the morning of May 27, Wood pulled back from his position in the line while other commands stretched to fill the gap. Brigadier-General Richard W. Johnson's division was ordered to support Wood in his efforts, in addition to a brigade on loan from another corps. Units in position along the line were ordered to make demonstrations to divert the attention of the Rebels from the point selected for the assault. Getting underway at 11:00 A.M., Howard had moved east for almost a mile when he wrongly assumed that he had passed the Confederate right flank. Forming his command for an assault, Wood's skirmishers soon returned to report Rebel works in the woods to the front. Howard then resumed his march for a mile further to the east, bringing the Northerners about two miles northeast of New Hope Church near the small settlement of Pickett's Mill. Unable to locate any Rebels in the area, Howard deduced that he was beyond Johnston's line and, after allowing his command a brief rest period, began preparations for his attack.[50]

Unknown to Howard, a morning reconnaissance made by Govan's Brigade of Cleburne's Division had detected his movements, and was at that moment preparing to receive his attack. Johnston, incorrectly assuming that Sherman was withdrawing to the east, ordered two unsuccessful assaults on the Union lines in an attempt to catch the Federals as they were withdrawing. One of these attacks fell upon the two divisions of the Fourth Corps that were occupying the line between Hooker and the Army of the Ohio. It was repulsed after what Thomas described as a "short and warm contest." At the same time, another Confederate attack fell upon the extreme right of Sherman's line, resulting in the Southerners overrunning the Federal skirmishers before their advance was stopped by the main Union line and reserves.[51]

Meanwhile, Howard was in the final stages of completing preparations for his attack on what he assumed to be the unprotected flank of the Confederate line. Wood's division, which was to execute the attack, was formed in a column of brigades. The lead brigade was that of William B. Hazen, followed by Colonel William H. Gibson's brigade and the brigade of Colonel Frederick Knefler. McLean's brigade was deployed into a clearing a short distance to the right in the hopes it would draw Rebel attention away from the main assault. Two brigades of Johnson's division were formed on the left of Wood's attack column to protect its flank. At 5:00 P.M., the Federal advance began. After traversing only a short distance, the Federals encountered opposition from several dismounted cavalry of Kelly's Division, who were deployed in the woods to guard the right flank of the Confederate line. Slowly pushing the cavalrymen before them, Hazen's brigade advanced across a small ravine and began to ascend the slope beyond. Looking upward, the men were greeted by the bone-chilling sight of the distinctive blue battle flags of Cleburne's Division floating in the breeze. Breasting the slope, they were met by a sheet of flame from Cleburne's line that dropped 500 of Hazen's brigade before forcing them to drop out of the engagement. The trailing brigades, taking Hazen's place in the action, also met a similar fate. Color Sergeant Ambrose D. Norton of the Fifteenth Ohio Infantry was killed, and his flag fell in the open area in front of Cleburne's line. Five Ohioans were mowed down in succession attempting to regain their colors.[52]

Sherman's maneuver was doomed from the moment Govan discovered Howard's march. In addition to the dismounted cavalry, the bulk of the repulse was handled by the Confederate brigades of Govan, Granbury, and Lowrey. After the Federal assault was defeated, heavy fighting ceased along the line, but skirmishing continued long after sunset. At 10:00 P.M., Cleburne discovered that many Federals who had gained shelter in the ravine were attempting to withdraw to their lines. Granbury's Brigade made a night attack on the ravine that resulted in the capture of 232 Union soldiers. Howard's casualties were heavy, with Wood reporting a loss in his division of 212 killed, 927 wounded, and 318 missing, for a total of 1,457. Some of the smaller Federal units were almost annihilated. One company of the Forty-First Ohio lost twenty of its twenty-two men, while the Forty-Ninth Ohio lost 203 of their 402 soldiers. The Eighty-Ninth Illinois left 154 of their members in front of Cleburne's line, prompting one Union soldier to record, "This is surely not war, it is butchery." Cleburne's losses were tallied at 35 killed and 363 wounded.[53]

Sherman's line was now stretched extremely thin, with two large and dangerous gaps. The first was between Hooker's right at New Hope Church and the left of Davis's division near Dallas; the second existed between the left of the Army of the Ohio near the church and the right of Howard's position near Pickett's Mill. Davis had posted a thin line of pickets across the first gap, and Mclean's brigade was placed in the rear of the second gap. Realizing that the Confederate line was too strong to be broken by assault, Sherman determined to straighten his line, plug the gaps, and work his way eastward to the railroad. Accordingly, Sherman issued orders to Davis and McPherson to shift eastward from their location at Dallas toward New Hope Church. As McPherson was in motion, Sherman planned to have the other two armies make a similar shift while the cavalry was sent forward to seize Allatoona Pass, giving him control of the railroad on the south bank of the Etowah. Guessing that the Federal commander would attempt such a shift, on May 28 Johnston ordered Hardee to conduct a reconnaissance to determine if the Federals were still in force in front of his left. Selecting Bate's Division for the mission, Hardee formed it into three columns so as to assault several points. Brigadier-General

Frank C. Armstrong's Brigade of cavalry was formed on Bate's left, and was to advance first. If the horsemen determined that the Union soldiers were in fact gone from their previous location, they were to fire several guns as a signal for Bate to spring forward and destroy the Northerners while they were on the march.[54]

When the Confederate advance began, the Army of the Tennessee was still behind its works on the Union right. McPherson's troops opened fire on the Rebel cavalry, and the resulting exchange of gunfire led Bate to assume that the shots he was hearing were the signal to advance. He lunged forward in an assault on the heavily fortified Union lines, and a vicious fight erupted that saw one Confederate division assault the position of two Union corps. Despite the hopelessness of the situation, Bate's troops fought bravely, overrunning the Federal skirmish line and temporarily capturing three guns of the First Iowa Battery. For almost 30 minutes, the Rebels stood in the open, firing at McPherson's line. Finally falling back, they rallied and returned to continue the assaults along the line. Once the engagement had been broken off, the bodies of 52 Southerners were found within the Union lines. Bate reported a total loss of 450, while Armstrong's cavalrymen suffered a loss of 167 in killed and wounded. Although Bate lost heavily, his attack had the effect of holding McPherson in his position and delaying Sherman's plan to shift his forces toward the railroad.[55]

On the evening of May 29, Johnston renewed his attacks upon McPherson's line in an attempt to hold him in place about Dallas and prevent his shift to the east. Going on throughout the night, and severe in the extreme, the attacks were made by a heavily reinforced skirmish line. "Braver men never shouldered a musket than those Rebels that came up to drive us out of our works," wrote one Wisconsin soldier. Another Union soldier wrote in his journal, "O God, what a night. They may tell of hell and its awful fires, but the boys who went thru the fight at Dallas ... are pretty well prepared for any events this side of eternity."[56]

Despite the Confederate efforts, McPherson was gradually able to disengage from Johnston's embrace and begin his eastward shift. The tactics employed by McPherson were to send details to the rear to prepare another line of works, then while posting a strong skirmish line, he would quickly and silently move his troops to the new position. Heavy Southern assaults were made on May 30 and 31st, but Sherman slowly began to draw his line together and move toward the railroad with his left. By the first of June, McPherson was in position at New Hope Church while Union cavalry seized Allatoona Pass. McPherson's movement freed Thomas and Schofield to begin their eastward push, all the while skirmishing with Wheeler's cavalry. As Sherman extended toward the railroad, Johnston was left with no alternative but to follow with the bulk of his infantry. Though slowed by heavy rains and opposition from the Rebels, on June 3 advance elements of Sherman's forces reached the rail line at the deserted little town of Acworth. After reuniting all of his troops, Sherman ordered a rest of several days for his weary troops, who now referred to the fighting around New Hope Church as "the hell hole," prompting one Union soldier to record on May 28 that "We have struck a hornet nest at the business end."[57]

Brigadier-General Gibson's after-action report of his Louisiana brigade at New Hope Church is below:

> At New Hope Church, I was ordered while on the march (by Col. E. H. Cunningham, of Lieutenant-General Hood's staff) to send out two regiments on the Pumpkin [Vine] Creek road to hold the enemy in check, who was reported to be advancing. I was soon ordered out with the brigade to develop him. I increased my skirmishers very heavily and advanced about a mile, driving the enemy's skirmishers with ease. My skirmishers were ordered to charge, which they did, chasing the enemy to his barricades and developing a strong position occupied by two lines of battle. A prisoner captured reported that he belonged to Geary's division, Hooker's corps, and that three divisions of that corps close nearby. I was ordered to retire to the division and to place my command in reserve. We had hardly taken post when the enemy advanced in great force, driving in my skir-

mishers and assailing with vigor our main lines. The battle lasted two hours, hotly and stubbornly contested, and resulted in the complete repulse of the enemy at all points. I have not witnessed a more gallant fight. He continues skirmishing since, but shows no disposition to charge.

During those and some slighter operations from the 7th of May I have lost in killed, wounded, and missing, out of 889 enlisted men, 34 killed, 150 wounded, and 19 missing; out of 85 officers, 4 killed and 13 wounded. Throughout the campaign I have found both officers and men prompt, energetic, intelligent, and devoted to duty.[58]

Johnston issued orders on June 3 that the Army of Tennessee was to withdraw the following night to a line running from Lost Mountain on the west, to the railroad on the east. Apparently, both he and Sherman were happy to have a slight lull in the campaign after the ferocious fighting in the Dallas area. In addition to the usual dangers of combat, the soldiers of both armies were forced to endure the heat, rain, foulest of odors from the unburied dead, the screams of the wounded, and continuous sharpshooting. In any event, the Battle of New Hope Church, conducted in a jungle-like atmosphere, had mercifully ended.

On June 13, Private R. A. Allen of the Fourth Louisiana Battalion Infantry had the unpleasant experience of writing to the parents of his friend and comrade, Private C. W. Lewis, to advise them of the death of their son in the fighting at New Hope Church. Below is the sad correspondence that all families, Northern and Southern, hoped never to receive.

On the Line, New Hope Church
June 4, 1864

Dear Sir:

It becomes my painful duty to inform you of the death of your son, C. W. Lewis. He was killed by the enemy's sharshooters on the 27 of May, having been pierced in the right side [by] 2 minnie balls at the same time, one entering the right side of his neck and ranging towards the left shoulder, the other penetrated his right side. He survived only about one hour, but was sensible to the last moment of his life, nor did he speak but a few words, said nothing about his wounds and pain nor about his friends or affairs. He died very easily without pain. I assisted to bury that night. He is buried near New Hope Church in a grave with two others of the Battalion. Being a mess mate and a particular friend of mine I deeply deplore his loss and sympathize with you in your bereavement, but while we mourn his loss, but trust in his eternal gain. He was much respected by his brother soldiers as a good soldier and a true patriot. He died like a hero at his post of duty falling for a holy cause....

With much regret I am sir,
Your Obit Serv't
R. A. Allen
Co. B, 4th La. Batt.
Gibson's Brigade
Army of Tenn.[59]

Johnston and Sherman would engage in two more battles that did not involve the Fourth Louisiana Battalion in active engagement. Therefore, they will be discussed in a condensed format. The first, at Kolb's Farm, occurred on June 22. On the night of June 18, Johnston, fearing envelopment, moved the Army of Tennessee to a new position astride Kennesaw Mountain to protect his supply line to Atlanta via the Western and Atlantic Railroad. The new Confederate position was an entrenched arc-shaped line to the west of Marietta, Georgia. Having encountered the entrenched Rebels astride Kennesaw Mountain stretching southward, Sherman fixed them in front and extended his right wing to envelop their flank and menace the railroad. Johnston countered by moving Hood's Corps from the left flank to the right on June 22. Arriving in his new position at Mt. Zion Church, Hood decided, on his own, to attack, though Stewart's Division was held in reserve and saw no fighting. Warned of Hood's intentions, Schofield and Hooker entrenched. Union artillery and swampy terrain thwarted Hood's attack and forced him to withdraw with costly casualties. Although victorious, Sherman's attempts at envelopment had momentarily failed.[60]

The second engagement was the Battle of Kennesaw Mountain on June 27. Having defeated Hood's troops at Kolb's Farm on June 22, Sherman was sure that Johnston had stretched his line precariously thin, and therefore, decided on a frontal attack with diversions on the flanks. On the morning of June 27, Sherman sent his troops forward after an artillery bombardment. Initially, they made some headway, overrunning Confederate pickets south of Burnt Hickory Road. But attacking an enemy that was heavily entrenched was an exercise in futility. The fighting ended by noon, with the Union forces suffering the staggering casualties of almost 3,000 blue-clad soldiers, versus 700 for the Confederates.[61]

Prior to these battles, tragedy struck the Army of Tennessee on June 14 with the death of Lieutenant-General Leonidas Polk. Polk, Johnston, and Hardee were eyeing the Union positions from atop Pine Mountain at 11 A.M. when they were spotted by Sherman, who was unaware of the identities of the party gathered in plain view. "How saucy they are!" Sherman exclaimed to Howard, before ordering Howard to make them take cover. Howard passed on Sherman's order to Captain Peter Simonson of the Fifth Indiana Battery, who promptly fired two projectiles toward the group. The Confederate generals separated from one another, when a third three-inch solid shot struck Polk in the left side and passed through his chest, ripping away his lungs and heart.[62] Though Polk, the former Episcopal Bishop of Louisiana, was not an outstanding military figure, he was one of the most popular generals in the Confederate service. His passing was mourned throughout the Confederacy.

Though temporary command of Polk's troops went to Major-General William W. Loring, it was Major-General Alexander P. Stewart, newly promoted to lieutenant-general, who was placed in command of Polk's Corps, also known as the Army of Mississippi, on July 7. Taking over command of Stewart's Division was Henry DeLamar Clayton, whom President Davis had promoted to major-general along with Edward Cary Walthall, who now commanded Cantey's Division. In addition, Brigadier-General John Calvin Brown had been placed in command of Hindman's Division after Hindman took a sick leave supposedly due to an eye injury, but mostly from resentment at having been passed over for corps command.[63]

With the repulse at Kennesaw Mountain, Sherman decided that instead of another costly frontal assault, he would attempt to go around Johnston's position in another flanking maneuver. Johnston again retreated on the night of July 2 from his Kennesaw Mountain position, and soon abandoned several more defensive positions to prevent being outflanked by Sherman. Soon he found his back virtually against Atlanta, and began to receive ever more desperate dispatches from President Davis, who was alarmed and angry at the amount of Confederate real estate Johnston had relinquished to Sherman. On July 17, per instructions of Davis, Johnston received the following message from General Samuel Cooper, adjutant of the Confederate army:

> Lieut. Gen. J. B. Hood has been commissioned to the temporary rank of general ... I am directed by the Secretary of War to inform you that as you have failed to arrest the advance of the enemy to the vicinity of Atlanta, far in the interior of Georgia, and express no confidence that you can defeat or repel him, you are hereby relieved from the command of the Army and Department of Tennessee, which you will immediately turn over to General Hood.[64]

The following day, Hood assumed command of the Army of Tennessee, while Johnston departed for Atlanta, where upon reuniting with his wife, the two traveled to Macon, Georgia. Johnston and Hood would never set eyes on one another again. At the urging of Hardee, Major-General Benjamin Franklin Cheatham was placed in acting command of Hood's Corps.

On the day that Johnston was being relieved from command of the Army of Tennessee, Private Joseph T. Hill, a musician in the Fourth Louisiana Battalion, composed the following eloquent letter to his brother and sisters in Franklin Parish, Louisiana:

Chapter 6 — Blizzard of Bad Tidings

Picket Lines
Chattahoochee River July 17, 1864

Dear Brother and Sisters,

Nearly eighteen months have elapsed and many a thought has occurred to you that I have long since been laid beneath the cold sod of some sister State in our glorious Confederacy. Yet it is not so, by the kind hand of Providence, which is ever ready to impart and administer to the trouble of man, I have been spared and the scenes which I have witnessed are almost indescribable. I have tarried, and borne them up to this time, with a profound confidence, and that spirit which enables man. Though deprived of the many encouraging letters from those most dear to me and almost entirely shut out from the society of the world, I have in every instance displayed the part of the true and genuine "Southern Soldier." The ties which bind me west of the "Father of Waters" have never been forgotten, but honored and cherished as the most precious Jewel that Heaven could bestow. Well do I remember that eventful day when I took my departure from that lovely and beautiful home in the far West, surrounded by all the magnificence and splendor which nature and art could display, and I too remember the countenances which shone brightly around me, and the bright and hopeful eyes which bespoke intercessions to my heart. Ah! Shall I ever thus be permitted to return to that lovely hearthstone again when all was so sanguine and hopeful, and there remain forever unmolested beneath the shady bowers of "Holly and Dogwood" a veteran hero in the revolution for Southern liberty and independence. This is beyond the power of man to tell, yet I have never been more hopeful of reaching that sunny home than I am now, and if earnest appeals and Prayers to God will avail anything my return will be safe and at an early period. This war in a great degree has been a true precept to demoralization, But thank God I have never suffered myself to become so weak and unmindful as to lose those manly virtues which leads to inspiration, rather than degradation, yet it is a fact too true to doubt, that a large number of our Soldiers have become lost to a Sense of honor and that piety which immortalizes the Soul. Ah! If I were deprived of this precious Jewel without a hope of regeneration, I would indeed be one of the most miserable beings on earth. I would pray to be banished from the earth and my name forever blotted from the memory of those who have been so earnest in their prayers for my protection and welfare during this unholy conflict with the vandal hordes of the North. I would not consider myself worthy a name of being one of the defenders of our Sunny land. Hope is the banner to which I cling, and I trust beneath its folds to thwart the efforts of all who may attempt to destroy that happiness spoken of by the inspired writer, "Moses," as being a declaration from God Himself.

Brother and Sisters, I am altogether a different youth now than when I left home. My mind, my thoughts, and my ways are wafted to a loftier mansion, one built not by the hands of man. Ah! That you could only witness the grand spectacles of our camp. Imagine every night when duties will permit, the weary and exhausted war-worn veterans assembling around a cheerful fire singing praises and offering up prayers for the perseverance of our noble army and early restoration of peace, and you will have a true picture of the interest and feelings now existing among many of our brave defenders, and I am proud to say it is almost daily increasing. The untiring energies of our chaplains will bear a name upon histories brightest pages. In their ministerial duties, their equals cannot be found, while on the other hand they keep us almost constantly supplied with "Tracts" and other religious matter.

I will now proceed to give you a brief sketch of events transpired since October 1862, which I suppose was the last news that you have had from me and I was at that time, if you remember, at Mrs. Words striving to obtain the hand of one of the earths fairest daughters. At the time I wrote you I doubted my success, but before departing for my command, there at Savannah, Georgia, she consented to be "mine." Indeed I was filled to over-flowing, with joy, and expected at an early day to lead my Prey to the Hymnal altar. I left her flushed with Hope and expected to return the next winter and consummate the nuptial, having obtained the consent of the "old folks" to that effect. In a short time after I joined my command at Savannah, we were ordered to North Carolina to check the efforts of the enemy in that quarter. We arrived at Wilmington in December and camped near the city. For several days we were busy preparing and arranging our camp and I neglected writing Margia as I now confess I should have done. The weather was extremely cold and the rain pouring down in perfect torrents upon us almost constantly. I contracted a disease [neuralgia] and was confined to my tent for more than two weeks unable to perform any duty. Immediately after I recovered enough to sit up I wrote her a long letter giving my reasons, etc., for negligence. She responded at an early day in a very sympathetic manner, but still the sentiment was not of that pure sublime nature which characterizes the female sex. The letter did in no degree discourage me. I entertained strong hopes of an early adjustment of the difficulty, and that our love would again reign supremely. We remained in North Carolina but a short time, the enemy having retreated and was threatening Savannah again. We were ordered back and arrived at Savannah in February and all rejoiced at being once more in our old encampment around the Empire City. Our correspondence became more brief as communication was now direct, and I began once more to think that the matter had been adjusted and that I would soon cast my anchor in a "Heaven of Bliss." But Ah! the fate of man is doomed to disappointment. While resting in Peace and quietude and dreaming of nothing but future prospects and the glories within, the strong arm of misfortune is stretched forth to wrestle from him [man] the prize which he sought through the purest of motives. Such was my case. On the 7th of April, 1863 (that day will ever remain fresh in my memory) I had retired to my tent unconscious of the fatal intelligence that the next train would bring from her whom I loved, honored, and cherished, above all others. During the afternoon of that eventful day, while enjoying a calm and sweet repose, I was amused by some of my friends and the fatal messenger which sealed my fate handed to me. I broke the seal with trembling hands, yet not apprehensive of its contents. I read on, line after line, and Ah! horrible misfortune, what met my eyes but this language, "Owing to present existing circumstances you must consider our engagement broken." I threw the fatal letter aside and replied immediately, asking her reasons for discarding me, and she never to this moment has assigned one reason for treating me in such a brutal manner. She wrote to me regular afterwards and I answered her letters in a very cool and indifferent manner up to the time we were ordered to Mississippi. After the campaign was over in that department we moved out from Jackson to Morton on the Southern Railroad. When I succeeded in procuring a short leave of absence for the avowed purpose of visiting her, which I did, but all in vain, another had wooed and won her and she had the audacity to ask me to stay and witness her marriage. I very respectfully declined and returned to camp as fast as steam would carry me. Thus ended my career with the little fascinating "Margia." She is now married. Married a Capt. Lee belonging to the 3rd Regiment Texas Cavalry. I am now fine and anxiously awaiting the day when Providence will smile on me and bless me with a "Rib," taken from a man.

I will not attempt to give you a full and decisive history of my experience in war matters since I left Savannah as time and space will not permit. Our campaign through Mississippi was the most severe that I have ever witnessed. The scarcity of water and the intense heat of summer carried away a great many of our brave defenders. We fought two battles at Jackson in which I was an active participant and in which we were successful in beating and driving back an overwhelming force of the enemy. In the last engagement at that place we slaughtered them dreadfully, but were finally forced to abandon the place on account of not having a force sufficient to prevent the enemy from flanking us. We retired to Morton and the enemy retraced their steps to Vicksburg. On the 25th day of August, 1863 we received marching orders for Tennessee. We were all anxious to arrive at the new field of future operation and not once apprehending any danger of the great impending Battle in that quarter. After seven days of long and warm travel in old boxcars we reached Chattanooga, the goal of our desires. It was indeed a charming spectacle to many. I will not attempt to paint in words sublime the magnificence of mountain scenery which was everywhere to be seen by the passer-by. We remained in Tennessee but a short time before we were engaged in the Battle of Chickamauga. We lost at least one-half of our Battalion in this battle either killed, wounded, or captured. The enemy retiring before our victorious columns, we pushed them back into Chattanooga with immense loss estimated at twenty-thousand. Our army was marched up and boldly confronted them in their fortifications. Yet evinced no disposition to attack them, Grant was then ordered up from Vicksburg with his army and assumed command, Rosecrans being relieved on account of being defeated at Chickamauga. After thoroughly recruiting his army and adding many legions to its already superior strength, and knowing too that ours had been decreased by the withdrawal of Longstreets Corps, he came out, attacked and drove our little army from every position. This was called the Battle of Missionary Ridge. Our loss was much greater in this engagement than the enemy. We fell back about thirty miles to Dalton where we constructed very comfortable quarters and remained unmolested until 7th of May 1864, when they came out and defiantly confronted us again near Dalton. Our army occupied a very strong position at this place and the men were anxious for the conflict. The Yankees made several desperate assaults along our lines, but only to meet with defeat each time. Finding it impossible to carry our position by assault, they moved to our left, thus causing Gen. Johnston to abandon his position and fall back in order to protect his communications. We have been retreating and fighting for nearly three months and have lost many valuable officers and men, and have largely decreased the Yankee Army.

I am now in the very heart of Georgia, only seven miles from Atlanta. I think the decisive Battle will take place in a short time. Our army is in fine spirits and perfectly sanguine of success. We have been successful everywhere so far this year. I entertain strong hopes of seeing you all again ere twelve months. Be of good cheer, God is on our side and will defend the just and right. Eph. Morgan was slightly wounded on the 15th of June. He is in Sumter County, Ala. Write by return Mes. Anderson. He will return in September. Send your letter either to Delhi or Monroe, La. and he will get it and bring it to me. Give me all the news. Give my love to all and tell Miss Rittie and Miss Laura that I am still living.

Your Brother,
J. T. H.[65]

Hood launched two separate battles against the Federal army shortly after assuming command. Due to the fact that the Fourth Louisiana Battalion was not engaged in these battles, they will be discussed in a condensed format. For excellent detailed information on these engagements, one need only to refer to the Notes and Bibliography sections of this work. The first, known as the Battle of Peachtree Creek, was fought on July 20. Under Johnston, the Army of Tennessee had retired south of Peachtree Creek, an east to west–flowing stream located about three miles north of Atlanta. Sherman divided his army into three columns for the assault on Atlanta with the Army of the Cumberland, under Thomas, moving from the north. Hood attacked Thomas after his army crossed Peachtree Creek. The determined assault threatened to overrun the Union troops at various locations but ultimately was repulsed. Hood was forced to fall back from the attack. Union losses were tallied at 1,710, while Confederate casualties were a disproportionate 4,796.[66]

The second engagement, known as the Battle of Atlanta, occurred on July 22. Following his repulse on July 20, Hood determined to attack McPherson's Army of the Tennessee. He withdrew his main army at night from Atlanta's outer line of defensive works to the inner line, enticing Sherman to follow. In the meantime, Hood had sent Hardee's Corps on a fifteen-mile march to hit the unprotected Union left and rear to the east of the city. Wheeler's cavalry was to operate farther out on Sherman's supply line, and Cheatham's Corps was to attack the Union front. Hood, however, miscalculated the time necessary to make the march, and Hardee was unable to attack until afternoon. Although Hood had outmaneuvered Sherman for the time being, McPherson was concerned about his left flank and sent his reserve troops, those of Dodge's corps, to that location. Two Confederate divisions ran into this reserve force and were repulsed. The Rebel attack stalled on the Union rear but began to roll up the left flank. Around the same time, Corporal Robert Coleman of the Fifth Confederate Infantry shot and killed McPherson when he rode out to observe the fighting. Determined Confederate attacks continued, but the Union forces were able to repulse the attempts. At 4:00 P.M., Cheatham's Corps broke through the Union front at the home of Augustus Hurt, but Sherman had massed twenty artillery pieces on a knoll near his headquarters to shell these Confederates and halt their drive. Logan's corps then led a counterattack that restored the Union line. The Union troops held, though the butcher's bill for this fight was 3,641 in Northern casualties. Confederate losses were pegged at a staggering 8,499, a testament to the severity of the fighting.[67]

In the lull following the Battle of Atlanta, Sherman nominated Howard to assume command of the Army and Department of the Tennessee to replace McPherson. The next day, Sherman received a telegram from Halleck advising him that Lincoln had approved the promotion of Howard. This, of course, set off a backlash of discontent among the generals that felt entitled to the promotion. The first was Logan, who rightly felt that he was passed over because he was not a West Pointer. The second was Hooker, who was outraged at Howard's promotion over himself, and requested to be relieved from serving under Sherman. This request was promptly granted, and Hooker departed for home. Major-General David Sloane Stanley was promoted to replace Howard in command of the Fourth Corps, and Major-General Henry W. Slocum was summoned from the District of Vicksburg to replace Hooker.[68]

Hood was also making changes in his army following the latest battle. They began on the afternoon of July 24, when he replaced chief-of-staff Brigadier-General William W. Mackall with Brigadier-General Francis A. Shoup as a result of Mackall's refusal to shake hands with Braxton Bragg, who was at Hood's headquarters on an official visit. In addition, Walker's Division was disbanded due to his death and the brigades of Mercer, Gist, and Stevens were assigned respectively to Cleburne, Maney, and Bate. Major-General Patton Anderson was placed in command of Hindman's Division to replace Brown, and Colonel Robert Beckham was named as Shoup's successor as chief-of-artillery for the whole army. Hood also obtained Major-General Martin Luther Smith as chief engineer for the army, and persuaded Davis to order Lieutenant-General Stephen Dill Lee to Atlanta to assume command of Hood's old corps. Cheatham was returned to command of his division. All in all, it was a very busy month structure-wise for both armies.[69]

Late in the morning of July 27, Sherman directed Howard to pull the Army of the Tennessee out of their trenches. Their new assignment was to march until they reached a point beyond the Confederate left on the Lick Skillet Road, which would enable Howard to flank Hood's line and "get hold of Hood's railroad" somewhere north of East Point. By doing this, the Confederate commander would have to choose between Atlanta and East Point. Reasoning that Hood would realize that if he remained in Atlanta he would be trapped, he would therefore have to evacuate the city and fall back on East Point. Howard gained permission from Sherman to have his divisions carefully unfold to "take their place on Thomas's right, moving up in succession" so that each would protect the flank of the preceding division. This cautious maneuvering by Howard resulted in only a partial deployment by nightfall, though the movement was resumed the following day. Wood's division fell into position near a small frame Methodist chapel called Ezra Church by the congregation that gathered there for worship services.[70]

Upon learning of the Federal maneuver at 4:00 A.M., Hood assumed that Sherman was now making an attempt on his railroad from the west. Hood then ordered Hardee's Corps to shift to the left and occupy the fortifications between the Peachtree Road and Decatur Road. Stephen Lee was ordered to move the divisions of Clayton and Brown to the Lick Skillet Road and deploy them in the morning to confront Howard's advance. Stewart was to pull Loring's and Walthall's divisions from the works on the northwest side of Atlanta and march out on the same road until he was well beyond the Union right flank. After being reinforced by the divisions of French and Bate, he was to attack the Federal right flank and destroy it on the morning of July 29. If Hood's plan is successful, it would cripple Sherman so badly that he would no longer be a threat to the city.[71]

By late morning on July 28, Howard had all of Blair's corps in position along a ridge facing east. Harrow's and Morgan Smith's divisions, formed in line of battle, were advancing southward until reaching another ridge a half-mile north of the Lick Skillet Road that ran westward from the church. Their skirmishers, who had encountered stiff resistance from dismounted Rebel cavalry, moved toward the road, which ran in a northwest direction from Atlanta. Upon hearing several artillery shots that rattled the trees, Howard ordered Logan to have his troops fortify their positions, which they swiftly did by erecting barricades of logs, rails, and pews taken from Ezra Church. Though Sherman was skeptical that Hood was about to launch an

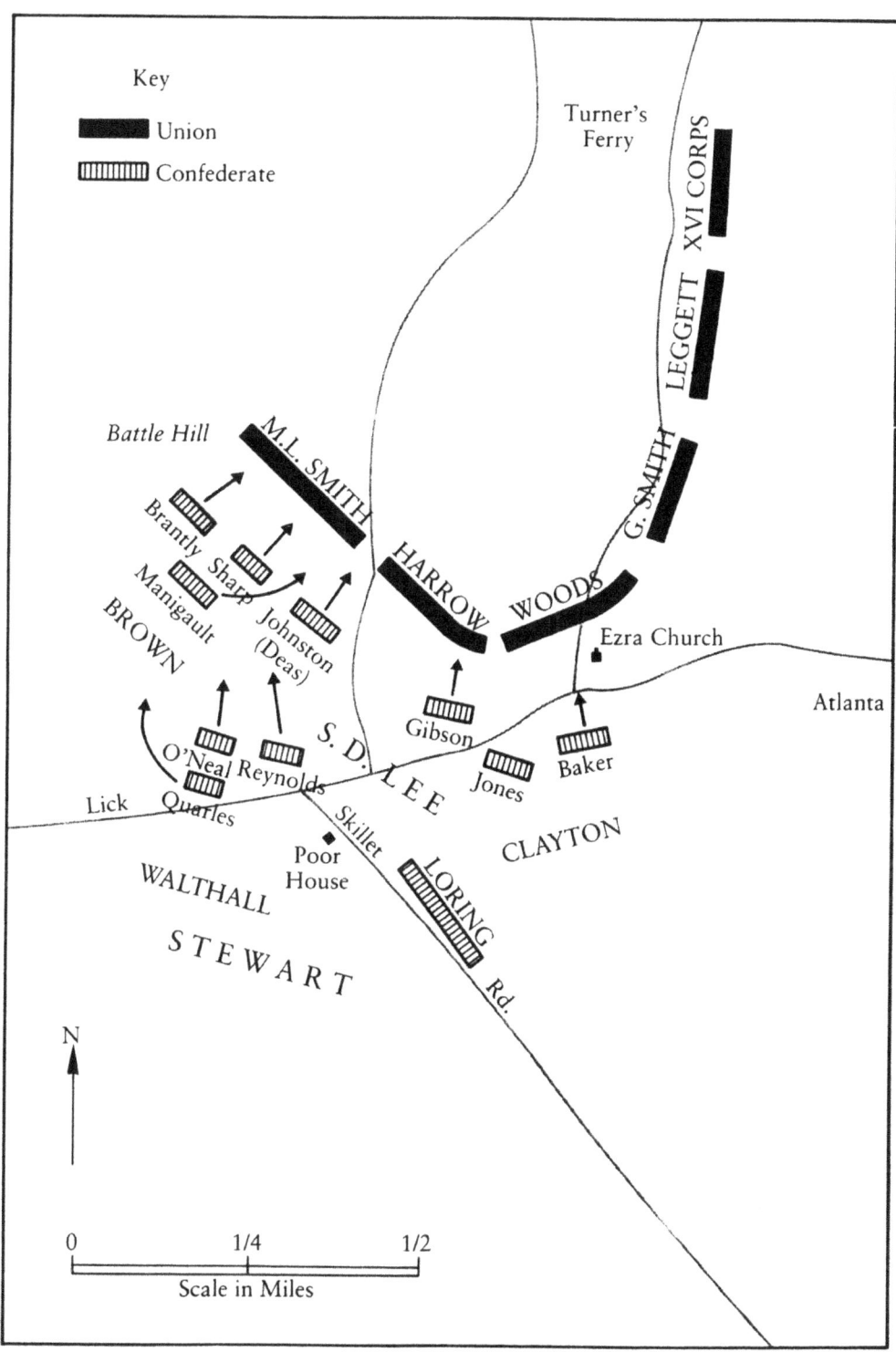

Map of Battle of Ezra Church (courtesy of Albert Castel, *Decision in the West: The Atlanta Campaign of 1864*, University Press of Kansas, 1992).

attack, he advised Howard to not worry about his right flank, as Davis's division would be approaching from the west at any time.

Off to the south, Lee was riding at the head of Brown's Division, followed by Clayton's Division, along the Lick Skillet Road. At 12:30 P.M., Morgan Smith's soldiers heard the fearful Rebel yell coming from the woods to the south. Knowing full well what that meant, the Federals knelt down behind their barricades and cocked their rifles. "Take steady aim and fire low at the word," the officers advised. Suddenly, the Union skirmish line came flying back in the face of three of Brown's brigades, who assaulted Smith's division. Twice they were repulsed, except on the extreme right where Brantly's Brigade seized a poorly defended hill before being driven back by a savage counterattack.[72]

Once he had seen Brown's assault waver, Lee instructed his inspector general, Lieutenant-Colonel E. H. Cunningham, to move Clayton's Division forward at once. Cunningham failed to notify Clayton or Gibson of the order, and instead ordered Gibson's Louisiana Brigade to attack. Although the Louisiana troops, as one put it the following day, "smell[ed] the biggest kind of rot," they advanced at the quick-step against Harrow's and Wood's troops around Ezra Church. Upon coming in sight of the Union works on top of a hill, they lie down and engage in a brutal fire fight for almost an hour. During this time, two-thirds of the left wing of Gibson's Brigade was "used up completely." After being requested by Gibson, Clayton sent in Baker's Brigade, which was "driven back in confusion" as soon as it came under fire. Correctly surmising that his troops were incapable of breaking the Federal line, Clayton called off the assault and withdrew Gibson's and Baker's embattled brigades. Despite these repulses, Lee ordered Manigault's Brigade to take the highest portion of the Union-held ridge. Leading his men forward, Manigault was forced to retreat on two separate attempts at capturing the ridge, before the attack was mercifully called off by Lee.[73]

Lee frantically tried to rally his command to no avail. Refusing to attempt the impossible again, many huddled in ravines or headed for the rear. Suddenly Stewart appeared with Loring's and Walthall's divisions, and was informed by Lee that Hood wanted him to attack the Federal right flank. Lee's reasons for advising Stewart of this are a mystery, as he had just received a message from Shoup directing him "to prevent the enemy from gaining the Lick Skillet Road, and not to attack unless the enemy exposes himself in attacking us." Stewart agreed to attempt the assault, deducing that he could not continue his march down the road if the Federals were in a position to seize it and cut him off from the rest of the army. Stewart then ordered Walthall's Division, which was in the van, to assault the Union right and hurl it back toward Ezra Church. Walthall formed his division between the road and the Poor House, with Cantey's Brigade on the left, Reynolds's Brigade on the right, and Quarles's Brigade behind Cantey's to act as a reserve and to protect his left flank. At 2:00 P.M., Walthall began his advance and, after a short distance, spotted the Federals "in strong position and large force on a hill." This was the hill that was briefly held by Brantly before he was forced back and, despite Walthall's impression, it was defended only by four regiments of Lightburn's brigade. Aware of the vulnerability and value of the hill that anchored his right, Howard summoned ten regiments from Blair and four from Dodge to reinforce Lightburn, as well as posting 26 artillery pieces to sweep the area to the west.[74]

Reynold's and O'Neal's forces attacked the position with vigor, charging repeatedly and maintaining a heavy fire at close range. Lightburn's men responded with the same amount of enthusiasm before being relieved by Dodge's troops. The support that Walthall was promised for his right failed to materialize, prompting Walthall to bring up Quarles's Brigade on his left after again being told by Lee he would immediately send a brigade to his right. Quarles's entrance into the fight unnerved Howard, who reinforced Smith with two of Dodge's regiments before calling on Sherman for help from the Army of the Cumberland. At first denying the request,

Sherman relented and sent one of Palmer's brigades to assist in the battle. By the time it arrived, it was no longer needed. Walthall, who still had not received the support on his right, was forced to retreat, though he did hold on long enough for Loring's Division to deploy behind him to counter a possible Union counterattack. Suddenly, Stewart was struck in the head by a deflected minié ball, causing him to topple from the saddle. A few minutes later, Loring was also hit, whereupon Walthall assumed command of both divisions. Soon, he received a message from Shoup that was addressed to Stewart, stating that Hood "desires you to hold the enemy, but not to do more fighting than necessary, unless you should get a decided advantage." For the Army of Tennessee, the Battle of Ezra Church was another defeat with appalling losses. The Confederate casualties were pegged at almost 3,000 men, with 480 being Gibson's Louisianans, including the commander of the Fourth Louisiana Battalion, Major Duncan Buie, being one of the wounded. Buie was replaced in his temporary command role with Captain Thomas Alexander Bisland of Company E. In sharp contrast, Union losses were 632 in killed, wounded, and missing.[75] A portion of Brigadier-General Randall Gibson's after-action report of the battle is below:

> I have the honor to report that after marching about two miles out of Atlanta upon the Lick Skillet road on the 28th of July I was ordered by Major-General Clayton, commanding division, to form my brigade in line of battle nearly parallel to the road. I was also informed that Holtzclaw's brigade and mine were to form the first line of battle and Baker's to constitute the reserve, and that it was designed to attack the enemy immediately. I proceeded to form my line in the woods, covered with a remarkably dense undergrowth, as rapidly as possible, and having it almost completed directed Major Austin, commanding skirmishers, to advance and to develop the enemy thoroughly. I then went to Holtzclaw's brigade, which was to move forward with mine (the formation of which Major-General Clayton was superintending) to get some special instructions and information with regard to certain points of importance. Having accomplished this I went at once in the direction of the brigade, when to my astonishment I found it had been moved forward without any order from me or notice to me, and as I have since learned by an order given by some staff officer upon the left of the brigade, and improperly repeated and obeyed by Colonel Leon von Zinken, commanding the left, who was not in my absence, the senior officer present with the brigade, and who should have awaited orders from some superior in command. I galloped through the woods to overtake the command, but heavy firing soon told me that it had struck the enemy in strong force. On reaching the brigade I found the enemy posted in strong works, and having discovered the extent of the line, sending out detachments to turn the left flank. Striking an overwhelming force in a position splendidly adapted for defense and difficult of assault, the brigade fought with much energy and obstinacy, but failed to dislodge the enemy. I at once communicated with Major-General Clayton, who ordered Baker's brigade up, and though the distance was only 400 or 500 yards, the undergrowth was so dense and difficult to march through that he did not reach me in time to carry the position by a combined charge. I moved my command into the ravine nearby and reformed, and under orders placed my line of battle upon the crest of the hill about 400 yards from the enemy's line. General Baker was posted upon my right.
>
> All the officers and men bore themselves with becoming gallantry. A report of casualties already forwarded shows my loss to have been severe.[76]

As the month of July drew to a close, the Confederate flag still flew defiantly over Atlanta. Sherman commenced a bombardment of the city that, if it could not force Atlanta's capitulation, would at least make life miserable for its inhabitants. On August 11, Sherman telegraphed Halleck that "I am too impatient for a siege," and began planning another of his grand flanking maneuvers to force Hood to either retreat or attack.[77] His plan called for first sending all surplus wagons, men, horses, and materials across the Chattahoochee River and loading the remaining wagons with one hundred rounds of ammunition per man, a fifteen-day supply of food, and enough forage to last for the same amount of time. By August 25, these preparations had been made and the Twentieth Corps fell back one-half mile toward the Chattahoochee, leaving behind only a picket line. They were followed by the Fourth Corps, which passed behind

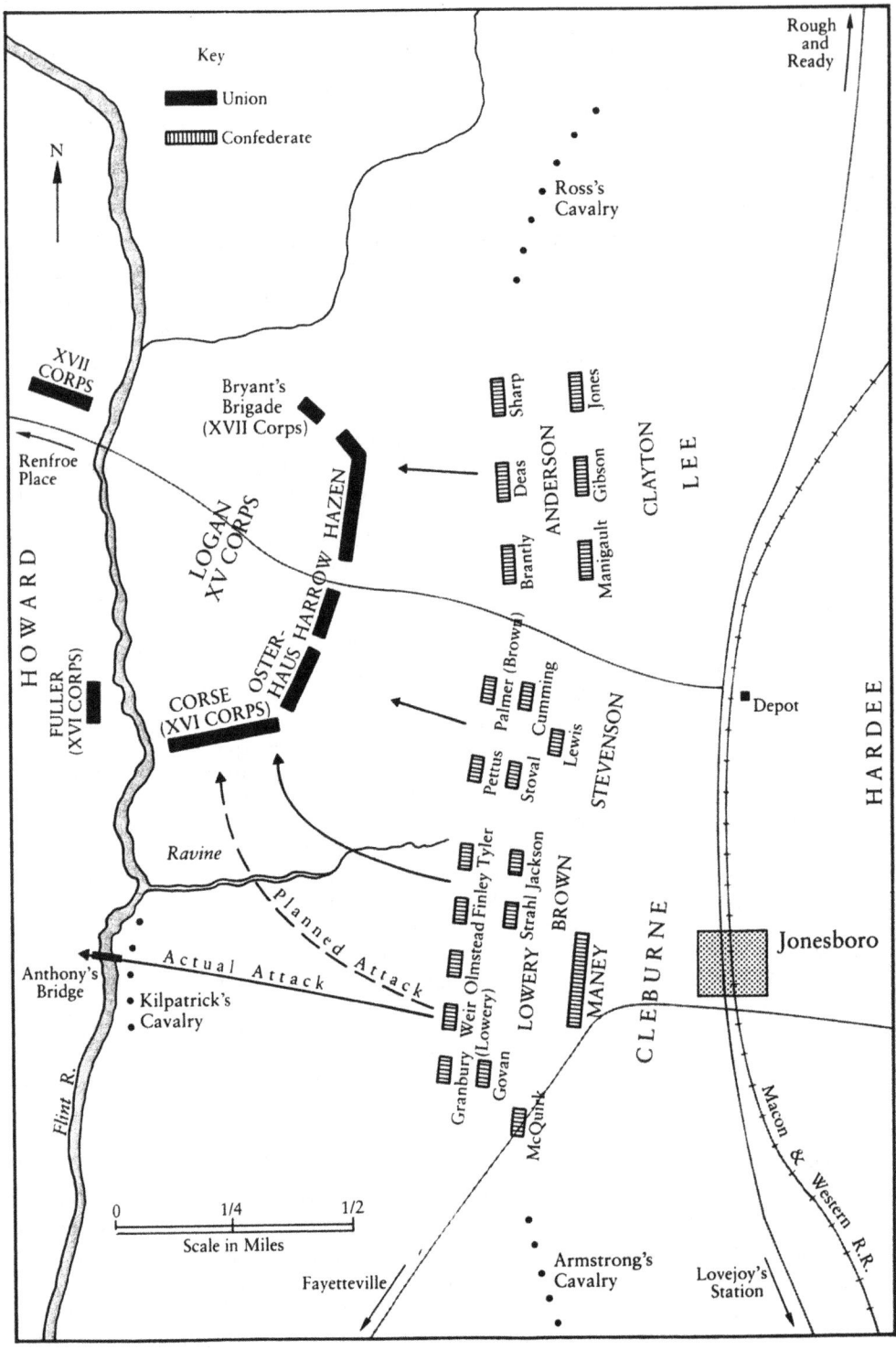

Map of Battle of Jonesboro — First Day (courtesy of Albert Castel, *Decision in the West: The Atlanta Campaign of 1864*, University Press of Kansas, 1992).

Chapter 6 — Blizzard of Bad Tidings

the Twentieth Corps and took up a position along the south bank of the Chattahoochee so as to cover the railroad bridge and adjoining crossings. On the morning of August 26, the Fourth Corps then moved to the Utoy Post Office area, deploying in a line of battle facing north so as to impede a Confederate attack on what now was the rear of the Federal army.[78]

The Confederates did not discover the pullback until daybreak on the 26th, when they sent forward skirmishers but did not pursue. Hood would have liked to believe that Sherman was retreating, but all he knew without doubt was that the Federals had moved the left wing of their army from the north and east of Atlanta. The right wing, as far as he knew, was still deployed west of the city. Hood was aware that this could possibly be another Union attempt to reach the Macon railroad by extending southward. To guard against this possibility, Hood ordered Maney to be ready to move his division at a moment's notice, and sent an identical order to Walthall. He also alerted Jackson's cavalry division to be vigilant on the left, and ordered the militia commanded by Smith to occupy the fortifications between the Peachtree Road and the railroad, held by Stevenson's Division, after dark. Stevenson's troops were to move to the rear.[79]

During the night, Sherman ordered the Army of the Tennessee and the Fourteenth Corps to abandon their trenches using the same tactics employed by the previous two corps. The following morning, Stewart's Corps occupied most of the lines abandoned by the Army of the Tennessee, and Lee's Corps took over the Fourteenth Corps trenches. Hood, concerned that an attack might be imminent upon his left, ordered Strahl's Brigade to the East Point area to reinforce Hardee, who had most of his corps in this location. He also instructed Jackson to have Armstrong's Brigade oppose any attempt at a Union crossing of Camp Creek in the direction of Rough and Ready, a small town on the Macon railroad three miles southeast of East Point. Hood was beginning to realize that Sherman was launching another large-scale flanking movement to the south, but could not figure out where, when, and how.[80]

While Atlantans rejoiced that the bombardment had finally been lifted, Sherman's army continued advancing southward. Though he was still trying to guess where Sherman would move and what he had in mind, Hood sent Reynold's Brigade to Jonesboro by train, and instructed Lewis's Brigade to follow as soon as the train returned. Brown, with the remainder of Bate's Division, was ordered to Rough and Ready to fortify the town and scout for raiders coming from the direction of the West Point railroad. Sherman, for some inexplicable reason, had his men wreck the West Point railroad on August 29, though it was already unusable. That evening, he issued orders for the following day: Howard was to march toward Jonesboro but halt four miles west of it at Renfroe Place; Thomas was to move the Fourth and Sixteenth corps via Shoal Creek Church to Couch's House, located three miles north of Renfroe Place on the Fayetteville Road; and Schofield, following Thomas, would proceed to Morrow's Mill and entrench facing East Point and Rough and Ready so as to be in position to protect the army's left flank. Then, on August 31, Howard would occupy Jonesboro and destroy the Macon railroad, cutting Atlanta's last logistical link to the remainder of the Confederacy and forcing Hood to either be starved out or give battle.[81]

Receiving reports on the evening of August 30 that the Federals were advancing on Jonesboro in force, Hood ordered Hardee to march his corps to Jonesboro that night, and ordered Lee to follow with his corps. Hood placed both corps under Hardee's command, and instructed the two Rebel generals to attack the Federals at Jonesboro as early as possible in the morning and drive them across the Flint River. Once accomplishing this objective, Lee's Corps would withdraw to Rough and Ready while Stewart's Corps and Smith's militia marched to East Point. Hood's plan was that the united forces would fall upon Sherman's left flank and, in conjunction with an advance by Hardee, sweep the Federals down the Flint River and the West Point railroad while the cavalry held the Twentieth Corps in place north of Atlanta. In the event the attack should fail, Hardee was to send Lee's Corps back under cover of darkness to Rough and

Ready, so it would be in position to protect a retreat to Lovejoy's Station, as Hood would have to evacuate Atlanta to save the army. At 11:30 P.M., Lee got his corps underway following behind Hardee's, which was being temporarily commanded by Cleburne. Due to difficulties in getting their troops to their assignments, Hardee and Lee were not in position for an attack until 2:00 P.M. on August 31. Lee's troops were justifiably exhausted, having slept little for 48 hours and having marched for over fifteen miles on rough roads with little food, resulting in hundreds falling out along the way.[82]

Hardee's front extended for one and a half miles, from just below Jonesboro to a small amount above it. His southern wing consisted of his own corps, with Cleburne in command, with Cleburne's Division under Lowrey on the left, Bate's Division under Brown on the right, and Cheatham's Division under Maney behind Lowrey. Lee's Corps composed the north wing, with Stevenson's Division on the left, Anderson's on the right, and Clayton's Division behind Anderson. Strahl's Brigade from Maney's command was used to bolster Brown's undersized division; Stovall's Georgians were posted in Stevenson's second line; and Manigault's Brigade was used to supplement Clayton, who was understrength with the detachment of Baker's Brigade to assist in defending Mobile, Alabama. A small battalion of engineers and dismounted cavalry under Colonel John McGuirk was deployed in Cleburne's left rear, Lewis's Brigade was assigned to Stevenson's Division to add to its weight, Reynolds's Brigade was in reserve, and Jackson's cavalry picketed the flanks and patrolled the railroad north and south of Jonesboro. Due to the horrendous straggling, Hardee had close to 20,000 soldiers in line of battle out of what should have been 26,000.

Hardee planned to attack en echelon from left to right, with Lowrey leading off, swinging Cleburne's Division northward so as to strike the Federal right flank. Brown would follow, with Maney advancing with him. Lee, when he heard the sounds of battle on the left, was to join in the assault with the objective of shattering the other Union flank with the combined power of Anderson's and Clayton's divisions while Stevenson engaged the enemy center. Hardee had instructed Lee and Cleburne of Hood's admonition "to go at the enemy with fixed bayonets," and they passed it on to the rank and file, though it was received with marked apathy.[83]

West of Jonesboro, the Union Fifteenth Corps had been in their entrenched position for 15 hours, Corse's division of the Sixteenth Corps had been on its right almost as long, and Bryant's brigade of the Seventeenth Corps had been on its left since 11:15 A.M. In most of the Federal sectors, their front was protected by abatis, palisades, or both, and batteries were planted everywhere so that they could deliver cross, as well as direct, fire. Also, a brigade of Kilpatrick's cavalry was deployed on the right behind a rail barricade along the east bank of the Flint River where, supported by a four gun battery on the opposite bank, it could guard a crossing known as Anthony's Bridge. Howard had almost 12,000 troops in line and 7,500 more in reserve, half of them on the right and the other half on the left. He could also call on the 1,000-man-strong First Missouri Engineers, who had just arrived to reinforce him from the Army of the Cumberland. In contrast to the Confederates, Howard's forces were well fed and rested, were strongly fortified, and exuded confidence.[84]

At 3:00 P.M., Hardee's artillery roared to life, and ten minutes later, Cleburne sent his skirmishers forward. Lee, mistakenly assuming the fire he heard was the beginning of Cleburne's assault, ordered his corps to charge the Union lines. The first line advanced quickly and in good order, until it was met with a sheet of .58-caliber slugs that stopped it cold. Some of the survivors took cover behind the captured barricades, while others either crouched behind the palisades fronting the main Federal works or fled in utter rout. The second line repeated the experience of the first and reacted identically. Officers desperately endeavored to rally their men for another charge, but they were met with refusals and contempt. Sensing that they had little to fear from the assault, Logan's blue-clads began firing slowly but with deadly accuracy. It was less a battle than sheer murder.[85]

Cleburne's attack got underway and degenerated into complete chaos. Granbury's Brigade began swinging to the north in an attempt to strike the right flank of the Federal salient, and came under fire from Kilpatrick's cavalry at Anthony's Bridge. Instead of ignoring the noisy but ineffectual fusilade, the Rebels detoured to the west to engage the Yankee cavalry. Kilpatrick's men crossed the easily waded river, and Granbury's Texans chased after them, followed by most of the remainder of Cleburne's Division, which was now heading away from the field of battle. On the right, Brown's assault from the south against the left of Corse's division lacked support on either flank and quickly folded beneath a murderous fire of grape and musketry. Huge numbers of Rebels, most from Finley's and Tyler's brigades, were cowering in a deep gully, while in the center, Maney's troops, which were to have joined in Brown's and Lowrey's attack, were facing the Union works all alone. Unsure as to the correct course of action, Maney ordered a halt and sent a messenger to Cleburne requesting instructions. While waiting for a response, he regrouped his troops in expectation of an order to attack. Lowrey, having recalled his errant troops, did the same, though after making a personal reconnaissance he had concluded that the Federal position was impregnable. But no new attack was ordered by Hardee, who, upon receiving information that Lee's Corps was demoralized and in danger of being driven from the field by a Union counterattack, ordered Cleburne to withdraw and sent Lowrey to reinforce Lee. The battle was over, and the Confederate effort to hurl Howard back across the Flint River had ended in disaster.

The casualty figures speak for themselves. Howard's losses came to a mere 172, while Hardee's totaled 2,200, of whom 1,400 belonged to Lee's Corps. Jackson's Brigade lost one-third of its strength and gained nothing for the effort, and Gibson's Louisianans, who lost fifty percent of their members at Ezra Church, suffered the same number of catastrophic losses as before. Among the Rebel wounded were Brigadier-General Alfred Cumming and Patton Anderson.[86]

A partial recording of General Gibson's after-action report for his Louisianans at the Battle of Jonesboro follows:

> After reaching Jonesborough on the morning of August 31, having made a night march, I was ordered to form line of battle west of the railway and prepare to attack the enemy. I supported Brigadier-General Deas' brigade, and in the charge followed his line at the distance of thirty or forty yards. His line struck the enemy's works and recoiled. My line moved forward with great enthusiasm and went beyond the fence into the thicket in which the enemy's rifle-pits were, when a few men, halting at the fence and lodging in the skirmish pits, began to fire, and soon the whole line fired, halted, and finally gave way. A few of the men got up to the works of the enemy and some inside them, where they found the enemy being re-enforced while their own commands were retiring, and they had consequently to abandon the posts they had won. I never saw a more gallant charge, or one that so fully promised success. The officers and men all behaved with great intrepidity in charging through an open field under a very heavy and well-directed fire. I can only account for the failure to take the position held by the enemy by the halting to destroy the fence and by the obstacles encountered in the dense growth of small trees causing a few to fire and breaking up the impetus with which they had been hurled upon the charge, and which should have carried them over the works. It is true the loss had been heavy in passing the open field, and the line had on this account grown thin, and there were no supports. I reformed a portion of the brigade near the enemy, but finally drew up in our works and prepared to go forward again. Brigadier-General Deas, commanding first line, ordered me to remain in the works until, by order of Major-General Clayton, I took position near the railway from which I had moved originally. I never saw a better spirit manifested than when called upon to reform for the purpose of making a second attack. Every officer and man was in his place and ready to advance.
>
> My loss was very heavy in this assault. In fifteen minutes I lost nearly half my command in killed and wounded.[87]

By nightfall of August 31, Hood, as well as Hardee, had abandoned plans for any further attack on the Army of the Tennessee. Unaware of the Confederate defeat at Jonesboro, Hood

Top: The inside of Atlanta. *Bottom:* Large Confederate Fort–Atlanta (both photographs courtesy of the Library of Congress).

Potter House — Atlanta (courtesy of the Library of Congress).

ordered Lee to march his corps back to Atlanta to reinforce Stewart in expectation of an attack on the city by Schofield and Thomas. Later that night, Hood received word that Union troops had cut the Macon railroad at Rough and Ready, and had crossed his last rail line in strength at several different points. Knowing that Atlanta was doomed, Hood ordered his staff to prepare for the Army of Tennessee's evacuation from Atlanta. Later, worse news followed bad with word that the Federals were now between Hardee and the rest of the Confederate Army. After receiving news of Hardee's defeat at Jonesboro, Hood finalized his plans for the abandonment of Atlanta. He, with the troops still in Atlanta, would move southeast on the McDonough Road, which ran parallel to, but several miles east of, the Macon and Western Railroad. Lee was instructed to position his corps to cover the retreating column against a thrust from the Federals along the railroad to the west. Hood's objective was Lovejoy's Station, located almost seven miles south of Jonesboro and some eleven miles west of McDonough. Once the Army of Tennessee could be reunited, it would be positioned to cover Macon and the prisoner-of-war camp at Andersonville. Meanwhile, the Rebels would destroy everything that they could not take with them from Atlanta.[88]

While the Southerners in Atlanta spent September 1 making preparations for the evacua-

Top: Confederate Fortifications — Atlanta. *Bottom:* Marietta Street — Atlanta (both photographs courtesy of the Library of Congress).

tion of the city, Hardee and his troops at Jonesboro braced themselves for Sherman's inevitable assault. Hardee expected Sherman to bring the full weight of his forces to bear upon his isolated corps, and deployed his troops accordingly, in a defensive position. Cleburne's Division was positioned on his right flank, with its right bent back across the railroad north of the town. Hardee's other divisions took position west of the railroad, facing Howard to the west. Only about 12,500 men held this two-mile line, and in some places the Confederates were six feet apart. Much of the line had few, if any, obstructions in their front to slow a Union assault. But Hardee was about to get a break from Sherman's foolish insistence on wasting time destroying the unusable railroad, and the morning of September 1 saw Union forces hard at work on this task.

View from Confederate Fort — Atlanta (courtesy of the Library of Congress).

Once the wrecking of the useless railroad was accomplished, Sherman planned to bring the Fourteenth Corps down the railroad from the north against Hardee's line, while the Fourth Corps moved on the left of the Fourteenth. While Howard and the Army of the Tennessee demonstrated against Hardee's left, the Northerners would envelop the right of the Confederate line with Thomas's two corps. Shortly after 4:00 P.M., the Federals launched their attack, only to suffer several repulses before overrunning the angle in Hardee's line and capturing most of the defenders there. Fate lifted the Confederate banner when Howard failed to make a serious advance, enabling the Rebels to pull together a defensive line and stem the assault at the angle. Before the Federals could regroup and the Fourth Corps could come up on the east, darkness brought a close to the fighting. Soon afterward, Hardee began to withdraw his forces out of their Jonesboro line, slipping away under cover of darkness without the Union troops realizing they had gone. Not until 6:00 A.M. on September 2 did Sherman learn that the Rebels had escaped from his front.[89]

During the night as Hardee retreated south from Jonesboro, Hood, with Stewart's Corps and the militia, filed out of Atlanta and marched southeast toward McDonough. Before departing, government warehouses were opened to anyone who could carry away their contents of bacon, blankets, clothing, and other items. What was not taken was put to the torch, along with five locomotives and eighty-one freight cars that were trapped in Atlanta when Sherman cut the rail lines to the south. Twenty-eight of the cars were filled with ammunition, and the resulting explosion leveled nearby buildings and reverberated across the countryside. Ironically, some of the soldiers who witnessed the destruction would see it recreated seventy-five years later on movie screens throughout the country in the film *Gone with the Wind*.[90]

Soon after daylight on September 2, Atlanta Mayor James M. Calhoun and other city officials rode north from the city carrying the white flag. At 11:00 A.M., the first Union troops entered Atlanta and raised the flags of the Sixtieth New York Infantry and the One Hundred

Railroad Station — Atlanta (courtesy of the Library of Congress).

Eleventh Pennsylvania Infantry over City Hall. General Slocum entered the city early in the afternoon and dispatched a message to Stanton in Washington. The first line read simply: "General Sherman has taken Atlanta."[91]

To the south, Sherman was attempting to organize a pursuit of Hardee's troops. He and the other Northerners at Jonesboro had heard the explosions emanating from the direction of Atlanta, but were unsure as to whether they indicated a battle between Hood and Slocum, an evacuation of the city, an accident, or something else entirely. Sherman reacted by sending Howard on the west side of the railroad and Thomas with the Fourth Corps directly south along the tracks, while ordering Schofield with the Twenty-Third Corps to move after Hardee on a route to the east. Sherman held the Fourteenth Corps at Jonesboro to bury the dead, take care of the wounded, and guard against a Confederate thrust from the north. Early that afternoon, the Federals encountered Hardee's new line almost a mile north of Lovejoy's Station, entrenched in a strong position along a ridge with both flanks resting on low, marshy ground. For several hours the Union army probed Hardee's line, but after a thorough reconnaissance revealed no weaknesses, Sherman abandoned all thought of attacking it. Later that evening, Stewart's Corps, followed by Lee's, wound their way into Lovejoy's Station. At last, Hood had reunited his army.[92]

Early on September 3, Sherman received official notice from Slocum that Atlanta had been abandoned and was now occupied by the Twentieth Corps. Sherman then made the decision to abandon any attempt to advance farther south for the time being. The next important point was Macon, located almost sixty-five miles away by rail. Thanks to his own orders, the railroad was wrecked south of Rough and Ready and would be unable to supply his army in an advance on the town even if they could find working cars and locomotives in Atlanta. Heavily influencing his decision to halt the campaign was the fact that his soldiers were exhausted after months of campaigning in the oppressive summer climate of the South and desperately needed rest. With these factors in mind, Sherman gave the order for his forces to pull back to, and occupy, Atlanta, while he contemplated his next move. After all, as he was to say in a dispatch to Halleck, "Atlanta is ours, and fairly won."[93]

ATLANTA, GA., CAMPAIGN ORDER OF BATTLE
May 3–September 8, 1864

Union Forces: Military Division of the Mississippi
Major-General William Tecumseh Sherman

Headquarters Guard
7th Company Ohio Sharpshooters: Lieutenant William McCrory
Chief of Artillery: Brigadier-General William Farquhar Barry

ARMY OF THE CUMBERLAND

Major-General George Henry Thomas

Army Headquarters
1st Ohio Cavalry — Co. I (Escort): Lieutenant Henry C. Reppert
Chief of Artillery: Brigadier-General John Milton Brannan

Fourth Corps
Major-General Oliver Otis Howard
Major-General David Sloane Stanley

First Division
Major-General David Sloane Stanley
Brigadier-General William Grose
Brigadier-General Nathan Kimball

First Brigade
Brigadier-General Charles Cruft
Colonel Isaac M. Kirby
21st Illinois Infantry: Major James E. Calloway
38th Illinois Infantry: Lt. Colonel William T. Chapman
31st Indiana Infantry: Colonel John T. Smith
81st Indiana Infantry: Lt. Colonel William C. Wheeler
1st Kentucky Infantry: Colonel David A. Enyart
2nd Kentucky Infantry: Lt. Colonel John R. Hurd
90th Ohio Infantry: Lt. Colonel Samuel N. Yeoman
101st Ohio Infantry: Colonel Isaac M. Kirby

Second Brigade
Brigadier-General Walter C. Whitaker
Colonel Jacob E. Taylor
59th Illinois Infantry: Colonel P. Sidney Post
96th Illinois Infantry: Colonel Thomas E. Champion
115th Illinois Infantry: Colonel Jesse H. Moore
35th Indiana Infantry: Lt. Colonel Augustus G. Tassin
84th Indiana Infantry: Lt. Colonel Andrew J. Neff
21st Kentucky Infantry: Colonel Samuel W. Price
23rd Kentucky Infantry: Lt. Colonel George W. Northup
40th Ohio Infantry: Colonel Jacob E. Taylor
45th Ohio Infantry: Captain John H. Humphrey
51st Ohio Infantry: Colonel Richard W. McClain
99th Ohio Infantry: Lt. Colonel John E. Cummins

Third Brigade
Brigadier-General William Grose
Colonel P. Sidney Post
Colonel John E. Bennett
75th Illinois Infantry: Colonel John E. Bennett
80th Illinois Infantry: Lt. Colonel William M. Kilgour
84th Illinois Infantry: Colonel Louis H. Waters
9th Indiana Infantry: Colonel Isaac C. B. Suman
30th Indiana Infantry: Lt. Colonel Orrin D. Hurd
36th Indiana Infantry: Lt. Colonel Oliver H. P. Carey
84th Indiana Infantry: Captain John C. Taylor
77th Pennsylvania Infantry: Colonel Thomas E. Rose

Artillery
Captain Peter Simonson
Captain Samuel M. McDowell
Captain Theodore S. Thomasson
Indiana Light Artillery—5th Battery: Captain Alfred Morrison
Pennsylvania Light Artillery—Battery B: Captain Samuel M. McDowell

Second Division
Brigadier-General John Newton

First Brigade
Brigadier-General Nathan Kimball
Colonel Francis T. Sherman
Colonel Emerson Opdycke
36th Illinois Infantry: Colonel Silas Miller
44th Illinois Infantry: Colonel Wallace W. Barrett
73rd Illinois Infantry: Major Thomas W. Motherspaw
74th Illinois Infantry: Colonel Jason Marsh
88th Illinois Infantry: Lt. Colonel George W. Smith
28th Kentucky Infantry: Lt. Colonel J. Rowan Boone
2nd Missouri Infantry: Colonel Bernard Laiboldt
15th Missouri Infantry: Colonel Joseph Conrad
24th Wisconsin Infantry: Lt. Colonel Theodore S. West

Second Brigade
Brigadier-General George Day Wagner
Colonel John W. Blake
100th Illinois Infantry: Colonel Frederick A. Bartleson
40th Indiana Infantry: Colonel John W. Blake
57th Indiana Infantry: Lt. Colonel George W. Lennard
28th Kentucky Infantry: Lt. Colonel J. Rowan Boone
26th Ohio Infantry: Lt. Colonel William H. Squires
97th Ohio Infantry: Colonel John Q. Gray

Third Brigade
Brigadier-General Charles Garrison Harker
Brigadier-General Luther Prentice Bradley
22nd Illinois Infantry: Lt. Colonel Francis Swanwick
27th Illinois Infantry: Lt. Colonel William A. Schmitt
42nd Illinois Infantry: Lt. Colonel Edgar D. Swain
51st Illinois Infantry: Colonel Luther P. Bradley
79th Illinois Infantry: Colonel Allen Buckner
3rd Kentucky Infantry: Colonel Henry C. Dunlap
64th Ohio Infantry: Lt. Colonel Robert C. Brown
65th Ohio Infantry: Lt. Colonel Horatio N. Whitbeck
125th Ohio Infantry: Lt. Colonel David H. Moore

Artillery
Captain Wilbur F. Goodspeed
Captain Charles C. Aleshire
1st Illinois Light Artillery—Battery M: Captain George W. Spencer
1st Ohio Light Artillery—Battery A: Lieutenant Charles W. Scovill

Third Division
Brigadier-General Thomas John Wood
Colonel P. Sidney Post

First Brigade
Brigadier-General August Willich
Colonel William H. Gibson
25th Illinois Infantry: Colonel Richard H. Nodine
35th Illinois Infantry: Lt. Colonel William P. Chandler

89th Illinois Infantry: Colonel Charles T. Hotchkiss
32nd Indiana Infantry: Colonel Frank Erdelmeyer
8th Kansas Infantry: Colonel John A. Martin
15th Ohio Infantry: Lt. Colonel Frank Askew
49th Ohio Infantry: Lt. Colonel Samuel F. Gray
15th Wisconsin Infantry: Lt. Colonel Ole C. Johnson

Second Brigade
Brigadier-General William Babcock Hazen
Colonel Oliver H. Payne
59th Illinois Infantry: Captain Samuel West
6th Indiana Infantry: Lt. Colonel Calvin D. Campbell
5th Kentucky Infantry: Colonel William W. Berry
6th Kentucky Infantry: Major Richard T. Whitaker
23rd Kentucky Infantry: Lt. Colonel James C. Foy
1st Ohio Infantry: Major Joab A. Stafford
6th Ohio Infantry: Colonel Nicholas L. Anderson
41st Ohio Infantry: Lt. Colonel Robert L. Kimberley
71st Ohio Infantry: Colonel Henry K. McConnell
93rd Ohio Infantry: Lt. Colonel Daniel Bowman
124th Ohio Infantry: Colonel Oliver H. Payne

Third Brigade
Brigadier-General Samuel Beatty
Colonel Frederick Knefler
79th Indiana Infantry: Colonel Frederick Knefler
86th Indiana Infantry: Colonel George F. Dick
9th Kentucky Infantry: Colonel George H. Cram
17th Kentucky Infantry: Colonel Alexander M. Stout
13th Ohio Infantry: Colonel Dwight Jarvis
19th Ohio Infantry: Colonel Charles F. Manderson
59th Ohio Infantry: Lt. Colonel Granville A. Farmbes

Artillery
Captain Cullen Bradley
Illinois Light Artillery — Bridges' Battery: Captain Lyman Bridges
Ohio Light Artillery — 6th Battery: Lieutenant Oliver H. P. Ayres

Artillery Brigade
Major Thomas W. Osborn
Captain Lyman Bridges
1st Illinois Light Artillery — Battery M: Captain George W. Spencer
Illinois Light Artillery — Bridges' Battery: Lieutenant Lyman A. White
Indiana Light Artillery — 5th Battery: Captain Alfred Morrison
1st Ohio Light Artillery — Battery A: Captain Wilbur F. Goodspeed
1st Ohio Light Artillery — Battery M: Captain Frederick Schultz
Ohio Light Artillery — 6th Battery: Captain Cullen Bradley
Pennsylvania Light Artillery-Battery B: Captain Jacob Ziegler

Fourteenth Corps
Major-General John McCauley Palmer
Brigadier-General Richard W. Johnson
Brigadier-General Jefferson Columbus Davis

First Division
Brigadier-General Richard W. Johnson
Brigadier-General John Haskell King
Brigadier-General William Passmore Carlin

First Division Provost Guard
16th United States Infantry — Co. D — 1st Battalion: Captain Charles F. Trowbridge

First Brigade
Brigadier-General William Passmore Carlin
Colonel Anson G. McCook
Colonel Marion C. Taylor
104th Illinois Infantry: Lt. Colonel Douglas Hapeman
42nd Indiana Infantry: Lt. Colonel William T. B. McIntire
88th Indiana Infantry: Lt. Colonel Cyrus E. Briant
15th Kentucky Infantry: Colonel Marion C. Taylor
2nd Ohio Infantry: Colonel Anson G. McCook
33rd Ohio Infantry: Lt. Colonel James H. M. Montgomery
94th Ohio Infantry: Lt. Colonel Rue P. Hutchins
10th Wisconsin Infantry: Captain Jacob W. Roby
21st Wisconsin Infantry: Lt. Colonel Harrison C. Hobart

Second Brigade
Brigadier-General John Haskell King
Colonel William L. Stoughton
Colonel Marshall F. Moore
11th Michigan Infantry: Colonel William L. Stoughton
69th Ohio Infantry: Colonel Marshall F. Moore
15th United States Infantry—1st and 3rd Battalions: Major Albert Tracy
15th United States Infantry—2nd Battalion: Major John R. Edie
16th United States Infantry—1st Battalion: Captain Alexander H. Stanton
16th United States Infantry—2nd Battalion: Captain Robert P. Barry
18th United States Infantry—1st and 3rd Battalions: Captain George W. Smith
18th United States Infantry—2nd Battalion: Captain William J. Fetterman
19th United States Infantry—1st and 2nd Battalions: Captain James Mooney

Third Brigade
Colonel Benjamin F. Scribner
Colonel Josiah Given
Colonel Marshall F. Moore
37th Indiana Infantry: Lt. Colonel William D. Ward
38th Indiana Infantry: Lt. Colonel Daniel F. Griffin
21st Ohio Infantry: Colonel James M. Neibling
74th Ohio Infantry: Colonel Josiah Given
78th Pennsylvania Infantry: Colonel William Sirwell
79th Pennsylvania Infantry: Colonel Henry A. Hambright
1st Wisconsin Infantry: Lt. Colonel George B. Bingham

Artillery
Captain Lucius H. Drury
1st Illinois Light Artillery—Battery C: Captain Mark H. Prescott
1st Ohio Light Artillery—Battery I: Captain Hubert Dilger

Second Division
Brigadier-General Jefferson Columbus Davis
Brigadier-General James Dada Morgan

First Brigade
Brigadier-General James Dada Morgan
Colonel Robert F. Smith
Colonel Charles M. Lum
10th Illinois Infantry: Colonel John Tillson
16th Illinois Infantry: Colonel Robert F. Smith
60th Illinois Infantry: Colonel William B. Anderson
10th Michigan Infantry: Colonel Charles M. Lum
14th Michigan Infantry: Colonel Henry R. Mizner
17th New York Infantry: Colonel William T. C. Grower

Second Brigade
Colonel John G. Mitchell
34th Illinois Infantry: Lt. Colonel Oscar Van Tassell
78th Illinois Infantry: Colonel Carter Van Vleck
98th Ohio Infantry: Lt. Colonel John S. Pearce
108th Ohio Infantry: Lt. Colonel Joseph Good
113th Ohio Infantry: Lt. Colonel Darius B. Warner
121st Ohio Infantry: Colonel Henry B. Banning

Third Brigade
Colonel Daniel McCook
Colonel Oscar F. Harmon
Colonel Caleb J. Dilworth
Lt. Colonel James W. Langley
85th Illinois Infantry: Colonel Caleb J. Dilworth
86th Illinois Infantry: Lt. Colonel Allen L. Fahnestock
110th Illinois Infantry: Lt. Colonel E. Hibbard Topping
125th Illinois Infantry: Colonel Oscar F. Harmon
22nd Indiana Infantry: Lt. Colonel William M. Wiles
52nd Ohio Infantry: Lt. Colonel Charles W. Clancy

Artillery
Captain Charles M. Barnett
2nd Illinois Light Artillery — Battery I: Lieutenant Alonzo W. Coe
Wisconsin Light Artillery — 5th Battery: Captain George Q. Gardner

Third Division
Brigadier-General Absalom Baird

First Brigade
Brigadier-General John Basil Turchin
Colonel Moses B. Walker
19th Illinois Infantry: Lt. Colonel Alexander W. Raffen
24th Illinois Infantry: Captain August Mauff
82nd Indiana Infantry: Colonel Morton C. Hunter
23rd Missouri Infantry: Colonel William P. Robinson
11th Ohio Infantry: Lt. Colonel Ogden Street
17th Ohio Infantry: Colonel Durbin Ward
31st Ohio Infantry: Colonel Moses B. Walker
89th Ohio Infantry: Colonel Caleb H. Carlton
92nd Ohio Infantry: Colonel Benjamin D. Fearing

Second Brigade
Colonel Ferdinand Van Derveer
Colonel Newell Gleason
75th Indiana Infantry: Lt. Colonel William O'Brien
87th Indiana Infantry: Colonel Newell Gleason
101st Indiana Infantry: Lt. Colonel Thomas Doan
2nd Minnesota Infantry: Colonel James George
9th Ohio Infantry: Colonel Gustave Kammerling
35th Ohio Infantry: Major Joseph L. Budd
105th Ohio Infantry: Lt. Colonel George T. Perkins

Third Brigade
Colonel George P. Este
10th Indiana Infantry: Lt. Colonel Marsh B. Taylor
74th Indiana Infantry: Lt. Colonel Myron Baker
10th Kentucky Infantry: Colonel William H. Hays
18th Kentucky Infantry: Lt. Colonel Hubbard K. Milward
14th Ohio Infantry: Major John W. Wilson
38th Ohio Infantry: Colonel William A. Choate

Artillery
Captain George Estep
Indiana Light Artillery — 7th Battery: Captain Otho H. Morgan
Indiana Light Artillery — 19th Battery: Lieutenant William P. Stackhouse

Artillery Brigade
Major Charles Houghtaling
1st Illinois Light Artillery — Battery C: Captain Mark H. Prescott
2nd Illinois Light Artillery — Battery I: Captain Charles M. Barnett
Indiana Light Artillery — 7th Battery: Captain Otho H. Morgan
Indiana Light Artillery — 19th Battery: Lieutenant William P. Stackhouse
Indiana Light Artillery — 20th Battery: Captain Milton A. Osborne
1st Ohio Light Artillery — Battery I: Captain Hubert Dilger
Wisconsin Light Artillery — 5th Battery: Captain George Q. Gardner

Twentieth Corps
Major-General Joseph Hooker
Major-General Henry Warner Slocum
Brigadier-General Alpheus Starkey Williams

Twentieth Corps Headquarters
15th Illinois Cavalry — Co. K (Escort): Captain William Duncan

First Division
Brigadier-General Alpheus Starkey Williams
Brigadier-General Joseph Farmer Knipe

First Brigade
Brigadier-General Joseph Farmer Knipe
Colonel Warren W. Packer
5th Connecticut Infantry: Colonel Warren W. Packer
3rd Maryland Infantry: Lieutenant David Gove
123rd New York Infantry: Colonel Archibald L. McDougall
141st New York Infantry: Colonel William K. Logie
46th Pennsylvania Infantry: Colonel James L. Selfridge

Second Brigade
Brigadier-General Thomas Howard Ruger
27th Indiana Infantry: Colonel Silas Colgrove
2nd Massachusetts Infantry: Colonel William Cogswell
13th New Jersey Infantry: Colonel Ezra A. Carman
107th New York Infantry: Colonel Nirom M. Crane
150th New York Infantry: Colonel John H. Ketcham
3rd Wisconsin Infantry: Colonel William Hawley

Third Brigade
Colonel James S. Robinson
Colonel Horace Boughton
82nd Illinois Infantry: Lt. Colonel Edward S. Salomon
101st Illinois Infantry: Lt. Colonel John B. Lesage
45th New York Infantry: Colonel Adolphus Dobke
143rd New York Infantry: Colonel Horace Boughton
61st Ohio Infantry: Colonel Stephen J. McGroarty
82nd Ohio Infantry: Lt. Colonel David Thomson
31st Wisconsin Infantry: Colonel Francis H. West

Artillery
Captain John D. Woodbury
1st New York Light Artillery — Battery I: Lieutenant Charles E. Winegar
1st New York Light Artillery — Battery M: Captain John D. Woodbury

Second Division
Brigadier-General John White Geary

First Brigade
Colonel Charles Candy
Colonel Ario Pardee, Jr.
5th Ohio Infantry: Colonel John H. Patrick
7th Ohio Infantry: Lt. Colonel Samuel McClelland
29th Ohio Infantry: Colonel William T. Fitch
66th Ohio Infantry: Lt. Colonel Eugene Powell
28th Pennsylvania Infantry: Lt. Colonel John Flynn
147th Pennsylvania Infantry: Colonel Ario Pardee, Jr.

Second Brigade
Colonel Adolphus Bushbeck
Colonel John T. Lockman
Colonel Patrick H. Jones
Colonel George W. Mindil
33rd New Jersey Infantry: Colonel George W. Mindil
119th New York Infantry: Colonel John T. Lockman
134th New York Infantry: Lt. Colonel Allan H. Jackson
154th New York Infantry: Colonel Patrick H. Jones
27th Pennsylvania Infantry: Lt. Colonel August Riedt
73rd Pennsylvania Infantry: Major Charles C. Cresson
109th Pennsylvania Infantry: Captain Frederick L. Gimber

Third Brigade
Colonel David Ireland
Colonel William Rickards, Jr.
Colonel George A. Cobham, Jr.
60th New York Infantry: Colonel Abel Goddard
78th New York Infantry: Colonel Herbert von Hammerstein
102nd New York Infantry: Colonel James C. Lane
137th New York Infantry: Lt. Colonel Koert S. Van Voorhis
149th New York Infantry: Colonel Henry A. Barnum
29th Pennsylvania Infantry: Colonel William Rickards
111th Pennsylvania Infantry: Colonel George A. Cobham, Jr.

Artillery
Captain William Wheeler
Captain Charles C. Aleshire
New York Light Artillery — 13th Battery: Captain William Wheeler
Pennsylvania Light Artillery — Battery E: Captain James D. McGill

Third Division
Major-General Daniel Butterfield
Brigadier-General William Thomas Ward

First Brigade
Brigadier-General William Thomas Ward
Colonel Benjamin Harrison
102nd Illinois Infantry: Colonel Franklin C. Smith
105th Illinois Infantry: Colonel Daniel Dustin
129th Illinois Infantry: Colonel Henry Case
70th Indiana Infantry: Colonel Benjamin Harrison
79th Ohio Infantry: Colonel Henry G. Kennett

Second Brigade
Colonel Samuel Ross
Colonel John Coburn

20th Connecticut Infantry: Colonel Samuel Ross
33rd Indiana Infantry: Major Levin T. Miller
85th Indiana Infantry: Colonel John P. Baird
19th Michigan Infantry: Colonel Henry C. Gilbert
22nd Wisconsin Infantry: Colonel William L. Utley

Third Brigade
Colonel James Wood, Jr.
33rd Massachusetts Infantry: Lt. Colonel Godfrey Rider, Jr.
136th New York Infantry: Lt. Colonel Lester B. Faulkner
55th Ohio Infantry: Colonel Charles B. Gambee
73rd Ohio Infantry: Major Samuel H. Hurst
26th Wisconsin Infantry: Lt. Colonel Frederick C. Winkler

Artillery
Captain Marco B. Gary
1st Michigan Light Artillery—Battery I: Captain Luther R. Smith
1st Ohio Light Artillery—Battery C: Lieutenant Jerome B. Stephens

Artillery Brigade
Major John A. Reynolds
1st Michigan Light Artillery—Battery I: Captain Luther R. Smith
1st New York Light Artillery—Battery I: Captain Charles E. Winegar
1st New York Light Artillery—Battery M: Captain John D. Woodbury
New York Light Artillery—13th Battery: Captain Henry Bundy
1st Ohio Light Artillery—Battery C: Captain Marco B. Gary
Pennsylvania Light Artillery—Battery E: Lieutenant Thomas S. Sloan
5th United States Artillery—Battery K: Captain Edmund C. Bainbridge

Unattached Units
Reserve Brigade
Colonel Joseph W. Burke
Colonel Heber LeFavour
100th Ohio Infantry: Colonel Joseph W. Burke
9th Michigan Infantry: Lt. Colonel William Wilkinson
22nd Michigan Infantry: Lt. Colonel Henry B. Dean

Pontoniers
Colonel George P. Buell
58th Indiana Infantry: Lt. Colonel Joseph Moore
Pontoon Battalion: Captain Patrick O'Connell

Siege Artillery
11th Indiana Artillery Battery: Captain Arnold Sutermeister

Ammunition Train Guard
1st Battalion Ohio Sharpshooters: Captain Gershom M. Barber

Cavalry Corps
Brigadier-General Washington Lafayette Elliott

Cavalry Corps Headquarters
4th Ohio Cavalry—Co. D: Captain Philip H. Warner

First Division
Brigadier-General Edward Moody McCook

First Brigade
Colonel Joseph B. Dorr
Colonel John T. Croxton
Lt. Colonel James P. Brownlow
8th Iowa Cavalry: Colonel Joseph B. Dorr

4th Kentucky Cavalry: Colonel John T. Croxton
2nd Michigan Cavalry: Lt. Colonel Benjamin Smith
1st Tennessee Cavalry: Colonel James P. Brownlow

Second Brigade
Colonel Oscar H. LaGrange
Lt. Colonel James W. Stewart
Lt. Colonel Horace P. Lamson
Lt. Colonel William H. Torrey
2nd Indiana Cavalry: Lt. Colonel James W. Stewart
4th Indiana Cavalry: Lt. Colonel Horace P. Lamson
1st Wisconsin Cavalry: Lt. Colonel William H. Torrey

Third Brigade
Colonel Louis D. Watkins
Colonel John K. Faulkner
4th Kentucky Cavalry: Colonel Wickliffe Cooper
6th Kentucky Cavalry: Major William H. Fidler
7th Kentucky Cavalry: Colonel John K. Faulkner

Artillery
18th Indiana Battery: Captain Moses M. Beck

Second Division
Brigadier-General Kenner Garrard

First Brigade
Colonel Robert H. G. Minty
4th Michigan Cavalry: Lt. Colonel Josiah B. Park
7th Pennsylvania Cavalry: Colonel William B. Sipes
4th United States Cavalry: Captain James B. McIntyre

Second Brigade
Colonel Eli Long
Colonel Beroth B. Eggleston
1st Ohio Cavalry: Colonel Beroth B. Eggleston
3rd Ohio Cavalry: Colonel Charles B. Seidel
4th Ohio Cavalry: Lt. Colonel Oliver P. Robie

Third Brigade (Mounted Infantry)
Colonel John T. Wilder
Colonel Abram O. Miller
98th Illinois Cavalry: Lt. Colonel Edward Kitchell
123rd Illinois Cavalry: Lt. Colonel Jonathan Biggs
17th Indiana Cavalry: Lt. Colonel Henry Jordan
72nd Indiana Cavalry: Colonel Abram O. Miller

Artillery
Chicago Board of Trade Battery: Lieutenant George I. Robinson

Third Division
Brigadier-General Judson Kilpatrick
Colonel Eli H. Murray
Colonel William W. Lowe

First Brigade
Lt. Colonel Robert Klein
Lt. Colonel Matthewson T. Patrick
Major J. Morris Young
3rd Indiana Cavalry — 4 Cos.: Major Alfred Gaddis
5th Iowa Cavalry: Major Harlon Baird

Second Brigade
Colonel Charles C. Smith

Lt. Colonel Fielder A. Jones
Major Thomas W. Sanderson
8th Indiana Cavalry: Lt. Colonel Fielder A. Jones
2nd Kentucky Cavalry: Major William H. Eifort
10th Ohio Cavalry: Major Thomas W. Sanderson

Third Brigade
Colonel Eli H. Murray
Colonel Smith D. Atkins
92nd Illinois Cavalry: Colonel Smith D. Atkins
3rd Kentucky Cavalry: Lt. Colonel Robert H. King
5th Kentucky Cavalry: Colonel Oliver L. Baldwin

Artillery
10th Wisconsin Artillery Battery: Captain Yates V. Beebe

ARMY OF THE TENNESSEE
Major-General James Birdseye McPherson
Major-General John Alexander Logan
Major-General Oliver Otis Howard

Army Headquarters
4th Co.—Ohio Cavalry (Escort): Captain John S. Foster
1st Ohio Cavalry—Co. B (Escort): Captain George F. Conn

Fifteenth Corps
Major-General John Alexander Logan
Brigadier-General Morgan Lewis Smith

First Division
Brigadier-General Peter Joseph Osterhaus
Brigadier-General Charles Robert Woods

First Brigade
Brigadier-General Charles Robert Woods
Colonel Milo Smith
26th Iowa Infantry: Colonel Milo Smith
30th Iowa Infantry: Lt. Colonel Aurelius Roberts
27th Missouri Infantry: Colonel Thomas Curly
76th Ohio Infantry: Colonel William B. Woods

Second Brigade
Colonel James A. Williamson
4th Iowa Infantry: Lt. Colonel Samuel D. Nichols
9th Iowa Infantry: Colonel David Carskaddon
25th Iowa Infantry: Colonel George A. Stone
31st Iowa Infantry: Colonel William Smyth

Third Brigade
Colonel Hugo Wangelin
3rd Missouri Infantry: Colonel Theodore Meumann
12th Missouri Infantry: Lt. Colonel Jacob Kaercher
17th Missouri Infantry: Major Francis Romer
29th Missouri Infantry: Colonel Joseph S. Gage
31st Missouri Infantry: Lt. Colonel Samuel P. Simpson
32nd Missouri Infantry: Major Abraham J. Seay

Artillery
Major Clemens Landgraeber
2nd Missouri Light Artillery—Battery F: Captain Louis Voelkner
Ohio Light Artillery—4th Battery: Captain George Froehlich

Second Division
Brigadier-General Morgan Lewis Smith
Brigadier-General Joseph Andrew Jackson Lightburn
Brigadier-General William Babcock Hazen

First Brigade
Brigadier-General Giles Alexander Smith
Colonel James S. Martin
Colonel Theodore Jones
55th Illinois Infantry: Lt. Colonel Theodore C. Chandler
111th Illinois Infantry: Colonel James S. Martin
116th Illinois Infantry: Lt. Colonel Anderson Froman
127th Illinois Infantry: Lt. Colonel Frank S. Curtiss
6th Missouri Infantry: Lt. Colonel Delos Van Deusen
8th Missouri Infantry: Lt. Colonel David C. Coleman
30th Ohio Infantry: Lt. Colonel George H. Hildt
57th Ohio Infantry: Colonel Americus V. Rice

Second Brigade
Brigadier-General Joseph Andrew Jackson Lightburn
Colonel Wells S. Jones
83rd Indiana Infantry: Colonel Benjamin J. Spooner
37th Ohio Infantry: Lt. Colonel Louis von Blessingh
47th Ohio Infantry: Colonel Augustus C. Parry
53rd Ohio Infantry: Colonel Wells S. Jones
54th Ohio Infantry: Lt. Colonel Robert Williams

Artillery
Captain Francis DeGress
1st Illinois Light Artillery — Battery A: Captain Peter P. Wood
1st Illinois Light Artillery — Battery B: Captain Israel P. Rumsey
1st Illinois Light Artillery — Battery H: Captain Francis DeGress

Third Division
Brigadier-General John Eugene Smith

Third Division Headquarters
4th Missouri Cavalry — Co. F (Escort): Lieutenant Alexander Mueller

First Brigade
Colonel Jesse I. Alexander
Colonel Joseph B. McCown
63rd Illinois Infantry: Colonel Joseph B. McCown
48th Indiana Infantry: Lt. Colonel Edward J. Wood
59th Indiana Infantry: Lt. Colonel Jefferson K. Scott
4th Minnesota Infantry: Lt. Colonel John E. Tourtellotte
18th Wisconsin Infantry: Lt. Colonel Charles H. Jackson

Second Brigade
Colonel Green B. Raum
13th Illinois Infantry (Detachment): Lieutenant Mark M. Evans
56th Illinois Infantry: Lt. Colonel John P. Hall
17th Iowa Infantry: Colonel Clark R. Wever
10th Missouri Infantry: Colonel Francis C. Deimling
24th Missouri Infantry — Co. E: Lieutenant Daniel Driscoll
80th Ohio Infantry: Lt. Colonel Pren Metham

Third Brigade
Brigadier-General Charles Leopold Matthies
Colonel Benjamin D. Dean

Colonel Jabez Banbury
93rd Illinois Infantry: Lt. Colonel Nicholas C. Buswell
5th Iowa Infantry: Colonel Jabez Banbury
10th Iowa Infantry: Lt. Colonel Paris P. Henderson
26th Missouri Infantry: Colonel Benjamin D. Dean

Artillery
Captain Henry Dillon
Wisconsin Light Artillery — 6th Battery: Lieutenant Samuel F. Clark
Wisconsin Light Artillery — 12th Battery: Captain William Zickerick

Cavalry
5th Ohio Cavalry: Colonel Thomas T. Heath

Fourth Division
Brigadier-General William Harrow

First Brigade
Colonel Reuben Williams
Colonel John M. Oliver
26th Illinois Infantry: Lt. Colonel Robert A. Gillmore
48th Illinois Infantry: Major Edward Adams
90th Illinois Infantry: Lt. Colonel Owen Stuart
12th Indiana Infantry: Colonel Reuben Williams
99th Indiana Infantry: Lt. Colonel John M. Berkey
100th Indiana Infantry: Lt. Colonel Albert Heath
15th Michigan Infantry: Lt. Colonel Frederick S. Hutchinson
70th Ohio Infantry: Captain Louis Love

Second Brigade
Brigadier-General Charles Carroll Walcutt
40th Illinois Infantry: Lt. Colonel Rigdon S. Barnhill
103rd Illinois Infantry: Colonel Willard A. Dickerman
97th Indiana Infantry: Colonel Robert F. Catterson
6th Iowa Infantry: Lt. Colonel Alexander J. Miller
46th Ohio Infantry: Lt. Colonel Isaac N. Alexander

Third Brigade
Colonel John M. Oliver
48th Illinois Infantry: Colonel Lucien Greathouse
99th Indiana Infantry: Colonel Alexander Fowler
15th Michigan Infantry: Lt. Colonel Austin E. Jaquith
53rd Ohio Infantry: Colonel Wells S. Jones
70th Ohio Infantry: Lt. Colonel Dewitt C. Loudon

Artillery
Major John T. Cheney
Captain Henry H. Griffiths
Captain Josiah H. Burton
1st Illinois Light Artillery — Battery F: Captain Josiah H. Burton
Iowa Light Artillery — 1st Battery: Captain Henry H. Griffiths

Sixteenth Corps (Left Wing)
Major-General Grenville Mellen Dodge
Brigadier-General Thomas Edward Greenfield Ransom

Sixteenth Corps Headquarters
1st Alabama Cavalry (Union): Colonel George E. Spencer
52nd Illinois Infantry — Co. A: Captain George E. Young

Second Division
Brigadier-General Thomas William Sweeney
Brigadier-General Elliott Warren Rice
Brigadier-General John Murray Corse

First Brigade
Brigadier-General Elliott Warren Rice
52nd Illinois Infantry: Lt. Colonel Edwin A. Bowen
66th Indiana Infantry: Lt. Colonel Roger Martin
2nd Iowa Infantry: Colonel James B. Weaver
7th Iowa Infantry: Lt. Colonel James C. Parrott

Second Brigade
Colonel Patrick E. Burke
Colonel August Mersy
Lt. Colonel Robert N. Adams
Lt. Colonel Jesse J. Phillips
9th Illinois Mounted Infantry: Lt. Colonel Jesse J. Phillips
12th Illinois Infantry: Lt. Colonel Henry Van Sellar
66th Illinois Infantry: Major Andrew K. Campbell
81st Ohio Infantry: Lt. Colonel Robert N. Adams

Third Brigade
Brigadier-General William Van Derveer
Colonel Moses M. Bane
Colonel Henry J. B. Cummings
Colonel Richard Rowett
7th Illinois Infantry: Colonel Richard Rowett
50th Illinois Infantry: Major William Hanna
57th Illinois Infantry: Lt. Colonel Frederick J. Hurlbut
39th Iowa Infantry: Colonel Henry J. B. Cummings

Artillery
Captain Frederick Welker
1st Michigan Light Artillery — Battery B: Captain Albert F. R. Arndt
1st Missouri Light Artillery — Battery H: Lieutenant Andrew T. Blodgett
1st Missouri Light Artillery — Battery I: Lieutenant John F. Brunner

Fourth Division
Brigadier-General James Clifford Veatch
Brigadier-General John Wallace Fuller
Brigadier-General Thomas Edward Greenfield Ransom

First Brigade
Brigadier-General John Wallace Fuller
Colonel John Norville
Lt. Colonel Henry T. McDowell
64th Illinois Infantry: Colonel John Morrill
18th Missouri Infantry: Lt. Colonel Charles S. Sheldon
27th Ohio Infantry: Lt. Colonel Mendal Churchill
39th Ohio Infantry: Colonel Edward F. Noyes

Second Brigade
Brigadier-General John Wilson Sprague
35th New Jersey Infantry: Colonel John J. Cladek
43rd Ohio Infantry: Colonel Wager Swayne
63rd Ohio Infantry: Lt. Colonel Charles E. Brown
25th Wisconsin Infantry: Colonel Milton Montgomery

Third Brigade
Colonel James H. Howe
Colonel William T. C. Grower
Colonel John Tillson
10th Illinois Infantry: Captain George C. Lusk

25th Indiana Infantry: Lt. Colonel John Rheinlander
17th New York Infantry: Major Joel O. Martin
32nd Wisconsin Infantry: Colonel Charles H. DeGroat

Artillery
Captain Jerome B. Burrows
Captain George Robinson
1st Michigan Light Artillery — Battery C: Captain George Robinson
Ohio Light Artillery — 14th Battery: Captain Jerome B. Burrows
2nd United States Artillery — Battery F: Lieutenant Albert M. Murray

Seventeenth Corps
Major-General Francis "Frank" Preston Blair, Jr.

Seventeenth Corps Headquarters
1st Ohio Cavalry — Co. M (Escort): Lieutenant Charles H. Schultz
9th Illinois Mounted Infantry — Co. G: Captain Isaac Clements
11th Illinois Cavalry — Co. G: Captain Stephen S. Tripp

Third Division
Brigadier-General Mortimer Dormer Leggett
Brigadier-General Charles Robert Woods

Third Division Headquarters
1st Ohio Cavalry — Co. D (Escort): Lieutenant James W. Kirkendall

First Brigade
Brigadier-General Manning Ferguson Force
Colonel George E. Bryant
20th Illinois Infantry: Lt. Colonel Daniel Bradley
30th Illinois Infantry: Colonel Warren Shedd
31st Illinois Infantry: Colonel Edwin S. McCook
45th Illinois Infantry: Lt. Colonel Robert P. Sealy
12th Wisconsin Infantry: Colonel George E. Bryant
16th Wisconsin Infantry: Colonel Cassius Fairchild

Second Brigade
Colonel Robert K. Scott
Lt. Colonel Greenberry F. Wiles
20th Ohio Infantry: Lt. Colonel John C. Fry
32nd Ohio Infantry: Colonel Benjamin F. Potts
68th Ohio Infantry: Lt. Colonel George E. Welles
78th Ohio Infantry: Greenberry F. Wiles

Third Brigade
Colonel Adam G. Malloy
17th Wisconsin Infantry: Lt. Colonel Thomas McMahon
Worden's Battalion Infantry: Major Asa Worden

Artillery
Captain William S. Williams
1st Illinois Light Artillery — Battery D: Captain Edgar H. Cooper
1st Michigan Light Artillery — Battery H: Captain Marcus D. Elliott
Ohio Light Artillery — 3rd Battery: Lieutenant John Sullivan

Fourth Division
Brigadier-General Walter Quintin Gresham
Brigadier-General Giles Alexander Smith
Colonel William Hall

Fourth Division Headquarters
11th Illinois Cavalry — Co. G (Escort): Captain Stephen S. Tripp

First Brigade
Colonel William L. Sanderson
Colonel Benjamin F. Potts
32nd Illinois Infantry: Colonel John Logan
53rd Illinois Infantry: Lt. Colonel John W. McClanahan
23rd Indiana Infantry: Lt. Colonel William P. Davis
53rd Indiana Infantry: Lt. Colonel William Jones
3rd Iowa Infantry—(3 Cos.): Captain Daniel McLennan
32nd Ohio Infantry: Captain William M. Morris
12th Wisconsin Infantry: Colonel George E. Bryant

Second Brigade
Colonel George C. Rogers
Colonel Isaac C. Pugh
Colonel John Logan
14th Illinois Infantry: Captain Carlos C. Cox
15th Illinois Infantry: Major Rufus C. McEathron
32nd Illinois Infantry: Lt. Colonel George H. English
41st Illinois Infantry: Major Robert H. McFadden

Third Brigade
Brigadier-General William Worth Belknap
Colonel William Hall
Colonel John Shane
11th Iowa Infantry: Lt. Colonel John C. Abercrombie
13th Iowa Infantry: Colonel John Shane
15th Iowa Infantry: Colonel William Worth Belknap
16th Iowa Infantry: Lt. Colonel Addison H. Sanders

Artillery
Captain Edward Spear, Jr.
Captain William Z. Clayton
2nd Illinois Light Artillery—Battery F: Lieutenant Walter H. Powell
Minnesota Light Artillery—1st Battery: Captain William Z. Clayton
1st Missouri Light Artillery—Battery C: Captain John L. Matthaei
Ohio Light Artillery—10th Battery: Captain Francis Seaman
Ohio Light Artillery—15th Battery: Lieutenant James Burdick

Army of the Ohio

Major-General John McAllister Schofield
Brigadier-General Jacob Dolson Cox

Army Headquarters
7th Ohio Cavalry—Co. G (Escort): Captain John A. Ashbury

Army Engineer Battalion
Captain Charles E. McAlester
Captain Oliver S. McClure

First Division
Brigadier-General Alvin Peterson Hovey

First Brigade
Colonel Richard F. Barter
120th Indiana Infantry: Lt. Colonel Allen W. Prather
124th Indiana Infantry: Colonel James Burgess
128th Indiana Infantry: Colonel Richard P. DeHart

Second Brigade
Colonel John C. McQuiston
Colonel Peter T. Swaine
123rd Indiana Infantry: Colonel John C. McQuiston

129th Indiana Infantry: Colonel Charles A. Zollinger
130th Indiana Infantry: Colonel Charles S. Parrish
99th Ohio Infantry: Lt. Colonel John E. Cummins

Artillery
Indiana Light Artillery — 23rd Battery: Lieutenant Luther S. Houghton
Indiana Light Artillery — 24th Battery: Captain Alexander Hardy

Second Division
Brigadier-General Henry Moses Judah
Brigadier-General Milo Smith Hascall

First Brigade
Brigadier-General Nathaniel Collins McLean
Brigadier-General Joseph Alexander Cooper
80th Indiana Infantry: Lt. Colonel Alfred D. Owen
91st Indiana Infantry: Colonel John Mehringer
13th Kentucky Infantry: Colonel William E. Hobson
25th Michigan Infantry: Lt. Colonel Benjamin F. Orcutt
45th Ohio Infantry: Colonel Benjamin P. Runkle
3rd Tennessee Infantry: Colonel William Cross
6th Tennessee Infantry: Colonel Joseph A. Cooper

Second Brigade
Brigadier-General Milo Smith Hascall
Colonel John R. Bond
Colonel William E. Hobson
107th Illinois Infantry: Lt. Colonel Francis H. Lowry
80th Indiana Infantry: Lt. Colonel Alfred D. Owen
13th Kentucky Infantry: Colonel William E. Hobson
23rd Michigan Infantry: Lt. Colonel Oliver L. Spaulding
45th Ohio Infantry: Colonel Benjamin P. Runkle
111th Ohio Infantry: Colonel John R. Bond
118th Ohio Infantry: Lt. Colonel Thomas L. Young

Third Brigade
Colonel Silas A. Strickland
14th Kentucky Infantry: Colonel George W. Gallup
20th Kentucky Infantry: Lt. Colonel Thomas B. Waller
27th Kentucky Infantry: Lt. Colonel John H. Ward
50th Ohio Infantry: Lt. Colonel George R. Elstner

Artillery
Captain Joseph C. Shields
Indiana Light Artillery — 22nd Battery: Captain Benjamin F. Denning
1st Michigan Light Artillery — Battery F: Captain Byron D. Paddock
Ohio Light Artillery — 19th Battery: Captain Joseph C. Shields

Third Division
Brigadier-General Jacob Dolson Cox
Colonel James William Reilly

First Brigade
Colonel James William Reilly
Colonel James W. Gault
112th Illinois Infantry: Colonel Thomas J. Henderson
16th Kentucky Infantry: Colonel James W. Gault
100th Ohio Infantry: Colonel Patrick S. Slevin
104th Ohio Infantry: Colonel Oscar W. Sterl
8th Tennessee Infantry: Colonel Felix A. Reeve

Second Brigade
Brigadier-General Mahlon Dickerson Manson
Brigadier-General Milo Smith Hascall
Colonel John S. Hurt
Colonel John S. Casement
Colonel Daniel Cameron
65th Illinois Infantry: Lt. Colonel William S. Stewart
63rd Indiana Infantry: Colonel Israel N. Stiles
65th Indiana Infantry: Lt. Colonel Thomas Johnson
24th Kentucky Infantry: Colonel John S. Hurt
103rd Ohio Infantry: Colonel John S. Casement

Third Brigade
Brigadier-General Nathaniel Collins McLean
Colonel Robert K. Byrd
Colonel Israel N. Stiles
11th Kentucky Infantry: Colonel S. Palace Love
12th Kentucky Infantry: Lt. Colonel Laurence H. Rousseau
1st Tennessee Infantry: Colonel Robert K. Byrd
5th Tennessee Infantry: Colonel James T. Shelley

Dismounted Cavalry Brigade
Colonel Eugene W. Crittenden
16th Illinois Cavalry: Captain Hiram S. Hanchett
12th Kentucky Cavalry: Lt. Colonel James T. Bramlette

Artillery
Major Henry W. Wells
Indiana Light Artillery—15th Battery: Captain Alonzo D. Harvey
1st Ohio Light Artillery—Battery D: Captain Giles J. Cockerill

Cavalry
Major-General George Stoneman
Colonel Horace Capron

Cavalry Headquarters
7th Ohio Cavalry—Co. D (Escort): Lieutenant Samuel Murphy

First Brigade
Colonel Israel Garrard
9th Michigan Cavalry: Colonel George S. Acker
7th Ohio Cavalry: Lt. Colonel George G. Miner

Second Brigade
Colonel James Biddle
Colonel Thomas H. Butler
16th Illinois Cavalry: Captain Hiram S. Hanchett
5th Indiana Cavalry: Colonel Thomas H. Butler
6th Indiana Cavalry: Lt. Colonel Courtland C. Mason
12th Kentucky Cavalry: Colonel Eugene W. Crittenden

Third Brigade
Colonel Horace Capron
14th Illinois Cavalry: Lt. Colonel David P. Jenkins
8th Michigan Cavalry: Lt. Colonel Elisha Mix
McLaughlin's Ohio Squadron: Major Richard Rice

Independent Brigade
Colonel Alexander W. Holeman
Lt. Colonel Silas Adams
1st Kentucky Cavalry: Lt. Colonel Silas Adams
11th Kentucky Cavalry: Lt. Colonel Archibald J. Alexander

Artillery
24th Indiana Artillery Battery: Captain Alexander Hardy

CONFEDERATE FORCES: ARMY OF TENNESSEE

April 30, 1864
General Joseph Eggleston Johnston

Army Headquarters
Guy Dreux's Louisiana Cavalry Company (Escort): Lieutenant O. Debreys
Holloway's Alabama Cavalry Company (Escort): Captain Edwin M. Holloway

Hardee's Corps
Lieutenant-General William Joseph Hardee

Corps Headquarters
Raum's Mississippi Cavalry Company (Escort): Captain W. C. Raum

Cheatham's Division
Major-General Benjamin Franklin Cheatham

Division Headquarters
2nd Georgia Cavalry — Co. G (Escort): Captain Thomas M. Merritt

Maney's Brigade
Colonel George C. Porter
1st and 27th Tennessee Infantry (Consolidated): Colonel Hume R. Field
4th Tennessee Infantry: Lt. Colonel Oliver A. Bradshaw
6th and 9th Tennessee Infantry (Consolidated): Lt. Colonel John W. Buford
41st Tennessee Infantry: Lt. Colonel James D. Tillman
50th Tennessee Infantry: Colonel Stephen H. Colms
24th Tennessee Battalion Infantry: Lt. Colonel Oliver A. Bradshaw

Strahl's Brigade
Brigadier-General Otho French Strahl
4th and 5th Tennessee Infantry (Consolidated): Colonel Jonathan J. Lamb
19th Tennessee Infantry: Colonel Francis M. Walker
24th Tennessee Infantry: Lt. Colonel Samuel E. Shannon
31st and 33rd Tennessee Infantry (Consolidated): Lt. Colonel Fountain E. P. Stafford

Wright's Brigade
Colonel John C. Carter
8th Tennessee Infantry: Colonel John H. Anderson
16th Tennessee Infantry: Captain Benjamin Randals
28th Tennessee Infantry: Colonel Sidney S. Stanton
38th Tennessee Infantry: Lt. Colonel Andrew D. Gwynne
51st and 52nd Tennessee Infantry: Lt. Colonel John G. Hall

Vaughan's Brigade
Brigadier-General Alfred Jefferson Vaughan, Jr.
11th Tennessee Infantry: Colonel George W. Gordon
12th and 47th Tennessee Infantry (Consolidated): Colonel William M. Watkins
29th Tennessee Infantry: Colonel Horace Rice
13th and 154th Tennessee Infantry (Consolidated): Colonel Michael Magevney, Jr.

Cleburne's Division
Major-General Patrick Ronayne Cleburne

Division Headquarters
Sanders' Company Tennessee Cavalry (Escort): Captain Calvin F. Sanders

Polk's Brigade
Brigadier-General Lucius Eugene Polk
1st and 15th Arkansas Infantry (Consolidated): Lt. Colonel William H. Martin
5th Confederate Infantry: Captain W. A. Brown

Chapter 6—Blizzard of Bad Tidings

2nd Tennessee Infantry: Colonel William D. Robison
35th Tennessee Infantry: Colonel Benjamin J. Hill
48th Tennessee Infantry (Nixon's): Captain Henry G. Evans

Govan's Brigade
Brigadier-General Daniel Chevilette Govan
2nd and 24th Arkansas Infantry (Consolidated): Colonel E. Warfield
5th and 13th Arkansas (Consolidated): Colonel John E. Murray
6th and 7th Arkansas Infantry (Consolidated): Colonel Samuel G. Smith
8th and 19th Arkansas Infantry (Consolidated): Colonel George F. Baucum
3rd Confederate Infantry: Captain M. H. Dixon

Lowrey's Brigade
Brigadier-General Mark Perrin Lowrey
16th Alabama Infantry: Lt. Colonel Frederick A. Ashford
33rd Alabama Infantry: Colonel Samuel Adams
45th Alabama Infantry: Colonel Harris D. Lampley
32nd Mississippi Infantry: Colonel William H. H. Tison
45th Mississippi Infantry: Colonel Aaron B. Hardcastle

Granbury's Brigade
Brigadier-General Hiram Bronson Granbury
6th Texas Infantry and 15th Texas Cavalry (Dismounted): Captain Rhoads Fisher
7th Texas Infantry: Captain J. H. Collett
10th Texas Infantry: Colonel Roger Q. Mills
17th and 18th Texas Cavalry (Dismounted): Captain George D. Manion
24th and 25th Texas Cavalry (Dismounted): Colonel Franklin C. Wilkes

Walker's Division
Major-General William Henry Talbot Walker

Division Headquarters
53rd Alabama Partisan Rangers—Co. G (Escort): Captain P. B. Mastin, Jr.

Jackson's Brigade
Brigadier-General John King Jackson
1st Georgia Confederate Infantry: Colonel George A. Smith
5th Georgia Infantry: Colonel Charles P. Daniel
47th Georgia Infantry: Colonel A. C. Edwards
65th Georgia Infantry: Captain William G. Foster
5th Mississippi Infantry: Colonel John Weir
8th Mississippi Infantry: Colonel John C. Wilkinson
2nd Georgia Battalion Sharpshooters: Major Richard H. Whitely

Gist's Brigade
Brigadier-General States Rights Gist
8th Georgia Battalion Infantry: Lt. Colonel Zachariah L. Watters
46th Georgia Infantry: Major Samuel J. C. Dunlop
16th South Carolina Infantry: Colonel James McCullough
24th South Carolina Infantry: Colonel Ellison Capers

Stevens's Brigade
Brigadier-General Clement Hoffman Stevens
25th Georgia Infantry: Colonel William J. Winn
29th Georgia Infantry: Lt. Colonel William D. Mitchell
30th Georgia Infantry: Major Henry Hendrick
66th Georgia Infantry: Colonel J. Cooper Nisbet
1st Georgia Battalion Sharpshooters: Major Arthur Schaaff
26th Georgia Battalion Sharpshooters: Major John W. Nisbet

Bate's Division
Major-General William Brimage Bate

Division Headquarters
Foules's Company Mississippi Cavalry: Captain Thomas M. Lenoir

Lewis's Brigade
2nd Kentucky Infantry: Colonel James W. Moss
4th Kentucky Infantry: Lt. Colonel Thomas W. Thompson
5th Kentucky Infantry: Lt. Colonel Hiram Hawkins
6th Kentucky Infantry: Major George W. Maxson
9th Kentucky Infantry: Colonel John W. Caldwell

Tyler's Brigade
37th Georgia Infantry: Lt. Colonel Joseph T. Smith
10th Tennessee Infantry: Major John O'Neill
15th and 37th Tennessee Infantry (Consolidated): Major John M. Wall
20th Tennessee Infantry: Lt. Colonel James J. Turner
4th Georgia Battalion Sharpshooters: Captain W. M. Carter

Finley's Brigade
1st Florida Cavalry (Dismounted) and 3rd Florida Infantry: Major Glover A. Ball
1st and 4th Florida Infantry (Consolidated): Lt. Colonel Edward Badger
6th Florida Infantry: Colonel Angus D. McLean
7th Florida Infantry: Lt. Colonel Tillman Ingram

Hood's Corps
Lieutenant-General John Bell Hood

Hindman's Division
Major-General Thomas Carmichael Hindman

Division Headquarters
Lenoir's Independent Company Alabama Cavalry (Escort): Captain Thomas M. Lenoir

Deas's Brigade
Brigadier-General Zachariah Cantey Deas
19th Alabama Infantry: Colonel Samuel K. McSpadden
22nd Alabama Infantry: Colonel Benjamin R. Hart
25th Alabama Infantry: Colonel George D. Johnston
39th Alabama Infantry: Lt. Colonel William C. Clifton
50th Alabama Infantry: Colonel John G. Coltart
17th Alabama Battalion Sharpshooters: Captain F. Nabers

Tucker's Brigade
Brigadier-General William Feimster Tucker
7th Mississippi Infantry: Lt. Colonel Benjamin F. Johns
9th Mississippi Infantry: Captain S. S. Calhoon
10th Mississippi Infantry: Captain Robert A. Bell
41st Mississippi Infantry: Colonel J. Byrd Williams
44th Mississippi Infantry: Lt. Colonel R. G. Kelsey
9th Mississippi Battalion Sharpshooters: Major William C. Richards

Manigault's Brigade
Brigadier-General Arthur Middleton Manigault
24th Alabama Infantry: Colonel Newton N. Davis
28th Alabama Infantry: Lt. Colonel William L. Butler
34th Alabama Infantry: Colonel Julius C. B. Mitchell
10th South Carolina Infantry: Colonel James F. Pressley
19th South Carolina Infantry: Lt. Colonel Thomas P. Shaw

Walthall's Brigade
Brigadier-General Edward Cary Walthall
24th and 27th Mississippi Infantry (Consolidated): Colonel Samuel Benton
29th, 30th and 34th Mississippi Infantry (Consolidated): Colonel William F. Brantly

Stevenson's Division
Major-General Carter Littlepage Stevenson

Brown's Brigade
Brigadier-General John Calvin Brown
3rd Tennessee Infantry: Lt. Colonel Calvin J. Clack
18th Tennessee Infantry: Lt. Colonel William R. Butler
26th Tennessee Infantry: Captain Abijah F. Boggess
32nd Tennessee Infantry: Major John P. McGuire
45th Tennessee Infantry and 23rd Tennessee Battalion Infantry: Colonel Anderson Searcy

Reynold's Brigade
Brigadier-General Alexander Welch Reynolds
58th North Carolina Infantry: Major Thomas J. Dula
60th North Carolina Infantry: Lt. Colonel James T. Weaver
54th Virginia Infantry: Colonel Robert C. Trigg
63rd Virginia Infantry: Captain Connally H. Lynch

Cumming's Brigade
Brigadier-General Alfred Cumming
34th Georgia Infantry: Major John M. Jackson
36th Georgia Infantry: Major Charles E. Broyles
39th Georgia Infantry: Lt. Colonel J. F. B. Jackson
56th Georgia Infantry: Colonel E. P. Watkins

Pettus's Brigade
Brigadier-General Edmund Winston Pettus
20th Alabama Infantry: Colonel James M. Dedman
23rd Alabama Infantry: Lt. Colonel Joseph B. Bibb
30th Alabama Infantry: Colonel Charles M. Shelley
31st Alabama Infantry: Colonel Daniel R. Hundley
46th Alabama Infantry: Captain George E. Brewer

Stewart's Division
Major-General Alexander Peter Stewart

Division Headquarters
10th Confederate Cavalry — Co. A (Escort): Captain John M. McKleroy

Stovall's Brigade
Brigadier-General Marcellus Augustus Stovall
40th Georgia Infantry: Colonel Abda Johnson
41st Georgia Infantry: Major Mark S. Nall
42nd Georgia Infantry: Colonel Robert J. Henderson
43rd Georgia Infantry: Major William C. Lester
52nd Georgia Infantry: Captain Rufus R. Asbury

Gibson's Brigade
Brigadier-General Randall Lee Gibson
1st Louisiana Infantry Regulars: Major S. S. Batchelor
13th Louisiana Infantry: Lt. Colonel Francis L. Campbell
16th and 25th Louisiana Infantry (Consolidated): Colonel Joseph C. Lewis
19th Louisiana Infantry: Lt. Colonel Hyder A. Kennedy
20th Louisiana Infantry: Major Samuel L. Bishop
4th Louisiana Battalion Infantry: Major Duncan Buie
14th Louisiana Battalion Sharpshooters: Major John E. Austin

Clayton's Brigade
Brigadier-General Henry DeLamar Clayton
18th Alabama Infantry: Colonel James T. Holtzclaw
32nd and 58th Alabama Infantry: Colonel Bushrod Jones
36th Alabama Infantry: Lt. Colonel Thomas H. Herndon
38th Alabama Infantry: Colonel A. R. Lankford

Baker's Brigade
Brigadier-General Alpheus Baker
37th Alabama Infantry: Lt. Colonel Alexander A. Greene
40th Alabama Infantry: Captain Elbert D. Willett
42nd Alabama Infantry: Lt. Colonel Thomas C. Lanier

Cavalry Corps
Major-General Joseph Wheeler

Martin's Division
Major-General William Thompson Martin

Morgan's Brigade
Brigadier-General John Tyler Morgan
1st Alabama Cavalry: Major A. H. Johnson
3rd Alabama Cavalry: Colonel Tyirie H. Mauldin
4th Alabama Cavalry: Colonel Alfred A. Russell
7th Alabama Cavalry: Colonel James C. Malone, Jr.
51st Alabama Cavalry: Lt. Colonel M. L. Kirkpatrick

Iverson's Brigade
Brigadier-General Alfred Iverson
1st Georgia Cavalry: Colonel Samuel W. Davitte
2nd Georgia Cavalry: Colonel Charles C. Crews
3rd Georgia Cavalry: Colonel Robert Thompson
4th Georgia Cavalry: Colonel Isaac W. Avery
6th Georgia Cavalry: Colonel John R. Hart

Kelly's Division
Brigadier-General John Herbert Kelly

Allen's Brigade
Brigadier-General William Wirt Allen
3rd Confederate Cavalry: Colonel P. H. Rice
8th Confederate Cavalry: Lt. Colonel John S. Prather
10th Confederate Cavalry: Captain T. G. Holt
12th Confederate Cavalry: Captain Charles H. Conner

Dibrell's Brigade
Colonel George Gibbs Dibrell
4th Tennessee Cavalry: Colonel William S. McLemore
8th Tennessee Cavalry: Captain Jefferson Leftwich
9th Tennessee Cavalry: Colonel Jacob B. Biffle
10th Tennessee Cavalry: Colonel William E. DeMoss
11th Tennessee Cavalry: Colonel Daniel W. Holman

Humes's Division
Brigadier-General William Young Conn Humes

Humes's Brigade
Colonel James T. Wheeler
1st Tennessee Cavalry: Major Joseph J. Dobbins
2nd Tennessee Cavalry: Captain John H. Kuhn
4th Tennessee Cavalry: Lt. Colonel Paul F. Anderson
5th Tennessee Cavalry: Colonel George W. McKenzie
9th Tennessee Battalion Cavalry: Major James H. Akin

Harrison's Brigade
Colonel Thomas Harrison
3rd Arkansas Cavalry: Colonel Amson W. Hobson
8th Texas Cavalry: Lt. Colonel Gustave Cook
11th Texas Cavalry: Colonel George R. Reeves

Grigsby's Brigade
Colonel J. Warren Grigsby
1st Kentucky Cavalry: Colonel J. R. Butler
2nd Kentucky Cavalry (Woodward's): Major Thomas W. Lewis
9th Kentucky Cavalry: Lt. Colonel Robert G. Stoner
Allison's Squadron Tennessee Cavalry: Captain John H. Allison
Dortch's Battalion Kentucky Cavalry: Captain John B. Dortch
Hamilton's Battalion Tennessee Cavalry: Major Joseph Shaw

Hannon's Brigade
Colonel Moses W. Hannon
53rd Alabama Cavalry: Lt. Colonel John F. Gaines
24th Battalion Alabama Cavalry: Major Robert B. Snodgrass

Artillery
Brigadier-General Francis Asbury Shoup

Hardee's Corps
Colonel Melancthon Smith

Hoxton's Battalion
Alabama Artillery Battery: Captain John Phelan
Marion Light Artillery (Florida): Lieutenant Thomas J. Perry
Mississippi Artillery Battery: Captain William B. Turner

Martin's Battalion
Bledsoe's Artillery Battery (Missouri): Lieutenant Charles W. Higgins
Ferguson's Artillery Battery (South Carolina): Lieutenant René T. Beauregard
Howell's Artillery Battery (Georgia): Lieutenant W. G. Robson

Hotchkiss's Battalion
Arkansas Artillery Battery: Captain Thomas J. Key
Semple's Artillery Battery (Alabama): Lieutenant Richard W. Goldthwaite
Warren Light Artillery (Mississippi): Lieutenant H. Shannon

Cobb's Battalion
Cobb's Artillery Battery (Kentucky): Lieutenant R. B. Matthews
Johnston Artillery (Tennessee): Captain John W. Mebane
Washington Light Artillery (Louisiana): Lieutenant William C. D. Vaught

Hood's Corps
Colonel Robert F. Beckham

Courtney's Battalion
Alabama Artillery Battery: Captain James Garrity
Alabama Artillery Battery: Captain Staunton H. Dent
Douglas's Artillery Battery (Texas): Lieutenant John H. Bingham

Eldridge's Battalion
Eufaula Artillery (Alabama): Captain McDonald Oliver
Louisiana Artillery Battery: Captain Charles E. Fenner
Mississippi Artillery Battery: Captain Thomas J. Stanford

Johnston's Battalion
Cherokee Artillery (Georgia): Captain Max Van Den Corput
Stephens Light Artillery (Georgia): Captain John B. Rowan
Tennessee Artillery Battery: Captain Lucius G. Marshall

Cavalry Corps
Lt. Colonel Felix H. Robertson
Ferrell's Artillery Battery (Georgia)
Huwald's Artillery Battery (Tennessee): Lieutenant D. Breck Ramsey
Tennessee Artillery Battery: Captain Benjamin F. White, Jr.
Wiggins's Artillery Battery (Arkansas): Lieutenant J. P. Bryant

Artillery Reserve
Lt. Colonel James H. Hallonquist

Palmer's Battalion
Alabama Artillery Battery: Captain Charles L. Lumsden
Georgia Artillery Battery: Captain Ruel W. Anderson
Georgia Artillery Battery: Captain Minor W. Harris

Waddell's Battalion
Alabama Artillery Battery: Captain Winslow D. Emery
Bellamy's Artillery Battery (Alabama): Lieutenant Francis O'Neal
Missouri Artillery Battery: Captain Overton W. Barret

Williams's Battalion
Barbour Artillery (Alabama): Captain Reuben F. Kolb
Jefferson Artillery (Mississippi): Captain Put Darden
Nottoway Artillery (Virginia): Captain William C. Jeffress

Detachments
Cantey's Brigade
Brigadier-General James Cantey
17th Alabama Infantry: Colonel Virgil S. Murphey
29th Alabama Infantry: Colonel John F. Conoley
37th Mississippi Infantry: Colonel Orlando S. Holland
Alabama Battalion Sharpshooters: Major J. S. Moreland

Engineer Troops
Third Regiment—Co. A: Major Stephen W. Presstman
Third Regiment—Co. B (Cheatham's Division): Captain H. N. Pharr
Third Regiment—Co. C (Stewart's Division): Captain A. W. Gloster
Third Regiment—Co. D: Captain Edmund Winston
Third Regiment—Co. F (Cleburne's Division): Captain W. A. Ramsey
Third Regiment—Co. G (Hindman's Division): Lieutenant Robert L. Cobb
Sappers and Miners: Captain A. W. Clarkson

ARMY OF MISSISSIPPI

June 10, 1864
Lieutenant-General Leonidas Polk

Loring's Division
Major-General William Wing Loring

First Brigade
Brigadier-General Winfield Scott Featherston
3rd Mississippi Infantry: Colonel Thomas A. Mellon
22nd Mississippi Infantry: Major Martin A. Oatis
31st Mississippi Infantry: Colonel Marcus D. L. Stephens
33rd Mississippi Infantry: Colonel Jabez L. Drake
40th Mississippi Infantry: Colonel Wallace B. Colbert
1st Mississippi Battalion Sharpshooters: Major James M. Stigler

Second Brigade
Brigadier-General John Adams
6th Mississippi Infantry: Colonel Robert Lowry
14th Mississippi Infantry: Lt. Colonel Washington L. Doss
15th Mississippi Infantry: Colonel Michael Farrell
20th Mississippi Infantry: Colonel William N. Brown
23rd Mississippi Infantry: Colonel Joseph M. Wells
43rd Mississippi Infantry: Colonel Richard Harrison

Third Brigade
Colonel Thomas M. Scott

27th Alabama Infantry: Colonel James Jackson
35th Alabama Infantry: Colonel Samuel S. Ives
49th Alabama Infantry: Lt. Colonel John D. Weeden
55th Alabama Infantry: Colonel John Snodgrass
57th Alabama Infantry: Colonel Charles J. L. Cunningham
12th Louisiana Infantry: Lt. Colonel Noel L. Nelson

Artillery Battalion
Major John Myrick
Barry's Artillery Battery (Tennessee)
Bouanchaud's Artillery Battery (Louisiana)
Cowan's Artillery Battery (Mississippi)

French's Division
Major-General Samuel Gibbs French

First Brigade
Brigadier-General Matthew Duncan Ector
29th North Carolina Infantry: Lt. Colonel Bacchus S. Proffitt
39th North Carolina Infantry: Colonel David Coleman
9th Texas Infantry: Colonel William H. Young
10th Texas Cavalry (Dismounted): Colonel C. R. Earp
14th Texas Cavalry (Dismounted): Colonel John L. Camp
32nd Texas Cavalry (Dismounted): Colonel Julius A. Andrews

Second Brigade
Brigadier-General Francis Marion Cockrell
1st Missouri Infantry: Captain Bradford Keith
2nd Missouri Infantry: Colonel Peter C. Flournoy
3rd Missouri Infantry: Colonel James McCown
4th Missouri Infantry: Captain Bradford Keith
5th Missouri Infantry: Colonel James McCown
6th Missouri Infantry: Colonel Peter C. Flournoy
1st and 3rd Missouri Cavalry (Dismounted): Colonel Elijah Gates

Third Brigade
Brigadier-General Claudius Wistar Sears
4th Mississippi Infantry: Colonel Thomas N. Adaire
35th Mississippi Infantry: Colonel William S. Barry
36th Mississippi Infantry: Colonel William W. Witherspoon
39th Mississippi Infantry: Lt. Colonel William E. Ross
46th Mississippi Infantry: Colonel William H. Clark
7th Mississippi Battalion Infantry: Captain W. A. Trotter

Artillery Battalion
Major George S. Storrs
Guibor's Artillery Battery (Missouri)
Hoskin's Artillery Battery (Mississippi)
Ward's Artillery Battery (Alabama)

Cantey's Division
Brigadier-General James Cantey

First Brigade
Brigadier-General Daniel Harris Reynolds
1st Arkansas Infantry
2nd Arkansas Infantry
4th Arkansas Infantry
9th Arkansas Infantry
25th Arkansas Infantry

Second Brigade
Colonel Virgil S. Murphey

1st Alabama Infantry
17th Alabama Infantry
26th Alabama Infantry
29th Alabama Infantry
37th Alabama Infantry

Artillery Battalion
Major William C. Preston
Selden's Artillery Battery (Alabama)
Tarrant's Artillery Battery (Alabama)
Yates's Artillery Battery (Mississippi)

Cavalry Division
Brigadier-General William Hicks "Red" Jackson

First Brigade
Brigadier-General Frank Crawford Armstrong
6th Alabama Cavalry: Colonel Charles H. Colvin
1st Mississippi Cavalry: Colonel R. A. Pinson
2nd Mississippi Cavalry: Major John J. Perry
28th Mississippi Cavalry: Major Joshua T. McBee
Ballentine's Regiment Mississippi Cavalry: Captain Edward E. Porter

Second Brigade
Brigadier-General Lawrence Sullivan Ross
3rd Texas Cavalry: Lt. Colonel Jiles S. Boggers
6th Texas Cavalry: Lt. Colonel Peter F. Ross
9th Texas Cavalry: Colonel Dudley W. Jones
27th Texas Cavalry: Colonel Edwin R. Hawkins

Third Brigade
Brigadier-General Samuel Wragg Ferguson
2nd Alabama Cavalry: Lt. Colonel John N. Carpenter
12th Mississippi Cavalry: Colonel William M. Inge
56th Alabama Cavalry: Colonel William Boyles
Miller's Regiment Mississippi Cavalry
Perrin's Regiment Mississippi Cavalry

Artillery Battalion
Croft's Artillery Battery (Georgia)
King's Artillery Battery (Missouri)
Watie's Artillery Battery (South Carolina)

CONFEDERATE FORCES: ARMY OF TENNESSEE

August 31, 1864
General John Bell Hood

Hardee's Corps
Lieutenant-General William Joseph Hardee

Cheatham's Division
Brigadier-General George Maney

Gist's Brigade
Colonel Ellison Capers
46th Georgia Infantry: Captain W. A. Davie
65th Georgia Infantry: Captain William G. Foster
16th South Carolina Infantry: Captain John W. Boling
24th South Carolina Infantry: Lt. Colonel Jesse S. Jones
2nd Georgia Battalion Sharpshooters: Major Richard H. Whitely
8th Georgia Battalion Sharpshooters: Lt. Colonel Zachariah L. Watters

Wright's Brigade
Brigadier-General John Carpenter Carter
8th Tennessee Infantry: Colonel John H. Anderson
16th Tennessee Infantry: Captain Benjamin Randals
28th Tennessee Infantry: Captain John B. Holman
38th Tennessee Infantry: Major Hamilton W. Cotter
51st and 52nd Tennessee Infantry (Consolidated): Major Thomas G. Randle

Maney's Brigade
Colonel George C. Porter
4th Tennessee and 24th Tennessee Battalion Infantry: Lt. Colonel Oliver A. Bradshaw
1st and 27th Tennessee Infantry: Captain William Ledbetter, Jr.
6th and 9th Tennessee Infantry: Lt. Colonel John L. Harris
19th Tennessee Infantry: Major James G. Deaderick
50th Tennessee Infantry: Colonel Stephen H. Colms

Strahl's Brigade
Colonel James D. Tillman
4th and 5th Tennessee Infantry: Major Henry Hampton
24th Tennessee Infantry: Lt. Colonel Samuel E. Shannon
31st Tennessee Infantry: Lt. Colonel Fountain E. P. Stafford
33rd Tennessee Infantry: Major Robert N. Payne
41st Tennessee Infantry: Captain A. M. Kieth

Vaughan's Brigade
Colonel Michael Magevney, Jr.
11th Tennessee Infantry: Colonel George W. Gordon
12th and 47th Tennessee Infantry: Lt. Colonel Josiah N. Wyatt
13th and 154th Tennessee Infantry: Major William J. Crook
29th Tennessee Infantry: Colonel Horace Rice

Cleburne's Division
Major-General Patrick Ronayne Cleburne

Lowrey's Brigade
Brigadier-General Mark Perrin Lowrey
16th Alabama Infantry: Colonel Frederick A. Ashford
33rd Alabama Infantry: Lt. Colonel Robert F. Crittenden
45th Alabama Infantry: Lt. Colonel Robert H. Abercrombie
5th Mississippi Infantry and 3rd Mississippi Battalion Infantry: Colonel John Weir
8th and 32nd Mississippi Infantry: Captain Andrew E. Moody

Govan's Brigade
Brigadier-General Daniel Chevilette Govan
1st and 15th Arkansas Infantry: Captain Felix G. Lusk
2nd and 24th Arkansas Infantry: Major A. T. Meek
5th and 13th Arkansas Infantry: Colonel Peter V. Green
6th and 7th Arkansas Infantry: Colonel Samuel G. Smith
8th and 19th Arkansas Infantry: Major David H. Hamiter
3rd Confederate Infantry: Captain M. H. Dixon

Granbury's Brigade
Brigadier-General Hiram Bronson Granbury
5th Confederate Infantry: Captain Aaron A. Cox
35th Tennessee Infantry: Colonel Benjamin J. Hill
6th Texas Infantry and 15th Texas Cavalry (Dismounted): Captain M. M. Houston
7th Texas Infantry: Captain John W. Brown
10th Texas Infantry: Lt. Colonel Robert B. Young
17th and 18th Texas Cavalry (Dismounted): Captain William H. Perry
24th and 25th Texas Cavalry (Dismounted): Major William A. Taylor
Nutt's Company Louisiana Cavalry: Captain L. M. Nutt

Mercer's Brigade
Colonel Charles H. Olmstead
1st Georgia Volunteer Infantry: Major Martin J. Ford
54th Georgia Infantry: Colonel Charlton H. Way
57th Georgia Infantry: Lt. Colonel Cincinnattus S. Guyton
63rd Georgia Infantry: Captain James T. Buckner

Bate's Division
Major-General John Calvin Brown

Division Headquarters
Breckinridge Guards Mississippi Cavalry: Captain James H. Buck

Jackson's Brigade
Brigadier-General Henry Rootes Jackson
1st Georgia Confederate Infantry: Captain William J. Whitsitt
25th Georgia Infantry: Captain A. H. Smith
29th Georgia Infantry: Lt. Colonel W. W. Billopp
30th Georgia Infantry: Major Henry Hendrick
66th Georgia Infantry: Captain Thomas L. Langston
1st Georgia Battalion Sharpshooters: Major Arthur Shaaff

Lewis's Brigade
Brigadier-General Joseph Horace Lewis
2nd Kentucky Infantry: Lt. Colonel Philip Lee
4th Kentucky Infantry: Lt. Colonel Thomas W. Thompson
5th Kentucky Infantry: Lt. Colonel George W. Connor
6th Kentucky Infantry: Major George W. Maxson
9th Kentucky Infantry: Colonel John W. Caldwell

Finley's Brigade
Lt. Colonel Daniel L. Kenan
1st Florida Cavalry (Dismounted) and 3rd Florida Infantry: Major Glover Alling Ball
1st and 4th Florida Infantry (Consolidated): Major Jacob A. Lash
6th Florida Infantry: Captain Henry B. Grace
7th Florida Infantry: Major Nathan S. Blount

Tyler's Brigade
Brigadier-General Thomas Benton Smith
37th Georgia Infantry: Lt. Colonel Joseph T. Smith
2nd Tennessee Infantry: Colonel William D. Robison
10th Tennessee Infantry: Colonel William Grace
15th and 37th Tennessee Infantry (Consolidated): Lt. Colonel R. Dudley Frayser
20th Tennessee Infantry: Lt. Colonel William M. Shy
30th Tennessee Infantry: Lt. Colonel James J. Turner
4th Georgia Battalion Sharpshooters: Captain B. M. Turner

Stewart's Corps
Lieutenant-General Alexander Peter Stewart

Loring's Division
Brigadier-General Winfield Scott Featherston

Featherston's Brigade
Colonel Marcus D. L. Stephens
3rd Mississippi Infantry: Lt. Colonel Samuel M. Dyer
22nd Mississippi Infantry: Major James M. Stigler
31st Mississippi Infantry: Captain Robert A. Collins
33rd Mississippi Infantry: Captain Moses Jackson
40th Mississippi Infantry: Captain W. L. Bassett
1st Mississippi Battalion Sharpshooters: Major James M. Stigler

Adams's Brigade
Brigadier-General John Adams
6th Mississippi Infantry: Colonel Robert Lowry
14th Mississippi Infantry: Major Robert J. Lawrence
15th Mississippi Infantry: Colonel Michael Farrell
20th Mississippi Infantry: Colonel William N. Brown
23rd Mississippi Infantry: Colonel Joseph M. Wells
43rd Mississippi Infantry: Colonel Richard Harrison

Scott's Brigade
Brigadier-General Thomas Moore Scott
27th, 35th and 49th Alabama Infantry (Consolidated): Colonel Samuel S. Ives
55th Alabama Infantry: Colonel John Snodgrass
57th Alabama Infantry: Colonel Charles J. L. Cunningham
12th Louisiana Infantry: Colonel Noel L. Nelson

French's Division
Major-General Samuel Gibbs French

Ector's Brigade
Colonel William H. Young
29th North Carolina Infantry: Lt. Colonel Bacchus S. Proffitt
39th North Carolina Infantry: Colonel David Coleman
9th Texas Infantry: Major James H. McReynolds
10th Texas Cavalry (Dismounted): Colonel C. R. Earp
14th Texas Cavalry (Dismounted): Colonel John L. Camp
32nd Texas Cavalry (Dismounted): Colonel Julius A. Andrews

First Missouri Brigade
Brigadier-General Francis Marion Cockrell
1st and 4th Missouri Infantry (Consolidated): Lt. Colonel Hugh A. Garland
2nd and 6th Missouri Infantry (Consolidated): Lt. Colonel Stephen Cooper
3rd and 5th Missouri Infantry (Consolidated): Colonel James McCown
1st Missouri Cavalry and 3rd Missouri Cavalry Battn. (Dismounted): Colonel Elijah Gates

Sear's Brigade
Brigadier-General Claudius Wistar Sears
4th Mississippi Infantry: Major Thomas P. Nelson
35th Mississippi Infantry: Colonel William S. Barry
36th Mississippi Infantry: Colonel William W. Witherspoon
39th Mississippi Infantry: Major R. J. Durr
46th Mississippi Infantry: Colonel William H. Clark
7th Mississippi Battalion Infantry: Captain J. D. Harris

Walthall's Division
Major-General Edward Cary Walthall

Quarles's Brigade
Brigadier-General William Andrew Quarles
1st Alabama Infantry: Captain Richard Williams
42nd Tennessee Infantry: Captain Austin M. Duncan
46th and 55th Tennessee Infantry (Consolidated): Lt. Colonel Gideon B. Black
48th Tennessee Infantry: Captain Henry G. Evans
49th Tennessee Infantry: Captain Robert H. McClelland
53rd Tennessee Infantry: Captain S. C. Orr

Cantey's Brigade
Colonel Edward A. O'Neal
17th Alabama Infantry: Captain William W. McMillan
26th Alabama Infantry: Captain J. W. White
29th Alabama Infantry: Captain Samuel Abernethy
37th Mississippi Infantry: Major Samuel H. Terral

Reynolds's Brigade
Brigadier-General Daniel Harris Reynolds
1st Arkansas Mounted Infantry: Captain R. P. Parks
2nd Arkansas Mounted Infantry: Lieutenant L. C. French
4th Arkansas Infantry: Captain Augustus Kile
9th Arkansas Infantry: Colonel Isaac L. Dunlop
25th Arkansas Infantry: Captain Edward C. Woodson

Lee's Corps
Lieutenant-General Stephen Dill Lee

Anderson's Division
Major-General Patton Anderson

Deas's Brigade
Brigadier-General Zachariah Cantey Deas
19th Alabama Infantry: Lt. Colonel George R. Kimbrough
22nd Alabama Infantry: Lt. Colonel Harry T. Toulmin
25th Alabama Infantry: Captain Napoleon B. Rouse
39th Alabama Infantry: Major Drewry H. Smith
50th Alabama Infantry: Captain Archibald D. Ray

Brantly's Brigade
Brigadier-General William Felix Brantly
24th Mississippi Infantry: Lt. Colonel William L. Lyles
27th Mississippi Infantry: Captain Joel R. Baugh
29th and 30th Mississippi Infantry (Consolidated): Lt. Colonel James B. Morgan
34th Mississippi Infantry: Captain Benjamin F. Houston

Manigault's Brigade
Brigadier-General Arthur Middleton Manigault
24th Alabama Infantry: Colonel Newton N. Davis
28th Alabama Infantry: Lt. Colonel William L. Butler
34th Alabama Infantry: Major John N. Slaughter
10th South Carolina Infantry: Captain B. B. McWhite
19th South Carolina Infantry: Colonel Thomas P. Shaw

Tucker's Brigade
Brigadier-General Jacob Hunter Sharp
7th and 9th Mississippi Infantry (Consolidated): Lt. Colonel Benjamin F. Johns
10th and 44th Mississippi Infantry (Consolidated): Lt. Colonel R. G. Kelsey
41st Mississippi Infantry: Colonel J. Byrd Williams
9th Mississippi Battalion Sharpshooters: Lieutenant John Thomas Oliver

Stevenson's Division
Major-General Carter Littlepage Stevenson

Brown's Brigade
Colonel Joseph B. Palmer
3rd Tennessee Infantry (Volunteers): Lt. Colonel Calvin J. Clack
18th Tennessee Infantry: Major William H. Joyner
26th Tennessee Infantry: Colonel Richard M. Saffell
32nd Tennessee Infantry: Major John P. McGuire
45th Tennessee and 23rd Tennessee Battalion (Consolidated): Colonel Anderson Searcy

Pettus's Brigade
Brigadier-General Edmund Winston Pettus
20th Alabama Infantry: Captain S. W. Davidson
23rd Alabama Infantry: Lt. Colonel Joseph B. Bibb
30th Alabama Infantry: Colonel Charles M. Shelley
31st Alabama Infantry: Major George W. Mattison
46th Alabama Infantry: Captain George E. Brewer

Cumming's Brigade
Brigadier-General Alfred Cumming
2nd Georgia State Troops: Colonel James Wilson
34th Georgia Infantry: Major John M. Jackson
36th Georgia Infantry: Captain Thomas Williams
39th Georgia Infantry: Captain William P. Milton
56th Georgia Infantry: Captain Benjamin F. Spearman

Reynolds's Brigade
Colonel Washington M. Hardy
58th North Carolina Infantry: Captain Samuel M. Silver
60th North Carolina Infantry: Major James T. Huff
54th Virginia Infantry: Captain James M. Boyd
63rd Virginia Infantry: Lt. Colonel Connally H. Lynch

Clayton's Division
Major-General Henry DeLamar Clayton

Stovall's Brigade
Brigadier-General Marcellus Augustus Stovall
1st Georgia State Troops: Captain William Tate
40th Georgia Infantry: Major Raleigh S. Camp
41st Georgia Infantry: Major Mark S. Nall
42nd Georgia Infantry: Colonel Robert J. Henderson
43rd Georgia Infantry: Captain H. R. Howard
52nd Georgia Infantry: Captain J. R. Russell

Baker's Brigade
Brigadier-General Alpheus Baker
37th Alabama Infantry: Captain C. Pennington
40th Alabama Infantry: Colonel John H. Higley
42nd Alabama Infantry: Captain William D. McNeill
54th Alabama Infantry: Colonel John A. Minter

Gibson's Brigade
Brigadier-General Randall Lee Gibson
1st Louisiana Infantry (Regulars): Lieutenant W. P. Grivot
4th Louisiana Infantry: Colonel Samuel E. Hunter
4th Louisiana Battalion Infantry: Captain William J. Powell
13th Louisiana Infantry: Lt. Colonel Francis L. Campbell
14th Louisiana Battalion Sharpshooters: Major John E. Austin
16th and 25th Louisiana Infantry (Consolidated): Colonel Joseph C. Lewis
19th Louisiana Infantry: Captain Camp Flournoy
20th Louisiana Infantry: Captain Alexander Dresel
30th Louisiana Infantry: Captain Henry P. Jones

Holtzclaw's Brigade
Brigadier-General James Thadeus Holtzclaw
18th Alabama Infantry: Lt. Colonel Peter F. Hunley
32nd and 58th Alabama Infantry (Consolidated): Colonel Bushrod Jones
36th Alabama Infantry: Lt. Colonel Thomas H. Herndon
38th Alabama Infantry: Captain Benjamin Lane Posey

Cavalry Corps
Major-General Joseph Wheeler

Martin's Division
Allen's Brigade
1st Alabama Cavalry: Lt. Colonel D. T. Blakey
3rd Alabama Cavalry: Colonel James Hagan
4th Alabama Cavalry: Colonel Alfred A. Russell

7th Alabama Cavalry: Captain George Mason
51st Alabama Cavalry: Colonel M. L. Kirkpatrick
12th Alabama Battalion Cavalry: Captain Warren S. Reese

Iverson's Brigade
1st Georgia Cavalry: Colonel Samuel W. Davitte
2nd Georgia Cavalry: Colonel Charles C. Crews
3rd Georgia Cavalry: Colonel Robert Thompson
4th Georgia Cavalry: Colonel Isaac W. Avery
6th Georgia Cavalry: Colonel John R. Hart

Humes's Division
Ashby's Brigade
1st (6th) Tennessee Cavalry: Colonel James T. Wheeler
2nd Tennessee Cavalry: Captain William M. Smith
5th Tennessee Cavalry: Colonel George W. McKenzie
9th Tennessee Battalion Cavalry: Major James H. Akin

Harrison's Brigade
3rd Arkansas Cavalry: Colonel Amson W. Hobson
4th Tennessee Cavalry: Lt. Colonel Paul F. Anderson
8th Texas Cavalry: Lt. Colonel Gustave Cook
11th Texas Cavalry: Colonel George R. Reeves

Kelly's Division
Anderson's Brigade
3rd Confederate Cavalry: Lt. Colonel John McCaskill
8th Confederate Cavalry: Lt. Colonel John S. Prather
10th Confederate Cavalry: Captain W. J. Vason
12th Confederate Cavalry: Captain Charles H. Conner
5th Georgia Cavalry: Colonel Edward Bird

Hannon's Brigade
53rd Alabama Cavalry: Lt. Colonel John F. Gaines
24th Alabama Battalion Cavalry: Major Robert B. Snodgrass

Dibrell's Brigade
4th Tennessee Cavalry: Colonel William S. McLemore
8th Tennessee Cavalry: Captain Jefferson Leftwich
9th Tennessee Cavalry: Captain James M. Reynolds
10th Tennessee Cavalry: Major John Minor
11th Tennessee Cavalry: Colonel Daniel W. Holman

Williams's Brigade
1st (3rd) Kentucky Cavalry: Colonel J. R. Butler
2nd Kentucky Cavalry (Woodward's): Major Thomas W. Lewis
9th Kentucky Cavalry: Colonel William C. P. Breckinridge
2nd Kentucky Battalion Cavalry: Captain John B. Dortch
Allison's Squadron and Hamilton's Battalion Cavalry (Consolidated): Major Joseph Shaw

Kelly's Division Reserves
4th Georgia Cavalry: Colonel Duncan L. Clinch
Sanders's Tennessee Battalion Cavalry: Captain Calvin F. Sanders

Jackson's Division
Brigadier-General William Hicks "Red" Jackson

Armstrong's Brigade
Brigadier — General Frank Crawford Armstrong
1st Mississippi Cavalry: Colonel R. A. Pinson
2nd Mississippi Cavalry: Major John J. Perry
28th Mississippi Cavalry: Major Joshua T. McBee
Ballentine's Mississippi Cavalry: Lt. Colonel William L. Maxwell

Ross's Brigade
Brigadier-General Lawrence Sullivan Ross
3rd Texas Cavalry: Lt. Colonel Jiles S. Boggess
6th Texas Cavalry: Lt. Colonel Peter F. Ross
9th Texas Cavalry: Lt. Colonel Thomas G. Berry
27th Texas Cavalry: Lt. Colonel John H. Broocks

Artillery
Colonel Robert F. Beckham

Hardee's Corps Artillery
Colonel Melancthon Smith

Hoxton's Artillery Battalion
Perry's Florida Artillery Battery: Captain Thomas J. Perry
Phelans's Alabama Artillery Battery: Lieutenant Nathaniel Venable
Turner's Mississippi Artillery Battery: Captain William B. Turner

Palmer's Artillery Battalion
Alabama Artillery Battery: Captain Charles L. Lumsden
Georgia Artillery Battery: Captain Ruel W. Anderson
Georgia Artillery Battery: Captain Minor W. Havis

Hotchkiss's Artillery Battalion
Captain Thomas J. Key
Key's Arkansas Artillery Battery: Lieutenant James G. Marshall
Goldthwaite's Alabama Artillery Battery: Captain Richard W. Goldthwaite
Swett's Mississippi Artillery Battery: Lieutenant Henry N. Steele

Martin's Artillery Battalion
Bledsoe's Missouri Artillery Battery: Captain Hiram M. Bledsoe
Ferguson's South Carolina Artillery Battery: Lieutenant René T. Beauregard
Howell's Georgia Artillery Battery: Captain Evan P. Howell

Cobb's Artillery Battalion
Major Robert Cobb
Gracey's Kentucky Artillery Battery: Captain Frank P. Gracey
Mebane's Tennessee Artillery Battery: Lieutenant J. W. Phillips
Slocomb's Louisiana Artillery Battery: Captain Cuthbert H. Slocomb

Lee's Corps Artillery
Lt. Colonel James H. Hallonquist

Eldridge's Artillery Battalion
Eufaula Alabama Artillery: Captain William J. McKenzie
Louisiana Artillery Battery: Captain Charles E. Fenner
Stanford's Mississippi Artillery Battery: Lieutenant James S. McCall

Williams's Artillery Battalion
Captain Reuben F. Kolb
Barbour Alabama Artillery: Lieutenant Robert Cherry
Jefferson Mississippi Artillery: Captain Put. Darden
Nottoway Virginia Artillery: Lieutenant Samuel B. Wingo

Courtney's Artillery Battalion
Dent's Alabama Artillery Battery: Captain Staunton H. Dent
Douglas's Texas Artillery Battery: Captain James P. Douglas
Garrity's Alabama Artillery Battery: Lieutenant Philip Bond

Johnston's Artillery Battalion
Captain John B. Rowan
Cherokee Georgia Artillery: Lieutenant Meshack L. McWhorter
Stephens Georgia Light Artillery: Lieutenant William L. Ritter
Tennessee Artillery Battery: Captain Lucius G. Marshall

Stewart's Corps Artillery
Lt. Colonel Samuel C. Williams

Waddell's Artillery Battalion
Captain Overton W. Barret
Alabama Artillery Battery: Captain Richard H. Bellamy
Alabama Artillery Battery: Captain Winslow D. Emery
Barret's Missouri Artillery Battery: Lieutenant William Brown

Myrick's Artillery Battalion
Cowan's Mississippi Artillery Battery: Lieutenant George H. Tompkins
Louisiana Artillery Battery: Captain Alcide Bouanchaud
Tennessee Artillery Battery: Captain Robert L. Barry

Storr's Artillery Battalion
Mississippi Artillery Battery: Captain James A. Hoskins
Missouri Artillery Battery: Captain Henry Guibor
Ward's Alabama Artillery Battery: Lieutenant George W. Weaver

Preston's Artillery Battalion
Selden's Alabama Artillery Battery: Lieutenant Charles W. Lovelace
Tarrant's Alabama Artillery Battery: Captain Edward Tarrant
Yates's Mississippi Artillery Battery: Lieutenant W. J. Shelton

Wheeler's Corps Artillery
Huwald's Tennessee Artillery Battery: Lieutenant D. Breck Ramsey
Ferrell's Georgia Artillery Battery: Lieutenant Nathan Davis
Tennessee Artillery Battery: Captain Almaria L. Huggins
Tennessee Artillery Battery: Captain Benjamin F. White, Jr.
Wiggins's Arkansas Artillery Battery: Lieutenant J. Wylie Calloway

Jackson's Cavalry Division Artillery
Croft's Georgia Artillery Battery: Captain Edward Croft
King's Missouri Artillery Battery: Captain Houston King
Waties's South Carolina Artillery Battery: Lieutenant R. B. Waddell

Chapter Seven

The Storm Breaks: The Close of the War

So, from the Charleston Convention to this point, I shared the fortunes of the Confederacy, and can say, as Grattan did of Irish freedom, that I sat by its cradle and followed its hearse.
—Lieutenant-General Richard Taylor regarding the close of the American Civil War, New York 1879

Once Sherman arrived in Atlanta on September 7, he established his headquarters at the home of the Neal family. Their son, Lieutenant Andrew J. Neal, had been killed in the bombardment of Atlanta while in the Confederate service as an artillerist. The home, a Corinthian-columned mansion, was located on the southwest corner of Washington and Mitchell streets across from the courthouse.[1] Once ensconced in his new headquarters, Sherman summoned Mayor Calhoun and entrusted him with a letter for Hood. In the communication, Sherman stated that all of the remaining inhabitants of Atlanta were to be expelled from the city. Those who wished to escape the war and travel north would be permitted to do so, and those that chose to stay in the South would be transported to Rough and Ready. Sherman proposed a ten-day truce in the area of Rough and Ready to effect his edict. In defense of his order, Sherman explained to Halleck that "war is war, and not popularity seeking. If they want peace they and their relatives must stop the war."[2]

The following day, Hood accepted Sherman's offer of a truce with the response, "I do not consider I have any alternative in the matter." Hood did strongly protest the order, answering Sherman that it "transcends, in studied and ingenious cruelty, all acts ever before brought to my attention in the dark history of this war." Sherman's reply to Hood summed up his feelings on the matter: "Talk thus to the marines, but not to me." His reply to the mayor and three members of the city council was even harsher in tone: "You might as well appeal against the thunderstorm as against these terrible hardships of war."[3] Beginning on September 12 and ending on September 21, a total of 709 adults (most of whom were women), 867 children, and 79 slaves were placed aboard wagons and ambulances and transported to Rough and Ready. From there, they were loaded aboard Confederate wagons that took them to Lovejoy's Station, where they were boarded on trains that moved them to Macon and other points farther south. A hastily constructed camp of log cabins was erected at Dawson, Georgia, to provide shelter for the newly homeless former residents of Atlanta.[4] While allowing his army time to rest and refit, Sherman spent his time in Atlanta sitting on the porch of his mansion headquarters in slippers, smoking cigars, reading newspapers, and plotting his next offensive move.[5]

While Sherman pondered in Atlanta, three of the Confederacy's leaders were not sitting idle. One was President Davis, who boarded a train in Richmond bound for Georgia, where he planned to inspect the Army of Tennessee and see if the alarming reports regarding the condition of the army were true. He also wanted to meet with Hood and his generals to determine the course of future operations to reverse the tide of the war in the western theater. The second leader was Hood, who, after evacuating the Union prisoners from Andersonville to prevent their repatriation by a Federal thrust and to relieve himself of the duty of having to protect the prisoner-of-war camp, was moving his army from Lovejoy's Station to Palmetto, a small village on the Montgomery and West Point Railroad. Hood's intentions on moving to Palmetto, located 24 miles southwest of Atlanta and close to the Chattahoochee, were to cut Sherman's communications, forcing him to abandon Atlanta, whereupon Hood would pounce on him as he retreated through northern Georgia. Hood's plan, as he related it to Davis, was

Lieutenant-General Richard Taylor (courtesy of the Library of Congress).

then to move into Tennessee and possibly Kentucky to regain the soil the Confederacy had been driven from earlier in the war. The third leader, and by far the most dangerous, was Nathan Bedford Forrest. Accompanied by 4,500 cavalry, Forrest was riding toward the Tennessee River under orders from Lieutenant-General Richard Taylor, the new commander of the Department of Alabama, Mississippi, and East Louisiana, to wreck the rail lines between Chattanooga and Nashville.[6]

Arriving at Palmetto on September 25 after a two-day stop in Macon, Davis reviewed the troops of his western army. Devoid of cheers, the review was punctuated by shouts of, "Give us Johnston! Give us our old commander!"[7] Davis then spent the remainder of the day in private conferences with Hood, Hardee, Lee, Stewart, and several of the division commanders. Though under pressure to relieve Hood as commander of the army, in a scene reminiscent of the Bragg era, he refused. Davis then gave Hood permission to lead the Army of Tennessee in a strike on Sherman's supply line. In a conciliatory move to those calling for Hood's removal, Davis appointed P. G. T. Beauregard to head a new Military Division of the West, combining Hood's and Taylor's troops, though Beauregard would have only the authority to advise, and not to order. Davis also allowed Hardee to escape from further serving under Hood by appointing him to command the coastal defenses of Florida, South Carolina, and Georgia. Cheatham was then elevated to command of Hardee's old corps on a recommendation from Hood.[8]

On September 29 through the 30th, the 40,000-strong Army of Tennessee crossed the Chattahoochee on pontoons near Campbellton, and by the evening of October 1 had advanced 8 miles beyond it toward Marietta. Aware of Hood's march northward, Sherman had sent two divisions to Chattanooga and one to Rome to guard against Hood's movement. Upon discovering on

October 2 that the Army of Tennessee was across the Chattahoochee and moving toward Marietta, Sherman set out in pursuit with all of his forces except the Twentieth Corps, which remained on garrison duty in Atlanta. For the next two weeks, Sherman attempted to overtake and smash Hood's army, while the Confederate commander repeatedly struck at the Western and Atlantic Railroad, tearing up all the track between Big Shanty and Acworth, as well as between Dalton and Tunnel Hill. A desperate assault by French's Division at Allatoona was repulsed at the cost of 1,000 gray-clad soldiers, while Stephen Lee made no attempt to attack Resaca after the garrison commander was unfazed by his demand that if he did not surrender, "no prisoners will be taken." Sherman managed to avoid all of the traps that Hood had set for him, and the damage done to the railroad was soon repaired, though Forrest did leave a large portion of the Nashville and Decatur Railroad in ruins before having to make a closely pursued escape back across the Tennessee River. Instead of a starving Federal army wildly retreating through north Georgia, it was Hood who was forced to withdraw toward Alabama in search of supplies for his troops.[9]

Sherman derived little satisfaction from his successful parrying of the Rebel thrusts at his communications, as he now had settled upon a plan for offensive operations. All that was required was for Grant to approve the plan, and he would be on his way "to the sea." Sherman's plan called for turning his back on Hood and making a grand march to the Atlantic seacoast of the Southern states. "I can make this march and make Georgia howl!" he declared to Grant. Grant liked his most-trusted lieutenant's plan, but was afraid that Hood would then be free to sweep through Tennessee and Kentucky. Sherman responded by stating that any advance into Tennessee would be met by Thomas, who would be left in Tennessee with "a force strong enough to prevent [Hood] reaching any country in which we have an interest." Grant was convinced. His sole condition for authorizing the expedition was that Thomas be left with enough troops to "take care of Hood and destroy him."[10]

The following ten days were a whirlwind of preparations. All of Sherman's field forces returned to Atlanta except the Twenty-Third Corps and the Fourth Corps, which went to Thomas in Tennessee. Trains departing Atlanta carried the sick and unfit soldiers of the Union Army, as well as surplus equipment and stores. The trains arriving brought new recruits, veterans returning from furloughs, and enormous quantities of munitions. In Atlanta, the Union engineers destroyed all buildings that could possibly be of any use to the Rebels once they departed. On November 16, Sherman marched out of Atlanta on the Decatur Road with 62,000 battle-hardened veterans, leaving behind them Atlanta, "smouldering and in ruins, the black smoke rising high in the air, and hanging like a pall over the ruined city," as he would recall in his memoirs.[11]

As Sherman was leaving Atlanta, Hood was crossing the Tennessee River at Florence, Alabama. Hood's plan, though it was really more of a fantasy, was to take Nashville before moving on to launch an invasion of Kentucky. If Sherman pursued him, he planned to give battle with his army and the fresh recruits he was sure he would pick up in the two states, then after defeating him, he would send some of his troops to Robert E. Lee in Virginia before advancing on Cincinnati. Should the Union commander defeat him in battle or fail to pursue him as planned, Hood reasoned that he would then join forces with Lee at Richmond and destroy Grant with their combined Confederate armies, then advance on Washington. Hood could see no alternatives if the dream of an independent South was to be recognized.[12]

On November 22 the Army of Tennessee crossed the boundary of the state for whom it was named, with Forrest leading the advance with his and Jackson's cavalry. Despite the added weight of Forrest's troopers, the army still numbered only 40,000, with 30,000 of that number infantry. To thwart his plans, Thomas had 55,000 Federals under arms, though only the Fourth Corps and Twenty-Third Corps under Schofield were in front of Hood at that time. The rest were either in Nashville or on the way there and, knowing this, Hood attempted to get between Thomas and Schofield and give battle to the separated Union forces. On November 28–29, Hood sent Lee's Corps to make a feint against Schofield's front at Columbia while sending Cheatham, Forrest, and Stewart swinging around to his rear at Spring Hill. Just in the nick of time, Stanley, with elements of the Fourth Corps, managed to reach there first and keep open the direct road to Nashville. Hood was still in position to cut off the Northerners from that city, and issued orders to that effect. For some unknown reason, the orders were not executed, and Schofield marched his troops past the Confederates on November 29 under cover of darkness.[13]

Justifiably frustrated, Hood set out in pursuit of Schofield, determined to destroy him before he could reach Nashville. The Fourth Louisiana Battalion was ordered to remain at Columbia to guard the crossing over the Duck River in the event that the Army of Tennessee was forced to retreat.[14] This deployment guarding the pontoon crossing would save the Fourth Louisiana Battalion from the carnage that was soon to befall the main army. Finding Schofield at Franklin, Tennessee, with his army deployed behind breastworks and their backs to the Harpeth River, Hood ordered a frontal assault despite the objections of Forrest, who advised him to flank the Federals from their position by sending a force across the shallow Harpeth southwest of Franklin. At 4:00 P.M., 18,000 Confederates moved forward in dense masses astride the Columbia Pike, with bands playing and flags waving in the breeze. This assault force was larger, and concentrated on a narrower front, than the one Robert E. Lee had thrown against Cemetery Ridge at Gettysburg on July 3, 1863. Soon they would suffer the same fate that occurred to their brethren in Pennsylvania more than a year earlier.

Hood was watching his troops advance across the level, open fields from his location on the side of Winstead Hill, just west of the pike and two miles south of Franklin. Federal rifle and artillery fire soon began to rip huge holes in their ranks, though they closed them rapidly and kept moving forward, screaming the Rebel yell as they did so. Along the pike, Cleburne's and Cheatham's divisions charged side by side, overrunning two brigades from the Fourth Corps that were deployed a half-mile in front of the main Union line. The survivors of the two brigades made a mad dash for the main line, closely pursued by Cheatham's Tennesseans, who went over the Federal works. A vicious counterassault by Colonel Emerson Opdycke's One Hundred Twenty-Fifth Ohio, who were waiting in reserve, aided by brigades of the Twenty-Third Corps, sent them reeling back out of the breastworks. To the east of the pike, Stewart's troops made charge after desperate charge, but were repulsed by a hailstorm of canister and musketry. Soon, the scene of battle grew dark, but the fighting still raged unabated. At 7:00 P.M., in response to a request from Cheatham for reinforcements, Hood sent in Major-General Edward Johnson's Division of Lee's Corps, which had begun to arrive on the battlefield. After five hours of some of the most brutal fighting of the entire war, the firing sputtered to a close. The Confederates that were able staggered and crawled to the rear, while the Federals withdrew and resumed their retreat to Nashville.[15]

Daybreak of the first day of December illuminated a horrid picture of death at Franklin. Gray-clad corpses were strewn among the fields south of the town, while in the ditches that fronted the Federal works, Southerners lay in piles. The butcher's bill for the Confederacy at the Battle of Franklin was 6,000 dead, with 700 more captured. This number was more than three times the number of casualties Lee suffered as a result of Pickett's charge at Gettysburg. A host of Rebel generals were among the killed, most notable of whom was Cleburne, whose loss to the Confederate cause was felt the most, and whose fiancée, Susan Tarleton, who lived in Mobile, Alabama, fainted upon hearing a newsboy cry on a nearby street the tidings of the battle at Franklin and of Cleburne's death. Generals Granbury, Strahl, Gist, and John Adams were also dead, and Brown, Manigault, Cockrell, Quarles, Scott, and John C. Carter were wounded. Cheatham's and Cleburne's divisions existed only in name, and majors and captains were now in charge of brigades, while captains and lieutenants replaced the fifty-five regimental commanders who had fallen. Brigades were now reduced to the size of regiments, while regiments were no more than companies. Union casualties numbered 2,300, of whom 1,000 were taken as prisoners of war. In Hood's vain attempt to prove his worthiness to command in the wake of the loss of Atlanta, he had destroyed the Confederacy's western army.[16]

With his weakened force, Hood staggered to the outskirts of Nashville and entrenched on the hills south of the city, waiting for Thomas to emerge from his fortifications there and give him battle. Two weeks later, on December 15, Thomas came forth and granted Hood's wish, throwing more Federal troops against the Confederate left flank than Hood had in his whole army. In a two-day battle waged in the cold, misting rain, Thomas routed the starved and frozen remnants of the once-proud Army of Tennessee on the afternoon of December 16, putting them to flight on the Granny White and Franklin pikes toward the Tennessee River. Stunned to see the Rebel army disintegrating before his eyes, Stephen Lee pulled his troops back to the Overton Hills, where he held firm until his entire corps could be placed into an orderly retreat. Still, the end had come so quickly that sixteen of Lee's artillery pieces were lost before the artillery horses could be brought up from the rear. When Hood's army crossed the river on Christmas Day of 1864, they numbered less than 20,000; all the others who had followed him on his journey to the Ohio River were now dead or prisoners of war. The road from Nashville was strewn with abandoned wagons, baggage, artillery, and small arms.[17]

With a rear guard commanded by Forrest, the Army of Tennessee struggled through a driving snow that pelted the ragged Confederate column, while ice-covered roads slashed the feet of the mostly barefoot Southerners. Their destination was Tupelo and Corinth, Mississippi. Gibson's Brigade was ordered to march the 1,000 Union prisoners to Corinth, which Private H. J. Lea of the Fourth Louisiana Battalion recalled years after the war: "I shall never forget that march back to Corinth, as the weather was terrible, the ground frozen, and we were poorly clad and many barefooted."[18]

Though Hood misled the government in Richmond into believing the battle at Franklin was a victory, the truth surfaced when Lieutenant-General Richard Taylor visited the army on January 9, 1865, and reported to Richmond the condition of the army. Hood requested to be relieved from command of the army, a request that was quickly granted by Jefferson Davis. The survivors of the Army of Tennessee rejoined General Joseph Johnston in the Carolinas (now restored to command by general-in-chief of all Confederate armies Robert E. Lee) where he was attempting to oppose Sherman's march to the sea.[19] Gibson's Louisiana Brigade was ordered to Mobile, Alabama, to assist in the defense of the Gulf Coast city, encamping in the suburbs of the city near Spring Hill before garrisoning Spanish Fort. At long last, the Fourth Louisiana Battalion bid farewell to the once-glorious Army of Tennessee, and was now nearer their beloved Louisiana and Mississippi. In February, the battalion was consolidated with the Twenty-Fifth Louisiana Infantry due to the appalling losses suffered by both units during the Atlanta Campaign.[20] Though no one could foresee this at the time, with the dawn of 1865 the war had now entered its final stages.

Lieutenant-General Taylor realized that with the Army of Tennessee out of the way, Union attention would turn to Mobile as a target of future operations. Taylor instructed Major-General Dabney Herndon Maury, the commander of the Confederate District of the Gulf, "to make steady and energetic preparations for the anticipated movement." In addition to Gibson's Brigade, Holtzclaw's Brigade and French's Division of the Army of Tennessee were also ordered to Mobile to assist in the defense.[21]

Though plans were being made by Grant and Halleck for an assault on Mobile in early 1865, the city itself was not the primary objective of the campaign. Grant wanted Major-General Edward Richard Sprigg Canby, commander of the Federal Department of the Gulf, to capture

Mobile if he could do so without a protracted siege, then advance on the industrial centers of Selma and Montgomery, Alabama. If Canby encountered much delay in capturing Mobile, Grant advised him to simply bypass the city. Grant also agreed to send 18,000 infantry and 5,000 cavalry from Tennessee to reinforce Canby's 26,000 troops, which were stationed at Barancas, Florida, and on Dauphin Island. After determining that the fortifications around Mobile were likely to withstand a lengthy siege, Canby decided to capture the Confederate works on the eastern shore and then move against Mobile by the Tensas and Alabama rivers, or cut it off from above. Going around Spanish Fort or Fort Blakely was not an option as the Rebel garrisons would be a threat to his supply line between Pensacola, Florida, and Montgomery. Though ordered by Grant to begin his operations in January, inclement weather forced the operations to begin in March, when Major-General Frederick Steele was instructed by Canby to advance on Pollard, Alabama, with the goal of cutting the railroad there and creating the impression of a march on Montgomery. Steele got his expedition underway on March 20, and on March 25 the remainder of Canby's forces began advancing on Spanish Fort and Blakely.[22]

Despite having only 9,000 soldiers to defend Mobile, Maury and Taylor were resolute in their determination to hold the city. Upon discovering Canby's advance on the city, additional measures were adopted to assist in the defense of Mobile. Colonel Thomas H. Taylor, the post commander, issued orders that all able-bodied men were to join local defense units or face expulsion from the city. Brigadier-General St. John Richardson Liddell, commanding Confederate forces on the eastern shore, advised Maury of the Federal landing at Fish River on March 20, and requested reinforcements. In response, Maury dispatched all of his infantry to Liddell, where they were placed south and east of Spanish Fort along D'Olive's Creek. Instead of advancing directly toward Spanish Fort, Canby began outflanking Liddell in the direction of Fort Blakely, prompting Liddell to withdraw most of his troops toward Blakely and to order Brigadier-General Gibson to assume command of Spanish Fort. To defend the fort, Gibson had 500 troops from his Louisiana Brigade, 950 (mostly young boys) from the Alabama Reserves, and 360 artillerist. Inside the redoubts at the fort, Gibson found 12 coehorn mortars, 6 heavy guns, and 14 fieldpieces. After conducting an inspection of the lines, Gibson set his men to work strengthening the existing works. In addition to digging rifle pits, the men built bombproofs behind the works to use as magazines, temporary hospitals, and living quarters. To stall the Union advance and buy additional time for his troops to dig in, Gibson ordered an attack on the Federal pickets on the morning of March 27. Lieutenant-Colonel Robert H. Lindsay led 550 men in the assault, breaking through the enemy skirmish line but falling back in the face of the main Union force forming in line of battle, though this action did serve to delay Canby's advance for several hours.[23]

Later that same day, the Federals began advancing their lines and by nightfall had completed the investment of Spanish Fort, prompting Gibson to send off all his horses and wagons under cover of darkness. Gibson requested cannon and rifle ammunition from Maury, and more entrenching tools from Liddell. He also requested to keep the Alabama Reserves, whom Liddell wanted to move to Fort Blakely, out of concern that the Federals would assault his lines the following morning. Liddell responded by allowing Gibson to retain the Reserves temporarily.[24]

The Union troops occupied the days of March 28 and 29th by advancing their skirmish line and erecting batteries. Though their lines lay from 1,000 to 1,200 yards from the Confederate trenches, at some places the Federal skirmishers had made their way to within 275 yards. Artillery fire from the Rebel guns played havoc on the Union lines during this time, in large part due to the placement of screens that were made from steel plates two feet by three feet square and one-half inch thick that were placed over each embrasure. These screens were secured to the inner faces of the embrasures so that they could be rapidly lowered and raised as the guns were run into battery or recoiled. After visiting Spanish Fort on March 28, Maury strengthened the garrison by ordering a regiment from Holtzclaw's Brigade at Blakely in relief of one of the Alabama Reserve regiments, as well as sending a detachment of sharpshooters armed with Whitworth rifles to Gibson. On March 30, only some sharpshooting and sporadic artillery fire was conducted by the opposing forces. Maury again inspected the fort on that day and, due to Gibson's 320 casualties up to that time, ordered the brigades of Holtzclaw and Colonel Julius A. Andrews to Spanish Fort from Blakely to relieve the remainder of the reserves. Gibson assigned Holtzclaw to command of the two brigades, which now composed his left wing.[25]

In response to the fire of Federal sharpshooters that downed several of his men, on March 31 Gibson requested 400 "Beauregard screens" to protect his own sharpshooters. These screens, designed by General P. G. T. Beauregard at Charleston, were wooden embrasures covered by sandbags. Deciding to take the offensive to protect his troops, Gibson ordered a bombardment of the closest enemy troops, and asked for volunteers to conduct a sortie against this force that night. After nightfall, 17 volunteers rushed the Federal rifle pits that lay almost 150 yards outside the Confederate lines, capturing one captain and 21 blue-clads before driving back the remainder of the Federal force with no loss of their own. Maury formally acknowledged the men for their "brilliant and successful sortie."[26]

As the siege progressed, life inside Spanish Fort became increasingly hazardous and difficult for the defenders. One soldier recalled the hardships of the siege: "Every day was full of incident, and it soon got so that we had no rest day or night. Artillery duels became of daily occurrence, our head logs were constantly knocked down upon us, bruising and crippling us; squads of sharpshooters devoted their especial attention to our port holes or embrasures and poured a steady stream of bullets through them from early morn till dewy eve."[27] In the areas where no communication trenches had been dug, the soldiers could only move about by crawling through the areas. Food was in abundance due to the donations of the citizens of Mobile, but still morale declined with each passing day, prompting Gibson to offer encouragement to the men by making frequent visits to the trenches, exposing himself to the murderous fire of the Federals.[28]

Gibson persistently asked for additional forces to augment the garrison, explaining to Maury that the huge gaps between the soldiers along the Confederate line were larger than those of the Confederate forces during the Atlanta Campaign. Extremely concerned for his men, Gibson attempted to place his troops in the safest positions allowed but still maintain the ability to react to a Union attack. Gibson also established a force of sharpshooters for each artillery piece that were ordered to maintain a steady fire on the Union skirmishers to prevent them from randomly shooting the Rebel artillerists. The fire was so constant that on April 5, the men had expended almost 54,000 rounds in two days, prompting Gibson to encourage the soldiers to scrounge for spent "solid shot, shell, bullets, and missiles" to send to the ordnance department in Mobile for recycling.[29]

With the unrelenting Federal bombardment of Gibson's men showing no decline in intensity, on April 4 it was taken to a new level. The citizens of Mobile could feel the concussions of the shells striking the earth and hear the reports of the heavy artillery in use. One citizen recorded: "This evening the firing is terrific, not a moment elapsing between the booming of heavy artillery."[30] Though it lasted for only two hours, Gibson and his artillery officers estimated that the Federals employed thirty to forty heavy guns and at least a dozen mortars in the bombardment. During the last days of the siege of Spanish Fort, the Federals increased their activities on Gibson's left flank, where the marshy, heavily wooded ground made it virtually impossible to erect earthworks for protection. The Union troops also began to move launches to the area so that they could operate on Bay Minette and the Apalachee River. A battery at Fort Blakely, aided by the Confederate gunboats *Nashville* and *Morgan*, attempted to relieve the pressure on Gibson's left, but the increasing number of Union guns drove the supports back. The *Nashville* was partially disabled and the other supports kept from the area during daylight hours

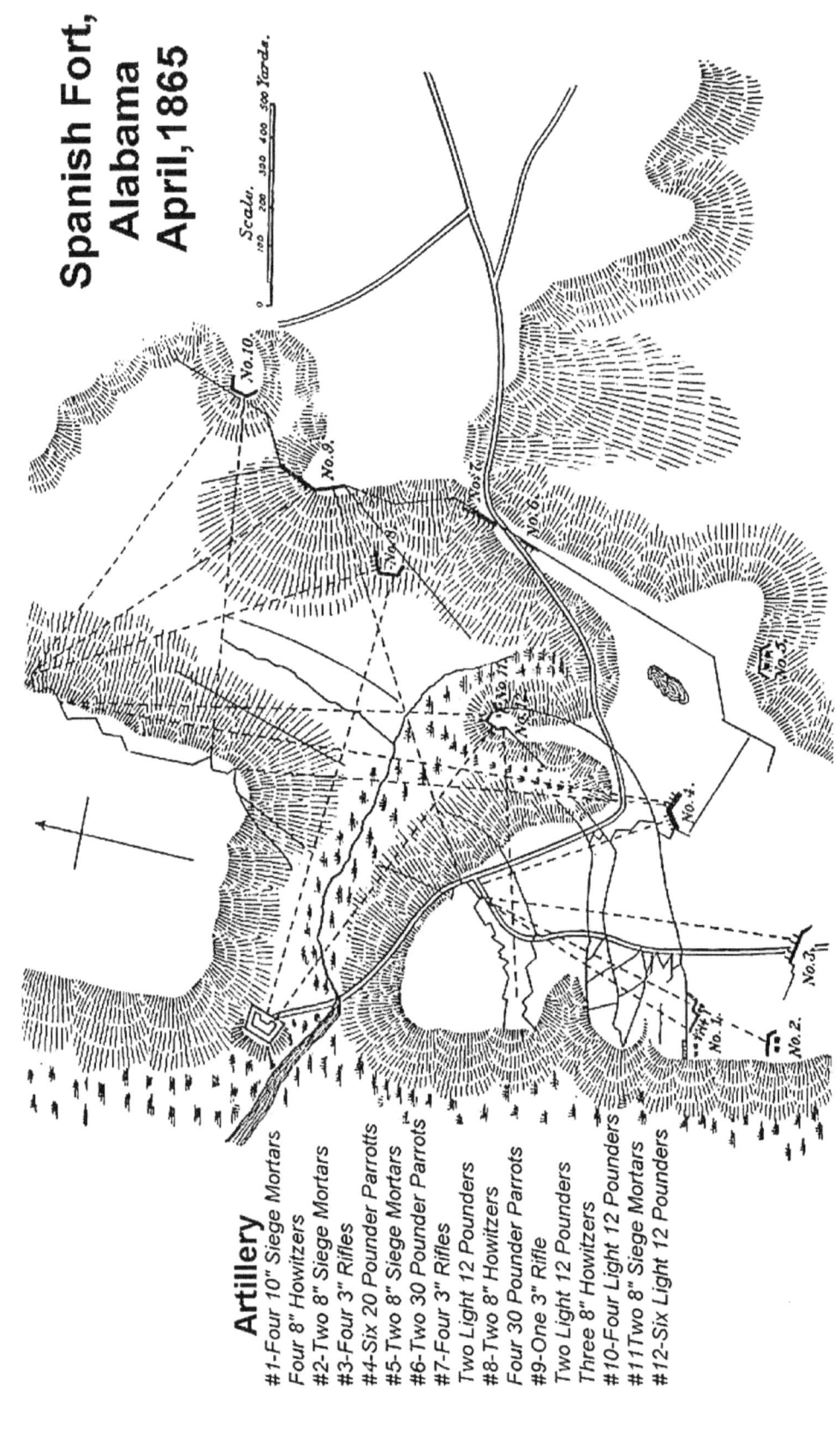

by the accurate fire from the Northern Parrott guns. Gibson had planned an attack on the Union troops opposite his left but canceled the operation when he was unable to enlist a gunboat to enfilade the enemy flank. To protect against a surprise attack, Gibson deployed extra manpower and two guns on his extreme left, until he was finally able to obtain the assistance of several Confederate navy picket boats to help watch his flank.[31]

By April 7, the Federals had managed to dig almost up to the main Rebel works at Spanish Fort and emplaced so much heavy artillery and mortars around the fort that the Confederate guns could only sporadically reply to the bombardment. Gibson responded by having his exhausted forces throw up additional bombproofs and traverses, as well as requesting engineer troops and hand grenades from Maury. A shortage of ammunition prompted Gibson to order his troops in the main line to stop all rifle fire, the exception being the sharpshooters in the advanced rifle pits. Gibson instructed his officers to ensure that the advanced pits were equipped with the Beauregard screens and were safe from an unexpected assault. Maury responded by sending Gibson several howitzers, hand grenades, and additional laborers to work on the fortifications on the night of April 7–8. Heavy activity by the Federals on the morning of April 8 prompted Gibson to order his skirmishers to maintain a steady fire on the Union work parties, and to order his officers to be vigilant for a surprise assault. Later that afternoon, he ordered the troops in Fort McDermott to open artillery fire on the enemy work party in their front, prompting the Federals to deliver a scorching fire on the fort that soon silenced the Confederate guns after disabling one piece and destroying an ammunition chest. Gibson then decided to determine the Union intentions by having his artillery open upon the enemy positions at sunset.[32] Gibson thought that "the moment had at length arrived when I could no longer hold the position without imminent risk of losing the garrison."[33]

Unknown to Gibson, Canby had also planned a bombardment that was to commence at sunset, having placed 53 siege guns in position and ordered his subordinates to be prepared to exploit any break in the Confederate defenses. Gibson's artillerists opened first at 5:30 P.M., but managed to throw only a few rounds before Canby's gunners silenced them with their superior weapons. The fire soon became so intense that the garrison was no longer safe even in their bombproofs, with the 15-inch mortars penetrating six feet of packed earth before exploding. One member of the garrison recalled that the troops watched these huge shells dropping into the works, but "we had to stand and take it. It was though the mouth of the pit had yawned and the uproar of the damned was about us. And it was not taking away from this infernal picture to see men, as I did, hopping about, raving distracted mad, the blood bursting from eyes and ears and mouth, driven stark crazy by concussion or some other cause."[34]

As darkness enveloped the scene, the Eighth Iowa Infantry advanced against the works on Gibson's left, driving the Texans of Andrews's Brigade from their position before capturing several hundred Rebels and overrunning 300 yards of entrenchments. The garrison's provost-guard launched a counterattack that arrested the Federal advance, forcing the Northern troops to throw up light trenches and await further developments. With the report of Holtzclaw that the troops under his command were not strong enough in number to push the enemy back, Gibson ordered the abandonment of the works to save the garrison from capture. Gibson ordered his old brigade to withdraw from the right flank, then posted some of the men to watch his left while the remainder were deployed to cover the retreat. Once the gunners had spiked their guns to prevent usage by the enemy, Gibson and the entire garrison, including the sick and wounded, assembled on the beach, where Gibson had the men remove their shoes and carry their weapons on their side away from the enemy. The garrison then filed silently along a wooden treadway that led from the rear of Spanish Fort across the marsh to a point on the Apalachee River opposite Battery Huger. Aided by the cover of darkness, the Rebels reached the end of the wooden planks without discovery by the Federals, where steamers transported the garrison from Battery Huger to Fort Blakely, though several of the men traveled across the marsh directly to the fort.[35] The citizens of Mobile were shocked by the fall of Spanish Fort, with one recording that "Still I had to believe the evidence of my own eyes, for our soldiers were passing by in squads, from an early hour, dirty, wet and completely worn out."[36]

Gibson's reported losses during the siege of Spanish Fort were heavy, with 73 killed, 350 wounded, and 6 missing. In the final bombardment and assault on his position, he lost 20 killed, 45 wounded, and 250 missing. On April 8 as many as 325 soldiers were possibly captured by Federal forces. Union losses were tallied at 52 killed, 575 wounded, and 30 missing.[37] Lieutenant-General Taylor praised the conduct of the garrison during the siege: "Gibson's stubborn defense and skillful retreat make this one of the best achievements of the war."[38] Also generous in praise was Maury: "It is not too much to say that no position was ever held by Confederate troops with greater hardihood and tenacity, nor evacuated more skillfully after hope of further defense was gone."[39] Gibson also expressed his admiration for the men of his command, stating that "If any credit shall attach to the defense of Spanish Fort, it belongs to the heroes whose sleep shall no more be disturbed by the cannon's roar. For two weeks, the less than 3,000-man garrison had held at bay almost 24,000 Union soldiers, qualifying it as one of the most admirable events of the whole war."[40]

While Canby's Federals lay siege to Spanish Fort, Liddell had instructed his troops to prepare the lines at Fort Blakely for an attack by the Northerners. Initially, Liddell's command consisted of Holtzclaw's Brigade, a small artillery force, and three brigades of Cockrell's Division, formerly French's. As the siege of Spanish Fort dragged on, Liddell had detached Holtclaw's Brigade and the brigade of Andrews to aid General Gibson. In exchange, he received the brigade of Alabama Reserve Troops. The First Mississippi Light Artillery reported to Liddell on April 1, swelling his ranks to 2,700 effectives. The position at Fort Blakely consisted of nine lunettes connected by rifle pits, and encompassed almost 3,000 yards, with advanced rifle pits, abatis, and land mines protecting the ground in front of the works. Liddell placed Sears's Mississippi Brigade, commanded by Colonel Thomas N. Adaire, on the left, Cockrell's Brigade, commanded by Colonel James McCown, in the center, and the Alabama Reserve troops on the right. Even with these dispositions, at some points, there were gaps of ten paces or more between the soldiers.[41]

The Federals commanded by Major-General Frederick Steele did not reach the vicinity of Fort Blakely until the morning of April 1, when the cavalrymen of his command encountered an outpost of Liddell's on the Stockton Road, about four miles to the north. The outpost was manned by 100 soldiers of the Forty-Sixth Mississippi Infantry commanded by Captain J. B. Hart. The Rebels fell back slowly in the face of the Federal troopers, until a charge with sabers drawn by the mounted troops drove the Confederates from their position, resulting in the capture of three officers and seventy-one enlisted men. The pursuing Federals chased the fleeing Mississippians almost to the main trenches at Blakely before being stopped cold by the Missourians of McCown, who were deployed in a ravine across the road. Determining that Steele would attempt to storm his lines during the day, Liddell ordered troops from the Missouri brigade posted in the advanced skirmish pits in his front, then instructed the Reserves to do likewise. The preparations were for naught, as Steele seems to have contented himself with dispersing Liddell's Stockton Road outpost.[42]

On the morning of April 2, the Confederate skirmishers on the Stockton Road attempted to drive in the Federal cavalry pickets. Brigadier-General John Parker Hawkins, commander of the First Division of United States Colored Troops, quickly formed his men into line of battle and advanced toward the sounds of firing, where through sheer weight of numbers his troops forced the Confederates back toward their main line. The Federals followed until they came within a half mile of the advanced rifle pits and artillery, where they began to entrench. Soon,

Steele's other division of white soldiers arrived and began to entrench to the left of Hawkin's troops. Fearing an attack was imminent, Liddell requested light artillery and mortars from Maury for use on his right flank, as well as requesting gunboat support to bombard the right flank of the Union soldiers. The ironclad *Huntsville* was near Liddell's position, but was unable to elevate her guns enough to fire over the bluff. In any event, the attack that Liddell was in fear of did not materialize.[43]

The investment of Fort Blakely was completed on April 3 with the addition of two divisions from the troops that were previously in front of Spanish Fort. From April 3 through April 8, the Federals occupied their time by advancing siege approaches to the fort and emplacing batteries, though Liddell's men maintained a steady fire from their batteries and skirmish pits to slow down the work. The ironclads *Huntsville* and *Nashville*, as well as the gunboat *Morgan*, aided in the defense of Fort Blakely by throwing the weight of their guns into the contest. Liddell's artillery fire was enhanced by the addition of wooden screens to protect the gunners, and the fact that the Federals at first had only a few light artillery pieces. In order to maintain an accurate rifle and artillery fire even after sundown, the Confederates used fireballs sent up by coehorn mortars to illuminate the area in front of their works. Though in intensity the siege of Fort Blakely did not equal the siege at Spanish Fort, both sides in the contest did conduct operations against each other's advanced rifle pits, although these actions produced no lasting success for either force. One such example occurred on the morning of April 7, when Union troops attacked the rifle pits held by the boy-soldiers of the Alabama Reserves, though the young Rebels were able to drive the attackers back. In retaliation, Liddell ordered a sortie against the Federals that began with a midnight bombardment of the Union lines, followed by a charge from the Second Alabama Reserves on the Federal pickets. When the Reserves had closed to within 40 yards of the pits, they were met with a scorching musketry fire that threw them back with a loss of 15 killed and 22 wounded.[44]

In conjunction with the bombardment of Spanish Fort on April 8, a heavy artillery fire was also directed at Fort Blakely. This was followed in the afternoon by a masked battery of heavy Parrott rifled guns that opened on the Confederate ships that were lying in the nearby Tensas River. The *Morgan* received several hits from the battery, the most serious located near the waterline, but the *Nashville* was unscathed in the attack, though both ships were forced to withdraw when they ran out of ammunition. To help cover the evacuation of Spanish Fort on April 8, Liddell ordered his artillerists and riflemen to fire on the Union positions. Following the fall of the fort, Canby began shifting his forces toward Fort Blakely and ordered Steele to make preparations for an assault on the position. The attack was launched at 5:30 P.M. when the four Union divisions that had occupied the trenches since April 3 began a simultaneous advance, rushing forward and sending Liddell's skirmishers fleeing toward the main Confederate line before carrying the entire line of entrenchments. Though 3,700 Confederates became prisoners of war, including generals Liddell, Thomas, and Cockrell, almost 200 men were able to escape to the safety of the naval squadron by swimming or floating on driftwood. Canby's losses were totaled at 105 killed and 466 wounded, though the entire Federal loss during the siege of Fort Blakely was 116 killed, 655 wounded, and 4 missing.[45]

With the fall of the second of Mobile's defensive forts, only Battery Huger and Battery Tracy prevented Canby from moving through the rivers to capture Mobile. Battery Huger was held by 200 troops of Companies B and K of the Twenty-Second Louisiana Infantry, and Company C of the First Mississippi Light Artillery, all under the command of Major Washington Marks. At Battery Tracy, 120 soldiers from Companies G, H, and I of the Twenty-Second Louisiana Infantry, commanded by Captain Ambrose A. Plattsmier, manned the five guns of the fort. Both batteries had fired their guns in support of Spanish Fort in the early days of the siege, but a severe shortage of ammunition led Maury to instruct the men to discontinue firing throughout the remainder. From March 31 to April 8, the two forts endured daily shelling from the Union Parrott gun battery located on Bay Minette, as well as the fire from the Federal naval fleet in Mobile Bay.[46] After the evacuation of Spanish Fort, Colonel Isaac W. Patton of the Twenty-Second Louisiana took his four companies that had been part of the garrison at the fort and assumed command of both Tracy and Huger. Maury instructed Patton to "Open all your guns upon the enemy, keep up an active fire, and hold your position until you receive orders to retire."[47] The Louisianans maintained an accurate, heavy fire against the Federal land batteries from April 9 through April 11, attempting to fire every round they had before abandoning the works. On the night of April 11, Maury dispatched a staff officer to Patton with orders to retire, which they accomplished with the aid of a steamer after spiking the guns.[48]

With the loss of his defensive positions, Maury began the evacuation of Mobile on the morning of April 10. Alarm bells broke the morning stillness, the signal for the local defense troops to turn out to assist with the preparations. The local troops and the regulars began loading ordnance and commissary stores aboard 18 steamers Maury had standing by at the city, while some of the supplies were loaded aboard the few remaining railroad cars in Mobile. A large portion of the Confederate troops departed that day enroute to Enterprise, Alabama, by way of Meridian, Mississippi, where they were to journey on to the Carolinas to join General Joseph E. Johnston's Confederate forces. Maury did keep a small infantry and cavalry force in the city to act as a rear guard. The sick and wounded soldiers who were too ill to be moved were placed in the Mobile City Hospital and the Marine Hospital, both under the care of the Sisters of Charity. The evacuation continued into April 11, when the few remaining officers and enlisted men disabled the remaining artillery and ammunition that could not be taken out of the city. Battery commanders were ordered to dump their ammunition into the water of the moats, and apply the torch to the gun carriages and bombproofs.[49]

Flag Officer Ebenezer Farrand of the Confederate naval squadron was also making preparations for the evacuation of Mobile. Due to the weak engines of the floating batteries *Tuscaloosa* and *Huntsville* that prevented them from steaming upriver against the current, Farrand ordered them sank in the main channel of the Mobile River, leaving him with only the gunboats *Nashville*, *Baltic*, and *Morgan*, and the steamers *Southern Republic* and *Black Diamond*. Accompanying the fleet were the former blockade runners *Heroine*, *Mary*, *Virgin*, and *Red Gauntlet*. Farrand's plan to ascend the Alabama River to Selma, Alabama, was dashed when he discovered that Union forces had captured that town and its naval station, prompting him to order his fleet up the Tombigbee River, where his men placed torpedoes near its junction with the Alabama River to prevent pursuit by enemy vessels.[50]

With evacuation of Mobile now complete, Maury left the city on April 12 with the rear guard of 300 Louisiana troops commanded by Lieutenant-Colonel Robert H. Lindsay, leaving General Gibson with the Twelfth Mississippi Cavalry and a small section of artillery to complete the destruction of government property that was left behind. Gibson and his force left the city at 11:00 a.m., after torching a mound of cotton bales piled up north of the city to prevent Union capture. Canby then ordered two divisions under Major-General Gordon Granger to occupy the city. A regiment from Granger's force moved into Mobile during the afternoon and raised the Stars and Stripes over the customshouse. Later, to the tune of the "Star Spangled Banner," a brigade moved in also and occupied the former Confederate works. Mobile was now the last in a long line of major Southern cities to fall to the Federals during the Civil War.[51]

Shortly after the fall of Mobile, some of Gibson's decimated command were reorganized due to the horrific losses incurred in defending the city. The Fourth Louisiana Battalion, now a battalion in name only, ceased to exist under the name it had proudly worn since the heady days of 1861, when the dream of Southern independence had shown brightest. A new regiment was formed bearing the name of the Pelican Regiment, in honor of the residence of her Louisiana members. Companies A, B, and D of the Fourth Louisiana Battalion became Company F in the new unit, while Companies C, E, and F became Company G.[52]

On the day that Fort Blakely fell, General Robert E. Lee surrendered the Army of Northern Virginia to Ulysses S. Grant at Appomattox, Virginia. On April 14, actor John Wilkes Booth crept into a box at Ford's Theatre in Washington and assassinated President Abraham Lincoln, prompting the ascension to the presidency of Vice-President Andrew Johnson. This was followed on April 26 by General Joseph E. Johnston's surrender of his Confederate forces to William T. Sherman at Greensboro, North Carolina, prompting Lieutenant-General Richard Taylor to order the halt of his forces then enroute to the Carolinas. On May 8, Taylor surrendered his command to Major-General Canby at Citronelle, Alabama. The men under his command were paroled at Meridian on May 10, 1865, and Ensign Austin W. Smith gave this account of their final days under arms: "On reaching a point about twenty miles east of Meridian we received orders to return for the purpose of surrender. On our arrival we were marched out on the commons, stacked our flags and arms and accouterments, and marched back to camp. The next day we marched in a body to the office, where we were given paroles, received transportation to our homes, and, one by one, broke ranks."[53]

As suddenly as it had erupted, the American Civil War had now sputtered to a conclusion, though its cost of over 600,000 American lives was staggering. On May 8, Randall L. Gibson delivered this farewell address to his Louisiana brigade before breaking camp for the final time:

FELLOW-SOLDIERS:

For more than four years we have shared together the fortunes of war. Throughout all the scenes of this eventful revolution you have been fully tried, and now retire with the consciousness of having achieved a character for discipline, for valor, and for unselfish patriotism of which you may be justly proud. There is nothing in your career to look back upon with regret. You have always been in front of the enemy; you have never feasted in soft places at the rear, nor fought your battles at comfortable firesides. Your banners are garlanded with the emblems of every soldierly virtue. More than twenty battle-fields have seen them unfurled. They were never lowered save over the bier of a comrade. Forget not the good and true men who have fallen. No sculptured marble may perpetuate the memory of their services, but you will wear their names ever green in your hearts, and they will be enshrined forever in the affections of the Southern people, in whose cause they fell.

Comrades, henceforth other duties will devolve upon you. Adversities can only strengthen the ties that bind you to your country and increase the obligations you owe to her interests and her honor. As soldiers, you have been among the bravest and most steadfast, and as citizens, be law abiding, peaceable, and industrious. You have not surrendered and will never surrender your self-respect and love of country. You separate not as friends, but brethren whom common hopes, mutual trials, and equal disasters have made kinsmen. Hereafter you shall recount to your children, with conscious pride, the story of these rugged days, and you will always greet a comrade of the old brigade with open arms. Having commanded a company and regiment in the brigade, I have known many of you from the very beginning of the struggle, have been with you through all its varied fortunes, and offer to each one of you a grateful and affectionate farewell. May God bless you.

R. L. GIBSON,
Brigadier-General, Commanding[54]

The remaining members of the Fourth Louisiana Battalion were surrendered by General Taylor under the name of the Pelican Regiment. For the survivors of the battalion whom had endured the carnage of the most brutal war in American history, the saga had now drawn to a close. The most difficult phase of the war was now at hand; the return as citizens to a land laid waste by four years of war. One original member of the Fourth Louisiana Battalion whom would not be returning to his war-ravaged home was Captain Henry Wirz, the commandant of Andersonville. With the Northern populace clamoring for retribution for the 13,000 deaths that occurred at the notorious prisoner-of-war camp from February of 1864 through its liberation in May of 1865, Wirz became the first person in American history to be put on trial for war-crimes. Charged with murder and conspiracy to destroy the lives of large numbers of Union prisoners, Wirz was tried before a military commission and found guilty of the charges brought against him. He was hanged on the grounds of the Old Capitol Prison in Washington, D.C., on November 10, 1865.

Sergeant-Major Robert W. Wells of the Fourth Louisiana Battalion penned the below correspondence soon after the close of the war to his sister in Virginia. In it, he describes his return to civilian life in Natchez, Mississippi.

Main St., Natchez, Miss
December 10, 1865

My Own Darling Sister,

I will not attempt to apologize to you for not complying with my promise to write to you immediately upon my arrival at this place. I will simply state my reasons for not doing so. In the first place, until a short time ago I have not been settled and would not write to you thinking it would be most satisfactory to hear from me after I have become engaged. In the next place I did not know where a letter would reach you, and you know that my letters are so precious that it would never do for one of them to be lost, but know I am engaged (what a candid confession for a young man to make) and know exactly where to address you so I will try to interest you in a few scratches of my pen.

I received your most welcome and interesting letter this morn and I assure you, dear May, that it gave me the greatest pleasure to hear from you and my darling Bess and all of my sweet little cousins at home. I received a letter from you some time since written from "Lapnarife," but did not answer it for the aforesaid reasons. Oh! how much I have missed each of you, my dear Sisters, and how badly I want to see you, not withstanding I am surrounded by my dear friends here, friends as warm and true to ever the light of Heaven shine upon. Yet, dear May, there is no love like a sisters love, no one can take her place in our hearts. I long to be with you again and live over some of the happy, happy days of yore! How I would love to spend the eve with all of you at Mr. Capin's. What a heap I would have to tell you of my treats and pleasures since I last saw you. I have had some of the former and many of the latter.

I will refer you to my letters to dear McK., giving full details of my trip to Winchester to this place. I made quite a protracted stay in Maryland, much more so than I had expected when I left home. I had many dear friends to visit over there that I could not get through any sooner, and besides, the young ladies were so attractive and offered me so many inducements to remain that I would have been there until now had I consulted my own pleasure. I was at no expense while there. My young lady friends supplied me with linen handkerchiefs, collars, neckties, socks, etc., while the older members of society furnished me with pocket money and paid my traveling expenses. What more did I want, and May, besides this, I think the gay society over there did a great deal towards healing the wounds so recently inflicted in my heart, but all things, according to the Scriptures, have end, just so did my pleasures in Maryland.

Stern duty compelled me to sever those sweet ties since I have been here. I have had just one romp of pleasure. My friends all gave me a warm reception and a most hearty welcome back to the city. May, if you could only see how kind and devoted they are all to me, you would not wonder at my being here at Natchez. The young ladies of the adjoining neighbors gave me a lively party in honor of my safe return from the war. I tell you I felt extremely large upon the occasion. It was given at Mrs. Vaughan's and a nicer time I never had. Some lady friends invited the company from the country, and I was commissioned to invite my friends from the city. How I did wish that Bess and yourself could have been present. I know you would have enjoyed yourselves hugely.

Tell my dear Bess that if she is not married in a year, you know that I am coming to Virginia for her and make her come to my home in the South. Take good care of her, May, and don't let her act imprudently. I am so sorry to hear that both of you have been unwell. I hope in this you have recovered and one of you are enjoying good health, and am also sorry to hear that Sister has been sick. I wrote to her about two weeks since and hope that she has received my letter. I think she ought to know better than to think that I would slight her in any way. You know me well enough to know that I would not do such a thing for anything in the world. I love all of my darling sisters too much to do anything to hurt their feelings.

I have written to McK twice since I arrived here, not because I love him more than I do either of you, but because I know that he will have opportunities of forwarding my letters to you, thus making one of my letters in the place of three or four. I have five letters to write but each of you have only one. I have no time but at night to write my letters, so I think under the circumstances you ought not to expect me to be so punctual. I intend to write to one of you every week and oftener if I have the time, and besides all this, I have my sweethearts to write to and you know that consumes some time.

I hope the Capt. will succeed in getting a comfortable situation, for if anyone deserves to be happy, it is he, for I think he is one of the best men I ever knew. I don't expect that I shall ever forget his kindness and devotion to me during my most pleasant visit with his happy home last summer. May, I shall always look back to that visit as one of the happiest of my life. How often do I think of the happy, happy times spent with my sweet friends at "Cabin Home," "Mountain Home" and "Moreland," and with my dear, dear friends, our cousins at Front Royal, our little group, to make my pleasure during the summer, although it seems to me but a fancy dream, and of Mrs. Capon. How much I enjoyed it, give my best love to my cousins there, and kiss each of them a dozen times for me, and tell them how much I want to see them.

Now, dear May, I must tell you what I am doing for myself and how I am passing off my time. On the 15th of November last, I entered the House of N. Frank as Salesman in the fancy dry goods department, at a salary of $70.00 per month. A few days afterwards, the proprietor came to me and gave me a very handsome compliment, viz that he was very much pleased with the manner in which I had conducted myself, and that he was satisfied that I was working to his interest, and in consequence he had ordered the workkeeper to allow me $100.00 for that month and to increase my salary on the 1st of the next, and so you can see what I am doing and what I intend to do. I am determined to make a fortune and to save it, possess "Metallic Charms," I will if my health is spared to me for a few years longer. I will show to some of my little friends that what we consider misfortunes at the time are nothing more than blessings in disguise. I think my little "life" scrape last summer will prove beneficial to me, for I am determined now to go to work with more energy than ever and show to all of you that I can be a man.

I have a very pleasant boarding house, a nice fellow for a roommate and altogether I have a very good time. My Landlady gave quite a nice little party a few nights since and gave me the privilege of inviting all my young friends, we had a delightful time. I expect to eat my Christmas dinner at Mrs. Vaughan's. I have had several invitations to dine out upon that occasion but prefer being at Mrs. Vaughn's. She is just as good and noble as ever, had a great many questions to ask of each of you, and says she will enjoy the photographs so much she has both of them in her album and thinks them quite pretty. I will not tell you the many compliments I've heard said them for fear of exciting your vanity. Suffice it to say both of them have been very much admired by many of my friends.

I have just received a letter from McK dated November 16th in which he says he has just returned from dear old Fauquier. I almost envy him his visits to the Cobbler neighborhood.

Now, dear May, as I have filled two sheets I must close. Please excuse the many glaring imperfectives of this letter. Give my best love to my cousins and also the Armstrongs. Tell cousin Phebe I will write to her in a few days. Love to all and F. R. and Fauquier when you see them. Kiss dear Bess for me and make her write to me and you write very soon, and may Heaven bless you in ever the prayer of your devoted Brother.

Rob[55]

MOBILE, ALA., CAMPAIGN ORDER OF BATTLE
March 17–April 12, 1865

Union Forces: Department of the Gulf
Major-General Edward Richard Sprigg Canby

Engineer Brigade
Brigadier-General Joseph Bailey
96th United States Colored Troops: Colonel John C. Cobb

97th United States Colored Troops: Colonel George D. Robinson
1st Company Pontoniers: Captain John J. Smith

Siege Train
Brigadier-General James Totten
1st Indiana Heavy Artillery: Colonel Benjamin F. Hays
New York Light Artillery — 18th Battery: Captain Albert G. Mack

Thirteenth Corps
Major-General Gordon Granger

Mortar Batteries
6th Michigan Heavy Artillery — Co. A: Captain Seldon F. Craig
6th Michigan Heavy Artillery — Co. K: Lieutenant Charles W. Wood

First Division
Brigadier-General James Clifford Veatch

First Brigade
Brigadier-General James Richard Slack
99th Illinois Infantry — 5 Cos: Lt. Colonel Asa C. Matthews
47th Indiana Infantry: Lt. Colonel John A. McLaughlin
21st Iowa Infantry: Lt. Colonel Salue G. Van Anda
29th Wisconsin Infantry: Lt. Colonel Bradford Hancock

Second Brigade
Brigadier-General Elias Smith Dennis
8th Illinois Infantry: Colonel Josiah A. Sheetz
11th Illinois Infantry: Colonel James H. Coates
46th Illinois Infantry: Colonel Benjamin Dornblaser

Third Brigade
Lt. Colonel William B. Kinsey
29th Illinois Infantry: Lt. Colonel John A. Callicott
30th Missouri Infantry — 4 Cos: Lt. Colonel William T. Wilkinson
161st New York Infantry: Major Willis E. Craig
23rd Wisconsin Infantry: Major Joseph E. Greene

Artillery
Captain George W. Fox
Massachusetts Light Artillery — 4th Battery: Lieutenant George W. Taylor
Massachusetts Light Artillery — 7th battery: Captain Newman W. Storer

Second Division
Brigadier-General Christopher Columbus Andrews

First Brigade
Colonel Henry Bertram
94th Illinois Infantry: Colonel John McNulta
19th Iowa Infantry: Lt. Colonel John Bruce
23rd Iowa Infantry: Colonel Samuel L. Glasgow
20th Wisconsin Infantry: Lt. Colonel Henry A. Starr
1st Missouri Light Artillery-Battery F: Captain Joseph Foust

Second Brigade
Colonel William T. Spicely
76th Illinois Infantry: Colonel Samuel T. Busey
97th Illinois Infantry: Lt. Colonel Victor Vifquain
24th Indiana Infantry: Lt. Colonel Francis A. Sears
69th Indiana Infantry — 4 Cos: Lt. Colonel Oran Perry

Third Brigade
Colonel Frederick W. Moore
37th Illinois Infantry: Colonel Charles Black

Chapter 7 — The Storm Breaks

20th Iowa Infantry: Lt. Colonel Joseph B. Leake
34th Iowa Infantry: Colonel George W. Clark
83rd Ohio Infantry: Lt. Colonel William H. Baldwin
114th Ohio Infantry: Colonel John H. Kelly

Artillery
Connecticut Light Artillery — 2nd Battery: Captain Walter S. Hotchkiss
Massachusetts Light Artillery — 15th Battery: Lieutenant Albert Rowse

Third Division
Brigadier-General William Plummer Benton

First Brigade
Colonel David P. Grier
28th Illinois Infantry: Lt. Colonel Richard Ritter
77th Illinois Infantry: Lt. Colonel John B. Reid
96th Ohio Infantry — 5 Cos: Lt. Colonel Albert H. Brown
35th Wisconsin Infantry: Colonel Henry Orff

Second Brigade
Colonel Henry M. Day
91st Illinois Infantry: Lt. Colonel George A. Day
50th Indiana Infantry — 5 Cos: Lt. Colonel Samuel T. Wells
29th Iowa Infantry: Colonel Thomas H. Benton, Jr.
7th Vermont Infantry: Colonel William C. Holbrook

Third Brigade
Colonel Conrad Krez
33rd Iowa Infantry: Colonel Cyrus H. Mackey
77th Ohio Infantry: Lt. Colonel William E. Stevens
27th Wisconsin Infantry: Captain Charles H. Cunningham
28th Wisconsin Infantry: Lt. Colonel Edmund B. Gray

Artillery
New York Light Artillery — 21st Battery: Captain James Barnes
New York Light Artillery — 26th Battery: Lieutenant Adam Beattie

Sixteenth Corps
Major-General Andrew Jackson Smith

Pontoniers
114th Illinois Infantry: Major John M. Johnson

First Division
Brigadier-General John McArthur

First Brigade
Colonel William L. McMillen
33rd Illinois Infantry: Colonel Charles E. Lippincott
26th Indiana Infantry: Colonel John G. Clark
93rd Indiana Infantry: Colonel DeWitt C. Thomas
10th Minnesota Infantry: Lt. Colonel Samuel P. Jennison
72nd Ohio Infantry: Lt. Colonel Charles G. Eaton
95th Ohio Infantry: Lt. Colonel Jefferson Brumback

Second Brigade
Colonel Lucius F. Hubbard
47th Illinois Infantry: Colonel David W. Magee
5th Minnesota Infantry: Lt. Colonel William B. Gere
9th Minnesota Infantry: Colonel Josiah F. Marsh
11th Missouri Infantry: Major Modesta J. Green
8th Wisconsin Infantry: Lt. Colonel William B. Britton

Third Brigade
Colonel William R. Marshall
12th Iowa Infantry: Major Samuel G. Knee
35th Iowa Infantry: Lt. Colonel William B. Keeler
7th Minnesota Infantry: Lt. Colonel George Bradley
33rd Missouri Infantry: Lt. Colonel William H. Heath

Artillery
Indiana Light Artillery — 3rd Battery: Captain Thomas J. Ginn
Iowa Light Artillery — 2nd Battery: Captain Joseph R. Reed

Second Division
Brigadier-General Kenner Garrard

First Brigade
Colonel John I. Rinaker
119th Illinois Infantry: Colonel Thomas J. Kinney
122nd Illinois Infantry: Lt. Colonel James F. Drish
89th Indiana Infantry: Lt. Colonel Hervey Craven
21st Missouri Infantry: Captain Charles W. Tracy

Second Brigade
Brigadier-General James Isham Gilbert
117th Illinois Infantry: Colonel Risdon M. Moore
27th Iowa Infantry: Major George W. Howard
32nd Iowa Infantry: Lt. Colonel Gustavus A. Eberhart
10th Kansas Infantry — 4 Cos: Lt. Colonel Charles S. Hills
6th Minnesota Infantry: Lt. Colonel Hiram P. Grant

Third Brigade
Colonel Charles L. Harris
58th Illinois Infantry — 4 Cos: Captain John Murphy
52nd Indiana Infantry: Lt. Colonel Zalmon S. Main
34th New Jersey Infantry: Colonel William Hudson Lawrence
178th New York Infantry: Lt. Colonel John B. Gandolfo
11th Wisconsin Infantry: Major Jesse S. Miller

Third Division
Brigadier-General Eugene Asa Carr

First Brigade
Colonel Jonathan B. Moore
72nd Illinois Infantry: Lt. Colonel Joseph Stockton
95th Illinois Infantry: Colonel Leander Blanden
44th Missouri Infantry: Captain Frank G. Hopkins
33rd Wisconsin Infantry: Lt. Colonel Horatio H. Virgin

Second Brigade
Colonel Lyman M. Ward
40th Missouri Infantry: Colonel Samuel A. Holmes
49th Missouri Infantry: Colonel David P. Dyer
14th Wisconsin Infantry: Major Eddt F. Ferris

Third Brigade
Colonel James L. Geddes
81st Illinois Infantry: Lt. Colonel Andrew W. Rogers
108th Illinois Infantry: Colonel Charles Turner
124th Illinois Infantry: Brevet Colonel John H. Howe
8th Iowa Infantry: Lt. Colonel William B. Bell

Artillery Brigade
Captain John W. Lowell
Illinois Light Artillery — Cogswell's Battery: Lieutenant William R. Elting

Chapter 7 — The Storm Breaks

2nd Illinois Light Artillery — Battery G: Lieutenant Perry Wilch
Indiana Light Artillery — 1st Battery: Captain Lawrence Jacoby
Indiana Light Artillery — 14th Battery: Captain Francis W. Morse
Ohio Light Artillery — 17th Battery: Captain Charles S. Rice

Column from Pensacola Bay, Florida
Major-General Frederick Steele

First Division
Brigadier-General John Parker Hawkins

First Brigade
Brigadier-General William Anderson Pile
73rd United States Colored Troops: Lt. Colonel Henry C. Merriam
82nd United States Colored Troops: Colonel Ladislas L. Zulavsky
86th United States Colored Troops: Lt. Colonel George E. Yarrington

Second Brigade
Colonel Hiram Scofield
47th United States Colored Troops: Lt. Colonel Ferdinand E. Peebles
50th United States Colored Troops: Colonel Charles A. Gilchrist
51st United States Colored Troops: Colonel A. Watson Webber

Third Brigade
Colonel Charles W. Drew
48th United States Colored Troops: Colonel Frederick M. Crandal
68th United States Colored Troops: Colonel J. Blackburn Jones
76th United States Colored Troops: Major William E. Nye

Cavalry
Lucas's Division
Brigadier-General Thomas John Lucas

First Brigade
Colonel Morgan H. Chrysler
1st Louisiana Cavalry: Lt. Colonel Algernon S. Badger
31st Massachusetts Mounted Infantry: Lt. Colonel Edward P. Nettleton
2nd New York Veteran Cavalry: Lt. Colonel Asa L. Gurney

Second Brigade
Lt. Colonel Andrew B. Spurling
1st Florida Cavalry: Captain Francis Lyons
2nd Illinois Cavalry: Major Franklin Moore
2nd Maine Cavalry: Major Charles A. Miller

Artillery
Massachusetts Light Artillery — 2nd Battery: Captain William Marland

First Division
Brigadier-General Joseph Farmer Knipe

First Brigade
Colonel Joseph Kargé
12th Indiana Cavalry: Major William H. Calkins
2nd New Jersey Cavalry: Lt. Colonel P. Jones Yorke
4th Wisconsin Cavalry: Colonel Webster P. Moore

Second Brigade
Colonel Gilbert M. L. Johnson
10th Indiana Cavalry: Major George R. Swallow
13th Indiana Cavalry: Lt. Colonel William T. Pepper
4th Tennessee Cavalry: Lt. Colonel Jacob M. Thornburgh

Artillery
Ohio Light Artillery—14th Battery: Captain William C. Myers

District of South Alabama
Brigadier-General Thomas Kilby Smith

Dauphin Island
Lt. Colonel Byron Kirby
3rd Maryland Cavalry—6 Cos: Captain Eli D. Grinder
6th Michigan Heavy Artillery—5 Cos: Captain Seymour Howell

Mobile Point
Lt. Colonel Charles E. Clarke
1st Michigan Light Artillery—Battery G: Lieutenant George L. Stillman
6th Michigan Heavy Artillery—3 Cos: Major Harrison Soulé

CONFEDERATE FORCES: DISTRICT OF THE GULF
March 10, 1865
Major-General Dabney Herndon Maury

Thomas's Brigade
Brigadier-General Bryan Morel Thomas
1st Alabama Infantry Reserves: Colonel Daniel E. Huger
2nd Alabama Infantry Reserves: Lt. Colonel Junius A. Law
21st Alabama Infantry: Lt. Colonel James M. Williams

Gibson's Brigade
Brigadier-General Randall Lee Gibson
1st, 16th and 20th Louisiana Infantry (Consolidated): Lt. Colonel Robert H. Lindsay
25th Louisiana Infantry and 4th Louisiana Battalion Infantry: Colonel Francis C. Zacharie
19th Louisiana Infantry: Major Camp Flournoy
4th, 13th and 30th Louisiana Infantry (Consolidated): Colonel Francis L. Campbell
14th Louisiana Battalion Sharpshooters: Colonel Francis L. Campbell

Holtzclaw's Brigade
18th Alabama Infantry: Captain A. C. Greene
32nd and 58th Alabama Infantry (Consolidated): Colonel Bushrod Jones
36th Alabama Infantry: Colonel Thomas H. Herndon
38th Alabama Infantry: Captain Charles E. Bussey

Taylor's Command
Colonel Thomas H. Taylor
City Battalion and Special Services—4 Cos: Major William Hartwell
Pelham Cadets Battalion: Captain P. Williams, Jr.

Sappers and Miners
Captain L. Hutchinson
Hutchinson's Company: Lieutenant R. Middleton
Vernon's Company: Lieutenant J. Armstrong

French's Division
Brigadier-General Francis Marion Cockrell

Cockrell's Brigade
Colonel James McCown
1st Missouri and 3rd Missouri Battn. Cavalry (Cons. and Dism.): Captain Joseph H. Neal
1st and 4th Missouri Infantry (Consolidated): Captain Charles L. Edmondson
2nd and 6th Missouri Infantry (Consolidated): Lt. Colonel Stephen Cooper
3rd and 5th Missouri Infantry (Consolidated): Captain Benjamin E. Guthrie
Steede's Mississippi Battalion Cavalry: Major Abner C. Steede
Abbay's Artillery Battery: Captain George F. Abbay

Ector's Brigade
Colonel David Coleman

29th North Carolina Infantry: Captain John W. Gudger
39th North Carolina Infantry: Major Paschal C. Hughes
9th Texas Infantry: Lt. Colonel Miles A. Dillard
10th Texas Cavalry (Dismounted): Captain Jacob Ziegler
14th Texas Cavalry (Dismounted): Lt. Colonel Abram Harris
32nd Texas Cavalry (Dismounted): Captain Nathan Anderson

Sears's Brigade
Colonel Thomas N. Adaire
4th Mississippi Infantry: Major Thomas P. Nelson
7th Mississippi Battalion Infantry: Captain Samuel D. Harris
35th Mississippi Infantry: Captain George W. Oden
36th Mississippi Infantry: Lt. Colonel Edward Brown
39th Mississippi Infantry: Captain C. W. Gallaher
46th Mississippi Infantry: Captain J. A. Barwick

Clanton's Brigade
Brigadier-General James Holt Clanton
3rd Alabama Infantry Reserves: Major Solomon T. Strickland
6th Alabama Cavalry: Lt. Colonel Washington T. Lary
8th Alabama Cavalry: Lt. Colonel Thomas L. Faulkner
Keyser's Detachment: Captain Joseph C. Keyser

Armistead's Cavalry Brigade
8th Alabama Cavalry: Colonel Charles P. Ball
16th Confederate Cavalry: Lt. Colonel Philip B. Spence
Lewis's Battalion Cavalry: Major William V. Harrell

Maury's Command
Colonel Henry Maury
15th Confederate Infantry: Colonel Henry Maury
Tobin's Artillery Battery: Captain Thomas F. Tobin

Artillery Reserves
Mobile Defenses — Left Wing
Colonel Charles A. Fuller

Artillery
Major Henry A. Clinch
1st Louisiana Artillery — Co. C: Captain John H. Lamon
1st Louisiana Artillery — Co. I: Captain Edward G. Butler
Coffin's Virginia Artillery: Lieutenant J. B. Humphreys
Alabama State Reserves: Captain William H. Homer
Alabama State Reserves: Lieutenant R. H. Bush
Barry's Artillery Battery: Lieutenant Richard L. Watkins
Young's Artillery Battery: Captain Alfred J. Young

Batteries
Lt. Colonel L. Hoxton
Dent's Artillery Battery: Captain Staunton H. Dent
Douglas's Battery: Lieutenant Ben. Hardin
Eufaula Artillery Battery: Lieutenant William H. Woods
Fenner's Artillery Battery: Lieutenant W. T. Cluverius
Garrity's Artillery Battery: Captain James Garrity
Rice's Artillery Battery: Captain T. W. Rice
Thrall's Artillery Battery: Captain James C. Thrall

Mobile Defenses-Right Wing
Colonel Melancthon Smith

Trueheart's Artillery Battalion
Captain Charles L. Lumsden

Lovelace's Artillery Battery: Lieutenant William M. Selden
Lumsden's Artillery Battery: Lieutenant A. C. Hargrove

Gee's Artillery Battalion
Major James T. Gee
Perry's Artillery Battery: Captain Thomas J. Perry
Phelan's Artillery Battery: Captain John Phelan
Turner's Artillery Battery: Captain William B. Turner
1st Alabama Artillery (Detachment): Lieutenant P. Lee Hammond

Cobb's Artillery Battalion
Captain Cuthbert H. Slocomb
Phillips's Artillery Battery: Captain J. W. Phillips
Ritter's Artillery Battery: Captain William L. Ritter
Slocomb's Artillery Battery: Lieutenant J. Ad. Chalaron

Grayson's Artillery Battalion
Captain John B. Grayson
Cowan's Artillery Battery: Captain James J. Cowan
Culpeper's Artillery Battalion: Lieutenant J. L. Moses
Tarrant's Artillery Battery: Captain Edward Tarrant
Winston's Artillery Battery: Captain William C. Winston

Batteries
Colonel William E. Burnet

Battery McIntosh
Major W. C. Capers
1st Louisiana Artillery — Cos. A and D
1st Mississippi Artillery — Co. L

Battery Tilghman
Green's Kentucky Battery: Lieutenant H. S. Quisenberry

Battery Gladden
Captain Richard C. Bond
2nd Alabama Artillery — Cos. C and E
1st Louisiana Artillery — Cos B and G

Battery Missouri
Captain James Gibney
22nd Louisiana Infantry — Cos. E and K
Holmes's Light Artillery Battery

Battery Buchanan
Crew of the Gunboat C. S. S. Gaines: Naval Captain P. U. Murphy
3rd Missouri Light Artillery: Lieutenant T. B. Catron

Picket Fleet
1st Mississippi Artillery — 4 Cos: Major Jefferson L. Wofford

The Biographical Register

It is indeed a desirable thing to be well descended, but the glory belongs to our ancestors. — Plutarch

A Guide to Using the Register

This biographical register for the citizen soldiers of the Fourth Louisiana Battalion Infantry has been designed to provide an accurate record of each soldiers' Confederate military service, pensions and land warrant applications, veterans' census, civilian life, spouses, children, and death and burial information. The information on some of the men is far from complete. Many records of the late Confederacy were destroyed during and at the close of the war. By no means do the authors wish to imply that all records have been located, and we encourage the admirers and descendants of these brave men to conduct their own research for further information. However, this register is an invaluable tool for beginning your Civil War–era ancestral/subject research.

Each soldier is listed in the company in which he served, last name first. This is followed by his beginning rank at enlistment, and, if promoted, each subsequent rank. His enlistment date and place of enlistment follow, in addition to his muster rolls and, if taken prisoner, his date and place of capture, parole, or forwarding to a Union military prison as a prisoner of war. If paroled and he reported for exchange, the date and place are also listed. Other elements included in some of the entries, according to the availability of information, are the date and place of his 1865 final parole, military medical history, physical description, residences, occupations, names of wives, number of children and genders, listing on Confederate enumerations, service in other units, and burial location.

Beside some soldiers' names is the notice "No War Dept. Record." This indicates that the U.S. War Dept. was unable to find a Confederate service record for this name. This is not, however, evidence that the person was not in the Confederate military service and assigned to the Fourth Louisiana Battalion Infantry. As late as February 10, 1932, the adjutant general of the U.S. War Department stated in correspondence to Louisiana Congressman Bolivar E. Kemp, "The collection of Confederate records in this Department is far from complete, and failure to find the entire record of a person thereon is by no means conclusive proof that he did not serve during some period not covered by the records on file." Hence the inclusion of these men's biographical data.

The removal and consolidation of numerous duplicate names has been accomplished with great care to prevent exclusion. In the event that two names could not definitively be ascertained as of the same person, both were left in the register. If the target subject or ancestor's surname has many spellings or pronunciations, the register should be scrutinized to determine if the soldier could be listed under an alternative surname spelling. All name variations found in the various records searched are listed next to the name of the soldier under "(aka)"—"also known as."

If the soldier was assigned to an elite group or position, such as Field and Staff, Color Bearer/Guard, Hospital Steward, Druggist, Surgeon, or Sergeant-Major, to name a few, a special section has been created for their biographical registry under their position name.

The terms used in the register are defined below, as well as position descriptions, so readers will have an idea of what function their ancestor/subject performed during those turbulent days. Bear in mind that all soldiers served when and where needed, at whatever position demanded immediate attention or service.

Term Definitions

Adjutant— Principal staff officer who is the organ of the commanding officer. Duties include supervising the encampment, transmitting orders, assigning details, and mounting guards. Reported to the lieutenant–colonel of the battalion exclusively.

Captain— Responsible for the supervision/direction of a battalion company, and the senior officer in the company. Reported to the battalion's major and lieutenant colonel.

Chaplain— Responsible for administering religious rites, burials and services to the battalion, as well as moral guidance to the soldiers. Reported to the commanding officer.

Color Guard/Bearers— Responsible for carrying and protecting the battalion flags/colors, especially in battle.

This was a position of honor, and was important for marking the front of the battalion in battle situations. In combat, where the men could not hear orders, they followed the flag. Rank and titles were almost always interchangeable. The Color Guard consisted of 1 Color Sergeant and up to 8 Color Corporals. The Color Corporal was almost always delegated as a member of the Color Guard, and the Color Sergeant was most like an Ensign. The General Guides were also Color Guard/Bearers.

Confederate Pension Application—A pension application for Confederate soldiers to receive a pension paid through the state in which the soldier resided at the time of application. Louisiana and most other Southern states began providing pensions in 1898.

Confederate Proof and Land Warrant Application—The Louisiana Legislature passed 3 acts to provide relief for Confederate soldiers or their widows. These were the Act 96 of 1884, Act 116 of 1886, and Act 55 of 1896. The legislative acts provided land warrants to soldiers or their widows who had been wounded, maimed, killed, or contracted diseases while in the Confederate States of America (CSA) military. The acts provided 160 acres of state lands (usually swamp) to eligible applicants.

Confederate Widow's Pension Application—A pension application for the widow of a Confederate veteran to receive a pension paid by the former Confederate state in which she resided at the time of application.

Druggist—Responsible for the production, acquisition, manufacture, and dosages of medicines prescribed by the battalion surgeons. Reported to the battalion surgeon or assistant surgeons.

General Guide—Consisting of a right and left guide, they were members of the Color Guard/Bearers. Responsible for carrying small guidon-type flags, they were placed on the extreme right and left flanks of the battalion when in battle motion to keep the soldiers from drifting too far to the left or right.

Hospital Steward—Responsible for the general administration of the battalion hospital including ventilation, lighting, heating, keeping hospital records, and maintaining hospital supplies as well as the supervision and discipline of the hospital attendants. Usually a noncommissioned officer who ranked above a first sergeant of a company. In battle, he would assist in the field hospital or a dressing station. On a march, he was responsible for hospital supplies and medicine chests.

Ordnance Sergeant—Responsible for ensuring that the battalion weapons were in proper working order and procurement of sufficient quantities of ammunition issued to the individual companies of the battalion.

Quartermaster—Responsible for providing quarters, clothing and pay for the battalion. A modern-day example would be a company's purchasing agent.

Sergeant Major—The senior enlisted soldier of the battalion, he had absolute, unrestricted access to the lieutenant-colonel or commanding officer. All noncommissioned or enlisted officers were under his command.

Skirmisher—A company or two would precede their battalion out front and would screen its advance or defense, or, as the war became more trench oriented, would serve as an early warning system for any enemy attack.

Surgeon/Assistant Surgeon—Responsible for the medical care of all soldiers in the battalion, including treating wounds, injuries or diseases, as well as prescribing medications. Surgeons were also responsible for the physical evaluation of recruits, and issuance of Medical Discharges to disabled or ill soldiers. Reported to the lieutenant—colonel of the battalion. Surgeons usually held the rank of major, with the assistant surgeon holding the rank of lieutenant. Assistant surgeons, in the best of situations, were doctors who had just graduated from medical school.

Battalion Infantry

COMMANDING GENERALS

Department

Beauregard, Pierre Gustave Toutant (aka Peter)— Private/Brigadier General/General—*Born:* May 28, 1818, to Jacques Toutant Beauregard and Ms. DeReggio, in St. Bernard Parish, Louisiana. *Religion:* Catholic. *Education:* Private school in New York City, known in the East as the French School. Graduated from West Point in 1838, second in a class of forty-five. After graduation, he received a commission as a 2nd Lieutenant in the Corps of Engineers. *Politics:* In 1858, he ran for Mayor of New Orleans, but was defeated by his Know-Nothing Party opponent. *Marriage/Family:* In September of 1841, he married Marie Laure Villere. They had three children: René, Henri, and Laure Villere. His wife died in March of 1850 while giving birth to their daughter. His wife is buried in the family cemetery in St. Bernard Parish. His second marriage was to Caroline Deslonde, also a Creole. They had no children. Caroline died on March 2, 1864, and is buried in St. John the Baptist Catholic Church Cemetery at Edgard, Louisiana. *Pre-War:* 2nd lieutenant in the corps of engineers, serving on the Louisiana Gulf coast. While in the Mexican-American War, he was an engineer officer on General Winfield Scott's staff, and was twice breveted for gallantry. After the war, he was in charge of the engineering department named the Mississippi and the Lake Defenses in Louisiana. He also repaired old forts and constructed new ones on the Florida coast and in the Mobile, Alabama, harbor. From 1853 to 1860, he was superintendent of the New Orleans customhouse, with the rank of captain. He was appointed superintendent of West Point as of January 23, 1861, but relinquished his position five days later. His superiors feared his Southern sympathies would make an unfavorable impression on the young male students. *During the War:* Resigned his U.S. army commission on February 20, 1861, and was appointed a brigadier-general in the Provisional Army of the Confederacy on March 1, 1861. Two days later, he was placed in command at Charleston, South Carolina, and demanded the evacuation of Fort Sumter in April of the same year. In June, he was second-in-command to General Joseph E. Johnston at the Battle of First Manassas. He was commissioned a full general in the Regular Confederate Army on July 21, 1861, and sent to the west. In 1862, when General Albert Sidney Johnston was killed at Shiloh, he assumed command. Facing a large Union army commanded by Major-General Henry Wager Halleck, Beauregard was forced to retreat to Corinth, Mississippi. When Beauregard took sick leave, he was superseded in command of the Army of Tennessee by General Braxton Bragg. Upon his return to duty, he was placed in charge of the defenses of South Carolina and the Georgia Coast. He performed with skill, especially during the defense of Charleston in 1863 and 1864. In May of 1864, he reluctantly supported General Robert E. Lee in Virginia. He served under General Joseph E. Johnston in the Carolinas in the closing weeks of the war, returning to New Orleans after the surrender. *Post-War:* President of two railroads. He and former Confederate general Jubal Anderson Early supervised the drawings of the infamous Louisiana Lottery. He was also for many years adjutant-general of the state of Louisiana. *Interesting:* He was the designer of the Confederate battle flag. The U.S. military installation, Camp Beauregard, located in Louisiana, is named in his honor. He was a member of the Aztec Club, a membership for Mexican-American War veterans. Spoke French before he spoke English. *Death and Burial:* Died in New Orleans on February 20, 1893, and buried in the Metairie Cemetery at Metairie, Jefferson Parish, Louisiana.

Johnston, Joseph Eggleston (aka Old Joe, Retreating Joe, Colonel)—Brigadier General/ General— *Born:* February 3, 1807, at Cherry Grove, near Farmville, Prince George County, Virginia, to Peter Johnston, a circuit-court judge and veteran of the Revolutionary War, and Mary Valentine Wood. Joseph Eggleston was named in honor of the captain under whom his father served in the war. Johnston had six older brothers. *Education:* Attended Abingdon Academy in Virginia, which his father helped to found. Graduated thirteenth in a class of forty-six in 1829 with an unblemished conduct record throughout his attendance. His favorite subjects were astronomy, military history, and French, in which he became fluent. Throughout his life, he enjoyed reading the novels of Sir Walter Scott. For a period of time, an eye infection prohibited him from night study. His classmate and later friend, Robert E. Lee, graduated second. *Marriage/Family:* Married Lydia McLane on July 10, 1845, at St. Paul's Episcopal Church in Baltimore, Maryland. Johnston was thirteen years her senior. Their wedding service was performed by Reverend Dr. William E. Wyatt. The union produced no children, though Dabney Maury noted in his recollections that General Johnston adored children. His wife, Lydia, died on February 22, 1887. *Pre-War:* He was commissioned a 2nd Lieutenant in the U.S. 4th Artillery — Co. C, and served primarily on garrison duty. In 1832, he participated in the Black Hawk War against the Indians in Illinois, where Johnston signed the treaty as a formal witness to the negotiations for surrender. In the 1830s and 1840s, he was on topographical duty and served on a series of expeditions to the western frontier. First Lieutenant Johnston submitted his resignation to the U.S. Army in May of 1837, but re-entered the army in 1838. He served with distinction in both Seminole Wars as a civilian topographical engineer. He served as an aide-de-camp to General Winfield Scott during the Seminole War. In the Second Seminole War at Jupiter Inlet, he was wounded, counting no less than thirty bullet holes in his clothing, including two in his cap. One bullet grazed his scalp, leaving him with a permanent scar. He was breveted captain for gallantry in the fierce battle at Jupiter Inlet, which was his last combat service of the Second Seminole War. Johnston was wounded in almost every battle in which he participated. In 1842, he returned to Florida and served as an assistant adjutant-general for six months. During the Mexican-American War, he was with General Winfield Scott at Vera Cruz. He also participated in the battles of Cerro Gordo, Contreras, Cherubusco, Molino del Rey, and Chapultepec. At the Battle of Cerro Gordo, Johnston was severely wounded by grapeshot, though the wounds were not life-threatening. He was breveted lieutenant-colonel while fighting there. Robert E. Lee wept and held Johnston's hand while giving him the sad news that his nephew, Preston, a lieutenant of artillery, was killed while manning his guns. Preston had been hit by a Mexican artillery shell and died during the night while at the Battle of Contreras. Lieutenant-Colonel Johnston was heartbroken, as he thought of Preston as his own son. At the Battle of Chalpultepec, a soldier from Johnston's battalion was the first to climb over the walls; soon the blue flag of the Voltiguer's Regiment, riddled with holes, flew from the parapet. Johnston was wounded again at the Battle of Chapultepec. For his actions, he was breveted to the rank of colonel. The War Department asserted that since he had entered the war as a captain, Johnston's two brevet promotions had made him first a major, then a lieutenant-colonel. Johnston appealed his case for colonelcy, but Secretary of War William L. Marcy denied his petition, with the Senate confirming his decision. He surveyed the U.S./Canadian border in the newly admitted state of Michigan, and in the 1850s, he served as a surveyor and was supervisor of river improvements in the west. He also participated as a 2nd Lieutenant of the First Cavalry Regiment in keeping the peace during the "Bleeding Kansas" troubles. On June 28, 1860, Johnston became quartermaster-general of the army with the rank of brigadier-general. His main responsibility was to manage supplies and accounts for the army. *During the War:* He resigned his U.S. army commission on April 22, 1861, to enter the service of the Confederacy when his native state of Virginia seceded. He was commissioned a brigadier-general in the Regular Army of the Confederacy in May of 1861, and was the only officer of the U.S. Army to join with the rank of brigadier-general. He was then placed in command at Harper's Ferry, and arrived there on May 23, 1861. He replaced General Stonewall Jackson, commanding in the Shenandoah Valley. He eluded the force under command of General Patterson, and marched to assist General Pierre Gustave Toutant Beauregard at the Battle of First Manassas. Johnston's performance there won him a promotion to full general on August 31, 1861, to rank from July 4. He assumed command on July 17, 1861, of the Army of Northern Virginia. His being ranked below Samuel Cooper, Albert Sidney Johnston, and Robert Edward Lee gave rise to a long-running feud with President Jefferson Davis. He opposed General McClellan in the Peninsular Campaign until being severely wounded at the Battle of Seven Pines in May of 1862, when the army command was transferred to Robert E. Lee. In that battle, he received a slight wound in the right shoulder from a musket-shot, before being unhorsed by a heavy fragment of shell which struck his breast. He recuperated in Richmond, though the wounds left him out of military duty for almost six months. On November 12, 1862, he reported for duty and was made commander of the Department of the West. In 1863, Johnston was in the unenviable position of attempting to reverse the situation at Vicksburg, while his subordinate, General Pemberton, was receiving contrary orders from Richmond. He commanded the Army of Tennessee from December 27, 1863, to July 18, 1864. President Davis ordered General John Bell Hood to replace Johnston in July of 1864, shortly before the Battle of Peachtree Creek. In February of 1865, he was restored to command of the remnants of the Army of Tennessee by Robert E. Lee to oppose Sherman's march through the Carolinas. He commanded the Department of South Carolina, Georgia, and Florida from February 25, 1865, through April 26, 1865. After General Lee's surrender at Appomattox Court House, General Johnston capitulated to Major-General William T. Sherman in Greensboro, North Carolina, on April 26, 1865. The details of the surrender were arranged at the house of James Bennett.

There was a previous surrender agreement made on April 18th, but it was discarded by the U.S. government. The terms of surrender granted to Lee were made the basis of the capitulation. *Post-War:* Johnston accepted employment briefly in 1865 with the National Express & Transportation Company. From May of 1866 to November of 1867, he was president of the Alabama and Tennessee River Railroad Company. A London-based insurance company hired him as manager of the Southern Department. He served in the U.S. House of Representatives from 1879 through 1881. He was appointed as the U.S. commissioner of railroads by President Grover Cleveland, and served from 1885 through 1891. *Interesting:* As a young boy, one of his favorite pastimes was re-enacting the Battle of King's Mountain. At the age of eight, his father gave him the military sword he had carried in the Revolutionary War, which became a prize possession to the son. He had a special relationship with U.S. Major-General George Brinton McClellan, who also graduated from West Point in 1846. Johnston and his wife attended McClellan's wedding in 1860. Although Johnston had several nicknames, he did not like being called Joe. He was a member of the Aztec Club, a membership for veterans of the Mexican-American War. *Interesting Quote:* Learning of his nephew Preston's death, he wrote to his brother Beverly: "I loved him more than my own heart."[1] He returned Preston's remains to Baltimore for burial. He wrote to Lizzie, Preston's sister, about his remains: "I couldn't bear that a Mexican foot should tread over them."[2] *Literary Works:* He authored, "Narrative of Military Operations," published in 1874. He also wrote several articles for the series of books, "Battles and Leaders of the Civil War." *Death and Burial:* Died in Washington, D.C., on March 21, 1891, of pneumonia which was contracted by standing in the rain at William Tecumseh Sherman's funeral. He is buried at Green Mount Cemetery in Baltimore, Maryland.

Pemberton, John Clifford (aka Old Pem)—Brigadier General/Major-General/Lieutenant General/Lieutenant Colonel. *Born:* Philadelphia, Pennsylvania, on August 10, 1814, to John Pemberton, a businessman, and Rebecca Clifford. *Education:* Private schools with tutors, before attending the University of Pennsylvania. Graduated from West Point in the class of 1837, finishing twenty-seventh out of a class of fifty. His best subjects were mathematics and horsemanship. *Marriage/Family:* Married Martha Thompson, of Norfolk, Virginia, on January 18, 1846, producing five children. Martha's nickname was "Pattie." She died on August 14, 1907. *Pre-War:* Commissioned a 2nd Lieutenant in the 4th U.S. Artillery, he fought the Seminoles in Florida from 1837 to 1839. He served at Fort Mackinac, Michigan, on the Canadian border from 1840 to 1842, as well as various other posts. He was promoted to 1st Lieutenant on March 19, 1842, and assigned to Fort Monroe, Virginia. During the Mexican-American War, he served as an aide-de-camp to Major-General William J. Worth in Zachary Taylor's army. He participated in the battles of Palo Alto, Resaca de la Palma, Vera Cruz, Monterrey, Cerro Gordo, Churubusco, Molino del Rey, Chapultepec, and Mexico City. He earned the brevet rank of captain on September 23, 1846, and major on September 8, 1847. He was twice wounded during the war. His brave performance in Mexico so impressed the citizens of Philadelphia that they presented him with a sword. In the 1840s and 1850s, he served at various posts in New York, Florida, and Louisiana. He became captain on September 16, 1850. In 1858, he was transferred to Fort Leavenworth, Kansas, and participated in the Utah Expedition against the Mormons. From 1858 through 1861, he dealt with the Indians in the northwest. The following year he was stationed at Fort Ridgely, Minnesota, where he remained until the outbreak of the Civil War. *During the War:* Resigned his U.S. commission on April 24, 1861. General Winfield Scott offered him a colonel's commission, but Pemberton declined, despite two of his brothers joining the U.S. Army. On April 28, 1861, he became a lieutenant-colonel in the Virginia State Army, where he received orders to organize Virginia's cavalry in Richmond. On May 8, 1861, he advanced to colonel and was ordered to Norfolk to train artillery units. His early Confederate service was as commander of the Department of South Carolina, Georgia, and Florida. He had Fort Wagner and Battery B built to protect Charleston, South Carolina. In January of 1862, he was engaged in the Battle of Port Royal Ferry, South Carolina, where he defeated the Federals. He was promoted to brigadier-general on June 17, 1861, major-general ranking from January 14, 1862, and lieutenant-general ranking from October 10, 1862. After his promotion, he was assigned to command of the Department of Mississippi and Eastern Louisiana. He was responsible for the defense of the Mississippi River between Vicksburg, Mississippi, and Port Hudson, Louisiana. General Joseph E. Johnston was his superior and commanded the Confederate western theater. When Major-General U.S. Grant was advancing on Vicksburg in April of 1863, Pemberton found himself overwhelmed with conflicting orders from President Jefferson Davis and General Joseph Johnston. Davis insisted that he hold Vicksburg at all costs, while Johnston insisted he abandon the city. Ultimately, Pemberton chose to follow Davis's orders. Pemberton was unable to receive supplies and reinforcements to withstand the ensuing forty-seven-day Federal siege of Vicksburg. Pemberton realized he was in a desperate situation, and after a stubborn defense, he accepted the inevitable. Surrender terms were negotiated on July 3, 1863, and the formal surrender occurred on July 4, 1863. Pemberton, born a Northerner, aroused the suspicions of the Southerners throughout his service, but particularly so when he surrendered the Confederate citadel and her garrison on the Union holiday. After his parole at Vicksburg, he resigned his commission on May 18, 1864, and was appointed by President Davis as a lieutenant-colonel of artillery, in which position he served until the end of the war. *Post-War:* His mother purchased a farm in Fauquier County, Virginia, where he resided. In 1876, he moved to Philadelphia, thereafter spending winters in Virginia and summers in Penllyn, Pennsylvania. *Interesting:* Prior to the Civil War, he was once arrested for nose-pulling at a party with a fellow officer when the officer spoke in an insolent manner about women. In 1853, he survived a threat on his life when an incident occurred regarding a corporal who did not salute him. Major Pemberton confined the corporal to his quarters. Three days later when Pemberton withdrew the charges, the corporal entered the room Pemberton was reading and smoking in, and saluted him sarcastically, stating, "It is owing to my being arrested a few days ago, major, that I am upon guard duty today."[3] After Corporal White thanked Pemberton for withdrawing the charges, he calmly and deliberately pulled out a pistol, pointed it at Pemberton's chest, and a fight ensued while Pemberton attempted to disarm White, who had a size advantage. He shoved the assailant to the floor and yelled, "Murderer!" for some time during the struggle, before a band member heard the noise and rushed in, followed by an officer.[4] Together, the band member and the officer pushed the gun to the floor and disarmed the hostile corporal. Corporal White was put in irons and taken away, and Pemberton's life was spared. *Death and Burial:* Died on July 13, 1881, in the village of Penllyn, Pennsylvania. Buried at Laurel Hill Cemetery in Philadelphia, Pennsylvania, with his wife. *Dedications:* In June of 1909, there was a statue erected in honor of Pemberton in the Vicksburg National Military Park in Vicksburg, Mississippi.

Taylor, Richard (aka Dick)—Colonel/Brigadier General/Major General/Lieutenant General—*Born:* January 27, 1826, at the family property, "Springfields," near Louisville, Kentucky, the only son of the twelfth president of the United States, Zachary Taylor, and Margaret "Peggy" Mackall Smith. Named for his grandfather, who served as an officer from Virginia in the Revolutionary War under George Washington. *Education:* Private schools in Kentucky and Massachusetts. Attended Yale College in 1843 and graduated in 1845. An avid reader of European military history. *Politics:* Served as a delegate to the Whigs' nominating convention at Donaldsonville, Louisiana, in 1851, then the American Know-Nothing Party, before joining the Democratic Party. From 1856 to 1861, served in the Louisiana State Senate. In 1860, he was chosen as a Louisiana delegate to the Democratic National Convention in Charleston, South Carolina. Served as a delegate to the Louisiana secession convention in January of 1861, where he immediately voted for secession, believing war was imminent. He was chairman of the Committee on Military and Naval Affairs. *Marriage/Family:* He met Louise Marie "Mimi" Myrthe Bringier while his father was campaigning for the presidency. Married in February of 1851, they had three daughters and two sons. Both sons tragically died of scarlet fever during the war. *Children:* Louise Margaret, Elizabeth (Betty M.), Zachary, Richard, and Myrthe Bianca. His wife died on March 16, 1875, at the age of forty-one. *Pre-War:* In 1848, he agreed to manage "Cypress Grove," the family cotton plantation, in Jefferson County, Mississippi. Due to raging flood-waters that destroyed the cotton crops, he urged his father to purchase "Fashion," a large sugar plantation in St. Charles Parish, Louisiana. When his father died on July 9, 1850, he inherited "Fashion" and 147 slaves. *During the War:* Appointed colonel of the 9th Louisiana Infantry by Louisiana Governor Thomas Overton Moore. Mustered in on July 6, 1861. Promoted to brigadier-general on October 21, 1861, upon his return from an illness, by order of President Jefferson Davis. He proceeded to Richmond, Virginia, to request Davis revoke his promotion because of fear it would be construed as favoritism, but Davis denied his request. When Brigadier-General William Henry Talbot Walker, commander of the Louisiana Brigade, was transferred to command of a Georgia Brigade, Taylor was assigned command of the Louisianans. During the spring of 1862, he led his brigade under Stonewall Jackson's command in the brilliant Shenandoah Valley Campaign. He was present at the battles of Front Royal on May 23, 1862, at Winchester on May 25, 1862, and at the Battle of Port Republic on June 9, 1862. He and his army joined General Robert E. Lee at the Seven Days' battles in Richmond, where he suffered severely with pains in his head, back, and temporary paralysis of his upper limbs. He suffered terribly throughout his life with rheumatoid arthritis. Upon witnessing the wounded and dead on the field at the Seven Days' battle, he amazingly struggled to get on his horse, joined the battle, and went into action. At the end of the battle, he experienced paralysis of his lower limbs and was taken to Richmond, where he had a month of rest and regained good health. While in Richmond, he learned of his promotion to major-general on July 28, 1862, due to Jackson's recommendation for his gallantry in the Shenandoah Valley. Upon his transfer to command of the District of West Louisiana in the summer of 1862, Taylor discovered huge beds of pure rock salt at Judge D.D. Avery's island in Vermilion Bay, south of New Iberia, Louisiana. Fortunately for the Confederacy, Judge Avery was devoted to the Confederate cause and placed his mine at Taylor's disposal. Many slaves were utilized to mine the salt, and a packing establishment was organized at New Iberia to cure beef. Taylor kept the island safe by posting infantry and artillery to protect the valuable resource from the enemy. The Union later sent a gunboat up the Petit Anse to shell the mine, but it became entangled in the marsh and the attempt was abandoned. In the Red River campaign, his most notable success was during the Battle of Mansfield, Louisiana, when the Confederates attacked the Union forces under Major-General Nathaniel Banks, driving the enemy from every position. On April 8, 1864, at Mansfield, the Confederates captured twenty-one pieces of artillery, twenty-five hundred prisoners, two hundred and fifty wagons, and many stands of colors. Taylor became unhappy with Lieutenant-General Edmund Kirby Smith, the commander of the Trans-Mississippi Department, feeling Smith was being stubborn in his refusal to send Major-General John George Walker's division to help attempt the recapture of New Orleans. Smith dismissed Taylor, and named Walker the new commander of the District of the West on the same day Congress issued a joint resolution recognizing Taylor's brilliant success in the battles of Mansfield and Pleasant Hill, Louisiana. Taylor was so angry at Smith that he asked to be relieved from duty. He was then promoted to lieutenant-general to rank from April 8, 1864, and assigned command of the Department of Alabama, Mississippi, and East Louisiana by President Davis. After General John Bell Hood requested to be relieved from command of the Army of Tennessee, Taylor briefly commanded Hood's defeated and demoralized army on January 23, 1865. After public and political demands for General Joseph E. Johnston to be reappointed to lead the Army of Tennessee, Johnston relieved Taylor and assumed command on February 23, 1865. Taylor surrendered to U.S. Major-General Edward Richard Sprigg Canby on May 4, 1865, at Citronelle, Alabama. At the end of the war, Taylor felt an obligation to protect the thousands of bales of Confederate cotton before transferring it to the United States. He said he "hated the very name of the article, as it was the source of much corruption to their people," but recognized that it was now Federal property.[5] *Post-War:* Taylor resided in New Orleans, Louisiana, and tried to improve his finances by securing a lease of the New Basin Canal from the state. He persisted with requests to U.S. President Andrew Johnson for permission to visit the imprisoned Jefferson Davis. He was concerned for Davis's feeble health and eventually his request was granted: he visited Davis at Fortress Monroe, Virginia. Taylor also sought and was granted permission for Jefferson Davis's family to visit him. After the war, he learned his estate had been confiscated by the U.S. government and sold, leaving him penniless. In the late 1850s, he owned several horses which he raced competitively. In early 1866, he was involved in the management of the Metairie Jockey Club. In December of 1868, he was elected the Boston Club's president, an office which he retained for five annual terms. In May of 1873, he went to Europe, where he was treated like an American prince. He met the Prince of Wales, who appointed him an honorary member of the Marlborough Club, which was designated for princes and their sons. He was also awarded a membership in the British Turf Club, where he went to various horse racing events before returning to New York. In 1871, he was elected to the board of trustees of the Peabody Educational Fund for the promotion of education of the poor in the South. In May of 1875, Taylor and his three daughters moved to Winchester, Virginia. In 1876, Taylor worked diligently to gain the support of Southern delegates during New Yorker Samuel J. Tilden's Democratic presidential campaign, though the outcome of his efforts was disappointing. *Interesting:* Confederate President Jefferson Davis married Taylor's sister, his first wife, Sara Knox Taylor, in 1835. Major-General Dabney Maury was a longtime family friend. Taylor took his servant and early playmate, Tom Strothers, whom he had an affection for, with him into war. When he returned to New Orleans, he was penniless. He sold his warhorse, which had carried him through many fierce battles, to get enough money to visit his family at Natchitoches, Louisiana. The horse would not move a hoof when the purchaser came to take him away, so attached was it to Taylor. When Taylor's wife died in 1875, Jefferson Davis consoled Richard Taylor and cried at her coffin. *Interesting Quote:* "Extinction of slavery was expected by all and regretted by none, although loss of slaves destroyed the value of land."[6] *Literary Works:* He authored, *Destruction and Reconstruction*, a military memoir, which was published a week before his death in 1879 by D. Appleton and Company. Several months before his death, he published an article in the North American Review. Entitled "A Statesman of the Colonial Era," it was a biographical sketch of George Mason. *Death and Burial:* He took holy communion on April 11, 1879, from an Episcopal clergyman and died of cardiac arrest at the New York home of his wealthy attorney friend, Samuel Latham Mitchell Barlow, on April 12, 1879. He is buried alongside his wife in the family crypt at Metairie Cemetery in New Orleans, Louisiana. It is said that dignitaries from both the South and the North attended his funeral, including some who had opposed him on the battlefield.

District

Evans, Nathan George (aka Shanks) — Brigadier General — *Born:* February 3, 1824, at Marion County, South Carolina, the third son of Thomas Evans and Jane Beverly Daniel of Virginia. *Education:* Graduated from Randolph-Macon College in 1841, at the age of eighteen. He entered West Point and graduated thirty-sixth in a class of thirty-eight in 1852. *Marriage/Family:* Married Ann Victoria Gary, sister of Confederate General Martin Witherspoon Gary, of Abbeville County, South Carolina, in 1860. It is unknown if the union produced any children. *Pre-War:* After graduating from West Point, he served on the frontier with the U.S. 2nd Dragoons. He was commissioned 1st lieutenant in the newly organized 2nd U.S. Cavalry in 1855, and was promoted to captain in 1856. Prior to his Civil War service, he fought the Indians in New Mexico and in Texas. At the battle of Wachita Village on October 1, 1858, his command defeated a large body of Comanche Indians. He personally killed two of their well-known chieftains in hand-to-hand combat. The legislature of South Carolina presented him with a sword for his bravery and success. *During the War:* On February 27, 1861, he resigned his commission as a captain in the U.S. Army. During the bombardment of Fort Sumter, he was assigned to duty as adjutant-general of the South Carolina troops. At First Manassas, he commanded a small brigade on the extreme left of the line. He detected the turning movement of the Union troops in time to redeploy his forces against McDowell, presenting a front to the enemy which went far towards saving the day for the Confederates. He was promoted to brigadier-general on October 21, 1861, after the Battle of Ball's Bluff. He commanded a brigade, which became known as the "Tramp Brigade." He was present at the battles of Second Manassas, South Mountain, and Sharpsburg, and was with General Joseph E. Johnston's army during the Vicksburg Campaign. From early 1863, he was in constant difficulties, being tried for intoxication and disobedience of orders, though acquitted both times. General Beauregard considered him incompetent, and removed him from command for a long period. His brigade inspection reports reflected unfavorably on him as well. He returned to duty in 1864, but fell from his horse and was painfully injured. In the spring of 1865, he was in the field for a few months. *Post-War:* After the Civil War, he settled in Midway, Alabama, where he served as a high school principal. *Interesting:* He earned his nickname because of his thin legs. *Death and Burial:* Died on November 23, 1868, and is buried in the Tabernacle Cemetery in Cokesbury, South Carolina.

Maury, Dabney Herndon—Brigadier General/Major General—*Born:* May 21, 1822, at Fredericksburg, Virginia, to Captain John Minor Maury of the U.S. Navy and Eliza Maury. His parents were first cousins. After the death of his father in 1828, Dabney and his brother lived with their paternal uncle, Matthew Fontaine Maury, an oceanographer. *Education:* Attended the University of Virginia from 1839 to 1841, studying law there and under a judge in Fredericksburg. He preferred a military career to practicing law and decided to enter West Point, where he graduated thirty-seventh in a class of fifty-nine. *Marriage/Family:* Married Nannie Rose Mason of King George County, Virginia, on March 10, 1852, in Stafford County, Virginia, producing four children. *Pre-War:* Served four years on the frontier in Texas, hunting and pursuing Indians. From 1847 to 1850, he was an assistant professor of geography, history, and ethics at West Point, and an assistant of infantry tactics from 1850 to 1852. In 1859, he wrote and published a standard manual, *Skirmish Drill for Mounted Troops.* He served in the Mexican-American War after being breveted 2nd Lieutenant in the Regiment of Mounted Rifles, later designated the 3rd U.S. Cavalry. He received a brevet to 1st Lieutenant for gallant and meritorious conduct at the battle of Cerro Gordo, where he was seriously wounded when a musket ball shattered his left arm, permanently crippling him. He returned to the U.S. to recuperate. From 1858 to 1860, he was superintendent of the Cavalry School at Carlisle, Pennsylvania. As a captain before the war, he served as an assistant adjutant-general of the Department of New Mexico. A census record shows he resided in Santa Fe, New Mexico, in 1860. He was in Topeka, Kansas when he received notice of an order, which stated, he was "stricken from the rolls of the army for entertaining treasonable designs against the government of the United States."[7] He was dismissed from the U.S. Army on June 25, 1861. *During the War:* Maury went to Richmond and was appointed a captain of cavalry in the Confederate Army in July of 1861, colonel of cavalry in the Virginia State forces, and a lieutenant-colonel in the Provisional Army. The War Department assigned him as an adjutant-general to General Joseph E. Johnston while at Manassas on July 19, and Maury was flabbergasted by Johnston's reaction to his arrival. After a brief conversation with Johnston, Maury returned to Richmond and asked to be transferred. Although Maury felt embarrassed by Johnston's reaction, they remained good friends. A little more than a month later, he was reassigned as adjutant-general to Major Theophilus "Granny" Hunter Holmes, commander of the Department of Fredericksburg, where he remained until February of 1862. He was promoted to colonel and assigned as chief-of-staff to Major-General Earl Van Dorn, commander of the Army of the West. After his performance at the Battle of Pea Ridge, Arkansas, on March 7 and 8th, 1862, he received a promotion to brigadier-general on March 18, 1862, to rank from March 12. He fought gallantly at the battles of Iuka and Corinth, and was appointed major-general on November 4, 1862. He took his division to Vicksburg, Mississippi, the following month, and saw action at Yazoo Pass and Steele's Bayou. After commanding north of Vicksburg at Snyder's Bluff for several months, Maury proceeded in early April of 1863 to support Major-General William Wing Loring's forces defending Fort Pemberton. On April 15, President Jefferson Davis ordered Maury to Knoxville, Tennessee. Less than two weeks later, however, the War Department ordered him to Mobile, Alabama, where he replaced Simon B. Buckner, as commander of the District of the Gulf on May 19, 1863, a post he held until the end of the war. In June of 1863, Maury's command was upgraded to a department, but it was redesignated as a district within the Department of Alabama, Mississippi, and East Louisiana in January of 1864. On July 26, Maury assumed temporary command in Meridian, Mississippi, of the Department of Alabama, Mississippi, and East Louisiana, and held the position until Lieutenant-General Richard Taylor assumed command on September 6. Federal forces moved against the eastern defenses of Mobile Bay in Maury's district in late March of 1865. After the capture of Spanish Fort on April 8, and Fort Blakely the following day, Maury ordered an evacuation of Mobile. He left the city with his army's rear guard on April 12, 1865. Maury and his men surrendered at Cuba Station, Alabama, on May 8, 1865. *Post-War:* After the war, like so many other Confederate generals, he was penniless. He visited New Orleans briefly and then returned to his family home in Fredericksburg. He established and taught at the Classical and Mathematical Academy for boys in Fredericksburg. He then moved to New Orleans to become an express agent. He purchased land in nearby St. Tammany Parish, approximately thirty minutes east of New Orleans, and operated a naval stores manufacturing company. When it failed, he returned to New Orleans. He wrote a school history of Virginia, and helped to organize the Southern Historical Society in 1868 to preserve the Confederacy's archival records. In 1873, the society relocated to Richmond, Virginia, and he served as the chair of its executive committee until 1886. He was a member of the executive committee of the National Guard Association until 1890. President Grover Cleveland appointed him as the U.S. Minister to Colombia, a position in which he served from 1885 to 1889. *Interesting:* For his brave services in Mexico, he was presented with a sword from the citizens and legislators of Fredericksburg, Virginia. He declined a $30,000 per year job as a supervisor of the infamous Louisiana Lottery. He gave up his business to be a volunteer nurse during a New Orleans yellow fever epidemic. In 1873, he assisted in organizing the Westmoreland Club of Richmond. General Joseph E. Johnston was a godfather to his granddaughter, and General Carter Littlepage Stevenson was a godfather to one of his sons, who was baptized at his headquarters in Vicksburg. His headquarters was bombarded by the Federals during the baptismal service. He was called Puss N' Boots, because his small body looked lost in the immense pair of cavalry boots he wore. *Literary Works:* He authored, *Recollections of a Virginian* in 1894, and *A Young People's History of Virginia and Virginians* in 1896. *Death and Burial:* Died at the home of his son in Peoria, Illinois, on January 11, 1900. He is buried in the Confederate Cemetery at Fredericksburg, Virginia. His headstone reads, "Gentleman, Patriot, and Soldier." *Dedications:* There was a statue erected in April of 1915 in honor of Maury at the Vicksburg National Military Park in Vicksburg, Mississippi.

Army

Bragg, Braxton—Brigadier General/Major General/General—*Born:* March 21, 1817, in Warrenton County, North Carolina, to Thomas Bragg, a carpenter, and Margaret Crossland. Bragg had eleven siblings. Two of his brothers were successful lawyers and were involved in politics. His brother, Thomas Bragg, Jr., served as governor of North Carolina from 1855 to 1859. His eldest brother, John Bragg, became a judge of Mobile, Alabama, and a member of the U.S. Congress. *Religion:* Episcopal. *Education:* Warrenton Male Academy. Shortly after his sixteenth birthday in 1833, he was accepted to West Point. Graduated in June of 1837, an impressive fifth in a class of fifty. Academically, he was a good student, though in March of 1836, Bragg and four other cadets jeopardized their military careers by playing cards, which was a serious offense that could have resulted in expulsion. The matter was resolved in February of 1837. *Politics:* Democrat. *Marriage/Family:* He met his wife, Elisa Brooks Ellis, in 1849 at a ball being held in his honor at a new school house in Thibodaux, Louisiana. They were married on June 7, 1849, at her family home, "Evergreen Plantation," in Thibodaux. The ceremony was officiated by Reverend John Sandel. John Duncan served as best man. They had no children. *Pre-War:* Appointed 2nd lieutenant in the 3rd U.S. Artillery in July of 1837, and fought the Seminole Indians in Florida. Participated in the Mexican-American War. Breveted captain at Fort Brown, major at Monterey, and lieutenant-colonel at Buena Vista. In 1849, he was temporary adjutant-general to General Edmund Pendleton. In 1855, he was offered the position of major in the 1st U.S. Regiment of Cavalry, but declined the appointment. In 1856, he resigned from the army as a lieutenant-colonel to become a planter in Louisiana. On February 8, 1856, he purchased a sugar plantation, "Bivouac," in Lafourche Parish. For the standards of the time, Bragg was considered a rich man. After December of 1860, he never returned or saw his home again, as it was confiscated and sold. From 1859 to 1861, he was commissioner of public works for the Second District of Louisiana, and was elected to the board. On December 12, 1860, Louisiana Governor Thomas O. Moore appointed Bragg a member of the state military board. On January 11, 1861, he persuaded the commander of the Baton Rouge U.S. arsenal to surrender. *During the War:* Promoted to brigadier-general in the Provisional Confederate Army on March 7, 1861, and assigned command of the coastal defenses from Pensacola, Florida, to Mobile, Alabama. After being promoted to major-general on September 12, 1861, he asked for, and was granted, a transfer north. He assumed command of Albert S. Johnston's 2nd Corps, which he led at the Battle of Shiloh. Upon General A.S. Johnston's death in that battle, he was appointed the same day to a full-general in the Regular Army to rank from April 6, 1862. In the latter part of June in 1862, he replaced General P.G.T. Beauregard as commander of the Army of Tennessee, due to Beauregard's ill-health. He led the Army of Tennessee in the Kentucky invasion from August to October of 1862. He was defeated by General Don Carlos Buell at the Battle of Perryville. He was forced to retreat when battling General William S. Rosecrans' army following the Battle of Murfreesboro in early January of 1863. In the spring of 1863, he was again sick, plagued with boils and very weak. In September of 1863, he was victorious at the Battle of Chickamauga. He besieged Rosecrans's army at Chattanooga, but in November of 1863 General U.S. Grant forced him to retire into Georgia, where he yielded command at his own request to General Joseph E. Johnston. Upon his resignation from command of the Army of Tennessee, he was assigned as military advisor to President Davis at Richmond in February of 1864. After General Lee's appointment as general-in-chief, Bragg saw service at Wilmington, North Carolina, under General Joseph E. Johnston. In March of 1865, he participated in the

Confederate victory at Bentonville, North Carolina. *Post-War:* Civil Engineer in New Orleans, Louisiana. Later, he became superintendent of harbor improvements in Mobile, Alabama. In the 1870s, he became commissioner of public works for the state of Alabama. He moved to Galveston, Texas, in 1874 and became chief engineer for the Gulf, Colorado, and Santa Fe Railroad. *Interesting:* His brother, John Bragg, also built the beautiful Bragg-Mitchell Mansion located in Mobile, Alabama. It was rumored that Braxton Bragg was born in jail while his mother was imprisoned on a charge of murdering a free Negro. A different account says that his mother, while pregnant, killed a free Negro but was at home in time for Braxton's birth. General Bragg was not a favorite among his comrades, but it has been noted that he was a favorite of President Jefferson Davis. He and William Tecumsah Sherman were very good friends throughout their lives. In October of 1847, it was reported that there was an assassination attempt on Bragg's life in which someone placed an eight-inch bomb shell, with a train leading off by which it was ignited, under his bed. Fortunately for Bragg, two of the missiles went through his bed without touching him and miraculously, he escaped injury. He suffered from fever, dyspepsia, boils, migraine headaches, nervousness, and rheumatism through his life. *Death and Burial:* He died from a stroke in Galveston, Texas, on September 27, 1876. He is buried at Magnolia Cemetery in Mobile, Alabama. *Dedications:* Bragg, Texas, was named for Bragg. Originally named Camp Bragg, the U.S. army's Fort Bragg in North Carolina was also named in his honor.

Hood, John Bell (aka Sam) — Captain/Colonel/Brigadier General/Major General/Lieutenant General — *Born:* June 1, 1831, in Owingsville, Bath County, Kentucky, to John W. Hood, a physician, and Theodosia French. *Religion:* Baptized on May 11, 1864, by Bishop, and Lieutenant-General, Leonidas Polk. *Education:* Attended local schools and was tutored. He entered West Point in 1849 and graduated in 1853 forty-fourth in a class of fifty-two. *Marriage/Family:* On April 30, 1868, he married Anna Marie Hennen, a native of New Orleans. Over the next ten years he would father eleven children, including three sets of twins: Lydia, Annabel, Ethel, Duncan, Odile, Ida, Oswald, Anna Gertrude, John Bell, Jr., and a set of twin girls. *Pre-War:* Received a commission as 2nd Lieutenant of the 4th U.S. Infantry in 1854. After serving in Missouri and California, he was promoted to 2nd Lieutenant on March 3, 1855, and assigned to Company G of the 2nd U.S. Cavalry on the Texas frontier. While on a reconnaissance patrol at Fort Mason, Texas, on July 20, 1857, he battled the Comanche Indians in hand-to-hand combat near Devil's River, Texas, and was wounded when an arrow pierced his left hand. He was promoted to 1st Lieutenant on August 8, 1858. He received orders to report to West Point in September of 1860 to serve as Chief Instructor of Cavalry. However, at his personal request to U.S. Adjutant-General Samuel Cooper, the order was rescinded, and he remained with the 2nd Cavalry Regiment. Hood resigned his U.S. commission as a 1st Lieutenant in the U.S. Army on April 17, 1861, in anticipation of the outbreak of the Civil War. Dissatisfied with his native state of Kentucky's neutrality, and impressed with the beauty of Texas, he declared Texas his home. *During the War:* He was commissioned a captain in the Confederate cavalry on March 16, 1861. On September 30, 1861, he was appointed colonel of the 4th Texas Infantry, superseding Robert T.P. Allen. He was promoted to brigadier-general to rank from March 3, 1862, and was given command of what became known as "Hood's Texas Brigade." Hood led the brigade in the Peninsular Campaign. He was engaged in the second Battle of Bull Run, the battles of Boonesborough, Fredericksburg, and Antietam. On June 27, 1862, during the Battle of Gaines Mill, where his brigade lost more than half its number, he was wounded. He was appointed major-general on the field to rank from October 10, 1862. Under Lieutenant-General James Longstreet, he was elevated to command of a division for his performance at Sharpsburg and Fredericksburg. In the fall of 1863, he was severely wounded a second time at the Battle of Gettysburg, losing the use of his arm. Two months later, he rejoined his command and was ordered to Tennessee to reinforce General-Braxton Bragg. During the second day's fighting at Chickamauga on September 20, 1863, seeing the line of his brigade waver, he rode to the front, and demanded the colors. The Texans rallied and charged, and Hood, at the head of the column, broke the Union line. During this battle, he was again seriously wounded, necessitating the amputation of his right leg. Appointed to lieutenant-general on February 1, 1864, to rank from September 20, 1863, he rejoined the Army of Tennessee. He was given command of a corps consisting of three divisions: Thomas C. Hindman's, Carter L. Stevenson's, and Alexander P. Stewart's. He led his corps during the Atlanta Campaign, and on July 18, 1864, was given command of the Army of Tennessee, replacing General Joseph E. Johnston. He received a temporary promotion of full general, although the promotion was never confirmed by the Confederate Congress. Defeated by Sherman at the battles of Peachtree Creek, Atlanta, Ezra Church, and Jonesboro, he was forced to evacuate Atlanta on September 1, 1864. Subsequently, Hood led his troops in the invasion of Tennessee. Although Union Major-General John M. Schofield withdrew before Hood, he was defeated at the bloody Battle of Franklin on November 30, 1864. At the Battle of Nashville on December 15 and 16th, 1864, he was soundly defeated by Union Major-General George H. Thomas. At his own request in January of 1865, he was relieved from command of the Army of Tennessee. Richard Taylor assumed temporary command of the Army of Tennessee. In May of 1865, he surrendered himself at Natchez, Mississippi. *Post-War:* Engaged in business as a commission-merchant in New Orleans, and was also president of the Louisiana branch of the Life Association of America, an insurance company. During the yellow fever epidemic of 1879, his wife and eldest child died within a few hours of each other, and Hood also succumbed to the disease. Hood would lose all of his modest fortune during the winter of 1878–1879 due to the yellow fever epidemic that had closed the New Orleans Cotton Exchange and wiped out almost every city insurance company. *Interesting:* With the remains of the Army of Tennessee, they retreated toward Tupelo, Mississippi, singing "The Yellow Rose of Texas." His ten orphaned children, all under the age of ten, were left destitute. They were ultimately adopted by seven different families in Louisiana, New York, Mississippi, Georgia, and Kentucky. *Interesting Quote:* In a conversation with Richmond diarist Mary Chesnut, Hood stated that he had declared to Jefferson Davis while with the Army of Tennessee in 1864, "Mr. President, why don't you come and lead us yourself? I would follow you to the death."[8] *Literary Works:* He authored, *Advance and Retreat, Personal Experiences in the United States and Confederate Armies*, published in 1880. *Death and Burial:* Died on August 31, 1879, of yellow fever, within days of his wife and eldest child. Hood, his wife, and three of the children are buried in the Hennen family tomb at Metairie Cemetery in New Orleans, Louisiana.

Johnston, Joseph Eggleston—(See Department section.)

Corps

Breckinridge, John Cabell—Brigadier General/Major General—*Born:* January 16, 1821, in Lexington, Kentucky, the only son of Joseph Cabell and Mary Clay Smith. His father, who died at age thirty-four, was a distinguished member of the Kentucky bar. *Education:* Graduated in 1838 from Centre College in Danville, Kentucky. Studied for six months at Princeton College in New Jersey, then returned to Kentucky to work under the future Whig governor, Judge William Owsley. Once completing his studies under the judge, he studied law at Transylvania University. *Religion:* Presbyterian. *Politics:* Elected Democratic vice-president of the U.S. at the age of thirty-five, and took the oath of office on March 4, 1857. Member of the Kentucky legislature from 1849 to 1851. A member of the U.S. House of Representatives from 1851 to 1855. In 1859, he was appointed to the U.S. Senate by the Kentucky legislature, and opposed war in the special session of 1861. Candidate for president in 1860, finished a distant second to Abraham Lincoln in the electoral college. *Marriage:* Married Mary Cyrene Burch of Scott County, Kentucky, on December 12, 1843, producing six children. She sewed a flag for a regiment in her husband's division. *Pre-War:* He left for the Mexican American War in 1847, and was commissioned a major in the 3rd Kentucky Volunteer Infantry. He witnessed more illness than battle, and returned home by July of 1848. *During the War:* Commissioned a Confederate brigadier-general on November 2, 1861, when his native state declared for the Union. Promoted to major-general to rank from April 14, 1862, commanding the Reserve Corps at Shiloh, and aided in the defense of Vicksburg in the summer of 1862. At the battle of Shiloh, he was struck by two spent bullets and several horses were shot from under him. He narrowly escaped death when a cannonball struck his horse and pinned him beneath it while skirmishing with the Federals in the Shenandoah Valley. He was ordered to assume command of the Army of Tennessee's 1st Brigade, 2nd Division, on November 16, 1861, during the Kentucky Campaign. When he arrived, he learned that General Bragg had retreated after the Battle of Perryville. Failing in an attack on Baton Rouge, he distinguished himself at the battle of Murfreesboro, Tennessee, again under Bragg's command. He fought bravely, though Union artillery fire forced the Confederates to retreat. Throughout the war, there was much contention between Bragg and Breckinridge. After Murfreesboro, he was ordered to aid in the relief of Vicksburg with Joseph E. Johnston in 1863. He participated in the Battle of Chickamauga in September of 1863 where, though victorious, the Confederates suffered heavy casualties. Following Chickamauga, he participated in the Battle of Chattanooga, where the Confederates were forced to withdraw. His son, Lieutenant Clift Breckinridge, was captured at the Battle of Missionary Ridge on November 25, 1863. His other son, Cabel, was an aide to his father. On February 15, 1864, he received orders relieving him of command in the Army of Tennessee. Approximately a month later, he was given command of the Department of Southwestern Virginia in 1864, and later accompanied General Jubal A. Early in his raid on Washington, D.C. On February 4, 1865, he was appointed by President Davis as Confederate secretary of war. In May of 1864, he led in the Battle of New Market against General Ulysses S. Grant, where the Confederates were superiorly outnumbered but won decisively, forcing a federal retreat. *Post-War:* When Breckinridge learned that Davis had finally been captured at Irwinville, Georgia, he was already moving south toward Florida, attempting to get out of the country. General William T. Sherman had personally advised Breckinridge to flee, explaining that the North felt very bitter toward the former U.S. vice-president who took up arms against the government. He sailed to Cardenas, Cuba, on June 11, 1865. From Cuba, he went to Europe, where he remained until 1869, then he moved on to Toronto, Canada, and asked for asylum. In Toronto, he was reunited with his family. On August 8, 1866, the family sailed to Great Britain, and they safely returned to Kentucky in 1869, where he resumed his law practice. He later managed the Piedmont and Arlington Insurance Company, and served as president of the proposed Elizabethtown, Lexington, and Big Sandy Railroad from 1869 to 1874. He owned several thoroughbred horses, and was president of the Lexington Racing Society, also known as the Kentucky Association. *Interesting Quote:* "I must not shield my son from the dangers of his comrades."⁹ *Death and Burial:* Died in Lexington on May 17, 1875, from cirrhosis of the liver, and is buried in the family plot at Lexington City Cemetery in Kentucky. *Dedication:* There is a statue of Breckinridge in the Vicksburg National Military Park in Vicksburg, Mississippi.

Cheatham, Benjamin Franklin (aka Frank) — Brigadier General/Major General — *Born:* October 20, 1820, at "Westover," the family plantation near Nashville, Tennessee, to Leonard Pope, a lawyer, planter, and military veteran, and Elizabeth Robertson. His father served with Andrew Jackson during the War of 1812. Benjamin had ten siblings. His maternal grandfather was James Robertson, founder of Nashville and historically referred to as the "Father of Tennessee." *Education:* Tutored at home by an accomplished Englishman before attending a boy's school in Nashville. Starting at age seventeen, he spent two years at college in Kentucky, from 1837 to 1839. *Politics:* In the fall of 1857, he was a Democratic candidate for mayor of Nashville, but failed to win the election. In 1872, he was an unsuccessful candidate for the U.S. Congress. *Marriage/Family:* Married Anna Bell Robertson in 1866 at First Presbyterian Church in Nashville; Chaplain Todd Quintard, an old army friend and the Episcopal bishop of Tennessee, officiated the ceremony. At Frank's request, Quintard baptized him the same year. After his marriage, the couple moved to Coffee County, Tennessee, to a farm owned by his in-laws. Their union produced five children, three boys and two girls: Benjamin Frank Cheatham Jr., Patton R., Joe Johnston, Medora, and Alice. A few weeks after his death, Anna received a four-year appointment as Postmistress of Nashville. She died of consumption in Nashville on January 14, 1888, at age 49. *Pre-War:* In the early 1840s, he joined a local militia company, the Nashville Blues. He rose in rank after five years of service to 1st lieutenant before resigning his commission. He later raised Company E of the First Tennessee Infantry, also known as the "Bloody First," and became captain. He served with distinction in the Mexican-American War as a captain in the 1st Tennessee Regiment. In September of 1846, he was slightly wounded during the Battle of Monterey. He was discharged from the U.S. Army in May of 1847. That same year, he returned to Nashville and resumed farming. He later raised the Third Tennessee Regiment and was elected colonel. They were mustered in on October 1, 1847, and mustered out of service, less than a year later, on July 24, 1848, at Memphis, Tennessee. In the fall of 1849, he traveled to California during the Gold Rush with six members of the Third Tennessee Regiment. He operated a merchandise store supplying gold-seekers, and a hotel/tavern in Stockton, California, named Hotel de Mexico, until returning to Tennessee in 1853, where he again resumed farming. That same year, he was appointed a major-general in the Tennessee Militia, commanding the 2nd Division. From 1855 to 1859, he was an area sales agent for a farm implements company. Like his father, he had a passion for training and breeding thoroughbred horses, and in 1860 became the owner of the Nashville Race Track. *During the War:* After Tennessee seceded, Governor Isham Harris appointed him a brigadier-general in the Provisional Army of Tennessee on May 9, 1861. He was commissioned a brigadier-general in the Confederate army on July 9, 1861, and his first Civil War combat experience was at the Battle of Belmont, Missouri, on November 7, 1861, where he led a bayonet charge that defeated the Union troops led by General U.S. Grant. His leadership skills in that battle won him a promotion to major-general on March 10, 1862. He was then ordered to join General Albert Sidney Johnston's army at Corinth, Mississippi. On April 6, 1862, he led the 2nd Division of the 1st Corps in an attack on the Hornet's Nest, where he was slightly wounded in the shoulder. It was reported by General Pierre Gustave Toutant Beauregard that Cheatham had three horses shot from under him during the two-day battle. At the Battle of Perryville, Kentucky, on October 8, 1862, Cheatham and his men destroyed three Union brigades and killed two Union generals. After participating in the Battle of Stone's River on December 31, 1862, he faced controversy when several reports alleged that he appeared intoxicated and unable to direct his men. When General Hood replaced General Joseph E. Johnston in 1864 as commander of the Army of Tennessee, Cheatham was placed in command of General Hardee's old corps. He saw action at Chickamauga, Missionary Ridge, Peachtree Creek, Atlanta, and Kennesaw Mountain. Cheatham led the Tennessee Division at Jonesboro. Controversy erupted when Hood accused Cheatham of failing to attack the Federal troops at Spring Hill, Tennessee, on November 29, 1864, and blamed Cheatham for the Confederate defeat at the Battle of Franklin the following day. Hood accused Cheatham of dereliction of duty, but a military court cleared Cheatham of the charges. Cheatham and his men bore the brunt of the Union assaults at the Battle of Nashville on December 15. He and the remnants of his command reported to General Joseph E. Johnston in January of 1865. Following Johnston's surrender to Sherman on April 26, 1865, at Durham's Station in North Carolina, Cheatham was paroled on May 1, 1865. *Post-War:* After the Civil War, he returned to Coffee County, Tennessee, to resume farming. From 1875 to 1879, he was appointed by his former chief-of-staff, and state governor, James D. Porter, as superintendent of state prisons in Tennessee. In October of 1885, President Grover Cleveland appointed him Postmaster of Nashville, a position he held until the time of his death. *Interesting:* He often used profanity and was a heavy drinker. It is noted that after a battle someone reported he fell off his horse while waving his hat rather too vigorously in a gesture to encourage his men. After his fall, a member of his staff had to ride beside him and hold him on his horse. His son, Benjamin Franklin Cheatham, Jr. (1867–1944), was a major-general in the U.S. Army, serving with distinction in the Spanish-American War and World War I. *Interesting Quote:* Toward the end of his life, he suffered delirium and it is noted that he said, "There go the troops, bring me my horse, I am going to the front."[10] *Death and Burial:* Died on September 4, 1886, at his brother Felix's home in Nashville of arteriosclerosis. At his funeral, his body was wrapped in a Confederate flag. His funeral procession extended more than a mile. He is buried at Mount Olivet Cemetery in Nashville, Tennessee. *Dedications:* A statue was erected in Nashville Centennial Park in 1903 in his honor and dedicated in 1909 by the Frank Cheatham Bivouac, United Confederate Veterans, and a chapter of the United Daughters of the Confederacy.

Hardee, William Joseph (aka Old Reliable)— Brigadier General/Major General/Lieutenant General—*Born:* October 12, 1815, in Camden, Georgia, to Major John Hardee, a veteran of the War of 1812, businessman, and state senator, and Sarah Ellis. *Religion:* He was confirmed in the Episcopal Church by Lieutenant General Leonidas Polk and his second wife, Mrs. Mary Hardee. He was a vestry man in the St. Paul Episcopal church in Selma, Alabama. *Education:* Tutored, then entered West Point in June of 1834. Graduated twenty-sixth in a class of forty-five in July of 1838. During 1840, upon receiving instructions from the Secretary of War, he attended the Royal Cavalry School in Paris, France, for twelve months. He received instruction in riding and cavalry tactics, and obtained his merit certificate on January 28, 1842. *Marriage/Family:* Married Elizabeth Drummett on November 16, 1840, producing four children: Anna Drummett, Sarah Florida (Sallie), William, and Elizabeth Douglas. His first wife, Elizabeth, died on June 10, 1853, of tuberculosis. He met his 2nd wife, Mary Frances Lewis, at Demopolis, Alabama, and was married on January 13, 1863. Major-General Patrick Ronayne Cleburne was the best man at his wedding. Mary died on April 6, 1875, at the age of 35 from tuberculosis. Ironically, both wives died of the same disease, in the same town, with the same attending physician. *Pre-War:* Prior to attending cavalry school, he was promoted to 1st lieutenant and served in the Seminole War in Florida until 1840. Due to his success as a regimental drillmaster, the U.S. War Department promoted him to captain on October 21, 1844. In May of 1848, he was ordered to Baltimore, Maryland, for duty as a recruiting officer. While fighting in the Mexican-American War, he was breveted twice to major, then to lieutenant-colonel, for gallantry and courage. During the war, he was captured at Matamoras while skirmishing at the Carricitos ranch. He was released and again assumed command of his company. He also participated in the battles of Contreras, Medllin, El Molino del Rey, La Rosia, the Siege of Vera Cruz, the capture of Mexico City, and other minor skirmishes. On June 17, 1856, he was ordered to report for duty as Commandant of Cadets at West Point. Hardee remained in Washington during the summer of 1855, serving as a member of a cavalry equipment board. *During the War:* When Georgia seceded from the Union, he resigned his lieutenant-colonel's commission on January 31, 1861. He was appointed a brigadier-general in the Confederate army on June 17, and major-general on October 7, 1861. He organized a brigade of Arkansas regiments and operated in Arkansas until he was ordered to join General Albert S. Johnston prior to the Battle of Shiloh. He commanded a wing of the Army of Tennessee during Bragg's invasion of Kentucky. At Murfreesboro, he was promoted to lieutenant-general on October 10, 1862. He commanded a corps at the Battle of Chattanooga, and served under General Joseph E. Johnston and John Bell Hood during the Atlanta campaign. He declined command of the Army of Tennessee, to replace General Bragg, after the Chattanooga campaign. He had a lack of confidence in General Hood that caused him to request a transfer from the Army of Tennessee after the battle of Jonesboro. He opposed Sherman in Georgia and the Carolinas at the end of the war. In the closing weeks of the conflict, he was again under Johnston, his old commander and friend. He yielded Savannah and Charleston to Sherman's army, and surrendered in North Carolina on April 26, 1865. *Post-War:* He engaged in planting at Selma, Alabama, and became one of the original board members of the Selma Fire and Marine Insurance Company. He also helped organize the Central Agricultural and Mechanical Association. He was president of the Selma and Meridian Railroad in 1866, but by 1868, the railroad was forced to give up its leases. *Interesting:* General Hardee suffered from dyspepsia throughout his life. His older brother, Thomas Ellis Hardee, was murdered in the streets of St. Mary's on August 30, 1839, and the assailant was never caught. His son, Willie Hardee, was also in the Civil War and died on March 24, 1865, at the Battle of Bentonville at age sixteen. He was buried in the St. Matthew's Episcopal Church Cemetery in Hillsboro, North Carolina. It is noted in one source that Willie Hardee, Jr., was an aide to his father while in Confederate service. However, there was an article in the January 1916 edition of *Confederate Veteran* magazine, written by Reverend G.C. Garrison of Texas, stating that young Will was never a member of his father's staff. The reverend stated he was at Hardee's headquarters during the last two years of the war, and was present with the company that escorted General Hardee to his wife's plantation in Demopolis, Alabama, at the end of the war. He was also a member of the Aztec Club, which was organized on October 13, 1847, originally composed of General Winfield Scott's veterans. *Literary Works:* Authored the standard textbook, *Hardee's Rifle and Light Infantry Tactics*, a new army tactics manual published in 1861 that saw use in both armies. *Death and Burial:* Died due to cancer of the stomach on November 6, 1873, and is buried at Live Oak Cemetery in Selma, Alabama. *Dedications:* The state of Georgia honored him with a sword, in recognition of his service in the Mexican-American War. Georgia Governor George W. Townes invited Noble Andrew Hardee to Milledgeville to receive the sword for his brother.

Hindman, Thomas Carmichael — Colonel/Brigadier General/Major General — *Born:* January 28, 1828, at Knoxville, Tennessee, to Thomas Carmichael Hindman, Sr., an Indian agent for the U.S. government, and Sallie Holt. When he was four years old, his parents moved to Jacksonville, Alabama. In 1841, the family moved to Ripley, Mississippi, and operated a large plantation. *Religion:* Presbyterian. *Education:* Local and private schools in Mississippi. Graduated with honors in 1846 from the Lawrenceville Classical and Commercial Institute in New Jersey. *Politics:* Active Democrat, opposed the Know-Nothing Party, and was a States'-Rights Democrat. Hindman was known for his eloquent speaking and when Jefferson Davis ran for governor of Mississippi in 1851, he supported him by speaking on his behalf in the northern counties of Mississippi. Member of the Mississippi House of Representatives for one term from 1853 to 1854. Elected to the Thirty-Sixth U.S. Congress, and re-elected from Arkansas in 1858 and 1860. He was offered a seat with the Thirty-Seventh U.S. Congress, but refused the seat to align himself with the Confederacy. He moved to Helena, Arkansas, in 1856, and practiced law with the associates of John C. Palmer and Judge M.T. Sanders under the firm name, Hindman, Palmer, and Sanders. When Henry M. Rector ran for governor of Arkansas in 1860, he campaigned for his election. In 1860, he was instrumental in securing the secession of Arkansas. *Marriage/Family:* Married Mary "Mollie" Watkins Biscoe on November 11, 1856, producing four children: Susan Nash, Biscoe, Thomas Carmichael, Jr., and Blanche Carlotta. *Pre-War:* Raised a company in his home county at age eighteen, which became part of the 2nd Mississippi Regiment. He rose in rank to 2nd Lieutenant and Captain. Served conspicuously during the Mexican-American War. At the close of the war, he returned to his father's plantation in Ripley, Mississippi. In 1848, he studied law for three years under the Honorable Orlando Davis. In 1851, he was admitted to the Tippah County Bar before opening a law practice in Ripley. *During the War:* Entered the Confederate Army as a colonel of the 2nd Arkansas Infantry. Promoted to brigadier-general on September 28, 1861, and major-general on April 14, 1862, to rank from April 4. At Woodsonville during the Kentucky Campaign, he drove the enemy back. General Hardee thanked Hindman and his command for their conduct and brilliant courage. At the Battle of Shiloh in 1862, he attacked the enemy, drawing him from two lines of works and capturing a number of prisoners. While fighting at Shiloh, he was injured when his horse was killed by a cannonball, disabling him when the horse fell. He displayed courage and skill which won him the confidence of his troops during this battle. He commanded the Trans-Mississippi Department from his headquarters in Little Rock, Arkansas, during the spring of 1862. He fought gallantly at the Battle of Prairie Grove, and in his report of the battle on December 9, 1862, he estimated the Federal loss at nearly 1,000 killed and wounded, 300 captured prisoners, 20 wagons, and 4 stands of colors. Hindman was accused of declaring martial law and adopting oppressive military regulations in Arkansas. After commanding the department for seventy days, he was replaced by Major-General Theophilus "Granny" Hunter Holmes. At Chickamauga he was wounded, confirmed when Hindman reported that he was injured on September 20, 1863, in an official report. On September 29, 1863, he was reprimanded for disobeying orders and not writing a report of the operations that occurred around McLemore's Cove in September of 1863. He was suspended from command and ordered to proceed to Atlanta with his personal staff to await further orders, though he was later reinstated. While participating in the Battle of Atlanta, he suffered an eye injury which incapacitated him from further field duty. There has been some controversy regarding his wound, as some sources claim he was only slightly wounded, and took sick leave because of a lack of promotion, and not because of his injury. *Post-War:* In the summer of 1865, he moved his family to Mexico and managed a coffee plantation, remaining there several years. They eventually returned to Helena, where he farmed and resumed his law practice. He was a strong opponent of the Arkansas Republican party. *Interesting:* His father was the first male child born in Knoxville, Tennessee, in 1793. Patrick R. Cleburne was the best man at Hindman's wedding. In 1855, during a terrible yellow fever epidemic in Helena, he and Cleburne, along with a Methodist preacher, offered their services to care for the sick. In Helena, Arkansas, in 1856, Hindman and Patrick R. Cleburne were involved in a gunfight with Know-Nothing Party members that nearly cost them their lives. During the gunfight, Hindman was wounded by a bullet to his right breast, while Cleburne was shot in the back. *Death and Burial:* On September 27, 1868, while sitting in his parlor reading a newspaper with his wife and children present, he was murdered when an unknown assassin fired a gunshot through the parlor window. There has been speculation it may have resulted from his outspoken stand in opposition to the carpetbag regime that existed during that time period. Buried in Maple Hill Cemetery in Helena, Arkansas.

Hood, John Bell — (See Army section.)

Lee, Stephen Dill — Captain/Major/Lieutenant Colonel/Colonel/Brigadier General/Major General/Lieutenant General — *Born:* September 22, 1833, at Charleston, South Carolina, to Thomas Lee, a physician, and Caroline Allison. It has been noted that he was distantly related to the Lee's of Virginia, but by the time of the Civil War, no one in either of the families knew of the linkage. Stephen's mother died when he was quite young, leaving him and a sister to be raised by their widowed father. He was named for one of his uncles with whom he became close. *Religion:* Member of the Baptist Church at age 40. *Education:* Attended a boarding school in North Carolina. Entered West Point at age seventeen, graduating seventeenth in a class of forty-six. in 1854. He excelled in artillery and cavalry studies. *Politics:* Democrat. Mississippi Democratic State Senator in 1878. Delegate to the Mississippi constitutional convention in 1890. When South Carolina seceded from the Union, he waited nearly two months before resigning his commission and returning to his home state to offer his military services to the Confederacy. One of his friends later asserted that Lee had taken the step with regret. *Marriage/Family:* Married Regina Blewett Harrison of Columbus, Mississippi, at her stately old mansion in Columbus, on February 9, 1865. They had one known son, Blewett Lee. The couple lived in the mansion after they were married, which is now a Museum and Historical Pilgrimage headquarters. *Pre-War:* Upon graduating from West Point, he was assigned to the U.S. 4th Artillery Regiment as a 1st lieutenant, and was adjutant of Florida and quartermaster during the Seminole War in 1857. He saw nearly seven years of service before resigning his U.S. commission in February of 1861. He served along the Kansas-Missouri borderland, and in Florida and Texas. Just prior to the Civil War, he was stationed at Fort Randall in the Dakota Territory. *During the War:* Resigned his U.S. commission on February 20, 1861. He entered the Confederacy as a captain and aide-de-camp to General P.G.T. Beauregard. He and Colonel Chestnut carried the summons to Union Major Robert Anderson demanding the surrender of Fort Sumter. When Major Anderson declined, they carried the orders to the field battery to open fire on the fort. He was with the delegation that formally accepted the capitulation terms of the fort. He served in the artillery throughout all the Virginia campaigns until Sharpsburg, and was promoted through grades to colonel. Appointed to brigadier-general on November 6, 1862. He was assigned to command General John C. Pemberton's artillery in Vicksburg, Mississippi, and fought at the Battle of Champion Hill in 1863. He was exchanged after the July 4, 1863, surrender of Vicksburg, Mississippi. He was then promoted to major-general on August 3, 1863, and placed in command of the Department of Mississippi, Alabama, and East Louisiana. On March 16, 1865, to rank from June 23, 1864, he was appointed to lieutenant-general and assumed command of Hood's old corps in the Army of Tennessee. He participated in the battles of Ezra Church and the first day at Jonesboro, before receiving orders from General Hardee to march back to Atlanta to cover the evacuation of the city in 1864. He saw action at the battles of Franklin and Spring Hill, where he was wounded in the foot in November of 1864. Lee was surrendered along with the rest of General Joseph E. Johnston's forces in North Carolina on April 26, 1865. *Post-War:* He resided in Mississippi, and was an insurance salesman and planter. In 1880, he became the first president of the newly established Agricultural and Mechanical College of Mississippi, now Mississippi State University, serving until 1889. He resigned from the university to become a member of the federal commission for the development of the Vicksburg National Military Park, in which he was deeply involved. He was the founder and president of the Mississippi Historical Society. In 1904, he was the highest ranking Confederate general still alive. He also helped found the United Confederate Veterans (UCV). During the last four years of his life, he became commander in chief of the UCV, a position he held until his death in Vicksburg, Mississippi. *Interesting:* William Dorsey Pender was his closest friend at West Point. Other close friends were Oliver Otis Howard, Custis Lee, John Pegram, and James Ewell Brown Stuart. He studied artillery and cavalry under Professor George H. Thomas. Robert E. Lee was a great influence in his life. He was the youngest of the lieutenant-generals of the Confederacy. *Interesting Quote:* "I am only chief because my comrades have gone before me."[11] *Literary Works:* Author of *The South since the War*. *Death and Burial:* Died on May 28, 1908, and buried in the Harrison family plot at Friendship Cemetery in Columbus, Mississippi. *Dedications:* In June of 1909, there was a statue erected of Lee in the Vicksburg National Military Park in Vicksburg, Mississippi.

Polk, Leonidas (aka Bishop)— Major General/Lieutenant General —*Born:* April 10, 1806, the second of twelve children, in Raleigh, North Carolina, to William Polk, a Revolutionary War major, successful planter, and businessman, and Sarah Hawkins. He was the nephew of the Eleventh President of the United States, James Knox Polk. *Education:* Attended preparatory schools. Attended the University of North Carolina, and graduated eighth from West Point in 1827. *Marriage/Family:* Married Frances Ann Devereux in May of 1830. They had eight children: Alexander Hamilton, Frances Devereux, Katherine, Sarah H., Susan R., Elizabeth Devereux, William Mecklenberg, and Rebecca L. *Pre-War:* Converted to Christianity under the influence of Episcopalian chaplain Charles Pettit McIlvaine. He resigned his U.S. army commission shortly after graduating from West Point, then attended the Virginia Theological Seminary. He was ordained a deacon in the Protestant Episcopal Church. Chaplain McIlvaine baptized cadet Polk forty days after his first conference at West Point. Reverend Polk served the Monumental Church in Richmond, Virginia, as assistant rector for a year in 1830, then traveled extensively in Europe. In 1838 he was appointed missionary bishop of the Southwest, which included Louisiana, Alabama, Mississippi, Arkansas, and the Indian Territory. In 1841 he became the first Protestant Episcopal bishop of Louisiana. Under his evangelical leadership, Episcopal churches were established at Shreveport, Plaquemine, Opelousas, Thibodaux, Napoleonville, and Donaldsonville. He ordained sixteen deacons and nineteen priests, and the number of churches grew from three to thirty-three. In 1842 he donated land in Maury County, Tennessee, and built St. John's Church. *During the War:* Although he was hesitant to give his military services to the war efforts, he gave in to the request of an old West Point friend, Jefferson Davis, and was appointed a major-general in the Provisional Army of the Confederacy on

June 25, 1861, to rank from that date. He also organized the Army of Mississippi, later a part of the Army of Tennessee. He participated in the engagement at Belmont, Missouri, where both he and General U.S. Grant claimed success. He was assigned to command of Department No. 2 until superseded by General Albert Sidney Johnston. Promoted to lieutenant-general to rank from October 10, 1862. He subsequently served as a corps commander in the Army of Tennessee, and saw action at Shiloh, Perryville, Murfreesboro, Chickamauga, and the early stages of the Atlanta campaign. While commanding at Murfreesboro, generals Polk, Cheatham, and Withers felt strongly they should retreat, while General Bragg, the commander of the Army of Tennessee, was determined to maintain their position despite the hazard. Polk urged the removal of General Bragg because he considered Bragg an incompetent commander. Much to Polk's surprise, Bragg removed Polk from command in the Army of Tennessee, and Polk received official notice on October 23, 1863. At the battle of Chickamauga, General Bragg cited Polk to be court-martialed for dilatory tactics there. Polk was removed from command during the controversy, but was later reinstated. Polk was killed during the Atlanta Campaign. *Interesting:* He preferred to be a planter more than a soldier. Albert Sidney Johnston was Polk's roommate at West Point. His nephew, Lucius Eugene Polk, was also a brigadier-general in the Army of Tennessee. His son, William, followed his father into the Civil War at age seventeen. William ended his military service as inspector-general of the Army of Tennessee. William later studied medicine at Tulane University and became dean of the Medical Department of Cornell University. He wrote a biography of his father. He was also elected President of the New York Academy of Medicine. Polk baptized General John B. Hood. Polk's son-in-law and aide, William Dudley Gale, (married to daughter Katherine) wrote to his wife about General Hood's baptism: "with two or three witnesses and by the light of a dim tallow candle."[12] Polk built his plantation, "Ashwood Hall," in Tennessee, and lived there until his brother, Andrew Jackson Polk, purchased it. Polk later bought "Leighton," a large plantation in southern Louisiana. Due to financial problems, Polk had to sell the large plantation, and later moved to New Orleans, Louisiana. In the 1850s he helped found the University of the South at Sewanee, Tennessee. When Polk was killed, in his pocket were three little volumes, prepared by Chaplain Quintard, entitled, "Balm for the Weary and Wounded," and were inscribed to generals Johnston, Hardee, and Hood, "with the compliments of General Leonidas Polk, June 12, 1864."[13] Two days later, Assistant Adjutant-General Douglas West delivered them. It has been noted in several sources that Polk did not like to take orders, especially from General Braxton Bragg. *Interesting quote:* "I buckle the sword over the gown."[14] *Death and Burial:* Though warned of danger, General Polk, along with generals Johnston and Hardee, was observing the enemy lines near Pine Mountain, Georgia, when Union artillerymen opened on them per orders from Union General William T. Sherman. An artillery shell struck his breast and went through his heart, killing him instantly, on June 14, 1864. Private Samuel Rush Watkins, of the Maury Grays, recalled, "While looking at them (the position of the enemy) with his field glass, a solid shot from the Federal guns struck him on his left breast, passing through his body and through his heart." Sam Watkins also wrote, "Every private soldier loved him. Second to Stonewall Jackson, his loss was the greatest the South ever sustained."[15] He was first buried in Marietta, Georgia, but later was reentered in the Christ Church (Episcopal) Cathedral in New Orleans in 1945. *Dedications:* Originally named Camp Polk, Fort Polk in Leesville, Louisiana, was named in honor of Leonidas Polk.

Walker, William Henry Talbot—Brigadier General/Major General—*Born:* November 26, 1816, in Augusta, Georgia, to Freeman Walker, a lawyer and member of the U.S. Senate. His mother is unknown. *Education:* Attended Richmond Academy, and graduated forty-sixth in a class of fifty at West Point in 1837. *Marriage/Family:* Married Mary Townsend of Albany, New York. *Pre-War:* Commissioned an officer in the 6th U.S. Infantry. Fought in the Seminole War in Florida in 1837 and 1838. He received three wounds in the Battle of Okeechobee on December 25, 1837. His wounds forced his resignation from the U.S. Army in 1838, though he rejoined the army in 1840. Breveted major for gallant conduct at Contreras and Churubusco during the Mexican-American War. Breveted lieutenant-colonel at the Battle of Molino del Rey, where he was again severely wounded and the surgeons feared he would die. Served on recruiting duty from 1849 to 1852. In 1854, he was appointed Commandant of Corps of Cadets at West Point. In 1855, he was appointed major and served on the frontier. He resigned his U.S. commission on December 20, 1860. *During the War:* Appointed a brigadier-general in the Confederate Army on May 25, 1861. He was stationed at Pensacola, Florida, under General Braxton Bragg, and in Northern Virginia. Bragg requested that Walker be transferred because of his feeble health. He was ordered to Manassas in the summer of 1861 to report for duty under General Joseph E. Johnston. He resigned on October 29, 1861, because of illness. He was at once commissioned major-general of the Georgia State Troops. He was appointed a brigadier-general in the Confederate Army to rank from February 9, 1863. Soon afterwards, he was promoted to major-general on May 23, 1863, to rank from that date due to General Joseph E. Johnston's recommendation and praise. Walker's division participated in the Siege of Jackson, Mississippi, in July of 1863, where he saw some skirmishing but suffered the majority of casualties from Union artillery fire. He was in charge of a division in the Army of Tennessee that consisted of Gist's, Wilson's, and Ector's brigades, before being placed in command of the reserve corps before Chickamauga. At the Battle of Chickamauga, it was reported that his losses were 1,477 wounded, killed, and missing. Killed during the Battle of Atlanta. *Interesting:* He could rarely sleep except in a sitting position. *Interesting Quote:* General Joseph E. Johnston stated Walker was, "The only officer in the West who is competent to command a brigade."[16] *Death and Burial:* On July 22, 1864, during the Atlanta Campaign, Walker was instantly killed by picket fire from a member of the Federal 16th Corps. Buried in the Walker Family Cemetery in Augusta, Georgia, with his wife. *Dedications:* Fort Walker, located in Grant Park at Fulton, Georgia, is named for Walker. There is also a monument dedicated in his honor at the outlet of Wilkinson Drive onto Glenwood, alongside the Interstate 20 interchange, in Atlanta. There was also a statue of Walker erected in October of 1913 in the Vicksburg National Military Park in Vicksburg, Mississippi.

Division

Clayton, Henry DeLamar, Sr.—Major/Colonel/Brigadier General/Major General—*Born:* March 7, 1827, in Pulaski County, Georgia, to Nelson Clayton, a native of North Carolina, farmer, and Georgia legislator, and Sara Carruthers. *Religion:* Episcopalian. *Education:* Attended Vineville Academy near Macon, Georgia. Graduated from Emory and Henry College with a Bachelor of Arts degree in 1848, and belonged to the Calliopean Literary Society, one of the two debating societies. *Politics:* Secessionist Democrat. Elected to the Alabama state legislature, representing Barbour County, from 1857 to 1861, where he was chairman of the state military committee at the outbreak of the Civil War. *Marriage/Family:* Married in 1850 to Victoria Virginia Hunter, a native of South Carolina, producing eight sons and four daughters. She authored, "White and Black under the Old Regime," published in 1899. She died in Eufaula, Alabama, on February 8, 1908. *Pre-War:* Studied law in Eufaula, Alabama, under John Shorter, who later became governor of the state. He was admitted to the bar in 1849, and opened a law practice in nearby Clayton, Alabama. *During the War:* He organized a militia company, the 1st Alabama Infantry, and was commissioned colonel on March 28, 1861, before being stationed at Pensacola, Florida. He later recruited the 39th Alabama Infantry, which he led in Bragg's Kentucky invasion. At the Battle of Murfreesboro, he was severely wounded, necessitating a leave of thirty days to recuperate. He was promoted to brigadier-general to rank from April 22, 1863, and major-general on July 7, 1864. He fought, and was again wounded, at the Battle of Chickamauga. He commanded a brigade during the Chattanooga Campaign, where they were heavily engaged. Assuming command of General Alexander P. Stewart's old division, he participated in the opening battles of the Atlanta Campaign and the invasion of Tennessee. He received praise from General Hood during the retreat from Nashville in late 1864, where his division and Brigadier-General Edmund Winston Pettus's brigade acted as the rear guard of the army until relieved by General Carter L. Stevenson. They fought at the battle of Bentonville, and surrendered with General Joseph E. Johnston in North Carolina in April of 1865. *Post-War:* Farmed and resumed his law practice. In May of 1866, he was elected judge of the Circuit Court of Alabama, and was re-elected in 1874 and 1880. Campaigned unsuccessfully for governor of Alabama in 1886, though later that year he became the 9th president of the University of Alabama. *Death and Burial:* Died in Tuscaloosa, Alabama, on October 3, 1889, and is buried next to his U.S. Congressman son, Henry DeLamar Clayton, Jr., in the Eufaula City Cemetery in Eufaula, Alabama.

Stewart, Alexander Peter (aka Old Straight)—Major/Brigadier General/Major General/Lieutenant General—*Born:* October 2, 1821, in Rogersville, Tennessee, to William A. Stewart of Delaware, and Elizabeth Decherd of Virginia. *Religion:* Presbyterian. *Education:* Attended Carrick Academy in Winchester, Tennessee. Graduated twelfth in a class of fifty-six from West Point in 1842. *Politics:* An old-line Whig who strongly opposed secession. *Marriage/Family:* Married Harriet Byron Chase on August 27, 1845, producing four sons: Robert Caruthers, Alphonso Chase, Alexander Peter, Jr., and Gustavus Woodson. *Pre-War:* Breveted 2nd Lieutenant in the 3rd U.S. Artillery. From 1843 to 1845, he taught mathematics as an assistant professor at West Point. Resigned his U.S. army commission in 1845 to accept a chair in mathematics and natural and experimental philosophy at Cumberland University in Lebanon, Tennessee. He resigned his chair in 1849 to accept a similar post at the University of Nashville. He was also city surveyor of Nashville, Tennessee. In 1856, he returned to Cumberland University as an educator. *During the War:* Volunteered for service in the Confederate States Army, though his initial assignment was organizing camps of instruction. Commissioned a major, he led the heavy artillery and water batteries at Columbus, Kentucky, and at the Battle of Belmont, Missouri. Promoted to brigadier-general on November 8, 1861, he led the 2nd Brigade under General Leonidas Polk. Promoted to major-general to rank from June 2, 1863. He gallantly commanded a division at the battles of Chickamauga and Chattanooga. He was a corps commander at the battle of Ezra Church, where he was wounded. When Leonidas Polk was killed at Pine Mountain, Georgia, Stewart was promoted to lieutenant-general on June 23, 1864, and succeeded to command of Polk's Corps, remaining in this position until the end of the war. Surrendered with General Joseph E. Johnston at Greensboro, North Carolina, on April 26, 1865, and was paroled in May of 1865. *Post-War:* Like many other Confederate generals, Stewart was poor at the end of the war. He resumed his professorship at Cumberland University. He later moved to St. Louis, Missouri, and worked in the insurance business from 1870 to 1874. In the latter year, he was elected chancellor of the University of Mississippi, resigning his chancellorship in 1886. He was later appointed a commissioner of the Chickamauga and Chattanooga National Military Park, serving until his death. *Death and Burial*: Died on August 30, 1908, in Biloxi, Mississippi. Buried at the Belle Fontaine Cemetery in St. Louis, Missouri.

Brigade

Adams, Daniel Weisiger—Lieutenant Colonel/Colonel/Brigadier General—*Born*: May 1, 1821, in Frankfort, Kentucky, to George Adams, a Federal judge, and Anna Mobrey. In 1825, his father moved the family to Natchez, Mississippi, where he became a distinguished politician. Daniel's older brother, William Wirt Adams, was also a brigadier-general in the Confederate States Army. *Education*: He read law and was admitted to the Mississippi State Bar. Although some sources claim he attended the University of Virginia, that appears to be an error. *Politics*: Elected State Senator from Jackson, Mississippi, and served in the 1852 session. He strongly opposed secession. *Marriage*: Twice married and fathered four children. His first wife was Mary Virginia Calloway and his second wife was Ann M. Bullis. His one known child, Daniel Weisiger Adams, Jr., was born in 1873 in Tensas Parish, Louisiana. *Pre-War*: He moved to New Orleans and was admitted to the Louisiana State Bar. In 1861, he was appointed by Governor Thomas O. Moore as one of three military board members to prepare Louisiana for Civil War. *During the War*: Before entering Confederate service, he served as a 2nd Lieutenant of the Mississippi State Troops. Upon the February 5, 1861, formation of the 1st Louisiana Regulars Infantry, he served as lieutenant-colonel and then colonel. The regiment was transferred on March 13, 1861, to Confederate service, and was ordered in April of 1861 to report for duty at Pensacola, Florida. At the Battle of Shiloh, when Brigadier-General Adley Hogan Gladden received a mortal wound from a cannon shot on April 6th, 1862, Adams assumed command as brigade commander before being severely wounded in the head by a rifle ball, resulting in the loss of his right eye. Colonel Zachariah Cantey Deas of the 22nd Alabama Regiment assumed temporary command while he recuperated. Adams was promoted to brigadier-general on May 23, 1862. He commanded a Louisiana Brigade at Perryville during the Kentucky campaign in 1862, and was praised by corps commander Lieutenant-General William J. Hardee for his leadership and gallantry. At the Battle of Murfreesboro in December of 1862, he received a second wound, and Colonel Randall Lee Gibson assumed command of the brigade while Adams recovered. Returning to duty, he commanded his brigade during the operations in and around Jackson, Mississippi, in the summer of 1863. During the Battle of Chickamauga on September 20, 1863, Adams's Brigade was attacked by Union General George Henry Thomas's Federal corps and forced to retreat. During the battle, he received a third wound and was captured by the Federals. After his exchange and upon regaining his health, he was given command of a cavalry brigade operating in northern Alabama in 1864. On September 24, 1864, General Richard Taylor ordered Adams to assume command of the District of Central Alabama. His main duties were gathering supplies, chasing deserters, and uncovering Federal collaborators. In the winter of 1864, he was ordered to assist John Bell Hood's Army of Tennessee with organizing a supply train and aiding with communications. In February of 1865, he was instructed to report to General Edmund Kirby Smith in the Trans-Mississippi Department. On March 11, 1865, the District of North Alabama was abolished and the District of Alabama was created. He was placed in command of the state of Alabama, excluding the District of the Gulf. In March and April of 1865, he led a command of Alabama State Troops under General Nathan B. Forrest in opposing General James Harrison Wilson's raid into Alabama. His soldiers fought in the Battle of Selma on April 2. He led the evacuation of Montgomery, Alabama, on April 11, and participated in an engagement in Columbus, GA, where he was forced to fall back before Wilson's Union forces on April 16, 1865. Adams received his parole at Meridian, Mississippi, on May 9, 1865. *Post-War*: Traveled to England, then returned to New Orleans, resuming his law practice and engaging in business. *Interesting*: In 1843, he killed Vicksburg newspaper editor James Hagan in a duel for criticizing his father's politics publicly. He was later acquitted of the murder charge. *Death and Burial*: Died in New Orleans, Louisiana, on June 13, 1872. He is buried near his brother, William Wirt, at Greenwood Cemetery in Jackson, Mississippi. *Dedications*: There is a statue of Daniel W. Adams in the Vicksburg National Military Park in Vicksburg, Mississippi.

Floyd, John Buchanan—Brigadier General—*Born*: June 1, 1806 at "Smithfield," his maternal grandparent's home in Montgomery County, Virginia. The eldest son of John Floyd, a planter, doctor, U.S. Congressman, and Governor of Virginia, and Letitia Preston. *Education*: His early education came from his intelligent mother, who had access to her husband's voluminous library. Graduated from South Carolina College in 1829 with a Bachelor of Arts degree, and was a member of the Euphradian Literary Society. *Politics*: In 1847, he was elected from his county as a Democratic delegate to the Virginia General Assembly, and was reelected the following year. The state legislature appointed Floyd for a three-year term beginning January 1, 1849, as governor of Virginia. When his term expired in 1852, he retired from politics and returned to his law practice in Abingdon, Virginia. He was later a presidential elector of the Democratic Party. He opposed the Know-Nothing Party, and won an election to the General Assembly in 1855. He was selected to deliver an important speech for future president James Buchanan at the Merchant's Exchange in New York City on October 2, 1856. In 1857, he was appointed secretary of war in Buchanan's administration and served for three years. His role as secretary of war became a very controversial one. Throughout his political career, he was a States'-Rights Democrat who was ardent in defending slavery and Southern rights, though he opposed secession. The year 1860 created much turmoil for Floyd due to several incidents that occurred. He was accused of transferring excessive amounts of weapons from Northern to Southern arsenals in preparation for war, which angered many Northerners. Another controversy erupted when he was accused of issuing "acceptances" that allowed contractors to borrow money against their promissary notes that he personally signed. A congressional committee implicated Floyd of wrong doing in 1861, when a contractor used the "acceptances" to obtain $870,000 worth of negotiable bonds from the Indian Trust Fund of the Interior Department. There was no evidence Floyd profited from the transaction, and after completing an investigation, the committee cleared Floyd of responsibility for the trust fund scandal. He resigned his position as secretary of war on December 29, 1860, when President Buchanan refused to restore Major Robert Anderson and his troops from Fort Sumter to Fort Moultrie. After leaving President Buchanan's administration, Floyd's allegiances changed and he supported secession. In 1868, the Supreme Court, by a divided bench, held the issue of "acceptances" in violation of the law, and of the limitations which it imposed on all officers of the government, therefore implying Floyd was involved in corruption. *Marriage/Family*: Married his cousin, Sally Buchanan Preston, in 1830, and though they had no children, they adopted Mary Wood Radford, who became Elizabeth Mary when she was baptized after her mother's death. Although unable to confirm, one source notes that John Preston Johnson was also adopted by the Floyds, and was killed in the Contreras battle during the Mexican-American War on August 19, 1847. Floyd's wife was born near Abingdon, Virginia, on February 14, 1802, and died there on May 7, 1879. *Pre-War*: Floyd established a law practice for a short time in Wytheville, Virginia, but relocated to Arkansas in 1836, where he practiced law and aspired to make a fortune in the cotton trade. In 1837, forty of his slaves were killed by a malignant fever and his own health was affected. Three years later, he returned to Abingdon, Virginia, and was nearly bankrupt. He resumed his career as an attorney and was successful enough to pay off his outstanding debts. *During the War*: Appointed a major-general in the Virginia State Line by the general assembly on May 17, 1862. After the secession of Virginia, he raised a brigade of volunteers and entered the Confederate military service. On May 23, 1861, he was promoted to brigadier-general to rank immediately. Under General Robert E. Lee, he commanded a brigade in western Virginia, and on August 11, 1861, he assumed command of the Army of Kanawha. They were involved in minor battles, defeating Union forces at Cross Lanes on August 26, and Colonel Tyler at Carnifax Ferry on September 10. He was congratulated by both President Davis and Secretary of War Judah P. Benjamin for his successes. He fought a battle with General William S. Rosecrans in September and at Gauley Bridge in October. He was ordered to serve in General Albert Sidney Johnston's Army of Tennessee. In February of 1862, they were ordered to Fort Donelson at Dover, Tennessee, where Floyd's reputation was again tarnished. Outnumbered by the Federals, and in fear for the safety of his men, he consulted with his junior officers, Gideon J. Pillow and Simon B. Buckner, regarding a surrender. General Pillow objected because it was against his convictions to surrender, and Floyd himself declined to surrender. General Buckner offered to take command and negotiate the surrender with Union General Ulysses S. Grant. Generals Floyd and Pillow transported their troops on two steamers and withdrew to Nashville, where the plan to save supplies was aborted. On March 11, 1862, Generals Floyd and Pillow were relieved from command by President Davis, without a court inquiry, for deserting their positions. Official records indicate that Floyd and Pillow were being relieved because they did not provide sufficient reports of the events that took place at Fort Donelson. His removal created panic among the citizens of southwestern Virginia, as they began to fear for their safety in anticipation of his removal. They wrote a letter to President Davis requesting Floyd's reinstatement, but Davis refused. The legislature of Virginia also did not approve of his removal, and commissioned him a major-general in the state militia two months after his removal. *Post-War*: He was directed to recruit and organize a division of troops for the state militia, raising 2,000 men and operating on the Big Sandy River until ill health forced his retirement. *Death and Burial*: Died on August 26, 1863, from Cancer of the stomach at the country estate of his adopted daughter, Mrs. Eliza Hughes, the wife of Judge Robert W. Hughes, near Abingdon. Buried at the Sinking Spring Cemetery in Abingdon. On his grave marker, there is nothing to indicate that he was a general, governor, or U.S. cabinet officer.

Gibson, Randall Lee—Colonel/Brigadier General—*Born*: September 10, 1832, near Versailles, Woodford County, Kentucky, to Tobias Gibson, a prosperous Louisiana sugar planter, and Louisiana Breckinridge Hart. *Education*: Received private tutoring at "Live Oaks," his father's plantation in Louisiana, in schools in Terrebonne Parish, Louisiana; and schools in Lexington, Kentucky. The family maintained a summer residence known as "Spring Hill," in Kentucky. Graduated with honors from Yale College in 1853. He read law in the firm of Clark and Bayne in New Orleans, Louisiana, and then completed his studies in the Law Department of the University of Louisiana, from which he graduated in 1855. *Politics*:

Elected to the U.S. House of Representatives in 1872, but denied his seat. Represented the First District of Louisiana from 1875 to 1883. In 1879, he assisted in establishing the Mississippi River Commission. Appointed by the Louisiana legislature to the U.S. Senate, he served from 1883 to 1892. *Marriage/Family*: Married Mary Montgomery in 1868, producing three sons: Montgomery, Tobias, Preston Johnston, and possibly one daughter after the war. *Pre-War*: From 1855 to 1858, Gibson traveled and studied in Germany, Russia, and Spain, where for six months he worked as attaché to the American embassy in Madrid. After returning to Louisiana, he practiced law and became a successful sugar planter and slaveholder in Thibodaux. *During the War*: Enlisted in Confederate service and was appointed aide-de-camp to Louisiana Governor Thomas O. Moore. In March of 1861, he was commissioned as a captain in the First Louisiana Artillery. Later that year, he became colonel of the Thirteenth Louisiana Infantry. He fought at Shiloh, Perryville, Murfreesboro, and Chickamauga. He requested a Court of Inquiry for a perceived slight made in General Braxton Bragg's report regarding his performance at the Battle of Shiloh. On January 11, 1864, he was promoted to brigadier-general and was distinguished during the Atlanta campaign and in Hood's invasion of Tennessee. On March 23, 1865, he was ordered by Major-General Dabney H. Maury to report with his brigade to Brigadier-General St. John R. Liddell at Blakely, Alabama. His last active military service was to assume immediate command of the defenses of Spanish Fort, near Mobile, Alabama. Colonel Francis L. Campbell assumed temporary command of Gibson's brigade. *Post-War*: Practiced law in New Orleans. President of the board of administration of Tulane University from 1882 to1892, the year of his death. *Interesting*: Member of the Peabody Education Fund, the Smithsonian Institution, and the Howard Memorial Library in New Orleans. His father was credited for naming the city of Houma, Louisiana. *Interesting Quote*: In Randall Lee Gibson's report pertaining to the defense of Spanish Fort, he writes: "If any credit be attached to the defense of Spanish Fort, it belongs to the heroes whose sleep shall no more be disturbed by the cannon's roar."[17] *Death and Burial*: Died at Hot Springs, Arkansas, on December 15, 1892. Buried at the Lexington City Cemetery in Kentucky. There is nothing on his grave marker noting his Confederate service, nor his time in the U.S. House and Senate. *Dedications*: In the administration building of Tulane University, "Gibson Hall," is named in his honor.

Harrison, George Paul, Jr.—2nd Lieutenant/Captain/Colonel—*Born*: March 19, 1841, at Monteith Plantation near Savannah, Georgia, to George Paul Harrison, Sr., a brigadier-general in the Georgia State Troops, rice planter, and state legislator, and Thurza Adelaide Guinn. *Education*: Attended Effingham Academy and Georgia Military Institute at Marietta, Georgia. *Marriage/Family*: Married four times. His first marriage was in Georgia to Miss Fannie Drake in April of 1863, producing one daughter, Mary Addie Harrison. His second marriage was to Mattie Ligon, the daughter of the Lieutenant-Governor of Alabama, Robert Fulwood Ligon, in 1886, producing no children. His third marriage was in 1896 to Frances Louise Witherspoon, who bore him a son, George Paul Harrison, III. His fourth marriage was in November of 1900 to Sarah Katherine Nunnally of Georgia, producing no children. *Pre-War*: In January of 1861, before completing his studies, he left the Georgia Military Institute to participate in the siege of Fort Pulaski on January 3, 1861, with the Georgia troops. Later that same month, he enrolled with the 1st Georgia Regulars as a 2nd lieutenant. In May of 1861, he returned to the institute, completed his courses, and graduated with first honors. *During the War*: Rejoined the First Georgia Regulars and accompanied them to Virginia, serving as the regimental adjutant until the winter of 1861–1862. In April of 1862, he was elected colonel of the 5th Georgia State Troops. He organized the 32nd Georgia Infantry in Savannah, Georgia, of which he was commissioned colonel on May 15, 1862. During 1862 and 1863, the newly organized regiment spent most of their active service garrisoning forts and defending Charleston, South Carolina. Harrison commanded and participated in the fighting at Grimball's Landing, Secessionville, and Fort Johnson. During the Federal assault on Fort Wagner on July 18, 1863, the 32nd Georgia was instrumental in reinforcing the garrison at a crucial time in the catastrophic Union defeat. At the bloody battle of Burden's Causeway in the summer of 1863, he was twice wounded. The strong leadership of Harrison resulted in the Federal defeat. Harrison described his brigade's performance in the battle as displaying great coolness and bravery. At the Battle of Olustee, also known as Ocean Pond, in Florida, he fought against the Abolitionists in February of 1864. During the battle, a detachment of the 32nd Georgia charged and captured three pieces of artillery. It has been cited that while at Olustee, he was wounded and his horse was shot from under him, though there are no official reports to substantiate this claim. In late 1864, he commanded the Confederate military post and prison at Florence, South Carolina, where he was responsible for almost 25,000 Union captives. He won the admiration of the Union prisoners because of the humane treatment they received while under his care. In 1865, he commanded a line on the Coosawatchie and fought in skirmishes at Honey Hill and Pocotaligo, South Carolina. In 1865, he was engaged with his brigade at River's Bridge, Broxton's Bridge, and led the skirmishes at Cheraw. He also covered Hardee's retreat at Averasboro, and participated in the Battle of Bentonville. Harrison surrendered in North Carolina with General Joseph E. Johnston and the remnants of the Army of Tennessee on April 26, 1865. Sources state that Harrison was promoted to brigadier-general in 1864, as well as February of 1865, however, there is no evidence to support these claims. Harrison signed himself as "colonel, commanding brigade" on his official correspondence as late as April of 1865. His superiors often referred to him as gallant, brave, and daring. *Post-War*: At the close of the war, he moved to Auburn and then Opelika, Alabama, where he became a successful lawyer and politician. He served as commandant of cadets at Auburn University. Afterward, he resumed his law practice in Opelika and engaged in planting. He served as a member of the State Constitutional Convention in 1875, and served in the State Senate from 1878 to 1884. He was also senate president for two years, from 1882 to 1884. He was a delegate to the Democratic National Convention in 1892. He was elected as a Democrat to the 53rd U.S. Congress to fill the vacancy caused by the resignation of William Calvin Oates. He was then reelected to the 54th Congress and served a full term from November 6, 1894, to March 3, 1897. When his term expired, he resumed his law practice in Opelika. In 1901, he was a delegate to the Alabama State Constitutional Convention. He was general counsel for the Western Railway of Alabama, and division counsel for the Central of Georgia Railway in 1893 and 1897. He was advisory counsel in Opelika for the Central of Georgia Railway in 1915, 1919, and 1920. He was a major-general commanding in the Alabama Division of the United Confederate Veterans. *Interesting*: After graduating from the Georgia Military Institute, he was detailed by Governor Joseph Brown to serve as commandant of cadets at the institute, which he did briefly. *Death and Burial*: Died on July 17, 1922, at Opelika. Buried at Rosemere Cemetery in Lee County, Alabama.

Mercer, Hugh Weedon—Colonel/Brigadier General—*Born*: November 27, 1808, at "The Sentry Box" in Fredericksburg, Virginia. He was the grandson of Revolutionary War veteran Hugh Mercer. *Education*: Graduated an impressive third in the class of 1828 from West Point. *Marriage/Family*: Married Mary Stites Anderson on February 5, 1834, producing two sons: Hugh Weedon and George Anderson. *Pre-War*: Served as an aide on the staff of Major-General Winfield Scott, and was promoted from 2nd lieutenant to 1st Lieutenant of artillery on October 10, 1834. During the nullification excitement in South Carolina, he was stationed at Charleston from 1832 to 1833, at Fort Oglethorpe, Georgia from 1833 to 1834, and was on quartermaster duty at Savannah, Georgia in 1834 to 1835. He resigned his U.S. army commission on April 30, 1835, and moved to Savannah, Georgia, where he was a cashier at the Planters Bank, holding that position until the outbreak of the Civil War. *During the War*: Upon Georgia seceding from the Union, he entered Southern service as a colonel of the 1st Georgia Volunteers. Promoted to brigadier-general on October 29, 1861. He commanded a brigade of Georgia regiments at Savannah, where he was stationed for the greater part of the war as post-commander. In the spring of 1863, they were ordered to Dalton, Georgia. He won special distinction in the battles around Marietta and at the battle of Kennesaw Mountain. During the Atlanta Campaign in 1864, his brigade lost 46 killed, 200 wounded, including himself, and 59 missing. On the day that General William H.T. Walker was killed, Mercer assumed Walker's command. General Mercer suffered from delicate health and General John B. Hood did not consider him a suitable division commander. On July 24, 1864, Hood disbanded Walker's Division and transferred Mercer's Brigade to Major-General Patrick R. Cleburne's Division. Cleburne shared Hood's opinion that Mercer was not an efficient commander, according to his report. On August 31, near Jonesboro, Georgia, he commanded a brigade for the last time. Against orders, Mercer made an impetuous charge across the Flint River in pursuit of the withdrawing Federals, in an attempt to drive the enemy from yet another line of fortifications. Though he was successful, he was relieved from duty that evening due to his physical inability to remain on the field. He accompanied General Hardee to Savannah after the battle of Jonesboro, and saw no further field duty. In April of 1865, it was reported by Union Major-General George H. Thomas, commanding the Department of the Cumberland, that Mercer was taken prisoner by U.S. General Wilson, who was not aware of the armistice in effect at that time. Mercer was paroled at Macon, Georgia, on May 13, 1865. *Post-War*: Resumed his pre-war career in the banking business. During 1869, he relocated to Baltimore, Maryland, and worked as a commission merchant for three years. In 1872, he moved to Baden-Baden, Germany, where he was hoping to improve his health. *Interesting*: His brigades were called "New Issue" and "Silver Fork Brigade," but the names were dropped. *Death and Burial*: Died on June 9, 1877. He is said to be buried at the Bonaventure Cemetery in Savannah, Georgia, but according to cemetery records in Germany, his body was never removed from the cemetery in Baden-Baden.

Smith, William Duncan—Major/Colonel/Brigadier General—*Born*: July 28, 1825, in Augusta, Georgia. *Education*: Attended West Point, graduating thirty-fifth in the class of 1846. *Pre-War*: Received a commission as a 2nd lieutenant in the 1st U.S. Dragoons. Fought in the Mexican-American War at Vera Cruz, Cerro Gordo, Contreras, and Churubusco. Severely wounded at the Battle of Molino del Rey. Performed garrison duty on the frontier after the Mexican War. Promoted to 1st lieutenant on August 8, 1851. From 1859 to 1861, he was on a leave of absence in Europe. *During the War*: After he returned from Europe, he resigned his U.S. army commission as captain of the 2nd Dragoons on January 28, 1861, to offer his services to the Confederacy. In the spring of 1861, Smith was acting assistant adjutant-general on the staff of Brigadier-General Alexander R. Lawton, who commanded the District of Georgia. He was commissioned a colonel in the 20th Georgia Infantry on July 14, 1861. After his promotion to brigadier-general on March 7, 1862, Smith was ordered to report to South Carolina for duty under John C. Pemberton, commanding the Department of South Carolina and Georgia. In June of 1862, Smith was placed in command of the First Military District of South Carolina, relieving General Hugh W. Mercer, who was transferred to Savannah, Georgia. Four days later, Pemberton ordered Smith to construct a battery near Thomas Grimball's plantation, where he could challenge the Union warships in the river, but Smith's troops were unable to drive the enemy back and withdrew. At the battle of Secessionville, South Carolina, he led a wing of General Nathan G. Evans's forces that defeated the Federals. Upon General Evans's arrival on June 14, 1862, Smith became second in command. On July 8, he was placed in charge of the First Military District of South Carolina again, with States Rights Gist commanding on James Island. *Death and Burial*: On October 4, 1862, at the age of thirty-seven, he succumbed to yellow fever and died at Charleston, South Carolina. He is buried at the Augusta City Cemetery in Augusta, Georgia. Inscribed on his tombstone is: "He Died for His Country."

Wilson, Claudius Charles—Captain/Colonel/Brigadier General—*Born*: October 1, 1831, in Springfield, Effingham County, Georgia, the son of Doctor Josiah Stewart Wilson and Eliza Mary Hines, both natives of Georgia. His instinctive ability to lead was most likely inherited from his two grandfathers, Major Josiah Thomas Wilson, a veteran of the War of 1812, and his great-grandfather, General Daniel Stewart Wilson, a veteran of the Revolutionary War who also served as a brigadier-general in the War of 1812. *Education*: Graduated with high honors from Emory College at Oxford, Georgia, in 1851. After reading and studying law under Colonel James M. Smith, he was admitted to the Savannah bar in 1852. *Marriage/Family*: Married Katherine McDuffie Morrison on September 14, 1852, producing four children: Joseph Henry, Claudia Cornelia, John Morrison, and Anna Belle. His wife died in May of 1904. *Pre-War*: In 1859, he was employed as solicitor-general for the Eastern Circuit Court of Georgia. Upon resigning in 1860, he practiced law with the firm of Norwood, Wilson, and Lester in Georgia. *During the War*: In 1861, he joined the Confederate Army as a captain of the 25th Georgia Infantry—Co. I, which he had been instrumental in raising and organizing. He was elected colonel of the regiment on September 2, 1861. After completing organizational functions, his command performed garrison duty on the South Carolina and Georgia coasts. During December of 1862, Wilson was given command of the 1st Georgia Brigade and was ordered to Wilmington, North Carolina, to support Major-General William Henry Chase Whiting in the New Berne Expedition. On January 14, 1863, the U.S.S. *Columbia* ran aground at Masonborough Inlet. Wilson took his brigade and two artillery batteries to the inlet to prevent the U.S. ship and her sailors from escaping. Lieutenant Joseph Pitty Couthouy of the U.S. Navy, formally surrendered the ship and her crew. Couthouy stated in his report that Wilson treated them "courteously, and expressed regret and mortification at the batteries having kept up their fire so long after the Federals displayed a white flag."[18] On February 4, 1863, Wilson's brigade was ordered back to Savannah, Georgia. Three months later, Wilson and his regiment became part of General William H.T. Walker's Brigade, and were ordered to North Mississippi to reinforce General Joseph E. Johnston in his attempt to relieve Vicksburg. Wilson and his men were lightly engaged in the Battle of Jackson, Mississippi, in May of 1863. Following the surrender of Vicksburg, he was ordered to Georgia. At the Battle of Chickamauga, Wilson's conduct was so impressive that he was recommended for a promotion to brigadier-general. He was requested to support Major-General Nathan Bedford Forrest and his cavalry unit in the early fighting on September 19. After receiving approval from Bragg and Walker, Wilson's and Brigadier-General Matthew Duncan Ector's Brigades fought fiercely. Wilson's leadership ability in that battle won him a promotion to brigadier-general on November 16, 1863. The Confederate Senate posthumously confirmed his promotion on February 17, 1864. *Death and Burial*: Wilson was denied the satisfaction of the promotion he so well deserved due to his death from typhoid fever on November 25, 1863, at Ringgold, Georgia. He was buried on December 1, 1863, in Laurel Oak Cemetery, but was later moved to Bonaventure Cemetery, both in Savannah, Georgia. *Dedications*: There was a statue of Wilson erected in August of 1915 in the Vicksburg National Military Park in Vicksburg, Mississippi.

FIELD AND STAFF

Lieutenant Colonel

McEnery, John (aka McEnerg)—Capt./Major/Lt. Col.—Enlisted: 6/4/1861 at Monroe, LA in Company B. Rolls for 6/4/1861 through 6/1862: Present, elected Capt. on 8/4/1861; Appointed Major in 3/1862 and Lt. Col. on 5/20/1862. Rolls for 6/1862 through 2/1863: Present. Rolls for 9/1864 through 2/28/1865: Absent, wounded at the Battle of Resaca, GA; Ordered to the Trans-Mississippi Dept. on 8/18/1864. Rolls for 3/1865 through 4/1865: Absent, on detached duty in Louisiana under Brig. Gen. Harry T. Hays, order and date not given. Official Rolls of Paroled Officers, C.S.A: Surrendered at New Orleans, LA on 5/26/1865; Paroled at Monroe, LA on 6/6/1865. *Born*: 3/31/1833 at Petersburg, VA to Henry O'Neil McEnery and Caroline H. Douglas. *Education*: Hanover College, Hanover, IN and Tulane University, New Orleans, LA. *Married*: Mary G. Thompson in 1858 at Monroe, Ouachita Parish, LA. *Occupations*: Appointed Registrar at Louisiana State Land Office in Ouachita Parish, LA in 1851 by President James Buchanan; Ouachita Parish Police Juror; Elected Judge in the 12th Louisiana Judicial District in 1865 but not seated by the U.S. Government; Elected as a Louisiana legislator in 1866 but not seated by the U.S. Government; Elected Louisiana governor in 1873 but not seated by the U.S. Government. *Religion*: Catholic. *Died*: 3/28/1891 at New Orleans, Orleans Parish, LA. *Buried:* Metairie Cemetery located at Metairie, Jefferson Parish, LA.

Zacharie, Francis C. — Pvt./1st Lt./Col.-(Temporary Commander) — *Enlisted:* 6/8/1861 at Richmond, VA as a Pvt. in the 1st Special Battalion Louisiana Infantry (Rightors) — Co. K. Rolls for 5/31/1861 through 6/30/1861: Present. Soldier also served as a 1st Lt. in the 9th Louisiana Infantry-Co. E. Regimental Return for 12/1861: Present at Camp Carondelet, LA. Soldier also served as a Col. in the 20th Louisiana Infantry, and commanded the 20th, 25th Louisiana Infantry, and 4th Louisiana Battalion Infantry (Consolidated) at Mobile, AL. Rolls of Prisoners of War, C.S.A: Surrendered at Citronelle, AL on 5/4/1865; Paroled at Meridian, MS on 5/10/1865.

Major

Bishop, Samuel L. — 1st Lt./Capt./Major/Lt. Col.-(Temporary Commander) — Enlisted: 12/21/1861 at New Orleans, LA as a 1st Lt. in Co. K. Rolls for 12/21/1861 through 2/1862: Present. Rolls for 3/1862 through 4/1862: Present, appointed Capt. on 4/25/1862 by order of Gen. Braxton Bragg. Rolls for 5/1862 through 4/1863: Present, commanding Co. D of the 13th and 20th Consolidated Louisiana Infantry. Rolls for 7/1863 through 10/31/1863: Absent, sick. Rolls for 11/1863 through 12/1863: Present, promoted to Major of the 20th Louisiana Infantry; Rank and pay dated back to 7/8/1863. Rolls for 1/1864 through 4/1864: Present. Rolls for 5/1864 through 8/31/1864: Commanding regiment. Rolls for 9/1864 through 2/1865: Absent, on detached service at Columbus, GA.

Buie, Duncan F. — Capt./Major — Enlisted: 8/1/1861 at Winnsboro, LA in Company C. Rolls for 7/1861 through 8/1861: Present, elected Capt. on 8/8/1861. Rolls for 9/1861 through 4/1862: Present. Rolls for 5/1862 through 6/1862: Present, promoted to Major on 5/30/1862. Rolls for 7/1862 through 8/1862: Present. Rolls for 9/1862 through 10/1862: Absent on furlough. Rolls for 1/1863 through 2/1863: Absent, commanding 47th Georgia Infantry at Red Bluff, S.C. since 2/24/1863. Rolls for 9/1864 through 2/28/1865: Absent, wounded at the Battle of the Poor House, GA on 7/28/1864. Rolls for 3/1865 through 4/1865: Absent, on detached duty at Columbus, GA. *Born:* 12/30/1828 at Burnt Prairie, Franklin Parish, LA to Neill Buie, born 1785 at Moore County, N.C. and Mary Elizabeth Jones (Buie), born 1798 in South Carolina. *Occupations:* School Teacher, Sheriff and Judge at Franklin Parish, LA. *Married:* Mary Eleanor "Molly" Dosson, born 1839 at Harrisonburg, LA, on 6/12/1855 at Chicot County, AR. *Died:* 3/23/1893 at Winnsboro, LA. *Buried:* Old Winnsboro Cemetery located at Winnsboro, Franklin Parish, LA.

Waddill, George C. (aka Waddell) — Capt./Major — Enlisted: 5/25/1861 at Richmond, LA in Company A; Elected Captain same day. Rolls for 5/25/1861 through 6/30/1861: Present or absent not stated. Rolls for 7/1861 through 8/1861: Present. Promoted from Capt. to Major in 9/1861. Captain Successor: W.J. Powell. Resigned in 12/1861. *Major Successor:* John McEnery.

Adjutant

Green, John W. — Cpl./Sgt./Adjutant — Enlisted: 5/25/1861 at Richmond, LA as a Cpl. in Company A. Rolls for 5/25/1861 through 8/1861: Present. Rolls for 9/1861 through 10/1861: Promoted to Sgt. on 9/1/1861; Promoted to Adjutant on 9/19/1861.

Streshley, William H. — 1st Lt./Adjutant — Enlisted: 8/15/1861 at Natchez, MS as a 1st Lt. in Company E. Regimental Return for 7/1862: Present or absent not stated. Regimental Return for 8/1862: Present or absent not stated at Camp Van Dorn, GA. Rolls for 9/1862 through 10/1862: Absent on furlough. Rolls for 1/1863 through 2/1863: Present. Rolls for 9/1864 through 4/1865: Absent, on detached duty at Marion, AL. *Born:* Virginia.

Surgeon

Bass, John H. — Pvt./Capt./Asst. Surgeon — Enlisted: 5/25/1861 at Richmond, LA in Company A. Rolls for 5/25/1861 through 6/1862: Present. Rolls for 11/1862 through 12/1862: Absent, on detached duty at Savannah, GA in charge of camp hospital. Rolls for 1/1863 through 4/1863: Present, promoted to Capt. and Asst. Surgeon on 2/11/1863. Rolls for 5/1863 through 9/1863: In hospital from wounds received at the Battle of Chickamauga, GA on 9/19/1863.

Bolen, Michael J. — Asst. Surg. — (No War Dept. Record)

Harley, H.H. — 1st Sgt./Hosp. Steward/Surgeon — Enlisted: 8/8/1861 at Winnsboro, LA in Company C. Rolls for 8/8/1861 through 6/1862: Present. Regimental Return for 8/1862: Hospital Steward. Rolls for 9/1862 through 10/1862: Absent, Acting Surgeon for Capt. Reed's Battery.

King, ? — Surgeon — Resigned on 12/1/1861. *Surgeon Successor:* Balitha Powell.

McEnery, H.O. — Pvt./Surgeon — Enlisted: 5/14/1862 at Monroe, LA in Company A. Federal Rolls of Prisoners of War: Received near Vicksburg, MS from the

Steamer Dacotah on 10/18/1862; Paroled prior to arrival. Rolls for 11/1862 through 12/1862: Promoted to C.S.A. Surgeon on 11/12/1862. Rolls for 1/1863 through 2/1863: Present. Transferred to the Trans-Mississippi Military Dept. of Louisiana in 9/1863.

McKisick, J.W. (aka McKissock) — Asst. Surgeon — Appointed Asst. Surgeon on 4/21/1863. Rolls for 9/1864 through 4/1865: Present.

Meng, James S. (aka Menge) — Surgeon — (No War Dept. Record) — Enlisted: 8/4/1861 at Natchez, MS in Company E. *Married:* Caroline H. _ on 12/11/1854 at Vidalia, Concordia Parish, LA. *Died:* 1/14/1891 at home at Vidalia, LA due to Pneumonia. *Buried:* Natchez, Adams County, MS. Confederate Widows Pension Application dated 4/13/1915 on file at the Louisiana State Archives-Microfilm Reel: CP1.96-Microdex 4-Sequence 28-Target Card: Meng, Caroline H.-Parish: Concordia-5 Pages.

Powell, Balitha — Surgeon — Regimental Returns for 7/1862 and 8/1862: Present or absent not stated at Camp Van Dorn, GA. Regimental Return for 9/1862: Present at Camp Van Dorn, GA. Rolls for 9/1862 through 10/1862: Appointed Surgeon on 2/19/1862 at Camp Van Dorn, VA; Transferred to Louisiana for Post Duty on 8/9/1862. Surgeon Successor: H.O. McEnery.

Sergeant Major

Middleton, John C. — Pvt./Sgt. Major/Jr. 2nd Lt. — Enlisted: 8/15/1861 at Natchez, MS in Company E. Rolls for 8/15/1861 through 6/1862: Present. Regimental Return for 9/1862: On furlough. Rolls for 11/1862 through 12/1862: Present. Rolls for 1/1863 through 2/1863: Present, promoted to Sgt. Major on 1/19/1863. Rolls for 12/1863 through 4/30/1864: Absent on furlough, elected Jr. 2nd Lt. of Company E on 12/21/1863. Rolls for 8/1864 through 4/1865: Present. Official Rolls of Paroled Officers, C.S.A: Surrendered at Citronelle, AL on 5/4/1865; Paroled at Meridian, MS on 5/10/1865.

Thompson, Alfred G. — Pvt./Sgt. Major/Pvt. — Enlisted: 6/4/1861 at Monroe, LA in Company B. Rolls for 6/4/1861 through 8/1861: Present. Rolls for 9/1861 through 10/1861: Present, promoted to Sgt. Major on 9/19/1861. Regimental Return for 8/1862: On furlough in Louisiana. Rolls for 9/1862 through 10/1862: Present. Rolls for 1/1863 through 2/1863: Reduced to Pvt. in Company B on 1/19/1863.

Wells, Robert W. — Pvt./Sgt. Major — Enlisted: 8/15/1861 at Natchez, MS in Company E. Rolls for 8/15/1861 through 10/1861: Present. Rolls for 11/1861 through 12/1861: Absent, sick at Richmond, VA. Rolls for 1/1862 through 2/1862: Present, last paid when absent sick at Richmond, VA. Rolls for 3/1862 through 10/1862: Present. Rolls for 1/1863 through 2/1863: Absent, sick in Mississippi. Rolls for 9/1/1864 through 4/1865: Absent, taken Prisoner of War near Atlanta, GA on 8/5/1864. Federal Rolls of Prisoners of War: Captured near Atlanta, GA on 8/5/1864; Received at the U.S. Military Prison, Louisville, KY from Nashville, TN on 8/12/1864. Forwarded to Camp Chase, OH on 8/13/1864; Paroled at Camp Chase, OH and transferred to Point Lookout, MD for Exchange on 3/18/1865. Exchanged at Boulware and Cox Wharf, James River, VA on 3/27/1865. Official Rolls of Paroled Officers, C.S.A: Surrendered at Citronelle, AL on 5/4/1865; Paroled at Winchester, VA on 6/21/1865. *Residence:* Natchez, Adams County, MS.

Quartermaster

Amis, Robert Emmett (aka Amie) — Pvt./Sgt./3rd Lt./2nd Lt./1st Lt./A.Q.M.-Enlisted: 5/25/1861 at Richmond, VA in Company A. Rolls for 5/25/1861 through 10/1861: Present, promoted from Sgt. to Jr. 2nd. Lt. on 9/25/1861. Rolls for 11/1861 through 12/1862: Present. Rolls for 1/1863 through 2/1863: Present, Acting A.Q.M. of the battalion. Rolls for 1/1864 through 2/1864: Absent without leave since 5/1862. On undated Roster: Elected 3rd Lt. in 9/1861; Promoted to 2nd Lt. in 9/1861. 3rd Lt. Successor: C.C. Briscoe. On Roster not dated: Promoted to 1st Lt. in 12/1861; Dropped from Rolls on 5/19/1864 due to prolonged absence. 1st Lt. Successor: D.M. Robinson. Confederate Widows Pension Application on file at the Louisiana State Archives-Microfilm Reel: CP1.3-Microdex 1-Sequence 18-Target Card: Amis, Fannie Turpin (Woodburn)-Parish: Madison-4 Pages.

Beek, Robert S. — Pvt./Q.M. Sgt. — Enlisted: 5/25/1861 at Richmond, LA in Company A. Rolls for 9/1861 through 10/1861: Present, promoted to Q.M. Sgt. on 9/14/1861. Rolls for 11/1861 through 2/28/1865: Present. Rolls for 3/1865 through 4/1865: Furloughed on 3/14/1865. Rolls of Prisoners of War, C.S.A: Surrendered at Citronelle, AL on 5/4/1865; Paroled at Tuscaloosa, AL on 5/19/1865.

Brockett, W.B. — 3rd Lt./2nd Lt./A.Q.M. — Enlisted: 5/25/1861 at Richmond, LA in Company A; Elected 3rd Lt. same day. Rolls for 7/1861 through 8/1861: Present. Regimental Returns for 7/1862 and 8/1862 at Camp Van Dorn, GA: Present or absent not stated. Rolls for 9/1862 through 10/1862: Present, appointed Quartermaster on 9/25/1861. 2nd Lt. Successor: Robert E. Amis. Rolls for 1/1863 through 2/1863: Present. Rolls for 9/1/1864 through 2/28/1865: Absent, ordered to the Trans-Mississippi Military Dept. on 8/18/1864.

Commissary

Eden, John P.—Pvt./Comm. Sgt.—Enlisted: 5/25/1861 at Richmond, LA in Company A. Rolls for 5/25/1861 through 8/1861: Present. Rolls for 9/1861 through 4/1862: Present, promoted to Commissary Sgt. on 9/1/1861. Rolls for 5/1862 through 6/1862: Present, on detached duty as Commissary Sgt. Rolls for 9/1862 through 2/1863: Present. Rolls for 1/1864 through 2/1864: Sick in quarters.

Henderson, Thomas—Pvt./Musician/Comm. Sgt.—Enlisted: 5/25/1861 at Richmond, LA. Rolls for 5/25/1861 through 10/1862: Present. Rolls for 1/1863 through 2/1863: Present, returned to Company A from Band on 1/20/1863. Rolls for 1/1864 through 2/1864: Absent with leave. Rolls for 8/1864 through 4/1865: Present, on extra daily duty as Battalion Commissary Sgt. Rolls of Prisoners of War, C.S.A: Surrendered at Citronelle, AL on 5/4/1865; Paroled at Meridian, MS on 5/10/1865. *Residence:* Stony Creek, Sussex County, VA.

Sidway, G.D.—Pvt./Commissary—Enlisted: 8/15/1861 at Natchez, MS in Company E. Rolls for 8/15/1861 through 6/1862: Present. Rolls for 11/1862 through 12/1862: Absent, on detached service at Savannah, GA in charge of camp. Rolls for 1/1863 through 2/1863: Absent, was in camp this morning, but now on duty at Savannah, GA. Rolls for 1/1864 through 2/1864: Absent on furlough since 2/8/1864. Rolls for 8/31/1864 through 2/28/1865: Absent, detailed on the staff of Maj. Gen. Benjamin F. Cheatham on 11/19/1864.

Ziegler, William H.—Pvt./Acting Comm. Sgt.—Enlisted: 5/25/1861 at Richmond, LA in Company A. Rolls for 5/25/1861 through 4/1862: Present. Regimental Return for 1/1862 and 9/1862: Assigned to Company Commissary. Rolls for 11/1862 through 2/1863: Present. Rolls for 1/1864 through 2/1864: Present, Acting Commissary Sgt. by order of Maj. Duncan Buie since 2/29/1864. Rolls for 8/31/1864 through 2/28/1865: Absent, detailed as Clerk for Division Hospital Commissary by order of Brig. Gen. Randall L. Gibson. Rolls for 3/1865 through 4/1865: Absent, detailed with Capt. Newman by order of Brig. Gen. Randall L. Gibson.

Ordnance

Dixon, John S.—Pvt./Ord. Sgt.—Enlisted: 5/25/1861 at Richmond, LA in Company A. Rolls for 5/25/1861 through 8/1862: Present. Rolls for 9/1862 through 10/1862: Absent on furlough. Rolls for 1/1863 through 4/1865: Present. Rolls of Prisoners of War, C.S.A: Surrendered at Citronelle, AL on 5/4/1865; Paroled at Meridian, MS on 5/13/1865. *Residence:* Adams County, MS.

Hospital Steward

Harley, H.H.—1st Sgt./Hosp. Steward/Surgeon—(See Surgeon)

Hines, Curtis T.—Hosp. Steward—(War Dept. Record for 31st La. Infantry-Co. C)-Rolls of Prisoners of War, C.S.A: Surrendered at New Orleans, LA on 5/26/1865; Paroled at Monroe, LA on 6/8/1865 and 6/12/1865. *Residence:* Ouachita Parish, LA. *Wife's Maiden Name:* McCormick, Frances S.W. Confederate Widows Pension Application on file at the Louisiana State Archives-Microfilm Reel: CP1.67-Microdex 3-Sequence 15-Target Card: Hines, Frances S.-Parish: Ouachita-5 Pages.

Hornsby, O.W.—Pvt./Hosp. Steward—Enlisted: 8/15/1861 at Natchez, MS in Company E. Rolls for 8/15/1861 through 9/1/1861: Present. Rolls for 9/1861 through 10/1861: Absent, sick at Richmond, VA. Rolls for 11/1861 through 12/1861: Discharged.

Marshall, Charles L.—Pvt./Hosp. Steward—Enlisted: 8/27/1862 at Vicksburg, MS in Company A. Rolls for 11/1862 through 12/1862: Present. Rolls for 1/1863 through 2/1863: Present, on extra duty in the Surgeon Dept. Rolls for 9/1864 through 2/28/1865: Present. Rolls for 3/1865 through 4/1865: Present. Rolls of Prisoners of War, C.S.A: Surrendered at Citronelle, AL on 5/4/1865; Paroled at Meridian, MS on 5/13/1865. *Residence:* Shreveport, Caddo Parish, LA.

Wheat, Moses—Pvt./Hosp. Steward—Enlisted: 8/8/1861 at Winnsboro, LA in Company C. Rolls for 8/8/1861 through 8/31/1861: Present. Rolls for 11/1861 through 12/1861: Present, on detached service at the date of last muster. Rolls for 1/1862 through 2/1862: Discharged on Surgeon's Certificate of Disability; Re-enlisted on 4/14/1862 at Winnsboro, LA. Rolls for 4/14/1862 through 4/30/1862: Present. Rolls for 5/1862 through 6/1862: Absent, sick in hospital at Charleston, S.C. Rolls for 9/1862 through 10/1862: Present. Rolls for 11/1862 through 12/1862: Absent, sick at Savannah, GA. Rolls for 1/1863 through 2/1863: Present, assigned as Hospital Steward. Federal Rolls of Prisoners of War: Captured and paroled at Yazoo City, MS on 7/13/1863 by order of Maj. Gen. Francis J. Herron. Description at capture-Hair: dark-Eyes: blue-Height: 5 ft. 6 in.

Battalion Druggist

Stewart, W.W.—Pvt./Battn. Druggist—Enlisted: 8/9/1861 at Carroll Parish, LA in Company D. Rolls for 8/9/1861 through 2/1862: Present. Rolls for 3/1862 through 4/1862: Present, appointed Battalion Druggist. Rolls for 5/1862 through 6/1862: Present. Rolls for 9/1862 through 10/1862: Absent on sick furlough. Rolls for 1/1863 through 2/1863: Discharged on 1/15/1863 due to Surgeon's Certificate of Disability.

Musician

Bauer, Theodore L. (aka Bower, Baur, J.) — Pvt.—/Musician-Rolls of Prisoners of War, C.S.A: Captured at Citronelle, AL on 5/4/1865; Paroled at Meridian, MS on 5/10/1865. *Residence:* Natchez, Adams County, MS. Soldier also served as a Pvt. with the Louisiana Pelican Infantry Regiment-Co. G. *Born:* 4/18/1849. *Died:* 3/7/1927. *Buried:* Natchez City Cemetery located at Natchez, Adams County, MS. Confederate Pension Application dated 1918 on file at the Mississippi Dept. of Archives and History-Target Card: Bauer, Theodore L. *County:* Adams.

Fetters, Thomas P. (aka Fatter) — Pvt./Musician — Enlisted: 6/4/1861 at Monroe, LA in Company B. Rolls for 6/4/1861 through 6/1862: Present. Regimental Return for 8/1862: In Government Service at Savannah, GA. Federal Rolls of Prisoners of War: Captured near Jackson, MS on 7/4/1863; Sent to Snyder's Bluff, MS on 7/30/1863. Received at Camp Morton, IN on 8/7/1863; Released on the U.S. Oath of Allegiance on 12/22/1863.

Haddox, Robert — Pvt./Musician — Enlisted: 5/25/1861 at Richmond, LA in Company A. Rolls for 5/25/1861 through 2/1863: Present. Rolls for 8/1864 through 2/1865: Absent, detached as Musician; Returned to Company A on 11/15/1864 but now absent on sick furlough. Rolls of Prisoners of War, C.S.A: Surrendered at Citronelle, AL on 5/4/1865; Paroled at Jackson, MS on 5/19/1865. *Residence:* Madison Parish, LA.

Hall, William F. — Pvt./Musician — Enlisted: 2/21/1862 at Winnsboro, LA in Company C. Rolls for 2/21/1862 through 2/1863: Present.

Harbison, M.P. (aka Harbinson) — Pvt./Musician — Enlisted: 8/9/1861 at Carroll Parish, LA in Company D. Rolls for 8/9/1861 through 4/1865: Present. Rolls of Prisoners of War, C.S.A: Surrendered at Citronelle, AL on 5/4/1865; Paroled at Meridian, MS on 5/10/1865. *Residence:* Carroll Parish, LA.

Henderson, Thomas — Pvt./Musician/Comm. Sgt.— (See Commissary Sgt.)

Hill, Joseph T. — Pvt./Musician — Enlisted: 9/9/1861 at Richmond, VA in Company C. Rolls for 9/9/1861 through 6/1862: Present. Rolls for 9/1862 through 10/1862: Absent on furlough. Rolls for 1/1863 through 2/1863: Present. Rolls for 9/1864 through 2/1865: Killed at Atlanta, GA on 8/11/1864. *Born:* 10/28/1841 at Greene County, AL to John Hill and Fanny Shaw. Soldier is recorded on the 1860 U.S. Census- *Residence:* Home of John Hill at Franklin Parish, LA.

Hober, John — Pvt./Musician — Enlisted: 3/24/1862 at Monroe, LA in Company F. Rolls for 3/24/1862 through 6/1862: Present. Rolls #1 for 9/1862 through 10/1862: Absent, detailed in Band. Rolls #2 for 9/1862 through 10/1862: Present. Rolls for 1/1863 through 2/1863: Present. Rolls for 8/31/1864 through 2/28/1865: Present, Musician. Rolls for 9/1/1864 through 2/28/1865: Returned to Company F on 11/15/1864. Rolls for 3/1865 through 4/1865: Present. Rolls of Prisoners of War, C.S.A: Surrendered at Citronelle, AL on 5/4/1865; Paroled at Meridian, MS on 5/10/1865. *Residence:* Monroe, Ouachita Parish, LA.

Holley, T.D. — Pvt./Musician — Enlisted: 6/4/1861 at Monroe, LA in Company B. Rolls for 6/4/1861 through 6/1862: Present. Rolls for 1/1864 through 4/1865: Absent, captured at the Battle of Chickamauga, GA on 9/19/1863. Federal Rolls of Prisoners of War: Captured near the Battle of Chickamauga, GA on 9/19/1863; Forwarded to the U.S. Military Prison, Louisville, KY on 10/1/1863. Transferred to Camp Douglas, IL on 10/4/1863; Enlisted in the U.S. Army (Infantry) on 4/18/1865.

Mason, John Thomas — Pvt./Musician — Enlisted: 5/25/1861 at Richmond, LA in Company A. Rolls for 5/25/1861 through 2/1862: Present. Rolls for 3/1862 through 4/1862: Discharged on Surgeon's Certificate of Disability on 3/26/1862. Regimental Return for 9/1862: In barracks at Savannah, GA. Rolls for 11/1862 through 12/1862: Present. Rolls for 1/1863 through 2/1863: Detailed as Musician. Rolls for 9/1864 through 2/1865: Returned to Company A on 11/15/1864. Rolls for 8/1864 through 2/28/1865: Absent, Musician; Returned to Company A for duty on 11/15/1864, now absent without leave. *Born:* Madison Parish, LA. *Married:* Arabella Jane McLemore. *Died:* 1913 in Delhi, Richland Parish, LA. *Buried:* Cemetery located on U.S. Hwy. 80 just east of Delhi, LA. Confederate Widows Pension Application on file at the Louisiana State Archives-Microfilm Reel: CP1.91-Microdex 2-Sequence 43-Target Card: Mason, Arabella J.-Parish: Richland-11 Pages.

Moore, Joseph Lawson — Pvt./Musician — Enlisted: 3/1/1862 at Natchez, MS in Company E. Rolls for 3/1/1862 through 2/1863: Present. Rolls for 9/1864 through 2/28/1865: Returned to Company E on 11/15/1864. Rolls for 8/1864 through 2/28/1865: Absent on furlough since 2/17/1864. Rolls for 3/1865 through 4/1865: Present. Rolls of Prisoners of War, C.S.A: Surrendered at Citronelle, AL on 5/4/1865; Paroled at Meridian, MS on 5/10/1865. *Residence:* Natchez, Adams County, MS. Confederate Widows Pension Application on file at the Louisiana State Archives-Microfilm Reel: CP1.100-Microdex 2-Sequence 11-Target Card: Moore, Mary Alice (McRae)-Parish: East Carroll-6 Pages.

Rushbrook, Samuel—Pvt./Musician-Enlisted: 8/9/1862 at Carroll Parish, LA in Company D. Rolls for 8/9/1862 through 2/1863: Present.

Chaplain

Scott, Winfrey Bond—Capt./Major/Chaplain (Gibson's Brigade)—Enlisted: 12/11/1861 at Camp Moore, LA in the 19th Louisiana Infantry-Co. D. Rolls for 12/11/1861 through 10/1862: Present. Rolls for 11/1862 through 12/1862: Absent on 30 day furlough since 12/9/1862. Rolls for 1/1863 through 10/1863: Present. Rolls for 11/1863 through 12/1863: Promoted to Major on 11/25/1863 due to the promotion of Major Hyder A. Kennedy to Lt. Col. Rolls for 1/1/1864 through 4/30/1864: Present. Rolls for 5/1/1864 through 8/31/1864: Leg amputated due to wounds received at the Battle of New Hope Church, GA; Died due to complications on 5/27/1864.

COLOR BEARERS/GUARD
Ensign

Smith, Austin Williams—Pvt./2nd Cpl./Ensign—Enlisted: 8/15/1861 at Natchez, MS in Company E. Rolls for 8/15/1861 through 12/1861: Present, promoted to 2nd Cpl. on 12/16/1861. Rolls for 1/1862 through 6/1862: Present. Rolls for 11/1862 through 12/1862: Absent, sick at Savannah, GA. Rolls for 1/1863 through 2/1863: Present, was in camp this morning but now on Picket Duty. Federal Rolls of Prisoners of War: Captured at the Battle of Chickamauga, GA on 9/20/1863; Received at the U.S. Military Prison, Louisville, KY on 10/1/1863. Forwarded to Camp Douglas, IL on 10/2/1863. Rolls of Prisoners of War, C.S.A: Surrendered at Citronelle, AL on 5/4/1865; Paroled at Meridian, MS on 5/10/1865. *Residence:* Natchez, MS. Soldier also served as an Ensign with the Louisiana Pelican Infantry Regiment-Co. G. *Buried:* Williams Family Cemetery located at Natchez, Adams County, MS.

Color Sergeant

Moreland, William Willis—Pvt./Color Sgt.-Enlisted: 2/15/1862 at Natchez, MS in Company D. Rolls for 2/15/1862 through 6/1862: Present. Regimental Returns for 7/1862 and 9/1862: Detailed to Color Guard. Rolls for 9/1862 through 10/1862: Absent on furlough. Rolls for 1/1863 through 2/1863: Present, promoted to Sgt. on 1/9/1863. Rolls for 12/31/1863 through 4/30/1864: Transferred to the C.S. Naval Service by order of the Secretary of War; Served as Second-Class Fireman aboard the C.S.S. Isondiga in 1864. Soldier also served with the 13th Mississippi Infantry. Confederate Pension Application on file at the Georgia Dept. of Archives and History-Name: Moreland, William Willis-County: Thomas. Also a Confederate Widows Pension Application on file-Name: Moreland, Sarah Ann-County: Thomas.

Pugh, William T.S.—Cpl./Sgt./Color Bearer—Enlisted: 5/25/1861 at Richmond, LA in Company A. Rolls for 5/25/1861 through 8/1861: Present. Rolls for 9/1861 through 10/1861: Present, promoted to Sgt. on 9/25/1861. Rolls for 11/1861 through 2/1862: Present. Rolls for 3/1862 through 4/1862: Present, promoted to Color Bearer on 10/2/1861. Rolls for 5/1862 through 2/1863: Present. Rolls for 1/1864 through 2/1864: Present, Color Bearer.

Color Corporal

Jackson, Sydney M.—Pvt./Color Cpl.—Enlisted: 5/25/1861 at Richmond, LA in Company A. Rolls for 5/25/1861 through 12/1862: Present, detailed to the Color Guard. Rolls for 1/1863 through 2/1863: Transferred to the 35th Mississippi Infantry-Co. F on 2/19/1863.

Phillips, Francis M.   Pvt./4th Cpl./Color Cpl. Enlisted: 8/8/1861 at Winnsboro, LA in Company C. Rolls for 8/8/1861 through 2/1865: Present. Rolls for 3/1865 through 4/1865: Present, on extra daily duty as

Austin Williams Smith (author's collection).

Color Cpl. Rolls of Prisoners of War, C.S.A: Surrendered at Citronelle, AL on 5/4/1865; Paroled at Meridian, MS on 5/10/1865. *Residence:* Winnsboro, Franklin Parish, LA. Soldier also served as a 4th Cpl. with the Louisiana Pelican Infantry Regiment-Co. G, the 3rd Louisiana Cavalry-Co. G, and the 9th Battalion Louisiana Cavalry. Confederate Pension Application on file at the Louisiana State Archives-Microfilm Reel: CP1.110-Microdex 1-Sequence 35-Target Card: Phillips, Francis M.-Parish: East Baton Rouge-9 Pages.

Color Bearer

Amis, Robert Emmett (aka Amie) — Pvt./Sgt./3rd Lt./Jr. 2nd Lt./1st Lt. — Enlisted: 5/25/1861 at Richmond, LA in Company A. Rolls for 5/25/1861 through 10/1861: Present, promoted from Sgt. to Jr. 2nd. Lt. on 9/25/1861. Rolls for 11/1861 through 12/1862: Present. Rolls for 1/1863 through 2/1863: Present, Acting A.Q.M. of the battalion. Rolls for 1/1864 through 2/1864: Absent without leave since 5/1862. On undated Roster: Elected 3rd Lt. in 9/1861, promoted to 2nd Lt. in 9/1861. 3rd Lt. Successor: C.C. Briscoe. On undated Roster: Promoted to 1st Lt. in 12/1861. Dropped from Rolls due to prolonged absence on 5/19/1864. 1st Lt. Successor: D.M. Robinson. Soldier also served as a Capt. with McNeil's Louisiana Cavalry-Co. E. Official Rolls of Paroled Officers, C.S.A: Surrendered at New Orleans, LA on 5/26/1865; Paroled at Monroe, LA on 6/6/1865. Confederate Widows Pension Application on file at the Louisiana State Archives-Microfilm Reel: CP1.3-Microdex 1-Sequence 18-Target Card: Amis, Fannie Turpin-Parish: Madison-4 Pages. *Wife's Maiden Name:* Fannie Turpin Woodburn.

Smith, Frank — Pvt./Color Bearer — Enlisted: 8/15/1861 at Natchez, MS in Company E. Rolls for 8/15/1861 through 2/1863: Present. Rolls for 1/1864 through 2/1864: Present. Rolls for 8/31/1864 through 2/28/1865: Discharged on 9/12/1864.

General Guides

Right

Hinman, Curtis P. — Cpl./Sgt./Right Gen. Guide — Enlisted: 5/25/1861 at Richmond, LA in Company A. Rolls for 5/25/1861 through 8/1861: Present. Rolls for 9/1861 through 10/1861: Present, appointed Sgt. on 9/20/1861. Rolls for 11/1861 through 12/1862: Present. Rolls for 1/1863 through 2/1863: Present, Acting Right General Guide for the battalion. Rolls for 1/1864 through 2/1864: Absent, in hospital at Macon, GA from wounds received at the Battle of Chickamauga, GA on 9/19/1863. Rolls for 8/1864 through 4/1865: Absent, detached duty at Macon, GA by order of Gen. Joseph E. Johnston.

Left

None Identified

COMPANY A: "MADISON INFANTRY," MADISON PARISH

Captain

Powell, William Jack (aka W.A.) — Pvt./Capt. — Enlisted: 5/25/1861 at Richmond, LA. Rolls for 5/25/1861 through 8/1861: Present. Rolls for 9/1861 through 10/1861: Present, promoted from Pvt. to Capt. on 10/18/1861. Rolls for 11/1861 through 2/1864: Present. Rolls for 8/31/1864 through 4/1865: Absent, on extra duty in Louisiana under orders since 9/1/1864. Confederate Pension Application dated 1914 on file at the Mississippi Dept. of Archives and History-Target Card: Powell, William A.-County: Amite.

Waddill, George C. — Capt./Major — (See Field and Staff)

Lieutenant

Amis, Robert Emmett (aka Amie, B.E.) — Pvt./Sgt./3rd Lt./2nd Lt./1st Lt./A.Q.M. — (See Color Bearers)

Briscoe, Claiborne C. — Sgt./3rd Lt. — Enlisted: 5/25/1861 at Richmond, LA. Rolls for 5/25/1861 through 2/1863: Present. On undated Roster: Elected 3rd Lt. in 3/1862. Killed at the Battle of Chickamauga, GA on 9/19/1863. 3rd Lt. *Successor:* D.M. Robinson.

Brockett, W.B. — 3rd Lt./2nd Lt./A.Q.M. — (See Field and Staff)

Couch, F.M. (aka J.M.) — 2nd Lt./1st Lt. — Enlisted: 5/25/1861 at Richmond, LA; Elected 2nd Lt. same day. Rolls for 5/25/1861 through 6/30/1861: Present or absent not stated. Rolls for 7/1861 through 2/1863: Present, promoted to 1st Lt. in 12/1861. Wounded at the Battle of Chickamauga, GA on 9/19/1863; Died on 9/24/1863. *1st Lt Successor:* D.M. Robinson. *Buried:* Oakland Cemetery located at Atlanta, Fulton County, GA.

Hamilton, S.W. — 1st Lt. — Enlisted: 5/25/1861 at Richmond, LA. Rolls for 5/25/1861 through 10/1861:

Present. Resigned in 12/1861 due to ill health. *Born:* 12/1816 at Paris, KY to William and Rebecca Ward Hamilton, the 5th of 7 children. *Occupation:* Doctor. *Residences:* Kentucky from 1816 to 1828, Missouri from 1828 to 1830, Tennessee from 1830 to 1832, Louisiana from 1848 to 1883, and Mississippi from 1836 to 1841 and from 1883 until his death.

Nance, Thomas R. (aka Hance, George) — Pvt./1st Sgt./2nd Lt. — Enlisted: 5/25/1861 at Richmond, LA. Rolls for 5/25/1861 through 6/1862: Present. Rolls for 11/1862 through 12/1862: Absent, sick at Savannah, GA. Rolls for 1/1863 through 2/1863: Present. Rolls for 1/1864 through 2/1864: Present, promoted from Pvt. to 1st Sgt. on 7/1/1864. Rolls for 8/31/1864 through 4/1865: Present. Rolls of Prisoners of War, C.S.A: Surrendered at Citronelle, AL on 5/4/1865; Paroled at Meridian, MS on 5/10/1865. Confederate Pension Application dated 1919 on file at the Mississippi Dept. of Archives and History-Target Card: Nance, George-County: Holmes.

Robinson, Dick M. (aka Robertson) — Pvt./3rd Lt./2nd Lt./1st Lt. — Enlisted: 5/25/1861 at Richmond, LA. Rolls for 5/25/1861 through 2/1864: Present, elected 3rd Lt. on 3/1/1863; Promoted to 2nd Lt. on 11/1/1863. Promoted to 1st Lt. on 5/17/1864. Rolls for 8/31/1864 through 2/28/1865: Absent on sick leave for 60 days since 2/1/1864. Rolls for 3/1865 through 4/1865: Present, signs Rolls as Company Commander. Official Rolls of Paroled Officers, C.S.A: Surrendered at Citronelle, AL on 5/4/1865; Paroled at Meridian, MS on 5/10/1865.

Wylly, Charles Spaulding — 1st Sgt./2nd Lt. — Enlisted: 5/25/1861 at Richmond, LA. Rolls for 5/25/1861 through 8/1861: Present, promoted to 2nd Lt. in Regular Service. Soldier also served as a 2nd Lt. with the 1st Georgia Infantry (Regulars)-Co. G. Confederate Pension Application on file at the Georgia Dept. of Archives and History-Name: Wylly, Charles Spaulding-County: Glynn.

Sergeant

Adams, Littleton T. (aka L.F.) — 1st Sgt. — Enlisted: 5/25/1861 at Richmond, LA. Rolls for 5/25/1861 through 2/1863: Present.

Curren, Robert N. (aka Curran) — Pvt./3rd Sgt. — Enlisted: 5/25/1861 at Richmond, LA. Rolls for 5/25/1861 through 10/1861: Present. Rolls for 11/1861 through 12/1861: Present, promoted to 3rd Sgt. on 12/22/1861. Rolls for 1/1862 through 2/1864: Present.

DeMoss, David H. (aka D.D.) — Pvt./Cpl./Sgt. — Enlisted: 5/25/1861 at Richmond, LA. Rolls for 5/25/1861 through 12/1863: Present. Rolls for 1/1864 through 2/1864: Present, promoted to Cpl. on 1/1/1864. Rolls for 8/31/1864 through 2/28/1865: Absent on 90 day furlough since 2/17/1865. Rolls for 3/1865 through 4/1865: Absent with leave by order of Maj. Gen. Dabney H. Maury. Rolls of Prisoners of War, C.S.A: Surrendered at Citronelle, AL on 5/4/1865; Paroled at Shreveport, LA on 6/7/1865. *Residence:* Homer, Claiborne Parish, LA.

Green, John W. — Cpl./Sgt./Adjutant — (See Field and Staff)

Hinman, Curtis P. — Cpl./Sgt./Right Gen. Guide — (See Color Bearers)

Pugh, William T.S. — Cpl./Sgt./Color Bearer — (See Color Bearers)

Scott, Robert T. (aka R.E.) — Sgt./Pvt. — Enlisted: 5/25/1861 at Richmond, LA. Rolls for 5/25/1861 through 8/1861: Present. Rolls for 9/1861 through 10/1861: Discharged without the knowledge or consent of the Company A Captain. Re-enlisted: 3/18/1862 at Vicksburg, MS. Rolls for 3/18/1862 through 2/1863: Present. Rolls for 1/1864 through 2/1864: Absent, sick in hospital by order of Surgeon Weir.

Wirz, Heinrich Hartmann (aka Wertz, Wirtz, Henry) — Pvt./Sgt. — Enlisted: 5/25/1861 at Richmond, LA. Detached duty in Richmond, VA; Wounded in right arm at the Battle of Seven Pines, VA. Promoted to Capt. and Asst. Adjt. Gen. on 6/12/1862 at Richmond, VA and ordered to report to Brig. Gen. John H. Winder for Provost Duty; Assigned to duty at the Tuscaloosa, AL and Richmond, VA Military Prisons. Received Presidential assignment as Confederate Government Plenipotentiary to the European governments in Paris, France and Berlin, Germany in late 1862; Returned to Richmond, VA in early 1864. Appointed Commandant of Andersonville, GA Confederate Military Prison on 3/27/1864. Federal Rolls of Prisoners of War: Captured at Andersonville, GA Military Prison on 5/7/1865; Transferred to the Old Capitol Prison, Washington, D.C. in 5/1865. Executed by hanging on 11/10/1865 at the Old Capitol Prison for War Crimes allegedly committed against Union prisoners. *Buried:* Mt. Olivet Cemetery. *Born:* 11/25/1823 at Zurich, Switzerland. *Fathers Name:* Abraham Wirtz. *Married:* Twice, second wife was Mrs. Wolf of Milliken's Bend, LA. *Children:* 5 — Paul and Louisa by his first wife, Cora by his second wife, and step-children Susie and Cornelius Wolf. *Occupations:* Textile Weaver, Mercantile Dealer, and Homeopathic Physician.

Witt, William H. (aka Whitt) — Pvt./5th Sgt. — Enlisted: 5/25/1861 at Richmond, LA. Rolls for 5/25/1861 through 6/1862: Present. Regimental Return for 7/1862: Under arrest at Savannah, GA. Rolls for 11/1862 through 4/1865: Present. Rolls of Prisoners of War, C.S.A: Surrendered at Citronelle, AL on 5/4/1865; Paroled at Meridian, MS on 5/10/1865. *Residence:* Shreveport, Caddo Parish, LA. Soldier also served as a 5th Sgt. with the Louisiana Pelican Infantry Regiment-Co. F.

Corporal

Bass, John Cortez— Pvt./Cpl.— Enlisted: 5/25/1861 at Richmond, LA. Rolls for 5/25/1861 through 2/1863: Present, promoted to Cpl. on 11/1/1862. Retired by Medical Examiner Board on 8/1/1864. Rolls of Prisoners of War, C.S.A: Surrendered at New Orleans, LA on 5/26/1865; Paroled at Monroe, LA on 6/9/1865. *Married:* Josephine Archibald on 3/15/1877 at Floyd, West Carroll Parish, LA. *Died:* 2/28/1919 at Lake Providence, LA due to Blindness and Old Age. *Buried:* Lake Providence Cemetery located at Lake Providence, East Carroll Parish, LA. Confederate Widows Pension Application dated 8/23/1922 on file at the Louisiana State Archives-Microfilm Reel: CP1.8-Microdex 2-Sequence 9-Target Card: Bass, Josephine A. (Archibald)-Parish: East Carroll-7 Pages.

Bridgers, Thomas E. (aka Bridges)— Pvt./Cpl.— Enlisted: 5/25/1861 at Richmond, LA. Rolls for 5/25/1861 through 12/1863: Present. Rolls for 1/1864 through 2/1864: Present, promoted to Cpl. on 1/1/1864. Rolls for 9/1864 through 10/1864: Absent on sick furlough since 9/1/1864. Rolls for 11/1864 through 12/1864: *Died:* 12/1864.

Buchta, John L.— Pvt./Cpl.— Enlisted: 5/25/1861 at Richmond, LA. Rolls for 5/25/1861 through 8/1861: Present. Rolls for 9/1861 through 10/1861: Present, promoted from Pvt. to Cpl. on 9/25/1861. Rolls for 11/1861 through 2/1863: Present. Federal Rolls of Prisoners of War: Deserted, took the U.S. Oath of Allegiance at Savannah, GA on 3/28/1865. Description at oath-Complexion: fair; Hair: brown; Eyes: hazel; Age: 24; Height: 5 ft. 6 in. *Occupation:* Tinsmith.

Burns, Hugh— Pvt./3rd Cpl.— Enlisted: 5/25/1861 at Richmond, LA. Rolls for 5/25/1861 through 6/1861: Present. Soldier also served as a 3rd Cpl./Pvt. with Miles Legion Louisiana Militia-Co. G. Enlisted: 4/18/1862 at Natchez, MS. Rolls for 4/18/1862 through 6/30/1862: Appointed 3rd Cpl. on 4/18/1862; Reduced to Pvt. on 6/30/1862. Federal Rolls of Prisoners of War: Captured at Port Hudson, LA on 7/9/1863; Paroled at Port Hudson, LA in 7/1863.

Compton, Charles S.— Pvt./4th Cpl.— Enlisted: 5/25/1861 at Richmond, LA. Rolls for 5/25/1861 through 12/1861: Present. Rolls for 1/1862 through 2/1862: Present, appointed 4th Cpl. on 1/1/1862. Rolls for 3/1862 through 2/1864: Present. Rolls for 8/31/1864 through 4/1865: Absent on furlough; Wounded at the Battle of Resaca, GA on 5/15/1864. *Died:* 1864. *Buried:* Confederate Cemetery located at Resaca, Gordon County, GA.

Crouth, D. Hardeman— Cpl.— Enlisted: 5/25/1861 at Richmond, LA. Rolls for 5/25/1861 through 8/1861: Present.

Dancy, William Stodard (aka Dancey, W.D.)— Pvt./Cpl.— Enlisted: 5/25/1861 at Richmond, LA. Rolls for 5/25/1861 through 12/1861: Present. Soldier also served as a Pvt. with the 2nd Tennessee Cavalry-Co. I. Confederate Widows Pension Application on file at the Tennessee State Library and Archives-Widows *Name:* Dancey, Fredonia Avent *County:* Shelby-Pension Number: W3501.

McEachern, Daniel H. (aka McEacham, McEachann, McEacharn)— Pvt./1st Cpl./Pvt.— Enlisted: 5/25/1861 at Richmond, LA. Rolls for 5/25/1861 through 8/1861: Present. Rolls for 9/1861 through 10/1861: Present, promoted from Pvt. to Cpl. on 9/20/1861. Rolls for 11/1861 through 6/1862: Present. Regimental Return for 9/1862: On furlough. Rolls for 11/1862 through 12/1862: Present, reduced to Pvt. from 1st Cpl. on 10/31/1862. Rolls for 1/1863 through 2/1863: Present.

Noland, James P. (aka Nolan, Nowlen)— Pvt./Cpl.— Enlisted: 5/25/1861 at Richmond, LA. Rolls for 5/25/1861 through 2/1863: Present. *Buried:* Myrtle Hill Cemetery located at Rome, Floyd County, GA.

Nunnery, Nathaniel— Pvt./4th Cpl.— Enlisted: 5/25/1861 at Richmond, LA. Rolls for 5/25/1861 through 12/1862: Present. Rolls for 1/1863 through 2/1863: Present, detailed on extra duty as Teamster on 2/25/1863. Rolls for 1/1864 through 4/1865: Present. Rolls of Prisoners of War, C.S.A: Surrendered at Citronelle, AL on 5/4/1865; Paroled at Monroe, LA and Meridian, MS on 5/10/1865. *Residence:* Morehouse Parish, LA. Soldier also served as a 4th Cpl. with the Louisiana Pelican Infantry Regiment-Co. F. *Buried:* Sacred Heart Catholic Church Cemetery located at the corner of West Francis St. and South Eugene St. at Rayville, Richland Parish, LA.

O'Riley, John (aka O'Rielly)— Pvt./4th Cpl.— Enlisted: 5/25/1861 at Richmond, LA. Rolls for 5/25/1861 through 2/1863: Present, promoted to 4th Cpl. on 1/1/1863. Rolls for 1/1864 through 4/1865: Absent, captured at the Battle of Chickamauga, GA on 9/19/1863. Federal Rolls of Prisoners of War: Captured near Chickamauga, GA on 9/19/1863; Received at the U.S. Military Prison, Louisville, KY on 10/1/1863. Forwarded to Camp Douglas, IL on 10/2/1863; Discharged from Camp Douglas, IL on 6/14/1865 in accordance with General Order #109, Adjutant General's Office, Washington, D.C. 6/6/1865. *Residence:* Madison Parish, LA.

Stephenson, George W.— Pvt./Cpl.— Enlisted: 5/25/1861 at Richmond, LA. Rolls for 5/25/1861 through 6/1862: Present. Rolls for 11/1862 through 12/1862: Absent, sick at Savannah, GA. Rolls for 1/1863 through 2/1863: Present. Rolls for 1/1864 through 2/1864: Present. Rolls for 3/1864 through 2/28/1865: Absent on 60 day furlough since 2/17/1865. Rolls for 3/1865 through 4/1865: Absent, sick in hospital at Lauderdale, MS.

Private

Allnut, James S. (aka **Allnutt**) — Pvt. — Enlisted: 8/27/1862 at Vicksburg, MS. Rolls for 8/27/1862 through 12/1862: Present. On C.S.A. General Hospital Register, Wilmington, N. C: Admitted on 1/5/1863; Released on 1/14/1863. Rolls for 1/14/1863 through 2/1864: Present. Federal Rolls of Prisoners of War: Captured near Atlanta, GA on 8/5/1864; Forwarded to the U.S. Military Prison, Louisville, KY on 8/12/1864. Transferred to Camp Chase, OH on 8/13/1864; Paroled at Camp Chase, OH on 2/12/1865. Forwarded to James River, VA for Exchange on 2/20–21/1865.

Allnut, William A. (aka **Allnutt**) — Pvt. — Enlisted: 7/1/1861 at Richmond, VA. Rolls for 7/1/1861 through 2/1863: Present.

Allnutt, Edward George — Pvt. — Enlisted: 1/22/1862 at Vicksburg, MS. Rolls for 1/22/1862 through 2/1864: Present. Federal Rolls of Prisoners of War: Captured near Atlanta, GA on 8/5/1864; Received at the U.S. Military Prison, Louisville, KY on 8/12/1864. Transferred to Camp Chase, OH on 8/13/1864; Paroled at Camp Chase, OH on 2/12/1865. Transferred to Point Lookout, MD; Received at James River, VA on 2/21/1865. Rolls for 3/1865 through 4/1865: Absent on parole furlough since 3/10/1865.

Amis, A.B. (aka **A.S.**) — Pvt. — Enlisted: 3/13/1862 at Vicksburg, MS. Rolls for 3/13/1862 through 12/1862: Present. Rolls for 1/1863 through 2/1863: Discharged on 1/10/1863 due to Substitution of James R. Lark; Transferred to Company F same day.

Amis, Robert E. (aka **B.E.**) — Pvt./Color Bearer/2nd Lt. — (See Color Bearers)

Anderson, Armstrong — Pvt. — Enlisted: 5/25/1861 at Richmond, LA. Rolls for 5/25/1861 through 6/1862: Present. Rolls for 11/1862 through 12/1862: Absent, sick at Savannah, GA. Rolls for 1/1863 through 2/1863: Present. Rolls for 1/1864 through 2/1864: Hospitalized from wounds received at the Battle of Chickamauga, GA on 9/19/1863. Rolls for 3/1864 through 4/1864: Retired by Medical Board on 3/18/1864.

Anderson, Petus A. (aka **Peter, A.P.**) — Pvt. — Enlisted: 5/25/1861 at Richmond, LA. Rolls for 5/25/1861 through 4/1862: Present. Rolls for 5/1862 through 6/1862: Absent, detached service at Ordnance Dept., Macon, GA. Rolls for 11/1862 through 2/1863: Present. Rolls for 1/1864 through 4/1865: Present, detailed as Brigade Carpenter by order of Brig. Gen. Randall L. Gibson. Rolls of Prisoners of War, C.S.A: Surrendered at Citronelle, AL on 5/4/1865; Paroled at Meridian, MS on 5/10/1865. *Residence:* Shreveport, Caddo Parish, LA.

Armstrong, Daniel — Pvt. — Enlisted: 5/25/1861 at Richmond, LA. Rolls for 5/25/1861 through 6/1862: Present. Regimental Return for 8/1862: Under arrest at Savannah, GA. Regimental Return for 9/1862: In barracks at Savannah, GA. Rolls for 11/1862 through 12/1862: Under arrest at Savannah, GA. Rolls for 1/1863 through 2/1863: Present. Rolls for 1/1864 through 2/1864: Absent, hospitalized at Savannah, GA from wounds received at the Battle of Chickamauga, GA on 9/19/1863. Rolls for 8/31/1864 through 4/1865: Absent, wounded at Chickamauga and in hospital at Savannah, GA. On List dated: Headquarters, Dept. of the South, Office of Provost Marshal General, Hilton Head, S.C. 3/22/1865-*Born:* Illinois-Last Residence: Savannah, GA-Remarks: Came into our lines on 2/18/1865 from Savannah, GA. Brief shows: Receipt for Rebel Prisoners sent north in custody of 2nd Lt. Jonathan H. Snow, 201st Pennsylvania Volunteer Infantry via the Steamer Fulton.

Balph, O.P. — Pvt. — Enlisted: 7/1/1861 at Richmond, VA. Rolls for 7/1/1861 through 2/1863: Present. Rolls for 1/1864 through 2/1864: Deserted from hospital in Georgia.

Barnum, Benjamin — Pvt. — Enlisted: 5/25/1861 at Richmond, LA. Rolls for 5/1861 through 2/1863: Present. On extra daily duty at Brigade Blacksmith since 9/1/1863 by order of Col. Claudius C. Wilson.

Barr, Herman B. — Pvt. — Enlisted: 5/25/1861 at Richmond, LA. Rolls for 5/25/1861 through 8/1861: Present. Soldier also served as a Pvt. with the 3rd Louisiana Cavalry (Harrison's)-Co. B. Rolls of Prisoners of War, C.S.A: Surrendered at New Orleans, LA on 5/26/1865; Paroled in 6/1865. *Residence:* Madison Parish, LA.

Barrell, Thomas (aka **Burrell**) — Pvt. — Enlisted: 5/25/1861 at Richmond. LA. Rolls for 5/25/1861 through 2/1862: Present. Rolls for 3/1862 through 4/1862: Absent, sick in Hospital at Augusta, GA. Rolls for 5/1862 through 6/1862: Discharged due to Surgeon's Certificate of Disability on 6/23/1862.

Barry, Dennis — Pvt. — Enlisted: 5/25/1861 at Richmond, LA. Rolls for 5/25/1861 through 10/1861: Present. Rolls for 11/1861 through 12/1861: Absent, left in hospital at Richmond, VA. Rolls for 1/1862 through 6/1862: Present. Regimental Return for 8/1862: Assigned as Hospital Nurse. Transferred to the C.S. Naval Service on 12/15/1862.

Beale, Jesse T. — Pvt. — Enlisted: 5/25/1861 at Richmond, LA. Rolls for 5/25/1861 through 10/1861: Present. Rolls for 11/1861 through 12/1861: Discharged without the knowledge or consent of the Company A Captain.

Beek, Robert S. (aka **Belk**) — Pvt./Q.M. Sgt. — (See Field and Staff)

Bridgers, A. — Pvt. — Enlisted: 11/30/1862 at Richmond, LA. Rolls for 11/1862 through 2/1863: Present.

Brooks, Samuel D.—Pvt.—Enlisted: 5/25/1861 at Richmond, LA. Rolls for 5/25/1861 through 2/1863: Present. Rolls for 1/1864 through 2/1864: Absent with leave by order of Gen. Joseph E. Johnston. Rolls for 8/31/1864 through 4/1865: Present. Rolls of Prisoners of War, C.S.A: Surrendered at Citronelle, AL on 5/4/1865; Paroled at Meridian, MS on 5/10/1865. *Residence:* Shreveport, Caddo Parish, LA.

Cain, John J. (aka Cane)—Pvt.—Enlisted: 3/18/1862 at Vicksburg, MS. Rolls for 3/18/1862 through 2/1864: Present. Federal Rolls of Prisoners of War: Captured at Resaca, GA on 5/16/1864; Sent to the U.S. Military Prison, Louisville, KY from Nashville, TN on 5/21/1864. Transferred to Camp Morton, IN on 5/22/1864; Released on the U.S. Oath of Allegiance on 5/10/1865. *Residence:* Madison Parish, LA. Description at oath-Complexion: dark-Hair: black-Eyes: blue-Height: 5 ft. 11½ in.

Campbell, Henry—Pvt.—Enlisted: 5/25/1861 at Richmond, LA. Rolls for 5/25/1861 through 2/1862: Present. Rolls for 3/1862 through 4/1862: Died on 3/4/1862.

Cane, John J.—Pvt.—Federal Rolls of Prisoners of War: Captured at Resaca, GA on 5/16/1864; Sent to Camp Morton, IN. Released on 5/10/1865 by order of O.C.G.P., issued on 5/5/1865.

Capehart, Francis M. (aka Cafehart, Caperhart, Caphart)—Pvt.—Enlisted: 8/27/1862 at Vicksburg, MS. Rolls for 8/27/1862 through 2/1863: Present. Federal Rolls of Prisoners of War: Captured at Yazoo City, MS on 7/13/1863; Sent to Memphis, TN on 7/20/1863. Received at Gratiot St. Military Prison, St. Louis, MO on 8/3/1863; Forwarded to Camp Morton, IN on 8/13/1863. Died at Camp Morton, IN on 2/1/1864 due to pneumonia. *Buried:* Crown Hill Cemetery located at Indianapolis, Marion County, IN.

Cassner, R.D.—Pvt.—Enlisted: 4/10/1862 at Vicksburg, MS. Rolls for 4/10/1862 through 6/1862: Present. Rolls for 11/1862 through 12/1862: Absent, sick at Savannah, GA. Rolls for 1/1863 through 2/1863: Present.

Cassner, Thomas P. (aka Casner)—Pvt.—Enlisted: 1/22/1862 at Vicksburg, MS. Rolls for 1/22/1862 through 2/1863: Present. *Died:* 5/22/1863 at Canton, MS. *Buried:* Canton City Cemetery located at Canton, Madison County, MS.

Chambers, Benjamin—Pvt.—Enlisted: 5/25/1861 at Richmond, LA. Rolls for 5/25/1861 through 2/1863: Present.

Chapman, John L.—Pvt.—Enlisted: 6/21/1861 at Richmond, VA.

Chatterson, John—Pvt.—Enlisted: 5/25/1861 at Richmond, LA. Rolls for 5/25/1861 through 6/1862: Present. Rolls for 11/1862 through 12/1862: Transferred to the C.S. Naval Service as Master-of-Arms on 12/15/1862. Federal Rolls of Prisoners of War: Captured on board the C.S.S. Atlanta at Wassaw Sound, GA on 6/17/1863. *Born:* 1838 in England.

Clark, Robert—Pvt.—Enlisted: 9/27/1862 at Vicksburg, MS. Rolls for 9/27/1862 through 2/1863: Present.

Crandell, S.W.—Pvt.—Enlisted: 9/27/1862 at Vicksburg, MS. Rolls for 11/1862 through 12/1862: Present. Rolls for 1/1863 through 2/1863: Present. Rolls for 1/1864 through 2/1864: Present.

Daniels, Thomas (aka Daniel)—Pvt.—Enlisted: 5/25/1861 at Richmond, LA. Rolls for 5/25/1861 through 10/1861: Present. Rolls for 11/1861 through 12/1861: Absent, sick and left in hospital at Richmond, VA. Rolls for 1/1862 through 2/1862: Died at Richmond, VA.

Daugherty, John D. (aka Dougherty)—Pvt.—Enlisted: 5/25/1861 at Richmond, LA. Rolls for 5/25/1861 through 6/1862: Present. Regimental Return for 8/1862: Under arrest at Savannah, GA. Regimental Return for 9/1862: In barracks at Savannah, GA. Rolls for 11/1862 through 2/1863: Present. *Died:* 5/22/1864. *Buried:* Confederate Cemetery located at Resaca, Gordon County, GA.

Daugherty, John M. (aka Dougherty)—Pvt.—Enlisted: 5/25/1861 at Richmond, LA. Rolls for 5/25/1861 through 2/1864: Present. On Federal 2nd Division, 20th Corps Hospital Register: Admitted on 5/15/1865 as a prisoner after the Battle of Resaca, GA due to a serious right lung injury; Simple dressing applied. *Died:* 1864. *Buried:* Confederate Cemetery located at Resaca, Gordon County, GA.

Dawson, Joseph S.—Pvt.—Enlisted: 5/25/1861 at Richmond, LA. Rolls for 5/25/1861 through 4/1862: Present.

Delaney, Thomas—Pvt.—Enlisted: 5/25/1861 at Richmond, LA. Rolls for 5/25/1861 through 6/1862: Present. Rolls for 11/1862 through 2/1863: Absent, on detached duty at Savannah, GA. Rolls for 1/1864 through 2/1864: On detached duty at Savannah, GA by order of Brig. Gen. Hugh W. Mercer since 10/6/1862; Assigned to Engineer Corps on 10/26/1863 by order of the Secretary of War.

DeShazo, C.J. (aka Deshays)—Pvt.—Enlisted: 9/27/1862 at Vicksburg, MS. Rolls for 9/27/1862 through 2/1863: Present. Federal Rolls of Prisoners of War: Captured and paroled at Vicksburg, MS on 7/4/1863.

Dixon, John S.—Pvt./Ord. Sgt.—(See Field and Staff)

Dixon, William Henry— Pvt.— Enlisted: 5/25/1861 at Richmond, LA. Rolls for 5/25/1861 through 10/1861: Present. Rolls for 11/1861 through 12/1861: Absent sick, left in hospital at Richmond, VA. Rolls for 1/1862 through 6/1862: Present. Regimental Return for 8/1862: Under arrest at Savannah, GA. Regimental Return for 9/1862: In barracks at Savannah, GA. Rolls for 11/1862 through 12/1862: Absent, sick at Savannah, GA. Rolls for 1/1863 through 4/1865: Present. Rolls of Prisoners of War, C.S.A: Surrendered at Citronelle, AL on 5/4/1865; Paroled at Meridian, MS on 5/10/1865. *Residence:* Natchez, Adams County, MS.

Eden, Anderson— Pvt.— Enlisted: 5/25/1861 at Richmond, LA. Rolls for 5/25/1861 through 6/1862: Present. Rolls for 11/1862 through 12/1862: Absent, sick at Savannah, GA. Rolls for 1/1863 through 2/1863: Present.

Eden, John P.— Pvt./Commissary Sgt.—(See Field and Staff)

Edwards, Jonathan M.— Pvt.— Enlisted: 5/25/1861 at Richmond, LA. Rolls for 5/25/1861 through 6/1862: Present.

Fankenbridge, William W.V. (aka Falkenberry, Fankenberg, Faulenberg, Faulkenberg, Faulkenbury, Fowburg)— Pvt.— Federal Rolls of Prisoners of War: Captured at Vidalia, LA on 2/28/1864; Sent to Vicksburg, MS on 4/25/1864. Forwarded to Memphis, TN on 4/27/1864; Received at the U.S. Military Prison, Alton, IL on 5/12/1864. Forwarded to the U.S. Military Prison, Louisville, KY on 5/15/1864; Transferred to Point Lookout, MD for Exchange on 2/17/1865. Federal Rolls of Prisoners of War: Captured at Richmond, VA on 4/3/1865. On U.S.A. General Hospital Register, Point Lookout, MD: Admitted on 5/6/1865; Released on the U.S. Oath of Allegiance on 7/25/1865. Forwarded to Washington, D.C. on 7/27/1865. On Register of Refugees and Rebel Deserters, Provost Marshal General's Office, Washington, D.C: Received on 7/29/1865; Transportation furnished to Natchez, MS. *Residence:* Concordia Parish, LA. Description at release-Complexion: florid-Hair: dark-Eyes: hazel-Height: 5 ft. 8½ in.

Ferrand, Horace— Pvt.— Enlisted: 5/14/1862 at Monroe, LA. Name on receipt given by Maj. N.C. Watts, C.S.A. Agent for Exchange, to Capt. H.M. Lazelle, U.S.A. Agent for Exchange, for prisoners of war received near Vicksburg, MS on 9/26/1862 who have hereby been paroled. *Remarks:* Exchanged at Aikens Landing, VA on 11/10/1862. Rolls for 11/1862 through 2/1863: Present. Rolls for 8/31/1864 through 2/28/1865: Present, detailed in Brigade Commissary Dept. by order of Brig. Gen. Randall L. Gibson. Rolls for 3/1865 through 4/1865: Present, assigned extra daily duty with Maj. Crouch by order of Gen. Gibson. Rolls of Prisoners of War, C.S.A: Surrendered at Citronelle, AL on 5/4/1865; Paroled at Meridian, MS on 5/10/1865. *Residence:* Caldwell Parish, LA. Soldier also served with the Louisiana Pelican Infantry Regiment-Co. F and the 20th Louisiana Infantry (Lovells)-Co. F. *Born:* 8/6/1838 at Caldwell Parish, LA to Alfred Ferrand and Louisa Landernau Ferrand. *Married:* Ann Eliza Filhiol on 8/25/1879 at Saint Matthew's Church at Monroe, Ouachita Parish, LA. *Children:* 1 Son-Eugene A. Ferrand. *Died:* 7/11/1910 at Colorado Springs, CO due to Apoplexy. *Buried:* Colorado Springs, CO. *Wife Born:* 8/21/1857 at Monroe, LA to Hypolite Filhiol of Monroe, LA and Debora Tufts Filhiol of Boston, MA. Wife Baptized: 5/14/1858 at Saint Matthew's Church at Monroe, LA. *Wife Died:* 6/16/1936 at Monroe, LA (Deaf and almost blind). Widows Pension amount: $60.00 per month. Confederate Widows Pension Application dated 12/6/1935 on file at the Louisiana State Archives-Microfilm Reel: CP1.48-Microdex 2-Sequence 17-Target Card: Ferrand, Ann Eliza-Parish: Ouachita-12 Pages.

Frisby, Daniel W. (aka Frisbey, D.L.)— Pvt.— Enlisted: 5/25/1861 at Richmond, LA. Rolls for 5/25/1861 through 2/28/1865: Present, placed on the Confederate Roll of Honor for gallantry and good conduct at the Battle of Chickamauga, GA per General Order #131 of the Adjutant and Inspector General's Office, Richmond, VA. Rolls for 3/1865 through 4/1865: Present, on daily extra duty as Provost Guard by order of Brig. Gen. Randall L. Gibson. Rolls of Prisoners of War, C.S.A: Surrendered at Citronelle, AL on 5/4/1865; Paroled at Meridian, MS on 5/10/1865. *Residence:* Shreveport, Caddo Parish, LA. Wounded: 4 times-Shot in jaw at the Battle of Chickamauga, GA, in left hip near Atlanta, GA on 6/23/1864, and in right shoulder and right hand at Spanish Fort, AL. *Born:* 2/3/1845 at Richmond, Madison Parish, LA. *Married:* No. *Children:* None. *Residence:* Louisiana for life. *Buried:* Blue Branch Cemetery located at Vernon Parish, LA. Soldier is recorded on the 1911 Census of Louisiana Confederate Soldiers and their Widows-*Residence:* Ward 6, Vernon Parish-Age: 66-Property Owned/Assessed: None-Employment: Farming-Infirmities: Kidney Trouble. Confederate Pension Application dated 7/17/1900 on file at the Louisiana State Archives-Microfilm Reel: CP1.51-Microdex 4-Sequence 5-Target Card: Frisby, Dan W.-Parish: Vernon-5 Pages. Also a Confederate Proofs and Land Warrant Application on file at the Louisiana State Archives-Name: Frisby, Daniel L.-Microfilm Reel: 1-Frame Number: 0451-Act: 116-Pages: 2-Parish: East Baton Rouge.

Gay, James— Pvt.— Enlisted: 5/25/1861 at Richmond, LA. Rolls for 5/25/1861 through 8/1861: Present.

Geety, James G.— Pvt.— Enlisted: 5/25/1861 at Richmond, LA. Rolls for 5/25/1861 through 6/1862: Present. Rolls for 11/1862 through 12/1862: Absent, sick at Savannah, GA. Rolls for 1/1863 through 2/1864: Present.

Gentry, Thomas S.—Pvt.—Enlisted: 5/25/1861 at Richmond, LA. Rolls for 5/25/1861 through 8/1861: Present. Rolls for 9/1861 through 12/1861: Discharged without the knowledge or consent of the Company A Captain.

Gibson, Preston J.—Pvt.—Enlisted: 5/25/1861 at Richmond, LA. Rolls for 7/1861 through 2/1863: Present. Rolls for 1/1864 through 2/1864: Sick in hospital at Jackson, MS by order of Surgeon Bolen.

Graves, James Q. (aka **J.K.**)—Pvt.—Enlisted: 3/18/1862 at Vicksburg, MS. Rolls for 3/1862 through 4/1862: Present. Rolls for 5/1862 through 6/1862: Present, on detached duty in Savannah, GA. Rolls for 11/1862 through 2/1863: Absent, sick in hospital at Whitesville, GA. Rolls for 1/1864 through 2/1865: Present. Rolls for 3/1865 through 4/1865: Absent, wounded at Spanish Fort, AL and sent to hospital. Rolls of Prisoners of War, C.S.A: Surrendered at Citronelle, AL on 5/4/1865; Paroled at Meridian. MS on 5/14/1865. *Residence:* Alexandria, Rapides Parish, LA. *Born:* 3/31/1832 at Orange, VA. *Married:* Laura E. Blanks on 1/13/1870. *Children:* 1 Son and 1 Daughter-Dr. James Q. Graves, Jr. and Daisy Graves Erskin. *Died:* 3/14/1913 at Columbia, LA due to Acute Nephritis. *Buried:* Columbia Hills Cemetery located at Columbia, Caldwell Parish, LA. Wife *Born:* 5/25/1851 at Columbia, LA. Wife *Died:* 1/21/1936. Widows Pension Amount: $60.00 per month in 1936. His son, Dr. James Q. Graves, Jr., was elected Surgeon of the Louisiana Division-Monroe, LA Camp of the Sons of Confederate Veterans in 1916. Confederate Widows Pension Application dated 8/5/1932 on file at the Louisiana State Archives-Microfilm Reel: CP1.57-Microdex 2-Sequence 10-Target Card: Graves, Laura (Banks)-Parish: Caldwell-21 Pages.

Guilfoil, Michael S. (aka **Gulfoil, Gilfoil**)—Pvt.—Enlisted: 5/25/1861 at Richmond, LA. Rolls for 5/1861 through 2/1864: Present. Rolls for 8/1864 through 4/1865: Absent, captured near Atlanta, GA on 8/5/1864. Federal Rolls of Prisoners of War: Captured at Atlanta, GA on 8/5/1864; Sent to Dept. of the Cumberland, Nashville, TN on 8/11/1864. Received at the U.S. Military Prison, Louisville, KY on 8/12/1864; Transferred to Camp Chase, OH on 8/14/1864. Died on 2/20/1865 due to pneumonia. *Buried:* Camp Chase Confederate Cemetery located at Columbus, Franklin County, OH.

Gustine, Samuel—Pvt.—Enlisted: 5/25/1861 at Richmond, LA. Rolls for 5/25/1861 through 2/1863: Present. On Register of C.S.A. Gen. Hospital #4, Wilmington, NC: Admitted on 12/27/1862; Returned to duty on 1/3/1863. Rolls for 1/1864 through 2/1864: Present. Rolls for 8/1864 through 2/1865: Absent, captured and slightly wounded in both arms near Atlanta, GA on 8/5/1864. Federal Rolls of Prisoners of War: Captured near Atlanta, GA on 8/5/1864; Forwarded to the U.S. Military Prison, Louisville, KY from Nashville, TN on 8/11/1864. Transferred to Camp Chase, OH on 8/14/1864; Paroled at Camp Chase, OH on 2/12/1865. Exchanged at Boulware and Cox Wharf, James River, VA on 2/20–21/1865. Rolls for 3/1865 through 4/1865: Present. Rolls of Prisoners of War, C.S.A: Surrendered at Citronelle, AL on 5/4/1865; Paroled at Meridian, MS on 5/10/1865. *Residence:* Shreveport, Caddo Parish, LA. *Born:* 1/26/1844 at New Orleans, LA. *Married:* Carrie E. Clark on 11/7/1880 at Van Zant County, TX. *Children:* 1 son. *Occupation:* Treasurer of Mitchell County, TX. *Father:* Dr. Lemuel Gustine of New Orleans, LA. *Died:* 12/11/1915 at his home in Colorado, TX. *Residences:* Colorado, Mitchell County, TX since 1872. Wife *Born:* 10/23/1851 at Marshall, TX. Wife *Died:* 12/6/1930 at her home at Colorado, Mitchell County, TX due to Cancer of the Uterus and Bladder. (His obituary appeared in the 10/1916 edition of Confederate Veteran magazine, and a letter regarding his military service was printed in the 11/1/1912 edition of the book, "Reminiscences of the Boys In Gray-1861–1865" by Mamie Yeary of the Pearl Witt Chapter #569-United Daughters of the Confederacy of McGregor, TX.) Confederate Widows Pension Application dated 1/7/1920 on file at the Texas State Library and Archives Commission-Widows Name: Gustine, Carrie E.-County: Mitchell-Pension Number: 36629.

Haddox, Henry—Pvt.—Enlisted: 9/27/1862 at Vicksburg, MS. Rolls for 11/1862 through 12/1862: Absent without leave. Rolls for 1/1863 through 2/1863: Present. Soldier also served as a Pvt. with the 2nd Tennessee Cavalry-Co. I. Confederate Pension Application dated 1903 on file at the Mississippi Dept. of Archives and History-Target Card: Haddox, Henry-County: Scott. Confederate Widows Pension Application on file at the Georgia Dept. of Archives and History-Name: Moore, Mrs. E.M. Haddox-County: Bibb.

Haddox, Robert—Pvt./Musician—(See Field and Staff)

Harvey, William H. (aka **Hervey**)—Pvt.—Enlisted: 8/27/1862 at Vicksburg, MS. Rolls for 8/27/1862 through 2/1863: Present, admitted to C.S.A. General Military Hospital, Wilmington, N.C. on 1/5/1863; Returned to duty on 1/7/1863. Rolls for 1/1864 through 2/1864: Absent, sick in hospital from wounds received at the Battle of Chickamauga, GA on 9/19/1863; Assigned to Quartermaster Dept. in the Trans-Mississippi Dept. at Arcadia, Bienville Parish, LA. Rolls for 8/1864 through 4/1865: Retired by Medical Board on 6/9/1864. Rolls of Prisoners of War, C.S.A: Surrendered at New Orleans, LA on 5/26/1865; Paroled at Shreveport, LA on 6/8/1865. *Residence:* Mount Lebanon, Bienville Parish, LA. *Married:* Agnes Noland on 4/25/1870 at Madison Parish, LA. *Died:* 4/21/1919 at Tallulah, LA due to Brights Disease. *Buried:* Tallulah, Madison Parish, LA. Confederate Widows Pension Application dated 6/7/1922 on file at the

Louisiana State Archives-Microfilm Reel: CP1.63-Microdex 1-Sequence 5-Target Card: Harvey, Agnes (Noland)-Parish: Madison-6 Pages. Also a Confederate Proofs and Land Warrant Application on file-Name: Harvey, William H.-Microfilm Reel: 1-Frame Number: 0417-Act: 116-Pages: 2-Parish: Madison.

Hathaway, John C.— Pvt.— Enlisted: 5/25/1861 at Richmond, LA. Rolls for 5/25/1861 through 4/1862: Present. Rolls for 5/1862 through 2/1863: Absent, on detached duty at Savannah, GA.

Henderson, Thomas— Pvt./Musician/Commissary Sgt.—(See Field and Staff)

Hickman, William F.T.— Pvt.— Enlisted: 5/25/1861 at Richmond, LA. Rolls for 5/25/1861 through 2/1864: Present. Rolls for 8/1864 through 2/1865: Absent, detached to Division Provost Guard by order of Maj. Gen. Alexander P. Stewart. Rolls for 3/1865 through 4/1865: Deserted in 1/1865. *Born:* 5/24/1835 at Pickens County, AL. *Married:* Yes. *Wife's Age:* 50 in 1904. *Children:* 5 — 3 Sons and 2 Daughters. *Occupation:* Farmer. *Residences:* Louisiana since 1870. *Died:* 5/27/1910. *Buried:* Friendship Cemetery located south of Haynesville, Claiborne Parish, LA. Three Confederate Pension Applications dated 2/29/1904, 6/15/1904 and 9/5/1906 on file at the Louisiana State Archives-Microfilm Reel: CP1.66-Microdex 3-Sequence 27-Target Card: Hickman, W.F.T.-Parish: Bienville-15 Pages.

Hitchings, Joseph (aka Hitchens)— Pvt.— Enlisted: 3/18/1862 at Vicksburg, MS. Rolls for 3/18/1862 through 4/1862: Present, sick in quarters. Rolls for 5/1862 through 6/1862: Present, on detached service at Savannah, GA. Rolls for 11/1862 through 2/1863: Absent without leave. Rolls for 1/1864 through 2/1864: Died while on detached duty in the Trans-Mississippi Military Dept. of Louisiana.

Horne, Pierce (aka Pearce)— Pvt.— Enlisted: 5/25/1861 at Richmond, LA. Rolls for 5/25/1861 through 8/1861: Present. Rolls for 9/1861 through 10/1861: Discharged without the knowledge or consent of the Company A Captain. Confederate Widows Pension Application on file at the Georgia Dept. of Archives and History-Name: Horne, Tallulah J.-County: Whitfield.

Jackson, Sydney M.— Pvt./Color Cpl.—(See Color Bearers)

James, Mark W.— Pvt.— Enlisted: 5/25/1861 at Richmond, LA. Rolls for 5/25/1861 through 2/1863: Present. Federal Rolls of Prisoners of War: Captured at the Battle of Missionary Ridge, TN on 11/25/1863; Received at the U.S. Military Prison, Louisville, KY on 12/7/1863 from Nashville, TN. Forwarded to Rock Island Barracks, IL on 12/8/1863; Enlisted in the U.S. Army for frontier service on 10/13/1864.

Lard, William— Pvt.—(No War Dept. Record)-*Buried:* Myrtle Hill Cemetery located at Rome, Floyd County, GA.

Lasley, William— Pvt.— Enlisted: 5/25/1861 at Richmond, LA. Rolls for 5/25/1861 through 6/30/1861: Present.

Leyon, Andrew (aka Liyon, Lyon)— Pvt.— Enlisted: 5/25/1861 at Richmond, LA. Rolls for 5/25/1861 through 1/1862: Present. Rolls for 3/1862 through 4/1862: Absent, sick in hospital at Augusta, GA. Rolls for 5/1862 through 6/1862: Present. Rolls for 11/1862 through 12/1862: Transferred to the C.S. Naval Service on 12/15/1862.

Linder, Samuel H.— Pvt.—(No War Dept. Record)-Soldier transferred to the 36th Mississippi Infantry-Co. A at Meridian, MS three weeks after enlistment on 10/10/1863. Wounded: Yes-Shell fragment in left leg below knee received at the Battle of Franklin, TN. *Born:* 12/2/1839 at Brookhaven, Lawrence County, MS. *Married:* Yes. *Wife's Age:* 52 in 1901. *Children:* None. *Occupation:* Farm Laborer. Two Confederate Pension Applications dated 7/10/1901 and 2/20/1905 on file at the Louisiana State Archives-Microfilm Reel: CP1.86-Microdex 2-Sequence 3-Target Card: Linder, Samuel H.-Parish: Caldwell-11 Pages.

Long, A.J. (aka Lono)— Pvt.-Enlisted: 1/22/1862 at Vicksburg, MS. Rolls for 1/22/1862 through 6/1862: Present. Rolls for 11/1862 through 12/1862: Absent, sick at Savannah, GA. Rolls for 1/1863 through 2/1863: Present. Rolls for 1/1864 through 2/1865: Present. Rolls for 3/1865 through 4/1865: Present, assigned daily extra duty as Provost Guard by order of Brig. Gen. Randall L. Gibson. Rolls of Prisoners of War, C.S.A: Surrendered at Citronelle, AL on 5/4/1865; Paroled at Meridian, MS on 5/10/1865. *Residence:* Claiborne County, MS. Soldier also served as a Pvt. with the Louisiana Pelican Infantry Regiment-Co. F.

Long, Thomas— Pvt.— Enlisted: 5/21/1861 at Richmond, LA. Rolls for 5/21/1861 through 6/30/1861: Present.

McEnery, H.O. (aka McEnary, McEnry, D.O.)— Pvt./Surgeon —(See Field and Staff)

McNeil, John W. (aka McNeal)— Pvt.— Enlisted: 5/25/1861 at Richmond, LA. Rolls for 5/25/1861 through 4/1862: Present. Rolls for 5/1862 through 6/1862: Present, on detached service at Savannah, GA. Regimental Returns for 7/1862 and 9/1862: At work on Gunboat at Savannah, GA. Rolls for 11/1862 through 2/1863: Absent, on detached service at Savannah, GA. Rolls for 1/1864 through 2/1864: Absent, on detached duty at Mobile, AL by order of Brig. General Hugh W. Mercer since 4/1862. Rolls for 8/1864 through 2/28/1865: Absent, detached on Gunboat at Savannah,

GA by order of Brig. Gen. Mercer. Rolls for 3/1865 through 4/1865: Deserted in 11/1864.

McPherson, James— Pvt.— Enlisted: 5/25/1861 at Richmond, LA. Rolls for 5/25/1861 through 6/30/1861: Present.

Magee, Zaborn D.— Pvt.— Soldier also served as a Pvt. with the Louisiana Pelican Regiment-Co. F, the 9th Battalion Louisiana Cavalry-Co. A, and the 3rd Louisiana Cavalry (Wingfield's)-Co. A. Enlisted: 5/13/1862 at Camp Moore, LA. Rolls for 3/1865 through 4/1865: Present, remarks: Assigned from the 3rd Louisiana Cavalry since last muster. Rolls of Prisoners of War, C.S.A: Surrendered at Citronelle, AL on 5/4/1865; Paroled at Meridian, MS on 5/10/1865. *Residence:* Washington Parish, LA. *Born:* 6/6/1841 at Washington Parish, LA. *Married:* Yes-twice. *Children:* 2–1 Son and 1 Daughter. *Occupation:* Truck Farmer. *Residences:* Louisiana since 1841. *Buried:* Zaborn Magee Cemetery located 1 mile west of Enon Baptist Church at Enon, Washington Parish, LA. Three Confederate Pension Applications dated 10/13/1898, 1/20/1900 and 9/13/1916 on file at the Louisiana State Archives-Microfilm Reel: CP1.88-Microdex 4-Sequence 8-Target Card: Magee, Z.D.-Parish: Washington-15 Pages.

Major, W.T., Jr.— Pvt.— Regimental Return for 8/1862: Re-enlisted on 8/20/1862 at Vicksburg, MS.

Marshall, Charles L.— Pvt./Hosp. Steward —(See Field and Staff)

Mason, John Thomas— Pvt./Musician —(See Field and Staff)

Mathews, Thompson B. (aka Matthews)— Pvt.— Enlisted: 5/25/1861 at Richmond, LA. Rolls for 5/25/1861 through 6/1862: Present. Regimental Return for 8/1862: Under arrest at Savannah, GA. Regimental Return for 9/1862: In barracks at Savannah, GA. Rolls for 11/1862 through 2/1865: Present. Rolls for 3/1865 through 4/1865: Absent, captured at Spanish Fort, AL on 4/8/1865 and Prisoner of War. Federal Rolls of Prisoners of War: Captured at Spanish Fort, AL on 4/8/1865; Forwarded to Ship Island, MS on 5/10/1865. Transferred to Vicksburg, MS on 5/1/1865; Paroled at Camp Townsend, MS on 5/6/1865.

Maus, Henry— Pvt.—(No War Dept. Record)-*Born:* 4/2/1838. *Died:* 3/11/1909. *Buried:* Evergreen Cemetery located at Gulfport, Harrison County, MS.

Miller, John— Pvt.— Enlisted: 5/25/1861 at Richmond, LA. Rolls for 5/25/1861 through 8/1861: Present. Rolls through 9/30/1861: Sick in camp.

Munford, John H. (aka Mumford)— Pvt.— Enlisted: 5/25/1861 at Richmond, LA. Rolls for 5/25/1861 through 6/30/1861: Present.

Neal, Robert— Pvt.— Enlisted: 5/25/1861 at Richmond, LA. Rolls for 5/25/1861 through 6/1862: Present. Regimental Return for 8/1862: Transferred on 8/1/1862 from camp.

Nunnery, Jacob— Pvt.—(No War Dept. Record)—*Buried:* Sacred Heart Catholic Church Cemetery located at the corner of West Francis St. and South Eugene St. at Rayville, Richland Parish, LA.

Nunnery, John M. (aka Nunnory)— Pvt.— Enlisted: 5/25/1861 at Richmond, LA. Rolls for 5/25/1861 through 2/1864: Present. Rolls for 8/31/1864 through 4/1865: Absent, wounded at the Battle of Jonesboro, GA and in hospital. Federal Rolls of Prisoners of War: Captured at the Battle of Jonesboro, GA on 9/12/1864; Admitted to U.S.A. General Hospital #1, Nashville, TN on 11/8/1864 due to a gunshot wound. Age: 21 yrs. Sent to the U.S. Military Prison, Louisville, KY on 5/10/1865; Released from the U.S. Military Prison, Louisville, KY on the U.S. Oath of Allegiance on 6/16/1865. *Residence:* Richmond, LA. Description at release-Complexion: dark-Hair: dark-Eyes: blue-Height: 5 ft. 10 in. *Born:* 11/10/1844. *Died:* 5/1/1917. *Buried:* Greenwood Cemetery located at the corner of City Park Ave. and Canal St. at New Orleans, Orleans Parish, LA. Soldier is recorded on the 1911 Census of Louisiana Confederate Soldiers and their Widows-*Residence:* Ward 7, Orleans Parish-Age: 67-Property Owned/Assessed: None-Employment: None-Infirmities: Wounds and loss of leg.

O'Riley, Charles— Pvt.— Enlisted: 5/25/1861 at Richmond, LA. Rolls for 5/25/1861 through 8/1861: Present.

O'Sullivan, Pat— Pvt.— Enlisted: 3/18/1862 at Vicksburg, MS. Rolls for 3/18/1862 through 6/1862: Present. Rolls for 11/1862 through 12/1862: Transferred to the C.S. Naval Service on 12/15/1862.

Owen, Jennings J.— Pvt.— Enlisted: 5/25/1861 at Richmond, LA. Rolls for 5/25/1861 through 12/1862: Present. Rolls for 1/1863 through 2/1863: Absent, on detailed duty in hospital at Wilmington, N.C. Rolls for 1/1864 through 4/1865: Absent, captured at the Battle of Missionary Ridge, TN on 11/25/1863. Federal Rolls of Prisoners of War: Captured at the Battle of Missionary Ridge, TN on 11/25/1863; Received at the U.S. Military Prison, Louisville, Ky from Nashville, TN on 12/7/1863. Forwarded to Rock Island Barracks, IL on 12/20/1863. On Roll dated Headquarters, Rock Island Barracks, IL 3/18/1864: Prisoner of War desires to take the U.S. Oath of Allegiance. *Remarks:* Conscripted into the C.S. Army and was under arrest when captured. Enlisted in the U.S. Army for frontier service on 10/4/1864 from Rock Island Barracks, IL.

Peterson, Peter A.— Pvt.— Enlisted: 5/25/1861 at Richmond, LA. Rolls for 5/25/1861 through 2/1862:

Present. Rolls for 3/1862 through 2/1864: On detached duty at Richmond, VA by order of the Secretary of War. Rolls for 8/31/1864 through 2/28/1865: Absent, detailed as Government Saddler at Richmond, VA by order of the Secretary of War. Rolls for 3/1865 through 4/1865: Absent, detailed at Richmond, VA by order of the Secretary of War.

Phillips, William E.—Pvt.—Enlisted: 5/25/1861 at Richmond, LA. Rolls for 5/25/1861 through 6/1862: Present. Rolls for 11/1862 through 12/1862: Absent without leave. Rolls for 1/1863 through 2/1863: Present. Rolls for 1/1864 through 2/1864: Deserted from hospital in Georgia.

Powers, James—Pvt.—Enlisted: 5/25/1861 at Richmond, LA. Rolls for 5/25/1861 through 8/1861: Present. Soldier also served as a Pvt. with the 5th Louisiana Infantry-Co. B. Enlisted: 5/10/1861 at New Orleans, LA. Rolls for 5/10/1861 through 7/1/1861: Present or absent not stated. Rolls for 9/1861 through 10/1863: Present. Rolls for 11/1863 through 4/1864: Absent, captured at Rappahannock Station, VA on 11/11/1863. Federal Rolls of Prisoners of War: Captured at Rappahannock, VA on 11/7/1863; Received at Point Lookout, MD from Washington, D.C. on 11/11/1863. Paroled at Point Lookout, MD on 3/10/1864 until Exchanged; Exchanged at City Point, VA on 3/15/1864. Rolls for 5/1864 through 10/1864: Present. Name on List dated Headquarters, 9th Army Corps Provost Marshal Office: Names of Confederates Prisoners who have been Paroled not to take up arms against the U.S. Govt. until regularly Exchanged. Total: 1614 at Burkesville Junction, VA on 4/14–17/1865. *Born:* Ireland. *Occupation:* shoemaker. *Residence:* New Orleans, LA. Age at enlistment: 18. Marital Status: single.

Pugh, Columbus—Pvt.—Enlisted: 5/25/1861 at Richmond, LA. Rolls for 5/25/1861 through 6/30/1861: Present. Soldier also served as a Sgt. with the 4th Louisiana Cavalry-Co. I. Rolls of Prisoners of War of Diverse Companies and Regiments Unattached, C.S.A: Surrendered at New Orleans, LA on 5/26/1865; Paroled at Monroe, LA on 6/6/1865. *Residence:* Bastrop, Morehouse Parish, LA.

Pugh, Joseph S.—Pvt.—Enlisted: 5/25/1861 at Richmond, LA. Rolls for 5/25/1861 through 8/1861: Present. Rolls for 9/1861 through 12/1861: Discharged without the knowledge or consent of the Company A Captain.

Robinson, William—Pvt.—Enlisted: 5/25/1861 at Richmond, LA for the duration of the war. Rolls for 5/25/1861 through 6/30/1861: Deserted.

Rosson, James M.—Pvt./Shoemaker—(No War Dept. Record)-Enlisted: 1861 at Richmond, LA; Paroled at Mobile, AL in 1865. *Born:* 1843 at Baton Rouge, LA. *Married:* Never. *Residences:* Louisiana for life. Confederate Pension Application dated 10/30/1924 on file at the Louisiana State Archives-Microfilm Reel: CP1.121-Microdex 4-Sequence 9-Target Card: Rosson, James M.-Parish: Iberville-9 Pages.

Rule, Nathaniel—Pvt.—Enlisted: 3/5/1862 at Vicksburg, MS. Rolls for 3/5/1862 through 1/1863: Present. Rolls for 1/1864 through 2/1864: Present. Rolls for 8/31/1864 through 4/1865: Absent, wounded at the Battle of New Hope Church, GA and on sick furlough.

Scott, Charles B.—Pvt.—Enlisted: 9/27/1862 at Vicksburg, MS. Rolls for 11/1862 through 2/1863: Present. On Register of C.S.A. General Military Hospital #4, Wilmington, N.C: Admitted on 1/5/1863; Returned to duty on 1/7/1863. *Died:* 9/27/1863. *Buried:* Oakland Cemetery located at Atlanta, Fulton County, GA.

Seaman, Henry (aka Seamen)—Pvt.—Enlisted: 5/25/1861 at Richmond, LA. Rolls for 1/1862 through 6/1862: Present. Rolls for 11/1862 through 12/1862: Absent, sick at Savannah, GA. Rolls for 1/1863 through 2/1863: Present. On Register of Floyd House and Ocmulgee Hospital, Macon, GA: Admitted on 11/29/1863 due to intermittent fever. Rolls for 1/1864 through 2/1864: Present. Rolls for 8/31/1864 through 2/28/1865: Absent, captured near Atlanta, GA on 8/5/1864. Federal Rolls of Prisoners of War: Captured near Atlanta, GA on 8/5/1864; Forwarded to the U.S. Military Prison, Louisville, KY from Nashville, TN on 8/12/1864. Transferred to Camp Chase, OH on 8/13/1864; Paroled at Camp Chase, OH on 2/12/1865. Exchanged at Boulware and Cox Wharf, James River, VA on 2/20–21/1865. Rolls for 3/1865 through 4/1865: Present. Rolls of Prisoners of War, C.S.A: Surrendered at Citronelle, AL on 5/4/1865; Paroled at Meridian, MS on 5/10/1865. *Residence:* Madison Parish, LA. Soldier also served as a Pvt. with the Louisiana Pelican Infantry Regiment-Co. F.

Semler, August T. (aka Semmler)—Pvt.—Enlisted: 3/18/1862 at Vicksburg, MS. Rolls for 3/18/1862 through 6/1862: Present. Rolls for 11/1862 through 12/1862: Absent, sick at Savannah, GA. Rolls for 1/1863 through 2/1863: Present. Rolls for 1/1864 through 2/1864: Absent, in hospital at Whitesville, GA by order of Surgeon H.O. McEnery. Rolls for 8/31/1864 through 2/28/1865: Absent, on sick furlough since 10/1/1864. Rolls for 3/1865 through 4/1865: Present. Rolls of Prisoners of War, C.S.A: Surrendered at Citronelle, AL on 5/4/1865; Paroled at Meridian, MS on 5/10/1865. *Residence:* Columbia, GA. Soldier also served as a Pvt. with the Louisiana Pelican Infantry Regiment-Co. F.

Shafer, Joseph T. (aka Shaffer, J.S., T.J.)—Pvt.—Enlisted: 5/25/1861 at Richmond, LA. Rolls for 5/25/

1861 through 6/1862: Present. Rolls for 11/1862 through 2/1863: Absent, on detached duty at Savannah, GA. *Died:* 9/11/1863 due to extended illness. *Buried:* Chatham Laurel Grove Cemetery located at Savannah, Chatham County, GA

Shay, Dennis W.— Pvt.— Enlisted: 5/28/1861 at Richmond, LA. Rolls for 5/28/1861 through 2/1862: Present. Rolls for 3/1862 through 4/1862: Died on 4/18/1862.

Simms, Benjamin— Pvt.— Enlisted: 5/25/1861 at Richmond, LA. Rolls for 5/25/1861 through 8/1861: Present.

Smith, Zachariah H. (aka Z.A.)— Pvt.— Enlisted: 5/25/1861 at Richmond, LA. Rolls for 5/25/1861 through 4/1862: Present. Rolls for 5/1862 through 2/1863: Absent, on detached service at Savannah, GA. Rolls for 1/1864 through 2/1864: Present. Rolls for 8/31/1864 through 4/30/1865: Absent, taken Prisoner of War on 8/5/1863. Federal Rolls of Prisoners of War: Captured near Atlanta, GA on 8/5/1864; Received at the U.S. Military Prison, Louisville, KY from Nashville, TN on 8/12/1864. Forwarded to Camp Chase, OH on 8/13/1864; Paroled at Camp Chase, OH on 2/12/1865. Name as signature to the U.S. Oath of Allegiance subscribed and sworn to at Camp Chase, OH on 5/13/1865. *Residence:* St. Louis, MO. Description at oath-Complexion: dark-Hair: black-Eyes: gray-Height: 5 ft. 8 in.

Stewart, Joseph M.— Pvt.— Enlisted: 5/25/1861 at Richmond, LA. Rolls for 5/25/1861 through 2/1863: Present. Rolls for 1/1864 through 2/1864: Present, on daily or extra duty as Teamster since 7/1862 by order of Lt. Col. John McEnery. Rolls for 8/31/1864 through 2/28/1865: Present, detailed as Brigade Teamster; On daily duty with Maj. Henshaw by order of Brig. Gen. Randall L. Gibson. Rolls of Prisoners of War, C.S.A: Surrendered at Citronelle, AL on 5/4/1865; Paroled at Meridian, MS on 5/10/1865. *Residence:* Shreveport, Caddo Parish, LA.

Sydner, John George (aka Syndnor, Sydnor, J.L.)— Pvt.— Enlisted: 5/25/1861 at Richmond, LA. Rolls for 5/25/1861 through 4/1862: Present.

Vallandingham, John (aka Valandingham)— Pvt.— Enlisted: 3/18/1862 at Vicksburg, MS. Rolls for 3/18/1862 through 6/1862: Present. Regimental Returns for 7/1862 and 8/1862: Absent on furlough in Louisiana. Rolls for 11/1862 through 12/1862: Discharged on 12/6/1862.

Vaughn, Rufus L.— Pvt.— Enlisted: 5/25/1861 at Richmond, LA. Rolls for 5/25/1861 through 4/1862: Present. Rolls for 5/1862 through 6/1862: Absent, wounded at the Battle of Secessionville, S.C. on 6/16/1862 and in hospital at Charleston, S.C. Regimental Return for 7/1862: In hospital at Savannah, GA. Rolls for 11/1862 through 2/1864: Present. Rolls for 8/31/1864 through 2/28/1865: Absent, sick in hospital at Montgomery, AL. Rolls for 3/1865 through 4/1865: Absent, sick. Rolls of Prisoners of War, C.S.A: Surrendered at Citronelle, AL on 5/4/1865; Paroled at Meridian, MS on 5/10/1865. *Residence:* Murfreesboro, Rutherford County, TN.

Vollman, Ferdinand (aka Volleman, Volliman, Vollinan, Wallman, Fred)— Pvt.— Enlisted: 5/25/1861 at Richmond, LA. Rolls for 5/25/1861 through 6/1862: Present. Rolls for 11/1862 through 2/1863: Absent, on detached service at Savannah, GA. Rolls for 1/1864 through 4/1865: Absent, captured at the Battle of Missionary Ridge, TN on 11/25/1863. Federal Rolls of Prisoners of War: Captured at the Battle of Missionary Ridge, TN on 11/25/1863; Received at the U.S. Military Prison, Louisville, KY from Nashville, TN on 12/7/1863. Sent to Rock Island Barracks, IL on 12/9/1863. Rolls of Prisoners of War at Rock Island Barracks, IL: Prisoner desires to take the U.S. Oath of Allegiance. *Remarks:* Wishes to go home, only support of his mother. Enlisted at Rock Island Barracks, IL in the U.S. Army for frontier service on 10/13/1864.

Waller, George— Pvt.— Enlisted: 5/25/1861 at Richmond, LA. Rolls for 5/25/1861 through 4/1862: Present. Rolls for 5/1862 through 6/1862: Present, on detached service at Savannah, GA. Rolls for 11/1862 through 2/1863: Absent, on detached service at Savannah, GA.

Weidle, William (aka Weeidle)— Pvt.— Enlisted: 5/25/1861 at Richmond, LA. Rolls for 3/1862 through 6/1862: Present. Rolls for 11/1862 through 12/1862: Transferred to the C.S. Naval Service on 12/15/1862.

Wells, Thomas— Pvt.— Enlisted: 5/25/1861 at Richmond, LA. Rolls for 5/25/1861 through 2/1863: Present. Rolls for 1/1864 through 2/1864: Absent, in hospital from wounds received at the Battle of Chickamauga, GA on 9/19/1863. Rolls for 8/31/1864 through 4/1865: Retired by Medical Board on 3/28/1864.

West, John H.— Pvt.— Enlisted: 5/25/1861 at Richmond, LA. Rolls for 5/25/1861 through 2/1863: Present. Rolls for 1/1864 through 4/1865: Absent, taken Prisoner of War at the Battle of Missionary Ridge, TN on 11/25/1863. Federal Rolls of Prisoners of War: Captured at the Battle of Missionary Ridge, TN on 11/25/1863; Received at the U.S. Military Prison, Louisville, KY from Nashville, TN on 12/7/1863. Forwarded to Rock Island Barracks, IL on 12/8/1863. Enlisted in the U.S. Naval Service at Rock Island Barracks, IL; Transferred to the Naval Rendezvous at Camp Douglas, Chicago, IL.

Wheatley, William— Pvt.— Enlisted: 5/25/1861 at

Richmond, LA. Rolls for 5/25/1861 through 2/1862: Present.

White, Milton—Pvt.—Enlisted: 5/25/1861 at Richmond, LA. Rolls for 5/25/1861 through 6/30/1861: Present.

White, Patrick—Pvt.—Enlisted: 5/25/1861 at Richmond, LA. Rolls for 5/25/1861 through 4/1862: Present. Rolls for 5/1862 through 6/1862: Present, sick in camp. Rolls for 11/1862 through 12/1862: Transferred to the C.S. Naval Service on 12/15/1862; Served as a Seaman on the C.S.S. Chicora and C.S.S. Isondiga and a Landsman on the C.S.S. Virginia II. Federal Rolls of Prisoners of War: Captured on Gunboat off Morris Island, S.C. on 9/7/1863; Sent to Point Lookout, MD. Received at Fort Warren, Boston Harbor, MA for Exchange on 9/23/1864; Exchanged on 10/1/1864.

Williams, Bryant—Pvt.—Enlisted: 3/18/1862 at Vicksburg, MS. Rolls for 4/1862 through 4/1865: Present. Rolls of Prisoners of War, C.S.A: Surrendered at Citronelle, AL on 5/4/1865; Paroled at Meridian, MS on 5/10/1865. *Residence:* Madison Parish, LA. Soldier also served as a Pvt. with the Louisiana Pelican Infantry Regiment-Co. F.

Williams, James—Pvt.—Enlisted: 5/25/1861 at Richmond, LA. Rolls for 5/25/1861 through 6/1862: Present. Rolls for 11/1862 through 12/1862: Absent, sick at Savannah, GA. Rolls for 1/1863 through 2/1864: Present.

Williams, Maurice—Pvt.—Enlisted: 5/25/1861 at Richmond, LA. Rolls for 5/25/1861 through 2/1863: Present. Rolls for 1/1864 through 2/1864: Present, on daily extra duty with the Division Prisoner Corps as of 11/20/1863 by order of Maj. Gen. Alexander P. Stewart. Rolls for 8/31/1864 through 2/28/1865: Present. Rolls for 3/1865 through 4/1865: Deserted at Mobile, AL in 4/1865.

Wilson, Jacob R.—Pvt.—Enlisted: 5/25/1861 at Richmond, LA. Rolls for 5/25/1861 through 4/1862: Present. Rolls for 5/1862 through 6/1862: Present, on extra duty in Battalion. Regimental Return for 7/1862: Detached in Commissary Dept. Regimental Return for 9/1862: Detached in Commissary Dept. Rolls for 11/1862 through 12/1862: Absent, on detached service at Savannah, GA in charge of commissary stores at camp. Rolls for 1/1863 through 2/1863: Present, on extra duty in Commissary Dept. Rolls for 1/1864 through 2/1864: Present. Rolls for 8/31/1864 through 2/28/1865: Absent, sick in hospital at Macon, GA since 5/15/1864. Rolls for 3/1865 through 4/1865: Absent due to disability; Detailed in hospital at Macon, GA. *Buried:* St. Louis Cemetery #1 located at Washington Ave. and Prytania St. at New Orleans, Orleans Parish, LA.

Young, Frank W.—Pvt.—Enlisted: 5/25/1861 at Richmond, LA. Rolls for 5/25/1861 through 4/1862: Present. Rolls for 5/1862 through 6/1862: Present, sick in hospital. Regimental Return for 8/1862: Died due to an accident disarming an unexploded shell on 8/13/1862. *Born:* Germany.

Ziegler, William H.—Pvt./Acting Comm. Sgt.—(See Field and Staff)

COMPANY B: "OUACHITA BLUES," OUACHITA PARISH

Captain

Hardy, Alanso B. (aka Hardee, Handy, Elanso, Alanso)—2nd Lt./1st Lt./Capt.—Enlisted: 6/4/1861 at Monroe, LA. Rolls for 6/4/1861 through 6/1862: Present. Elected Captain on 8/4/1863. Rolls for 1/1864 through 2/1864: Absent with leave for 25 days beginning 2/11/1864. Federal Rolls of Prisoners of War: Deserted and took the U.S. Oath of Allegiance at Memphis, TN on 5/13/1865. *Residence:* Monroe, Ouachita Parish, LA.

McEnery, John (aka McEnerg)-Capt./Major/Lt. Col.—(See Field and Staff)

Marks, Frank N. (aka E.N.)—1st Lt./Capt.—Enlisted: 6/4/1861 at Monroe, LA. Rolls for 6/4/1861 through 12/1861: Present, elected 1st Lt. on 8/4/1861. Rolls for 1/1862 through 2/1862: Present, elected Capt. on 2/7/1862. Rolls for 3/1862 through 6/1862: Present, promoted to Capt. in 3/1862. Regimental Return for 7/1862 and 8/1862: Present or absent not stated. Regimental Return for 9/1862: Present. Killed at the Battle of Chickamauga, GA on 9/19/1863.

Lieutenant

Collins, Samuel W. (aka S.R.)—1st Sgt./2nd Lt.—Enlisted: 6/4/1861 at Monroe, LA. Rolls for 6/4/1861 through 12/1861: Present. Rolls for 1/1862 through 2/1862: Present, promoted to 2nd Lt. on 2/17/1862. Rolls for 3/1864 through 4/1864: Present. Rolls for 5/1864 through 6/1864: Present, promoted to 2nd Lt. on 5/16/1864. Federal Rolls of Prisoners of War: Captured at Atlanta, GA on 8/5/1864; Received at the U.S. Military Prison, Louisville, KY on 8/12/1864 from Nashville, TN. Forwarded to Johnson's Island, OH on 8/13/1864; Released on the U.S. Oath of Allegiance on 6/15/1865. *Residence:* Trenton, LA. Description at oath-Complexion: light-Hair: dark-Eyes: blue-Height: 5 ft. 11 in. Wounded: No. *Born:* 9/28/1833 near Greenville, Butler County, AL. *Married:* Mary

Jane Nash on 10/18/1865 near Trenton, LA. *Children:* 3 Daughters-Pearl Collins and Mrs. O.M. Elwee (All Schoolteachers). *Occupation:* Farmer. Residences: Ouachita Parish and Jackson Parish, LA for 54 yrs. *Died:* 9/25/1902 at his home near Nash, Jackson Parish, LA due to Kidney Ailment. *Buried:* Salem Church Cemetery located on the Eros/Vernon Hwy., 2 miles southwest of Eros, Vernon Parish, LA. *Wife Died:* 6/27/1929 at 5:00 P.M. Widows Pension amount: $30.00 per month. Confederate Pension Application dated 11/9/1898 on file at the Louisiana State Archives-Microfilm Reel: CP1.30-Microdex 1-Sequence 7-Target Card: Collins, S.W.-Parish: Jackson-4 Pages. Also a Confederate Widows Pension Application dated 8/15/1903 on file-Microfilm Reel: CP1.29-Microdex 4-Sequence 29-Target Card: Collins, Mary Jane (Nee Nash)-Parish: Jackson-11 Pages.

Hardy, Thomas J. (aka Hardee, T.B.) — 3rd Lt./2nd Lt./1st Lt. — Enlisted: 6/4/1861 at Monroe, LA. Rolls for 6/4/1861 through 12/1861: Present. Rolls for 1/1862 through 2/1862: Present, elected 2nd Lt. on 2/17/1862. Rolls for 3/1862 through 6/1862: Present. Regimental Returns for 7/1862 and 8/1862: Present or absent not stated. Regimental Return for 9/1862: Present at Fort Jackson, Savannah, GA. Rolls for 1/1864 through 2/1864: Absent without leave in the Trans-Mississippi Dept. since 6/24/1863. Name on List dated: Provost Marshall Office, Port Hudson, LA 4/17/1864 of Prisoners and Refugees forwarded to Brig. Gen. John Bowen, Provost Marshal General, Dept. of the Gulf, from Port Hudson, LA on 4/17/1864. Name on List of Deserters sent down from the Red River to the New Orleans defenses, Office of the Provost Marshal, #48 Baronne St., New Orleans, LA on 4/21/1864.

Sergeant

Applewhite, William (aka Applewhyte) — Cpl./3rd Sgt./1st Sgt. — Enlisted: 6/4/1861 at Monroe, LA. Rolls for 6/4/1861 through 6/30/1861: Present. Rolls for 7/1861 through 8/1861: Present, Discharged. Rolls for 3/1862 through 4/1862: Re-enlisted on 3/24/1862 at Monroe, LA. Rolls for 3/24/1862 through 4/30/1862: Present. Rolls for 5/1862 through 6/1862: Promoted to 3rd Sgt. on 5/24/1862; Died on 6/27/1862.

Burke, J.T. — Sgt. — Enlisted: 6/4/1861 at Monroe, LA. Rolls for 6/4/1861 through 2/1864: Present.

Douglas, Thomas J. (aka Douglass) — Pvt./1st Sgt./Pvt. — Enlisted: 6/4/1861 at Monroe, LA. Rolls for 6/4/1861 through 12/1861: Present. Rolls for 1/1862 through 2/1862: Present, promoted to 1st Sgt. on 2/17/1862. Rolls for 3/1862 through 4/1862: Present, reduced to Pvt. on 3/26/1862. Rolls for 5/1862 through 6/1862: Present. Regimental Return for 8/1862: Under confinement at Savannah, GA. Federal Rolls of Prisoners of War: Captured near Jackson, MS in 7/1863; Sent to Snyder's Bluff, MS on 7/30/1863. Received at Camp Morton, IN on 8/7/1863; Enlisted in the U.S. 12th Michigan Battalion in 8/1863.

Dunham, J. Thomas — 5th Sgt./Pvt. — Enlisted: 6/4/1861 at Monroe, LA. Rolls for 6/4/1861 through 2/1862: Present. Rolls for 3/1862 through 4/1862: Present, reduced to Pvt. on 3/18/1862. Rolls for 5/1862 through 6/1862: Present.

Fuller, John N. (aka Fuler, J.M., J.H.) — Pvt./Orderly Sgt. — Enlisted: 3/6/1862 at Monroe, LA. Rolls for 3/6/1862 through 6/1862: Present. Rolls for 1/1864 through 2/1864: Present. Federal Rolls of Prisoners of War: Captured at Atlanta, GA on 8/5/1864; Forwarded to the U.S. Military Prison, Louisville, KY from Nashville, TN on 8/12/1864. Transferred to Camp Chase, OH on 8/13/1864; Paroled at Camp Chase, OH on 2/12/1865. Exchanged at Boulware and Cox Wharf, James River, VA on 2/20–21/1865. Rolls of Prisoners of War, C.S.A: Surrendered at Citronelle, AL on 5/4/1865; Paroled at Monroe, LA on 6/9/1865. *Residence:* Ouachita Parish, LA. *Married:* Ida J. Robinson on 11/9/1869 at Forksville, Ouachita Parish, LA. *Children:* 6–3 Sons, J.N., R.R. and N.M. and 3 Daughters, Lotta Fuller Smith, Addie Fuller and Maud Fuller Wright. *Died:* 12/24/1893 at Forksville, LA due to a fall from a horse. *Buried:* Forksville, LA. *Wife Died:* 4/10/1927. Widows Pension amount: $90.00 per quarter. Confederate Widows Pension Application dated 12/5/1912 on file at the Louisiana State Archives-Microfilm Reel: CP1.51-Microdex 4-Sequence 32-Target Card: Fuller, Ida J.-Parish: Ouachita-6 Pages.

Holley, George J. — Pvt./Sgt. — Enlisted: 6/4/1861 at Monroe, LA. Rolls for 6/4/1861 through 2/1862: Present. Rolls for 3/1862 through 6/1862: Present, appointed Sgt. on 3/18/1862. Rolls for 1/1864 through 2/1864: Absent, sent to hospital on 2/14/1864. Rolls for 8/30/1864 through 2/28/1865: Captured near Atlanta, GA on 8/5/1864. Federal Rolls of Prisoners of War: Captured near Atlanta, GA on 8/5/1864; Sent to the U.S. Military Prison, Louisville, KY from Nashville, TN on 8/14/1864. Forwarded to Camp Chase, OH on 8/14/1864; Paroled at Camp Chase, OH on 2/12/1865. Exchanged at Boulware and Cox Wharf, James River, VA on 2/20–21/1865. Rolls for 3/1865 through 4/1865: Absent on parole furlough since 3/10/1865.

McClendon, Davis J. (aka McClenden, F.J., T.J.) — Sgt. — Enlisted: 6/4/1861 at Monroe, LA. Rolls for 6/4/1861 through 2/1864: Present. Rolls for 8/1864 through 4/1865: Absent, wounded and sent to hospital near Atlanta, GA on 8/25/1864.

Morris, William Everett (aka W.B.) — 3rd Sgt./Pvt. — Enlisted: 6/4/1861 at Monroe, LA. Rolls for 6/4/1861 through 6/31/1861: Present. Rolls for 7/1861 through 8/1861: Discharged due to disability on

9/1/1861. Rolls for 3/1862 through 6/1862: Present; Re-enlisted on 3/24/1862 at Monroe, LA. Rolls for 9/1862 through 10/1862: Absent, reduced from 3rd Sgt. to Pvt. on 9/15/1862; Sick in Oglethorpe Hospital. Rolls for 11/1862 through 12/1862: Absent, sick in hospital at Augusta, GA. Rolls for 1/1863 through 2/1863: Present, confined in Guard House. Federal Rolls of Prisoners of War: Captured at Edwards Depot, MS on 5/17/1863; Sent to Memphis, TN on 5/25/1863. Forwarded to Camp Morton, IN and escaped three months later; Rejoined unit in Tennessee. *Born:* 3/10/1839 at Alabama. *Married:* Sarah Elizabeth Lockhart on 6/23/1864 at Danville, TN. *Children:* 7–5 Sons and 2 Daughters. *Occupation:* Boardinghouse. *Died:* 10/7/1912 in Shreveport, Caddo Parish, LA due to Paralysis and Old Age. *Buried:* Greenwood Cemetery located off Hwy. 169 near Greenwood, Caddo Parish, LA. *Wife's Age:* 62 as of 1912. *Wife Died:* 7/9/1929. Confederate Pension Application dated 7/31/1909 on file at the Louisiana State Archives-Microfilm Reel: CP1.101-Microdex 2-Sequence 12-Target Card: Morris, William E.-Parish: Caddo-7 Pages. Also a Confederate Widows Pension Application dated 12/20/1912 on file-Microfilm Reel: CP1.101-Microdex 2-Sequence 11-Target Card: Morris, Sarah E. (Lockhart)-Parish: Caddo-4 Pages.

Ray, John B.—Pvt./Sgt.—Enlisted: 9/23/1862 at Monroe, LA. Rolls for 1/1864 through 2/28/1865: Present. Rolls of Prisoners of War, C.S.A: Surrendered at Citronelle, AL on 5/4/1865; Paroled at Meridian, MS on 5/10/1865. *Residence:* Monroe, LA. Soldier also served as a 4th Sgt. with the Louisiana Pelican Infantry Regiment-Co. G. *Born:* 1/10/1845 at Monroe, Ouachita Parish, LA. Residences: Louisiana for life-Monroe and New Orleans. Confederate Pension Application dated 4/7/1921 on file at the Louisiana State Archives-Microfilm Reel: CP1.115-Microdex 4-Sequence 14-Target Card: Ray, John B.-Parish: Orleans-5 Pages. Also a Confederate Proofs and Land Warrant Application on file-Name: Ray, John B.-Microfilm Reel: 2-Frame Number: 0492-Act: 116 — Pages: 2-Parish: Orleans.

Stokes, Isaiah C. (aka A.C.)—Pvt./1st Sgt.—Enlisted: 6/4/1861 at Monroe, LA. Rolls for 6/4/1861 through 2/1862: Present. Rolls for 3/1862 through 4/1862: Present, appointed 1st Sgt. on 3/26/1862. Rolls for 5/1862 through 6/1862: Present.

Thomas, Benjamin F.—Sgt.—Enlisted: 6/4/1861 at Monroe, LA. Rolls for 6/4/1861 through 4/1862: Present. Rolls for 5/1862 through 6/1862: Absent, wounded at the Battle of Secessionville, S.C. and in hospital at Augusta, GA. Regimental Returns for 7/1862 and 8/1862: Wounded, in hospital at Augusta, GA. Rolls for 1/1863 through 4/1865: Absent, taken Prisoner of War at the Battle of Chickamauga, GA on 9/19/1863. Federal Rolls of Prisoners of War: Captured at the Battle of Chickamauga, GA on 9/19/1863; Received at the U.S. Military Prison, Louisville, KY from Nashville, TN on 10/1/1863. Forwarded to Camp Douglas, IL on 10/2/1863; Discharged at Camp Douglas, IL on 6/14/1865.

Corporal

Daniels, Robert F. (aka B.F.)—Pvt./Cpl.—Enlisted: 3/6/1862 at Monroe, LA. Rolls for 3/6/1862 through 6/1862: Present. Federal Rolls of Prisoners of War: Captured at Bayou Teche, LA on 4/20/1863; Sent to New Orleans, LA for Exchange. Rolls for 1/1864 through 2/1864: Present. Rolls for 8/31/1864 through 4/1865: Absent, wounded and captured near Atlanta, GA on 7/28/1864. On Federal 1st Division, 15th Army Corps Hospital Register: Admitted on 7/29/1864 near Atlanta, GA due to gunshot wound in left knee; Died on 8/3/1864 due to complications from amputation.

Fetters, John N. (aka Feters, Phetters)—4th Cpl./Pvt.—Enlisted: 6/4/1861 at Monroe, LA. Rolls for 6/4/1861 through 2/1862: Present. Rolls for 3/1862 through 4/1862: Present, reduced from 4th Corpl. to Pvt. on 4/6/1862 upon being detailed to work in Ordnance Dept. Rolls for 5/1862 through 2/1864: Absent, on detached service at Augusta, GA since 3/25/1862 by order of Brig. Gen. Alexander R. Lawton. Rolls for 8/31/1864 through 4/1865: Absent, detailed in Ordnance Dept., Macon, GA on 3/26/1862 by order of Gen. Lawton. Federal Rolls of Prisoners of War: Captured at Macon, GA on 4/20–21/1865 by the U.S. 1st Brigade, 2nd Cavalry Division; Released on the U.S. Oath of Allegiance at Nashville, TN on 5/12/1865. Surrendered at Macon, GA on 4/27/1865. Residence: Hamilton County, OH. Description at oath-Complexion: fair-Hair: brown-Eyes: blue-Height: 5 ft. 10 in. Endorsement shows: Rolls of Prisoners of War, C.S.A., who voluntarily surrendered themselves, took the U.S. Oath of Allegiance, and were allowed to return to their homes.

Friend, G.A.—Cpl.—Enlisted: 6/4/1861 at Monroe, LA. Rolls for 6/4/1861 through 4/1865: Present. Rolls of Prisoners of War, C.S.A: Surrendered at Citronelle, AL on 5/4/1865; Paroled at Meridian, MS on 5/10/1865. *Residence:* Natchitoches Parish, LA.

Herring, Robert Charles (aka Harron, Herron)—Pvt./Cpl.—Enlisted: 6/4/1861 at Monroe, LA. Rolls for 6/4/1861 through 2/1862: Present. Rolls for 3/1862 through 4/1862: Present, appointed Cpl. on 4/6/1862. Rolls for 5/1862 through 6/1862: Present. Federal Rolls of Prisoners of War: Captured near Jackson, MS in 7/1863; Sent to Snyder's Bluff, MS on 7/30/1863. Forwarded to Camp Morton, IN 8/7/1863; Enlisted in the U.S. 12th Michigan Battalion in 8/1863.

Honeycutt, John B. (aka J.H.)—Pvt./2nd Cpl.—Enlisted: 6/4/1861 at Monroe, LA. Rolls for 6/4/1861 through 2/1862: Present. Rolls for 3/1862 through

6/1862: Present, appointed 2nd Cpl. on 4/6/1862; Wounded at the Battle of Secessionville, S.C. on 6/16/1862. Rolls for 1/1864 through 4/1865: Absent, captured at the Battle of Chickamauga, GA on 9/19/1863. Federal Rolls of Prisoners of War: Captured at Chickamauga, GA on 9/20/1863; Forwarded to the U.S. Military Prison, Louisville, KY on 10/1/1863. Received at Camp Douglas, IL on 10/4/1863; Discharged on 6/14/1865 in accordance with General Order #109 of the Adjutant General's Office, Washington, D.C. 6/6/1865. *Wounded:* Yes-Right hand at the Battle of Secessionville, S.C. resulting in partial paralysis. *Born:* 4/16/1841 at Union Parish, LA. *Married:* 3 times-To 3rd wife Mae Griggs, the widow of Confederate soldier L.W. Griggs, on 12/28/1902 at Calhoun, Ouachita Parish, LA. *Children:* 9–5 Sons and 4 Daughters. *Occupation:* Farmer. *Residence:* Louisiana. *Died:* 12/10/1924 at Calhoun, LA due to old age. *Buried:* Calhoun, LA. Wife's Age: 55. Widows Pension amount: $90.00 per quarter. Confederate Pension Application dated 3/1/1907 on file at the Louisiana State Archives-Microfilm Reel: CP1.69-Microdex 1-Sequence 4-Target Card: Honeycutt, John B.-Parish: Ouachita-6 Pages. Also a Confederate Widows Pension Application dated 12/31/1924 on file-Microfilm Reel: CP1.69-Microdex 1-Sequence 9-Target Card: Honeycutt, Mae G.-Parish: Ouachita-4 Pages.

Kearney, Michael—2nd Cpl./Pvt.—Enlisted: 6/4/1861 at Monroe, LA. Rolls for 6/4/1861 through 4/1862: Present, reduced from 2nd Cpl. to Pvt. on 4/6/1862. Rolls for 5/1862 through 6/1862: Present. On undated List of Confederate Prisoners sent down for Exchange on 5/26/1863: Received on 5/29/1863. Rolls for 1/1864 through 2/1864: Present.

Nash, Julius E.—Cpl./Pvt.—Enlisted: 6/4/1861 at Monroe, LA. Rolls for 6/4/1861 through 2/1864: Present. Rolls for 8/31/1864 through 2/28/1865: Absent on 60 day furlough in Louisiana since 2/14/1865. Rolls for 3/1865 through 4/1865: Absent without leave since 4/17/1865 in Louisiana. Rolls of Prisoners of War of Diverse Companies and Regiments Unattached, C.S.A: Surrendered at Citronelle, AL on 5/4/1865; Paroled at Monroe, LA on 6/8/1865. *Residence:* Ouachita Parish, LA.

Private

Adams, John—Pvt.—Enlisted: 6/4/1861 at Monroe, LA. Rolls for 6/4/1861 through 6/1862: Present. Regimental Return for 7/1862: Absent without leave. Federal Rolls of Prisoners of War: Captured at Chattanooga, TN on 10/18/1863; Received at the U.S. Military Prison, Louisville, KY on 11/5/1863. Rolls of Confederate Deserters who took the U.S. Oath of Allegiance on 10/31/1863: Released on the U.S. Oath of Allegiance to go north of the Ohio River until further orders. *Residence:* Allegheny County, PA. Description at parole-Complexion: dark-Hair: black-Eyes: black-Height: 5 ft. 9 in.

Allen, R.A.—Pvt.—Enlisted: 3/6/1862 at Monroe, LA. Rolls for 3/6/1862 through 2/1864: Present. Soldier was present at the Battle of New Hope Church, GA on 5/27/1864, but later died near Atlanta, GA.

Arthur, William C. (aka W.H.)—Pvt.-Enlisted: 6/4/1861 at Monroe, LA. Rolls for 7/1861 through 8/1861: Died on 7/24/1861. *Buried:* Hollywood Cemetery located at Idlewild St. and Cherry St. at Richmond, Henrico County, VA; Enter cemetery gate from Albermale St. and bear right to the Confederate section.

Aultman, James (aka Altman)—Pvt.—Enlisted: 6/4/1861 at Monroe, LA. Rolls for 6/4/1861 through 6/30/1861: Present. Rolls for 7/1861 through 8/1861: Discharged due to disability.

Bates, William S. (aka Batey)—Pvt.—Enlisted: 6/4/1861 at Monroe, LA. Rolls for 6/4/1861 through 6/1862: Present. Rolls for 7/1862 through 8/1862: Present, transferred from Co. B to Co. D on 8/12/1862. Federal Rolls of Prisoners of War: Captured at Jackson, MS in 7/1863; Sent to Snyder's Bluff, MS on 7/30/1863. Received at Camp Morton, IN on 8/7/1863.

Beasley, J.H.—Pvt.—Enlisted: 6/4/1861 at Monroe, LA. Rolls for 7/1861 through 8/1861: Deceased.

Bickers, J. Ross (aka Bichers)—Pvt.—Enlisted: 6/4/1861 at Monroe, LA. Rolls for 6/4/1861 through 8/1861: Present.

Bond, William A.—Pvt.—Enlisted: 6/4/1861 at Monroe. LA. Rolls for 6/4/1861 through 2/1862: Present. Rolls for 3/1862 through 4/1862: Died in hospital at Augusta, GA on 4/24/1862.

Brooks, Elkanah H.—Pvt.—Enlisted: 9/17/1862 at Monroe, LA. Rolls for 1/1863 through 2/1863: Absent, sent to hospital on 2/22/1863 by order of Dr. Bass. Federal Rolls of Prisoners of War: Captured near Atlanta, GA on 8/5/1864; Received at the U.S. Military Prison, Louisville, KY from Nashville, TN on 8/12/1864. Forwarded to Camp Chase, OH on 8/13/1864; Paroled at Camp Chase, OH on 2/12/1865. Received at James River, VA from Point Lookout, MD on 2/20–21/1865 and Exchanged. Rolls for 2/28/1865 through 4/30/1865: Absent on parole furlough. Wounded: Yes, 2 times-left side at Jackson, MS and right leg at Chattanooga, TN. *Born:* 10/22/1844 at Macon County, AL. *Married:* Annie E. Robinson on 10/4/1871 at Farmerville, Union Parish, LA. *Children:* 6 Sons-Thomas D., James L., Benjamin F., Robert L., Samuel T. and 1 Daughter-Sallie Brooks Gaar. *Residence:* Louisiana since 1860. *Died:* 6/21/1918 at his home due to Heart Failure. *Buried:* Mount Zion Church Cemetery, located 4 miles east of Calhoun,

LA on U.S. Hwy. 80 in Ouachita Parish, LA. *Wife's Age:* 66. *Wife Died:* 11/18/1927. Widows Pension amount: $90.00 per quarter. Confederate Pension Application dated 9/25/1911 on file at the Louisiana State Archives-Microfilm Reel: CP1.18-Microdex 1-Sequence 9-Target Card: Brooks, E.H.-Parish: Ouachita-6 Pages. Also a Confederate Widows Pension Application dated 7/24/1918 on file-Microfilm Reel: CP1.18-Microdex 1-Sequence 9-Target Card: Brooks, Annie E. (Robinson)-Parish: Ouachita-4 Pages.

Brooks, J.M.C.—Pvt.—Enlisted: 3/6/1862 at Monroe, LA. Rolls for 3/6/1862 through 6/1862: Present. Rolls for 1/1864 through 4/1865: Absent, wounded at the Battle of Chickamauga, GA on 9/19/1863; Sent to hospital from battlefield.

Brooks, William—Pvt.—Enlisted: 6/4/1861 at Monroe, LA. Rolls for 7/1861 through 8/1861: Discharged due to disability.

Bullock, C.M.—Pvt.—Enlisted: 6/4/1861 at Monroe, LA. Rolls for 6/4/1861 through 2/1865: Present. Federal Rolls of Prisoners of War: Captured at Spanish Fort, AL on 4/8/1865; Received at Ship Island, MS on 4/10/1865. Transferred to Vicksburg, MS on 5/1/1865; Paroled at Camp Townsend, MS on 5/6/1865.

Bullock, Doctor L. (aka **Bulock**)—Pvt.—Enlisted: 6/4/1861 at Monroe, LA. Rolls for 6/4/1861 through 6/1862: Present. Federal Rolls of Prisoners of War: Captured near Jackson. MS in 7/1863; Sent to Snyder's Bluff, MS on 7/30/1863. Received at Camp Morton, IN on 8/7/1863; Died at Camp Morton, IN on 12/22/1863. *Buried:* Crown Hill Cemetery located at Indianapolis, Marion County, IN.

Bullock, L.D.—Pvt.—Enlisted: 3/6/1862 at Monroe, LA. Rolls for 3/6/1862 through 6/1862: Present. Died in hospital at Savannah, GA on 10/4/1863.

Burnett, Zachariah H. (aka **Burnnett**)—Pvt.—Enlisted: 6/4/1861 at Monroe, LA. Rolls for 6/4/1861 through 6/1862: Present. Regimental Return for 8/1862: In hospital at Whitesville, GA; Died on 7/27/1862. *Buried:* Laurel Grove Cemetery located at Savannah, Chatham County, GA.

Cabanis, W.D. (aka **Cabanis, Cabiness, W.B.**)—Pvt.—Enlisted: 6/4/1861 at Monroe, LA. Rolls for 7/1861 through 8/1861: Exchanged for I.B. Williams in 1861.

Clark, John—Pvt.—Enlisted: 6/4/1861 at Monroe, LA. Rolls for 6/4/1861 through 10/1861: Present. Rolls for 11/1861 through 12/1861: Discharged due to Surgeon's Certificate of Disability at Richmond, VA. On U.S. Marine General Hospital Register, New Orleans, LA: Admitted on 6/13/1865 from a steamboat due to gunshot wound to the back side and front; Transferred to Sedgwick Hospital on 6/22/1865. Released on 8/10/1865 due to Imbecility. Age at release: 23. Confederate Widows Pension Application dated 1920 on file at the Mississippi Dept. of Archives and History-Target Card: Clark, Eliza-County: Jackson.

Connelly, Thomas (aka **Conley, Conelly, Connoly**)—Pvt.—Enlisted: 6/4/1861 at Monroe, LA. Rolls for 6/4/1861 through 6/1862: Present. Federal Rolls of Prisoners of War: Captured near Chickamauga, GA on 9/19/1863; Forwarded to Louisville, KY on 10/1/1863 for Exchange. Died at the U.S. Military Prison Hospital, Nashville, TN on 10/5/1863 due to Intermittent Fever.

Cox, Stephen St. Louis—Pvt.—Enlisted: 6/4/1861 at Monroe, LA. Rolls for 6/4/1861 through 2/1864: Present. Federal Rolls of Prisoners of War: Captured near Atlanta, GA on 8/5/1864; Received at the U.S. Military Prison, Louisville, KY on 8/12/1864 from Nashville, TN. Forwarded to Camp Chase, OH on 8/13/1864; *Died* at Camp Chase, OH on 2/7/1865. *Buried:* Camp Chase Confederate Cemetery located at Columbus, Franklin County, OH.

Davis, John D. (aka **Darrs**)—Pvt.—Enlisted: 6/4/1861 at Monroe, LA. Rolls for 6/4/1861 through 2/1864: Present. Federal Rolls of Prisoners of War: Captured near Atlanta, GA on 8/5/1864; Received at the U.S. Military Prison, Louisville, KY on 8/12/1864. Forwarded to Camp Chase, OH on 8/13/1864; Paroled at Camp Chase, OH on 2/12/1865. Transferred to Point Lookout, MD; Exchanged at Boulware and Cox Wharf, James River, VA on 2/21/1865. Rolls for 3/1865 through 4/1865: Absent on parole furlough since 3/10/1865.

Dean, E.P. (aka **Deen**)—Pvt.—Enlisted: 6/4/1861 at Monroe, LA. Rolls for 6/4/1861 through 6/1862: Present. Federal Rolls of Prisoners of War: Captured near Jackson, MS on 7/17/1863; Sent to Snyder's Bluff, MS on 7/30/1863. Received at Camp Morton, Indianapolis, IN on 8/7/1863; *Died* on 9/19/1863. *Buried:* Crown Hill Cemetery located at Indianapolis, Marion County, IN.

Dew, John (aka **Drew**)—Pvt.—Enlisted: 6/4/1861 at Monroe, LA. Rolls for 6/4/1861 through 8/1861: Present. Rolls for 9/1861 through 10/1861: Died at Princeton, Mercer County, VA. Rolls for 11/1861 through 12/1861: Died at Princeton, VA on 11/23/1861.

Dillard, L K. (aka **J.K.**)—Pvt.—Enlisted: 6/4/1861 at Monroe, LA. Rolls for 6/4/1861 through 6/1862: Present. Rolls for 1/1864 through 2/1864: Sent to hospital at Lauderdale Springs, MS on 7/25/1863 by Capt. John McEnery; Deserted from hospital on 9/20/1863.

Dillon, J.H. (aka **Dillow**)—Pvt.—Enlisted: 6/4/1861 at Monroe, LA. Rolls for 6/4/1861 through 12/1861: Present. Rolls for 1/1862 through 2/1862: Discharged at Richmond, LA while in hospital.

Doughty, John (aka Daughty) — Pvt. — Enlisted: 6/4/1861 at Monroe, LA. Rolls for 6/4/1861 through 6/1862: Present. Name on report dated: U.S. Provost Marshals Office, Northern District, Dept. of the South, Charleston, S.C. 3/15/1865, of C.S. Deserters Received on 2/18/1865. *Born:* Ireland-*Last Residence:* South Carolina-Age: 35 years-Eyes: gray-Hair: dark-Complexion: dark-Height: 5 ft. 7 in. Remarks: Took the U.S. Oath of Allegiance and discharged.

Dunlavey, James (aka Dunlasy) — Pvt. — Enlisted: 6/4/1861 at Monroe, LA. Rolls through 6/1862: Present. Regimental Return for 9/1862: Hospitalized.

Essig, Daniel John (aka Essigs, B.J.) — Pvt. — Enlisted: 6/4/1861 at Monroe, LA. Rolls for 6/4/1861 through 4/1862: Present. Rolls for 5/1862 through 6/1862: Absent, sick in hospital at Macon, GA. Rolls for 1/1864 through 2/1864: Present. In hospital at Selma, AL due to wounds received at the Battle of Atlanta, GA in 1864. *Born:* 8/1/1838. *Married:* Minnie Maxey on 12/31/1873 at Liberty, Amite County, MS. *Children:* 4 Daughters. *Occupation:* Tombstone Salesman. *Residences:* Bienville Parish and Claiborne Parish, LA since 1853. *Died:* 7/29/1917 at Homer, Claiborne Parish, LA due to Brights Disease. *Buried:* Old Homer Cemetery located at Homer, LA. *Wife Died:* 10/5/1940 after being bedridden for 2 yrs. Widows Pension amount: $60.00 per month. Confederate Pension Application dated 3/31/1913 on file at the Louisiana State Archives-Microfilm Reel: CP1.46-Microdex 2-Sequence 30-Target Card: Essig, D.J. Parish: Claiborne-6 Pages. Also a Confederate Widows Pension Application dated 8/31/1917 on file-Microfilm Reel: CP1.46-Microdex 2-Sequence 31-Target Card: Essig, Mannie-Parish: Claiborne-9 Pages. Wife's Maiden Name: Mannie Maxey.

Faust, M.M. — Pvt. — Enlisted: 6/4/1861 at Monroe, LA. Rolls for 6/4/1861 through 2/1862: Present. Rolls for 3/1862 through 4/1862: Absent, sick at hospital in Augusta, GA. Rolls for 5/1862 through 6/1862: Present. Rolls for 1/1864 through 2/1864: Absent, wounded at the Battle of Chickamauga, GA on 9/19/1863; Sent to hospital from battlefield. Rolls for 3/1864 through 4/1865: Retired by Medical Board on 7/8/1864.

Fetters, Thomas P. (aka Fatter, T.B.) — Pvt./Musician — (See Field and Staff)

Flowers, Jesse (aka Flower) — Pvt. — Enlisted: 6/4/1861 at Monroe, LA. Rolls for 6/4/1861 through 6/1862: Present. On Register of Floyd House and Ocmulgee Hospital, Macon, GA: Admitted on 11/14/1863. Rolls for 1/1864 through 2/1864: Absent, wounded at the Battle of Chickamauga, GA on 9/19/1863; Sent to hospital from battlefield. Rolls for 5/31/1864 through 4/1865: Absent, confined in the Georgia State Penitentiary by order of Gen. Joseph E. Johnston.

Flynn, F.M. — Pvt. — Enlisted: 6/4/1861 at Monroe, LA. Rolls for 6/4/1861 through 2/1865: Present. Rolls for 3/1865 through 4/1865: Absent, wounded at Spanish Fort, AL on 3/27/1865 and hospitalized. Rolls of Prisoners of War, C.S.A: Surrendered at Citronelle, AL on 5/4/1865; Paroled at Meridian, MS on 5/10/1865. *Residence:* Wetumpka, Elmore County, AL.

Flynn, Michael (aka Flinn) — Pvt. — Enlisted: 6/4/1861 at Monroe, LA. Rolls for 6/4/1861 through 2/1862: Present. Rolls for 3/1862 through 4/1862: Absent, sick in hospital at Augusta, GA. Rolls for 5/1862 through 6/1862: Present. Rolls for 1/1864 through 2/1864: Present. Rolls for 8/31/1864 through 4/1865: Absent, sick in hospital at Lagrange, GA.

Folmer, B.F. (aka Falmer, Folmar) — Pvt. — Enlisted: 6/4/1861 at Monroe, LA. Rolls for 6/4/1861 through 6/1862: Present. Rolls for 1/1864 through 2/1864: Absent, wounded at the Battle of Chickamauga, GA on 9/19/1863; Sent to hospital from battlefield. Rolls for 8/31/1864 through 4/1865: Absent, wounded at the Battle of Chickamauga, GA on 9/19/1863 and in hospital.

Garrett, Isaiah L. (aka J.L.) — Pvt. — Enlisted: 9/23/1862 at Monroe, LA. Rolls for 1/1864 through 2/1865: Present. Rolls for 3/1865 through 4/1865: Absent, captured at Spanish Fort, AL on 4/8/1865. Federal Rolls of Prisoners of War: Captured at Spanish Fort, AL on 4/8/1865; Sent to Ship Island, MS on 4/10/1865. Transferred to Vicksburg, MS on 5/1/1865; Paroled at Camp Townsend, MS on 5/6/1865. *Born:* 1/1/1845 to Isaiah Garrett and Narcissa Grayson Garrett. *Occupations:* Farmer and Ouachita Parish, LA Clerk of Court, Postmaster and Sheriff. *Residence:* Ouachita Parish, LA. *Died:* 11/16/1897. *Buried:* Tennille Cemetery located 1 mile east of the University of Louisiana-Monroe on Desiard St. at Monroe, Ouachita Parish, LA.

George, R.B. — Pvt. — Enlisted: 3/6/1862 at Monroe, LA. Rolls for 3/1862 through 6/1862: Present. Rolls for 1/1864 through 2/1864: Present, sick in camp. Rolls for 8/1864 through 4/1865: Present. Rolls of Prisoners of War, C.S.A: Surrendered at Citronelle, AL on 5/4/1865; Paroled at Meridian, MS on 5/10/1865. *Residence:* Monroe, Ouachita Parish, LA. Soldier also served as a Pvt. with the Louisiana Pelican Infantry Regiment-Co. F. *Wounded:* Yes, shot through left thigh in a picket fight near Atlanta, GA. *Born:* 12/9/1829 at Troup County, GA. *Married:* Yes, 4 times. *Wife's Age:* 55 as of 1905. *Children:* 3–2 Sons and 1 Daughter. *Occupation:* Livestock Farmer. *Residence:* Ouachita Parish, LA since 1855. Confederate Pension Application dated 5/15/1905 on file at the Louisiana State Archives-Microfilm Reel: CP1.54-Microdex 2-Sequence 8-Target Card: George, R.B.-Parish: Lincoln-8 Pages.

Gleason, David — Pvt. — Enlisted: 6/4/1861 at Monroe, LA. Rolls for 6/4/1861 through 6/30/1861: On furlough since services of Company B were accepted.

Rolls for 3/30/1862 through 4/30/1862: Absent, sick in hospital at Savannah, GA.

Gleason, John—Pvt.—Enlisted: 6/4/1861 at Monroe, LA. Rolls for 6/4/1861 through 4/1862: Present. Rolls for 5/1862 through 6/1862: Killed at the Battle of Secessionville, S.C. on 6/16/1862.

Grayson, James Stuart—Pvt.—Enlisted: 6/4/1861 at Monroe, LA. Rolls for 6/4/1861 through 2/1864: Present. Rolls #1 for 8/1864 through 2/1865: Present. Rolls #2 for 8/1864 through 2/1865: Absent, furloughed from hospital in 1864 for 30 days, absent since without leave. Rolls of Prisoners of War, C.S.A: Surrendered at Citronelle, AL on 5/4/1865; Paroled at Monroe, LA on 6/12/1865. *Residence:* Ouachita Parish, LA. *Born:* 11/7/1824. *Died:* 3/1869 near the residence of Capt. J. P. Crosley on the west bank of the Ouachita River at Ouachita Parish, LA due to murder and robbery committed by U.S. Soldiers John Phelps and Eugene Reary. (His obituary appeared in the 3/31/1869 edition of the Ouachita-Telegraph newspaper)

Guynn, Edward Wade (aka Guinn)—Pvt.—Enlisted: 6/4/1861 at Monroe, LA. Rolls for 3/1865 through 4/1865: Absent, in hospital at Lauderdale Springs, MS. *Wounded:* Yes, shot in right thigh and flesh wound in back of skull four miles from Atlanta, GA on 7/28/1864, and shot in shin near Columbus, MS in 4/1865. *Born:* 12/1/1836 near Montgomery, Montgomery County, AL. *Married:* Josephine Sims on 8/6/1865 at Union Parish, LA. *Wife's Age:* 52 as of 1899. *Children:* 4—2 Sons and 2 Daughters. *Occupation:* Farmer. *Died:* 3/23/1901 at his home in Union Parish, LA due to Rheumatism. *Buried:* Liberty Church Cemetery in Union Parish, LA. Confederate Pension Application dated 1/2/1899 on file at the Louisiana State Archives-Microfilm Reel: CP1.60-Microdex 2-Sequence 1-Target Card: Guinn, Edward W.-Parish: Union-6 Pages. Also a Confederate Widows Pension Application dated 11/20/1902 on file-Microfilm Reel: CP1.60-Microdex 2-Sequence 3-Target Card: Guinn, Samantha J.-Parish: Union-3 Pages. Also an additional Confederate Widows Pension Application on file-Microfilm Reel: CP1.152-Microdex 1-Sequence 35-Target Card: Guinn, Samantha Josephine (Sirus)-Parish: Union-6 Pages. Wife married prior: Henry Sims.

Hammond, W.D.—Pvt.—Enlisted: 6/4/1861 at Monroe, LA. Rolls for 6/4/1861 through 10/1861: Present. Rolls for 11/1861 through 12/1861: Discharged on Surgeon's Certificate of Disability on 12/13/1861.

Hardy, Covington—Pvt.—Enlisted: 3/6/1862 at Monroe, LA. Rolls for 3/6/1862 through 6/30/1862: Present.

Harris, Richard—Pvt.—Enlisted: 6/4/1861 at Monroe, LA. Rolls for 6/4/1861 through 6/30/1861: Present. Rolls for 7/1861 through 8/1861: Present, discharged due to disability on 9/1/1861.

Holley, G. James (aka Holly)—Pvt.—Enlisted: 3/6/1862 at Monroe, LA. Rolls for 3/6/1862 through 4/30/1862: Present. Rolls for 5/1862 through 6/1862: Absent, sick in hospital at Savannah, GA. Rolls for 1/1864 through 2/1865: Absent, captured at the Battle of Chickamauga, GA on 9/19/1863. Federal Rolls of Prisoners of War: Captured at Chickamauga, GA on 9/19/1863; Forwarded to the U.S. Military Prison, Louisville, KY on 10/1/1863. Transferred to Camp Douglas, IL on 10/4/1863; Discharged on 6/14/1865 in accordance with General Order #109, Adjutant Generals Office, Washington, D.C. 6/6/1865.

Holley, Thomas D. (aka Holly, F.D., T.D.)—Pvt./Musician—(See Field and Staff)

Howe, John—Pvt.—Enlisted: 6/4/1861 at Monroe, LA. Rolls for 6/4/1861 through 4/1862: Present. Rolls for 1/1864 through 4/1865: Absent, captured at Missionary Ridge, TN on 11/25/1863. Federal Rolls of Prisoners of War: Captured at the Battle of Missionary Ridge, TN on 11/25/1863; Forwarded to the U.S. Military Prison, Louisville, KY from Nashville, TN on 12/7/1863. Transferred to Rock Island Barracks, IL on 12/13/1863; Enlisted in the U.S. Army for frontier service on 10/31/1864.

Huber, Lewis (aka Hoover, Heubert, Louis)—Pvt.—Enlisted: 6/4/1861 at Monroe, LA. Rolls for 6/4/1861 through 6/1862: Present. On Federal List of Rebel Deserters: Captured at Lookout Valley, TN on 11/17/1863; Forwarded to the U.S. Military Prison, Louisville, KY on 11/24/1863. Released on the U.S. Oath of Allegiance on 11/25/1863 and sent north.

Jackson, Silas J.—Pvt.—Enlisted: 6/4/1861 at Monroe, LA. Rolls for 6/4/1861 through 6/1862: Present. Federal Rolls of Prisoners of War: Captured near Chickamauga, GA on 9/19/1863; Received at the U.S. Military Prison, Louisville, KY on 10/1/1863. Forwarded to Camp Douglas, IL on 10/2/1864; Discharged from Camp Douglas, IL on 6/14/1865 in accordance with General Order #109, Adjutant Generals Office, Washington, D.C. 6/6/1865. *Residence:* Ouachita Parish, LA.

Johnson, Robert W.—Pvt.—Enlisted: 6/4/1861 at Monroe, LA. Rolls for 6/4/1861 through 6/1862: Present. Federal Rolls of Prisoners of War: Captured near Jackson, MS in 7/1863; Sent to Snyder's Bluff, MS on 7/30/1863. Received at Camp Morton, IN on 8/7/1863; Enlisted in the U.S. Military Service in 8/1863.

Justice, Thomas W. (aka F.W., T.J., T.M.)—Pvt.—Enlisted: 6/4/1861 at Monroe, LA. Rolls for 6/4/1861 through 6/1862: Present. Federal Rolls of Prisoners of War: Captured at Graysville, GA on 11/26/1863; Sent to the U.S. Military Prison, Louisville, KY from Nashville, TN on 12/10/1863. Forwarded to Rock Island Barracks, IL on 12/11/1863; Enlisted at Rock Island Barracks, IL in the U.S. Army for frontier service on 10/13/1864.

Lawrence, G.W. (aka Laurance)—Pvt.—Enlisted: 6/4/1861 at Monroe, LA. Rolls for 6/4/1861 through 6/1862: Present.

Lawrence, M.F. — Pvt. — Enlisted: 3/1/1863 at Monroe, LA. Rolls for 1/1864 through 2/1864: Present.

Lewis, C.W. (aka C.D.) — Pvt. — Enlisted: 6/4/1861 at Monroe, LA. Rolls for 6/4/1861 through 6/1862: Present. Rolls for 1/1864 through 2/1864: Present. Killed at the Battle of New Hope Church, GA on 5/27/1864. *Buried:* In a common grave with two other members of the Fourth Louisiana Battalion near New Hope Church, GA.

McClendon, James — Pvt. — Enlisted: 3/4/1862 at Monroe, LA. Rolls for 3/4/1862 through 6/1862: Present, wounded at the Battle of Secessionville, S.C. on 6/16/1862. Rolls for 1/1864 through 2/1864: Present. Rolls for 8/1864 through 2/28/1865: Absent, captured near Atlanta, GA on 8/15/1864. Federal Rolls of Prisoners of War: Captured near Atlanta, GA on 8/5/1864; Sent to the U.S. Military Prison, Louisville, KY from Nashville, TN on 8/12/1864. Transferred to Camp Chase, OH on 8/14/1864; Paroled at Camp Chase, OH on 2/12/1865. Exchanged at Boulware and Cox Wharf, James River, VA on 2/20–21/1865. Rolls for 3/1865 through 4/1865: Absent on parole furlough since 3/10/1865.

McClendon, P.H. (aka McLendon) — Pvt. — Enlisted: 3/6/1862 at Monroe, LA. Rolls for 3/6/1862 through 6/1862: Present. Rolls for 1/1864 through 4/1865: Absent, captured at the Battle of Missionary Ridge, TN on 11/25/1863. Federal Rolls of Prisoners of War: Captured at Missionary Ridge, TN on 11/25/1863; Forwarded to the U.S. Military Prison, Louisville, KY from Nashville, TN on 12/6/1863. Sent to Rock Island Barracks, IL on 12/9/1864; Paroled at Rock Island Barracks, IL and transferred for Exchange. Exchanged at Boulware and Cox Wharf, James River, VA on 3/10–12/1865.

McClendon, Travis J. — Pvt. — Enlisted: 6/4/1861 at Monroe, LA. Rolls for 6/1861 through 4/1862: Present. Rolls #1 for 5/1862 through 6/1862: Absent, wounded at the Battle of Secessionville, S. C and hospitalized at Charleston, S.C. Roll #2 for 5/1862 through 6/1862: Present. Rolls for 1/1864 through 4/1865: Absent, captured at the Battle of Chickamauga, GA on 9/19/1863. Federal Rolls of Prisoners of War: Captured at the Battle of Chickamauga, GA on 9/20/1863; Sent to the U.S. Military Prison, Louisville, KY on 10/1/1863. Transferred to Camp Douglas, IL on 10/4/1863; Paroled and forwarded to City Point, VA for Exchange on 3/14/1865. Exchanged at Boulware and Cox Wharf, James River, VA on 3/18 — 21/1865. *Born:* 12/6/1836 in Alabama. *Married:* Mattie Robinson. *Children:* 7 — 3 Sons and 4 Daughters. *Occupation:* Farmer. *Died:* 3/2/1923. *Buried:* Hasley Cemetery located at West Monroe, Ouachita Parish, LA by Peters Funeral Home of Monroe, LA. *Wife's Age:* 64 in 1909. Confederate Pension Application dated 10/10/1909 on file at the Louisiana State Archives-Microfilm Reel: CP1.93-Microdex 3-Sequence 16-Target Card: McClendon, Travis-Parish: Ouachita-11 Pages.

McCrary, William (aka McCrarey) — Pvt. — Enlisted: 6/4/1861 at Monroe, LA. Rolls for 6/1861 through 8/1861: Present. Rolls for 9/1861 through 10/1861: Present or absent not stated. Rolls for 11/1861 through 12/1861: Discharged on Surgeon's Certificate of Disability on 12/13/1861. Soldier also served as a Pvt. with the 31st Louisiana Infantry-Co. G. Rolls of Prisoners of War, C.S.A: Surrendered at New Orleans, LA on 5/26/1865; Paroled at Monroe, LA on 6/9/1865 and 6/12/1865. *Residence:* Ouachita Parish, LA. *Born:* 7/16/1840 at Marion County, GA. *Occupation:* Farmer. *Residence:* Union Parish, LA since 1858. Confederate Pension Application dated 11/17/1913 on file at the Louisiana State Archives-Microfilm Reel: CP1.93-Microdex 4-Sequence 32-Target Card: McCrary, William-Parish: Union-6 Pages.

McCue, Luke (aka McKew) — Pvt. — Enlisted: 6/4/1861 at Monroe, LA. Rolls for 6/4/1861 through 6/1862: Present. Federal Rolls of Prisoners of War: Captured near Jackson, MS on 7/17/1863; Sent to Snyder's Bluff, MS on 7/30/1863. Transferred to Camp Morton, IN on 8/7/1863; Released on the U.S. Oath of Allegiance on 5/22/1865. Description at release-Complexion: florid-Hair: black-Eyes: blue-Height: 5 ft. 4¾ in. *Residence:* St. Louis, MO.

McGuire, Thomas (aka Maguire) — Pvt. — Enlisted: 6/4/1861 at Monroe, LA. Rolls for 6/4/1861 through 4/1865: Present. Rolls of Prisoners of War, C.S.A: Surrendered at Citronelle, AL on 5/4/1865; Paroled at Meridian, MS on 5/10/1865. *Residence:* Monroe, Ouachita Parish, LA. Soldier also served as a Pvt. with the Louisiana Pelican Infantry Regiment-Co. F.

McInalty, Patrick — Pvt. — Enlisted: 6/4/1861 at Monroe, LA. Rolls for 6/4/1861 through 6/1862: Present. Regimental Return for 9/1862: Hospitalized.

Magee, H.L. — Pvt. — Enlisted: 4/26/1864; Sent to Company B from the 1st Louisiana Cavalry. Rolls of Prisoners of War, C.S.A: Surrendered at Citronelle, AL on 5/4/1865; Paroled at Meridian, MS on 5/10/1865. *Residence:* Washington Parish, LA. Soldier also served as a Pvt. with the Louisiana Pelican Infantry Regiment-Co. F.

Mansfield, Lawrence (aka Lawerence) — Pvt. — Enlisted: 6/4/1861 at Monroe, LA. Rolls for 6/4/1861 through 6/1862: Present. Federal Rolls of Prisoners of War: Captured near Jackson, MS on 7/17/1863; Sent to Snyder's Bluff, MS on 7/30/1863. Transferred to Camp Morton, IN on 8/7/1863; Released on the U.S. Oath of Allegiance on 5/22/1865. Description at release-Complexion: dark-Hair: dark-Eyes: gray-Height: 5 ft. 3¼ in. *Residence:* St. Louis, MO.

Marsh, Thomas A. — Pvt. — Enlisted: 6/4/1861 at Monroe, LA. Rolls for 6/1861 through 6/1862: Present. Rolls for 1/1864 through 2/1864: Sent to hospital at Lauderdale Springs, MS on 7/25/1863 by Dr. McEnery; Deserted from hospital on 9/20/1863. Rolls of Prisoners of War, C.S.A: Surrendered at Citronelle, AL on 5/4/1865; Paroled at Monroe, LA on 6/15/1865. *Residence:* Union Parish, LA. *Born:* 5/21/1840 at Perry County, AL. *Married:* Twice-2nd wife Sarah E. Conley on 3/18/1879. *Children:* 7–3 Sons and 4 Daughters. (Oldest son killed by a train) *Occupation:* Farmer. *Residences:* Union Parish and Vernon Parish, LA since 1850. *Died:* 2/17/1914 at Carmenia, LA due to Heart Failure. *Wife Born:* 1849 in Alabama. Wife's Age: 64. Confederate Widows Pension Application dated 8/7/1911 on file at the Louisiana State Archives-Microfilm Reel: CP1.90-Microdex 3-Sequence 43-Target Card: Marsh, Sarah E.-Parish: Sabine-18 Pages. Also an additional Confederate Widows Pension Application dated 6/6/1931 on file-Microfilm Reel: CP1.90-Microdex 3-Sequence 16-Target Card: Marsh, Sarah E.-Parish: Vernon-6 Pages.

Massey, J.H. (aka Massie) — Pvt. — Enlisted: 6/4/1861 at Monroe, LA. Rolls for 6/4/1861 through 6/1862: Present. Regimental Return for 8/1862: Absent in hospital at Whitesville, GA. Rolls for 1/1864 through 2/1864: Absent, wounded at the Battle of Chickamauga, GA on 9/19/1863; Sent to hospital from the battlefield. Rolls for 8/31/1864 through 2/28/1865: Absent, in hospital at Montgomery, AL since 9/29/1864. Rolls for 3/1865 through 4/1865: Absent in hospital, wounded at the Battle of Chickamauga, GA on 9/19/1863.

Mills, George W. — Pvt. — Enlisted: 6/4/1861 at Monroe, LA. Rolls for 6/4/1861 through 6/1862; Present. Rolls for 1/1864 through 4/1865: Absent, captured at the Battle of Missionary Ridge, TN on 11/25/1863. Federal Rolls of Prisoners of War: Captured at Missionary Ridge, TN on 11/25/1863; Sent to the U.S. Military Prison, Louisville, KY from Nashville, TN on 12/6/1863. Transferred to Rock Island Barracks, IL on 12/9/1863; Enlisted in the U.S. Army for frontier service on 10/14/1864.

Montrose, E.A. (aka A.E.) — Pvt. — Enlisted: 6/4/1861 at Monroe, LA. Rolls for 6/4/1861 through 12/1861: Present.

Odom, Robert J.W. — Pvt. — Enlisted: 6/4/1861 at Monroe, LA. Rolls for 6/4/1861 through 2/1862: Present. Rolls for 3/1862 through 4/1862: Present, detailed to work on Gun Boat at Savannah, GA. Rolls for 5/1862 through 6/1862: Present. Rolls for 1/1864 through 2/1864: Present. *Buried:* Philyaw Cemetery located at Miller County, AR.

O'Donnell, Patrick (aka O'Donald) — Pvt. — Enlisted: 6/4/1861 at Monroe, LA. Rolls for 6/4/1861 through 2/1862: Present.

Packer, Alexander N. — Pvt. — Enlisted: 6/4/1861 at Monroe, LA. Rolls for 6/4/1861 through 6/1862: Present, wounded at the Battle of Secessionville, S.C. on 6/16/1862. Regimental Return for 7/1862: Sick in Alabama, wounded. Regimental Return for 9/1862: Detailed as Teamster. *Died:* 5/29/1863 at Canton, MS.

Buried: Canton City Cemetery located at Canton, Madison County, MS.

Poindexter, W.S. — Pvt. — Enlisted: 6/4/1861 at Monroe, LA. Rolls for 6/4/1861 through 6/30/1861: Present. Rolls for 7/1861 through 8/1861: Discharged due to disability.

Pratt, Leander J. (aka E.J.) — Pvt. — Enlisted: 6/4/1861 at Monroe, LA. Rolls for 6/4/1861 through 2/1864: Present. Rolls for 8/31/1864 through 2/28/1865: Absent, captured near Atlanta, GA on 8/5/1864. Federal Rolls of Prisoners of War: Captured near Atlanta, GA on 8/5/1864; Received at the U.S. Military Prison, Louisville, KY on 8/12/1864. Forwarded to Camp Chase, OH on 8/13/1864; Died on 11/5/1864 due to Congestive Chill. *Buried:* Camp Chase Confederate Cemetery located at Columbus, Franklin County, OH.

Puckett, A.P. — Pvt. — Enlisted: 6/4/1861 at Monroe, LA. Rolls for 6/4/1861 through 2/1862: Present. Rolls for 3/1862 through 4/1862: Present, detailed to work on Gun Boat at Savannah, GA. Rolls for 5/1862 through 6/1862: Present. Rolls for 1/1864 through 2/1864: Present. Rolls for 8/31/1864 through 4/1865: Absent, assumed to have been captured near Nashville, TN.

Pulliam, C.M. (aka Pullim, Pullman) — Pvt. — Enlisted: 6/4/1861 at Monroe, LA. Rolls for 6/4/1861 through 6/1862: Present.

Ramey, H.M. — Pvt. — Enlisted: 6/4/1861 at Monroe, LA. Rolls for 6/4/1861 through 6/1862: Present.

Ray, L.C. — Pvt. — Enlisted: 3/6/1862 at Monroe, LA. Rolls for 3/6/1862 through 4/1865: Present. Rolls of Prisoners of War, C.S.A: Surrendered at Citronelle, AL on 5/4/1865; Paroled at Meridian, MS on 5/10/1865. *Residence:* Monroe, Ouachita Parish, LA. Soldier also served as a Pvt. with the Louisiana Pelican Infantry Regiment-Co. F.

Rayford, Harrison C. (aka Ragland, Raiford, Railford) — Pvt. — Enlisted: 3/6/1862 at Monroe, LA. Rolls for 3/6/1862 through 6/1862: Present. Rolls for 1/1864 through 4/1865: Absent, captured at the Battle of Missionary Ridge, TN on 11/25/1863. Federal Rolls of Prisoners of War: Captured at the Battle of Missionary Ridge, TN on 11/25/1863; Received at the U.S. Military Prison, Louisville, KY from Nashville, TN on 12/7/1863. Forwarded to Rock Island Barracks, IL on 12/11/1863; Died at Rock Island Barracks, IL on 2/11/1865 due to Pneumonia. *Buried:* Rock Island Confederate Cemetery located at Rock Island, IL.

Roberts, Luke — Pvt. — Enlisted: 4/12/1862 at Monroe, LA. Rolls for 5/1862 through 6/1862: Died in hospital at Charleston, S.C. on 6/22/1862.

Robinson, John L. — Pvt. — Enlisted: 6/4/1861 at Monroe, LA. Rolls for 6/4/1861 through 6/1862: Present. Rolls for 1/1864 through 2/1864: Absent, detailed as Teamster on 2/14/1863 by order of Capt. Powell, Commanding Battalion. Rolls for 8/31/1864 through 4/1865: Present. Rolls of Prisoners of War, C.S.A: Surrendered at Citronelle, AL on 5/4/1865; Paroled at Meridian, MS on 5/10/1865. *Residence:* Monroe, Ouachita Parish, LA. *Born:* 11/25/1837 in Georgia. *Married:* Never. *Children:* None. *Residences:* Louisiana since 1869, Arkansas and Kansas prior. Confederate Pension Application dated 12/17/1909 on file at the Louisiana State Archives-Microfilm Reel: CP1.120-Microdex 2-Sequence 6-Target Card: Robinson, John L.-Parish: Ouachita-6 Pages.

Robinson, J.L.B. (aka J.E.B.) — Pvt. — Enlisted: 6/4/1861 at Monroe, LA. Rolls for 6/4/1861 through 2/1862: Present. Rolls for 3/1862 through 6/1862: Absent, on sick furlough at home near Monroe, LA. Rolls for 1/1864 through 4/1865: Present. Rolls of Prisoners of War, C.S.A: Surrendered at Citronelle, AL on 5/4/1865; Paroled at Meridian, MS on 5/10/1865. *Residence:* Monroe, Ouachita Parish, LA. *Died:* 5/10/1898. Confederate Widows Pension Application dated 1903 on file at the Arkansas History Commission-Widows Name: Robinson, Mrs. L.A. Residences: Clark County, AR. *Wife Died:* 6/16/1933.

Robinson, S.W. — Pvt. — Enlisted: 3/6/1862 at Monroe, LA. Rolls for 3/6/1862 through 4/1862: Present. Rolls for 5/1862 through 6/1862: Absent, wounded at the Battle of Secessionville, S.C. and in hospital at Charleston, S.C. Regimental Return for 7/1862: Sick in Georgia, wounded. Regimental Return for 8/1862: Sick in hospital at West Point, GA, wounded.

Ryan, Edward D. (aka Rion) — Pvt. — Enlisted: 6/4/1861 at Monroe, LA. Rolls for 6/4/1861 through 2/1862: Present. Rolls for 3/1862 through 4/1862: Present, under arrest at Savannah, GA. Rolls for 5/1862 through 6/1862: Present.

Sheppard, Andrew C. (aka Shephard, Shepherd) — Pvt. — Enlisted: 6/4/1861 at Monroe, LA. Rolls for 6/4/1861 through 6/1862: Present. Rolls for 1/1864 through 4/1865: Absent, captured at the Battle of Chickamauga, GA on 9/19/1863. Federal Rolls of Prisoners of War: Captured near Chickamauga, GA on 9/19/1863; Forwarded to the U.S. Military Prison, Louisville, KY on 10/1/1863. Transferred to Camp Douglas, IL on 10/2/1863; Enlisted in the 5th U.S. Volunteer Infantry on 4/18/1863. *Died:* 11/14/1901 due to Pneumonia. *Married:* Martha J. Williams on 12/31/1874 near Sparta, Bienville Parish, LA. *Buried:* Castor Church Cemetery located at Castor, Bienville Parish, LA. Confederate Widows Pension Application dated 10/6/1915 on file at the Louisiana State Archives-Microfilm Reel: CP1.126-Microdex 3-Sequence 4-Target Card: Sheppard, Martha J. (Williams)-Parish: Webster-5 Pages.

Sheppard, B.F. — Pvt. — Enlisted: 6/4/1861 at Monroe, LA. Rolls for 6/4/1861 through 8/1861: Present. Rolls for 9/1861 through 10/1861: Discharged at Richmond, VA without the knowledge of the Company B Captain.

Sheppard, Richard M. — Pvt. — Enlisted: 6/4/1861 at Monroe, LA. Rolls for 6/4/1861 through 6/30/1861: Absent on furlough since Company B organization. Soldier also served as a Pvt. with the 12th Louisiana Infantry-Co. H. Enlisted: 2/27/1862 at Monroe, LA. Rolls for 11/1862 through 2/1863: Present. Rolls for 7/1863 through 8/1863: Absent without leave since 8/27/1863. Rolls for 9/1863 through 10/1863: Absent, placed under arrest at Canton, MS on 9/13/1862 by order of Col. Thomas M. Scott.

Sherring, Edward — Pvt. — Enlisted: 6/4/1861 at Monroe, LA. Rolls for 6/4/1861 through 6/1862: Present. Rolls for 1/1864 through 2/1864: Present.

Shively, William — Pvt. — Enlisted: 3/6/1862 at Monroe, LA. Rolls for 3/6/1862 through 6/1862: Present. Died from wounds received at the Battle of Chickamauga, GA. Placed on the Confederate Roll of Honor for gallantry and good conduct at the Battle of Chickamauga, GA per General Order #131 of the Inspector and Adjutant General's Office, Richmond, VA.

Sikes, Joseph J. — Pvt.-Federal Rolls of Prisoners of War: Captured at Chattanooga, TN on 10/18/1863; Forwarded to the U.S. Military Prison, Nashville, TN. Released on the U.S. Oath of Allegiance on 10/31/1863.

Smith, James — Pvt. — Enlisted: 6/4/1861 at Monroe, LA. Rolls for 6/4/1861 through 6/1862: Present.

Smith, William A. — Pvt. — Enlisted: 4/14/1862 at Monroe, LA. Rolls for 1/1864 through 2/1864: Absent, wounded at Jackson, MS on 7/17/1863; Sent to hospital same day by order of Dr. McEnery. Rolls for 3/1865 through 4/1865: Retired by the Medical Board on 7/8/1864. Rolls of Prisoners of War of Diverse Companies and Regiments Unattached, C.S.A: Surrendered at New Orleans, LA on 5/26/1865; Paroled at Monroe, LA on 6/9/1865. *Residence:* Ouachita Parish, LA. *Buried:* Smith Family Cemetery located at St. Helena Parish, LA; On Hwy. 38 east from Easleyville, turn north on Parish Rd. 1 and travel 2 miles before turning left on the gravel road. Confederate Widows Pension Application dated 1920 on file at the Mississippi Dept. of Archives and History-Target Card: Easley, Letha-County: Pike.

Stinson, R. James — Pvt. — Enlisted: 6/4/1861 at Monroe, LA. Rolls for 6/4/1861 through 4/1862: Present. Rolls for 5/1862 through 4/1865: Absent, detailed to work on Gunboat at Savannah, GA on 5/20/1862 by order of the Secretary of War.

Stokes, James Thomas — Pvt. — Enlisted: 5/17/1861 at Monroe, LA. Rolls for 1/1864 through 2/1864: Present. Rolls for 8/31/1864 through 2/28/1865: Absent, wounded near Atlanta, GA on 8/15/1864 and hospitalized. Rolls for 3/1865 through 4/1865: Absent on 60 day furlough since 3/20/1865. Soldier also served as a Pvt. with the 2nd Louisiana Infantry-Co. C. Enlisted: 5/11/1861 at New Orleans, LA. Rolls for 5/11/1861 through 12/1861: Present. Rolls for 1/1862 through 4/1862: Absent, sick at Williamsburg, VA. Rolls for 5/1862 through 6/1862: Sick at Richmond, VA. Rolls for 7/1862 through 8/1862: Transferred to the Fourth Louisiana Battalion Infantry-Co. B on 8/1/1862. Rolls for 3/1865 through 4/1865: Absent on 60 day furlough since 3/10/1865. *Married:* Mary E. Bayless on 12/23/1865 at Farmerville, Union Parish, LA. *Religion:* Baptist. *Died:* 10/18/1899 at his home in Charlieville, Richland Parish, LA due to Swamp Fever. *Buried:* Alto, Richland Parish, LA. *Wife's Age:* 67 as of 1912. Confederate Widows Pension Application dated 6/8/1912 on file at the Louisiana State Archives-Microfilm Reel: CP1.133-Microdex 2-Sequence 16-Target Card: Stokes, Mary E. (Bayless)-Parish: Richland-4 Pages.

Sullivan, Michael — Pvt. — Enlisted: 6/4/1861 at Monroe, LA. Rolls for 6/4/1861 through 6/1862: Present. Federal Rolls of Prisoners of War: Captured near Jackson, MS in 7/1863; Received at Snyder's Bluff, MS on 7/30/1863. Forwarded to Camp Morton, IN on 8/7/1863. On undated Roll of Prisoners of War at Camp Morton, IN: Prisoner desires to take the U.S. Oath of Allegiance. Remarks: Enlisted at Monroe, LA on 6/4/1861, desires to take the Oath and go to Arkansas to remain loyal. Case doubtful. Paroled at Camp Morton, IN; Forwarded to Point Lookout, MD via the Baltimore and Ohio Rail Road for Exchange. Exchanged at Boulware and Cox Wharf, James River, VA on 3/22/1865.

Sunderland, James O. (aka Sumerland, Sundolan, Joseph, J.C.) — Pvt. — Enlisted: 6/4/1861 at Monroe, LA. Rolls for 6/4/1861 through 6/1862: Present. Federal Rolls of Prisoners of War: Captured at Lookout Valley, TN on 11/17/1863; Received at the U.S. Military Prison, Louisville, KY from Nashville, TN on 11/24/1863. Released on the U.S. Oath of Allegiance and paroled on 11/25/1863 and sent north of the Ohio River by order of Brig. Gen. Jeremiah T. Boyle. Description at release-Complexion: dark-Hair: dark-Eyes: black-Height: 5 ft. 5 in.

Thomas, J.C.C. — Pvt. — Enlisted: 5/6/1862 at Monroe, LA. Rolls for 5/6/1862 through 6/1862: Present. On Floyd House and Ocmulgee Hospital Register, Macon, GA: Admitted on 11/7/1863; Returned to duty on 11/17/1863. Rolls for 1/1864 through 2/1864: Present. Rolls for 8/31/1864 through 2/28/1865: Absent, sick in hospital since 1/27/1865. Rolls for 3/1865 through 4/1865: Present. Rolls of Prisoners of War, C.S.A: Surrendered at Citronelle, AL on 5/4/1865; Paroled at Meridian, MS on 5/10/1865. *Residence:* Monroe, Ouachita Parish, LA. Soldier also served as a Pvt. with the Louisiana Pelican Infantry Regiment-Co. F.

Thomas, William C. — Pvt. — Enlisted: 6/4/1861 at Monroe, LA. Rolls for 6/4/1861 through 6/1862: Present. On Floyd House and Ocmulgee Hospital Register, Macon, GA: Admitted on 12/18/1863. Rolls for 1/1864 through 2/1864: Absent, sick in hospital at Macon, GA since 12/17/1863. On Floyd House and Ocmulgee Hospital Register, Macon, GA: Admitted on 2/8/1864; Furloughed for 45 days. Rolls for 8/31/1864 through 4/1865: Present. Rolls of Prisoners of War, C.S.A: Surrendered at Citronelle, AL on 5/4/1865; Paroled at Meridian, MS on 5/10/1865. *Residence:* Monroe, Ouachita Parish, LA. *Died:* 1/14/1902. Buried: Little Rock National Cemetery at Little Rock, Benton County, AR.

Thompkin, L.T. — Pvt. — Enlisted: 6/4/1861 at Monroe, LA. Rolls for 6/4/1861 through 6/30/1861: Absent on furlough since Company B organization.

Thompkins, B.F. (aka Tompkins) — Pvt. — Enlisted: 6/4/1861 at Monroe, LA. Rolls for 6/4/1861 through 6/30/1861: Absent on furlough since Company B organization.

Thompson, Alfred G. — Pvt./Sgt. Major/Pvt. — (See Field and Staff)

Thompson, George W. — Pvt. — Enlisted: 3/6/1862 at Monroe, LA. Rolls for 4/1862 through 2/1864: Present. Rolls for 8/31/1864 through 2/28/1865: Absent, wounded near Marietta, GA on 5/22/1864. Rolls for 3/1865 through 4/1865: Absent without leave in Louisiana.

Thompson, J.N. — Pvt. — Enlisted: 3/6/1862 at Monroe, LA. Rolls for 3/6/1862 through 6/1862: Present. Regimental Return for 7/1862: Sick at Savannah, GA. Regimental Return for 8/1862: Sick at Whitesville, GA. Rolls for 1/1864 through 2/1864: Present. Rolls for 8/31/1864 through 2/28/1865: Absent, wounded at the Battle of New Hope Church, GA on 5/25/1864. Rolls for 3/1865 through 4/1865: Absent, wounded and in hospital at Macon, GA.

Thompson, John M. — Pvt. — Enlisted: 6/4/1861 at Monroe, LA. Rolls for 6/4/1861 through 6/30/1861: Present. Rolls for 7/1861 through 8/1861: Present, admitted into Company B on 8/16/1861. Rolls for 9/1861 through 2/1864: Present. Rolls for 8/31/1864 through 2/28/1865: Absent, wounded at the Battle of New Hope Church, GA on 5/25/1864. Rolls for 3/1865 through 4/1865: Absent, wounded at the Battle of New Hope Church, GA and in hospital.

Turner, Franklin — Pvt. — Enlisted: 6/4/1861 at Monroe, LA. Rolls for 6/4/1861 through 6/1862: Present. Rolls for 1/1864 through 4/1865: Absent, captured at the Battle of Missionary Ridge, TN on 11/25/1863. Federal Rolls of Prisoners of War: Captured at Graysville, GA on 11/26/1863; Received at the U.S. Military Prison, Louisville, KY from Nashville, TN on 12/10/1863. Forwarded to Rock Island Barracks, IL on 12/11/1863. Enlisted in the U.S. Navy at Rock Island Barracks, IL and transferred to the Naval Rendezvous at Camp Douglas, IL on 1/25/1864.

Turner, L.A.—Pvt.—Enlisted: 6/4/1861 at Monroe, LA. Rolls for 6/4/1861 through 6/30/1861: Absent on furlough since the Company B organization. Soldier also served as a Pvt. with the 6th Louisiana Cavalry-Co. F.

Warren, James—Pvt.—Enlisted: 6/4/1861 at Monroe, LA. Rolls for 6/4/1861 through 8/1861: Present. Rolls for 9/1861 through 10/1861: Present or absent not stated. Rolls for 11/1861 through 12/1861: Died at Peterstown, VA on 11/29/1861.

White, Thomas J.—Pvt.—Enlisted: 6/4/1861 at Monroe, LA. Rolls for 6/4/1861 through 6/1862: Present. Regimental Return for 8/1862: Died at Crawford County, GA.

Williams, Archie—Pvt.-(No War Dept. Record)—Enlisted: 3/20/1862 at Monroe, LA. *Wounded:* No. *Born:* 7/25/1849 in Georgia. *Married:* Yes. *Children:* 5 Daughters. *Occupation:* Farmer. *Residences:* Louisiana since 1850. Wife's Age: 50 as of 1907. Pension amount: $24.00 per month. (Letter dated 6/9/1913 to the Pension Board from Ouachita Parish, LA residents Isaac T. Hamilton and Israel I. Gantt stating that Archie Williams is a Negro and they have known him many years. Another letter dated 6/14/1917 from the Pension Board advised Williams to provide his side of the controversy and to show proof that he was in the army as a regular enlisted soldier.) Confederate Pension Application dated 5/20/1907 on file at the Louisiana State Archives-Microfilm Reel: CP1.147-Microdex 4-Sequence 30-Target Card: Williams, Archie-Parish: Ouachita-10 Pages.

Williams, B.F. (aka F.B.)—Pvt.—Enlisted: 6/4/1861 at Monroe, LA. Rolls for 6/4/1861 through 6/1862: Present. Rolls for 1/1864 through 2/1864: Absent, sent to hospital at Atlanta, GA on 11/4/1863 by order of Dr. Bolen.

Williams, J.B. (aka I.B.)—Pvt.—Enlisted: 6/4/1861 at Monroe, LA. Rolls for 6/4/1861 through 4/1862: Present. Rolls for 5/1862 through 6/1862: Killed at the Battle of Secessionville, S.C. on 6/16/1862.

Williams, J.N. (aka J.W.)—Pvt.—Enlisted: 6/4/1861 at Monroe, LA. Rolls for 6/4/1861 through 8/1861: Present. Soldier also served as a Pvt. with the 31st Louisiana Infantry-Co. F.

Williams, Thomas G.—Pvt.—Enlisted: 6/4/1861 at Monroe, LA. Rolls for 6/4/1861 through 6/1862: Present. Rolls for 1/1864 through 2/1864: Absent, wounded in left ankle at Jackson, MS on 7/15/1863; Sent to hospital the same day by Dr. McEnery. Medical Discharge due to left leg amputation 6 inches below knee due to ankle wound. *Born:* Caldwell Parish, LA. *Married:* Yes, wives deceased. *Children:* 2-1 Son and 1 Daughter. (Did not know their locations as of 1898) *Occupation:* School Teacher. Residences: Louisiana except from 1886 to 1890 when in Missouri. Confederate Pension Application dated 10/4/1898 on file at the Louisiana State Archives-Microfilm Reel: CP1.148-Microdex 3-Sequence 22-Target Card: Williams, Thomas G.-Parish: Caldwell-5 Pages.

Willis, John Y. (aka G.W.)—Pvt.—Enlisted: 6/4/1861 at Monroe, LA. Rolls for 6/4/1861 through 6/1862: Present. Regimental Return for 9/1862: Hospitalized. Federal Rolls of Prisoners of War: Captured at Greenup County, KY or Lookout Valley, TN on 11/13/1863; Received at the U.S. Military Prison, Louisville, KY from Nashville, TN on 11/24/1863. Released from Louisville, KY on 11/25/1863; Sent north of the Ohio River as a C.S. Army Deserter. Description at release-Complexion: fair-Hair: sandy-Eyes: blue-Height: 5 ft. 6 in.

Witcher, William J. (aka Wicher)—Pvt.—Enlisted: 6/4/1861 at Monroe, LA. Rolls for 6/4/1861 through 6/1862: Present. Regimental Return for 9/1862: Hospitalized. Rolls for 1/1864 through 2/1864: Present. Rolls for 8/31/1864 through 4/1865: Absent, taken Prisoner of War at Atlanta, GA on 8/5/1864. Federal Rolls of Prisoners of War: Captured near Atlanta, GA on 8/5/1864; Received at the U.S. Military Prison, Louisville, KY from Nashville, TN on 8/12/1864. Forwarded to Camp Chase, OH on 8/13/1864; Paroled at Camp Chase, OH and transferred to Point Lookout, MD on 3/18/1865 for Exchange. Exchanged at Boulware Wharf, VA on 3/27/1865.

COMPANY C: "FRANKLIN LIFE GUARD," FRANKLIN PARISH

Captain

Buie, Duncan—Capt./Major—(See Field and Staff)

Ward, J. Lawrence (aka L.R.)—1st Lt./Capt.—Enlisted: 8/8/1861 at Winnsboro, LA; Elected 1st Lt. same day. Rolls for 8/8/1861 through 6/1862: Present, promoted to Capt. on 5/20/1862. 1st Lt. Successor: S.R. Norris. Regimental Return for 7/1862: Present or absent not stated. Regimental Return for 8/1862: Present. Rolls for 9/1862 through 2/1863: Present. Rolls for 8/31/1864 through 4/1865: Absent without leave since 10/1/1863 in Louisiana.

Lieutenant

Doyal, Isaac—2nd Sgt./2nd Lt.—Enlisted: 8/8/1861 at Winnsboro, LA. Rolls for 8/8/1861 through 10/1861: Present. Rolls for 11/1861 through 12/1861: Present, elected 2nd Lt. on 11/11/1861. Rolls for 1/1862 through

10/1862: Present. Rolls for 11/1862 through 12/1862: Absent, under arrest at Savannah, GA. Rolls for 1/1863 through 2/1863: Present.

Hammond, Wiley F.—Pvt./2nd Lt.—Enlisted: 8/8/1861 at Winnsboro, LA. Rolls for 8/8/1861 through 6/1862: Present. Rolls for 9/1862 through 2/1863: Absent, sick at Augusta, GA; Elected 2nd Lt. in 8/1863. Killed at the Battle of Resaca, GA on 5/22/1864.

Hooter, John W.—2nd Lt.—Enlisted: 8/8/1861 at Winnsboro, LA; Appointed 2nd Lt. same day.

Mock, William T.—Pvt./Cpl./4th Sgt./2nd Lt.—Enlisted: 8/8/1861 at Winnsboro, LA. Rolls for 8/9/1861 through 8/31/1861: Present. Rolls for 11/1861 through 12/1861: Present, appointed Cpl. on 11/20/1861. Rolls for 1/1862 through 10/1862: Present. Rolls for 11/1862 through 12/1862: Absent, sick at Savannah, GA; Appointed 4th Sgt. on 11/1/1862. Rolls for 1/1863 through 2/1863: Present. Elected 2nd Lt. on 7/17/1863. Rolls for 8/31/1864 through 2/28/1865: Absent, detailed on recruiting service in east Louisiana on 2/14/1865 by order of Lt. Gen. Richard Taylor. Rolls for 3/1865 through 4/1865: Absent on recruiting service in east Louisiana by order of Brig. Gen. Randall L. Gibson.

Norris, Samuel R. (aka L.R.)—3rd Lt./2nd Lt./1st Lt.—Enlisted: 8/8/1861 at Winnsboro, LA. Rolls for 8/8/1861 through 6/1862: Present. Rolls for 9/1862 through 12/1862: Absent, under arrest at Savannah, GA. Rolls for 1/1863 through 2/1863: Present. On Register of Floyd House and Ocmulgee Hospital, Macon, GA: Admitted on 12/1/1863; Remarks: City Hall. Rolls for 8/31/1864 through 4/1865: Present, under arrest and confinement. Official Rolls of Paroled Officers, C.S.A: Surrendered at Citronelle, AL on 5/4/1865; Paroled at Meridian, MS on 5/10/1865. Soldier also served as a 1st Lt. with the Louisiana Pelican Infantry Regiment-Co. G.

West, William J.—3rd Sgt./Jr. 2nd Lt.—Enlisted: 8/8/1861 at Winnsboro, LA. Rolls for 8/8/1861 through 6/1862: Present, elected 3rd Sgt. on 6/20/1862 and promoted to Jr. 2nd Lt. on 6/21/1862. Regimental Return for 7/1862: Present or absent not stated. Regimental Return for 8/1862: Present. Rolls for 9/1862 through 10/1862: Absent on furlough. Rolls for 11/1862 through 12/1862: Absent, sick at Savannah, GA. Rolls for 1/1863 through 2/1863: Present. Resigned in 7/1863. Jr. 2nd Lt. Successor: W.T. Mock.

Sergeant

Harley, H.H. (aka Harly)—1st Sgt./Hospital Steward/Surg.—(See Field and Staff)

Kenton, Phillip C.—Cpl./Sgt.—Enlisted: 8/8/1861 at Winnsboro, LA. Rolls for 8/8/1861 through 2/1863: Present. Rolls for 8/31/1864 through 2/28/1865: Wounded at the Battle of Chickamauga, GA on 9/19/1863 and on retired list in Louisiana. Rolls for 3/1865 through 4/1865: On retired papers in Louisiana since 8/1/1864. Confederate Proofs and Land Warrant Application on file at the Louisiana State Archives-Name: Kenton, Phillip C.-Microfilm Reel: 1-Frame Number: 0014-Act: 116-Pages: 3-Parish: Franklin.

Leavell, Jonathan Quincy Adams (aka Leavill)—Sgt.-Federal Rolls of Prisoners of War: Captured at Columbia, TN on 12/24/1864; Forwarded to Camp Chase, OH. Released on the U.S. Oath of Allegiance on 5/13/1865.

Morgan, Ephraim (aka Morgun, B.)—Pvt./2nd Sgt.—Enlisted: 8/8/1861 at Winnsboro, LA. Rolls for 8/8/1861 through 12/31/1861: Present, appointed 2nd Sgt. on 11/20/1861. Rolls for 1/1862 through 4/1862: Present. Rolls for 5/1862 through 6/1862: Present or absent not stated. Regimental Return for 7/1862: Sick at Somerville, S.C. Regimental Return for 9/1862: On furlough. Rolls for 9/1862 through 12/1862: Present, appointed 1st Sgt. to fill vacancy created by Sgt. Harley's promotion on 11/1/1862. Rolls for 1/1863 through 2/1863: Present. On 1st Mississippi C.S.A. General Hospital Register, Jackson, MS: Admitted on 7/13/1863; Sent to General Hospital on 7/14/1863. Rolls for 8/1864 through 2/1865: Present. Rolls for 3/1865 through 4/1865: Absent in hospital at Columbus, GA. Rolls of Prisoners of War, C.S.A: Surrendered at Citronelle, AL on 5/4/1865; Paroled at Meridian, MS on 5/16/1865. *Residence:* Franklin Parish, LA.

Stoker, William H.P. (aka Stocker)—Pvt./5th Sgt.—Enlisted: 8/8/1861 at Winnsboro, LA. Rolls for 8/8/1861 through 4/1862: Present. Rolls for 5/1862 through 6/1862: Present, appointed to 5th Sgt. on 6/22/1862. Rolls for 9/1862 through 2/1863: Present. Rolls for 8/31/1864 through 4/1865: Absent, taken Prisoner of War on 9/19/1863. Federal Rolls of Prisoners of War: Captured at the Battle of Chickamauga, GA on 9/19/1863; Received at the U.S. Military Prison, Louisville, KY from Nashville, TN on 10/1/1863. Forwarded to Camp Douglas, IL on 10/2/1863; Discharged from Camp Douglas, IL on 6/14/1865 in accordance with General Orders #109, Adjutant General Office, Washington, D.C. 6/6/1865. *Residence:* Franklin Parish, LA.

Tucker, Jesse B.—1st Cpl./5th Sgt.—Enlisted: 8/8/1861 at Winnsboro, LA. Rolls for 8/8/1861 through 2/1863: Present, appointed from 1st Cpl. to 5th Sgt. on 12/1/1862. On 1st Mississippi C.S.A. Hospital Register, Jackson, MS: Admitted on 7/13/1863; Sent to General Hospital on 7/14/1863.

Vanderburg, Joshua S.—Sgt.—Enlisted: 8/8/1861 at Winnsboro, LA. Rolls for 8/8/1861 through 6/1862: Present. Rolls for 9/1862 through 10/1862: Present, sick in camp. Rolls for 11/1862 through 12/1862: Absent, on detached service in charge of the camp at Savannah, GA. Rolls for 1/1863 through 2/1863: Present.

Whatley, Elisha—Pvt./5th Sgt.—Enlisted: 8/8/1861 at Winnsboro, LA. Rolls for 8/8/1861 through 12/1861: Present, appointed to 5th Sgt. on 11/20/1861. Rolls for 1/1862 through 6/1862: Present. Rolls for 9/1862 through 10/1862: Absent without leave. Rolls for 11/1862 through 12/1862: Discharged due to furnishing a lawful Substitution at Wilmington, N.C. *Married:* Louise M. Frazier on 7/13/1869 at Catahoula Parish, LA. *Children:* Yes. *Died:* 10/4/1877 at Bayou Robert, Rapides Parish, LA due to Congestion. *Buried:* Spring Hill Church Cemetery located at Rapides Parish, LA. *Wife's Age:* 54 in 1907. *Wife's Residences:* Louisiana since 1863. Confederate Widows Pension Application dated 4/22/1907 on file at the Louisiana State Archives-Microfilm Reel: CP1.145-Microdex 4-Sequence 32-Target Card: Whatley, Louise M. (Frazier)-Parish: Vernon-2 Pages.

Corporal

Blackman, William V. (aka W.S.)—Pvt./1st Cpl.—Enlisted: 8/8/1861 at Winnsboro, LA. Rolls for 8/8/1861 through 6/1862: Present. Rolls for 9/1862 through 10/1862: Absent on furlough. Rolls for 11/1862 through 12/1862: Appointed 1st Cpl. on 11/1/1862. Rolls for 1/1863 through 4/1865: Present. Rolls of Prisoners of War, C.S.A: Surrendered at Citronelle, AL on 5/4/1865; Paroled at Meridian, MS on 5/10/1865. *Residence:* Winnsboro, Franklin Parish, LA. Soldier also served as a 1st Cpl. with the Louisiana Pelican Infantry Regiment-Co. G.

Doyal, John W.—Pvt./Cpl.—Enlisted: 8/8/1861 at Winnsboro, LA. Rolls for 8/8/1861 through 2/28/1865: Present. Rolls for 3/1865 through 4/1865: Absent, detailed as a Nurse in hospital at Lauderdale, MS by order of the Medical Board. Rolls of Prisoners of War, C.S.A: Surrendered at Citronelle, AL on 5/4/1865; Paroled at Meridian, MS on 5/10/1865. *Residence:* Winnsboro, Franklin Parish, LA.

Moore, Joseph H.—Cpl.—Enlisted: 8/8/1861 at Winnsboro, LA. Rolls for 8/8/1861 through 8/31/1861: Present.

Slaughter, Hudson H. (aka H.A., Hut)—Pvt./4th Cpl.—Enlisted: 8/8/1861 at Winnsboro, LA. Rolls for 8/8/1861 through 10/1862: Present. Rolls for 11/1862 through 12/1862: Present, appointed to 4th Cpl. on 12/1/1862. Rolls for 1/1863 through 2/1863: Present. *Wounded:* Yes-Shot in left side near spine, left arm and left hand at the Battle of Atlanta, GA resulting in finger amputation. Soldier also served with the 27th Mississippi Infantry-Co. E. *Born:* Summerville, Pickens County, AL. *Married:* Yes. *Children:* 1 Son-L.H. Slaughter. *Occupation:* Farmer. *Residence:* Franklin Parish, LA since 1859. *Died:* 5/15/1928 at Bastrop, Morehouse Parish, LA. Pension amount: $90.00 per quarter. Confederate Pension Application dated 5/28/1910 on file at the Louisiana State Archives-Microfilm Reel: CP1.128-Microdex 4-Sequence 3-Target Card: Slaughter, Hudson H.-Parish: Franklin-14 Pages.

Stokes, C. Lester—Cpl.—Enlisted: 8/8/1861 at Winnsboro, LA. Rolls for 8/8/1861 through 2/28/1865: Present. Rolls for 3/1865 through 4/1865: Absent, taken Prisoner of War on 4/8/1865. Federal Rolls of Prisoners of War: Captured at Spanish Fort, AL on 4/8/1865; Received at Ship Island, MS on 4/10/1865. Forwarded to Vicksburg, MS on 5/1/1865; Paroled at Camp Townsend, MS on 5/6/1865. Rolls of Prisoners of War, C.S.A: Surrendered at Citronelle, AL on 5/4/1865; Paroled at Meridian, MS on 5/10/1865. *Residence:* Winnsboro, Franklin Parish, LA.

Private

Allen, Daniel—Pvt.—Enlisted: 8/8/1861 at Winnsboro, LA. Rolls for 11/1861 through 12/1861: Deceased.

Aultman, Martin V. (aka Alltman, Merlin)—Pvt.—Enlisted: 9/21/1861 at Richmond, VA. Rolls for 9/21/1861 through 2/1863: Present. Federal Rolls of Prisoners of War: Captured at Chattanooga, TN on 10/21/1863; Received at the U.S. Military Prison, Louisville, KY on 11/5/1863. Released on the U.S. Oath of Allegiance from Louisville, KY in 11/1863 and sent north by order of Brig. Gen. Jeremiah T. Boyle.

Barfield, George W.—Pvt.—Enlisted: 8/8/1861 at Winnsboro, LA. Rolls for 8/1861: Discharged on Surgeons Certificate of Disability on 8/30/1861. Soldier also served as a Pvt. with the 8th Louisiana Infantry-Co. E. Enlisted: 2/22/1862 at Winnsboro, LA. Rolls for 3/1862 through 11/1862: Absent, sick in hospital at Lynchburg, VA. Rolls through 12/31/1862: Discharged on Surgeons Certificate of Disability at Lynchburg, VA in 12/1862. Age at enlistment: 16. Married at enlistment: No. *Residence:* Winnsboro, Franklin Parish, LA.

Beavell, Ranton D. (aka Bevel, Bevin, Bewinn, Berrimo, Rardan, Rubon)—Pvt.—Enlisted: 4/14/1862 at Winnsboro, LA. Rolls for 5/1862 through 6/1862: Absent, sick in hospital at Charleston, S.C. Rolls for 9/1862 through 2/1863: Present. On Macon, GA Hospital Register: Admitted on 11/28/1863. Federal Rolls of Prisoners of War: Captured near Atlanta, GA on 8/5/1864; Received at the U.S. Military Prison, Louisville, KY from Nashville, TN on 8/12/1864. Transferred to Camp Chase, OH on 8/13/1864; Died on 11/28/1864 at Camp Chase, OH due to Smallpox.

Begley, Jacob—Pvt.—Enlisted: 2/27/1862 at Winnsboro, LA. Rolls for 2/27/1862 through 6/1862: Present.

Rolls for 9/1862 through 10/1862: Absent on furlough. Rolls for 11/1862 through 2/1863: Present.

Bills, Louis (aka Bilss, Lewis)—Pvt.—Enlisted: 9/21/1861 at Richmond, VA. Rolls for 9/21/1861 through 6/1862: Present. Rolls for 9/1862 through 10/1862: Absent without leave. Rolls for 11/1862 through 12/1862: Present. Rolls for 1/1863 through 2/1863: Absent, in prison at Savannah, GA.

Blackman, John S.—Pvt.—Enlisted: 8/8/1861 at Winnsboro, LA. Rolls for 8/8/1861 through 2/28/1865: Present. Rolls for 3/1865 through 4/1865: Absent, sick in hospital.

Blake, John—Pvt.—Enlisted: 8/8/1861 at Winnsboro, LA. Rolls for 8/8/1861 through 4/1865: Present. Rolls of Prisoners of War, C.S.A: Surrendered at Citronelle, AL on 5/4/1865; Paroled at Meridian, MS on 5/10/1865. *Residence:* Winnsboro, Franklin Parish, LA.

Boughton, Samuel Strothers (aka Broughton, Boughten)—Pvt.—Enlisted: 3/17/1862 at Fort Pillow, AR. Rolls for 8/31/1864 through 4/1865: Absent, wounded on 7/28/1864 at Atlanta, GA and in hospital at Lauderdale, MS. Rolls of Prisoners of War, C.S.A: Surrendered at Citronelle, AL on 5/4/1865; Paroled at Meridian, MS on 5/10/1865. *Residence:* Franklin Parish, LA. Soldier also served as a Pvt. with the Louisiana Pelican Infantry Regiment-Co. G. *Born:* 12/13/1838. *Died:* 1/20/1879. *Buried:* Archibald Family Cemetery located at Archibald, Richland Parish, LA.

Bowden, Andrew Jackson, Sr. (aka H.J.)—Pvt.—Enlisted: 4/14/1862 at Winnsboro, LA. Rolls for 4/14/1862 through 2/1865: Present. Federal Rolls of Prisoners of War: Captured at Spanish Fort, AL on 4/8/1865; Received at Ship Island, MS on 4/10/1865. Transferred to Vicksburg, MS on 5/1/1865; Paroled at Camp Townsend, MS on 5/6/1865. *Born:* 1846. *Married:* Sally Adams on 12/5/1867 at Franklin Parish, LA. *Died:* 8/6/1904. *Buried:* Franklin-Bowden Cemetery located off Hwy. 562 between Fort Necessity and Extension, Franklin Parish, LA.

Bowman, William Camsby—Pvt.—Enlisted: 8/8/1861 at Winnsboro, LA. Rolls for 8/8/1861 through 10/1862: Present. Rolls for 11/1862 through 12/1862: Transferred to the C.S. Naval Service as Seaman on 12/15/1862; Assigned to the C.S.S. Atlanta in 1863. *Born:* 1845 in North Carolina. Buried: Graceland Orange Grove Cemetery located at Lake Charles, Calcasieu Parish, LA. Soldier also served with the 34th North Carolina Infantry. Confederate Pension Application on file at the Louisiana State Archives-Microfilm Reel: CP1.15-Microdex 4-Sequence 42-Target Card: Bowman, William C.-Parish: Calcasieu-6 Pages. Also a Confederate Widows Pension Application on file-Microfilm Reel: CP1.15-Microdex 4-Sequence 41-Target Card: Bowman, Sarah N.-Parish: Calcasieu-2 Pages.

Branagin, Barney (aka Bramegin, Branaghan, Branegan, Branegin, Brannegan)—Pvt.—Enlisted: 8/8/1861 at Winnsboro, LA. Rolls for 8/8/1861 through 6/1862: Present. Rolls for 9/1862 through 12/1862: Absent, sick at Augusta, GA. On C.S.A. Hospital Register, Wilmington, N.C: Admitted on 1/11/1863, furloughed on 1/20/1863; Returned to duty on 1/21/1863. Federal Rolls of Prisoners of War: Captured near Resaca, GA on 5/16/1864; Received at the U.S. Military Prison, Louisville, KY from Nashville, TN on 5/20/1864. Forwarded to Camp Morton, IN on 5/21/1864; Released from Camp Morton, IN on 5/18/1865 on the U.S. Oath of Allegiance. *Residence:* Cleveland, OH. Description at release-Complexion: florid-Hair: black-Eyes: blue-Height: 5 ft. 6½ in.

Broadway, Benjamin Franklin—Pvt.—Enlisted: 9/21/1861 at Richmond, VA by Capt. Duncan Buie. Rolls for 9/21/1861 through 2/1862: Present. Rolls for 3/1862 through 4/1862: Medical Discharge at Camp Hope, GA on 4/5/1862 due to severe rheumatism that affected hips, legs and feet. Soldier also served as a Pvt. with the 31st Louisiana Infantry-Co. C. Enlisted: 4/21/1862 at Delhi, LA.

Brock, Charles J. (aka C.S.)—Pvt.—Enlisted: 8/8/1861 at Winnsboro, LA. Rolls for 11/1861 through 12/1861: Medical Discharge in 12/1861 due to Surgeon's Certificate of Disability.

Brock, Elhanon V.—Pvt.—Enlisted: 8/8/1861 at Winnsboro, LA. Rolls for 11/1861 through 12/1861: Discharged in 12/1861 by Surgeon's Certificate of Disability. Soldier also served as a Pvt. with the 31st Louisiana Infantry-Co. C. Enlisted: 5/14/1862 at Delhi, LA. Rolls for 5/14/1862 through 2/1863: Present. Federal Rolls of Prisoners of War: Captured and paroled at Vicksburg, MS on 7/4/1863. Reported in camp for Exchange at Vienna, LA on 3/29/1864.

Brown, Joseph F.—Pvt.—Enlisted: 9/21/1861 at Richmond, VA. Rolls for 11/1861 through 12/1861: Deceased.

Bullard, William L.—Pvt.—Enlisted: 9/21/1861 at Richmond, VA. Rolls for 11/1861 through 12/1861: Recruit, discharged on Surgeon's Certificate of Disability. Soldier also served as a Pvt. with the 25th Louisiana Infantry-Co. B. Enlisted: 3/29/1862 at Warsaw, LA. Rolls for 5/1862 through 6/1862: Present. Rolls for 11/1862 through 12/1862: Killed at the Battle of Murfreesboro, TN.

Carroll, Francis—Pvt.—Enlisted: 4/14/1862 at Winnsboro, LA. Rolls for 5/1862 through 6/1862: Absent, wounded at the Battle of Secessionville, S.C. on 6/16/1862 and in hospital at Charleston, S.C. Rolls for 9/1862 through 10/1862: Absent on sick furlough. Rolls for 11/1862 through 2/1863: Absent on sick furlough in Louisiana.

Cathey, James B. — Pvt. — Enlisted: 8/8/1861 at Winnsboro, LA. Rolls for 8/8/1861 through 6/1862: Present. Rolls for 9/1862 through 2/1863: Absent, sick at Augusta, GA. Rolls for 8/31/1864 through 4/1865: Present. Rolls of Prisoners of War, C.S.A: Surrendered at Citronelle, AL on 5/4/1865; Paroled at Meridian, MS on 5/10/1865. *Residence:* Winnsboro, Franklin Parish, LA.

Cathey, John W. — Pvt. — Enlisted: 8/8/1861 at Winnsboro, LA. Rolls for 8/8/1861 through 12/1862: Present. Rolls for 1/1863 through 2/1863: Absent, sick in hospital at Savannah, GA. On Floyd House and Ocmulgee Hospital Register, Macon, GA: Admitted on 10/19/1863 due to Debility; Released from hospital on 10/19/1863.

Chandler, M.M. — Pvt. — Enlisted: 9/25/1862 at Winnsboro, LA. Rolls for 9/25/1862 through 2/1863: Present. *Born:* 5/8/1831. *Died:* 4/24/1892. *Buried:* Douglas Cemetery located on the Ruston/Sibley Hwy. at Lincoln Parish, LA.

Choat, William Franklin — Pvt. — Enlisted: 8/8/1861 at Winnsboro, LA. Rolls for 8/8/1861 through 2/1863: Present. *Born:* 1842 at Franklin Parish, LA to Isaac W. Choat and Catherine McAlister. *Married:* Samantha Ann Green Thomason on 6/29/1864 at Franklin Parish, LA. (She was the widow of John D. Thomason, who was killed in battle during the war) *Children:* 2 Sons-Isaac "Ike" Lewis, William Thomas and 1 Daughter: Henrietta Ann "Annie."

William Franklin Choat (courtesy of Shawn Choat Martin).

Connor, M. — Pvt. — Enlisted: 12/31/1862 at Savannah, GA. Rolls for 11/1862 through 12/1862: Present, substitution for E.W. Whatley. Rolls for 1/1863 through 2/1863: Absent without leave.

Costley, Benjamin L. (aka Castin) — Pvt. — Enlisted: 8/8/1861 at Winnsboro, LA. Rolls for 8/8/1861 through 2/1863: Present.

Crane, Patrick Huston — Pvt. — Enlisted: 2/27/1862 at Winnsboro, LA. Rolls for 2/27/1862 through 2/1863: Present. Federal Rolls of Prisoners of War: Captured at the Battle of Missionary Ridge, TN on 11/25/1863; Received at the U.S. Military Prison, Louisville, KY from Nashville, TN on 12/5/1863. Forwarded to Rock Island Barracks, IL on 12/6/1863; Enlisted in the U.S. Army for frontier service on 10/6/1864. Rolls of Prisoners of War, C.S.A: Surrendered at Citronelle, AL on 5/4/1865; Paroled at Meridian, MS on 5/10/1865. *Residence:* Winnsboro, Franklin Parish, LA.

Crane, William H.A. (aka W.A.H.) — Pvt. — Enlisted: 8/8/1861 at Winnsboro, LA. Rolls for 8/8/1861 through 12/1862: Present. Rolls for 1/1863 through 2/1863: Absent, in prison at Savannah, GA. On Register of Floyd House and Ocmulgee Hospital, Macon, GA: Admitted on 9/27/1863. Rolls for 8/1864 through 4/1865: Present.

Daniels, ? — Pvt. — Enlisted: 4/18/1865 at Meridian, MS. Rolls for 3/1865 through 4/1865: Absent without leave since 4/24/1865.

Davidson, William — Pvt. — Enlisted: 8/8/1861 at Winnsboro, LA. Rolls for 11/1861 through 12/1861: Discharged on Surgeon's Certificate of Disability.

Davis, M. — Pvt. — Enlisted: 8/9/1861 at Carroll Parish, LA. Rolls for 8/9/1861 through 8/31/1861: Present. Regimental Return for 9/1862: In barracks at Savannah, GA.

Deal, Andrew Jackson — Pvt. — Enlisted: 8/8/1861 at Winnsboro, LA. Rolls for 8/8/1861 through 2/1863: Present. Rolls for 8/31/1864 through 2/28/1865: Present, taken Prisoner of War at the Battle of Chickamauga, GA on 9/19/1863. Rolls for 3/1865 through 4/1865: Absent, wounded on 4/4/1865 at Spanish Fort, AL and hospitalized. Name on Federal Register of Sick and Wounded Prisoners of War at City Hospital, Mobile, AL. Rolls of Prisoners of War, C.S.A: Surrendered at Citronelle, AL on 5/4/1865; Paroled at Mobile, AL on 5/11/1865. *Residence:* Leak County, MS. *Wounded:* Yes, 2 times at Spanish Fort, AL-Shell fragment in left arm resulting in amputation and right cheek by a spent minié ball resulting in partial facial paralysis and partial blindness in right eye. *Born:* 1840 at Dale County, AL. *Married:* Yes. *Children:* 4–2 Sons and 2 Daughters. *Wife's Age:* 54 as of 1898. *Occupation:* Farmer. *Residences:* Union Parish and Lincoln Parish, LA since 1893. Confederate Pension Application dated 12/7/1898 on file at the Louisiana State

Archives-Microfilm Reel: CP1.37-Microdex 1-Sequence 17-Target Card: Deal, Andrew J.-Parish: Lincoln-4 Pages.

Dorman, William L. (aka Dowman, Darman, W.D.) — Pvt. — Enlisted: 9/9/1861 at Richmond, VA. Rolls for 9/9/1861 through 4/1862: Present. Rolls for 5/1862 through 6/1862: Absent, sick in hospital at Charleston, S.C. Rolls for 9/1862 through 12/1862: Present. Rolls for 1/1863 through 2/1863: Absent, in prison at Savannah, GA. Federal Rolls of Prisoners of War: Captured at the Battle of Missionary Ridge, TN on 11/25/1863; Received at the U.S. Military Prison, Louisville, KY from Nashville, TN on 12/5/1863. Forwarded to Rock Island Barracks, IL on 12/9/1863; Enlisted in the U.S. Army for frontier service on 10/6/1864. Rolls for 8/31/1864 through 4/1865: Absent, taken Prisoner of War on 11/25/1863.

Drew, Michael (aka Dreer) — Pvt. — Enlisted: 8/8/1861 at Winnsboro, LA. Rolls for 8/8/1861 through 6/1862: Present. Regimental Return for 8/1862: Under confinement at Savannah, GA. Rolls for 9/1862 through 2/1863: Present. Federal Rolls of Prisoners of War: Captured near the Battle of Chickamauga, GA on 9/19/1863; Forwarded to the U.S. Military Prison, Louisville, KY from Camp Douglas, IL on 10/2/1863. Discharged from Camp Douglas, IL on 6/14/1865. *Residence:* Franklin Parish, LA.

Elliott, D. Wansley — Pvt. — Enlisted: 8/8/1861 at Winnsboro, LA. Rolls for 8/8/1861 through 8/31/1861: Present. Rolls for 11/1861 through 12/1861: Present, on detached service at the date of last muster. Rolls for 1/1862 through 4/1865: Present. Rolls of Prisoners of War, C.S.A: Surrendered at Citronelle, AL on 5/4/1865; Paroled at Meridian, MS on 5/10/1865. *Residence:* Winnsboro, Franklin Parish, LA. Soldier also served as a Pvt. with the Louisiana Pelican Infantry Regiment-Co. G.

Elliott, Tavnor H. — Pvt. — Enlisted: 8/8/1861 at Winnsboro, LA. Rolls for 8/8/1861 through 8/31/1861: Present. Rolls for 11/1861 through 12/1861: Discharged on Surgeon's Certificate of Disability.

Etier, John — Pvt. — Enlisted: 8/8/1861 at Winnsboro, LA. Rolls for 8/8/1861 through 8/31/1861: Present. Rolls for 11/1861 through 12/1861: Deceased. *Born:* 1845. *Died:* 10/17/1861. *Buried:* Hollywood Cemetery located at the corner of Idlewild St. and Cherry St. at Richmond, Henrico County, VA; Enter the gate from Albemarle St. and bear right to the Confederate Section.

Fife, B.P. — Pvt. — Enlisted: 4/14/1862 at Winnsboro, LA. Rolls for 4/14/1862 through 2/1863: Present. *Died:* 9/3/1863. *Buried:* Clarke/Quitman Memorial Confederate Cemetery located on Hwy. 45, 1 mile south of Quitman, Clarke County, MS.

Fife, John Mayfield — Pvt. — Enlisted: 8/8/1861 at Winnsboro, LA. Rolls for 8/8/1861 through 2/1862: Present. Rolls for 3/1862 through 4/1862: Discharged on Surgeon's Certificate of Disability on 4/11/1862 and Final Statement given. *Born:* 9/9/1833 at Claiborne County, MS. *Parents:* John Mayfield Fife, Sr. and Emilla Brocus. *Occupations:* Farmer and Rancher in Texas and Louisiana. *Died:* Franklin Parish, LA.

Fife, R.C. — Pvt. — Enlisted: 4/14/1862 at Winnsboro, LA. Rolls for 4/14/1862 through 10/1862: Present. Rolls for 11/1862 through 2/1863: Absent without leave.

Fife, Saxton Shaw — Pvt. — Enlisted: 4/14/1862 at Winnsboro, LA. Rolls for 4/14/1862 through 2/1863: Present. *Born:* 1/4/1836 at Claiborne County, MS. *Parents:* John Mayfield Fife, Sr. and Emilla Brocus. *Died:* 6/15/1922 at Pattison, Claiborne County, MS. *Buried:* Hendrick Family Cemetery located at Claiborne County, MS.

Fife, W. — Pvt. — Enlisted: 4/14/1862 at Winnsboro, LA. Rolls for 4/14/1862 through 2/1863: Present.

Flynn, Michael (aka Flinn) — Pvt. — Enlisted: 6/4/1861 at Monroe, LA. Rolls for 6/4/1861 through 2/1862: Present. Rolls for 3/1862 through 4/1862: Absent, sick at hospital in Augusta, GA. Rolls for 5/1862 through 6/1862: Present. Rolls for 1/1864 through 2/1864: Present. Rolls for 8/31/1864 through 4/1865: Absent, sick in hospital at Lagrange, GA.

Flynn, George L. — Pvt. — Enlisted: 8/8/1861 at Winnsboro, LA. Rolls for 8/8/1861 through 8/31/1861: Present. Rolls for 11/1861 through 12/1861: Discharged on Surgeon's Certificate of Disability.

D. Wansley Elliott (courtesy of Robert "Bob" Archibald).

Haibrook, Allen M. (aka Halbrook) — Pvt. — Enlisted: 8/8/1861 at Winnsboro, LA. Rolls for 11/1861 through 12/1861: Discharged on Surgeon's Certificate of Disability.

Hall, William F. — Pvt./Musician — (See Field and Staff)

Hampton, Wade — Pvt. — Enlisted: 8/8/1861 at Winnsboro, LA. Rolls for 8/8/1861 through 2/1863: Present.

Hanson, Elbert M. (aka Hensen, E.W.) — Pvt. — Enlisted: 8/8/1861 at Winnsboro, LA. Rolls for 8/8/1861 through 2/1863: Present. Rolls for 8/1864 through 4/1865: Absent, Prisoner of War since 9/19/1863. Federal Rolls of Prisoners of War: Captured at the Battle of Chickamauga, GA on 9/20/1863; Forwarded to the U.S. Military Prison, Louisville, KY from Nashville, TN on 10/1/1863. Transferred to Camp Douglas, IL on 10/4/1863; Paroled at Camp Douglas, IL in 1865. Sent to City Point, VA for Exchange on 3/14/1865; Exchanged at Boulware and Cox Wharf, James River, VA on 3/18 – 21/1865.

Herlong, George W. (aka Herling) — Pvt. — Enlisted: 8/8/1861 at Winnsboro, LA. Rolls for 8/8/1861 through 6/1862: Present. Rolls for 9/1862 through 2/1863: Absent, on detached service at Savannah, GA since 10/6/1862. Rolls for 8/1864 through 2/1865: Present. Rolls for 3/1865 through 4/1865: Absent, sick in hospital at Enterprise, MS. Rolls of Prisoners of War, C.S.A: Surrendered at Citronelle, AL on 5/4/1865; Paroled at Meridian, MS on 5/10/1865. *Residence:* Jefferson County, MS. *Born:* 4/8/1838. *Died:* 11/28/1904. *Buried:* Hazelhurst City Cemetery located at Hazelhurst, Copiah County, MS. Confederate Widows Pension Application dated 1916 on file at the Mississippi Dept. of Archives and History-Target Card: Herlong, Emily L.-County: Copiah.

Herrin, David J. (aka D.F.) — Pvt. — Enlisted: 8/8/1861 at Winnsboro, LA. Rolls for 11/1861 through 12/1861: Present, on detached service at date of last muster. Rolls for 1/1862 through 2/1862: Discharged on Surgeon's Certificate of Disability.

Hicks, Elias A. (aka Hix) — Pvt. — Enlisted: 2/28/1862 at Winnsboro, LA. Rolls for 2/28/1862 through 2/1863: Present.

Hill, Benjamin — Pvt. — Enlisted: 8/8/1861 at Winnsboro, LA. Rolls for 8/8/1861 through 6/1862: Present. Rolls for 9/1862 through 10/1862: Absent, in prison at Oglethorpe Barracks, Savannah, GA. Rolls for 11/1862 through 2/1863: Present.

Hindman, Charles M. — Pvt. — Enlisted: 8/8/1861 at Winnsboro, LA. Rolls for 8/8/1861 through 6/1862: Present. Rolls for 9/1862 through 10/1862: Present, detached on Provost Guard. Rolls for 11/1862 through 2/1863: Present. Rolls for 8/1864 through 4/1865: Absent, Prisoner of War since 11/25/1863. Federal Rolls of Prisoners of War: Captured at the Battle of Missionary Ridge, TN on 11/25/1863; Sent from Nashville, TN to the U.S. Military Prison, Louisville, KY on 12/6/1863. Received at Rock Island Barracks, IL on 12/9/1863; Enlisted in the U.S. Army for frontier service on 10/31/1864.

Jacks, James H. — Pvt. — Enlisted: 8/8/1861 at Winnsboro, LA. Rolls for 8/8/1861 through 12/31/1861: Discharged due to disability on 8/30/1862.

Jordan, W.H. — Pvt. — Enlisted: 8/8/1861 at Winnsboro, LA. Rolls for 8/8/1861 through 2/1863: Present. Soldier also served as a Sgt. with the 8th Louisiana Cavalry-Co. C. Rolls of Prisoners of War, C.S.A: Surrendered at New Orleans, LA on 5/26/1865; Paroled at Natchitoches, LA on 6/9/1865. *Residence:* DeSoto Parish, LA.

Lassiter, Irvin — Pvt. — Enlisted: 8/8/1861 at Winnsboro, LA. Rolls for 8/8/1861 through 8/31/1861: Present. Rolls for 11/1861 through 12/1861: Deceased.

Lee, R.A. — Pvt. — Enlisted: 9/21/1861 at Richmond, VA. Rolls for 11/1861 through 12/1861: Deceased.

Lenard, Henry (aka Leonard, Hugh, High) — Pvt. — Enlisted: 8/8/1861 at Winnsboro, LA. Rolls for 8/8/1861 through 2/1863: Present. Rolls for 8/31/1864 through 4/1865: Present; Prisoner of War since 11/25/1863. Federal Rolls of Prisoners of War: Captured near the Battle of Missionary Ridge, TN on 11/25/1863; Received at the U.S. Military Prison, Louisville, KY from Nashville, TN on 12/6/1863. Forwarded to Rock Island Barracks, IL on 12/9/1863; Paroled at Rock Island Barracks, IL and transferred for Exchange on 3/6/1865. Received and Exchanged at Boulware and Cox Wharf, James River, VA on 3/11–12/1865.

McDonald, William B. — Pvt. — Enlisted: 8/8/1861 at Winnsboro, LA. Rolls for 8/8/1861 through 8/31/1861: Present. Rolls for 11/1861 through 12/1861: Discharged on Surgeon's Certificate of Disability. *Born:* 1/20/1845. *Died:* 5/4/1882. *Buried:* McDonald Family Cemetery located on the Wiggers family property off Buie Loop Rd. at Fort Necessity, Franklin Parish, LA.

McDougal, Anguish — Pvt. — Enlisted: 8/8/1861 at Winnsboro, LA. Rolls for 8/8/1861 through 12/1862: Present. Rolls for 1/1863 through 2/1863: Absent on sick furlough. Rolls for 8/1864 through 4/1865: Absent, taken Prisoner of War at the Battle of Missionary Ridge, TN on 11/25/1863.

McGinnis, Patrick (aka Maginis, McGennis, Peter, B.) — Pvt. — Enlisted: 9/21/1861 or 10/2/1861 at Richmond, VA. Rolls for 11/1861 through 12/1862: Present. On C.S.A. General Military Hospital #4 Register, Wilmington, N. C: Admitted on 12/23/1862; Returned to duty on 1/2/1863. Rolls for 1/1863 through 2/1863: Absent on picket duty. On Floyd and Ocmulgee Hospital Register, Macon, GA: Admitted on 10/21/1863. Rolls for 8/1864 through 2/28/1865: Present, detailed on Medical Board by order of Brig. Gen. Randall L. Gibson. Rolls for 3/1865 through 4/1865: Absent on daily duty. Rolls of Prisoners of War, C.S.A: Surrendered at Citronelle, AL on 5/4/1865; Paroled at Meridian, MS on 5/10/1865. *Residence:* Winnsboro, Franklin Parish, LA. Soldier also served as a Pvt. with the Louisiana Pelican Infantry Regiment-Co. G.

Masters, James— Pvt.— Enlisted: 8/8/1861 at Winnsboro, LA. Rolls for 8/8/1861 through 2/1863: Present.

Mathews, Lazarus— Pvt.— Enlisted: 8/8/1861 at Winnsboro, LA. Rolls for 8/8/1861 through 6/1862: Present. Regimental Return for 8/1862: Under confinement at Savannah, GA. Rolls for 9/1862 through 10/1862: Present, detailed on Picket Guard. Rolls for 11/1862 through 12/1862: Transferred to the C.S. Naval Service as a Seaman on 12/15/1862. Federal Rolls of Prisoners of War: Captured on board the C.S.S. Atlanta at Wassaw Sound, GA on 6/17/1863. *Born:* 1839 in Louisiana.

Meharg, John P. (aka Mahearge, Maherge)— Pvt.— Enlisted: 8/6/1861 at Winnsboro, LA. Rolls for 8/6/1861 through 6/1862: Present. Rolls for 9/1862 through 11/1862: Absent, sick at Augusta, GA. Rolls for 8/31/1864 through 10/1/1864: Absent without leave since 8/1/1864.

Meyer, John (aka Mayer, Myer)— Pvt.-(No War Dept. Record)-Soldier also served with the Louisiana Pelican Infantry Regiment. *Born:* 1/28/1826 in France. *Married:* Yes-Wife deceased as of 1911. *Children:* 1-Deceased as of 1906. *Residences:* Franklin Parish, LA since 1857. Confederate Pension Application dated 9/24/1906 on file at the Louisiana State Archives-Microfilm Reel: CP1.97-Microdex 1-Sequence 27-Target Card: Meyer, John-Parish: Franklin-6 Pages.

Miller, Collins— Pvt.— Enlisted: 8/8/1861 at Winnsboro, LA. Rolls for 8/8/1861 through 8/31/1861: Present. Rolls for 11/1861 through 12/1861: Deceased.

Mills, Irvin— Pvt.— Enlisted: 4/14/1862 at Winnsboro, LA. Rolls for 5/1862 through 6/1862: Absent, sick in hospital at Charleston, S.C. Regimental Return for 7/1862: Deceased.

Mills, J.W.— Pvt.— Enlisted: 3/14/1862 at Winnsboro, LA. Rolls for 3/14/1862 through 4/1862: Present.

Mock, Alonzo M. (aka Mauk)— Pvt.— Enlisted: 8/8/1861 at Winnsboro, LA. Rolls for 8/8/1861 through 2/1863: Present. Rolls for 8/31/1864 through 2/28/1865: Absent, missing since the retreat from Tennessee. Federal Rolls of Prisoners of War: Captured near Jonesboro, GA on 8/31/1864; Forwarded to the Provost Marshal, Dept. of the Cumberland for Exchange. Exchanged at Rough and Ready, GA on 9/19–22/1864 by order of Maj. Gen. William T. Sherman, Commanding the Military District of the Mississippi. Federal Rolls of Prisoners of War: Captured at Columbia, TN on 12/24/1864; Forwarded to the U.S. Military Prison, Louisville, KY from Nashville, TN on 1/3/1865. Transferred to Camp Chase, OH on 1/11/1865; Released on the U.S. Oath of Allegiance on 5/13/1865. Description at release-Complexion: dark-Hair: light-Eyes: blue-Height: 5 ft. 7 in.-*Residence:* Franklin Parish, LA. *Born:* 1838 at Franklin Parish, LA. *Married:* Yes-wife deceased as of 1899. *Children:* 1 Daughter. Confederate Pension Application dated 4/5/1899 on file at the Louisiana State Archives-Microfilm Reel: CP1.99-Microdex 2-Sequence 11-Target Card: Mock, Alonzo-Parish: Lincoln-4 Pages.

Montgomery, J.D.— Pvt.— Enlisted: 4/14/1862 at Winnsboro, LA. Rolls for 5/1862 through 6/1862: Wounded at the Battle of Secessionville, S. C on 6/16/1862; Died on 6/21/1862 at Charleston, S.C. *Buried:* Magnolia Cemetery located at Charleston, Charleston District, S.C.

Morris, G.E. (aka G.C., G.W.)— Pvt.— Enlisted: 4/14/1862 at Winnsboro, LA. Rolls for 5/1862 through 6/1862: Absent, sick in hospital at Charleston, S.C. Regimental Return for 7/1862: Sick at Columbia, S.C. Regimental Return for 8/1862: Died in camp on 8/6/1862.

Mounger, John A.— Pvt.— Enlisted: 8/8/1861 at Winnsboro, LA. Rolls for 8/8/1861 through 8/31/1861: Present. Rolls for 11/1861 through 12/1861: Transferred out of the battalion.

Murrays, George C. (aka Murry, Murray, Maurice)— Pvt.— Enlisted: 4/14/1862 at Winnsboro, LA. Rolls for 4/14/1862 through 6/1862: Present. Regimental Return for 8/1862: Sick at Charleston, S.C. Rolls for 9/1862 through 10/1862: Present, detailed on Picket Guard. Rolls for 11/1862 through 12/1862: Absent, sick at Savannah, GA. Rolls for 1/1863 through 2/1863: Absent, on picket duty. Federal Rolls of Prisoners of War: Captured near Jackson, MS on 7/4/1863; Forwarded to Snyder's Bluff, MS on 7/30/1863. Transferred to Camp Morton, IN on 8/7/1863; Released on the U.S. Oath of Allegiance on 9/2/1863.

Nelson, William— Pvt.— Enlisted: 4/14/1862 at Winnsboro, LA. Rolls for 4/14/1862 through 9/1862: Present. Rolls for 11/1862 through 12/1862: Absent, sick at Savannah, GA. Rolls for 1/1863 through 2/1863: Discharged on Surgeon's Certificate of Disability.

Norris, Samuel J.— Pvt.— Enlisted: 8/8/1861 at Winnsboro, LA. Rolls for 8/8/1861 through 8/31/1861: Present. Rolls for 11/1861 through 12/1861: Deceased.

Orr, Peter— Pvt.— Enlisted: 8/8/1861 at Winnsboro,

LA. Rolls for 8/8/1861 through 2/1863: Present. Died from wounds received at the Battle of Chickamauga, GA on 9/19/1863. Placed on the Confederate Roll of Honor for gallantry and good conduct at the Battle of Chickamauga, GA per General Order #131 of the Inspector and Adjutant General's Office, Richmond, VA.

Parker, K.—Pvt.-Rolls of Prisoners of War, C.S.A: Surrendered at Citronelle, AL on 5/4/1865; Paroled at Natchitoches, LA on 6/15/1865. *Residence:* Franklin Parish, LA.

Porter, Rodney (aka Radden)—Pvt.—Enlisted: 8/8/1861 at Winnsboro, LA. Rolls for 8/8/1861 through 2/1862: Present. Rolls for 5/1862 through 6/1862: Absent, wounded at the Battle of Secessionville, S.C. on 6/16/1862 and in the hospital at Columbia, S.C. Rolls for 9/1862 through 2/1863: Present. Rolls for 8/31/1864 through 4/1865: Absent, taken Prisoner of War at the Battle of Chickamauga, GA on 9/19/1863. Federal Rolls of Prisoners of War: Captured near the Battle of Chickamauga, GA on 9/19/1863; Received at the U.S. Military Prison, Louisville, KY on 10/1/1863. Transferred to Camp Douglas, IL on 10/2/1863; Forwarded to New Orleans, LA for Exchange on 5/4/1865. Rolls of Prisoners of War, C.S.A: Transferred to the Commissioner for Exchange on 5/23/1865 from New Orleans, LA by order of Maj. Gen. Edward R.S. Canby.

Ragan, John W.—Pvt.—Enlisted: 8/8/1861 at Winnsboro, LA. Rolls for 8/8/1861 through 2/1862: Present. Rolls for 3/1862 through 4/1862: Absent, sick in hospital at Augusta, GA. Rolls for 5/1862 through 6/1862: Killed at the Battle of Secessionville, S.C. on 6/16/1862.

Ragan, Thomas C.—Pvt.—Enlisted: 8/8/1861 at Winnsboro, LA. Rolls for 8/8/1861 through 8/31/1861: Present. Rolls for 11/1861 through 12/1861: Died on 10/15/1861. *Buried:* Hollywood Cemetery located at Idlewild St. and Cherry St. at Richmond, Henrico County, VA; Enter from Albemarle St. and bear right to the Confederate Section.

Randolph, Benjamin A.—Pvt.—Enlisted: 4/14/1862 at Winnsboro, LA. Rolls for 5/1862 through 6/1862: Absent, sick in hospital at Atlanta, GA. Rolls for 9/1862 through 10/1862: Present. Rolls for 11/1862 through 12/1862: Absent, sick at Savannah, GA. Rolls for 1/1863 through 2/1863: Present. Rolls for 8/31/1864 through 4/1865: Present. Roll of Prisoners of War, C.S.A: Surrendered at Citronelle, AL on 5/4/1865; Paroled at Meridian, MS on 5/10/1865. *Residence:* Winnsboro, Franklin Parish, LA. Soldier also served as a Pvt. with the Louisiana Pelican Infantry Regiment-Co. G. Confederate Widows Pension Application dated 1916 on file at the Mississippi Dept. of Archives and History-Target Name: Randolph, Massey Haddox-County: Harrison.

Rasberry, Richard J.—Pvt.—Enlisted: 8/8/1861 at Winnsboro, LA. Rolls for 8/8/1861 through 8/31/1861: Present. Rolls for 11/1861 through 12/1861: Discharged on Surgeon's Certificate of Disability. Soldier also served as a Pvt. with the 31st Louisiana Infantry-Co.C. *Born:* 12/5/1837 at Greene County, AL. *Married:* Yes. *Children:* 6–4 Sons and 2 Daughters. *Occupation:* Farmer. *Residences:* Claiborne Parish, Franklin Parish, and Bossier Parish, LA since 1856. Two Confederate Pension Applications dated 5/16/1911 and 10/11/1911 on file at the Louisiana State Archives-Microfilm Reel: CP1.115-Microdex 3-Sequence 10-Target Card: Rasberry, Richard J.-Parish: Claiborne-17 Pages.

Reed, Ira—Pvt.—Enlisted: 8/8/1861 at Winnsboro, LA. Rolls for 8/8/1861 through 12/1861: Present. Rolls for 1/1862 through 2/1862: Discharged on Surgeon's Certificate of Disability.

Riley, John Hampton (aka J.P.)—Pvt.—Enlisted: 8/8/1861 at Winnsboro, LA. Rolls for 8/8/1861 through 2/1863: Present. Rolls for 8/31/1864 through 2/28/1865: Absent, taken Prisoner of War on 8/5/1864. Federal Rolls of Prisoners of War: Captured near Atlanta, GA on 8/5/1864; Received at the U.S. Military Prison, Louisville, KY from Nashville, TN on 8/12/1864. Forwarded to Camp Chase, OH on 8/13/1864; Paroled at Camp Chase, OH on 2/12/1865. Exchanged at Boulware and Cox Wharf, James River, VA on 2/20–21/1865. Rolls for 3/1865 through 4/1865: Absent on furlough of Exchange in Louisiana. *Born:* 6/15/1844 at County Tipperary, Ireland. Emigrated to the U.S. in 1851 at age 7 to live with his uncle, Patrick E. Gilfoil, at Omega, LA. Confederate Pension Application dated 6/23/1921 on file at the Louisiana State Archives-Microfilm Reel: CP1.118-Microdex 3-Sequence 28-Target Card: Riley, John H.-Parish: Madison-5 Pages.

Roach, Anthony (aka Andrew)—Pvt.—Enlisted: 9/21/1861 at Richmond, LA. Rolls for 9/21/1861 through 2/1863: Present. Rolls for 8/31/1864 through 4/30/1865: Absent, taken Prisoner of War on 9/19/1863. Federal Rolls of Prisoners of War: Captured at the Battle of Chickamauga, GA on 9/19/1863; Forwarded to the U.S. Military Prison, Louisville, KY on 10/1/1863. Transferred to Camp Douglas, IL on 10/2/1863; Died on 12/16/1863. *Buried:* Oakwoods Cemetery Confederate Mound located at Chicago, Cook County, IL.

Roberts, Robert—Pvt.—Enlisted: 8/8/1861 at Winnsboro, LA. Rolls for 8/8/1861 through 2/1863: Present. Rolls for 8/31/1864 through 2/28/1865: Taken Prisoner of War on 11/25/1863. Federal Rolls of Prisoners of War: Captured at the Battle of Missionary Ridge, TN on 11/25/1863; Received at the U.S. Military Prison, Louisville, KY from Nashville, TN on 12/7/1863. Forwarded to Rock Island Barracks, IL on 12/11/1863; Paroled at Rock Island Barracks, IL and transferred for Exchange on 3/6/1865. Exchanged at Boulware and Cox Wharf, James River, VA on 3/10–12/1865. Rolls for 3/1865 through 4/1865: Absent on furlough due to not having been Exchanged.

Savage, Moses—Pvt.-Federal Rolls of Prisoners of War: Captured near Atlanta, GA on 8/3/1864; Forwarded to Camp Chase, OH from the U.S. Military Prison, Louisville, KY on 8/13/1864.

Scott, John W.—Pvt.—Enlisted: 8/8/1861 at Winnsboro, LA. Rolls for 8/8/1861 through 2/1865: Present. On Mobile, AL Hospital Register: Admitted on 3/17/1865. Rolls for 3/1865 through 4/1865: Absent, sick in hospital at Lauderdale, MS. Rolls of Prisoners of War of Unattached Men, C.S.A: Surrendered at Citronelle, AL on 5/4/1865; Paroled at Jackson, MS on 5/19/1865. *Residence:* Franklin Parish, LA. *Born:* 10/4/1834. *Died:* 1/20/1868. *Buried:* Scott Cemetery located on Hwy. 129 at Monterey, Concordia Parish, LA.

Shackleford, Andrew J.—Pvt.—Enlisted: 8/8/1861 at Winnsboro, LA. Rolls for 8/8/1861 through 8/31/1861: Present. Rolls for 11/1861 through 12/1861: Died on 11/6/1861. *Buried:* Hollywood Cemetery located at the corner of Idlewild St. and Cherry St. at Richmond, Henrico County, VA; Enter the gate from Albemarle St. and bear right to the Confederate Section.

Sherrouse, Charles M. (aka Shereuse)—Pvt.—Enlisted: 3/18/1863 at Savannah, GA. Rolls for 8/31/1864 through 2/28/1865: Absent without leave since 10/25/1864. Rolls of Prisoners of War of Men Belonging to Commands East of the Mississippi River, C.S.A: Surrendered at Citronelle, AL on 5/4/1865; Paroled at Natchitoches, LA on 6/6/1865. *Residence:* Franklin Parish, LA. *Born:* 10/2/1845 at Franklin Parish, LA. *Married:* Yes. *Children:* 2 Daughters. *Occupation:* Traveling Salesman/Agent. *Wife's Age:* 68 as of 1911. He was a resident of the Beauvoir Confederate Soldier's Home at Biloxi, Harrison County, MS. *Residences:* Louisiana and Jackson County, MS. Confederate Pension Application dated 8/18/1911 on file at the Louisiana State Archives-Microfilm Reel: CP1.126-Microdex 4-Sequence 5-Target Card: Sherrouse, C.M.-Parish: Orleans-10 Pages. Also a Confederate Pension Application dated 1920 on file at the Mississippi Dept. of Archives and History-Target Card: Sherrouse, Charles M.-County: Jackson.

Smith, William J.—Pvt.—Enlisted: 8/8/1861 at Winnsboro, LA. Rolls for 8/8/1861 through 8/31/1861: Present. Rolls for 11/1861 through 12/1861: Present, on detached service. Rolls for 1/1862 through 10/1862: Present. Rolls for 11/1862 through 12/1862: Transferred to the C.S. Naval Service on 12/15/1862 for duty on the C.S.S. Atlanta.

Smith, William R.—Pvt.—Enlisted: 8/8/1861 at Winnsboro, LA. Rolls for 8/8/1861 through 8/31/1861: Present. Rolls for 11/1861 through 12/1861: Present, on detached service. Rolls for 1/1862 through 4/1862: Discharged on Surgeon's Certificate of Disability on 3/10/1862 and Final Statement given. *Born:* 4/15/1820. *Died:* 7/5/1908. *Buried:* Concord Methodist Church Cemetery located on Hwy. 4, 15 miles east of Jonesboro, Jackson Parish, LA.

Spurlock, Allen—Pvt.-Federal Rolls of Prisoners of War: Captured near Atlanta, GA on 8/3/1864; Received at the U.S. Military Prison, Louisville, Ky. Forwarded to Camp Chase, OH on 8/13/1864.

Taylor, John C.—Pvt.—Enlisted: 8/8/1861 at Winnsboro, LA. Rolls for 8/8/1861 through 8/31/1861: Present. Rolls for 11/1861 through 12/1861: Present, on detached service at the date of last muster. Rolls for 1/1862 through 2/1862: Present. Rolls for 3/1862 through 4/1862: Absent, sick in hospital at Augusta, GA. Rolls for 5/1862 through 10/1862: Present. Rolls for 11/1862 through 12/1862: Transferred to the C.S. Naval Service as a Landsman on 12/15/1862 for duty on the C.S.S. Savannah, C.S.S. Richmond and the C.S.S. Atlanta. Federal Rolls of Prisoners of War: Captured on board the C.S.S. Atlanta at Wassaw Sound, GA on 6/17/1863. *Wounded:* No. *Born:* 10/4/1835 at Dallas County, AL. *Married:* Mary __ on 11/17/1866 about 7 miles from Mansfield, DeSoto Parish, LA. *Children:* 6–3 Sons and 3 Daughters. *Residence:* DeSoto Parish, LA since 1867. *Died:* 9/7/1908 at DeSoto Parish, LA due to Consumption. *Buried:* Grove Hill Cemetery located in Ward 7, DeSoto Parish, LA. *Wife's Age:* 66 as of 1909. *Wife's Residences:* Louisiana for life. Confederate Pension Application dated 8/29/1907 on file at the Louisiana State Archives-Microfilm Reel: CP1.135-Microdex 4-Sequence 26-Target Card: Taylor, John C.-Parish: DeSoto-6 Pages. Also a Confederate Widows Pension Application dated 4/9/1909 on file-Microfilm Reel: CP1.135-Microdex 4-Sequence 42-Target Card: Taylor, Mary-Parish: DeSoto-2 Pages.

Thomason, Hamilton—Pvt.—Enlisted: 10/2/1861 at Richmond, VA. Rolls for 11/1861 through 12/1861: Deceased. *Father:* Elisha Thomason.

Waller, Archibald P.—Pvt.—Enlisted: 8/8/1861 at Richmond, LA or 8/9/1861 at DeSoto Parish, LA. Rolls for 8/8/1861 through 8/31/1861: Present. Rolls for 11/1861 through 12/1861: Present, on detached service at the date of last muster. Rolls for 1/1862 through 10/1862: Present. Rolls for 11/1862 through 12/1862: Transferred to the C.S. Naval Service as a Seaman on 12/15/1862 for duty on the C.S.S. Chicora for 1863/1864.

Ward, Isaac M.—Pvt.—Enlisted: 8/8/1861 at Winnsboro, LA. Rolls for 8/8/1861 through 2/1863: Present.

Washburn, Winston A.—Pvt.—Enlisted: 8/8/1861 at Winnsboro, LA or 8/9/1861 at DeSoto Parish, LA. Rolls for 8/8/1861 through 8/31/1861: Present. Rolls for 11/1861 through 12/1861: Deceased.

Wheat, Moses—Pvt./Hospital Steward—(See Field and Staff)

White, Alexander—Pvt.—Enlisted: 8/8/1861 at

Winnsboro, LA. Rolls for 8/8/1861 through 8/31/1861: Present. Rolls for 11/1861 through 12/1861: Discharged on Surgeon's Certificate of Disability.

Whitney, John M.—Pvt.—Enlisted: 8/8/1861 at Winnsboro, LA. Rolls for 8/8/1861 through 8/31/1861: Present. Rolls for 11/1861 through 12/1861: Discharged on Surgeon's Certificate of Disability.

Williams, Ezra F.—Pvt.—Enlisted: 8/8/1861 at Winnsboro, LA. Rolls for 8/8/1861 through 8/31/1861: Present. Rolls for 11/1861 through 12/1861: Discharged on Surgeon's Certificate of Disability.

Williams, Matthew—Pvt.—Enlisted: 8/8/1861 at Winnsboro, LA. Rolls for 8/8/1861 through 8/31/1861: Present. Rolls for 11/1861 through 12/1861: Deceased.

Wilson, A.J.—Pvt.—Enlisted: 8/8/1861 at Winnsboro, LA. Rolls for 8/8/1861 through 2/1862: Present. Rolls for 3/1862 through 4/1862: Absent without leave. Record of Events: Pvt. A.J. Wilson received recruiting papers to raise a company on 2/5/1862 and has not been heard of since his departure on 3/20/1862. Company C was stationed on Skidway Island, Camp Adams, S. C; When heard of last he was at Stevenson, TN since last muster in 1862. Company C had moved twice: 1st move on 3/17/1862 from Camp Zelia, Skidway Island S.C. to the Isle of Hope, S.C.-2nd move on 4/21/1862 from the Isle of Hope, S.C. to Camp Marion, S.C. Total Distance: 13 miles. Rolls for 5/1862 through 6/1862: Absent without leave. Regimental Return for 8/1862: Absent without leave in Tennessee. On C.S.A. General Hospital Register, Shreveport, LA: Admitted on 3/3/1865; Returned to duty on 3/19/1865.

Womack, W.H.—Pvt.—Enlisted:8/8/1861 at Winnsboro, LA. Rolls for 8/8/1861 through 8/31/1861: Present. Rolls for 11/1861 through 12/1861: Discharged on Surgeon's Certificate of Disability.

Young, James R.—Pvt.—Enlisted: 8/8/1861 at Winnsboro, LA. Rolls for 8/8/1861 through 8/31/1861: Present. Rolls for 11/1861 through 12/1861: Discharged on Surgeon's Certificate of Disability.

COMPANY D: "CARROLL REBELS," CARROLL PARISH

Captain

Coleman, Edward L.—Capt.—Enlisted: 8/9/1861 at Carroll Parish, LA; Elected Capt. same day. Rolls for 8/9/1861 through 6/1862: Present. Rolls for 9/1862 through 10/1862: Absent in Savannah, GA on Court Martial. Rolls for 1/1863 through 2/1863: Present. On undated Roster: Killed in action at the Battle of Chickamauga, GA on 9/18/1863; Capt. Successor: L.C. Stevens. *Buried:* Confederate Cemetery located at Marietta, Cobb County, GA. *Parents:* Colonel J.B. Coleman and Catherine Ellis Coleman of Port Gibson, MS.

Stowers, Louis Edward (aka **Stoners, Stowen, Stevens, Lewis**)—1st Lt./Capt.—Enlisted: 8/9/1861 at Carroll Parish, LA. Rolls for 8/9/1861 through 12/1861: Present. Rolls for 1/1862 through 2/1862: Present or absent not stated. Rolls for 3/1862 through 2/1863: Present. Federal Rolls of Prisoners of War: Captured at the Battle of Missionary Ridge, TN on 11/25/1863; Transferred to Nashville, TN from the General Field Hospital, Bridgeport, AL on 12/11/1863. Received at the U.S. Military Prison, Louisville, KY from Nashville, TN on 12/20/1863; Transferred to Fort Delaware, DE on 1/15/1864; Paroled at Fort Delaware, DE on 10/6/1864. Forwarded to Point Lookout, MD on 10/11/1864; Exchanged at Boulware and Cox Wharf, James River, VA on 10/15/1864. Rolls for 10/15/1864 through 2/28/1865: Present. Rolls for 3/1865 through 4/1865: Absent, captured at Spanish Fort, AL on 4/8/1865. Federal Rolls of Prisoners of War: Captured at Spanish Fort, AL on 4/8/1865; Received at Ship Island, MS on 4/10/1865. Forwarded to New Orleans, LA on 4/30/1865; Exchanged on 5/1/1865. Official Rolls of Paroled Officers, C.S.A: Surrendered at Citronelle, AL on 5/4/1865; Paroled at Jackson, MS on 5/11/1865. *Residence:* Lake Providence, East Carroll Parish, LA. *Born:* 8/31/1836. *Died:* 12/19/1872. *Buried:* Wintergreen Cemetery located at Port Gibson, Claiborne County, MS.

Lieutenant

Anderson, R.—Jr. 2nd Lt.—Enlisted: 8/9/1861 at Carroll Parish, LA. Rolls for 8/9/1861 through 8/31/1861: Present. On undated Roster: Elected Jr. 2nd Lt. on 8/9/1861, promoted to 2nd Lt. in 10/1861. Resigned in 10/1861. Jr. 2nd Lt. Successor: J.W. McClendon.

Brown, J.R.—Pvt./2nd Lt.—Enlisted: 8/9/1861 at Carroll Parish, LA. Rolls for 8/9/1861 through 4/1864: Present. Rolls for 5/1864 through 6/1864: Present, promoted to 2nd Lt. on 5/6/1864. Rolls for 8/31/1864 through 2/28/1865: Absent on leave. Rolls for 3/1865 through 4/1865: Present. Official Rolls of Paroled Officers, C.S.A: Surrendered at Citronelle, AL on 5/4/1865; Paroled at Meridian, MS on 5/11/1865.

Lott, Arthur J. (aka **Litt**)—2nd Lt.—Enlisted: 8/9/1861 at Carroll Parish, LA; Elected 2nd Lt. same day. Rolls for 8/9/1861 through 8/31/1861: Absent. Resigned in 10/1861. 2nd Lt. Successor: R. Anderson. Soldier also served as a Capt. with the independent Louisiana cavalry company Carroll Dragoons. On List dated Parish of Carroll, LA: Enlisted 3/19/1862 in the C.S. Army for the duration of the war or term of service; $50.00 Bounty paid.

McClendon, J.W. (aka McClenden, W.) — Pvt./2nd Lt./1st Lt.— Enlisted: 8/9/1861 at Carroll Parish, LA. Rolls for 8/1861 through 12/1861: Present, promoted to 2nd Lt. in 11/1861. Rolls for 1/1862 through 2/1862: Present or absent not stated. Rolls for 3/1862 through 4/1862: Absent on recruiting furlough. Rolls for 5/1862 through 6/1862: Present. Regimental Returns for 7/1862 and 8/1862: Present or absent not stated. Rolls for 9/1862 through 4/1864: Present, dropped from Rolls on 5/1/1864 due to prolonged absence.

Middleton, Jonathan C.— Pvt./Sgt. Major/Jr. 2nd Lt.—(See Field and Staff)

Sergeant

Breazeale, John James (aka Brazile, Brazeale, Braziel, Brazle) — 3rd Sgt./Pvt.— Enlisted: 8/9/1861 at Carroll Parish, LA. Rolls for 8/9/1861 through 12/1862: Present. Rolls for 1/1863 through 2/1863: Present, reduced to Pvt. at his own request on 1/9/1863. Rolls for 3/1863 through 8/1863: Present. Federal Rolls of Prisoners of War: Captured at the Battle of Missionary Ridge, TN on 11/25/1863; Sent to the U.S. Military Prison, Louisville, KY on 12/7/1863 from Nashville, TN. Transferred to Rock Island Barracks, IL on 12/8/1863; Hospitalized at Rock Island Barracks, IL from 3/1864 through 8/1864. Enlisted in the U.S. Army for frontier service on 10/6/1864.

Brown, Charles— Cpl./4th Sgt./Pvt.— Enlisted: 8/9/1861 at Carroll Parish, LA. Rolls for 8/9/1861 through 12/1862: Present. Rolls for 1/1863 through 2/1863: Present, reduced to Pvt. at his own request on 1/9/1863. Rolls for 10/10/1863 through 4/1865: Absent, sick in hospital at Madison, GA.

Cloman, J.W. (aka Clowman, G.W.)—1st Sgt./Pvt.— Enlisted: 8/9/1861 at Carroll Parish, LA. Rolls for 8/9/1861 through 2/1862: Present. Rolls for 3/1862 through 4/1862: Absent with leave at Savannah, GA. Rolls for 5/1862 through 10/1862: Present. Rolls for 1/1863 through 2/1863: Present, under arrest in camp. Rolls for 12/31/1863 through 4/30/1864: Present. Rolls for 8/31/1864 through 4/1865: Absent, wounded near Atlanta, GA on 7/28/1864 and in hospital at Macon, GA.

Feltenburg, H.— Pvt./Sgt.— Enlisted: 8/9/1861 at Carroll Parish, LA. Rolls for 8/9/1861 through 4/30/1864: Present. Rolls for 8/31/1864 through 4/1865: Absent on furlough since 2/17/1865.

Fox, George D. (aka G.R.) — Sgt./Pvt.— Enlisted: 8/9/1861 at Carroll Parish, LA. Rolls for 8/9/1861 through 2/1863: Present. Federal Rolls of Prisoners of War: Captured near Jackson, MS on 7/4/1863; Received at Snyder's Bluff, MS on 7/30/1863. Forwarded to Camp Morton, IN 8/7/1863; Released on the U.S. Oath of Allegiance from Camp Morton, IN on 5/20/1865 in accordance with the issuance of General Order #85 on 5/8/1865. *Residence:* Alliance, OH. Description at oath-Complexion: dark-Hair: dark-Eyes: dark-Height: 5 ft. 7 in.

Johns, David— Pvt./2nd Cpl./1st Sgt.— Enlisted: 8/9/1861 at Carroll Parish, LA. Rolls for 8/9/1861 through 6/1862: Present. Rolls for 9/1862 through 10/1862: Sick, in hospital at Savannah, GA. Rolls for 1/1863 through 2/1863: Present, promoted to 1st Sgt. from 2nd Cpl. on 12/31/1862. Rolls for 12/31/1862 through 4/30/1864: Absent, wounded at the Battle of Missionary Ridge, TN on 11/25/1863; Sick in hospital at Macon, GA. Rolls for 8/31/1864 through 2/28/1865: Incarcerated in the Georgia State Penitentiary by order of Gen. Joseph E. Johnston. Rolls for 3/1865 through 4/1865: Absent, convicted of manslaughter and sent to the penitentiary.

Mills, Sebron W. (aka Selburn) — 6th Sgt./Pvt.— Enlisted: 8/8/1861 at Carroll Parish, LA. Rolls for 8/8/1861 through 10/1862: Present, reduced to Pvt. at his own request on 1/9/1863. Federal Rolls of Prisoners of War: Captured at Warren County, MS on 7/11/1863; Sent to Memphis, TN on 7/17/1863. Forwarded to Gratiot St. Military Prison, St. Louis, MO on 7/26/1863; Transferred to Camp Morton, IN on 8/26/1863. Received at Camp Morton, IN on 8/27/1863. *Born:* 8/1/1838 at Pike County, GA. *Married:* M.E. O'Neal on 2/14/1866 at Douglas, LA. *Children:* 9–5 Sons and 4 Daughters. *Residence:* Louisiana since 1842. *Died:* 1/18/1919 at Calhoun, LA due to Paralysis. *Buried:* Indian Village Cemetery located 4 miles from Calhoun, Ouachita Parish, LA on Louisiana Hwy. 144. Confederate Pension Application dated 1/18/1912 on file at the Louisiana State Archives-Microfilm Reel: CP1.98-Microdex 3-Sequence 16-Target Card: Mills, S.W.-Parish: Ouachita-6 Pages. Also a Confederate Widows Pension Application dated 2/28/1919 on file-Microfilm Reel: CP1.98-Microdex 3-Sequence 15-Target Card: Mills, Mrs. M.E.-Parish: Ouachita-3 Pages.

Moon, Samuel A.— Pvt./Sgt.— Enlisted: 8/9/1861 at Carroll Parish, LA. Rolls for 8/9/1861 through 6/1862: Present. Rolls for 9/1862 through 10/1862: Absent on picket duty at Savannah, GA. Rolls for 1/1863 through 2/1863: Present. Rolls for 12/31/1863 through 4/30/1864: Absent, sick in hospital at Newman, GA. Rolls for 8/1864 through 2/1865: Absent, sick in hospital at Thompson, GA. Rolls for 3/1865 through 4/1865: Absent, sick in hospital at Opelika, AL. Confederate Pension Application on file at the Georgia Dept. of Archives and History-Name: Moon, Sam A.-County: Monroe.

Rollins, M.B.— Pvt./Sgt.— Enlisted: 8/9/1861 at Carroll Parish, LA. Rolls for 8/9/1861 through 10/1862: Present. *Born:* 1834. *Died:* 12/27/1862. *Buried:* Oakdale Cemetery located at Wilmington, New Hanover County, N.C.

Upshaw, William Elisha— Pvt./Sgt.— Enlisted: 8/9/1861 at Carroll Parish, LA. Rolls for 8/9/1861 through

6/1862: Present. Rolls for 9/1862 through 10/1862: Absent, on picket duty at Savannah, GA. Rolls for 1/1863 through 2/1863: Present, promoted to Sgt. on 1/9/1863. Discharged: 1863. Residence at enlistment: Spearsville, Union Parish, LA. Soldier also served as a Pvt. with the 2nd Louisiana Battalion Heavy Artillery-Co. F. *Born:* 2/29/1833 in Walton County, GA to Richard Upshaw and Rebecca Elder Upshaw. *Grandfather:* Leroy Upshaw, a Revolutionary War veteran who served as a Capt. in the militia of Amherst County, VA. *Siblings:* Pvt. Jonathan W. Upshaw of Co. D. *Married:* Laura Ann Rockett Hunt (*Born:* 6/13/1831-*Died:* 1/13/1867) on 5/9/1864 at Union Parish, AR and Julia Ann Gardner (*Born:* 12/23/1836-*Died:* 11/23/1903) on 2/1/1868. *Religion:* Baptist (Was charged with non-attendance by the Spearsville, LA Baptist Church in 4/1864, but attended in 5/1864 and requested forgiveness) *Died:* 1/8/1882. *Buried:* Spearsville City Cemetery located at Union Parish, LA.

Walker, S.G. — Pvt./4th Sgt./2nd Sgt. — Enlisted: 8/9/1861 at Carroll Parish, LA. Rolls for 8/9/1861 through 2/1863: Present, promoted to 4th Sgt. on 1/9/1863. Rolls for 12/31/1863 through 4/30/1864: Absent on 60 day sick furlough since 3/29/1864. Rolls for 8/31/1864 through 4/1865: Present. Rolls of Prisoners of War, C.S.A: Surrendered at Citronelle, AL on 5/4/1865; Paroled at Meridian, MS on 5/10/1865. *Residences:* DeSoto Parish, LA and Raleigh, N.C. Soldier also served as a 2nd Sgt. with the Louisiana Pelican Infantry Regiment-Co. A.

Ward, Hyram — Sgt. — Enlisted: 8/9/1861 at Carroll Parish, LA. Rolls for 8/9/1861 through 8/31/1861: Present; Remarks: Sick in hospital at Bristol, VA. (Remarks cancelled)

Corporal

Birdsell, A. — 1st Cpl./Pvt. — Enlisted: 8/9/1861 at Carroll Parish, LA. Rolls for 8/9/1861 through 6/1862: Present. Rolls for 9/1862 through 10/1862: Absent, on Picket Duty at Savannah, GA. Rolls for 1/1863 through 2/1863: Present, reduced to Pvt. by his own request on 1/9/1863. Federal Rolls of Prisoners of War: Captured near Jackson, MS in 7/1863; Sent to Snyder's Bluff, MS on 7/30/1863.

Deyo, A.C. — Pvt./4th Cpl. — Enlisted: 8/9/1861 at Carroll Parish, LA. Rolls for 8/9/1861 through 6/1862: Present, appears as 4th Cpl. Rolls for 9/1862 through 4/30/1864: Absent, on detached duty at Savannah, GA since 10/6/1862; Transferred to the Engineer Corps by order of the Secretary of War.

Foreman, George — Cpl./Pvt. — Enlisted: 8/9/1861 at Carroll Parish, LA. Rolls for 8/9/1861 through 4/1862: Present. Rolls for 5/1862 through 6/1862: Absent, sick in hospital at Charleston, S.C. Rolls for 9/1862 through 4/30/1864: Present, detailed as Teamster. Federal Rolls of Prisoners of War: Captured near Marietta, GA on 7/3/1864; Received at the U.S. Military Prison, Louisville, KY from Nashville, TN on 7/13/1864. Transferred to Camp Morton, IN on 7/14/1863; Released on the U.S. Oath of Allegiance on 2/21/1865.

Gilbert, W.F. (aka W.T.) — Pvt./1st Cpl. — Enlisted: 8/9/1861 at Carroll Parish, LA. Rolls for 8/9/1861 through 10/1862: Present. On Register of C.S.A. General Military Hospital #4, Wilmington, N. C: Admitted on 12/27/1862 due to Catarrhus; Returned to duty on 1/2/1863. Rolls for 1/1863 through 2/1863: Present, promoted to 1st Cpl. on 1/9/1863.

Howell, Lewis M. (aka L.H., L.N.) — Pvt./Cpl. — Enlisted: 8/9/1861 at Carroll Parish, LA. Rolls for 8/9/1861 through 4/1862: Present. Rolls for 5/1862 through 6/1862: Absent, sick in hospital at Macon, GA. Rolls for 9/1862 through 10/1862: On Guard Duty around camp. Rolls for 1/1863 through 4/1864: Present. Rolls for 8/1864 through 2/28/1865: Absent, captured near Atlanta, GA on 8/5/1864. Federal Rolls of Prisoners of War: Captured near Atlanta, GA on 8/5/1864; Forwarded to the U.S. Military Prison, Louisville. KY on 8/12/1864. Transferred to Camp Chase, OH on 8/14/1864; Paroled at Camp Chase, OH on 2/12/1865. Exchanged at Boulware and Cox Wharf, James River, VA on 2/20-21/1865. Rolls for 3/1865 through 4/1865: Present. Rolls of Prisoners of War, C.S.A: Surrendered at Citronelle, AL on 5/4/1865; Paroled at Meridian, MS on 5/10/1865. *Residence:* Union Parish, LA.

Martin, W.H. (aka N.H.) — Pvt./Cpl. — Enlisted: 8/9/1861 at Carroll Parish, LA. Rolls for 8/9/1861 through 6/1862: Present. Regimental Return for 8/1862: Absent with leave. Rolls for 1/1863 through 2/1863: Absent in hospital at Savannah, GA. Rolls for 9/1862 through 10/1862: Present, reduced to Pvt. and fined 1 months pay on 8/1/1862 by order of a Battalion Court Martial.

Mealy, J.L. — Pvt./Cpl. — Enlisted: 3/12/1862 at Carroll Parish, LA. Rolls for 3/12/1862 through 6/1862: Present. Regimental Return for 9/1862: On furlough. Rolls for 9/1862 through 10/1862: Absent without leave. Rolls for 1/1863 through 2/1863: Present.

Moultry, Y. (aka Moultrie) — Pvt./Cpl. — Enlisted: 8/9/1861 at Carroll Parish, LA. Rolls for 8/9/1861 through 6/1862: Present. Rolls for 9/1862 through 10/1862: Absent on furlough. Rolls for 1/1863 through 2/1863: Present, promoted to Cpl. on 1/9/1863.

Osbanks, Charles (aka Osback, Osbanks) — Cpl. — Enlisted: 8/9/1861 at Carroll Parish, LA. Rolls for 8/9/1861 through 4/1862: Present. Rolls for 5/1862 through 6/1862: Absent, taken Prisoner of War by the enemy on 6/14/1862 while on picket duty. Regimental Return for 7/1862: Taken Prisoner of War on 6/14/1862 by the enemy. Regimental Return for 8/1862: Absent without leave. Regimental Return for 9/1862: Absent without leave and assumed to be a Deserter.

Rice, Reuben H.—Pvt./Cpl.—Enlisted: 8/9/1861 at Carroll Parish, LA. Rolls for 8/9/1861 through 4/1865: Present. Rolls of Prisoners of War, C.S.A: Surrendered at Citronelle, AL on 5/4/1865; Paroled at Meridian, MS on 5/10/1865. *Residence:* Carroll Parish, LA. *Born:* 11/7/1837. *Died:* 2/11/1913. *Buried:* Rice Family Cemetery located 4.5 miles south of Magnolia, Pike County, MS. His obituary appeared in the 9/1913 edition of Confederate Veteran magazine. Confederate Pension Application dated 1904 on file at the Mississippi Dept of Archives and History-Target Name: Rice, Reuben H.-County: Pike. Also a Confederate Widows Pension Application dated 1913 on file-Target Name: Rice, Elizabeth Pasthenia-County: Pike.

Private

Bagley, M. (aka A.)—Pvt.—Enlisted: 8/9/1861 at Carroll Parish, LA. Rolls for 8/9/1861 through 2/1863: Present.

Berry, H.L.—Pvt.—Enlisted: 8/9/1861 at Carroll Parish, LA. Rolls for 8/9/1861 through 4/1862: Present. Rolls for 5/1862 through 6/1862: Mortally wounded at the Battle of Secessionville, S.C. on 6/16/1862; Died at Charleston, S.C. on 6/18/1862.

Bond, J.J.—Pvt.—Enlisted: 9/16/1862 at Savannah, GA. Rolls for 9/16/1862 through 10/1862: Present. Deserted on 1/9/1863.

Braswell, J. (aka T.)—Pvt.—Enlisted: 8/9/1861 at Carroll Parish, LA. Rolls for 8/9/1861 through 2/1862: Present. *Died:* 4/24/1862 at Augusta, GA.

Braswell, Robert B.—Pvt.—Enlisted: 8/9/1861 at Carroll Parish, LA. Rolls for 8/9/1861 through 2/1863: Present. Federal Rolls of Prisoners of War: Captured near Jackson, MS in 7/1863; Sent to Snyder's Bluff, MS on 7/30/1863. Received at Camp Morton, IN on 8/7/1863; Released upon the U.S. Oath of Allegiance on 5/18/1865. *Residence:* Columbia, AR. Description at release-Complexion: florid-Hair: sandy-Eyes: blue-Height: 5 ft. 9¼ in.

Breazeale, A.J. (aka Brazeal)—Pvt.—Enlisted: 4/22/1862 at Camp Moore, LA. Rolls for 4/22/1862 through 4/1865: Present. Rolls of Prisoners of War, C.S.A: Surrendered at Citronelle, AL on 5/4/1865; Paroled at Meridian, MS on 5/10/1865. *Residence:* Union Parish, LA. Soldier also served as a Pvt. with the Louisiana Pelican Infantry Regiment-Co. G.

Childers, R.W. (aka Childress)—Pvt.—Enlisted: 8/9/1861 at Carroll Parish, LA. Rolls for 8/9/1861 through 12/1861: Present. Rolls for 1/1862 through 2/1862: Absent, at home on sick furlough. Rolls for 3/1862 through 4/1862: Present. Rolls for 5/1862 through 6/1862: Mortally wounded at the Battle of Secessionville, S.C. on 6/16/1862; Died at Charleston, S.C. on 6/23/1862.

Christopher, J. (aka Christopher)—Pvt.—Enlisted: 8/9/1861 at Carroll Parish, LA.

Collins, J.B. (aka J.T., J.G.)—Pvt.—Enlisted: 8/9/1861 at Carroll Parish, LA. Rolls for 8/9/1861 through 6/1862: Present. Regimental Return for 8/1862: Absent without leave, Deserted. Regimental Return for 9/1862: Absent without leave, assumed to have Deserted.

Considine, T. (aka Constantine)—Pvt.—Enlisted: 10/15/1861 at Richmond, VA. Rolls for 9/1862 through 10/1862: Present, transferred from Nelson's Light Artillery on 8/20/1862 to serve for the duration of the war. Rolls for 1/1863 through 2/1863: Present. Federal Rolls of Prisoners of War: Captured near Jackson, MS in 7/1863; Sent to Snyder's Bluff, MS on 7/30/1863.

Cook, A.J.—Pvt.—Enlisted: 8/9/1861 at Carroll Parish, LA. Rolls for 8/9/1861 through 12/1861: Present. Rolls for 1/1862 through 2/1862: Died in camp on 1/4/1862. Confederate Widows Pension Application dated 1918 on file at the Mississippi Dept. of Archives and History-Target Card: Cook, Fannie A.-County: Walthall.

Corkern, O.P. (aka Corkene)—Pvt.—Enlisted: 12/3/1862 at Saint Tammany Parish, LA. Rolls for 3/1865 through 4/1865: Present. Rolls of Prisoners of War, C.S.A: Surrendered at Citronelle, AL on 5/4/1865; Paroled at Meridian, MS on 5/10/1865. *Residence:* Washington Parish, LA.

Cosh, M. (aka Cash)—Pvt.—Enlisted: 8/9/1861 at Carroll Parish, LA. Rolls for 8/9/1861 through 8/31/1861: Absent.

Cosh, R. (aka Cash)—Pvt.—Enlisted: 8/9/1861 at Carroll Parish, LA. Rolls for 8/9/1861 through 8/31/1861: Absent.

Crow, James W.H.—Pvt.—Enlisted: 8/9/1861 at Carroll Parish, LA. Rolls for 8/9/1861 through 4/1864: Present. Federal Rolls of Prisoners of War: Captured near Atlanta, GA on 8/5/1864; Received at the U.S. Military Prison, Louisville, KY from Nashville, TN on 8/12/1864. Forwarded to Camp Chase, OH on 8/13/1864; Paroled at Camp Chase, OH on 2/12/1865. Transferred to Point Lookout, MD; Exchanged at Boulware and Cox Wharf, James River, VA on 2/20–21/1865.

Cunningham, T.L. (aka J.S., D.L.)—Pvt.—Enlisted: 8/9/1861 at Carroll Parish, LA. Rolls for 8/9/1861 through 2/1862: Present. Rolls for 5/1862 through 6/1862: Absent, sick in hospital at Macon, GA. Rolls for 3/1862 through 4/1862: Present. Regimental Return for 7/1862: Sick at Macon, GA. Regimental Return for 8/1862: Died at Macon, GA on 8/1862.

Delaney, J. — Pvt. — Enlisted: 10/15/1861 at Richmond, VA. Rolls for 9/1862 through 10/1862: Absent, transferred from Nelson's Light Artillery on 8/20/1862 to serve for the duration of the war; Under arrest in Savannah, GA Jail. Rolls for 1/1862 through 2/1862: Absent, in jail at Savannah, GA.

Denning, William G. (aka Dennin, Denin, Dennan) — Pvt. — Enlisted: 10/15/1861 at Richmond, VA; Transferred from Nelson's Light Artillery on 8/20/1862 to serve for the duration of the war. Rolls for 8/20/1862 through 4/30/1864: Present. Federal Rolls of Prisoners of War: Captured near Marietta, GA on 7/3/1864; Received at the U.S. Military Prison, Louisville, KY on 7/13/1864. Transferred to Camp Morton, IN on 7/13/1864; Released on the U.S. Oath of Allegiance at Camp Morton, Indianapolis, IN on 6/21/1865. Remarks: Captured at Kenesaw Mountain, GA on 7/3/1864. Description at release-Complexion: light-Hair: dark-Eyes: blue-Height: 5 ft. 7¼ in. *Residence:* Mobile, Mobile County, AL.

Dickson, Rodger H. — Pvt. — Enlisted: 8/9/1861 at Carroll Parish, LA. Rolls for 8/9/1861 through 6/1862: Present. Rolls for 9/1862 through 4/30/1864: Absent on detached duty at Savannah, GA since 10/6/1862; Assigned to the Division Engineer Corps by order of the Secretary of War. Rolls of Prisoners of War, C.S.A: Surrendered at Citronelle, AL on 5/4/1865; Paroled at Monroe, LA on 6/6/1865. *Residence:* Jefferson County, MS.

English, William — Pvt. — Enlisted: 8/9/1861 at Carroll Parish, LA. Rolls for 8/9/1861 through 8/31/1861: Present. Soldier also served as a Pvt./Capt. with the independent Louisiana cavalry company Captain Miller's Mounted Rifles. Enlisted: 9/1/1862 at Lynchburg, VA. Rolls for 9/1/1862 through 12/31/1862: Present.

Farrar, W.H.H. — Pvt. — Enlisted: 7/9/1861 at Carroll Parish, LA. Rolls for 7/9/1861 through 2/1862: Present. Rolls for 3/1862 through 4/1862: Died in camp on 3/20/1862.

Fleming, John — Pvt. — Enlisted: 9/1/1862 at Savannah, GA. Rolls for 9/1/1862 through 4/1865: Present. Rolls of Prisoners of War, C.S.A: Surrendered at Citronelle, AL on 5/4/1865; Paroled at Meridian, MS on 5/10/1865. *Residence:* Murfreesboro, Rutherford County, TN. Soldier also served as a Pvt. with the Louisiana Pelican Infantry Regiment-Co. G.

Flynn, James F. (aka Flyn, Flinn) — Pvt. — Enlisted: 5/12/1863 at Jackson, MS. Rolls for 12/31/1863 through 4/30/1864: Transferred to the C.S. Naval Service by order of the Secretary of War. *Died:* 12/25/1864 at New Orleans, LA. *Buried:* Cypress Grove Cemetery located at New Orleans, Orleans Parish, LA.

Gallman, J.T. (aka Gollman) — Pvt. — Enlisted: 8/9/1861 at Carroll Parish, LA. Rolls for 8/9/1861 through 2/1862: Present. Rolls for 3/1862 through 4/1862: Died in camp on 4/1/1862.

Giles, W.B. — Pvt. — Enlisted: 8/9/1861 at Carroll Parish, LA. Rolls for 8/9/1861 through 6/1862: Present. Regimental Return for 7/1862: Sick at Savannah, GA.

Harbison, M.P. (aka Harbinson) — Pvt./Musician — (See Field and Staff)

Hart, W.W. — Pvt. — Enlisted: 8/8/1861 at Carroll Parish, LA. Rolls for 8/8/1861 through 6/1862: Present. Rolls for 9/1862 through 10/1862: Absent, on detached service constructing breastworks since 10/6/1862. Rolls for 1/1863 through 2/1863: Absent on detached service.

Helm, L.R. (aka Helon) — Pvt. — Enlisted: 4/12/1862 at Carroll Parish, LA. Rolls for 12/1863 through 2/1865: Present. Rolls for 3/1865 through 4/1865: Absent, captured at Spanish Fort, AL on 4/8/1865. Federal Rolls of Prisoners of War: Captured at Spanish Fort, AL on 4/8/1865; Sent to Ship Island, MS on 4/10/1865. Transferred to Vicksburg, MS on 5/1/1865.

Hughes, A. — Pvt. — Enlisted: 8/9/1861 at Carroll Parish, LA. Rolls for 8/9/1861 through 10/1862: Present.

James, R. — Pvt. — Enlisted: 8/8/1861 at Carroll Parish, LA. Rolls for 8/8/1861 through 8/31/1861: Present.

Kelly, L.H. — Pvt. — Enlisted: 8/9/1861 at Carroll Parish, LA. Rolls for 8/9/1861 through 8/31/1861: Present.

Lear, Charles — Pvt. — Enlisted: 8/15/1861 at Richmond, VA. Rolls for 9/1862 through 10/1862: Present, transferred from Nelson's Light Artillery on 8/20/1861 to serve for the duration of the war. Rolls for 1/1863 through 2/1863: Present.

McCarty, W. — Pvt. — Enlisted: 8/9/1861 at Carroll Parish, LA. Rolls for 8/9/1861 through 8/31/1861: Present.

McDonald, A. — Pvt. — Enlisted: 8/9/1861 at Carroll Parish, LA. Rolls for 8/9/1861 through 4/1862: Present. Rolls for 5/1862 through 6/1862: Absent, taken as a Prisoner of War while on picket duty. Regimental Return for 7/1862: Taken as a Prisoner of War by the enemy on 6/14/1862. Regimental Return for 8/1862:

Absent without leave. Regimental Return for 9/1862: Absent without leave and assumed to have Deserted.

Martin, Thomas — Pvt. — Enlisted: 10/15/1861 at Richmond, VA. Regimental Return for 8/1862: Transferred from Nelson's Light Artillery. Rolls for 9/1862 through 10/1862: Absent, transferred from Nelson's Light Artillery in 8/1862 for the duration of the war; Under arrest in Savannah, GA Jail. Rolls for 1/1863 through 2/1863: Absent, in jail at Savannah, GA.

Meehan, Thomas (aka Maher, Mesham) — Pvt. — Enlisted: 8/9/1861 at Carroll Parish, LA. Rolls for 8/9/1861 through 4/1862: Present. Rolls for 5/1862 through 6/1862: Absent, wounded at the Battle of Secessionville, S.C. on 6/16/1862; In hospital at Charleston, S.C. Regimental Return for 8/1862: Sick at Columbia, S.C. Rolls for 9/1862 through 10/1862: Discharged by order of the Surgeon of College Hospital, Columbia, S.C.

Miller, Perkins Poole (aka Perk) — Pvt. — Enlisted: 8/9/1861 at Carroll Parish, LA. Rolls for 8/9/1861 through 2/28/1865: Present. Rolls for 3/1865 through 4/1865: Absent, captured at Spanish Fort, AL. Federal Rolls of Prisoners of War: Captured at Spanish Fort, AL on 4/8/1865; Forwarded to Ship Island, MS on 4/10/1865. Transferred to Vicksburg, MS on 5/1/1865; Paroled at Camp Townsend, MS on 5/6/1865. Rolls of Prisoners of War, C.S.A: Surrendered at Citronelle, AL on 5/4/1865; Paroled at Meridian, MS on 5/10/1865. *Residence:* Monroe, Ouachita Parish, LA. Description at enlistment-Complexion: red-Hair: sandy red and short-Goatee: red-Eyes: blue with heavy eyebrows-Weight: 160-Height: 5' 10"-Speech: slow-Disposition: genial with "fire" about him. *Born:* 1835. *Occupation:* Farmer. *Residences:* Mississippi and Union Parish, LA; Elm Mott, McLennan County, TX since 1884. *Died:* 10/2/1911. *Buried:* Travis State Cemetery located at 909 Navasota St. at Austin, Travis County, TX. Confederate Pension Application dated 11/27/1899 on file at the Texas State Library and Archives Commission-Name: Miller, Perkins-Pension Number: 05805-County: McLennan.

Mondey, C. — Pvt. — Enlisted: 8/9/1861 at Carroll Parish, LA. Rolls for 8/9/1861 through 8/31/1861: Present.

Mooney, P. — Pvt. — Enlisted: 8/9/1861 at Carroll Parish, LA. Rolls for 8/9/1861 through 6/1862: Present. Rolls for 9/1862 through 10/1862: On Guard Duty around camp. Rolls for 1/1863 through 2/1863: Present.

Moreland, W.W. — Pvt./Color Sgt. — (See Color Bearers)

Osterhaut, A. (aka Osterhout, Osterhauh) — Pvt. — Enlisted: 8/9/1861 at Carroll Parish, LA for the duration of the war. Rolls for 8/9/1861 through 8/31/1861: Present. Soldier also served as a Pvt. with the independent Louisiana cavalry company Carroll Dragoons. On List dated Parish of Carroll, LA: Enlisted 3/19/1862 in the C.S. Army for the duration of the war or term of service; $50.00 Bounty paid.

Owen, John J. (aka J.S.) — Pvt. — Enlisted: 8/9/1861 at Carroll Parish, LA. Rolls for 8/9/1861 through 4/1862: Present. Rolls for 5/1862 through 6/1862: Died at Camp Mercer, GA on 5/9/1862.

Puckett, P.B. — Pvt. — Enlisted: 3/12/1862 at Carroll Parish, LA. Rolls for 3/12/1862 through 6/1862: Present. Rolls for 9/1862 through 10/1862: Absent without leave. Rolls for 1/1863 through 2/1863: Absent on sick furlough.

Putcher, Adam — Pvt. — Enlisted: 8/9/1861 at Carroll Parish, LA. Rolls for 8/9/1861 through 2/1863: Present. Rolls for 12/31/1863 through 4/1865: Absent, captured at the Battle of Chickamauga, GA on 9/19/1863. Federal Rolls of Prisoners of War: Captured at the Battle of Chickamauga, GA on 9/19/1863; Received at the U.S. Military Prison, Louisville, KY on 10/1/1863. Forwarded to Camp Douglas, IL on 10/2/1863; Died at Camp Douglas, IL on 2/27/1865 due to Pneumonia. *Buried:* Oakwoods Cemetery Confederate Mound located at Chicago, Cook County, IL.

Reardon, M. (aka Rearidon, Rearden) — Pvt. — Enlisted: 9/1/1862 at Savannah, GA. Rolls for 9/1/1862 through 10/1862: Absent, on Picket Duty at Savannah, GA. Rolls for 1/1863 through 4/1865: Present, placed on the Confederate Roll of Honor for gallantry and good conduct at the Battle of Chickamauga, GA per General Order #131 of the Adjutant and Inspector General's Office, Richmond, VA. Rolls of Prisoners of War, C.S.A: Surrendered at Citronelle, AL on 5/4/1865; Paroled at Meridian, MS on 5/10/1865. *Residence:* Shreveport, Caddo Parish, LA.

Robb, B.F. — Pvt. — Enlisted: 8/9/1861 at Carroll Parish, LA. Rolls for 8/9/1861 through 6/1862: Present. Rolls for 9/1862 through 10/1862: On extra duty at Camp Hospital. Rolls for 1/1863 through 2/1863: Absent, in hospital at Savannah, GA.

Robinson, Wiley (aka Robison) — Pvt. — Enlisted: 8/9/1861 at Carroll Parish, LA. Rolls for 8/9/1861 through 2/1863: Present.

Rushbrook, Samuel B. (aka S.D.) — Pvt./Musician — (See Field and Staff)

Saxon, B.F. — Pvt. — Enlisted: 8/9/1861 at Carroll Parish, LA. Rolls for 8/9/1861 through 2/1863: Present.

Scarborough, W.J. (aka Scarbrough, W.H.) — Pvt. — Enlisted: 8/8/1861 at Carroll Parish, LA. Rolls for 8/8/1861 through 4/1862: Present. Rolls #1 for 5/1862 through 6/1862: Present. Rolls #2 for 5/1862 through 6/1862: Wounded at the Battle of Secessionville, S.C. on 6/16/1862 and in hospital at Charleston, S.C. Rolls for 9/1862 through 10/1862: Absent, wounded in battle and on sick furlough. Rolls for 11/1862 through 12/1862: Absent, sick in camp at Savannah, GA. Rolls #1 for 1/1863 through 2/1863: Was in camp this morning, now on Guard Duty. Rolls #2 for 1/1863 through 2/1863: Absent on sick furlough. Rolls for 1/1864 through 4/1865: Absent, taken Prisoner of War at the Battle of Missionary Ridge, TN on 11/25/1863. Federal Rolls of Prisoners of War: Captured at the Battle of Missionary Ridge, TN on 11/25/1863; Received at the U.S. Military Prison, Louisville, KY from Nashville, TN on 12/7/1863. Forwarded to Rock Island Barracks, IL on 12/11/1863. On Roll dated Headquarters, Rock Island Barracks, IL 3/18/1864: Desires to take the U.S. Oath of Allegiance. Name appears as signature to the U.S. Oath of Allegiance subscribed and sworn to at Rock Island Barracks, IL on 4/28/1865. *Residence:* Natchez, Adams County, MS. Description at oath-Complexion: light-Hair: black-Eyes: brown-Height: 5 ft. 6½ in. Age at oath: 22 yrs.

Scott, R.D.—Pvt.—Enlisted: 8/29/1862 at Mobile, AL. Rolls for 9/1862 through 2/1863: Present. On List dated Parole Camp, Enterprise, MS 11/8/1863: Forwarded to Richmond, VA for Exchange on 11/10/1863. Rolls for 3/1863 through 12/31/1863: Absent without leave from 8/22/1863 through 9/17/1863 and for 12/10/1863 through 12/31/1863.

Seaborn, O.—Pvt.—Enlisted: 9/1/1862 at Savannah, GA. Rolls for 9/1/1862 through 2/1863: Present.

Smith, J.L.—Pvt.—Enlisted: 8/9/1861 at Carroll Parish, LA. Rolls for 8/9/1861 through 2/1862: Present. Rolls for 3/1862 through 4/1862: Absent on furlough. Rolls for 5/1862 through 6/1862: Absent, wounded at the Battle of Secessionville, S.C. on 6/16/1862 and in hospital at Charleston, S.C. Rolls for 9/1862 through 10/1862: Absent on sick furlough, wounded at the Battle of Secessionville, S.C. Rolls for 1/1863 through 2/1863: Absent on sick furlough.

Stewart, W.W.—Pvt./Battalion Druggist—(See Field and Staff)

Stroud, F.—Pvt.—Enlisted: 8/9/1861 at Carroll Parish, LA. Rolls for 8/9/1861 through 2/1863: Present.

Stroud, J.—Pvt.—Enlisted: 8/9/1861 at Carroll Parish, LA. Rolls for 8/9/1861 through 10/1862: Present. Rolls for 1/1863 through 2/1863: Present.

Turner, Edward Bowman—Pvt.—Enlisted: 8/9/1861 at Carroll Parish, LA. Rolls for 8/9/1861 through 12/1861: Present. Rolls for 1/1862 through 2/1862: Absent, at home on sick furlough. Rolls for 3/1862 through 4/1862: Absent on sick furlough. Rolls for 5/1862 through 6/1862: Absent, sick at home; Furlough expired and absent without leave. Regimental Return for 7/1862: Absent without leave in Louisiana. Regimental Return for 8/1862: Deserted, absent without leave. Regimental Return for 9/1862: Absent without leave and assumed to have Deserted. *Born:* 11/2/1833. *Died:* 10/1/1888. *Buried:* Grace Episcopal Church Cemetery located on Hwy. 10 in downtown Saint Francisville, West Feliciana Parish, LA.

Upshaw, Jonathan W. (aka Upshard)—Pvt.—Enlisted: 8/9/1861 at Carroll Parish, LA. Rolls for 8/9/1861 through 4/1862: Present. Rolls for 5/1862 through 6/1862: Absent, wounded in leg at the Battle of Secessionville, S.C. on 6/18/1862 and in hospital at Charleston, S.C. *Died:* 7/18/1862 due to complications from leg amputation. *Born:* 1840 in Walton County, GA to Richard Upshaw and Rebecca Elder Upshaw. *Residence:* Spearsville, Union Parish, LA. *Religious Affiliation:* Baptist. *Siblings:* Sgt. William E. Upshaw of Co. D. (His obituary appeared in the 7/29/1862 edition of the Christian Index of Union Parish, LA.

Vines, Jackson David—Pvt.—Enlisted: 8/9/1861 at Carroll Parish, LA. Rolls for 8/9/1861 through 4/1865: Present. Rolls of Prisoners of War, C.S.A: Surrendered at Citronelle, AL on 5/4/1865; Paroled at Meridian, MS on 5/10/1865. *Residence:* Union Parish, LA. Soldier also served as a 1st Sgt. with the Louisiana Pelican Infantry Regiment-Co. F. *Wounded:* Twice-In abdomen at the Battle of Atlanta, GA and in right hip at Spanish Fort, AL. *Born:* 1/22/1838 at Edgefield District, S.C. *Married:* Sarah E. Smith-*Born:* 1840 in Alabama, Cynthia Rusinger, and Nancy (Fannie) Russell *Born:* 1854 in Arkansas, married on 11/23/1889 at Monroe, Ouachita Parish, LA. *Children:* 5 Sons-Joseph, William, Henry, Seburn, and __, and 1 Daughter-Mollie. *Occupation:* Farmer. *Residences:* Union Parish, LA for 20 yrs., Winn Parish, LA for 39 yrs., and DeSoto Parish, LA for 10 yrs. *Died:* 10/29/1899 at Longstreet, DeSoto Parish, LA due to Heart Failure. *Buried:* Longstreet, LA. *3rd Wife's Age:* 44 as of 1899. Soldier is recorded on the 1870 U.S. Census: *Residence:* Marion, Union Parish, LA-Wife: Sarah. Soldier is also recorded on the 1880 U.S. Census: *Residence:* Bossier Parish, LA-Wife: Nancy. Confederate Pension Application dated 3/1/1899 on file at the Louisiana State Archives-Microfilm Reel: CP1.142-Microdex 1-Sequence 35-Target Card: Vines, Jackson-Parish: DeSoto-4 Pages. Also a Confederate Widows Pension Application dated 2/14/1916 on file-Microfilm Reel: CP1.142-Microdex 1-Sequence 36-Target Card: Vines, Nancy (Russell)-Parish: Franklin-3 Pages.

Vines, John—Pvt.—Enlisted: 8/9/1861 at Carroll Parish, LA. Rolls for 8/9/1861 through 12/1861: Present. Rolls for 1/1862 through 2/1862: Died in camp on 1/30/1862. Rolls for 1/1863 through 2/1863: Absent, in hospital at Savannah, GA. *Born:* 1820.

Wescott, O.F.—Pvt.—Enlisted: 8/9/1861 at Carroll Parish, LA. Rolls for 8/9/1861 through 6/1862: Present. Rolls for 9/1862 through 10/1862: Present, at work constructing breastworks; Detached service on 10/6/1862. Rolls for 1/1863 through 2/1863: Absent on detached service. Rolls for 12/31/1863 through 4/30/1864: Absent, on detached duty with the Engineer Corps at Savannah, GA since 10/6/1862 by order of the Secretary of War.

COMPANY E: "NATCHEZ RIFLES," ADAMS COUNTY, MISSISSIPPI

Captain

Bisland, Thomas Alexander—1st Lt./Capt.— Enlisted: 8/15/1861 at Natchez, MS; Elected 1st Lt. same day. Rolls for 8/15/1861 through 10/1861: Present. Rolls for 11/1861 through 12/1861: Present, elected Capt. on 11/25/1861. Rolls for 1/1862 through 2/1863: Present. On 1st Mississippi C.S.A. Hospital Register, Jackson, MS: Admitted on 8/1/1863; Returned to duty on 10/5/1863. Admitted on 12/22/1863; Returned to duty on 2/28/1864. Rolls for 8/31/1864 through 4/1865: Absent on detached duty in east Louisiana and Mississippi. *Buried:* Pine Ridge Church Cemetery located at Adams County, MS.

Davis, Alfred Vidal—Capt.—Enlisted: 8/15/1861 at Natchez, MS; Elected Capt. same day. Resigned in Virginia in 11/1861. *Born:* 9/7/1826. *Died:* 5/13/1899. *Buried:* Natchez City Cemetery located at Natchez, Adams County, MS.

Lieutenant

Bell, William D. (aka W.B.)—4th Sgt./1st Sgt./2nd Lt.—Enlisted: 8/15/1861 at Natchez, MS. Rolls for 8/15/1861 through 10/1861: Present. Rolls for 11/1861 through 12/1861: Present, elected to 1st Sgt. on 12/16/1861. Rolls for 1/1862 through 8/1863: Present. Rolls for 9/1863 through 10/1863: Present, promoted to 2nd Lt. in 9/1863. Rolls for 11/1863 through 4/1865: Present. Rolls of Prisoners of War, C.S.A: Surrendered at Citronelle, AL on 5/4/1865; Paroled at Meridian, MS on 5/10/1865. Wounded: No, struck in shin by breastwork splinters from an exploding shell. *Born:* 12/4/1838 at Lanseville, OH. *Married:* Never. *Occupation:* Blacksmith. *Residences:* Bayou Vidal, Madison Parish, LA since 1879 and Newellton, Tensas Parish, LA since 1886. Confederate Pension Application dated 7/30/1902 on file at the Louisiana State Archives-Microfilm Reel: CP1.9-Microdex 3-Sequence 20-Target Card: Bell, William D.-Parish: Tensas-6 Pages.

Blackburn, Cary B.—2nd Lt.—Enlisted: 8/15/1861 at Natchez, MS. Rolls for 8/15/1861 through 10/1861: Present, elected 2nd Lt. on 8/15/1861. Resigned in 12/1861. 2nd Lt. Successor: A.E. Newton.

Dicks, John A.—Pvt./Jr. 2nd Lt.—Enlisted: 3/1/1862 at Natchez, MS. Rolls for 3/1/1862 through 10/1863: Present. Rolls for 11/1863 through 12/1863: Present, elected Jr. 2nd Lt. on 12/15/1863. Rolls for 1/1864 through 4/1865: Present. *Born:* 9/18/1845. *Died:* 3/9/1914. *Buried:* Natchez City Cemetery located at Natchez, Adams County, MS. He wrote to the 1/1895 edition of Confederate Veteran magazine attempting to contact any surviving Union soldiers who were in a group of 1200 prisoners that were marched out of Columbia, TN, a day in advance of Lt. Gen. John B. Hood's retreat in 12/1864, of which he was a guard.

Fox, Benjamin D.—Jr. 2nd Lt./1st Lt.—Enlisted: 8/15/1861 at Natchez, MS. Rolls for 8/15/1861 through 9/1/1861: Sick in camp. Rolls for 9/1861 through 10/1861: Present. Rolls for 11/1861 through 12/1861: Promoted to 1st Lt. on 11/26/1861; Absent on furlough. Rolls for 3/1862 through 4/1862: Present. Regimental Returns for 7/1862 through 9/1862: Present or absent not stated. Rolls for 11/1862 through 2/1863: Present.

Middleton, Jonathan C.—Pvt./Sgt. Major/Jr. 2nd Lt.—(See Field and Staff)

Newton, Algera Emmett (aka H., L.E.)—Cpl./1st Sgt./2nd Lt./1st Lt.—Enlisted: 8/15/1861 at Natchez, MS. Rolls for 8/15/1861 through 10/1861: Present, appointed 1st Sgt. on 9/1/1861. Rolls for 11/1861 through 12/1861: Present, promoted to 2nd Lt. on 11/21/1861. Rolls for 1/1862 through 2/1862: Present or absent not stated. Rolls for 3/1862 through 4/1862: Absent on recruiting furlough, sick at home. Rolls for 5/1862 through 6/1862: Present. Rolls for 11/1862 through 12/1862: Absent, on detached service. Rolls for 1/1863 through 2/1863: Absent, assigned to the staff of Col. Harrison. Rolls for 1/1864 through 2/1864: Absent, taken as a Prisoner of War. Federal Rolls of Prisoners of War: Captured near Vicksburg, MS on 10/6/1863; Received at Johnson's Island, OH from Memphis, TN on 10/26/1863. Paroled at Fortress Monroe, VA by order of Col. Hoffman on 10/12/1864. Rolls for 8/31/1864 through 2/28/1865: Present. Rolls for 3/1865 through 4/1865: Absent on furlough since 4/16/1865. Rolls of Prisoners of War, C.S.A: Surrendered at Citronelle, AL on 5/4/1865; Paroled at Jackson, MS on 5/15/1865. *Residence:* Jefferson County, MO. *Born:* 1/11/1842. *Died:* 1/3/1907. *Buried:* Natchez City Cemetery located at Natchez, Adams County, MS.

Roach, Eugene—Pvt./3rd Lt./Jr. 2nd Lt.—Enlisted: 8/15/1861 at Natchez, MS. Rolls for 8/15/1861 through 9/1/1861: Present. Rolls for 9/1861 through 10/1861: Absent, at home on furlough. Rolls for 11/1861 through 12/1861: Promoted to Lt. in another Company. Soldier also served as a Jr. 3rd Lt./Jr. 2nd Lt. with the Chalmette Regiment Louisiana Militia-Co. D. On undated Roll: Ordered into the service of the State of Louisiana. *Mar-

ried: Annie McLean on 10/23/1866 at Christ Church at New Orleans, LA. *Died:* 4/20/1893 at New Orleans, LA due to Typhoid Fever. *Buried:* Girod Street Cemetery located at New Orleans, Orleans Parish, LA. Confederate Widows Pension Application dated 7/14/1908 on file at the Louisiana State Archives-Microfilm Reel: CP1.119-Microdex 1-Sequence 3-Target Card: Roach, Annie (McLean)-Parish: Orleans-10 Pages.

Sthreshley, William H. (aka Streshley, Sthrseley) — 1st Lt./Adjutant — (See Field & Staff)

Sergeant

Bennett, George B. (aka Bennet) — Pvt./5th Sgt. — Enlisted: 8/15/1861 at Natchez, MS. Rolls for 9/1861 through 10/1861: Present, appointed 5th Sgt. on 9/1/1861. Rolls for 11/1861 through 4/1865: Present. Rolls of Prisoners of War, C.S.A: Surrendered at Citronelle, AL on 5/4/1865; Paroled at Meridian, MS on 5/10/1865. *Residence:* Charleston, Jefferson County, VA. *Died:* 1887. *Buried:* Block 16-Lot 5 at the Masonic Cemetery located at Nashville, Washington County, IL.

Carkeet, John (aka Carvutt, Cracksett, Carcutt) — Pvt./2nd Cpl./4th Sgt. — Enlisted: 8/15/1861 at Natchez, MS. Rolls for 8/15/1861 through 10/1861: Present. Rolls for 11/1861 through 12/1861: Present, promoted to 2nd Cpl. on 11/26/1861 and 4th Sgt. on 12/16/1861. Rolls for 1/1862 through 2/1863: Present. Federal Rolls of Prisoners of War: Captured at Chattanooga, TN on 11/25/1863; Received at the U.S. Military Prison, Louisville, KY from Nashville, TN for Exchange on 12/8/1863. Forwarded to Rock Island Barracks, IL on 12/9/1863; Took the U.S. Oath of Allegiance on 8/15/1864. Remarks: Deserted. *Residence:* Adams County, MS. Description at oath-Complexion: fair-Hair: light-Eyes: blue-Height: 5 ft. 7 in. Age at oath: 27. *Born:* 4/4/1832. *Died:* 3/6/1908. *Buried:* Natchez City Cemetery located at Natchez, Adams County, MS.

Carpenter, Allen D. (aka A.E., A.B., A.G.) — 2nd Sgt./Pvt. — Enlisted: 8/15/1861 at Natchez, MS. Rolls for 8/15/1861 through 4/1862: Present. Rolls for 5/1862 through 6/1862: Absent, wounded at the Battle of Secessionville, S.C. on 6/16/1862 and in hospital at Augusta, GA. Rolls for 11/1862 through 2/1864: Present. Federal Rolls of Prisoners of War: Captured at Resaca, GA on 5/16/1864; Received at the U.S. Military Prison, Louisville, KY on 5/21/1864 from Nashville, TN. Forwarded to Camp Morton, IN on 5/22/1864; Released on the U.S. Oath of Allegiance on 6/12/1865. *Residence:* Natchez, MS. Description at oath-Complexion: light-Hair: dark-Eyes: dark-Height: 5 ft. 11 in. *Born:* 3/12/1837. *Died:* 3/8/1902. *Buried:* Natchez City Cemetery located at Natchez, Adams County, MS.

Fanning, M. — Pvt./Sgt. — Enlisted: 8/15/1861 at Natchez, MS. Rolls for 8/15/1861 through 4/1865: Present. Rolls of Prisoners of War, C.S.A: Surrendered at Citronelle, AL on 5/4/1865; Paroled at Meridian, MS on 5/10/1865. *Residence:* Natchez, Adams County, MS.

Griffith, John T. — 3rd Sgt. — Enlisted: 8/15/1861 at Natchez, MS. Rolls for 8/15/1861 through 6/1862: Present. Rolls for 11/1862 through 12/1862: Absent, sick in camp at Savannah, GA. Rolls for 1/1863 through 2/1863: Absent, sick in hospital at Guyton Station, GA. Killed at the Battle of Jackson, MS.

Lawrence, S.C. (aka Laurence, G.C.) — Pvt./Sgt. — Enlisted: 8/15/1861 at Natchez, MS. Rolls for 8/15/1861 through 9/1/1861: Temporarily disabled by injuries received on the Railroad near Knoxville, TN on 8/19/1861. Rolls for 9/1861 through 10/1861: Absent, sick in Richmond, VA. Rolls for 11/1861 through 12/1861: Discharged and collected pay. Rolls for 1/1862 through 2/1862: Discharged in Richmond, VA; Re-enlisted on 1/1/1862. Rolls for 3/1862 through 2/1863: Present. Rolls for 1/1864 through 2/1864: Present. Rolls for 8/31/1864 through 4/30/1865: Absent, sick in hospital since 4/28/1864.

Lemunyan, H.D. (aka Lemungan, Lamunyan, J.D., S.D.) — Pvt./Sgt. — Enlisted: 8/15/1861 at Natchez, MS. Rolls for 8/15/1861 through 6/1862: Present. Rolls for 11/1862 through 12/1862: Absent, sick in camp at Savannah, GA. Rolls for 1/1863 through 2/1863: Absent, on picket duty at Ogeechee River Bridge, GA. Rolls for 1/1864 through 2/28/1865: Present. Rolls for 3/1865 through 4/1865: Absent, wounded at Spanish Fort, AL on 4/4/1865.

Penny, J.K. — Pvt./1st Cpl./Sgt. — Enlisted: 8/15/1861 at Natchez, MS. Rolls for 8/15/1861 through 12/1862: Present. Rolls for 1/1863 through 2/1863: Sick in camp. (On 2/21/1863, he was the speaker and presenter at a ceremony in which the battalion members presented Lt. Col. John McEnery with a sword).

Perryman, William J. (aka Perham) — Pvt./2nd Cpl./1st Sgt. — Enlisted: 8/15/1861 at Natchez, MS. Rolls for 8/15/1861 through 10/1861: Present. Rolls for 11/1861 through 12/1861: Present, appointed 2nd Cpl. on 11/26/1861. Rolls for 1/1862 through 4/1862: Present, wounded at the Battle of Secessionville, S.C. on 6/16/1862. Rolls for 11/1862 through 12/1862: Absent on sick leave. Rolls for 1/1863 through 2/1863: Present. Rolls for 1/1864 through 4/1865: Absent, taken Prisoner of War at the Battle of Missionary Ridge, TN on 11/25/1863. Federal Rolls of Prisoners of War: Captured at Chattanooga, TN on 11/25/1863; Received at the U.S. Military Prison, Louisville, KY from Nashville, TN on 12/7/1863. Forwarded to Rock Island Barracks, IL on 12/9/1863; Transferred on 3/2/1865 for Exchange.

Pheir, William (aka Phain, Pfard, Phair) — Pvt./Sgt. — Enlisted: 8/15/1861 at Natchez, MS. Rolls for 8/15/1861 through 2/1863: Present. Federal Rolls of

Prisoners of War: Captured at Chattanooga, TN on 11/25/1863; Forwarded to the U.S. Military Prison, Louisville, KY from Nashville, TN on 12/8/1863. Transferred to Rock Island Barracks, IL on 12/9/1863. On Roll dated Headquarters, Rock Island Barracks, IL 3/18/1864: Prisoner desires to take the U.S. Oath of Allegiance. Remarks: Deserted from the C.S. Army. Released from Rock Island Barracks, IL on 5/17/1865 under General Order #109 on 5/9/1865. *Residence:* Memphis, Shelby County, TN.

Williams, J.T.—1st Sgt./Pvt.—Enlisted: 8/15/1861 at Natchez, MS. Rolls for 8/15/1861 through 9/1/1861: Sick in camp. Rolls for 9/1861 through 10/1861: Absent, sick at Richmond, VA. Rolls for 11/1861 through 12/1861: Discharged and collected pay. Later became captain of a Louisiana cavalry company.

Corporal

Buckels, J.F.—Pvt./Cpl.—Enlisted: 8/15/1861 at Natchez, MS. Rolls for 8/15/1861 through 6/1862: Present. Rolls for 11/1862 through 12/1862: Absent, detailed as Wagoner at Wilmington, N.C. Rolls for 1/1863 through 2/1863: Absent at Fort Boggs, GA. Rolls for 1/1864 through 2/1864: Absent on furlough.

Clements, James (aka Clement)—Pvt./4th Cpl.—Enlisted: 8/15/1861 at Natchez, MS. Rolls for 8/15/1861 through 2/1862: Present. Rolls for 11/1862 through 2/1863: Absent, on detached service at Savannah, GA. Rolls for 1/1864 through 2/1864: Present. Federal Rolls of Prisoners of War: Captured near Atlanta, GA on 8/5/1864; Received at the U.S. Military Prison, Louisville, KY from Nashville, TN on 8/12/1864. Forwarded to Camp Chase, OH on 8/13/1864; Released on the U.S. Oath of Allegiance on 5/13/1865. Description at oath-Complexion: dark-Hair: dark-Eyes: blue-Height: 5 ft. 11½ in.

Corrin, Thomas (aka Carrin, Curren)—Pvt./Cpl.—Enlisted: 8/15/1861 at Natchez, MS. Rolls for 8/15/1861 through 4/1862: Present. Rolls for 5/1862 through 6/1862: Absent, detailed to work on Gunboat at Savannah, GA. Rolls for 11/1862 through 12/1862: Absent, sick in camp at Savannah, GA; Returned from working on Gunboat on 11/27/1862. Rolls for 1/1863 through 2/1863: Present. On Register of C.S.A. General Military Hospital #4, Wilmington, N.C: Admitted on 2/7/1863; Released on 2/20/1863.

Love, T.R.—Pvt./Cpl.—Enlisted: 3/1/1862 at Natchez, MS. Rolls for 3/1/1862 through 6/1862: Present. Rolls for 11/1862 through 12/1862: Absent, sick in camp at Savannah, GA. Rolls for 1/1863 through 2/1863: Absent, on picket duty at Ogeechee River Bridge, GA. Rolls for 1/1864 through 2/1864: Present. Rolls for 8/31/1864 through 2/28/1865: Killed at the Battle of Jonesboro, GA on 8/31/1864.

Patterson, George—4th Cpl./Pvt.—Enlisted: 8/15/1861 at Natchez, MS. Rolls for 8/15/1861 through 4/1862: Present. Rolls for 5/1862 through 6/1862: Absent, sick in hospital at Augusta, GA. Regimental Return for 7/1862: Sick at Augusta, GA. Regimental Return for 9/1862: On furlough. Rolls for 11/1862 through 12/1862: Absent, reduced to Pvt. on 11/15/1862; Sick at Savannah, GA. Rolls for 1/1863 through 2/1863: Absent, sick at Guyton Station, GA. Discharged in 1863.

Smith, J. Davidson, Dr.—Cpl./Pvt.—Enlisted: 8/15/1861 at Natchez, MS. Rolls for 8/15/1861 through 12/1862: Present. Rolls for 1/1863 through 2/1863: Was in camp this morning, but now on Picket Duty. Rolls for 1/1864 through 2/1864: Deserted. *Born:* 9/27/1841. *Died:* 1/10/1863. *Buried:* Routh Cemetery located at Natchez, Adams County, MS.

Smith, W.J.—Pvt./Cpl.—Enlisted: 8/15/1862 at Natchez, MS. Rolls for 11/1862 through 12/1862: Absent, sick at Savannah, GA. Rolls for 1/1863 through 2/1863: Present. Rolls for 1/1864 through 2/28/1865: Present. Rolls for 3/1865 through 4/1865: Absent, taken Prisoner of War on 4/7/1865.

Stewart, Charles A. (aka C.H.)—Pvt./3rd Cpl./1st Cpl.—Enlisted: 8/15/1861 at Natchez, MS. Rolls for 8/15/1861 through 10/1861: Present, appointed 1st Cpl. on 9/1/1861. Rolls for 11/1861 through 2/1863: Present. On M.D.O. Hospital Register, Chattanooga, TN: Admitted on 9/21/1863; Sent to General Hospital on 9/23/1863. Rolls for 1/1864 through 2/1864: Absent, wounded at the Battle of Chickamauga, GA on 9/19/1863. Rolls of Prisoners of War of Furloughed and Detailed Men, C.S.A: Surrendered at Citronelle, AL on 5/4/1865; Paroled at Shreveport, LA on 6/7/1865. *Residence:* Natchez, Adams County, MS.

Thomas, Oreon E.—Pvt./4th Cpl.—Enlisted: 8/15/1861 at Natchez, MS. Rolls for 8/15/1861 through 6/1862: Present. Regimental Return for 9/1862: On furlough. Rolls for 11/1862 through 12/1862: Present, promoted to 4th Cpl. on 11/15/1862. Rolls for 1/1863 through 2/1863: Absent, on picket duty at Ogeechee River Bridge, GA. Killed at the Battle of Chickamauga, GA on 9/19/1863.

Turner, William D.—Pvt./2nd Cpl.—Enlisted: 3/1/1862 at Natchez, MS. Rolls for 3/1/1862 through 2/1863: Present. On C.S.A. General Military Hospital #4 Register, Wilmington, N. C: Admitted on 2/6/1863; Returned to duty on 2/8/1863. Rolls for 1/1864 through 4/1865: Present. Rolls of Prisoners of War, C.S.A: Surrendered at Citronelle, AL on 5/4/1865; Paroled at Meridian, MS on 5/10/1865. *Residence:* Natchez, MS. Soldier also served as a 2nd Cpl. with the Louisiana Pelican Infantry Regiment-Co. G.

Walton, Albert W. (aka H.W.)—Pvt./Cpl.—Enlisted: 8/15/1861 at Natchez, MS. Rolls for 8/15/1861 through 2/1864: Present. Rolls for 8/31/1864 through 4/1865: Absent, sick in hospital since 7/4/1864. Federal Rolls of Prisoners of War: Captured at Egypt Station, MS on 12/28/1864; Transferred from Memphis, TN to the U.S. Military Prison, Alton, IL on 1/17/1865. On U.S. Post and Prison Hospital Register, Alton, IL: Admitted on 2/12/1865; Released from hospital on 2/19/1865. On U.S. Post and Prison Hospital Register, Alton, IL: Admitted on 3/15/1865; Died on 3/23/1865 due to Chronic Diarrhea. *Buried:* Confederate Cemetery, Alton, IL.

Private

Alexander, Charles F.—Pvt.—Enlisted: 5/12/1863 at Natchez, MS. Rolls for 1/1864 through 2/1864: Absent, sick in hospital since 2/23/1864. Rolls for 8/31/1864 through 2/28/1865: Absent on sick furlough, wounded on 7/25/1864. Rolls for 3/1865 through 4/1865: Absent, wounded on 7/25/1864.

Ashba, William (aka Ashby, Ashbu)—Pvt.—Enlisted: 3/1/1862 at Natchez, MS. Rolls for 5/1862 through 6/1862: Absent, sick in Augusta, GA or Columbia, S.C. Rolls for 11/1862 through 2/1863: Present. Federal Rolls of Prisoners of War: Captured at Adams County, MS on 1/12/1864. *Remarks:* Desires to take the U.S. Oath of Allegiance on 2/6/1864 and go north.

Babbitt, Charles Walter—Pvt.—Enlisted: 8/15/1861 at Natchez, MS; Absent, sick at Temperance Hall Hospital, Richmond, VA on 8/15/1861 through 9/1/1861. Rolls for 9/1861 through 6/1862: Present. Rolls for 8/1862: Absent with leave in Mississippi. Rolls for 9/1862: Absent, serving at James Island, S.C. Rolls for 11/1862 through 2/1863: Absent on detached service at Charleston, S.C. Promoted to 1st Lt. of Engineers in the Army of Northern Virginia on 8/1/1863. *Buried:* Natchez City Cemetery located at Natchez, Adams County, MS.

Ballance, Girard—Pvt.—Enlisted: 3/1/1862 at Natchez, MS. Rolls for 3/1/1862 through 2/1863: Present. Killed at the Battle of Chickamauga, GA. Placed on the Confederate Roll of Honor for gallantry and good conduct at the Battle of Chickamauga, GA per General Order #131 of the Adjutant and Inspector General's Office, Richmond, VA.

Bauer, Theodore L. (aka Bower, Baur, J.)—Pvt./Musician—(See Field and Staff)

Benbrook, Lewis—Pvt.-Rolls for 8/15/1861 through 9/1/1861: Sick in camp. Discharged in 1861. *Buried:* Kingston Cemetery located at Adams County, MS.

Blackburn, Cary B.—2nd Lt.—Enlisted: 8/15/1861 at Natchez, MS; Elected 2nd Lt. same day. Rolls for 8/15/1861 through 10/1861: Present. Resigned in 12/1861 to become a Surgeon. 2nd Lt. Successor: A.E. Newton.

Boyd, Joseph Colpin (aka Conklin)—Pvt.—Enlisted: 9/1/1862 at Natchez, MS. Rolls for 11/1862 through 12/1862: Absent, sick in hospital at Savannah, GA. Rolls for 1/1863 through 2/1863: Absent, on sick leave at Natchez, MS. Rolls for 1/1864 through 2/1864: Present. Rolls for 8/31/1864 through 4/1865: Absent, sent to hospital on 5/14/1864. *Born:* 7/18/1842. *Died:* 4/20/1919. *Buried:* Harrisonburg City Cemetery located at Harrisonburg, Catahoula Parish, LA. Confederate Pension Application on file at the Louisiana State Archives-Microfilm Reel: CP1.16-Microdex 1-Sequence 5-Target Card: Boyd, Joseph C.-Parish: Catahoula-11 Pages.

Buck, J.H. (aka J.A.)—Pvt.—Enlisted: 8/15/1861 at Natchez, MS. Discharged due to injuries received on the railroad near Knoxville, TN on 8/19/1861.

Buckles, James Monroe (aka Buckels)—Pvt.—Enlisted: 5/1/1862 at Natchez, MS. Rolls for 5/1/1862 through 2/1863: Present. Federal Rolls of Prisoners of War: Captured at Chattanooga, TN on 11/4/1863; Sent to the U.S. Military Prison, Louisville, KY from Nashville, TN on 11/14/1863. Took the U.S. Oath of Allegiance on 11/17/1863 at Louisville, KY and sent north of the Ohio River. Description at oath-Complexion: light-Hair: light-Eyes: blue-Height: 5 ft. 8 in. *Born:* 4/1/1842. Residences: Franklin County, MS. *Died:* 1/2/1922. *Buried:* Union Baptist Church located on Rt. 178, 3 miles southeast of Roxie, Franklin County, MS. He was a resident of Beauvoir Confederate Soldier's Home located at Biloxi, Harrison County, MS. Confederate Pension Application dated 1910 on file at the Mississippi Dept. of Archives and History-Target Card: Buckels, J.M. County: Franklin. Also a Confederate Widows Pension Application dated 1941 on file-Target Card: Buckles, Mrs. J.M.-County: Adams.

Butler, Robert M.—Pvt.—Enlisted: 8/15/1861 at Natchez, MS. Rolls for 8/15/1861 through 12/1861: Present. Rolls for 1/1862 through 2/1862: Absent on sick furlough. Rolls for 3/1862 through 4/1862: Discharged due to Surgeon's Certificate of Disability. *Born:* 7/6/1840 in Louisiana. *Died:* 4/21/1889. *Buried:* Natchez City Cemetery located at Natchez, Adams County, MS.

Calcote, John L.—Pvt.—Enlisted: 8/15/1861 at Natchez, MS. Rolls for 8/15/1861 through 12/1861: Present. Rolls for 1/1862 through 4/1862: Absent on sick furlough. Rolls for 5/1862 through 6/1862: Discharged on Surgeon's Certificate of Disability. Rolls for 1/1864 through 2/1864: Absent without leave since 9/1/1863. *Born:* 1844. *Died:* 1925. *Buried:* Hamburg (Yellow Fever) Cemetery located at Hamburg, Franklin County, MS. Confederate Pension Application dated 1913 on file at the Mississippi Dept. of Archives and History-Target Card: Calcote, J.L.-County: Franklin.

Campbell, Ben P.—Pvt.—Enlisted: 8/15/1861 at Natchez, MS. Rolls for 8/15/1861 through 4/1862: Present. Rolls for 5/1862 through 6/1862: Killed at the Battle of Secessionville, S.C. on 6/16/1862.

Campbell, Robert—Pvt.—Enlisted: 8/15/1861 at Natchez, MS. Rolls for 8/15/1861 through 4/1862: Present. Rolls for 5/1862 through 9/1862: Absent, detailed to work on Gun Boat at Savannah, GA. Rolls for 11/1862 through 2/1863: Absent, on detached service at Charleston, S.C. Rolls for 1/1864 through 2/1864: Present. Rolls for 8/31/1864 through 2/28/1865: Discharged by order of the Mobile, AL City Court.

Clay, John C. (aka H.)—Pvt.—Enlisted: 1/16/1862 at Mobile, AL. Rolls for 3/1862 through 4/1862: Present, transferred from Company E to Company D on 4/15/1862. Rolls for 5/1862 through 6/1862: Present. Regimental Return for 7/1862: Discharged.

Cockrell, T.J. (aka Cocknells, P.J.)—Pvt.—Enlisted: 10/12/1864 at Brookhaven, MS. Rolls for 10/12/1864 through 2/1865: Present. Federal Rolls of Prisoners of War: Captured at Spanish Fort, AL on 4/8/1865; Received at Ship Island, MS on 4/10/1865. Transferred to Vicksburg, MS on 5/1/1865; Paroled at Camp Townsend, MS on 5/6/1865. *Buried:* Confederate Cemetery located at Higginsville, Lafayette County, MO.

Cockrell, William S. (aka Cockrill, Cockerell, W.T., W.F.)—Pvt.—Enlisted: 8/15/1862 at Natchez, MS. Rolls for 11/1862 through 12/1862: Absent, sick in camp at Savannah, GA. Rolls for 1/1863 through 2/1863: Present. Federal Rolls of Prisoners of War: Captured at the Battle of Missionary Ridge, TN on 11/25/1863; Received at the U.S. Military Prison, Louisville, KY from Nashville, TN on 12/7/1863. Forwarded to Rock Island, IL on 12/29/1863; Transferred to City Point, VA on 3/2/1865 and Exchanged. *Born:* 5/17/1839. *Married:* Mary Ann Curteain on 4/23/1874 at Adams County, MS. *Children:* 1 Son-Samuel J. Cockrell and 1 Daughter-Katie Cockrell Tilton. *Died:* 12/4/1893 at Natchez, Adams County, MS due to Pneumonia. *Buried:* Natchez City Cemetery located at Natchez, Adams County, MS. *Wife Died:* 6/24/1927. *Wife's Residences:* Louisiana since 1916. Louisiana Widows Pension amount: $90.00 per quarter. Confederate Widows Pension Application dated 5/21/1921 on file at the Louisiana State Archives-Microfilm Reel: CP1.29-Microdex 1-Sequence 25-Target Card: Cockrell, Mary S. (Ann) (Curteain)-Parish: East Baton Rouge-7 Pages. Also a Confederate Widows Pension Application dated 1915 on file at the Mississippi Dept. of Archives and History-Target Card: Cockrell, Mary Ann-County: Wilkinson.

Cooney, John C. (aka J.H.)—Pvt.—Enlisted: 8/15/1861 at Natchez, MS. Rolls for 8/15/1861 through 2/1863: Present. Rolls for 1/1864 through 2/1864: Absent on furlough since 2/4/1864. Rolls of Prisoners of War, C.S.A: Surrendered at Citronelle, AL on 5/4/1865; Paroled at Alexandria, LA on 6/13/1865. *Residence:* Rapides Parish, LA.

Corbert, John—Pvt.-(No War Dept. Record)-*Born:* 4/4/1832. *Died:* 3/6/1906. Buried: Natchez City Cemetery located at Natchez, Adams County, MS.

Course, Charles F. (aka C.T.)—Pvt.—Enlisted: 8/15/1861 at Natchez, MS. Rolls for 8/15/1861 through 2/1863: Present. Rolls for 1/1864 through 2/1864: Absent, wounded at the Battle of Chickamauga, GA on 9/19/1863. Rolls for 8/31/1864 through 2/28/1865: Absent, sick in hospital since 8/6/1864. Rolls for 3/1865 through 4/1865: Absent, sick in hospital since 9/19/1863. Rolls of Prisoners of War, C.S.A: Surrendered at Citronelle, AL on 5/4/1865; Paroled at Gainesville, AL on 5/13/1865. *Residence:* Columbus, Lowndes County, MS.

Dey, M.M.—Pvt.—Enlisted: 8/15/1861 at Natchez, MS. Rolls for 8/15/1861 through 2/1864: Present. Rolls for 8/31/1864 through 2/28/1865: Absent, wounded on 7/28/1864 and on sick furlough. Rolls for 3/1865 through 4/1865: Absent, wounded near Atlanta, GA on 7/28/1864. Rolls of Prisoners of War, C.S.A: Surrendered at Citronelle, AL on 5/4/1865; Paroled at Jackson, MS on 5/19/1865. *Residence:* Adams County, MS.

Dicks, James G.—Pvt.—Enlisted: 3/1/1862 at Natchez, MS. Rolls through 4/1862: Present. Rolls for 5/1862 through 6/1862: Absent, sick in hospital at Columbia, S.C. Regimental Return for 7/1862: Discharged. Rolls for 1/1864 through 2/1864: Discharged. *Born:* 1839 at Adams County, MS. *Died:* 10/1/1867. *Buried:* Pine Ridge Church Cemetery located at Adams County, MS.

Dicks, Thomas G.—Pvt.—Enlisted: 3/1/1862 at Natchez, MS. Rolls for 3/1/1862 through 4/1862: Present. Rolls for 5/1862 through 6/1862: Absent, sick in hospital at Columbia, S.C. Regimental Return for 7/1862: Discharged. Rolls for 1/1864 through 2/1864: Discharged. *Born:* 9/16/1839. *Died:* 3/9/1925. *Buried:* Pine Ridge Church Cemetery located at Adams County, MS.

Dixon, John—Pvt.—Enlisted: 3/1/1862 at Natchez, MS. Rolls for 3/1/1862 through 6/1862: Present. Regimental Return for 9/1862: Died in camp on 9/5/1862.

Dougherty, O.R. (aka Daugherty)—Pvt.—Enlisted: 8/15/1861 at Natchez, MS. Rolls for 8/15/1861 through 9/1/1861: Absent, sick with measles at Petersburg, VA. Rolls for 9/1861 through 10/1861: Present. Rolls for 11/1861 through 12/1861: Absent, sick at Richmond, VA. Rolls for 1/1862 through 2/1862: Discharged and paid at Richmond, VA. *Buried:* Natchez City Cemetery located at Natchez, Adams County, MS.

Dufour, Charles—Pvt.—Enlisted: 8/15/1861 at

Natchez, MS. Rolls for 8/15/1861 through 6/1862: Present. Rolls for 11/1862 through 12/1862: Absent, sick in camp at Savannah, GA. Rolls for 1/1863 through 2/1863: Discharged on 2/11/1863.

Ellis, Henry—Pvt.—Enlisted: 8/15/1861 at Natchez, MS. Rolls for 8/15/1861 through 9/1/1861: Present. Rolls for 9/1861 through 10/1862: Present or absent not stated; Crippled from gunshot wound to thigh. Rolls for 11/1861 through 12/1861: Discharged and collected pay.

Farrar, Thornton H.—Pvt.—(No War Dept. Record) *Born:* 9/24/1843. *Died:* 3/4/1917. *Buried:* Greenwood Lodge Cemetery located 10 miles north of Woodville, Wilkinson County, MS.

Fondren, Meek M.—Pvt.—Enlisted: 5/25/1861 at Richmond, LA. Rolls for 5/25/1861 through 6/1862: Present. Rolls for 11/1862 through 2/1863: Absent, on detached service at Savannah, GA. Rolls for 1/1864 through 4/1865: Absent, assigned to duty in the Engineer Corps at Savannah, GA on 10/6/1863 by order of the Secretary of War. *Born:* 6/17/1836. *Died:* 9/14/1917. *Buried:* Maypearl Cemetery located at Ellis County, TX.

Fox, William H.H. (aka W.K.I.)—Pvt.—Enlisted: 3/1/1862 at Natchez, MS. Rolls for 3/1/1862 through 6/1862: Present. Rolls for 11/1862 through 2/1863: Absent, on detached service at Savannah, GA. Rolls for 1/1864 through 2/1864: Absent, assigned to duty in the Engineer Corps at Savannah, GA on 11/6/1863 by order of the Secretary of War. Rolls for 8/31/1864 through 4/1865: Absent, assigned to duty in the Engineer Corps on 10/6/1863 by order of the Secretary of War. *Born:* 10/23/1840. *Died:* 1/29/1936. *Buried:* Natchez City Cemetery located at Natchez, Adams County, MS. Confederate Pension Application dated 1925 on file at the Mississippi Dept. of Archives and History-Target Card: Fox, William H.H.-County: Adams.

Gahan, William C. (aka Grayham)—Pvt.—Enlisted: 3/1/1862 at Natchez, MS. Rolls for 3/1/1862 through 2/1864: Present. Rolls for 8/1864 through 2/1865: Absent, Prisoner of War since 8/5/1864. Federal Rolls of Prisoners of War: Captured near Atlanta, GA on 8/11/1864; Forwarded to the U.S. Military Prison, Nashville, TN on 8/11/1864. Received at the U.S. Military Prison, Louisville, KY on 8/12/1864; Transferred to Camp Chase, OH on 8/14/1864. Paroled at Camp Chase, OH on 2/12/1865; Exchanged at Boulware and Cox Wharf, James River, VA on 2/20/1865. Rolls for 3/1865 through 4/1865: Present. Rolls of Prisoners of War, C.S.A: Surrendered at Citronelle, AL on 5/4/1865; Paroled at Meridian, MS on 5/10/1865. *Residence:* Natchez, Adams County, MS. *Born:* 3/12/1844. *Died:* 11/20/1930. *Buried:* Natchez City Cemetery located at Natchez, MS.

Green, Elias—Pvt.—Enlisted: 8/15/1861 at Natchez, MS. Rolls for 8/15/1861 through 9/1/1861: Present. Rolls for 9/1861 through 10/1861: Present, sick in hospital due to injuries received at Knoxville, TN. Rolls for 11/1861 through 12/1861: Discharged and paid.

Green, Michael J.—Pvt.—Enlisted: 4/26/1862 at Natchez, MS. Rolls for 5/1862 through 6/1862: Present. Rolls for 11/1862 through 12/1862: Deserted.

Green, Thomas—Pvt.—Enlisted: 8/15/1861 at Natchez, MS. Rolls for 8/15/1861 through 2/1863: Present. Rolls for 1/1864 through 2/1864: Deserted. Federal Rolls of Prisoners of War: Captured at Chattanooga, TN on 11/24/1863; Received at the U.S. Military Prison, Louisville, KY from Nashville, TN on 12/8/1863. Transferred to Rock Island Barracks, IL on 12/11/1863; Enlisted in the U.S. Army for frontier service on 10/14/1864. Remarks: Deserted.

Guice, Thomas Reed (aka T.C.)—Pvt.—Enlisted: 8/15/1861 at Natchez, MS. Rolls for 8/15/1861 through 4/1862: Present. Rolls for 5/1862 through 6/1862: Absent at Augusta, GA, wounded at the Battle of Secessionville, S.C. Rolls for 11/1862 through 12/1862: Absent on sick leave. Rolls for 1/1863 through 2/1864: Present. Rolls for 8/1864 through 4/1865: Left sick in hospital since 5/15/1864. Confederate Widows Pension Application dated 1916 on file at the Mississippi Dept. of Archives and History: Target Card: Guice, Vernie E.-County: Claiborne.

Harris, Daniel G.—Pvt.—Enlisted: 3/1/1862 at Natchez, MS. Rolls for 3/1/1862 through 4/1862: Present. Rolls for 5/1862 through 2/1863: Absent, on detached service at Savannah, GA. Rolls for 1/1864 through 2/1865: Absent, Prisoner of War since 7/28/1864. Rolls for 3/1865 through 4/1865: Dropped from Rolls; Took the U.S. Oath of Allegiance while a Prisoner of War. Federal Rolls of Prisoners of War: Captured near Atlanta, GA on 7/28/1864; Sent to the U.S. Military Prison, Louisville, KY from Nashville, TN on 8/7/1864. Received at Camp Chase, OH on 8/11/1864; Released on the U.S. Oath of Allegiance on 5/8/1865 or 5/11/1865. *Residence:* Natchez, Adams County, MS.

Harris, Green S.—Pvt.—Enlisted: 3/1/1862 at Natchez, MS. Rolls for 3/1862 through 4/1862: Discharged on Surgeon's Certificate of Disability. Buried: Benville Union Cemetery located at Mt. Sterling, Brown County, IL.

Hart, C.—Pvt.—Enlisted: 8/15/1861 at Natchez, MS. Rolls for 8/15/1861 through 2/1862: Present. Rolls for 3/1862 through 4/1862: Present, sick in quarters. Rolls for 5/1862 through 2/1863: Present. Rolls for 1/1864 through 2/1864: Absent, taken Prisoner of War at the Battle of Missionary Ridge, TN on 11/25/1863.

Hornsby, Benjamin Franklin—Pvt.-(No War Dept. Record)—Enlisted: 3/1/1862 at Natchez, MS. Rolls of Prisoners of War, C.S.A: Surrendered at New

Orleans, LA on 5/26/1865; Paroled at Clinton, LA in 1865. *Born:* 9/8/1841 at Adams County, MS. *Married:* Juliet Mullins on 5/21/1919 at Saint Helena Parish, LA. *Occupation:* Blacksmith. *Residence:* Louisiana since 1872. *Died:* 3/13/1924 at Saint Helena Parish, LA due to Old Age. *Buried:* Mullins Family Cemetery located south of Pine Grove, Saint Helena Parish, LA. *Wife Born:* 8/16/1870 at Saint Helena Parish, LA. *Wife Died:* 10/17/1957 at the East Louisiana State Hospital at Jackson, West Feliciana Parish, LA. Soldier also served as a Pvt. with the 1st Mississippi Light Artillery and the 11th Arkansas Cavalry-Co. I. Confederate Pension Application dated 1/18/1913 and on file at the Louisiana State Archives-Microfilm Reel: CP1.69-Microdex 3-Sequence 1-Target Card: Hornsby, Benjamin F.-Parish: St. Helena-13 Pages.

Hornsby, O.W.—Pvt./Hospital Steward—(See Field and Staff)

Hornsby, W.W.—Pvt.—Enlisted: 8/15/1861 at Natchez, MS. Rolls for 8/15/1861 through 9/1/1861: Present. Rolls for 9/1861 through 12/1861: Died at Jackson River Depot, VA on 10/24/1861 due to Disease.

House, Alfred Henry (aka Albert)—Pvt.—Enlisted: 3/1/1862 at Natchez, MS. Rolls for 3/1/1862 through 2/1864: Present. Rolls for 8/1864 through 4/1865: Absent, Prisoner of War since 7/5/1864. Federal Rolls of Prisoners of War: Captured near Chattanooga, TN on 7/5/1864; Sent to the U.S. Military Prison, Louisville, KY from Nashville, TN on 7/13/1864. Transferred to Camp Douglas, IL on 7/16/1864; Discharged on 6/16/1865 in accordance with General Order #109 of the Adjutant General's Office, Washington, D.C. 6/6/1865. *Born:* 3/14/1845 at Adams County, MS. *Died:* 3/8/1922. *Buried:* Natchez City Cemetery located at Natchez, Adams County, MS. He was a resident of the Beauvoir Confederate Soldier's Home located at Biloxi, Harrison County, MS.

Howe, Charles M.—Pvt.—Enlisted: 3/1/1862 at Natchez, MS. Rolls for 3/1/1862 through 2/1864: Present. Rolls for 8/1864 through 4/1865: Prisoner of War since 7/5/1864. Federal Rolls of Prisoners of War: Captured at Chattanooga, TN on 7/5/1864; Forwarded to the U.S. Military Prison, Louisville, KY from Nashville, TN on 7/13/1864. Transferred to Camp Douglas, IL on 7/16/1864; Discharged on 6/16/1865 in accordance with General Order #109 of the Adjutant General's Office, Washington, D.C. 6/6/1865. *Born:* 10/14/1846. *Died:* 8/17/1891. *Buried:* Natchez City Cemetery located at Natchez, Adams County, MS.

Howe, William—Pvt.—Enlisted: 8/15/1861 at Natchez, MS. Rolls for 8/15/1861 through 2/1863: Present. Killed at the Battle of Jackson, MS in 7/1863.

Hubbard, Alonzo R. (aka Hurberd)—Pvt.—Enlisted: 8/15/1861 at Natchez, MS. Rolls for 8/15/1861 through 2/1863: Present. Rolls for 1/1864 through 2/1864: Absent, on furlough since 2/20/1864. Rolls for 8/1864 through 4/1865: Absent, captured on 8/5/1864. Federals Rolls of Prisoners of War: Captured near Atlanta, GA on 8/5/1864; Forwarded to the U.S. Military Prison, Louisville, KY on 8/12/1864. Transferred to Camp Chase, OH on 8/14/1864; Paroled at Camp Chase, OH on 2/12/1865 for Exchange. Exchanged at Boulware and Cox Wharf, James River, VA on 2/20–21/1865.

Ireland, George A.—Pvt.—Enlisted: 8/15/1861 at Waterloo, MS. Rolls for 8/15/1861 through 6/1862: Present. Rolls for 11/1862 through 2/1863: Absent, in jail at Savannah, GA. Rolls for 1/1864 through 2/1864: Deserted. Federal Rolls of Prisoners of War: Captured at Chattanooga, TN on 11/24/1863; Sent to the U.S. Military Prison, Louisville, KY from Nashville, TN on 12/7/1863. Forwarded to Rock Island Barracks, IL on 12/9/1863; Enlisted in the U.S. Naval Service at Rock Island Barracks, IL and transferred to the Naval Rendezvous, Camp Douglas, Chicago, IL on 1/25/1864.

Ireland, Thomas—Pvt.—Enlisted: 3/1/1862 at Natchez, MS. Rolls for 3/1/1862 through 2/1864: Present. Federal Rolls of Prisoners of War: Captured at Atlanta, GA on 9/1/1864. On U.S. 2nd Division, 20th Army Corps Hospital Register: Admitted on 9/6/1864; Sent to General Hospital on 9/13/1864. Transferred to General Field Hospital, Dept. of the Cumberland, Atlanta, GA due to left hand finger amputation; Sent to Barracks on 10/7/1864. Forwarded to the U.S. Military Prison, Louisville, KY from Nashville, TN on 10/28/1864; Received at Camp Douglas, IL on 11/1/1864. Released on the U.S. Oath of Allegiance on 6/13/1865. *Residence:* Jefferson Parish, LA. Description at release-Complexion: fair-Hair: light-Eyes: blue-Height: 5 ft. 5 in. *Residence:* Natchez, Adams County, MS. *Buried:* Natchez City Cemetery located at Natchez, MS.

Keep, T.F.—Pvt.—Enlisted: 8/5/1861 at Natchez, MS. Rolls for 8/5/1861 through 9/1/1861: Absent, sick at the residence of Mr. Enders at Richmond, VA.

Ketteringham, Frank K.—Pvt.—Enlisted: 3/1/1862 at Natchez, MS. Rolls for 3/1/1862 through 6/1862: Present. Rolls for 11/1862 through 2/1863: Absent, on detached service since 11/21/1862. Rolls for 1/1864 through 4/1865: Absent, assigned to duty in the Engineers Corps by order of the Secretary of War on 10/6/1863. Confederate Pension Application dated 1916 on file at the Mississippi Dept. of Archives and History-Target Card: Ketteringham, Frank-County: Adams.

Kittrell, G. (aka Keptnell)—Pvt.—Enlisted: 5/10/1862 at Washington County, GA. Rolls for 8/31/1864 through 2/28/1865: Present. Federal Rolls of Prisoners of War: Captured at Spanish Fort, AL on 4/8/1865; Received at Ship Island, MS on 4/10/1865. Transferred from Ship Island, MS to Vicksburg, MS on 5/1/1865.

On Rolls of Federal Headquarters for Exchange of Prisoners, Camp Townsend, MS: Received on 5/6/1865. Rolls of Prisoners of War, C.S.A: Surrendered at Citronelle, AL on 5/4/1865; Paroled at Meridian, MS on 5/10/1865. *Residence:* Washington County, GA.

Lanier, Joseph H. — Pvt. — Enlisted: 8/15/1861 at Natchez, MS. Rolls for 8/15/1861 through 4/1862: Present. Killed at the Battle of Secessionville, S.C. on 6/16/1862.

Lanier, R.J. — Pvt. — Enlisted: 8/15/1861 at Natchez, MS. Rolls for 8/15/1861 through 6/1862: Present. Rolls for 11/1862 through 12/1862: Absent, sick in camp at Savannah, GA. Rolls for 1/1863 through 2/1863: Present. Rolls for 1/1864 through 2/1864: Absent, sick in hospital since 9/5/1863. Rolls for 8/31/1864 through 2/28/1865: Absent, assumed to be a Prisoner of War. Rolls for 3/1865 through 4/1865: Absent, Prisoner of War since 7/1/1864. Federal Rolls of Prisoners of War: Captured near Rodney, MS on 7/19/1864; Confined in the U.S. Military Prison, Natchez, MS on 8/6/1864. Received at New Orleans, LA on 9/10/1864; Transferred to Ship Island, MS on 10/5/1864. Forwarded to Fort Columbus, N.Y. Harbor on 11/16/1864; Sent to Elmira, N.Y. on 11/19/1864. Paroled at Elmira, N.Y. on 2/9/1865; Sent to James River, VA for Exchange. Received and Exchanged at Boulware and Cox Wharf, James River, VA on 2/20–21/1865.

Lewell, John Quincy Adams (aka Level) — Pvt. — Enlisted: 8/8/1861 at Winnsboro, LA. Rolls for 8/8/1861 through 8/31/1861: Present. Rolls for 11/1861 through 12/1861: Discharged on Surgeon's Certificate of Disability. Rolls for 1/1862 through 6/1862: Present. Rolls for 9/1862 through 10/1862: Present, detailed this morning on Picket Guard. Rolls for 11/1862 through 2/1863: Present. Rolls for 8/31/1864 through 2/28/1865: Absent, missing since retreat from Tennessee. Federal Rolls of Prisoners of War: Captured near Columbia, TN on 12/24/1864; Received at the U.S. Military Prison, Louisville, KY from Nashville, TN on 1/3/1865. Forwarded to Camp Chase, OH on 2/9/1865; Released on the U.S. Oath of Allegiance on 5/13/1865. *Residence:* Franklin Parish, LA. Description at release: Complexion: florid-Hair: dark-Eyes: blue-Height: 5 ft. 9 in.

McAlister, Charles L. (aka McAllister, C.G.) — Pvt. — Enlisted: 8/15/1861 at Natchez, MS. Rolls for 8/15/1861 through 9/1/1861: Absent, sick in camp. Rolls for 9/1861 through 12/1862: Present. Rolls for 1/1863 through 2/1863: Absent, in hospital at Charleston, S.C. Rolls for 1/1864 through 4/1865: Absent, taken Prisoner of War at Missionary Ridge, TN on 11/25/1863. Federal Rolls of Prisoners of War: Captured at the Battle of Missionary Ridge, TN on 11/25/1863; Sent to the U.S. Military Prison, Louisville, KY from Nashville, TN on 12/7/1863. Transferred to Rock Island Barracks, IL on 12/9/1863. *Buried:* Natchez City Cemetery located at Natchez, Adams County, MS.

McDonald, John — Pvt. — Enlisted: 8/15/1861 at Natchez, MS. Rolls for 8/15/1861 through 9/1/1861: Absent, sick at Saint Charles Hospital, Richmond, VA. Rolls for 9/1861 through 4/1862: Present. Rolls for 5/1862 through 6/1862: Absent, detailed to work on Gunboat at Savannah, GA. Regimental Return for 7/1862: At work in Savannah, GA. Regimental Returns for 8/1862 and 9/1862: On Gunboat at Savannah, GA. Rolls for 11/1862 through 12/1862: Absent, sick in camp at Savannah, GA; Returned from working on Gunboat on 11/27/1862. Rolls for 1/1863 through 2/1863: Present. Rolls for 1/1864 through 2/1864: Absent, wounded at the Battle of Chickamauga, GA on 9/19/1863. Rolls for 8/31/1864 through 2/28/1865: Present. Rolls for 3/1865 through 4/1865: Absent, in hospital from wounds received at the Battle of Chickamauga, GA.

McGehee, J.P. — Pvt.-Rolls of Prisoners of War, C.S.A: Surrendered at Citronelle, AL on 5/4/1865; Paroled at Meridian, MS on 5/10/1865. *Residence:* Franklinton, Washington Parish, LA. Soldier also served as a Pvt. with the Louisiana Pelican Infantry Regiment-Co. G.

McGehee, M.M. — Pvt.-Rolls of Prisoners of War, C.S.A: Surrendered at Citronelle, AL on 5/4/1865; Paroled at Meridian, MS on 5/10/1865. *Residence:* Franklinton, Washington Parish, LA. Soldier also served as a Pvt. with the Louisiana Pelican Infantry Regiment-Co. G.

Maulding, E.W. — Pvt. — Enlisted: 8/15/1861 at Natchez, MS. Rolls for 9/1861 through 2/1863: Present. Rolls for 1/1864 through 2/1864: Deserted.

Meng, James S. — Surgeon — (See Field and Staff)

Middleton, W. Clark — Pvt. — Enlisted: 8/15/1861 at Natchez, MS. Rolls for 8/15/1861 through 9/1/1861: Absent, sick with typhoid fever at Temperance Hall Hospital, Richmond, VA. Died in Virginia in 9/1861.

Miller, John — Pvt. — Enlisted: 8/15/1861 at Natchez, MS. Rolls for 9/1861 through 10/1861: Present. Rolls for 11/1861 through 12/1861: Discharged.

Moore, Joseph Lawson — Pvt./Musician — (See Field and Staff)

Mosby, W.B. (aka Moseby) — Pvt. — Enlisted: 3/1/1862 at Natchez, MS. Rolls for 3/1/1862 through 6/1862: Present. Rolls for 11/1862 through 12/1862: Absent with leave at Charleston, S.C. Rolls for 1/1863 through 2/1863: Present. Rolls for 1/1864 through 2/1864: Transferred to the 5th Mississippi Infantry on 1/1/1863.

Mulkey, John W. (aka Mulky, G.W.) — Pvt. — Enlisted: 8/15/1861 at Natchez, MS. Rolls for 8/15/1861 through 4/1862: Present. Rolls for 5/1862 through 6/1862: Absent at Augusta, GA; Wounded at the Battle of Secessionville, S.C. on 6/16/1862. Rolls for 11/1862 through 12/1862: Transferred to the C.S. Marine Corps on 12/15/1862; Served as Coal-Heaver on board the C.S.S. Atlanta and the C.S.S. Georgia. Federal Rolls of Prisoners of War: Captured on board the C.S.S. Atlanta at Wassaw Sound, GA on 6/17/1863. *Born:* 1843 in Mississippi.

Nickels, Henry A. (aka Nickles, Nichols) — Pvt. — Enlisted: 8/15/1861 at Natchez, MS. Rolls for 8/15/1861 through 2/1862: Present. Rolls for 3/1862 through 4/1862: Absent, detailed as Hospital Nurse. Rolls for 5/1862 through 6/1862: Absent, sick in hospital at Charleston, S.C. Rolls for 11/1862 through 12/1862: Transferred to the C.S. Marine Corps on 12/15/1862. Federal Rolls of Prisoners of War: Captured at Wassaw Sound, GA on board the C.S.S. Atlanta on 6/17/1863. *Born:* England. Age at enlistment: 20 yrs.

O'Brien, John (aka O'Brient) — Pvt. — Enlisted: 8/15/1861 at Natchez, MS. Rolls for 8/15/1861 through 6/1862: Present. Rolls for 11/1862 through 12/1862: Absent, sick in camp at Savannah, GA. Rolls for 1/1863 through 2/1863: Present. Rolls for 1/1864 through 2/1864: Present. Rolls for 8/31/1864 through 4/1865: Absent, assumed to be a Prisoner of War since 8/31/1864.

Phillips, Richard J. (aka Philips, K.J.) — Pvt. — Enlisted: 8/15/1861 at Natchez, MS. Rolls for 8/15/1861 through 2/1864: Present. Rolls for 8/31/1864 through 2/28/1865: Killed in prison at Indianapolis, IN. Federal Rolls of Prisoners of War: Captured near Resaca, GA on 5/16/1864; Forwarded to the U.S. Military Prison, Louisville, KY from Nashville, TN on 5/20/1864. Transferred to Camp Morton, IN on 5/22/1864; Shot by a sentinel on 9/29/1864. *Buried:* Green Lawn Cemetery, Indianapolis, Marion County, IN.

Pickens, A.H. (aka Pickings) — Pvt. — Enlisted: 3/1/1862 at Natchez, MS. Rolls for 3/1/1862 through 2/1863: Present. Rolls for 1/1864 through 2/1864: Absent, sick in hospital since ?/12/1863. Rolls for 8/31/1864 through 2/28/1865: Died at Natchez, MS in 1864.

Pickins, David A. (aka Pickens, A.D.) — Pvt. — Enlisted: 8/15/1861 at Natchez, MS. Rolls for 8/15/1861 through 4/1862: Present. Rolls for 5/1862 through 12/1862: Absent, sick in hospital at Charleston, S.C. Rolls for 1/1863 through 2/1863: Present. Rolls for 1/1864 through 2/1864: Absent, wounded in right hand at the Battle of Chickamauga, GA on 9/19/1863. Rolls for 8/31/1864 through 4/1865: Absent, detailed in hospital at Columbus, GA. Rolls of Prisoners of War, C.S.A: Surrendered at Citronelle, AL on 5/4/1865; Paroled at 16th Army Corps Headquarters, Montgomery, AL on 5/22/1865. *Born:* Near Wescow, Fayette County, TN. *Married:* Never. *Children:* None. *Residence:* New Orleans, LA since 1870. Confederate Pension Application dated 6/9/1902 on file at the Louisiana State Archives-Microfilm Reel: CP1.110-Microdex 3-Sequence 14-Target Card: Pickins, David A.-Parish: Orleans-4 Pages.

Plantz, Charles L.F. (aka Platz, Pleintz) — Pvt. — Enlisted: 8/15/1861 at Natchez, MS. Rolls for 8/15/1861 through 2/1862: Present. Rolls for 3/1862 through 6/1862: Present, detailed as Hospital Nurse for the Battalion. Rolls for 11/1862 through 12/1862: Absent, sick in camp at Savannah, GA. Rolls for 1/1863 through 2/1863: Present. Rolls for 1/1864 through 2/1864: Present. Federal Rolls of Prisoners of War: Captured near Jonesboro, GA on 8/31/1864; Exchanged on 9/20—22/1864 by order of Maj. Gen. William T. Sherman, Commanding Military Dept. of the Mississippi at Rough and Ready, GA. Rolls for 8/31/1864 through 4/1865: Present. Rolls of Prisoners of War, C.S.A: Surrendered at Citronelle, AL on 5/4/1865; Paroled at Meridian, MS on 5/10/1865. *Residence:* Natchez, Adams County, MS. Soldier also served as a Pvt. with the Louisiana Pelican Infantry Regiment-Co. G and the Louisiana State Militia-Orleans Guard Battalion-Co. H. *Married:* Marie Despommier on 9/11/1869 at Notre Dame Church at New Orleans, LA. *Died:* 11/7/1890 at New Orleans, LA due to Apoplexy. *Buried:* Old Girod St. Cemetery located at New Orleans, Orleans Parish, LA. *Wife Born:* 8/1/1851 at Saint James Parish, LA. Two Confederate Widows Pension Applications dated 12/2/1926 and 5/30/1928 on file at the Louisiana State Archives-Microfilm Reel: CP1.111-Microdex 2-Sequence 13-Target Card: Plantz, Marie (Despommier)-Parish: Orleans-14 Pages.

Powers, Patrick Michael — Pvt. — Enlisted: 5/1/1862 at Natchez, MS. Rolls for 5/1/1862 through 2/1863: Present. Rolls for 1/1864 through 4/1865: Absent, taken Prisoner of War at the Battle of Missionary Ridge, TN on 11/25/1863. Federal Rolls of Prisoners of War: Captured at the Battle of Missionary Ridge, TN on 11/25/1863; Forwarded to the U.S. Military Prison, Louisville, KY from Nashville, TN on 12/7/1863. Transferred to Rock Island Barracks, IL on 12/11/1863. On Roll dated Headquarters, Rock Island Barracks, IL 3/18/1864: Prisoner desires to take the U.S. Oath of Allegiance. Remarks: Deserted from the C.S. Army and wishes to go home; Released on the U.S. Oath of Allegiance on 5/17/1865. *Residence:* Natchez, MS. *Buried:* Natchez City Cemetery located at Natchez, Adams County, MS.

Rehwinkel, R. (aka Rehiwinkle, Rehwinkle, Rehnwinkle) — Pvt. — Enlisted: 8/15/1861 at Natchez, MS. Rolls for 8/15/1861 through 6/1862: Present. Rolls for 11/1862 through 12/1862: Transferred to the C.S. Marine Corps on 12/15/1862. Also served as a Seaman on board the C.S.S. Isondiga.

Reynolds, J.W. — Pvt. — Enlisted: 8/15/1861 at Natchez, MS. Rolls for 8/15/1861 through 2/1863: Present. Rolls for 1/1864 through 2/1864: Absent, sick in hospital since 12/1/1863.

Rhodes, A.F. (aka A.T.) — Pvt. — Enlisted: 8/15/1861 at Natchez, MS. Rolls for 8/15/1861 through 9/1/1861: Present. Rolls for 9/1861 through 10/1861: Absent, sick at Richmond, VA. Rolls for 11/1861 through 12/1861: Discharged and collected pay.

Rife, J.W. — Pvt. — Enlisted: 8/15/1861 at Natchez, MS. Rolls for 8/15/1861 through 6/1862: Present. Rolls for 11/1862 through 12/1862: Transferred to the C.S. Marine Corps on 12/15/1862. Served as a Seaman on board the C.S.S. Isondiga.

Riggs, G.A.A. — Pvt. — Enlisted: 8/15/1861 at Natchez, MS. Rolls for 8/15/1861 through 9/1/1861: Disabled by internal injuries received on the Railroad near Knoxville, TN on 8/19/1861. Rolls for 9/1861 through 10/1861: Absent, sick at Richmond, VA. Rolls for 11/1861 through 12/1861: Discharged and collected pay.

Saul, Charles (aka Sauls, Saules) — Pvt. — Enlisted: 8/15/1861 at Camp Moore, LA. Rolls for 8/15/1861 through 9/1/1861: Absent, sick in camp with measles. Rolls for 9/1861 through 10/1861: Present. Rolls for 11/1861 through 2/1862: Absent, sick at Richmond, VA. Rolls for 3/1862 through 2/28/1865: Present. Rolls for 3/1865 through 4/1865: Absent, taken Prisoner of War at Spanish Fort, AL on 4/7/1865. Federal Rolls of Prisoners of War: Captured at Spanish Fort, AL on 4/8/1865; Received at Ship Island, MS on 4/10/1865. Forwarded to Vicksburg, MS on 5/1/1865; Paroled at Camp Townsend, MS on 5/6/1865.

Sawyer, C.M. — Pvt. — Enlisted: 3/1/1862 at Natchez, MS. Rolls for 3/1/1862 through 4/1862: Present. Rolls for 5/1862 through 6/1862: Absent, sick in hospital at Charleston, S.C. Rolls for 11/1862 through 12/1862: Absent, sick in camp at Savannah, GA. Rolls for 1/1863 through 2/1863: Absent, on detached service at Charleston, S.C. since 2/15/1863. Rolls for 1/1864 through 2/1864: Absent, sick in hospital since 9/10/1862. Rolls for 8/31/1864 through 2/28/1865: Absent, sick in hospital at Montgomery, AL. Rolls for 3/1865 through 4/1865: Absent, sick in hospital at West Point, MS since 7/28/1864.

Scheuber, Charles (aka Schember, Schuber, Schurber) — Pvt. — Enlisted: 4/10/1862 at Natchez, MS. Rolls for 4/10/1862 through 12/1862: Present. Rolls for 1/1863 through 2/1863: Was in camp this morning, but now on duty at Fort Boggs, GA. Rolls for 1/1864 through 2/1864: Present. Rolls for 8/31/1864 through 4/1865: Absent, taken Prisoner of War on 7/5/1864. Federal Rolls of Prisoners of War: Captured near Chattahoochee, GA on 7/5/1864; Received at the U.S. Military Prison, Louisville, KY from Nashville, TN on 7/15/1864. Forwarded to Camp Douglas, IL on 7/18/1864. On Roll dated Camp Douglas, IL 2/15/1865: Applied to take the U.S. Oath of Allegiance. Remarks: Claims to have been loyal and enlisted to avoid conscription; Captured and desires to take the U.S. Oath of Allegiance. Released on the U.S. Oath of Allegiance from Camp Douglas, IL on 5/4/1865. *Residence:* Adams County, MS. Description at oath-Complexion: dark-Hair: black-Eyes: black-Height: 5 ft. 7 in.

Scheuber, William H. (aka Schuber, Schuver) — Pvt.-Federal Rolls of Prisoners of War: Captured at Chattahoochee, GA on 7/5/1864; Transferred to Camp Douglas, IL on 7/17/1864 from Louisville, KY. Released by order of the U.S. President on 5/4/1865.

Scothorn, Henry L. (aka Scotthorn, H.O.) — Pvt. — Enlisted: 8/15/1861 at Natchez, MS. Rolls for 8/15/1861 through 6/1862: Present. Rolls for 11/1862 through 12/1862: Absent, detailed as Teamster at Savannah, GA. Rolls for 1/1863 through 2/1863: Absent, was in camp this morning, but now on duty at Fort Boggs, GA. *Born:* 8/4/1841. *Died:* 4/21/1908. *Buried:* Union Baptist Church located on Hwy. 178, 3 miles southeast of Roxie, Franklin County, MS.

Scott, Thomas J. — Pvt. — Enlisted: 8/15/1861 at Natchez, MS. Rolls for 8/15/1861 through 9/1/1861: Present. Rolls for 9/1861 through 10/1861: Deceased. Rolls for 11/1861 through 12/1861: Died at Jackson River Depot, VA on 10/22/1861 due to Dropsy. *Married:* Malinda Jenkins in 10/1858 at Enos Church, Washington Parish, LA. *Buried:* Amite City Cemetery located at Amite, Tangipahoa Parish, LA. *Wife Born:* 1829. Two Confederate Widows Pension Applications dated 11/16/1900 and 11/22/1911 on file at the Louisiana State Archives-Microfilm Reel: CP1.125-Microdex 1-Sequence 33-Target Card: Scott, Malinda (Jenkins)-Parish: Tangipahoa-6 Pages.

Seltzer, Charles B. (aka Setzer, Shaver, C.D., J.R.) — Pvt. — Enlisted: 8/15/1861 at Natchez, MS. Rolls for 8/15/1861 through 6/1862: Present. Rolls for 11/1862 through 12/1862: Absent, sick in camp at Savannah, GA. Rolls for 1/1863 through 2/1863: Absent, was in camp this morning, but now on duty at Fort Boggs, GA. Rolls for 1/1864 through 2/1864: Absent, detailed as Division Teamster on 2/17/1864. Rolls for 8/31/1864 through 4/1865: Present. Rolls of Prisoners of War, C.S.A: Surrendered at Citronelle, AL on 5/4/1865; Paroled at Meridian, MS on 5/10/1865. *Residence:* Thornsville, GA.

Shepherd, William Albert (aka Sheppard) — Pvt. — Enlisted: 8/15/1861 at Natchez, MS. Rolls for 8/15/1861 through 9/1861: Present. Rolls for 9/1861 through 10/1861: Absent, sick in hospital at Jackson River Depot, VA. Rolls for 11/1861 through 12/1861: Discharged and collected pay. Rolls for 11/1862 through 12/1862: Present. Rolls for 1/1863 through 2/1863: On extra daily duty as Nurse at camp hospital. Rolls for 1/1864 through 2/28/1865: Absent, sick in hospital at West Point, MS. Rolls for 3/1865 through 4/1865: Absent, detailed in hospital. Rolls of Prisoners of War of West Point, MS Hospital Attendants and Patients, C.S.A: Surrendered at Citronelle, AL on 5/4/1865;

Paroled at Meridian, MS on 5/14/1865. *Residence:* Natchez, Adams County, MS. *Born:* 1844. *Died:* 8/27/1914. *Buried:* Oaklawn Cemetery located at Tulsa, Tulsa County, OK in Section 2, Block 140, Grave 1 under a Confederate Iron Cross headstone. Confederate Pension Application on file at the Oklahoma State Archives-Name: Shepherd, William Albert-Application: 4188-Reel: 10.

Sidway, G.D.—Pvt./Commissary—(See Field and Staff)

Smith, Alfred W.—Pvt.—Enlisted: 5/1/1862 at Natchez, MS. Rolls for 5/1/1862 through 6/1862: Absent, sick in hospital at Augusta, GA. Rolls for 11/1862 through 12/1862: Absent, sick at Savannah, GA. Rolls for 1/1863 through 2/1863: Present. Rolls for 1/1864 through 4/1865: Absent, taken Prisoner of War on 9/19/1863. Federal Rolls of Prisoners of War: Captured at the Battle of Chickamauga, GA on 9/19/1863; Received at Camp Douglas, IL on 10/4/1863. Discharged on 6/14/1865 in accordance with General Order #109, Adjutant Generals Office, Washington, D.C. 6/6/1865. *Residence:* Natchez, Adams County, MS. Confederate Widows Pension Application dated 1916 on file at the Mississippi Dept. of Archives and History-Target Card: Smith, Celeste Virginia-County: Adams.

Smith, Austin Williams—Pvt./2nd Cpl./Color Bearer—(See Color Bearers)

Smith, Frank—Pvt./Color Bearer—(See Color Bearers)

Smith, R.T. (aka R.J.)—Pvt.—Enlisted: 1/16/1862 at Mobile, AL. Rolls for 1/16/1862 through 4/1862: Present. Rolls for 5/1862 through 6/1862: Absent, detailed to work on Gunboat at Savannah, GA. Rolls for 11/1862 through 12/1862: Absent, returned to camp from working on Gunboat on 11/27/1862. Rolls for 1/1863 through 2/1863: Present or absent not stated. Rolls for 1/1864 through 2/1864: Absent, on daily or extra duty with Howell's Battalion since 10/25/1863. On Register of Rebel Deserters and Refugees, Provost Marshal Generals Office, Washington, D. C: Received on 4/7/1865 from City Point, VA; Took the U.S. Oath of Allegiance and transportation ordered to New York City, N.Y. Status: Deserter from the C.S. Army.

Smith, Samuel—Pvt.—Enlisted: 4/11/1861 at Pensacola, FL. Rolls for 3/1865 through 4/1865: Present. Rolls of Prisoners of War, C.S.A: Surrendered at Citronelle, AL on 5/4/1865; Paroled at Meridian, MS on 5/10/1865. *Residence:* Natchez, Adams County, MS. Soldier also served as a Pvt. with the Louisiana Pelican Infantry Regiment-Co. G.

Spangler, Adam H. (aka Spankler)—Pvt.—Enlisted: 8/15/1861 at Natchez, MS. Rolls for 8/15/1861 through 9/1/1861: Present. Rolls for 9/1861 through 10/1861: Absent, sick in hospital. Rolls for 11/1861 through 12/1861: Discharged and collected pay in 12/1861.

Spurlock, W. J.—Pvt.—Enlisted: 3/1/1862 at Natchez, MS. Rolls for 3/1/1862 through 2/1863: Present. Rolls for 1/1864 through 2/1864: Present. Killed at the Battle of Ezra Church, GA on 7/28/1864.

Stead, James J.—Pvt.—Enlisted: 8/15/1861 at Natchez, MS. Rolls for 8/15/1861 through 2/1863: Present. Rolls for 1/1864 through 2/1864: Present. Killed at the Battle of Ezra Church, GA on 7/28/1864.

Stockman, John Roane (aka Stopman)—Pvt.—Enlisted: 8/15/1861 at Natchez, MS. Rolls for 8/15/1861 through 4/1862: Present. Rolls for 5/1862 through 6/1862: Absent, wounded at the Battle of Secessionville, S.C. on 6/16/1862 and absent at Columbia, S.C. Rolls for 11/1862 through 2/1863: Present. Rolls for 1/1864 through 4/1865: Absent, detailed as Clerk to Brig. Gen. William B. Taliaferro on 4/30/1863. Rolls of Prisoners of War, C.S.A: Surrendered at Goldsboro, N.C. on 4/26/1865; Paroled at Greensboro, N.C. on 4/26/1865. *Buried:* Natchez City Cemetery located at Natchez, Adams County, MS.

Strachan, William (aka Strachen, Stracher, Strather)—Pvt.—Enlisted: 8/15/1861 at Natchez, MS. Rolls for 8/15/1861 through 2/1863: Present. Rolls for 1/1864 through 2/1864: Deserted on 11/24/1863. Federal Rolls of Prisoners of War: Captured at Chattanooga, TN on 11/24/1863; Received at the U.S. Military Prison, Louisville, KY from Nashville, TN on 12/8/1863. Forwarded to Rock Island, IL on 12/9/1863. On Roll dated Headquarters, Rock Island Barracks, IL 3/18/1864: Prisoner desires to take the U.S. Oath of Allegiance. Remarks: Coward. Native of Scotland. Released on 5/16/1865 by General Order #109, Adjutant General Office, Washington, D.C., issued on 5/9/1865. *Residence:* St. Louis, MO.

Strickland, Drary H.—Pvt.-Federal Rolls of Prisoners of War: Captured near Atlanta, GA on 8/3/1864; Transferred to Camp Chase, OH from the U.S. Military Prison, Louisville, KY on 8/13/1864.

Taylor, Fred C.—Pvt.—Enlisted: 8/15/1861 at Natchez, MS. Rolls for 8/15/1861 through 4/1862: Present. Rolls for 5/1862 through 6/1862: Absent at Augusta, GA, wounded at the Battle of Secessionville, S.C. on 6/16/1862. Regimental Returns for 7/1862 and 8/1862: Sick at Augusta, GA. Regimental Return for 9/1862: Sick furlough. Rolls for 11/1862 through 12/1862: Absent on sick leave. Rolls for 1/1863 through 2/1863: Absent on sick leave at Natchez, MS. Rolls for 1/1864 through 2/1864: Absent, sick in hospital since 9/20/1863. Wounded at the Battle of Resaca, GA. *Died:* 6/3/1864. *Buried:* Oakland Cemetery located at Atlanta, Fulton County, GA.

Truly, Richard H.—Pvt.-(No War Dept. Record)-

Born: 1833 at Jefferson County, MS. *Died:* 1904. *Buried:* Jefferson County, MS.

Tyree, Jesse James (aka Tyler) — Pvt. — Enlisted: 8/15/1861 at Natchez, MS. Rolls for 8/15/1861 through 9/1/1861: Sick, in camp disabled due to rupture on 9/13/1861. Rolls for 10/1861 through 12/1862: Present. Rolls for 1/1863 through 2/1863: Present, on extra duty as Teamster. Rolls for 1/1864 through 4/1865: Present. Rolls of Prisoners of War, C.S.A: Surrendered at Citronelle, AL on 5/4/1865; Paroled at Meridian, MS on 5/10/1865. *Residence:* Natchez, MS. *Born:* 2/25/1844. *Died:* 4/17/1889. *Buried:* Natchez City Cemetery located at Natchez, Adams County, MS.

Underwood, J.H. — Pvt. — Enlisted: 8/15/1861 at Natchez, MS. Rolls for 8/15/1861 through 2/1864: Present. Rolls for 8/31/1864 through 2/28/1865: Absent, in hospital at Montgomery, AL due to wound received on 8/31/1864. Rolls for 3/1865 through 4/1865: Present. Rolls of Prisoners of War, C.S.A: Surrendered at Citronelle, AL on 5/4/1865; Paroled at Meridian, MS on 5/10/1865. *Residence:* Natchez, Adams County, MS.

Waddill, John M. (aka Wardell, Waddell) — Pvt. — Enlisted: 8/15/1861 at Natchez, MS. Rolls for 8/15/1861 through 2/1862: Present. Rolls for 3/1862 through 4/1862: Absent, sick in hospital in quarters. Rolls for 5/1862 through 12/1862: Present. Rolls for 1/1863 through 2/1863: Was in camp, but now absent on Picket Duty. Rolls for 1/1864 through 2/1864: Deserted on 7/16/1863 at Jackson, MS. Soldier also served with the 136th North Carolina Heavy Artillery. Confederate Widows Pension Application on file at the Georgia Dept. of Archives and History-Name: Waddell, Virginia T.-County: Fulton.

Walters, J. Louis (aka Walter) — Pvt. — Enlisted: 8/15/1861 at Natchez, MS. Rolls for 8/15/1861 through 2/1864: Present. Rolls for 8/31/1864 through 4/1865: Absent, taken Prisoner of War on 8/5/1864. Federal Rolls of Prisoners of War: Captured near Atlanta, GA on 8/5/1864; Received at the U.S. Military Prison, Louisville, KY from Nashville, TN on 8/12/1864. Forwarded to Camp Chase, OH on 8/13/1864.

Walters, Thomas (aka Walter) — Pvt. — Enlisted: 8/15/1861 at Natchez, MS. Rolls for 8/15/1861 through 2/1863: Present. Rolls for 1/1864 through 2/1864: Absent without leave since 7/16/1863. Rolls for 3/1865 through 4/1865: Absent, taken Prisoner of War on 7/16/1863. Federal Rolls of Prisoners of War: Captured near Jackson, MS on 7/18/1863; Sent to Snyder's Bluff, MS on 7/30/1863. Received at Vicksburg, MS on 7/31/1863; Transferred to Camp Morton, IN on 8/7/1863. Rolls of Prisoners of War at Camp Morton, IN: Prisoner desires to take the U.S. Oath of Allegiance. Remarks: Enlisted at Natchez, MS on 8/15/1861, desires to take the oath and go to Ohio and remain a loyal citizen; Case doubtful. Name appears as signature to a U.S. Oath of Allegiance subscribed and sworn to at Camp Morton, IN on 5/23/1865. *Residence:* Rolla, MO. Description at oath-Complexion: dark-Hair: black-Eyes: hazel-Height: 5 ft. 5½ in.

Ward, Charles R. (aka C.E., C.W.) — Pvt. — Enlisted: 8/15/1861 at Natchez, MS. Rolls for 8/15/1861 through 2/1862: Present. Rolls for 3/1862 through 6/1862: Absent, on detached service at Richmond, VA. Regimental Return for 7/1862: At work at Richmond, VA. Regimental Return for 8/1862 and 9/1862: Government service at Richmond, VA. Rolls for 11/1862 through 2/1864: Absent, on detached service at Richmond, VA by order of the Secretary of War since 4/30/1862. Rolls for 8/31/1864 through 4/1865: Present. Rolls of Prisoners of War, C.S.A: Surrendered at Citronelle, AL on 5/4/1865; Paroled at Meridian, MS on 5/10/1865. *Residence:* Richmond, Henrico County, VA. Soldier also served as a Pvt. with the Louisiana Pelican Infantry Regiment-Co. G. *Born:* 10/10/1841. *Married:* Winnie Tyree on 5/6/1866 at Vicksburg, MS. *Children:* 1 Son-James W. Ward. *Died:* 12/2/1902 at Natchez, MS due to Illness. *Buried:* Natchez City Cemetery located at Natchez, Adams County, MS. *Wife Died:* 5/28/1922. Confederate Widows Pension Application dated 7/14/1912 on file at the Louisiana State Archives-Microfilm Reel: CP1.143-Microdex 4-Sequence 38-Target Card: Ward, Winnie (Tyree)-Parish: Orleans-7 Pages.

Wardlow, G.B. (aka Wardlew, Wardlaw, G.D.) — Pvt. — Enlisted: 8/15/1861 at Natchez, MS. Rolls for 8/15/1861 through 6/1862: Present. Regimental Return for 8/1862: Absent with leave in Mississippi. Rolls for 11/1862 through 12/1862: Present. On C.S.A. General Military Hospital #4 Register, Wilmington, N. C: Admitted on 1/22/1863 due to pneumonia; Died on 1/27/1863. Rolls for 1/1863 through 2/1863: Died in hospital at Wilmington, N.C. on 1/27/1863.

Weir, Joseph T. — Pvt. — Enlisted: 8/15/1861 at Natchez, MS. Rolls for 8/15/1861 through 2/1862: Present. Rolls for 3/1862 through 6/1862: Present, detailed as Teamster for battalion. Regimental Returns for 7/1862 through 9/1862: Teamster. Rolls for 11/1862 through 12/1862: Present, Orderly for Col. Harrison. Rolls for 1/1863 through 2/1863: Present. Rolls for 1/1864 through 2/1864: Absent, sick in hospital since the Battle of Chickamauga, GA on 9/19/1863. *Born:* 3/23/1843. *Died:* 3/19/1914. *Buried:* Natchez City Cemetery located at Natchez, Adams County, MS.

Welch, James J. (aka Welsh, J.F.) — Pvt. — Enlisted: 8/15/1861 at Natchez, MS. Rolls for 8/15/1861 through 2/1864: Present. Rolls for 8/31/1864 through 4/1865: Absent, taken Prisoner of War on 8/5/1864. Federal Rolls of Prisoners of War: Captured near Atlanta, GA on 8/5/1864; Received at the U.S. Military Prison, Louisville, KY from Nashville, TN on 8/12/1864. Sent to Camp Chase, OH on 8/13/1864; Paroled at Camp Chase, OH and transferred to Point Lookout, MD for

Exchange on 3/18/1865. Exchanged at Boulware and Cox Wharf, James River, VA on 3/27/1865. Rolls of Prisoners of War, C.S.A: Surrendered at Citronelle, AL on 5/4/1865; Paroled at Montgomery, AL on 5/22/1865. *Born:* 2/15/1842. *Died:* 1/4/1904. *Buried:* Natchez City Cemetery located at Natchez, Adams County, MS.

Wells, Robert W.—Pvt./Sgt. Major—(See Field and Staff)

White, John P.—Pvt.—Enlisted: 3/12/1862 at New Orleans, LA. Rolls for 8/31/1864 through 2/28/1865: Absent, missing since 12/16/1864 and assumed to have been taken Prisoner of War. Rolls for 3/1865 through 4/1865: Absent, taken Prisoner of War on 8/5/1864. Federal Rolls of Prisoners of War: Captured near Columbia, TN on 12/22/1864; Received at the U.S. Military Prison, Louisville, KY from Nashville, TN on 1/2/1865. Transferred to Camp Chase, OH on 1/4/1865. Name appears as signature to the U.S. Oath of Allegiance subscribed and sworn to at Camp Chase, OH on 5/13/1865. Description at oath-Complexion: florid-Hair: dark-Eyes: dark-Height: 5 ft. *Residence:* Orleans Parish, LA.

Whitehead, D.O.—Pvt.—Enlisted: 5/2/1862 at Natchez, MS. Rolls for 5/2/1862 through 6/1862: D.O. and J.A. Whitehead were mustered in by Lt. Newton, and were to have joined Company E on 5/10/1862, but were forbidden to leave the State of Mississippi by Brig. Gen. Charles G.U. Dahlgren of the Mississippi State Troops. Gen. Dahlgren said that he had been so instructed by Gen. Pierre G.T. Beauregard. Regimental Return for 7/1862: Detained by order of Brig. Gen. Dahlgren. Rolls for 11/1862 through 12/1862: Absent, sick at Savannah, GA. Rolls for 1/1863 through 2/1863: Absent on sick leave.

Whitehead, J.A. (aka G.A.)—Pvt.—Enlisted: 5/2/1862 at Natchez, MS. Rolls for 5/2/1862 through 6/1862: D.O. and J.A. Whitehead were mustered in by Lt. Newton, and were to have joined Company E on 5/10/1862, but were forbidden to leave the State of Mississippi by Brig. Gen. Charles G.U. Dahlgren of the Mississippi State Troops. Gen. Dahlgren said that he had been so instructed by Gen. Pierre G.T. Beauregard. Regimental Return for 8/1862: Detained by order of Brig. Gen. Dahlgren. Rolls for 11/1862 through 2/1863: Present. Rolls for 1/1864 through 2/1864: Absent without leave since 8/10/1863.

COMPANY F: "OUACHITA REBELS," OUACHITA PARISH

Captain

Conner, Thomas N.—1st Lt./Capt.—Enlisted: 3/24/1862 at Monroe, LA; Appointed 1st Lt. on 3/25/1862. Rolls for 4/1862 through 2/1863: Present. Rolls for 3/1863 through 4/1863: Present, promoted to Capt. on 4/24/1863. Rolls for 3/1864 through 4/1864: Present. Rolls for 8/31/1864 through 2/27/1865: Absent with leave. Rolls for 3/1865 through 4/1865: Absent without leave. *Born:* 1/1/1829. *Died:* 2/20/1899. *Buried:* Old Monroe City Cemetery located at Monroe, Ouachita Parish, LA.

Walker, James H.—Capt.—Enlisted: 3/24/1862 at Monroe, LA; Appointed Capt. on 3/25/1862. Rolls for 3/24/1862 through 4/30/1862: Sick in quarters. Rolls for 5/1862 through 6/1862: Present, wounded in left lung at the Battle of Secessionville, S.C. on 6/16/1862. Regimental Return for 7/1862 and 8/1862: Present or absent not stated. Rolls for 9/1862 through 2/1863: Absent on sick furlough since 10/28/1862. Resigned on 4/24/1863. Captain Successor: T.N. Conner. *Born:* 4/22/1832 near Greensboro, Green County, GA. *Married:* Yes. *Children:* 6 Daughters. *Occupation:* School Teacher, Justice of the Peace and Bookkeeper. *Residences:* Morehouse Parish, Ouachita Parish, Claiborne Parish and Bienville Parish, LA for life except for short time teaching school at Magnolia, Columbia County, AR. *Wife's Age:* 65 as of 1899. Three Confederate Pension Applications dated 12/26/1899, 6/29/1906 and 12/28/1908 on file at the Louisiana State Archives-Microfilm Reel: CP1.142-Microdex 4-Sequence 43-Target Card: Walker, James H.-Parish: Bienville-14 Pages. Also a Confederate Proofs and Land Warrant Application on file-Name: Walker, James H.-Microfilm Reel: 1-Frame Number: 0446-Act: 116-Pages: 2-Parish: Claiborne.

Lieutenant

Herron, Daniel B. (aka Herring)—2nd Lt./1st Lt.—Enlisted: 3/24/1862 at Monroe, LA. Rolls for 3/24/1862 through 4/1862: Absent, on detached duty at Montgomery, AL. Rolls for 5/1862 through 12/1862: Present. Promoted to 1st Lt. on 4/24/1863. Rolls for 1/1864 through 2/1864: Present, on Picket Duty. Rolls for 3/1864 through 4/1864: Absent without leave since 3/8/1864. Soldier also served as a 2nd Lt. with the 4th Louisiana Cavalry-Co. G. Official Rolls of Paroled Officers, C.S.A: Surrendered at New Orleans, LA on 5/26/1865; Paroled at Monroe, LA on 6/7/1865.

Land, James B. (aka J.O.)—1st Sgt./Jr. 2nd Lt.—Enlisted: 3/24/1862 at Monroe, LA. Rolls for 3/24/1862 through 6/1862: Present, promoted to Jr. 2nd Lt. on 5/24/1862. Rolls for 9/1862 through 2/1863: Present. Rolls for 3/1864 through 4/1864: Present. Rolls for 8/31/1864 through 2/28/1865: Present or absent not stated. Rolls for 3/1865 through 4/1865: Absent, on detached service in east Louisiana by order of Brig. Gen. Randall L. Gibson.

Sanford, William D., Sr.—Sr. 2nd Lt.—Enlisted: 3/24/1862 at Monroe, LA; Elected 2nd Lt. same day. Rolls for 3/24/1862 through 4/30/1862: Present. Rolls for 5/1862 through 6/1862: Died on 5/19/1862. 2nd Lt. Successor: Herron, D.B.

Voorhees, John V.C. (aka Vorhees)—Pvt./5th Sgt./Jr. 2nd Lt.—Enlisted: 3/24/1862 at Monroe, LA. Rolls for 3/24/1862 through 4/30/1862: Absent, sick in hospital at Augusta, GA. Rolls for 5/1862 through 6/1862: Present, promoted to 5th Sgt. on 5/24/1862. Rolls for 9/1862 through 10/1862: Present. Rolls for 11/1862 through 12/1862: Absent, at work on Gunboat at Savannah, GA. Rolls for 1/1863 through 2/1863: Present. Elected Jr. 2nd Lt. on 4/24/1863. Rolls for 3/1864 through 4/1864: Absent, captured at Natchez, MS. Rolls for 8/31/1864 through 2/28/1865: Present or absent not stated. Rolls for 3/1865 through 4/1865: Absent, Prisoner of War. Federal Rolls of Prisoners of War: Captured at Big Black, MS on 11/16/1863; Received at Camp Morton, IN on 11/23/1863. Rolls of Prisoners of War at Camp Morton, IN: Prisoner desires to take the U.S. Oath of Allegiance. Remarks: Enlisted on 3/24/1861 at Monroe, LA and commissioned Jr. 2nd Lt. on 6/16/1862; Desires to take the U.S. Oath of Allegiance. Citizen of New York and proposes to remain loyal, Oath recommended. Transferred to Camp Chase, OH on 1/27/1864. Rolls of Prisoners of War at Camp Chase, OH: Prisoner desires to take the U.S. Oath of Allegiance on 6/10/1864. Remarks: Deserter from the C.S. Army, should be released.

Sergeant

Bullock, William C.—Pvt./5th Sgt.—Enlisted: 3/24/1862 at Monroe, LA. Rolls for 3/24/1862 through 6/1862: Present. Rolls for 9/1862 through 10/1862: Absent, on picket duty at Savannah, GA. Rolls for 11/1862 through 4/1864: Present, promoted to 5th Sgt. on 11/2/1862. Federal Rolls of Prisoners of War: Captured near Atlanta, GA on 8/5/1864; Received at the U.S. Military Prison, Louisville, KY from Nashville, TN on 8/12/1864. Sent to Camp Chase, OH on 8/13/1864; Paroled at Camp Chase, OH on 2/12/1865. Transferred to Point Lookout, MD on 2/20–21/1865. Rolls for 3/1865 through 4/1865: Present. Rolls of Prisoners of War, C.S.A: Surrendered at Citronelle, AL on 5/4/1865; Paroled at Meridian, MS on 5/10/1865. *Residence:* Monroe, Ouachita Parish, LA.

Butland, George C.—Pvt./4th Sgt.—Enlisted: 3/24/1862 at Monroe, LA. Rolls for 3/24/1862 through 8/1862: Present. Rolls for 9/1862 through 10/1862: Present, promoted to 4th Sgt. on 9/16/1862. Rolls for 11/1862 through 2/1863: Absent, detached to work on Gunboat at Savannah, GA. Rolls for 3/1864 through 4/1864: Transferred to the C.S. Naval Service on 4/12/1864.

Foster, Jonathan H. (aka E.)—Pvt./4th Cpl./Sgt.—Enlisted: 8/22/1862 at Monroe, LA. Rolls for 8/22/1862 through 10/1862: Present. Rolls for 11/1862 through 12/1862: Present, promoted to 4th Cpl. on 11/5/1862. Rolls for 1/1863 through 2/1863: Present on Picket Duty. Federal Rolls of Prisoners of War: Captured near Jackson, MS on 7/4/1863; Sent to Snyder's Bluff, MS on 7/30/1863. Forwarded to Camp Morton, IN on 8/7/1863; Died at Camp Morton, IN on 1/29/1865 due to Inflammation of the Lungs. *Buried:* Crown Hill Cemetery located at Indianapolis, Marion County, IN.

Hazelton, William A.—Pvt./Sgt./Pvt.—Enlisted: 3/24/1862 at Monroe, LA. Rolls for 3/1862 through 4/1862: Present, promoted to Sgt. on 4/24/1862. Rolls for 5/1862 through 2/1863: Present.

Herron, Thomas C.—Sgt./Pvt.-Co. F—Enlisted: 3/24/1862 at Monroe, LA. Rolls for 3/24/1862 through 4/30/1862: Present. Rolls for 5/1862 through 2/1863: Died on 5/9/1862.

Jarrett, Henry T.—Pvt./4th Cpl./3rd Cpl./Sgt.—Enlisted: 3/24/1862 at Monroe, LA. Rolls for 3/24/1862 through 10/1862: Present, promoted to 4th Cpl. on 10/19/1862. Rolls for 11/1862 through 12/1862: Present, promoted to 3rd Cpl. on 11/5/1862. Rolls for 1/1863 through 2/1863: Present. Federal Rolls of Prisoners of War: Captured at the Battle of Missionary Ridge, TN on 11/25/1863; Received at the U.S. Military Prison, Louisville, KY on 12/7/1863. Forwarded to Rock Island Barracks, IL on 12/9/1863; Paroled at Rock Island Barracks, IL and transferred for Exchange on 3/6/1865. Exchanged at Boulware and Cox Wharf, VA on 3/10–12/1865.

Rampy, Thomas F.—Sgt.—Enlisted: 3/24/1862 at Monroe, LA. Rolls for 3/24/1862 through 4/30/1862: Present. Rolls for 5/1862 through 6/1862: Present, sick in hospital at Charleston, S.C. Rolls for 9/1862 through 12/1862: Present. Rolls for 1/1863 through 2/1863: Absent, in hospital at Savannah, GA. Rolls for 3/1864 through 4/1864: Absent without leave since 12/1/1863.

Swofford, William R.—Sgt.—Enlisted: 3/24/1862 at Monroe, LA. Rolls for 3/24/1862 through 4/30/1862: Died on 4/23/1862.

White, Virginius F.—Pvt./1st Sgt.—Enlisted: 3/24/1862 at Monroe, LA. Rolls for 3/24/1862 through 2/1863: Present. Rolls for 3/1864 through 4/1865: Absent, captured at the Battle of Missionary Ridge, TN on 11/25/1863. Federal Rolls of Prisoners of War: Captured at the Battle of Missionary Ridge, TN on 11/25/1863; Received at the U.S. Military Prison, Louisville, KY from Nashville, TN on 12/7/1863. Forwarded to Rock Island Barracks, IL on 12/9/1863; Enlisted at Rock Island Barracks, IL in the U.S. Army for frontier service on 10/31/1864.

Corporal

Graves, James L.—1st Cpl./Pvt.—Enlisted: 3/24/1862 at Monroe, LA. Rolls for 3/24/1862 through 4/30/1862: Absent, on detached service at Montgomery, AL. Rolls for 5/1862 through 6/1862: Absent, sick in hospital at Macon, GA. Regimental Return for 8/1862: Absent with leave. Rolls for 9/1862 through 10/1862: Present, resigned as 1st Cpl. on 10/18/1862. Rolls for 11/1862 through 2/1863: Present. On Register of C.S.A. General Military Hospital #4, Wilmington, N. C: Admitted on 1/9/1863; Returned to duty on 1/12/1863. Rolls of Prisoners of War, C.S.A: Surrendered at Citronelle, AL on 5/4/1865; Paroled at Monroe, LA on 6/6/1865. *Residence:* Monroe, Ouachita Parish, LA. *Born:* 9/19/1833 at Newton County, GA. *Married:* Twice. *Wife's Age:* 28 as of 1907. *Children:* 3 Daughters-Bessie, Madeline and Hilda. *Buried:* Old Monroe City Cemetery located at Monroe, Ouachita Parish, LA. Confederate Pension Application dated 4/21/1907 on file at the Louisiana State Archives-Microfilm Reel: CP1.57-Microdex 2-Sequence 7-Target Card: Graves, James L.-Parish: Ouachita-4 Pages.

Hudson, William B. (aka W.D.)—Pvt./Cpl.—Enlisted: 3/24/1862 at Monroe, LA. Rolls for 3/24/1862 through 4/1862: Present, sick in quarters. Rolls for 5/1862 through 2/1865: Present. Rolls for 3/1865 through 4/1865: Absent, wounded in hospital at Lauderdale, MS. Rolls of Prisoners of War, C.S.A: Surrendered at Citronelle, AL on 5/4/1865; Paroled at Meridian, MS on 5/10/1865. *Residence:* Monroe, Ouachita Parish, LA.

Lea, Henry J., Sr. (aka Lee)—Pvt./Cpl.—Enlisted: 3/24/1862 at Monroe, LA. Rolls for 3/24/1862 through 2/1863: Present. On Register of Floyd House and Ocmulgee Hospital, Macon, GA: Admitted on 11/18/1863. Rolls for 3/1864 through 4/1864: Present. Rolls for 8/31/1864 through 2/28/1865: Absent on furlough since 2/21/1865 by order of Col. Taylor. Rolls for 3/1865 through 4/1865: Absent on furlough since 2/1865. *Born:* 1/16/1844 at Morehouse Parish, LA. *Married:* Eva Dawes on 7/19/1903 at Monroe, Ouachita Parish, LA. *Children:* 1 Daughter-Eva Lea Boyce. *Residences:* Louisiana for life-Franklin Parish, LA from 1865 except 1870, 1871, and 1872 in Richland Parish, LA. *Occupation:* Clerk of Court. *Died:* 2/26/1923 at Winnsboro, Franklin Parish, LA due to Kidney Ailment. *Buried:* Old Winnsboro City Cemetery located between Pine St. and West St. in Winnsboro, Franklin Parish, LA. Soldier wrote numerous articles for Confederate Veteran magazine detailing his activities during the war. *Wife Born:* 2/23/1877 at Mount Pleasant, Caldwell Parish, LA. *Wife Died:* 7/4/1959 in Alabama. Widows Pension amount: $60.00 per month. Confederate Pension Application dated 6/8/1916 on file at the Louisiana State Archives-Microfilm Reel: CP1.82-Microdex 2-Sequence 34-Target Card: Lea, H.J.-Parish: Franklin-9 Pages. Also two Confederate Widows Pension Applications dated 5/31/1927 and 11/17/1936 on file-Microfilm Reel: CP1.82-Microdex 2-Sequence 32-Target Card: Lea, Eva Dawes-Parish: Franklin & Bossier-71 Pages.

McDuffie, James—2nd Cpl./1st Cpl.—Enlisted: 3/24/1862 at Monroe, LA. Rolls for 3/24/1862 through 4/30/1862: Absent, on detached service at Savannah, GA. Rolls for 5/1862 through 6/1862: Present. Rolls for 9/1862 through 10/1862: Present, promoted to 1st Cpl. on 10/18/1862. Rolls for 11/1862 through 2/1863: Present. Federal Rolls of Prisoners of War: Captured at the Battle of Champion Hill, MS on 5/17/1863; Sent to Memphis, TN on 5/25/1863.

Matthews, John E.—3rd Cpl./2nd Cpl.—Enlisted: 3/24/1862 at Monroe, LA. Rolls for 5/1862 through 12/1862: Present, promoted to 2nd Cpl. on 11/5/1862. Rolls for 1/1863 through 4/1864: Present. Rolls for 8/1864 through 4/1865: Absent, captured near Atlanta, GA on 8/5/1864. Federal Rolls of Prisoners of War: Captured near Atlanta, GA on 8/5/1864; Forwarded to the U.S. Military Prison, Louisville, KY from Nashville, TN on 8/11/1864. Sent to Camp Chase, OH on 8/14/1864; Paroled at Camp Chase, OH on 2/12/1865. Exchanged at Boulware and Cox Wharf, James River, VA on 2/20–21/1865. Rolls of Prisoners of War, C.S.A: Surrendered at Citronelle, AL on 5/4/1865; Paroled at Shreveport, LA on 6/16/1865. *Residence:* Bossier Parish, LA. *Born:* 1830. *Died:* 2/21/1892. *Buried:* Travis State Cemetery located at 909 Navasota St. at Austin, Travis County, TX.

Shores, William H. (aka Sears, Sheres)—Pvt./2nd Cpl./Pvt.—Enlisted: 3/24/1862 at Monroe, LA. Rolls for 3/24/1862 through 6/1862: Present. Rolls for 9/1862 through 10/1862: Present, promoted to 2nd Cpl. on 9/16/1862. Rolls for 11/1862 through 12/1862: Present, reduced to Pvt. from 2nd Cpl. on 11/2/1862. Rolls for 1/1863 through 2/1863: Present. Federal Rolls of Prisoners of War: Captured near Atlanta, GA on 8/5/1864; Forwarded to Camp Chase, OH from the U.S. Military Prison, Louisville, KY on 8/13/1864.

Simmons, John H. (aka Simmonds, J.B., J.W.)—Pvt./Cpl.—Enlisted: 3/24/1862 at Monroe, LA. Rolls for 5/1862 through 6/1862: Absent, sick in hospital at Macon, GA. Rolls for 9/1862 through 10/1862: Present. Rolls for 11/1862 through 12/1862: Absent, in camp at Savannah, GA. Rolls for 1/1863 through 2/1863: Present. Federal Rolls of Prisoners of War: Captured near Atlanta, GA on 8/5/1864; Received at Camp Chase, OH from the U.S. Military Prison, Louisville, KY on 8/13/1864.

Stewart, James T.—3rd Cpl./Pvt.—Enlisted: 3/24/1862 at Monroe, LA. Rolls for 3/24/1862 through 6/1862: Present. Rolls for 9/1862 through 10/1862: Present, resigned as 3rd Cpl. on 9/15/1862. Rolls for 11/1862 through 12/1862: Absent, in camp at Savannah, GA. Rolls for 1/1863 through 2/1863: Certificate of Discharge given on 1/19/1863.

Private

Andrews, Warren A.—Pvt.—Enlisted: 3/24/1862 at Monroe, LA. Rolls for 3/24/1862 through 6/1862: Present. Rolls for 9/1862 through 10/1862: Present, detailed to work on Gunboat on 9/13/1862. Rolls for 3/1862 through 4/1862: Absent, sick at Montgomery, AL. Rolls for 11/1862 through 2/1863: Detailed to work in Savannah, GA on Gunboat. Rolls for 3/1864 through 2/28/1865: Present. Rolls for 3/1865 through 4/1865: Absent, sick in hospital at Mobile, AL since 3/26/1865. Rolls of Prisoners of War, C.S.A: Surrendered at Citronelle, AL on 5/4/1865; Paroled at Meridian, MS on 5/16/1865. *Residence:* Ouachita Parish, LA.

Atwell, William G.—Pvt.—Enlisted: 3/24/1862 at Monroe, LA. Rolls for 3/24/1862 through 6/1862: Present. Rolls for 9/1862 through 10/1862: Present, detailed to work on Artillery batteries around Savannah, GA on 10/6/1862. Rolls for 11/1862 through 2/1863: Absent, at work on defenses around Savannah, GA. Rolls for 3/1864 through 4/1864: Absent without leave since 12/1/1863. Rolls of Prisoners of War of Diverse Companies and Regiments, Unattached: Surrendered at New Orleans, LA on 5/26/1865; Paroled at Monroe, LA on 6/9/1865. *Residence:* Ouachita Parish, LA.

Babin, Benjamin Franklin—Pvt.—Enlisted: 5/25/1861 at Camp Moore, LA. Rolls for 5/25/1861 through 8/30/1861: Elected 2nd Lt. in 11th Louisiana Infantry-Co. F on 8/15/1861 and enlisted in the regiment on 8/18/1861 at Camp Moore, LA; Transferred to the 11th Louisiana Infantry on 10/31/1861. Soldier also served as a Pvt./Jr. 2nd Lt. in the 2nd Louisiana Cavalry-Cos. I and K. Federal Rolls of Prisoners of War: Captured at Pointe Coupee Parish, LA on 3/30/1864; Exchanged at Red River Landing, LA on 7/22/1864. Rolls of Prisoners of War, C.S.A: Surrendered at New Orleans, LA on 5/26/1865; Paroled at Alexandria, LA on 6/4/1865. *Married:* Clemence E. Soniat on 10/24/1871 at Saint Mary's Church, New Orleans, Orleans Parish, LA. *Children:* 1 Daughter-Maud I. Babin. *Died:* 5/21/1876 at Caldwell County, TX due to Tuberculosis and Dysentery. *Buried:* Sour Well, Caldwell County, TX. *Wife Died:* 5/1915. Confederate Widows Pension Application dated 10/30/1914 on file at the Louisiana State Archives-Microfilm Reel: CP1.5-Microdex 3-Sequence 21-Target Card: Babin, Clemence E.-Parish: Orleans-10 Pages.

Ballew, Charles G.—Pvt.—Enlisted: 3/24/1862 at Monroe, LA. Rolls for 3/24/1862 through 4/1862: Died on 4/25/1862.

Baygents, J.W. (aka Buggents)—Pvt.—Enlisted: 3/24/1862 at Monroe, LA. Rolls for 3/24/1862 through 6/1862: Present. Rolls for 9/1862 through 10/1862: Absent on Picket Duty at Savannah, GA. Rolls for 11/1862 through 2/1863: Present.

Bayle, J.M. (aka I.H.)—Pvt.—Enlisted: 3/24/1862 at Monroe, LA. Rolls for 3/24/1862 through 6/1862: Present. Rolls for 9/1862 through 10/1862: Absent on Picket Duty at Savannah, GA. Rolls for 11/1862 through 2/1863: Present.

Bonnett, David G.—Pvt.—Enlisted: 3/24/1862 at Monroe, LA. Rolls for 3/24/1862 through 4/30/1862: Present. Rolls for 5/1862 through 6/1862: Died on 5/3/1862.

Bostick, Arthur H. (aka Bostic, Bostwick, A.S., A.T.)—Pvt.—Enlisted: 3/24/1862 at Monroe, LA. Rolls for 3/24/1862 through 6/1862: Present. Rolls for 9/1862 through 10/1862: Absent on Picket Duty at Savannah, GA. Rolls for 11/1862 through 4/1864: Present. Federal Rolls of Prisoners of War: Captured near Atlanta, GA on 8/5/1864; Received at the U.S. Military Prison, Louisville, KY from Nashville, TN on 8/12/1864. Sent to Camp Chase, OH on 8/13/1864; Paroled at Camp Chase, OH on 2/12/1865. Transferred to Point Lookout, MD for Exchange; Received at James River, VA on 2/20–21/1865.

Boyett, Young R.—Pvt.—Enlisted: 3/24/1862 at Monroe, LA. Rolls for 5/1862 through 6/1862: Died on 5/19/1862.

Brown, William D.—Pvt.—Enlisted: 3/24/1862 at Monroe, LA. Rolls for 3/24/1862 through 4/30/1862: Present. Rolls for 6/1862 through 7/1862: Died on 6/4/1862 due to being knocked off a train while traveling. *Married:* Elizabeth _ on 9/6/1855 at Ouachita Parish, LA. *Wife's Age:* 68 as of 1898. Confederate Widows Pension Application dated 12/12/1898 on file at the Louisiana State Archives-Microfilm Reel: CP1.19-Microdex 2-Sequence 11-Target Card: Brown, Elizabeth-Parish: Ouachita-4 Pages.

Bryant, Martin (aka Maryin)—Pvt.—Enlisted: 3/24/1862 at Monroe, LA. Rolls for 3/24/1862 through 4/1864: Present. Rolls for 7/28/1864 through 4/1865: Absent, sick in hospital. Rolls of Prisoners of War, C.S.A: Surrendered at Citronelle, AL on 5/4/1865; Paroled at Meridian, MS on 5/12/1865. *Residence:* Monroe, Ouachita Parish, LA. *Wounded:* Yes, minié ball in left hip at the Battle of Chickamauga, GA and minié ball in left ankle at Shiloh, S.C. near Charleston. *Born:* 5/7/1834 at Talladega County, AL. *Married:* Mary Long on 1/15/1866 at Lapine, Ouachita Parish, LA. *Children:* 2 Sons. *Residence:* Louisiana for life, Ouachita Parish, LA for 40 yrs. *Occupation:* Farmer. *Died:* 4/20/1902 at Ouachita Parish, LA due to effects of Old Wounds. *Buried:* Antioch Church Cemetery located at Ouachita Parish, LA. *Wife's Age:* 52 as of 1898. Confederate Pension Application dated 12/20/1898 on file at the Louisiana State Archives-Microfilm Reel: CP1.20-Microdex 4-Sequence 1-Target Card: Bryant, Martin-Parish: Ouachita-8 Pages. Also a Confederate Widows Pension Application dated 12/11/1902 on file-Microfilm Reel: CP1.20-Microdex 4-Sequence 4-Target Card: Bryant, Mary (Long)-Parish: Ouachita-2 Pages.

Cason, Charles A. (aka Casing, Cayson)—Pvt.—Enlisted: 3/24/1862 at Monroe, LA. Rolls for 3/24/1862 through 2/1863: Present. Federal Rolls of Prisoners of War: Captured at the Battle of Missionary Ridge, TN on 11/25/1863; Received at the U.S. Military Prison, Louisville, KY from Nashville, TN on 12/5/1863. Forwarded to Rock Island, IL on 12/9/1863; Released on the U.S. Oath of Allegiance on 10/11/1864. *Residence:* Ouachita Parish, LA. Description at oath-Complexion: light-Hair: light-Eyes: gray-Height: 5 ft. 11 in. Age at oath: 19 yrs.

Colton, J.R. (aka Coulter, J.B.)—Pvt.—Enlisted: 3/24/1862 at Monroe, LA. Rolls for 3/24/1862 through 6/1862: Absent, sick in hospital at Augusta, GA.

Condren, John—Pvt.—Enlisted: 3/24/1862 at Monroe, LA. Rolls for 3/24/1862 through 12/1862: Present. Rolls for 1/1863 through 2/1863: Present, confined in Guard House.

Coulston, Elijah—Pvt.—Enlisted: 3/24/1862 at Monroe, LA. Rolls for 3/24/1862 through 4/30/1862: Absent, sick in hospital at Montgomery, AL. Rolls for 5/1862 through 2/1863: Present.

Dowdy, James G.—Pvt.—Enlisted: 3/24/1862 at Monroe, LA. Rolls for 3/24/1862 through 6/1862: Present. Rolls for 9/1862 through 10/1862: Absent on Picket Duty at Savannah, GA. Rolls for 11/1862 through 12/1862: Present. Rolls for 1/1863 through 2/1863: Absent, left as Nurse in hospital at Wilmington, N.C. Rolls for 3/1864 through 4/1865: Present. Rolls of Prisoners of War, C.S.A: Surrendered at Citronelle, AL on 5/4/1865; Paroled at Meridian, MS on 5/10/1865. *Residence:* Monroe, Ouachita Parish, LA.

Dyer, William—Pvt.—Enlisted: 3/24/1862 at Monroe, LA. Rolls for 3/24/1862 through 2/1863: Present.

Fay, John—Pvt.—Enlisted: 3/24/1862 at Monroe, LA. Rolls for 3/24/1862 through 10/1862: Present. Rolls for 11/1862 through 12/1862: Absent, in camp at Savannah, GA. Rolls for 1/1863 through 2/1863: Absent, in hospital at Augusta, GA.

Friend, Benjamin F.—Pvt.—Enlisted: 3/6/1862 at Monroe, LA. Rolls for 3/6/1862 through 6/1862: Present. Rolls for 1/1864 through 2/1864: Present. Federal Rolls of Prisoners of War: Captured at Atlanta, GA on 8/5/1864; Forwarded to Nashville, TN on 8/11/1864. Transferred to the U.S. Military Prison, Louisville, KY on 8/12/1864; Sent to Camp Chase, OH on 8/13/1864. Paroled at Camp Chase, OH on 2/12/1865; Transferred to Point Lookout, MD for Exchange. Received and Exchanged at Boulware and Cox Wharf, James River, VA on 2/20–21/1865.

Gladden, Charles S. (aka Gladen)—Pvt.—Enlisted: 3/24/1862 at Monroe, LA. Rolls for 3/24/1862 through 4/1862: Present. Rolls for 5/1862 through 6/1862: Died on 7/25/1862.

Grant, Franklin J. (aka Graves)—Pvt.—Enlisted: 3/24/1862 at Monroe, LA. Rolls for 3/24/1862 through 6/1862: Present. Rolls for 9/1862 through 10/1862: Absent with leave. Rolls for 11/1862 through 12/1862: Present. Rolls for 1/1863 through 2/1863: Absent, left as Nurse at hospital in Savannah, GA. On Register of C.S.A. General Military Hospital #4, Wilmington, N.C: Admitted on 1/9/1863 due to Neuralgia; Returned to duty on 2/16/1863. Rolls of Prisoners of War, C.S.A: Surrendered at Citronelle, AL on 5/4/1865; Paroled at Monroe, LA on 6/7/1865. *Residence:* Ouachita Parish, LA.

Graves, Robert—Pvt.—Enlisted: 3/24/1862 at Monroe, LA. Rolls for 3/24/1862 through 6/1862: Present. Regimental Return for 8/1862: Sick. Rolls for 9/1862 through 10/1862: Absent on sick furlough. Rolls for 11/1862 through 2/1863: Present.

Heckford, John (aka Hackford)—Pvt.—Enlisted: 3/24/1862 at Monroe, LA. Rolls for 3/24/1862 through 2/1863: Present. Rolls of Prisoners of War, C.S.A: Surrendered at Citronelle, AL on 5/4/1865; Paroled at Monroe, LA on 6/9/1865. *Residence:* Ouachita Parish, LA.

Herron, John E. (aka J.R.)—Pvt.—Enlisted: 5/15/1862 at Monroe, LA. Rolls for 5/15/1862 through 6/30/1862: Present. Rolls for 9/1862 through 10/1862: Absent with leave. Rolls for 11/1862 through 12/1862: Present. Rolls for 1/1863 through 2/1863: Absent, sick in hospital at Wilmington, N.C. On C.S.A. General Hospital #4 Register, Wilmington, N. C: Admitted on 1/22/1863 due to wound received at Toss Sail Sound, N. C; Released on 1/29/1863. Rolls for 8/1864 through 4/1865: Present. Rolls of Prisoners of War, C.S.A: Surrendered at Citronelle, AL on 5/4/1865; Paroled at Meridian, MS on 5/10/1865. *Residence:* Monroe, Ouachita Parish, LA. Soldier also served as a Pvt. with the Louisiana Pelican Infantry Regiment—Co. G. *Wounded:* No, but split foot with an axe while building breastworks at Top Sail Sound, N.C. *Born:* 1837 at Yazoo County, MS. *Married:* Mary E. Johnson on 2/25/1858 at Ouachita Parish, LA. *Children:* 4–3 Sons and 1 Daughter. *Residences:* Ouachita Parish, LA from 1854 and Morehouse Parish, LA since 1870. *Died:* 10/22/1900 at Bastrop, Morehouse Parish, LA due to effects of exposure during the war. *Buried:* New Bastrop City Cemetery located at Bastrop, LA. *Wife's Age:* 54. Confederate Pension Application dated 9/30/1898 on file at the Louisiana State Archives-Microfilm Reel: CP1.66-Microdex 3-Sequence 6-Target Card: Herron, John E.-Parish: Ouachita-4 Pages. Also a Confederate Widows Pension Application dated 8/9/1902 on file-Microfilm Reel: CP1.66-Microdex 3-Sequence 7-Target Card: Herron, Mary E.-Parish: Morehouse-3 Pages. Also a Confederate Proofs and Land Warrant Application on file-Name: Herron,

John E.-Microfilm Reel: 2-Frame Number: 0670-Act: 116-Pages: 4-Parish: Morehouse.

Herron, Stephen J.— Pvt.— Enlisted: 3/24/1862 at Monroe, LA. Rolls for 3/24/1862 through 4/30/1862: Present. Rolls for 5/1862 through 6/1862: Died on 5/9/1862.

Hicks, John— Pvt.— Enlisted: 3/24/1862 at Monroe, LA. Rolls for 3/24/1862 through 4/30/1862: Present. Rolls for 5/1862 through 6/1862: Died on 6/16/1862.

Hober, John (aka Hoffer)— Pvt./Musician—(See Field and Staff)

Holloway, John— Pvt.— Enlisted: 3/24/1862 at Monroe, LA. Rolls for 3/24/1862 through 4/1862: Present.

Honeycutt, Ebenezer (aka Honeycut)— Pvt.— Enlisted: 3/24/1862 at Monroe, LA. Rolls for 3/24/1862 through 4/1862: Present, sick in quarters.

Hopper, J.H. (aka Hoffer)— Pvt.— Enlisted: 4/9/1862 at Monroe, LA. Rolls for 3/1862 through 2/1863: Present.

Hopper, Thomas— Pvt.— Enlisted: 3/24/1862 at Monroe, LA. Rolls for 3/24/1862 through 2/1863: Present.

Howard, John— Pvt.— Enlisted: 3/24/1862 at Monroe, LA. Rolls for 3/24/1862 through 4/30/1862: Present. Rolls for 5/1862 through 6/1862: Died on 5/4/1862.

Johnson, John R.— Pvt.— Enlisted: 3/24/1862 at Monroe, LA. Rolls for 3/24/1862 through 2/1863: Present. Confederate Widows Pension Application on file at the Georgia Dept. of Archives and History — Name: Johnson, Elizabeth E.-County: Chatham.

Lammonds, John A. (aka Lammondo)— Pvt.— Enlisted: 3/24/1862 at Monroe, LA. Rolls for 3/24/1862 through 4/30/1862: Present, sick in hospital at Montgomery, AL. Rolls for 5/1862 through 2/1863: Present.

Lammons, D.R.— Pvt.— Enlisted: 3/24/1862 at Monroe, LA. Rolls for 3/24/1862 through 4/30/1862: Present. Rolls for 5/1862 through 6/1862: Absent, sick in hospital at Columbia, S.C. Rolls for 9/1862 through 2/1863: Present.

Lammons, J.M.— Pvt.— Enlisted: 10/1/1862 at Monroe, LA. Rolls for 10/1/1862 through 2/1863: Present.

Lark, James R.— Pvt.— Enlisted: 3/24/1862 at Monroe, LA. Rolls for 1/1863 through 2/1863: Present or absent not stated, transferred from Company A to Company F on 1/10/1863. Rolls for 3/1864 through 4/1864: Present. Rolls for 8/31/1864 through 2/28/1865: Absent, captured near Atlanta, GA on 8/5/1864. Federal Rolls of Prisoners of War: Captured near Atlanta, GA on 8/5/1864; Received at the U.S. Military Prison, Louisville, KY on 8/12/1864 from Nashville, TN. Forwarded to Camp Chase, OH on 8/13/1864; Died due to Smallpox on 11/28/1864. *Buried:* Camp Chase Confederate Cemetery located at Columbus, Franklin County, OH.

Leturno, Louis (aka Letterno)— Pvt.— Enlisted: 3/24/1862 at Monroe, LA. Rolls for 3/24/1861 through 6/1862: Present. Rolls for 9/1862 through 10/1862: Absent, on Picket Duty at Savannah, GA. Rolls for 11/1862 through 2/1863: Present.

Levins, R.— Pvt.— Enlisted: 4/13/1865 at Meridian, MS; Remarks: Absent without leave since 4/15/1865.

Lolley, Arwell Harvey (aka Lolly, Arvell)— Pvt.— Enlisted: 3/24/1862 at Monroe, LA. Rolls for 3/24/1862 through 2/1863: Present. Confederate Widows Pension Application on file at the Louisiana State Archives-Microfilm Reel: CP1.86-Microdex 4-Sequence 38-Target Card: Lolley, Amanda-Parish: Ouachita-4 Pages.

Lyles, James M. (aka Lysles)— Pvt.— Enlisted: 3/24/1862 at Monroe, LA. Rolls for 3/24/1862 through 2/1863: Present. Rolls for 8/31/1864 through 4/1865: Present. Rolls of Prisoners of War, C.S.A: Surrendered at Citronelle, AL on 5/4/1865; Paroled at Meridian, MS on 5/10/1865. *Residence:* Ouachita Parish, LA.

Marsh, Fred (aka Marsch)— Pvt.— Enlisted: 3/24/1862 at Monroe, LA. Rolls for 3/24/1862 through 2/1863: Present. Rolls for 3/1865 through 4/1865: Absent, missing since the evacuation of Mobile, AL and assumed to have Deserted.

Miller, H.— Pvt.— Enlisted: 3/24/1862 at Monroe, LA. Rolls for 3/24/1862 through 2/1863: Present. Federal Rolls of Prisoners of War: Captured at the Battle of Champion Hill, MS on 5/17/1863; Forwarded to Memphis, TN on 5/25/1863.

Miller, William H.— Pvt.— Enlisted: 3/24/1862 at Monroe, LA. Rolls for 3/24/1862 through 4/1862: Present. Rolls for 5/1862 through 6/1862: Absent, sick in hospital at Macon, GA. Rolls for 9/1862 through 10/1862: Present. Rolls for 11/1862 through 12/1862: Died in hospital at Wilmington, N.C. on 12/28/1862.

Morgan, Reuben C.— Pvt.— Enlisted: 3/24/1862 at Monroe, LA. Rolls for 3/24/1862 through 4/1862: Present. Rolls for 5/1862 through 6/1862: Absent, sick in hospital at Savannah, GA. Regimental Return for 7/1862: Sick furlough. Regimental Return for 8/1862: Absent without leave. Rolls for 9/1862 through 10/1862: Present, sick in quarters. Rolls for 11/1862 through 12/1862: Absent, sick in camp at Savannah, GA. Rolls for 1/1863 through 2/1863: Present.

Morris, Josiah — Pvt. — Enlisted: 3/24/1862 at Monroe, LA. Rolls for 3/24/1862 through 4/1862: Present. Rolls for 5/1862 through 6/1862: Died on 6/19/1862.

Morris, Thomas J. — Pvt. — Enlisted: 3/24/1862 at Monroe, LA. Rolls for 3/24/1862 through 10/1862: Present. Rolls for 11/1862 through 12/1862: Absent, in camp at Savannah, GA. Rolls for 1/1863 through 2/1863: Present.

Mullins, George W. (aka Mullen, Mullens) — Pvt. — Enlisted: 3/24/1862 at Monroe, LA. Rolls for 3/24/1862 through 10/1862: Present. Rolls for 11/1862 through 12/1862: Absent, in camp at Savannah, GA. Rolls for 1/1863 through 2/1863: Present, confined in Guard House. Federal Rolls of Prisoners of War: Captured at the Battle of Champion Hill, MS on 5/7/1863; Sent to Memphis, TN on 5/25/1863. Transferred to Fort Delaware, DE on 6/15/1863; Forwarded to Point Lookout, MD from Fort Columbus, N.Y. Harbor on 9/26/1863. Paroled at Point Lookout, MD in 1863 for Exchange; Exchanged at Boulware and Cox Wharf, James River, VA on 2/14–15/1865. Rolls of Prisoners of War, C.S.A: Surrendered at Citronelle, AL on 5/4/1865; Paroled at Monroe, LA on 6/9/1865. *Residence:* Ouachita Parish, LA.

Mullins, T.S. (Mullens) — Pvt. — Enlisted: 3/24/1862 at Monroe, LA. Rolls for 3/24/1862 through 4/30/1862: Present. Rolls for 5/1862 through 6/1862: Died on 6/12/1862.

Nash, W.A. — Pvt. — Enlisted: 3/24/1862 at Monroe, LA. Rolls for 3/24/1862 through 4/1862: Died on 4/25/1862.

Nelson, M.R. — Pvt. — Enlisted: 3/24/1862 at Monroe, LA. Rolls for 3/24/1862 through 4/1864: Present. Rolls for 8/31/1864 through 4/1865: Absent, sick in hospital since 5/16/1864.

Osburn, Noble R. (aka Osbourn, Osborne, Osborn, N.P.) — Pvt. — Enlisted: 3/24/1862 at Monroe, LA. Rolls for 3/24/1862 through 2/1863: Present. Rolls for 3/1864 through 4/1865: Present. Rolls of Prisoners of War, C.S.A: Surrendered at Citronelle, AL on 5/4/1865; Paroled at Meridian, MS on 5/10/1865. *Residence:* Monroe, Ouachita Parish, LA. Soldier also served as a Pvt. with the Louisiana Pelican Infantry Regiment-Co. G. *Died:* 1/27/1908. Confederate Pension Application dated 1902 on file at the Arkansas History Commission-Name: Osborn, N.R.-*Residence:* Clark County, AR. Also a Confederate Widows Pension Application dated 1908 on file-Widows Name: Osborn, Lucinda-*Residence:* Clark County, AR.

Parker, Henry A. (aka Parke, A.H.) — Pvt. — Enlisted: 3/24/1862 at Monroe, LA. Rolls for 4/30/1862 through 6/1862: Absent, sick in hospital at Montgomery, AL. Rolls for 9/1862 through 2/1863: Present. Rolls for 3/1864 through 4/1865: Absent, captured at the Battle of Chickamauga, GA on 9/19/1863. Federal Rolls of Prisoners of War: Captured near the Battle of Chickamauga, GA on 9/19/1863; Received at the U.S. Military Prison, Louisville, KY on 10/1/1863. Forwarded to Camp Douglas, IL on 10/2/1863; Released from Camp Douglas, IL on 6/15/1865 in accordance with General Order #109, Adjutant Generals Office, Washington, D.C. 6/6/1865.

Peebles, Shelton — Pvt. — Enlisted: 3/24/1862 at Monroe, LA. Rolls for 3/24/1862 through 4/30/1862: Present. Rolls for 5/1862 through 6/1862: Died on 5/9/1862.

Pinner, Adam N. — Pvt. — Enlisted: 3/24/1862 at Monroe, LA. Rolls for 3/24/1862 through 10/1862: Present. Rolls for 11/1862 through 12/1862: Absent, in camp at Savannah, GA. Rolls for 1/1863 through 4/1865: Present. Rolls of Prisoners of War, C.S.A: Surrendered at Citronelle, AL on 5/4/1865; Paroled at Meridian, MS on 5/10/1865. *Residence:* Rutherford County, N.C.

Pistole, Edward — Pvt. — Enlisted: 3/24/1862 at Monroe, LA. Rolls for 3/24/1862 through 6/1862: Present. Rolls for 9/1862 through 10/1862: Absent with leave. Rolls for 11/1862 through 12/1862: Absent, in camp at Savannah, GA. Rolls for 1/1863 through 2/1863: Present on Picket Duty.

Rials, Samuel L. (aka Rails) — Pvt. — Enlisted: 3/24/1862 at Monroe, LA. Rolls for 3/24/1862 through 4/30/1862: Present. Rolls for 5/1862 through 6/1862: Absent, sick in hospital at Macon, GA. Rolls for 9/1862 through 10/1862: Present. Rolls for 11/1862 through 12/1862: Absent, in camp at Savannah, GA. Rolls for 1/1863 through 2/1863: Present, sick in quarters. On Register of C.S.A. General Military Hospital #4, Wilmington, N. C: Admitted on 2/5/1863; Returned to duty on 2/20/1863.

Rice, E.P. — Pvt. — Enlisted: 3/24/1862 at Monroe, LA. Rolls for 3/24/1862 through 4/30/1862: Present. Rolls for 5/1862 through 6/1862: Died on 5/9/1862.

Riley, Sion — Pvt. — Enlisted: 3/24/1862 at Monroe, LA. Rolls for 3/24/1862 through 4/30/1862: Present. Rolls for 5/1862 through 6/1862: Absent, sick in hospital at Columbus, S.C.

Rounsavall, Isaac E. (aka J.E.) — Pvt. — Enlisted: 3/24/1862 at Monroe, LA. Rolls for 3/24/1862 through 10/1862: Present. Rolls for 11/1862 through 12/1862: Absent, in camp at Savannah, GA. Rolls of Prisoners of War of Diverse Companies and Regiments Unattached, C.S.A: Surrendered at New Orleans, LA on 5/26/1865; Paroled at Monroe, LA on 6/7/1865. *Residence:* Ouachita Parish, LA.

Sessions, Rufus D. — Pvt. — Enlisted: 3/24/1862 at Monroe, LA. Rolls for 3/24/1862 through 12/1862: Present. Rolls for 1/1863 through 2/1863: Absent on working party at Fort Boggs, GA. On Register of C.S.A. General Hospital, Shreveport, LA: Admitted on 3/31/1864; Returned to duty on 4/9/1864.

Smith, Thomas—Pvt.-Federal Rolls of Prisoners of War: Captured near Atlanta, GA on 8/5/1864; Received at the U.S. Military Prison, Louisville, KY. Forwarded to Camp Chase, OH on 8/13/1864.

Sullivan, Timothy—Pvt.—Enlisted: 6/6/1862 at Monroe, LA. Rolls for 6/6/1862 through 12/1862: Present. Rolls for 1/1863 through 2/1863: Absent, on working party at Fort Boggs, GA.

Varner, Eli F. (aka Verner, Warner, V.F.)—Pvt.—Enlisted: 3/24/1862 at Monroe, LA. Rolls for 3/24/1862 through 2/1863: Present. Rolls for 3/1864 through 4/1865: Absent, captured at the Battle of Missionary Ridge, TN on 11/25/1863. Federal Rolls of Prisoners of War: Captured at the Battle of Missionary Ridge, TN on 11/25/1863; Received at the U.S. Military Prison, Louisville, KY from Nashville, TN on 12/7/1863. Sent to Rock Island Barracks, IL on 12/13/1863; Paroled at Rock Island Barracks, IL and transferred for Exchange on 3/6/1865. Exchanged at Boulware and Cox Wharf, James River, VA on 3/10–12/1865.

Walker, Robert L.—Pvt.—Enlisted: 3/24/1862 at Monroe, LA. Rolls for 3/24/1862 through 2/1863: Present. Placed on the Confederate Roll of Honor for gallantry and good conduct at the Battle of Chickamauga, GA per General Order #131 of the Adjutant and Inspector General's Office, Richmond, VA.

Ward, Felix—Pvt.—Enlisted: 3/24/1862 at Monroe, LA. Rolls for 3/24/1862 through 4/30/1862: Present. Rolls for 5/1862 through 6/1862: Discharged on 5/9/1862. Soldier also served as a Pvt. with the 3rd Louisiana Cavalry-Co. E. Rolls of Prisoners of War of Diverse Companies and Regiments Unattached, C.S.A: Surrendered at New Orleans, LA on 5/26/1865; Paroled at Monroe, LA on 6/9/1865. *Residence:* Ouachita Parish, LA. *Wounded:* Yes-Left shoulder with three buck and one minié ball at the Battle of Chickamauga, GA. *Born:* 1846 at Bibb County, AL. *Married:* Yes. *Children:* 3–2 Sons-J.W. Ward, _ and 1 Daughter-Rilda Ward Johnson. *Occupation:* Farmer. *Residences:* Louisiana since 1859. *Died:* 3/23/1918. Three Confederate Pension Applications dated 10/13/1898, 11/23/1899 and 9/2/1900 on file at the Louisiana State Archives-Microfilm Reel: CP1.143-Microdex 4-Sequence 25-Target Card: Ward, Felix-Parish: Bienville-17 Pages.

Warren, John—Pvt.—Enlisted: 3/24/1862 at Monroe, LA. Rolls for 3/24/1862 through 6/1862: Present. Rolls for 9/1862 through 10/1862: Absent, on picket duty at Savannah, GA. Rolls for 11/1862 through 12/1862: Present. Rolls for 1/1863 through 2/1863: Present, on Guard Duty around camp. Rolls for 3/1864 through 4/1865: Absent, taken Prisoner of War at the Battle of Chickamauga, GA on 9/19/1863. Federal Rolls of Prisoners of War: Captured at the Battle of Chickamauga, GA on 9/19/1863. On General Field Hospital Register, Army of the Cumberland, Stevenson, AL: Admitted on 9/25/1863 due to gunshot wound in left arm. Received at the U.S. Military Prison, Louisville, KY from Nashville, TN on 11/13/1863; Transferred to Camp Morton, IN on 11/14/1863. Died at Camp Morton, IN on 12/28/1863. *Buried:* Green Lawn Cemetery, Indianapolis, Marion County, IN.

Wilson, O.—Pvt.—Enlisted: 3/24/1862 at Monroe, LA. Rolls for 3/24/1862 through 4/1864: Present. Rolls for 8/31/1864 through 2/28/1865: Discharged on 10/1/1864.

Womack, John P. (aka Wommack)—Pvt.—Enlisted: 3/24/1862 at Monroe, LA. Rolls for 3/24/1862 through 6/1862: Present. Rolls for 9/1862 through 10/1862: Absent with leave. Rolls for 11/1862 through 2/1863: Present.

Woodson, J.M.—Pvt.—Enlisted: Weedowed, AL on 9/13/1863. Rolls for 3/1865 through 4/1865: Present, assigned to duty in Company F by order of Brig. Gen. Randall L. Gibson. Rolls of Prisoners of War, C.S.A: Surrendered at Citronelle, AL on 5/4/1865; Paroled at Meridian, MS on 5/10/1865. *Residence:* Talladega, Talladega County, AL.

Chapter Notes

CHAPTER 1

1. U.S. Bureau of the Census, *Seventh United States Census, 1850*, Table V, p. 475; U.S. Bureau of the Census, *Eighth United States Census, 1860, Population*, p. 194.
2. *Executive Documents Printed by Order of the House of Representatives during the First Session of the Thirty-Sixth Congress, 1859–1860*, Serial 49 (Washington, DC, 1860), pp. 163–168, 278.
3. *New Orleans Daily-Picayune*, February 16, 1860.
4. *New Orleans Daily-Crescent*, January 19, 1860.
5. Ibid., January 21, 1860. Reported that the resolution was laid over and two days later editorially endorsed the resolution. It seems to have died in committee, as the *Louisiana Acts, 1860*, contains no joint resolution of this nature.
6. *New Orleans Daily-Crescent*, January 24, 1860.
7. *New Orleans Daily-Picayune*, March 7, 1860.
8. Ibid.
9. Ibid.
10. Ibid
11. Ibid.
12. Ibid., *Fifth Resolution of the Louisiana Convention*.
13. *New Orleans Daily-Crescent*, May 2, 1860.
14. *New Orleans Daily-Picayune*, April 25, 1860.
15. Dwight L. Dumond, *The Secession Movement, 1860–1861* (New York: Macmillan, 1931), p. 52.
16. James K. Greer, "Louisiana Politics, 1845–1860," *Louisiana Historical Quarterly* (New Orleans), 13 (1930): 468.
17. *New Orleans Daily-Picayune*, June 5, 1860.
18. Ibid., June 7, 1860.
19. Greer, "Louisiana Politics, 1845–1860," p. 474.
20. *New Orleans Daily-Picayune*, December 5, 1860 (official election returns). For a map of Louisiana illustrating the 1860 election, see Willie Malvin Caskey, *Secession and Restoration of Louisiana* (Cambridge, MA: Da Capo Press, 1970), p. 14.
21. Greer, "Louisiana Politics, 1845–1860," p. 620. See also Caskey, *Secession and Restoration of Louisiana*, pp. 12–13.
22. Dwight Lowell Dumond, ed., *Southern Editorials on Secession* (New York: Century Company, 1931), pp. xix, xx.
23. *New Orleans Daily-Picayune*, December 11, 1860.
24. Governor's message, *Documents of the Second Session of the Fifth Legislature of Louisiana, 1861* (Baton Rouge, 1861). Cited hereafter as *Louisiana Legislature Documents*.
25. *Acts Passed by the Fifth Legislature of the State of Louisiana, Second Session, 1861* (Baton Rouge, 1861), pp. 3–4. The acts of the special session are printed with those of the regular session. Cited hereafter as *Louisiana Acts*. *New Orleans Daily-Picayune*, December 11–12, 1860.
26. *Louisiana Legislature Documents, 1861*, Special Report of the Military Board, February 14, 1861.
27. *Louisiana Acts*, 1861, pp. 5–7. *New Orleans Daily-Picayune*, December 13, 1860.
28. *New Orleans Daily-Picayune*, December 29, 1860, and January 1, 1861, reports such meetings in the parishes of East Baton Rouge, Plaquemines, Pointe Coupee, Concordia, Claiborne, and Natchitoches.
29. National Historical Society, *Official Records of the War of the Rebellion* (Harrisburg, PA: Author, 1985), Ser. 1, 1:490.
30. Ibid., Report of Major Josiah Gorgas, CSA chief of ordnance, Ser. 4, 1:292.
31. *Memoirs of General W. T. Sherman* (Philadelphia: Norwood Editions, 1981), 1:182–183.
32. National Historical Society, *Official Records of the War of the Rebellion*, p. 495.
33. Greer, "Louisiana Politics, 1845–1860," pp. 634–638.
34. *Official Journal of the Proceedings of the Convention of the State of Louisiana, 1861*, pp. 13–14. Cited hereafter as *Journal of the Louisiana Convention, 1861*.
35. *New Orleans Daily-Picayune*, January 26, 1861.
36. Ibid., *Journal of the Louisiana Convention*, 1861, p. 15.
37. *Journal of the Louisiana Convention*, 1861, pp. 17–18, 231. The Louisiana Ordinance of Secession is also found in National Historical Society, *Official Records of the War of the Rebellion*, Ser. 4, 1:80.
38. Ibid., pp. 19–24, 241. *New Orleans Daily-Picayune*, January 30–31, 1861.
39. Ibid., pp. 235–237.
40. Caskey, *Secession and Restoration of Louisiana*, pp. 34–35.
41. Ibid., p. 34.
42. *Journal of the Louisiana Convention*, 1861, p. 51.
43. *Louisiana Acts*, 1861, p. 10.
44. *Journal of the Louisiana Convention*, 1861, pp. 75–76.
45. Ibid., pp. 283–285.
46. Ibid. p. 281.
47. Ibid., pp. 289–291.
48. *The Statutes at Large of the Provisional Government*

of the Confederate States of America (Richmond, 1864), pp. 43–44, 47–52; National Historical Society, *Official Records of the War of the Rebellion*, p. 135.
49. Ibid., pp. 221–222, 747–748.
50. Ibid., p. 748.
51. *New Orleans Daily-Crescent*, September 30, 1861; National Historical Society, *Official Records of the War of the Rebellion*, p. 753.
52. Ibid.
53. Ibid.
54. *Louisiana Acts*, 1861, p. 173.
55. *Annual Cyclopaedia*, (New York: 1861), 1:432.
56. William H. Tunnard, *The History of the Third Regiment Louisiana Infantry* (Baton Rouge, 1866), pp. 31–33.
57. *New Orleans Daily-Picayune*, July 14, 1861.
58. Diary of John W. McNeil, Call Number 2C484, Folder 9, Confederate States of America Collection, Center for American History, University of Texas at Austin.
59. U.S. Bureau of the Census, *Eighth United States Census, 1860*, "Madison Parish, Louisiana," CM-653, Reel 413:5, RG29; National Historical Society, *The Official Records of the War of the Rebellion*, Ser. 1, 3:711.

CHAPTER 2

1. Austin W. Smith, "Service with the Fourth Louisiana Battalion," *Confederate Veteran* (Wilmington, NC: Broadfoot Publishing, 1986), 19:542–543.
2. Ibid.
3. Diary of John W. McNeil, Call Number 2C484, Folder 9, Confederate States of America Collection, Center for American History, University of Texas at Austin.
4. Letter of D. Wansley Elliott, Robert Archibald Family Papers, Archibald, Richland Parish, Louisiana.
5. Smith, "Service with the Fourth Louisiana Battalion," pp. 542–543.
6. Clement A. Evans, ed., *Confederate Military History—West Virginia, Volume III* (Wilmington, NC: Broadfoot Publishing, 1988), pp. 45–47; Jacob D. Cox, *Battles and Leaders of the Civil War: From Sumter to Shiloh* (Secaucus, NJ: Castle Books: 1983), p. 126.
7. Cox, *Battles and Leaders of the Civil War: From Sumter to Shiloh*, p. 147.
8. Ibid, p.146; Evans, *Confederate Military History—West Virginia*, pp. 45–47.
9. Diary of John W. McNeil.
10. Evans, *Confederate Military History—West Virginia*, pp. 45–47; Cox, *Battles and Leaders of the Civil War: From Sumter to Shiloh*, p. 148.
11. Diary of John W. McNeil.
12. Evans, *Confederate Military History—West Virginia*, pp. 45–47; Cox, *Battles and Leaders of the Civil War: From Sumter to Shiloh*, p. 148.
13. Austin W. Smith, "Service with the Fourth Louisiana Battalion," pp. 542–543.
14. Ibid.; H. J. Lea, "With the Fourth Louisiana Battalion," *Confederate Veteran* (Wilmington, NC: Broadfoot Publishing, 1986), 27:339–340; National Historical Society, *Official Records of the War of the Rebellion — Supplements* (Harrisburg, PA: Author, 1985), 23:808–817.
15. Diary of John W. McNeil.
16. Ibid.; National Historical Society, *Official Records of the War of the Rebellion* (Harrisburg, PA: Author, 1985), Ser. 1, 14:539.
17. Michael B. Ballard, *Pemberton: The General Who Lost Vicksburg* (Jackson: University Press of Mississippi, 1999), pp. 86–87.
18. National Historical Society, *Official Records of the Union and Confederate Navies* (Harrisburg, PA: Author, 1985), 12:825.
19. Okon E. Uya, *From Slavery* (New York: Oxford University Press, 1997), p. 14; Daniel Ammen, *The Old and the New Navy* (Philadelphia: J. B. Lippincott, 1891), p. 65.
20. Diary of John W. McNeil.
21. H. J. Lea, "The Fourth Louisiana Battalion at the Battle of Secessionville, S.C.," *Confederate Veteran* (Wilmington, NC: Broadfoot Publishing, 1986), 31:14–16.
22. Sifakis, Stewart, *Who Was Who in the Civil War* (New York: Facts on File, 1988), pp. 49–50; *Biographical Register of the Officers and Graduates of the U.S. Military Academy 1802–1867, Volume 1* (Boston: Houghton, Mifflin & Company, 1891).
23. National Historical Society, *Official Records of the War of the Rebellion*, p. 45.
24. Ibid., pp. 45–47,. 46.
25. H. J. Lea, "The Fourth Louisiana Battalion at the Battle of Secessionville, S.C.," *Confederate Veteran* (Wilmington, NC: Broadfoot Publishing, 1986), 31:14–16; National Historical Society, "Report of Lt. Colonel John McEnery," *Official Records of the War of the Rebellion*, 14:100–101.
26. National Historical Society, *Official Records of the War of the Rebellion*, p. 52.
27. Ibid., p. 54.
28. H. C. Clarke, *The Confederate States Almanac and Repository of Useful Knowledge for 1862*, (Vicksburg, MS: Author, 1861); Rod Gragg, "A Bloody Half-Hour," *Civil War Times Illustrated*, January/February 1994, pp. 48–51.
29. Ibid., p. 50.; Herbert W. Beecher, *History of the First Light Battery Connecticut Volunteers, 1861–1865* (New York: A. T. De La Mare, 1908), p. 144.
30. National Historical Society, *Official Records of the War of the Rebellion*, p. 91.
31. Ibid., pp. 93–96.
32. Ibid., p. 98.
33. *Charleston Mercury*, June 17, 1862.
34. National Historical Society, *Official Records of the War of the Rebellion*, p. 59.
35. Ibid., p. 94.
36. Ibid., p. 65.
37. Ibid., p. 71.
38. Katcher, Philip, *Great Gambles of the Civil War* (Secaucus, NJ: Castle Books, 2003), p. 186.
39. Ibid.
40. Ibid.
41. John Niven, *Connecticut for the Union* (New Haven, CT: Yale University Press, 1965), p. 148.
42. Ibid.
43. Ibid.
44. National Historical Society, *Official Records of the War of the Rebellion*, pp. 72–73.
45. Carolyn P. Schriber, "A Scratch with the Rebels," *Civil War Times Illustrated*, January/February 1994, p. 49.
46. *New York Times*, June 28, 1862.
47. *Flint Wolverine Citizen*, July 12, 1862.
48. Gragg, "A Bloody Half-Hour," p. 55.
49. National Historical Society, *Official Records of the War of the Rebellion*, pp. 100–101; Lea, "The Fourth Louisiana Battalion at the Battle of Secessionville, S.C.," pp. 14–16.
50. *Charleston Mercury*, June 19, 1862.
51. National Historical Society, *Official Records of the War of the Rebellion*, pp. 100–101.
52. H. J. Lea, "The Fourth Louisiana Battalion at the Battle of Secessionville, S.C.," pp. 14–16.
53. *Charleston Mercury*, June 19, 1862.

54. Katcher, *Great Gambles of the Civil War*, pp. 189–190.
55. Ibid., pp. 190–191.
56. National Historical Society, *Official Records of the War of the Rebellion*, pp. 100–101.
57. Katcher, *Great Gambles of the Civil War*, p. 190.
58. Patrick Brennan, *Secessionville, Assault on Charleston* (Campbell, CA: Savas Publishing Company, 1996), pp. 264–265.
59. National Historical Society, *Official Records of the War of the Rebellion*, pp. 100–101.
60. Diary of John W. McNeil.
61. Niven, *Connecticut for the Union*, p. 149.
62. National Historical Society, *Official Records of the War of the Rebellion*, pp. 52–53.
63. Ibid., pp. 979–1013; Michael Burlingame, *The Inner World of Abraham Lincoln* (Urbana: University of Illinois Press, 1994), p. 197.
64. Diary of John W. McNeil.
65. R. D. Lawrence, "The Battle of Secessionville," *Confederate Veteran* (Wilmington, NC: Broadfoot Publishing, 1986), 30:368–370; Smith, "Service with the 4th Louisiana Battalion," pp. 542–543; Lea, "With the Fourth Louisiana Battalion" pp. 339–340; Lea, "The Fourth Louisiana Battalion at the Battle of Secessionville, S.C.," pp. 14–16.
66. National Historical Society, *Official Records of the War of the Rebellion — Supplements*, pp. 808–817.

CHAPTER 3

1. Samuel Carter III, *The Final Fortress: The Campaign for Vicksburg 1862–1863* (New York: St. Martin's Press, 1980), p. 3.
2. Bruce Catton, *The Coming Fury* (New York: Doubleday and Company, 1961), pp. 438–441.
3. Carl Sandburg, *Abraham Lincoln, The Prairie Years* (New York: Harcourt Brace, 1926), pp. 78, 83–87.
4. C. C. Buel and R. U. Johnson, eds., *Battles and Leaders of the Civil War* (Secaucus, NJ: Castle Books, 1956), 2:24.
5. Ibid., pp. 24–25.
6. Ibid.
7. Edward Pollard, *The Lost Cause* (New York: Gramercy Publishing, 1989), p. 324.
8. David Dixon Porter, "Opening of the Lower Mississippi," in Buel and Johnson, eds., *Battles and Leaders of the Civil War*, pp. 42–47.
9. National Historical Society, *Official Records of the Union and Confederate Navies* (Harrisburg, PA: The National Historical Society, 1985), Ser. 1, 18:491–493.
10. Ibid.
11. Ibid.
12. Ibid.
13. Shelby Foote, *The Civil War* (New York: Random House, 1974). 1:547.
14. Earl S. Miers, *Web of Victory* (Baton Rouge: Louisiana State University Press, 1984), pp. 32–33.
15. Carter, *The Final Fortress: The Campaign for Vicksburg 1862–1863*, p. 73.
16. Ibid., p. 74.
17. Foote, *The Civil War*, p. 556.
18. Diary of John W. McNeil, Call Number 2C484, Folder 9, Confederate States of America Collection, Center for American History, University of Texas at Austin.
19. National Historical Society, *Official Records of the War of the Rebellion* (Harrisburg, PA: The National Historical Society, 1985), Ser. 1, 17:469.
20. Ibid.
21. Liddell Hart, *Sherman: Soldier, Realist, American* (New York: Dodd Publishers, 1929), p. 165.
22. Diary of John W. McNeil.
23. Carter, *The Final Fortress: The Campaign for Vicksburg 1862–1863*, p. 106.
24. Ulysses S. Grant, *Personal Memoirs* (New York: Library of America, 1990), 1:432–433.
25. Carter, *The Final Fortress: The Campaign for Vicksburg 1862–1863*, p. 107.
26. Shelby Foote, *The Beleaguered City — The Vicksburg Campaign* (New York: The Modern Library, 1995), p. 96.
27. Diary of John W. McNeil.
28. Carter, *The Final Fortress: The Campaign for Vicksburg 1862–1863*, p. 157.
29. National Historical Society, *Official Records of the War of the Rebellion*, Ser. 1, 24:730.
30. Carter, *The Final Fortress: The Campaign for Vicksburg 1862–1863*, p. 182.
31. National Historical Society, *Official Records of the War of the Rebellion*, p. 923.
32. Ibid., p. 833.
33. Ibid.
34. Ibid., p. 919.
35. Walter Branham Capers, *The Soldier Bishop Ellison Capers* (Montville, NJ: Sprinkle Publications, 2000), p. 60.
36. Diary of John W. McNeil.
37. Joseph E. Johnston, *Narrative of Military Operations* (Indianapolis: Indiana University Press, 1959), p. 172; National Historical Society, *Official Records of the War of the Rebellion*, Part 1, p. 215.
38. Ibid., pp. 239, 260.
39. Carter, *The Final Fortress: The Campaign for Vicksburg 1862–1863*, p. 190.
40. National Historical Society, *Official Records of the War of the Rebellion*, p. 215.
41. Grant, *Personal Memoirs*, pp. 507–508.
42. National Historical Society, *Official Records of the War of the Rebellion*, p. 785.
43. Ibid., p. 786.
44. Ibid.; Dunbar Rowland, *The Official and Statistical Register of the State of Mississippi 1908* (Jackson: Brandon Printing Company, 1908), pp. 893–894.
45. National Historical Society, *Official Records of the War of the Rebellion*, Part 3, p. 305.
46. Ibid., p. 309.
47. Ibid., Part 1, p. 775.
48. Ibid., pp. 775, 777, 782.
49. Ibid., pp. 775, 782.
50. Ibid., p. 729.
51. Ibid., Part 3, p. 308.
52. Ibid., Part 1, pp. 753, 757.
53. Ibid., Part 2, p. 284.
54. Ibid., Part 1, p. 765.
55. Ibid., pp. 753, 759, 786.
56. Ibid., p. 753.
57. Ibid.
58. Letter, *Brumback to Wife*, Files of Vicksburg National Military Park, May 20, 1863.
59. Ibid.; National Historical Society, *Official Records of the War of the Rebellion*, p. 754.
60. Ibid., pp. 754, 759, 766, 768, 770.
61. Ibid., p. 756.
62. Ibid., p. 638.
63. Ibid., pp. 729, 775, 777, 782.
64. Ibid., p. 729.
64. Ibid., p. 786.
65. Ibid., pp. 729, 775, 777, 782.

66. Ibid., p. 786.
67. Frederick Grant, "A Boy's Experiences at Vicksburg" (1912; reprint, New York: MOLLUS), Ser. 3, pp. 92–93.
68. National Historical Society, *Official Records of the War of the Rebellion*, p. 751.
69. Diary of John W. McNeil.
70. National Historical Society, *Official Records of the War of the Rebellion*, p. 754.
71. Ibid., pp. 754, 759.
72. Lowell Harrison, "Jackson ... Is a Ruined Town," *Civil War Times Illustrated*, 15, no. 10 (February 1997): 7.
73. Ibid.
74. Ibid., p. 45.
75. Ibid.
76. Ibid.
77. Ibid., pp. 45–46.
78. Ibid., p. 47.
79. Ibid.
80. Ibid.
81. Diary of John W. McNeil.
82. Harrison, "Jackson ... Is a Ruined Town," p. 47.

Chapter 4

1. H. J. Lea, "With the Fourth Louisiana Battalion," *Confederate Veteran* (Wilmington, NC: Broadfoot Publishing, 1986), 27:339–340; National Historical Society, *Official Records of the War of the Rebellion* (Harrisburg, PA: Author, 1985), Ser. 1, 30, Part 4, pp. 529, 538, 547.
2. William S. Rosecrans, "The Chattanooga Campaign," *National Tribune*, March 6, 1882; National Historical Society, *Official Records of the War of the Rebellion*, Part 3, p. 36.
3. Steven E. Woodworth, *A Deep Steady Thunder: The Battle of Chickamauga* (Fort Worth, TX: Ryan Place Publishers, 1996), pp. 20–21.
4. Ibid., p. 24.
5. Ibid., p. 25.
6. Ibid., p. 26.
7. Ibid., pp. 26–27.
8. St. John Richardson Liddell, *Liddell's Record* (Morningside Publishers, 1985), pp. 139–140.
9. Peter Cozzens, *This Terrible Sound: The Battle of Chickamauga* (Chicago: University of Illinois Press, 1992), pp. 78–79.
10. National Historical Society, *Official Records of the War of the Rebellion*, Part 2, p. 31.
11. Cozzens, *This Terrible Sound: The Battle of Chickamauga*, pp. 109–113,
12. National Historical Society, *Official Records of the War of the Rebellion*, pp. 247–250.
13. Cozzens, *This Terrible Sound: The Battle of Chickamauga*, p. 105.
14. National Historical Society, *Official Records of the War of the Rebellion*, Part 1, pp. 114, 605.
15. Cozzens, *This Terrible Sound: The Battle of Chickamauga*, pp. 123, 125; I. B. Walker, "Chickamauga — Going into Action with Hands Full of Bacon and Coffee," *National Tribune*, July 2, 1891.
16. Ibid.
17. G. W. R. Bell, "Reminiscences of Chickamauga," *Confederate Veteran* (Wilmington, NC: Broadfoot Publishing, 1986), 12:71; National Historical Society, *Official Records of the War of the Rebellion*, Part 2, p. 528.
18. Ibid.
19. Cozzens, *This Terrible Sound: The Battle of Chickamauga*, pp. 128–129.
20. Jeremiah Donahower, "Narrative of the Civil War," Jeremiah Donahower Papers, Minnesota Historical Society, 2:112–113; Alexis H. Reed Diary, September 19, 1863, Second Minnesota Infantry File, Chickamauga/Chattanooga National Military Park; National Historical Society, *Official Records of the War of the Rebellion*, Part 1, pp. 428, 432, 434; Part 2, p. 524.
21. Cozzens, *This Terrible Sound: The Battle of Chickamauga*, p. 131.
22. National Historical Society, *Official Records of the War of the Rebellion*, Part 1, pp. 416, 418, 422, 571; Part 2, p. 248.
23. Freeman Cleaves, *Rock of Chickamauga: The Life of General George H. Thomas* (Norman: University of Oklahoma Press, 1948), pp. 158–159.
24. National Historical Society, *Official Records of the War of the Rebellion*, Part 1, pp. 124–125, 250.
25. Cozzens, *This Terrible Sound: The Battle of Chickamauga*, p. 135.
26. Ibid., pp. 136–138.
27. National Historical Society, *Official Records of the War of the Rebellion*, Part 2, pp. 248–249.
28. A. B. Clay, "The Battle of Chickamauga," *Confederate Veteran* (Wilmington, NC: Broadfoot Publishing, 1986), 19:329–330.
29. National Historical Society, *Official Records of the War of the Rebellion*, 31, Part 3, p. 827.
30. Ibid., 30, Part 2, p. 78; Cozzens, *This Terrible Sound: The Battle of Chickamauga*, pp. 141, 143.
31. Woodworth, *A Deep Steady Thunder: The Battle of Chickamauga*, pp. 38–40; National Historical Society, *Official Records of the War of the Rebellion*, 30, Part 1, pp. 56, 76, 487, 713, 982.
32. Ibid., pp. 40–44.
33. Ibid., pp. 43–44.
34. National Historical Society, *Official Records of the War of the Rebellion*, pp. 73, 497–498, 607, 838.
35. Woodworth, *A Deep Steady Thunder: The Battle of Chickamauga*, p. 47.
36. Ibid., p. 49.
37. Ibid., p. 50.
38. Ibid.
39. Ibid., pp. 50–51.
40. Ibid., p. 52.
41. W. J. McMurray, "The Gap of Death at Chickamauga," *Confederate Veteran* (Wilmington, NC: Broadfoot Publishing, 1986), 2:329.
42. Woodworth, *A Deep Steady Thunder: The Battle of Chickamauga*, pp. 53–54.
43. National Historical Society, *Official Records of the War of the Rebellion*, p. 799; "Statement of General Reynolds," p. 5, Thomas Papers, RG 94, National Archives.
44. Ibid., p. 634.
45. R. M. Collins, *Chapters from the Unwritten History of the War between the States* (St. Louis: Nixon-Jones Printing Company, 1893), p. 153.
46. William W. Heartsill, *Fourteen Hundred and Ninety-One Days in the Confederate Army, a Journal Kept by W. W. Heartsill, for Four Years, One Month, and One Day* (Jackson, TN: McCowat-Mercer Press, 1954), p. 152.
47. Benjamin McGee, *History of the Seventy-second Indiana Volunteer Infantry* (LaFayette, IN: S. Vatter and Company, 1882), p. 180.
48. Alva Griest Journal, p. 101, Harrisburg Civil War Roundtable Collection, United States Army Military History Institute.
49. National Historical Society, *Official Records of the War of the Rebellion*, p. 135; Woodworth, *A Deep Steady Thunder: The Battle of Chickamauga*, p. 59.
50. National Historical Society, *Official Records of the*

War of the Rebellion, Part 2, p. 287; G. Moxley Sorrel, *Recollections of a Confederate Staff Officer* (New York: Neale, 1905), p. 192.

51. National Historical Society, *Official Records of the War of the Rebellion*, pp. 32–33, 287–288.

52. Ibid., pp. 33, 52; Cozzens, *This Terrible Sound: The Battle of Chickamauga*, p. 300.

53. Cozzens, pp. 302–303.

54. Ibid., pp. 305–309.

55. Woodworth, *A Deep Steady Thunder: The Battle of Chickamauga*, pp. 65–66; National Historical Society, *Official Records of the War of the Rebellion*, Part 2, pp. 142, 240.

56. Woodworth, *A Deep Steady Thunder: The Battle of Chickamauga*, pp. 66–67.

57. Ibid., pp. 67, 69.

58. National Historic Society, *Official Records of the War of the Rebellion*, pp. 199, 209, 215, 216; W. W. Herr, "Kentuckians at Chickamauga," *Confederate Veteran* (Wilmington, NC: Broadfoot Publishing, 1986), 2:294–295.

59. R. Gerald McMurtry, "Confederate General Ben Hardin Helm: Kentucky Brother-in-Law of Abraham Lincoln," *Filson Club Historical Quarterly*, 32, no. 4 (October 1958): 311–313.

60. National Historical Society, *Official Records of the War of the Rebellion*, pp. 142, 240–241, 245; Daniel Harvey Hill, "Chickamauga — The Great Battle of the West," *Battles and Leaders of the Civil War* (Secaucus, NJ: Castle Books, 1956), 3:639.

61. National Historical Society, *Official Records of the War of the Rebellion*, p. 245; A. M. Speer to Henry V. N. Boynton, October 20, 1894, and Elison Capers to Marcus Wright, June 19, 1891, both in the Historical Files of Chickamauga, Chattanooga National Military Park.

62. St. John Richardson Liddell, *Liddell's Record* (Dayton, OH: Morningside Publishers, 1985), pp. 144–145; National Historical Society, *Official Records of the War of the Rebellion*, pp. 242, 245.

63. R. J. Redding to Henry V. N. Boynton, October 24, 1894, Historical Files of Chickamauga, Chattanooga National Military Park; National Historical Society, *Official Records of the War of the Rebellion*, pp. 242, 245.

64. National Historical Society, *Official Records of the War of the Rebellion*, p. 246.

65. Ibid., Elison Capers to Henry V. N. Boynton, June 19, 1891, A. M. Speer to Henry V. N. Boynton, October 26, 1894, all in Historical Files of Chickamauga, Chattanooga National Military Park; National Historical Society, *Official Records of the War of the Rebellion*, pp. 246, 249.

66. Woodworth, *A Deep Steady Thunder: The Battle of Chickamauga*, p. 70.

67. Ibid., pp. 71–72.

68. Francis A. Kiene, *A Civil War Diary: The Journal of Francis A. Kiene, 1861–1864*, edited by Ralph E. Kiene, Jr. (Kansas City: Year Book House, 1974), p. 18.

69. National Historical Society, *Official Records of the War of the Rebellion*, Part 1, p. 417; Part 2, p. 166; Woodworth, *A Deep Steady Thunder: The Battle of Chickamauga*, p. 75.

70. Woodworth, pp. 75–77.

71. Ibid., pp. 77–80.

72. National Historical Society, *Official Records of the War of the Rebellion*, Part 1, p. 984; Part 2, p. 166; Alexander D. Bache to Rosecrans, January 12, 1864, Rosecrans Papers, University of California at Los Angeles; John McElroy, "Army of the Cumberland and the Great Central Campaign," *National Tribune*, October 4, 1906.

73. Woodworth, *A Deep Steady Thunder: The Battle of Chickamauga*, pp. 83–84.

74. Ibid., pp. 84–86.

75. John Bell Hood, *Advance and Retreat* (Edison, NJ: The Blue and Gray Press, 1985), pp. 63–67; "Major Abner W. Wilkins," *Confederate Veteran* (Wilmington, NC: Broadfoot Publishing, 1986), 16:78; Cozzens, *This Terrible Sound: The Battle of Chickamauga*, p. 412.

76. Woodworth, *A Deep Steady Thunder: The Battle of Chickamauga*, pp. 86–87.

77. Ibid., pp. 87–88; Cozzens, *This Terrible Sound: The Battle of Chickamauga*, pp. 413–416.

78. National Historical Society, *Official Records of the War of the Rebellion*, Part 2, p. 504; "Personne," "Correspondence of the *Charleston Courier*," November 4, 1863.

79. Woodworth, *A Deep Steady Thunder: The Battle of Chickamauga*, pp. 91–95.

80. James Longstreet, *From Manassas to Appomattox, Memoirs of the Civil War in America* (Philadelphia: J. B. Lippincott, 1896), p. 452; Cozzens, *This Terrible Sound: The Battle of Chickamauga*, p. 456.

81. James Cooper, "Memoirs," Civil War Collection, Tennessee State Library and Archives, p. 35.

82. Woodworth, *A Deep Steady Thunder: The Battle of Chickamauga*, pp. 97–98.

83. National Historical Society, *Official Records of the War of the Rebellion*, pp. 533–534.

84. Thomas Livermore, *Numbers and Losses in the Civil War: 1861–1865* (Boston: Riverside Press, 1901), p. 69; Cozzens, *This Terrible Sound: The Battle of Chickamauga*, p. 534.

CHAPTER 5

1. Carl Sandburg, *Abraham Lincoln: The War Years* (New York: Harcourt, Brace, and Company, 1939), 2:426–427.

2. Ulysses S. Grant, "Chattanooga," *Battles and Leaders of the Civil War* (Secaucus, NJ: Castle Books, 1956), 3:679–680.

3. For a detailed account of the events preceding Rosecrans's removal from command, see William S. McFeely, *Grant: A Biography* (New York: W. W. Norton, 1981), p. 142; James H. Wilson, *Under the Old Flag: Recollections of Military Operations in the War for the Union, the Spanish War, the Boxer Rebellion, etc.* (New York: D. Appleton, 1912), 2:260; Ulysses S. Grant, *Personal Memoirs of U.S. Grant* (New York: Charles Webster, 1885), 2:17–18.

4. Diary of John W. McNeil, Call Number 2C484, Folder 9, Confederate States of America Collection, Center for American History, University of Texas at Austin.

5. *Savannah Republican,* October 11, 1863; October 12, 1863; October 16, 1863.

6. Peter Cozzens, *The Shipwreck of Their Hopes: The Battles for Chattanooga* (Chicago: University of Illinois Press, 1994), pp. 23–26; Wiley Sword, *Mountains Touched with Fire* (New York: St. Martin's Press, 1995), pp. 29–33.

7. Thomas Lawrence Connelly, *Autumn of Glory: The Army of Tennessee, 1862–1865* (Baton Rouge: Louisiana State University Press, 1971), p. 241; National Historical Society, *Official Records of the War of the Rebellion* (Harrisburg, PA: National Historical Society, 1985), Ser. 1, 52, Part 2, 538.

8. Ibid., pp. 241–249; Sword, *Mountains Touched with Fire*, p. 32.

9. Ibid., pp. 33–34; National Historical Society, *Official Records of the War of the Rebellion*, Part 4, p. 744.

10. Connelly, *Autumn of Glory: The Army of Tennessee, 1862–1865,* pp. 239, 246, 247, 249, 252, 253.
11. Diary of John W. McNeil.
12. McFeely, *Grant: A Biography,* pp. 137–138.
13. Cozzens, *The Shipwreck of Their Hopes: The Battles for Chattanooga,* pp. 44–47.
14. National Historical Society, *Official Records of the War of the Rebellion,* 31, Part 1, pp. 712, 713, 716, 738.
15. Ibid., pp. 717, 729.
16. Ibid., 31, Part 2, pp. 543, 545, 603, 604, 613; Part 4, p. 749; Part 4, pp. 616, 644.
17. Ibid., 30, Part 2, pp. 547, 606; Part 4, pp. 649, 707, 716, 725.
18. Ibid., Part 2, pp. 547, 551; Part 4, p. 739.
19. Ibid., Part 4, pp. 749, 753, 756, 760, 761, 762; Part 2, p. 606; 31, Part 3, pp. 576, 593, 594.
20. Ibid., pp. 593, 594, 601, 607; Sword, *Mountains Touched with Fire,* pp. 75–76.
21. Ibid., 62, Part 2, pp. 557–558.
22. Ibid., p. 77.
23. Ibid., pp. 77–78.
24. Cozzens, *The Shipwreck of Their Hopes: The Battles for Chattanooga,* pp. 53–57; Sword, *Mountains Touched with Fire,* p. 60.
25. W. A. McClendon, *Recollections of War Times by an Old Veteran While under Stonewall Jackson and Lieut. Gen. James Longstreet* (Carrollton, MS: Pioneer Publishing Company, 1905), p. 194; Robert L. Kimberley and Ephraim S. Holloway, *The Forty-first Ohio Veteran Volunteer Infantry in the War of the Rebellion, 1861–1865* (Huntington, WV: Blue Acorn Press, 1999), pp. 60–63; National Historical Society, *Official Records of the War of the Rebellion,* 31, Part 1, pp. 78, 84–86.
26. Cozzens, *The Shipwreck of Their Hopes: The Battles for Chattanooga,* pp. 63–65.
27. Sword, *Mountains Touched with Fire,* pp. 127–144.
28. National Historical Society, *Official Records of the War of the Rebellion,* Part 2, p. 571; Part 3, pp. 139–140.
29. Ibid., Part 2, pp. 67, 571; Part 3, p. 58; William F. Smith, *Sketch of Military Operations* (New York: C. F. Thomas and Company), pp. 194–195.
30. National Historical Society, *Official Records of the War of the Rebellion,* Part 2, pp. 32, 40, 64.
31. Ibid., Part 2, p. 41.
32. Ibid., p. 32.
33. Ibid., pp. 65, 94, 128, 254.
34. Ibid., p. 104.
35. Ibid., pp. 251, 254; Sword, *Mountains Touched with Fire,* p. 178.
36. William R. Glison Diary, November 22, 1863, Historical Files of Chickamauga, Chattanooga National Military Park.
37. National Historical Society, p. 254.
38. Ibid., pp. 65, 128, 129, 254, 255, 263, 280, 287.
39. *Mobile Daily Register and Advertiser,* December 11, 1863; R. Lockwood Tower, ed., *A Carolinian Goes to War: The Civil War Narrative of Arthur Middleton Manugault, Brigadier General, C.S.A.* (Columbia: University of South Carolina Press, 1992), pp. 130–131; William R. Glison Diary; John Hoffman, *The Confederate Collapse at the Battle of Missionary Ridge: The Reports of James Patton Anderson and His Brigade Commanders* (Dayton, OH: Morningside House, 1985), pp. 35, 36, 38.
40. John K. Shellenberger, "With Sheridan's Division at Missionary Ridge," *Sketches of War History 1861–1865* (Cincinnati: Robert Clarke Company, 1903), p. 50; National Historical Society, *Official Records of the War of the Rebellion,* pp. 65, 251, 255, 279, 280, 281, 285, 287, 295, 297, 298; *Mobile Daily Register and Advertiser,* December 11, 1863; Hoffman, *The Confederate Collapse at the Battle of Missionary Ridge: The Reports of James Patton Anderson and His Brigade Commanders,* pp. 35, 58, 68; Stephen H. Helmer, Letter, November 26, 1863, Civil War Miscellany Collection, United States Army Military History Institute.
41. National Historical Society, *Official Records of the War of the Rebellion,* pp. 65, 251, 255, 279, 280, 281, 285, 287, 295, 297, 298.
42. National Historical Society, *Official Records of the War of the Rebellion,* p. 65; Thomas J. Wood, "The Battle of Missionary Ridge," *Sketches of War History 1861–1865* (Cincinnati: Robert Clarke Company, 1903), 2:29.
43. Wood, "The Battle of Missionary Ridge."
44. National Historical Society, *Official Records of the War of the Rebellion,* pp. 129, 137, 189, 347, 348.
45. Ibid., pp. 105, 106, 347, 664, 666, 670, 673, 674, 718, 745, 746, 759; Mattie Lou Teague Crow, ed., *The Diary of a Confederate Soldier, John Washington Inzer, 1834–1928* (Huntsville, AL: Strode Publishers, 1977), pp. 40–41; Tower, *A Carolinian Goes to War: The Civil War Narrative of Arthur Middleton Manugault, Brigadier General, C.S.A.,* pp. 133–134; Hoffman, *The Confederate Collapse at the Battle of Missionary Ridge: The Reports of James Patton Anderson and His Brigade Commanders,* p. 36.
46. National Historical Society, *Official Records of the War of the Rebellion.,* pp. 31, 32, 154, 155, 571, 589, 590; Robert Underwood Johnson and Clarence Clough Buel, eds., *Battles and Leaders of the Civil War, Volume 3: The Tide Shifts* (Secaucus, NJ: Castle Books, 1956), pp. 715–716.
47. National Historical Society, *Official Records of the War of the Rebellion,* pp. 13, 14, 32, 42, 43, 346, 347, 572.
48. Ibid., pp. 572, 573, 589, 590, 597, 629, 636, 646, 654.
49. Ibid., pp. 58, 67, 573, 597, 643; William Wrenshall Smith, "Holocaust Holiday," *Civil War Times Illustrated,* 18, no. 6 (October 1979), p. 35; Zella Armstrong, *The History of Hamilton County and Chattanooga, Tennessee* (Jefferson City, TN: Overmountain Press, 1993), 2:41.
50. National Historical Society, *Official Records of the War of the Rebellion,* pp. 664, 674, 675, 678, 692, 708, 709, 747.
51. Ibid., pp. 41, 42, 102, 103, 105, 106, 107, 314, 329, 674n.
52. Ibid., pp. 315, 390, 391, 392; Edward E. Betts, *Map of the Battlefields of Chattanooga and Wauhatchie, September 27–28, 1863* (Washington, DC: Chickamauga and Chattanooga National Park Commission, 1901), Alabama Department of Archives and History.
53. National Historical Society, *Official Records of the War of the Rebellion,* pp. 718–719.
54. Ibid., pp. 315, 690, 692, 693, 694.
55. Ibid., pp. 392. 393, 690, 698, 699; Richard Eddy, *History of the Sixtieth Regiment New York State Volunteers* (Philadelphia: Author, 1864) pp. 306, 307.
56. National Historical Society, *Official Records of the War of the Rebellion,* pp. 674, 704, 705, 717, 719, 720, 723.
57. Ibid., pp. 156, 159, 165, 396, 441, 446, 446, 717; Ibid., p. 307.
58. Ibid., pp. 332, 395, 396, 425, 444, 705; *Alabama Historical Quarterly* (Montgomery, AL); 17:187.
59. National Historical Society, *Official Records of the War of the Rebellion,* pp. 436, 695, 719, 720, 721, 731, 732.
60. Ibid., pp. 678, 721, 723.
61. Ibid., pp. 317, 696, 726, 732, 734; Arnold Gates, ed., *The Rough Side of War: The Civil War Journal of Chesley A. Mosman, 1st Lieutenant, Company D, 59th Illinois Volunteer Infantry Regiment* (Bellevue, WA: Basin Publishing Company, 1987), p. 127.
62. National Historical Society, *Official Records of the*

War of the Rebellion, pp. 32, 67, 43, 44, 112; Johnson and Buel, eds., *Battles and Leaders of the Civil War,* 3:723.

63. National Historical Society, *Official Records of the War of the Rebellion,* pp. 677, 722; Thomas Lawrence Connelly, *Autumn of Glory: The Army of Tennessee, 1862–1865* (Baton Rouge: Louisiana State University Press, 1971), pp. 251, 273; Nathaniel Chears Hughes, Jr., *General William J. Hardee: Old Reliable* (Baton Rouge: Louisiana State University Press, 1965), pp. 171, 172; Judith Lee Hallock, *Braxton Bragg and Confederate Defeat* (Tuscaloosa: University of Alabama Press, 1991), 2:136.

64. National Historical Society, *Official Records of the War of the Rebellion,* pp. 13, 14, 748, 749, 757.

65. Ibid., pp. 574, 631; Sword, *Mountains Touched with Fire,* p. 243.

66. Ibid., pp. 243–247.

67. Wood, "The Battle of Missionary Ridge," p. 34.

68. Ibid.

69. Ibid.

70. Johnson and Buel, eds., *Battles and Leaders of the Civil War,* 3:724; National Historical Society, *Official Records of the War of the Rebellion,* pp. 87, 209.

71. Peter Cozzens, *The Shipwreck of Their Hopes: The Battles for Chattanooga* (Chicago: University of Illinois Press, 1994), pp. 248–249.

72. Ibid.

73. Ibid., pp. 249–251.

74. Ibid., pp. 253–254.

75. Wood, "The Battle of Missionary Ridge," p. 35.

76. Sword, *Mountains Touched with Fire,* pp. 268–269.

77. Ibid., p. 268.

78. National Historical Society, *Official Records of the War of the Rebellion,* p. 459; John McClenahan, *Memoirs,* Historical Files of Chickamauga, Chattanooga National Military Park.

79. Sword, *Mountains Touched with Fire,* pp. 270–274.

80. National Historical Society, *Official Records of the War of the Rebellion,* pp. 264, 266, 267, 278; Alexis Cope, *The Fifteenth Ohio Volunteers and Its Campaigns, War of 1861–1865* (Salem, MA: Higginson Book Company, 1998), pp. 381–382.

81. National Historical Society, *Official Records of the War of the Rebellion,* pp. 199, 230, 234, 281, 282, 508, 509, 513; Robert L. Kimberley and Ephraim S. Holloway, *The Forty-First Ohio Veteran Volunteer Infantry in the War of the Rebellion, 1861–1865* (Cleveland: W. R. Smellie, 1897), pp. 69–70.

82. Johnson and Buel, eds., *Battles and Leaders of the Civil War,* 3:725.

83. Ibid.

84. Ibid.

85. Sword, *Mountains Touched with Fire,* pp. 285–288.

86. Ibid.

87. Tower, *A Carolinian Goes To War: The Civil War Narrative of Arthur Middleton Manugault, Brigadier General, C.S.A.,* pp. 139–143.

88. Ibid., p. 140; Hoffman, *The Confederate Collapse at the Battle of Missionary Ridge: The Reports of James Patton Anderson and his Brigade Commanders,* pp. 43, 64; National Historical Society, *Official Records of the War of the Rebellion,* p. 299.

89. Ibid.

90. Hoffman, The Confederate Collapse at the Battle of Missionary Ridge: The Reports of James Patton Anderson and his Brigade Commanders, pp. 37, 42, 53, 54, 55, 63; National Historical Society, Official Records of the War of the Rebellion, pp. 301, 513, 515, 519, 523, 526, 528, 535; Joseph S. Fullerton, *Report on the Chickamauga and Chattanooga National Park Commission on the Claim of Gen. John B. Turchin and Others That in the Battle of Chattanooga His Brigade Captured the Position on Missionary Ridge Known as De Long Place, and the Decision of the Secretary of War Thereon* (Washington, DC: Government Printing Office, 1896), p. 10; Sword, Mountains Touched with Fire, pp. 292–293.

91. Hoffman, *The Confederate Collapse at the Battle of Missionary Ridge: The Reports of James Patton Anderson and His Brigade Commanders,* pp. 43, 55.

92. Ibid.; Sword, *Mountains Touched with Fire,* pp. 292–293.

93. *Ibid.,* pgs. 49–51; National Historical Society, *Official Records of the War of the Rebellion,* pp. 535, 538, 540, 541, 546; David Bittle Floyd, *History of the Seventy-fifth Regiment Indiana Volunteers, Its Organization, Campaigns, and Battles (1862–1865)* (Philadelphia: Lutheran Publishing Society, 1893), p. 240.

94. Sword, *Mountains Touched with Fire,* pp. 292–293.

95. National Historical Society, *Official Records of the War of the Rebellion,* 31, Part 2, pp. 189, 291, 293, 296, 662, 740, 741; 52, Part 1, pp. 96–98.

96. Ibid., 31, Part 2, pp. 291, 293, 296, 742; 52, Part 1, pp. 97–98; James Henry Haynie, *The Nineteenth Illinois, A Memoir of a Regiment of Volunteer Infantry Famous in the Civil War of Fifty Years Ago for Its Drill, Bravery, and Distinguished Service* (Chicago: M. A. Donohue Company, 1912), p. 281; Kimberley and Holloway, *The Forty-First Ohio Veteran Volunteer Infantry in the War of the Rebellion, 1861–1865,* p. 71.

97. National Historical Society, *Official Records of the War of the Rebellion,* 31, Part 2, pp. 665, 740, 742.

98. Ibid., p. 208; *The MacArthurs of Milwaukee* (Milwaukee: Milwaukee County Historical Society, 1979), pp. 6–7.

99. National Historical Society, *Official Records of the War of the Rebellion,* 31, Part 2, pp. 231, 665, 742; 52, Part 1, p. 98; Robert Watson Journal, November 25, 1863, Historical Files of Chickamauga, Chattanooga National Military Park.

100. Sword, *Mountains Touched with Fire,* pp. 306–310.

101. Ibid.

102. Mattie Lou Teague Crow, ed., *The Diary of a Confederate Soldier, John Washington Inzer 1834–1928* (Huntsville, AL: Strode Publishers, 1977), pp. 42–46.

103. Charles A. Willison, *Reminiscences of a Boy's Service with the 76th Ohio* (Huntington, WV: Blue Acorn Press, 1995), p. 77.

104. National Historical Society, *Official Records of the War of the Rebellion,* 31, Part 2, pp. 14, 148, 171, 459, 474, 480, 602, 608.

105. Sword, *Mountains Touched with Fire,* p. 311.

106. Ibid., p. 312.

107. Ibid.

108. National Historical Society, *Official Records of the War of the Rebellion,* 31, Part 2, pp. 191, 742; 32, Part 1, p. 98.

109. Ibid., 31, Part 2, p. 679.

110. Ibid., pp. 666, 679.

111. Ibid., pp. 36, 81, 88; "Statement of the Strength of the Army of Tennessee in the Engagements before Chattanooga, the Losses in Those Engagements, the Strength of the Army on Its Arrival at Dalton, Its Strength on the 20th Inst., and the Increase of Effective Strength Since the Retreat and to the 20th of December," Confederate Collection, Tennessee State Library and Archives.

112. Samuel B. Watkins, *"Co. Aytch," Maury Gray's First Tennessee Regiment* (New York: Benchmark Books, 2004), pp. 120–121.

113. National Historical Society, *Official Records of the War of the Rebellion,* pp. 14, 122, 326, 599, 757.

114. Ibid., pp. 35, 71, 72; John Y. Simon, ed., *The Pa-

pers of Ulysses S. Grant (Carbondale: Southern Illinois University Press, 1969), 9:496.
115. Ibid.
116. National Historical Society, *Official Records of the War of the Rebellion,* Part 2, p. 682; Part 3, pp. 754, 764.
117. Judith Lee Hallock, *Braxton Bragg and Confederate Defeat* (Tuscaloosa: University of Alabama Press, 1991), 2:149; Sword, *Mountains Touched with Fire,* p. 354.
118. National Historical Society, *Official Records of the War of the Rebellion,* pp. 873–874.

CHAPTER 6

1. National Historical Society, *Official Records of the War of the Rebellion* (Harrisburg, PA: National Historical Society, 1985), Ser. 1, 31, Part 3, pp. 856–857.
2. Ibid.
3. Albert Castel, *Decision in the West: The Atlanta Campaign of 1864* (Lawrence: University Press of Kansas, 1992), p. 31.
4. Ibid., p. 32.
5. National Historical Society, *Official Records of the War of the Rebellion,* 32, Part 2, pp. 530–535, 548–549, 591–592, 603–604; Elbert D. Willett, *History of Company B* (Anniston, AL: Norwood Publishing, 1902), p. 53.
6. Castel, *Decision in the West: The Atlanta Campaign of 1864,* pp. 39, 43, 44, 47.
7. Ibid., pp. 47–49.
8. National Historical Society, *Official Records of the War of the Rebellion,* 32, Part 1, pp. 256–259, 265–270; Part 2, pp. 370, 431; Robert Underwood Johnson and Clarence Clough Buel, eds., "The Sooy Smith Expedition," *Battles and Leaders of the Civil War* (Secaucus, NJ: Castle Books, 1956), 3:416–418; Robert Selph Henry, *"First with the Most" Forrest* (Indianapolis: Bobbs-Merrill Company, 1944), pp. 22–23.
9. National Historical Society, *Official Records of the War of the Rebellion,* Part 1, pp. 423–426, 449–453, 456–461, 476–477; Part 2, pp. 458–459, 461, 475, 480–482, 798–799, 808.
10. Letter of Robert W. Wells, February 14, 1864, Louisiana State University (LSU) Special Collections, LSU Libraries, Baton Rouge, LA, Mss. 1032.
11. Letter of J. J. Prewitt, Robert Archibald Family Papers, Archibald, Richland Parish, Louisiana.
12. National Historical Society, *Official Records of the War of the Rebellion,* Part 3, p. 13.
13. Castel, *Decision in the West: The Atlanta Campaign of 1864,* pp. 64–65.
14. Ulysses S. Grant, *Personal Memoirs* (New York: Library of America, 1990), 2:144–223.
15. Ibid., pp. 118–119; William T. Sherman, *Memoirs of General W. T. Sherman* (New York: Charles L. Webster and Company, 1891), 2:5–7.
16. Robert Gibbons, "Life at the Crossroads of the Confederacy: 1864–1865," *Atlanta Historical Bulletin,* 23 (1979): 11–15; Paul D. Lack, "Law and Disorder in Confederate Atlanta," *Georgia Historical Quarterly,* 56 (1982): 171–189.
17. Steve Davis, "The Great Snowball Battle of 1864," *Civil War Times Illustrated,* 15, no. 3 (February 1976): 32–35; William Bentley, "The Great Snowball Battle," *Civil War Times Illustrated,* 5, no. 9 (January 1967): 22–23.
18. Davis, "The Great Snowball Battle of 1864"; Bentley, "The Great Snowball Battle."
19. Castel, *Decision in the West: The Atlanta Campaign of 1864,* pp. 79–90.
20. Ibid., pp. 90–94.
21. Philip L. Secrist, *The Battle of Resaca* (Macon, GA: Mercer University Press, 1998), p. 13.
22. Ibid., p. 14.
23. Ibid.
24. Ibid., pp. 15–16.
25. Castel, *Decision in the West: The Atlanta Campaign of 1864,* pp. 131–136.
26. National Historical Society, *Official Records of the War of the Rebellion,* 38, Part 3, pp. 722, 761, 874–875.
27. Castel, *Decision in the West: The Atlanta Campaign of 1864,* pp. 150–151.
28. Ibid., pp. 156, 159–161; National Historical Society, *Official Records of the War of the Rebellion,* Part 1, pp. 734–736; Part 2, pp. 581–582, 610–611, 675–678; Jacob D. Cox, *Military Reminiscences of the Civil War* (New York: Charles E. Scribner, 1900), 1:432–436; 2:189–191, 219–220.
29. Castel, *Decision in the West: The Atlanta Campaign of 1864,* pp. 163–164.
30. Ibid., pp. 164–166.
31. National Historical Society, *Official Records of the War of the Rebellion,* Part 3, pp. 32, 92–93, 142–143, 190–191, 219–220; Part 4, p. 185; Philip L. Secrist, *The Battle of Resaca* (Macon, GA: Mercer University Press, 1998), pp. 24–29.
32. National Historical Society, *Official Records of the War of the Rebellion,* pp. 173, 175, 186, 188–190, 199, 709–710.
33. Ibid., Part 1, pp. 190–191, 422; William B. Hazen, *A Narrative of Military Service* (Boston: Ticknor and Company, 1885), p. 252.
34. National Historical Society, *Official Records of the War of the Rebellion,* Part 2, pp. 112–317, 321–24, 340–464; Part 3, pp. 812–813; Part 4, pp. 191, 194; Castel, *Decision in the West: The Atlanta Campaign of 1864,* pp. 174–175.
35. National Historical Society, *Official Records of the War of the Rebellion,* Part 2, pp. 28–29, 40–41, 59–60, 86–87, 511; Part 3, pp. 615, 813, 817–818, 825, 832, 842, 845, 848, 851; Bromfield L. Ridley, *Battles and Sketches of the Army of Tennessee* (Mexico, MO: Missouri Printing and Publishing Company, 1906), pp. 295–301.
36. National Historical Society, *Official Records of the War of the Rebellion,* Part 3, p. 859.
37. Castel, *Decision in the West: The Atlanta Campaign of 1864* (Lawrence: University Press of Kansas, 1992), p. 179.
38. Ibid., pp. 180–181.
39. National Historical Society, *Official Records of the War of the Rebellion,* Part 3, pp. 854–856.
40. Castel, *Decision in the West: The Atlanta Campaign of 1864,* pp. 207–221.
41. National Historical Society, *Official Records of the War of the Rebellion,* Part 3, pp. 616, 625, 705, 818, 947–948; Part 4, pp. 303–304, 739, 742.
42. Castel, *Decision in the West: The Atlanta Campaign of 1864,* p. 221.
43. Richard M. McMurry, "The Hell Hole," *Civil War Times Illustrated,* 11, no. 10 (February 1973): 36; H. J. Lea, "In The Battle of New Hope Church," *Confederate Veteran,* 31:61–62.
44. McMurry, "The Hell Hole."
45. Ibid., p. 37.
46. Ibid.
47. Ibid.
48. Ibid., p. 38.
49. Ibid.
50. Ibid.
51. Ibid.
52. Ibid.
53. Ibid., p. 40.

54. Ibid.
55. Ibid., pp. 41–42.
56. Ibid., p. 42.
57. Ibid., pp. 42–43.
58. National Historical Society, *Official Records of the War of the Rebellion*, Part 3, p. 855.
59. Letter of R. A. Allen, June 4, 1864, Historical Files of Kennesaw Mountain National Battlefield Park.
60. Castel, *Decision in the West: The Atlanta Campaign of 1864*, pp. 290–295.
61. Ibid., pp. 307–319.
62. Ibid., pp. 275–276; Sherman, *Memoirs of General W. T. Sherman*, 2:52–53; Oliver Otis Howard, *Autobiography of Oliver Otis Howard* (New York: Baker and Taylor Company, 1907), 1:563–564.
63. National Historical Society, *Official Records of the War of the Rebellion*, 38, Part 5, p. 868; 52, Part 2, pp. 646–647; Gilbert E. Govan and James W. Livingood, *A Different Valor: The Story of General Joseph E. Johnston, C.S.A* (New York: Bobbs-Merrill, 1956), p. 293.
64. National Historical Society, *Official Records of the War of the Rebellion*, 38, Part 5, p. 885.
65. Letter of Joseph T. Hill, July 17, 1864, Robert Archibald Family Papers, Archibald, Richland Parish, Louisiana.
66. Castel, *Decision in the West: The Atlanta Campaign of 1864*, pp. 365–383.
67. Ibid., pp. 383–414.
68. National Historical Society, *Official Records of the War of the Rebellion*, Part 3, p. 40; Part 5, pp. 260, 272–274, 276–277; Mrs. John A. Logan, *Reminiscences of a Soldier's Wife: An Autobiography* (New York, Charles Scribner's Sons, 1913), pp. 170–171; Sherman, *Memoirs of General W. T. Sherman*, 2:86–87.
69. Castel, *Decision in the West: The Atlanta Campaign of 1864*, pp. 422–423.
70. Ibid., pp. 424–428.
71. National Historical Society, *Official Records of the War of the Rebellion*, Part 1, pp. 75–76; Part 3, pp. 631–632, 688, 762, 872, 953; Part 5, pp. 255, 260–261, 264–265, 909, 912–917.
72. Castel, *Decision in the West: The Atlanta Campaign of 1864*, p. 428.
73. Ibid., p. 430.
74. Ibid., pp. 431–433; National Historical Society, *Official Records of the War of the Rebellion*, Part 3, pp. 632, 763, 872; Part 5, pp. 919–920.
75. Castel, *Decision in the West: The Atlanta Campaign of 1864*, pp. 431–433; National Historical Society, *Official Records of the War of the Rebellion*, Part 1, pp. 77–78, 633, 650; Part 3, pp. 40–41, 104, 148, 167–168, 222–223, 228–229, 247–248, 281–282, 762–763, 767–768, 775–794, 799–900, 802–803, 807, 821, 872, 926–928, 931–932, 939–940, 942–943; Part 5, pp. 279–280, 918–921.
76. National Historical Society, *Official Records of the War of the Rebellion*, Part 3, pp. 856–857.
77. Sherman, *Memoirs of General W. T. Sherman*, 2:101–102.
78. National Historical Society, *Official Records of the War of the Rebellion*, Part 1, pp. 79–80, 164, 212–213; Part 2, pp. 18–19.
79. Castel, *Decision in the West: The Atlanta Campaign of 1864*, p. 486.
80. Ibid., p. 487.
81. Ibid., pp. 489–492.
82. Ibid., pp. 496, 499.
83. National Historical Society, *Official Records of the War of the Rebellion*, Part 3, pp. 682–683, 700, 708, 727, 735, 741, 743–744, 755, 764, 773, 821–822, 824, 857.
84. Ibid., Part 3, pp. 44–45, 108–109; Part 5, pp. 728, 743–744; Cox, *Military Reminiscences of the Civil War*, 2:282; Oliver Otis Howard, "The Battles about Atlanta," *Atlantic Monthly*, 37 (1876): 563–564.
85. National Historical Society, *Official Records of the War of the Rebellion*, Part 3, pp. 764–765, 773–774, 822, 824, 835, 857–858; *Mobile Daily Advertiser and Register*, September 20, 1864.
86. Castel, *Decision in the West: The Atlanta Campaign of 1864*, pp. 502–503.
87. National Historical Society, *Official Records of the War of the Rebellion*, Part 3, pp. 857–858.
88. Castel, *Decision in the West: The Atlanta Campaign of 1864*, pp. 505, 507, 509.
89. Ibid., pp. 512–522.
90. National Historical Society, *Official Records of the War of the Rebellion*, pp. 633, 695, 765, 906, 991–992; Noble C. Williams, *Southern Life during the War* (Atlanta, 1902), p. 34; Franklin M. Garrett, *Atlanta and Environs: A Chronicle of Its People and Events* (New York: Lewis Historical Publishing Company, 1954), p. 633; *New York Herald*, September 16, 1864.
91. Castel, *Decision in the West: The Atlanta Campaign of 1864*, pp. 527–529; *New York Herald*, September 8, 1864; *Cincinnati Daily Commercial*, September 13, 1864; *New York Times*, September 15, 1864.
92. National Historical Society, *Official Records of the War of the Rebellion*, Part 1, pp. 82, 216, 251–252, 261–262, 299, 384, 451–452, 455, 465, 470, 933; Part 3, pp. 46, 696; Part 5, pp. 764–765, 771–772, 774–776, 784, 1016; Thomas Ward Osborn, *The Fiery Trail: A Union Officer's Account of Sherman's Last Campaign* (Knoxville: University of Tennessee Press, 1986), p. 37.
93. National Historical Society, *Official Records of the War of the Rebellion*, Part 1, p. 82; Part 5, pp. 777, 789; Sidney C. Kerksis, "The Siege and Capture of Atlanta," *The Atlanta Papers* (Dayton, OH: Morningside Bookshop, 1980), p. 128; Castel, *Decision in the West: The Atlanta Campaign of 1864* (Lawrence: University Press of Kansas, 1992), pp. 533–534.

Chapter 7

1. Franklin M. Garrett, *Atlanta and Environs: A Chronicle of Its People and Events* (New York: Lewis Historical Publishing Company, 1954), p. 639.
2. National Historical Society, *Official Records of the War of the Rebellion* (Harrisburg, PA: National Historical Society, 1985), Ser. 1, 38, Part 5, pp. 794, 822, 839; 39, Part 2, pp. 414–422.
3. Ibid.
4. Ibid., 39, Part 2, p. 481; 38, Part 3, p. 993.
5. Albert Castel, *Decision in the West: The Atlanta Campaign of 1864* (Lawrence: University Press of Kansas, 1992), p. 550.
6. National Historical Society, *Official Records of the War of the Rebellion*, 38, Part 5, pp. 1023–1024; 39, Part 2, pp. 818–819, 836; Robert Selph Henry, *"First with the Most" Forrest*, (Indianapolis: Bobbs-Merrill, 1944), pp. 345–350.
7. Castel, *Decision in the West: The Atlanta Campaign of 1864*, p. 551.
8. Ibid., pp. 551–552.
9. National Historical Society, *Official Records of the War of the Rebellion*, *Official Records of the War of the Rebellion*, 39, Part 1, p. 507; Part 2, pp. 464, 517–518, 532, 540; Stanley F. Horn, *The Army of Tennessee* (Norman: University of Oklahoma Press, 1941), pp. 375–378; John

Allen Wyeth, *Life of Lieutenant-General Nathan Bedford Forrest* (Dayton, OH: Morningside Bookshop, 1975), pp. 488–513.

10. William T. Sherman, *Memoirs of General W. T. Sherman* (New York: Charles L. Webster and Company, 1891), 2:152–167.

11. Ibid.

12. John Bell Hood, *Advance and Retreat* (New York: Krauss Reprint Company, 1969), pp. 266–269.

13. Ibid., pp. 278, 281–282; Horn, *The Army of Tennessee*, pp. 383–384.

14. H. J. Lea, "The Fourth Louisiana Battalion at the Battle of Secessionville, S.C.," *Confederate Veteran* (Wilmington, NC: Broadfoot Publishing, 1986), 31: 14–16; "Service with the Fourth Louisiana Battalion," *Confederate Veteran* (Wilmington, NC: Broadfoot Publishing, 1986), 19:542–543.

15. Castel, *Decision in the West: The Atlanta Campaign of 1864*, pp. 556–557.

16. Ibid.

17. Horn, *The Army of Tennessee*, pp. 394–418.

18. H. J. Lea, "With the Fourth Louisiana Battalion," *Confederate Veteran* (Wilmington, NC: Broadfoot Publishing, 1986), 27:339–340.

19. Horn, *The Army of Tennessee*, pp. 422–423.

20. Arthur W. Bergeron, Jr., *Confederate Mobile* (Baton Rouge: Louisiana State University Press, 2000), p. 168; Arthur W. Bergeron, Jr., *Guide to Louisiana Confederate Military Units 1861–1865* (Baton Rouge; Louisiana State University Press, 1989), pp. 157–158.

21. Bergeron, *Confederate Mobile*, pp. 167–168.

22. National Historical Society, *Official Records of the War of the Rebellion*, 45, Part 2, p. 506; 48, Part 1, p. 580; 49, Part 1, pp. 91–92, 593; Christopher Columbus Andrews, *History of the Campaign of Mobile* (New York: Van Nostrand, 1867), pp. 21, 31–32; Herman Hattaway and Archer Jones, *How the North Won: A Military History of the Civil War* (Chicago: University of Illinois Press, 1991), p. 662.

23. National Historical Society, *Official Records of the War of the Rebellion*, 49, Part 1, pp. 313–314, 1045; Part 2, pp. 1129, 1153, 1157; Dabney H. Maury, "Defense of Mobile in 1865," *Southern Historical Society Papers* (New York: Kraus Reprint Company, 1978), 3:4; General Order Number 11, Headquarters District of the Gulf, March 21, 1865 and Order of the Mobile Mayor's Office, as printed in the *Mobile Advertiser and Register*, March 21–22, 1865; P. D. Stephenson, "Defense of Spanish Fort," *Southern Historical Society Papers* (New York: Kraus Reprint Company, 1978), p. 121.

24. National Historical Society, *Official Records of the War of the Rebellion*, 49, Part 1, pp. 314–315; Part 2, pp. 1162–1163; Andrews, *History of the Campaign of Mobile*, pp. 49–50; Gibson to Liddell, March 27, 1865, in Randall Lee Gibson Papers, Louisiana State University Department of Archives and Manuscripts, Hill Memorial Library, Baton Rouge, Louisiana; Randall Lee Gibson to John McGrath, September 26, 1884, Randall Lee Gibson Letters, Tulane University Special Collections Division, Howard-Tilton Memorial Library, New Orleans, Louisiana.

25. Bergeron, *Confederate Mobile*, pp. 176–177.

26. Ibid., p. 177; General Order Number 17, Paragraph IV, Headquarters District of the Gulf, April 1, 1865, in Randall Lee Gibson Papers, Louisiana State University Department of Archives and Manuscripts, Hill Memorial Library, Baton Rouge, Louisiana.

27. Stephenson, "Defense of Spanish Fort," pp. 122–123.

28. Bergeron, *Confederate Mobile*, p. 178.

29. Ibid., p. 178.

30. Andrews, *History of the Campaign of Mobile*, p. 137; Thad Holt, Jr., *Miss Waring's Journal: 1863–1865* (Chicago: Wyvern Press of S. F. E., 1964), p. 12.

31. National Historical Society, *Official Records of the War of the Rebellion*, *Official Records of the War of the Rebellion*, Part 1, pp. 316, 319–320; Part 2, pp. 1184, 1192, 1200, 1209–1210; Randall L. Gibson to Dabney H. Maury, April 2, 1865 in Randall Lee Gibson Papers, Louisiana State University Department of Archives and Manuscripts, Hill Memorial Library, Baton Rouge, Louisiana.

32. Bergeron, *Confederate Mobile*, pp. 179–180.

33. National Historical Society, *Official Records of the War of the Rebellion*, Part 1, p. 316; Part 2, p. 1218.

34. Ibid., Part 1, pp. 96, 316; Stephenson, "Defense of Spanish Fort," pp. 123–125.

35. Bergeron, *Confederate Mobile*, p. 181.

36. Holt, *Miss Waring's Journal: 1863–1865*, p. 13.

37. National Historical Society, *Official Records of the War of the Rebellion*, Part 1, pp. 102, 317–318.

38. Richard Taylor, *Destruction and Reconstruction* (New York: Longmans, Green and Company, 1955), p. 270.

39. Stephenson, "Defense of Spanish Fort," p. 130.

40. National Historical Society, *Official Records of the War of the Rebellion*, Part 1, p. 318.

41. Dabney H. Maury, "Defense of Mobile in 1865," *Southern Historical Society Papers* (New York: Kraus Reprint Company, 1978), 3:8; James Bradley, *The Confederate Mail Carrier* (Westminster, MD: Heritage Books, 1990), p. 224; Edward W. Tarrant, "Siege and Capture of Fort Blakely," *Confederate Veteran* (Wilmington, NC: Broadfoot Publishing, 1986), 23:457.

42. National Historical Society, *Official Records of the War of the Rebellion*, Part 1, p. 311; Part 2, pp. 1185–1188; Andrews, *History of the Campaign of Mobile*, p. 91; Bradley, *The Confederate Mail Carrier*, pp. 224–225; R. S. Bevier, *History of the 1st and 2nd Missouri Confederate Brigades: 1861–1865* (St. Louis: Bryan, Brand and Company, 1879), p. 262.

43. National Historical Society, *Official Records of the War of the Rebellion*, Part 1, pp. 282, 287; Part 2, p. 1190; Bradley, *The Confederate Mail Carrier*, p. 225.

44. National Historical Society, *Official Records of the War of the Rebellion*, Part 1, pp. 261, 264, 283, 320–321; Part 2, pp. 282, 284; Bradley, *The Confederate Mail Carrier*, p. 225; Andrews, *History of the Campaign of Mobile*, p. 171.

45. National Historical Society, *Official Records of the War of the Rebellion*, Part 1, pp. 97–98, 101–102, 321–322; Part 2, pp. 1217, 1222–1223; Andrews, *History of the Campaign of Mobile*, p. 188; Jeanie Mort Walker, *Life of Capt. Joseph Fry, the Cuban Martyr* (Hartford, CT: J. B. Burr Publisher, 1874), pp. 180–184; Maury, "Defense of Mobile in 1865," 3:8; Bradley, *The Confederate Mail Carrier*, p. 225; Edward W. Tarrant, "Siege and Capture of Fort Blakely," *Confederate Veteran* (Wilmington, NC: Broadfoot Publishing, 1986), 23:457–458; Bevier, *History of the 1st and 2nd Missouri Confederate Brigades: 1861–1865*, pp. 265–267; St. John Richardson Liddell, *Liddell's Record* (Dayton: Morningside Publishers, 1985), p. 196.

46. Bergeron, *Confederate Mobile*, pp. 187–188.

47. Ibid., p. 188.

48. Ibid.

49. Ibid., p. 189; Holt, *Miss Waring's Journal: 1863–1865*, pp. 13–14; Oscar H. Lipscomb, "The Administration of John Quinlan, Second Bishop of Mobile, 1859–1883" (M. A. thesis, Catholic University of America, 1959), p. 92.

50. Bergeron, *Confederate Mobile*, p. 190; William Rix,

Incidents of Life in a Southern City during the War (Mobile: Iberville Historical Society Papers, 1865), p. 21.

51. Rix, *Incidents of Life in a Southern City during the War*, p. 24. Maury to Surget Correspondence, April 15, 1865, Department of the Gulf Records, Louisiana Historical Association Collection; Maury, "Defense of Mobile in 1865," 3:8; Holt, *Miss Waring's Journal: 1863–1865,* p. 15; Peter Joseph Hamilton, *A Little Boy in Confederate Mobile* (Mobile: Colonial Mobile Book Shop, 1947), p. 26; Benjamin B. Cox, "Mobile in the War between the States," *Confederate Veteran* (Wilmington, NC: Broadfoot Publishing, 1986), 24:210–211; National Historical Society, *Official Records of the War of the Rebellion,* Part 1, pp. 143–144, 146, 175.

52. Bergeron, *Guide to Louisiana Confederate Military Units 1861–1865,* pp. 157–158.

53. "Service with the Fourth Louisiana Battalion," *Confederate Veteran* (Wilmington, NC: Broadfoot Publishing, 1986), 19:542–543.

54. National Historical Society, *Official Records of the War of the Rebellion,* Part 1, pp. 319–320.

55. Letter of Robert W. Wells, December 10, 1865, Louisiana State University (LSU) Special Collections, LSU Libraries, Baton Rouge, LA, Mss. 1032.

Biographical Register Notes

1. Craig L. Symonds, *Joseph E. Johnston: A Civil War Biography* (New York: W. W. Norton Company, 1992), p. 66.
2. Ibid., p. 71.
3. Michael B. Ballard, *Pemberton: The General Who Lost Vicksburg* (Jackson: University Press of Mississippi, 1991), pp. 77–78.
4. Ibid.
5. Richard Taylor, *Destruction and Reconstruction* (New York: Longmans, Green and Company, 1955), p. 288.
6. Ibid.
7. Dabney Herndon Maury, *Recollections of a Virginian in the Mexican, Indian and Civil Wars* (New York: Charles Scribner's Sons, 1894). p. 137.
8. Mary Boykin Chesnut, *Mary Chesnut's Civil War* (New Haven, CT: Yale University Press, 1981), p. 565.
9. James C. Kotter, *The Breckinridges of Kentucky 1760–1981* (Lexington: University Press of Kentucky, 1986), p. 122.
10. Christopher Losson, *Tennessee's Forgotten Warriors: Frank Cheatham and His Confederate Division* (Knoxville: University of Tennessee Press, 1989), p. 277.
11. *Confederate Veteran* (Wilmington, NC: Broadfoot Publishing, 1986), 16:384.
12. William R. Polk, *Polk's Folly* (New York: Doubleday, 2000), p. 300.
13. Albert Castel, *Decision in the West: The Atlanta Campaign of 1864* (Lawrence: University Press of Kansas, 1992), pp. 276–277.
14. Joseph H. Parks, *General Leonidas Polk: The Fighting Bishop* (Baton Rouge: Louisiana State University Press, 1962), p. 170.
15. Samuel R. Watkins, *"Co. Aytch," Maury Gray's 1st Tennessee Regiment* (Dayton, OH: Morningside Bookshop, 1992), p. 139.
16. National Historical Society, *Official Records of the War of the Rebellion*, 24, Part 1, p. 190.
17. Ibid., 49, Part 1, pp. 319–320.
18. National Historical Society, *Official Records of the Union and Confederate Navies in the War of the Rebellion* (Harrisburg, PA: National Historical Society, 1985), Ser. 1, 8, p. 435.

Bibliography

Allardice, Bruce A. *More Generals in Gray*. Baton Rouge: Louisiana State University Press, 1995.

Arnold, James R. *Grant Wins the War: Decision at Vicksburg*. New York: John Wiley & Sons, 1997.

Ayres, Thomas. *Dark and Bloody Ground: The Battle of Mansfield and the Forgotten Civil War in Louisiana*. Dallas: Taylor Publishing Company, 2001.

Bearss, Edwin C. *The Vicksburg Campaign, Volume 2*. Dayton, OH: Morningside House, 1985.

Bergeron, Arthur W., Jr. *Confederate Mobile*. Baton Rouge: Louisiana State University Press, 1991.

_____. *Guide to Louisiana Confederate Military Units 1861–1865*. Baton Rouge: Louisiana State University Press, 1989.

Boatner, Mark M., III. *The Civil War Dictionary*. New York: David McKay Co., 1988.

Booth, Andrew B. *Records of Louisiana Confederate Soldiers and Louisiana Confederate Commands*. Spartanburg, SC: Reprint Company Publishers, 1984.

Bowers, John. *Chickamauga and Chattanooga: The Battles That Doomed the Confederacy*. New York: HarperCollins Publishers, 1994.

Bragg, Jefferson Davis. *Louisiana in the Confederacy*. Baton Rouge: Louisiana State University Press, 1941.

Brennan, Patrick L. *Secessionville: Assault on Charleston*. Campbell, CA: Savas Publishing Company, 1996.

Brinsfield, John W., William C. Davis, Benedict Maryniak, and James I. Roberston, Jr. *Faith in the Fight: Civil War Chaplains*. Mechanicsburg, PA: Stackpole Books, 2003.

Castel, Albert. *Decision in the West: The Atlanta Campaign of 1864*. Lawrence: University Press of Kansas, 1992.

Chesnut, Mary Boykin. *A Diary from Dixie*. Cambridge: Harvard University Press, 1980.

Coleman, Kenneth, and Charles Stephen Gurr. *Dictionary of Georgia Biography*. Athens: University of Georgia Press, 1983.

Confederate Veteran magazine, Vols. 1–40. Wilmington, NC: Broadfoot Publishing, 1986.

Connelly, Thomas Lawrence. *Autumn of Glory: The Army of Tennessee, 1862–1865*. Baton Rouge: Louisiana State University Press, 1971.

Conrad, Glen R. *A Dictionary of Louisiana Biography, Volumes I and II*. New Orleans: Louisiana Historical Association, 1988.

Cozzens, Peter. *The Shipwreck of Their Hopes: The Battles for Chattanooga*. Urbana: University of Illinois Press, 1994.

_____. *This Terrible Sound: The Battle of Chickamauga*. Urbana: University of Illinois Press, 1992.

Daniel, Larry J. *Soldiering in the Army of Tennessee*. Chapel Hill: University of North Carolina Press, 1991.

Davis, William C., and Julie Hoffman. *The Confederate General, Volumes I–VI*. Harrisburg, PA: National Historical Society, 1991.

Durham, Walter T. *Volunteer 49er's: Tennessee and the California Gold Rush*. Nashville: Vanderbilt University Press, 1997.

Dyer, John P. *Gallant Hood*. New York: Smithmark Publishers, 1995.

Eicher, John H., and David Eicher. *Civil War High Commands*. Stanford, CA: Stanford University Press, 2001.

Elliott, Sam Davis. *Soldier of Tennessee: General Alexander P. Stewart and the Civil War in the West*. Baton Rouge: Louisiana State University Press, 1956.

Encyclopedia of the Confederacy. New York: Simon and Schuster, 1993.

Evans, Clement A. *Confederate Military History, Volumes. I–XII*. Atlanta: Confederate Publishing Co., 1899.

Faust, Patricia L. *Historical Times Illustrated Encyclopedia of the Civil War*. New York: Harper and Row Publishers, 1986.

Garraty, John A., and Mark C. Carnes. *American National Biography, Volumes I–XXIV*. New York: Oxford University Press, 1999.

Givan, Gilbert E., and James W. Livingood. *A Different Valor: The Story of General Joseph E. Johnston*. New York: Bobbs & Merrill Company, 1956.

Heidler, David S., and Jeanne T. Heidler. *Encyclopedia of the American Civil War*. Santa Barbara: ABC/CLIO, 2000.

Hood, John Bell. *Advance and Retreat*. Edison, NJ: Blue and Gray Press, 1985.

Horn, Stanley J. *The Army of Tennessee.* Norman: University of Oklahoma Press, 1952.

Hughes, Nathaniel Chears, Jr. *General William J. Hardee: Old Reliable.* Baton Rouge: Louisiana State University Press, 1965.

Johnson, Clint. *Civil War Blunders.* Winston-Salem, NC: John F. Blair Publishers, 1997.

Johnston, Joseph E. *Narrative of Military Operations.* Bloomington: Indiana University Press, 1959.

Klotter, James C. *Breckinridges of Kentucky, 1760–1981.* Lexington: University Press of Kentucky, 1986.

Kneebone, John T., Jefferson Looney, Brent Tartar, and Sandra Gioia Treadway. *Dictionary of Virginia Biography, Volumes I–II.* Richmond: Library of Virginia, 1998.

Losson, Christopher. *Tennessee's Forgotten Warriors.* Knoxville: University of Tennessee Press, 1989.

Malone, Dumas. *Dictionary of American Biography, Volumes I–XX.* New York: Charles Scribner's & Sons, 1934.

Marks, Henry S. *Who Was Who in Alabama.* Huntsville, AL: Strode Publishers, 1972.

Marvel, William. *Andersonville: The Last Depot.* Chapel Hill: University of North Carolina Press, 1994.

McDonough, James Lee, and James Pickett Jones. *War So Terrible: Sherman and Atlanta.* New York: W. W. Norton and Company, 1987.

McMurry, Richard M. *Atlanta 1864: Last Chance for the Confederacy.* Lincoln: University of Nebraska Press, 2000.

_____. *John Bell Hood and the War for Southern Independence.* Lexington: University Press of Kentucky, 1982.

McWhiney, Grady. *Braxton Bragg and Confederate Defeat.* Tuscaloosa: University of Alabama Press, 1991.

Northen, William J. *Men of Mark in Georgia, Volumes I–VII.* Spartanburg, SC: Reprint Company Publishers, 1974.

Owen, Richard, and James Owen. *Generals at Rest: The Grave Sites of the 425 Official Confederate Generals.* Shippensburg, PA: White Mane Publishing Company, 1997.

Parks, Joseph H. *General Leonidas Polk, CSA: The Fighting Bishop.* Baton Rouge: Louisiana State University Press, 1962.

Polk, William R. *Polk's Folly.* New York: Doubleday, 2000.

Powell, William S. *Dictionary of North Carolina Biography, Volumes I–VI.* Chapel Hill: University of North Carolina Press, 1979.

Richardson, James D. *A Compilation of Messages and Papers of the Confederacy.* Nashville: U.S. Publishing Company, 1905.

Scaife, William R. *The Campaign for Atlanta.* Atlanta: Author, 1985.

Sifakis, Stewart. *Who Was Who in the Civil War.* New York: Facts on File, 1988.

Speer, Lonnie R. *Portals to Hell: Military Prisons of the Civil War.* Mechanicsburg, PA: Stackpole Books, 1997.

Sword, Wiley. *Mountains Touched with Fire: Chattanooga Besieged, 1863.* New York: St. Martin's Press, 1995.

Symonds, Craig L. *Joseph Eggleston Johnston, a Civil War Biography.* New York: W. W. Norton and Company, 1992.

Taylor, Richard. *Destruction and Reconstruction.* Edited by Richard B. Harwell. New York: Longmans, Green and Company, 1955.

Tyler, Lyon Gardiner. *Encyclopedia of Virginia Biography, Volumes I–V.* New York: Lewis Historical Publication Company, 1915.

Wakelyn, Jon L. *Biographical Dictionary of the Confederacy.* Westport, CT: Greenwood Press, 1977.

Warner, Ezra J. *Generals in Blue: Lives of the Union Commanders.* Baton Rouge: Louisiana State University Press, 1964.

_____. *Generals in Gray: Lives of the Confederate Commanders.* Baton Rouge: Louisiana State University Press, 1959.

Watkins, Samuel R. *The Diary of Sam Watkins, a Confederate Soldier.* New York: Benchmark Books, 2004.

Williams, T. Harry. *P. G. T. Beauregard: Napoleon in Gray.* Baton Rouge: Louisiana State University Press, 1955.

Wilson, James Grant, and John Fiske. *Appleton's Cyclopeadia of American Biography, Volumes I–VI.* Detroit: Gale Research Company, 1968.

Winters, John D. *The Civil War in Louisiana.* Baton Rouge: Louisiana State University Press, 1963.

Woodworth, Steven E. *A Deep Steady Thunder: The Battle of Chickamauga.* Fort Worth, TX: Ryan Place Publishers, 1996.

_____. *Jefferson Davis and His Generals.* Lawrence: University Press of Kansas, 1990.

Woodworth, Steven E. *Six Armies in Tennessee: The Chickamauga and Chattanooga Campaigns.* Lincoln: University of Nebraska Press, 1998.

Index

Acworth, Georgia 174, 229
Adaire, Col. Thomas N. 236
Adairsville, Georgia 169
Adams, Brig.-Gen. Daniel Weisiger: board member 10; brigade of 91, 115; biography of 266
Adams, Pvt. John 290
Adams, Brig.-Gen. John Adams 63, 67, 230
Adams, Sgt. Littleton T. 277
Adams County, Mississippi 16
Adams Point, mentioned in journal 24, 27
Adjutant and Inspector General's Office 97
Advance Guard 30
Alabama and Florida Railroad 61
Alabama Reserve Troops 232, 233, 236, 237
Alabama River 232, 238
Alabama, state of 7, 8, 61, 77, 229; brigade from 126, 136, 161, 168; northeastern 162; regiments 171
Alexander, Pvt. Charles F. 318
Alexander Family 83
Alexander's Bridge 80, 81
Alexandria-American 8
Allatoona, Georgia 169, 170, 172, 229
Allatoona Pass 173, 174
Allen, Pvt. Daniel 300
Allen, Henry Watkins 6
Allen, Pvt. R. A. 175, 290
Allnut, Pvt. James S. 279
Allnut, Pvt. William A. 279
Allnutt, Pvt. Edward George 279
Amis, Pvt. A. B. 279
Amis, A.Q.M. Robert Emmett 272, 276, 279
Anaconda Plan 43
Anderson, Pvt. Armstrong 279
Anderson, Maj.-Gen. James Patton 180, 187; brigadier general 121, 128, 129, 132; division of 133, 134, 186
Anderson, Pvt. Petus A. 279
Anderson, Lt. R. 308
Anderson, Lt. R. W., battery of 133

Andersonville, Georgia, prisoner of war camp at 189, 228, 239
Andrews, Col. Julius A., brigade of 233, 235, 236
Andrews, Pvt. Warren A. 330
Anthony's Bridge 186, 187
Antietam 87
Apalachee River 233, 235
Appamattox, Virginia 239
Applewhite, Sgt. William 288
Archibald, Louisiana 17, 159
C.S.S. *Arkansas* 47, 48
Arkansas, state of 7, 15, 43, 44, 53
Arkansas River 56
Armstrong, Pvt. Daniel 279
Armstrong, Brig.-Gen. Frank Crawford, brigade of 83, 174, 185
Army of Mississippi 163, 165, 176
Army of Northern Virginia 78, 80, 90, 116, 117, 161, 239; flags of 95
Army of Tennessee 61, 73, 76, 77, 78, 80, 89, 90, 91, 95, 113, 114, 115, 118, 122, 126, 127, 132, 137, 138, 156, 157, 161, 165, 167, 169, 175, 176, 179, 183, 189, 228, 229, 230, 231; brigades in Mississippi 67; losses at Chickamauga 97
Army of the Cumberland 76, 78, 80, 90, 93, 112, 116, 123, 125, 128, 131, 162, 165, 170, 172, 179, 182, 186; losses at Chickamauga 97
Army of the Ohio 77, 162, 165, 171, 172, 173
Army of the Potomac 112, 160, 161
Army of the Potomac Engineer Brigade 39
Army of the Tennessee 161, 162, 165, 174, 179, 180, 185, 187, 191
Arthur, Pvt. William C. 290
Ascension Parish, Louisiana 7, 9
Ashba, Pvt. William 318
Assumption Parish, Louisiana 7, 9
Athens, Georgia 162
C.S.S. *Atlanta*, mentioned in journal 58, 72
Atlanta Campaign 138, 163, 169, 231, 233
Atlanta, Georgia 78, 114, 115, 138, 158, 161, 162, 163, 167, 169, 172,

175, 176, 179, 180, 183, 185, 186, 189, 191, 192, 227, 228, 229, 231; mentioned in journal 73, 113; mentioned in letter 179
Atlanta-Marietta Road 170
Atlantic and Western Railroad 120
Atwell, Pvt. William G. 330
Augusta, Georgia: mentioned in journal 52; mentioned in letter 159
Aultman, Pvt. James 290
Autry, Col. James Lockhart 46

Babbitt, Charles, mentioned in letter 158
Babbitt, Pvt. Charles Walter 318
Babin, Pvt. Benjamin Franklin 330
Bagley, Pvt. M. 311
Baird, Brig.-Gen. Absalom 84, 85, 120, 129, 130; division of 89, 128, 132, 165, 166
Baker, Brig.-Gen. Alpheus, brigade of 161, 168, 170, 171, 182, 183, 186
Bald Hill 163, 165
Baldwin, George T. 17
Ballance, Pvt. Girard 97, 318
Ballew, Pvt. Charles G. 330
Balph, Pvt. O. P. 279
C.S.S. *Baltic* 238
Baltimore and Ohio Railroad 18
Baltimore, Maryland, democratic convention 8
Barancas, Florida 232
Barfield, Pvt. George W. 300
Barnum, Pvt. Benjamin 279
Barr, Pvt. Herman B. 279
Barrell, Pvt. Thomas 279
Barry, Pvt. Dennis 279
Bartilson, Col. Matthias H. 63
Bass, Cpl. John Cortez 278
Bass, Asst.-Surg. John H. 271
Bate, Brig.-Gen. William Brimage 88, 89, 128, 129, 133, 134, 135, 136, 137, 180; division of 161, 165, 172, 173, 174, 180, 185, 186
Bates, Pvt. Williams S. 290
Baton Rouge, Louisiana 5, 6, 8, 10, 11, 13, 45

349

Battery Cheves, mentioned in journal 72, 73
Battery Huger 235, 237, 238
Battery Simkins, mentioned in journal 72
Battery Thunderbolt 61; mentioned in journal 26, 58, 59, 72, 73
Battery Tracy 237, 238
Battle of Resaca de la Palma 163
Bauer, Pvt. Theodore L. 274, 318
Bay Minette, Alabama 233, 238
Baygents, Pvt. J. W. 330
Bayle, Pvt. J. M. 330
Baynard, Mrs., mentioned in letter 159
Bayou Pierre, Mississippi 60
Beale, Pvt. Jesse T. 279
Beasley, Pvt. J. H. 290
Beatty, Brig.-Gen. Samuel, brigade of 130
Beaufort, South Carolina 28, 41
Beauregard, General Pierre Gustave Toutant 48, 60, 61, 62, 115, 228, 233, 235; Fort Sumter 14; mentioned in journal 28, 40, 51, 52, 58, 67; biography of 251
Beavell, Pvt. Ranton D. 300
Beckham, Col. Robert 180
Beek, Q. M. Sgt. Robert S. 272, 279
Begley, Pvt. Jacob 300
Bell, John 9
Bell, Lt. William D. 315
Benbrook, Pvt. Lewis 318
Benham, Brig.-Gen. Henry Washington 22, 29, 30, 31, 35, 37, 38, 39
Benjamin, Judah Philip, senator 10, 11, 12, 13
Bennett, Sgt. George B. 316
U.S.S. *Benton* 60
Berry, Pvt. H. L. 311
Bickers, Pvt. J. Ross 290
Big Black River 44, 62, 69, 71
Big Folly Creek 32
Big Shanty, Georgia 229
Bills, Pvt. Louis 301
Billy Goat Hill 123, 127
Bird, Ted, mentioned in letter 160
Bird's Mill 137
Bird's Mill Road 128, 133
Birdsell, Cpl. A. 310
Bishop, Lt.-Col. Samuel L. 271
Bisland, Capt. Thomas Alexander 183, 315
Black Diamond, steamer 238
Blackburn, Lt. Cary B. 315, 318
Blackman, Pvt. John S. 301
Blackman, Cpl. William V. 300
Blair, Maj.-Gen. Francis "Frank" Preston, Jr. 182; corps of 180
Blake, Pvt. John 301
Bloody Pond 89
Bolen, Asst.-Surg. Michael J. 271
Bolton, Mississippi 69
Bolton Station 69
Bond, Pvt. J. J. 311
Bond, Pvt. William A. 290
Bonneau, Capt. F. N. 32

Bonnett, Pvt. David G. 330
Boomer, Col. George B., brigade of 65
Booth, John Wilkes, actor 239
Bossier-Banner 8
Bostick, Pvt. Arthur H. 330
Botetourt Artillery 60
Boughton, Pvt. Samuel Strothers 301
Bowden, Pvt. Andrew Jackson, Sr. 301
Bowen, Brig.-Gen. John Stevens 60
Bowman, Pvt. William Camsby 301
Bowman House 62
Boyd, Pvt. Joseph Colpin 318
Boyett, Pvt. Young R. 330
Boynton, Lt.-Col. James S. 79
Bragg, Gen. Braxton 54, 61, 73, 76, 77, 78, 79, 80, 81, 82, 83, 85, 86, 87, 88, 89, 90, 91, 93, 96, 97, 114, 115, 116, 117, 118, 119, 120, 122, 123, 126, 127, 128, 129, 130, 133, 134, 135, 136, 137, 138, 180, 228; military board member 10; mentioned in journal 40, 49, 52, 72; confronted by Forrest 112; biography of 257
Branagin, Pvt. Barney 301
Brandon Station, Mississippi 71
Brandy Station, Virginia 160
Brannan, Brig.-Gen. John Milton 82, 83, 84, 85, 94
Brantly, Brig.-Gen. William Felix, brigade of 182
Braswell, Pvt. Robert B. 311
Breasley, Col., mentioned in journal 49
Breazeale, Pvt. A. J. 311
Breazeale, Sgt. John James 309
Breckinridge, Maj.-Gen. John Cabell 71, 91, 93, 122, 127, 129, 137; candidate for president 7, 8, 9; division of 70, 78, 128; corps of 126; biography of 259
Bridgeport 116, 117, 118, 119
Bridgers, Pvt. A. 279
Bridgers, Cpl. Thomas E. 278
Briscoe, Lt. Claiborne C. 276
Broadway, Pvt. Benjamin Franklin 301
Brock, Pvt. Charles J. 301
Brock, Pvt. Elhanon V. 301
Brock, John, Jr. 86
Brock, John, Sr., cornfield of 86
Brock, Roland 86
Brockett, W. B.: election to third-lieutenant 15; mentioned in journal 20; biography of 272, 276
Brookhaven Light Artillery 62, 63, 65
Brookhaven, Mississippi 67
Brooks, Pvt. Elkanah H. 290
Brooks, Pvt. J. M. C. 291
Brooks, Pvt. Samuel D. 280
Brooks, Pvt. William 291
Brotherton Cornfield 87, 88, 89, 94
Brotherton Ridge 94

Brotherton Road 82, 84, 85, 86, 88, 89
Brotherton Woods 94
Brown, Sgt. Charles 309
Brown, Lt. Isaac Newton 47
Brown, Lt. J. R. 308
Brown, John 5, 6
Brown, Brig.-Gen. John Calvin 180, 185, 186, 187, 230; brigade of 86, 89, 127, 168, 171; division of 176, 180, 182
Brown, Pvt. Joseph F. 301
Brown, Pvt. William D. 330
Brown's Ferry 116, 119, 120, 122, 123; expedition of 117, 118
Bruinsburg, Mississippi 60
Bryant, Col. George E., brigade of 186
Bryant, Pvt. Martin 330
Buchanan Administration 7
Buchta, Cpl. John L. 278
Buck, Pvt. J. H. 318
Buckels, Cpl. J. F. 317
Buckland, Brig.-Gen. Ralph Pomeroy 64
Buckles, Pvt. James Monroe 318
Buckner, Maj.-Gen. Simon Bolivar 80, 81, 114, 115; corps of 78, 79, 90; division of 117
Buie, Major Duncan 168, 183; planter 15; mentioned in letter 17; mentioned in journal 50, 51; biography of 271, 298
Bullard, Pvt. William L. 301
Bullock, Pvt. C. M. 291
Bullock, Pvt. L. D. 291
Bullock, Sgt. William C. 328
Burke, Sgt. J. T. 288
Burnett, Pvt. Zachariah H. 291
Burns, Cpl. Hugh 278
Burnside, Maj.-Gen. Ambrose Everett 77, 78, 117, 118
Burnt Hickory, Georgia 170, 171
Burnt Hickory Road 176
Butland, Sgt. George C. 328
Butler, Maj.-Gen. Benjamin F. "Beast" 35, 44, 45, 46
Butler, Paymaster, mentioned in journal 55, 56
Butler, Pvt. Robert M. 318
Butler, Lt.-Col. William L. 121
Butterfield, Maj.-Gen. Daniel 171; division of 167, 168, 170
Buzzard Roost Gap 165
Buzzard Roost Pass 165

Cabanis, Pvt. W. D. 291
Cain, Pvt. John J. 280
Cairo, Illinois 43, 45, 46, 53, 54
Calcote, Pvt. John L. 318
Calhoun, Georgia 162, 163, 167
Calhoun, Mayor James M. 191, 227
Calhoun, John C. 10
Calvert's Battery 127
Camp Adams, mentioned in journal 24, 25
Camp Beauregard, North Carolina 41
Camp Chimborazo, Virginia, mentioned in journal 23, 24

Camp City Lines, Georgia 41
Camp Creek 163, 165, 166, 167, 185
Camp Hope, mentioned in journal 25
Camp McCoy, Virginia, mentioned in journal 20, 21, 22, 23
Camp Mercer, Georgia 23, 28; mentioned in journal 26
Camp Moore, Louisiana 14, 15; mentioned in letter 17
Camp Saw Mill, Virginia, mentioned in journal 23
Camp Street, New Orleans 10
Camp Two, Que Vie, mentioned in letter 159
Camp Van Dorn, Georgia 41, 48, 49, 50, 51
Camp Walker, Georgia, mentioned in journal 51, 52
Camp Walker, Louisiana 14
Campbell, Pvt. Ben P. 319
Campbell, Lt. James 34
Campbell, Pvt. Robert 319
Campbellton, Georgia 228
Canal Street 45
Canby, Maj.-Gen. Edward Richard Sprigg 231, 232, 235, 236, 237, 238, 239
Cantey, Brig.-Gen. James: brigade of 163, 165, 167, 182; division of 176
Canton, Mississippi 62, 67
Canton Road 70
Capehart, Pvt. Francis M. 280
Capin, Mr., mentioned in letter 240
Capitol Building, Washington 15
Capon, Mrs., mentioned in letter 240
Captain Dawson's Company, mentioned in journal 25
Carkeet, Sgt. John 316
Carlin, Brig.-Gen. William Passmore 88; brigade of 87, 136
Carpenter, Sgt. Allen D. 316
Carroll, Pvt. Francis 301
Carroll Rebels 16
Carter, Brig.-Gen. John Carpenter 230
Cartersville, Georgia 170
Cary Street, Richmond 16
Cason, Pvt. Charles A. 331
Cassner, Pvt. R. D. 280
Cassner, Pvt. Thomas P. 280
Cassville, Georgia 169
Cathey, Pvt. James B. 302
Cathey, Pvt. John W. 302
Catoosa Station 90
Cemetery Ridge 230
Chalaron, Lt. J. A. 133; cannon of 134
Chalmette, Louisiana 45
Chambers, Pvt. Benjamin 280
Champion, Col. 126
Champion, Matilda 69
Champion, Sid 69
Champion Hill, battle of 69
Chancellorsville, battle of 124
Chandler, Pvt. M. M. 302
Chandler, Lt.-Col. William P. 130

Chapman, Col. Charles 84
Chapman, Pvt. John L. 280
Charleston and Savannah Railroad, mentioned in journal 52
Charleston Battalion 32
Charleston Harbor 28
Charleston, South Carolina 6, 28, 30, 41, 48, 60, 61, 233; convention at 7, 8, 227; Fort Sumter 14; mentioned in journal 24, 26, 29, 40, 52, 58, 59, 72, 73, 113
Charleston, steamer, mentioned in journal 58
Charrone, Col., mentioned in journal 23
Chattahoochee River 177, 183, 185, 228, 229
Chattanooga Creek 122, 125, 126, 127, 135
Chattanooga, steamer 119
Chattanooga, Tennessee 73, 77, 78, 79, 80, 82, 90, 95, 96, 97, 112, 113, 116, 117, 118, 119, 120, 123, 138, 156, 162, 163, 228; mentioned in journal 115; mentioned in letter 178
Chattanooga Valley 121, 122, 125, 126, 127, 129, 135; mentioned in journal 113
Chatterson, Pvt. John 280
Cheat Mountain, Virginia 18
Cheatham, Maj.-Gen. Benjamin Franklin 79, 87, 89, 115, 127, 161, 176, 180, 228, 230; division of 86, 90, 91, 128, 165, 186, 230; corps of 179; biography of 260
Cherokee Battery 167
Cherokee Indian, language of 73
Chesapeake Bay 43
Chesnut, Col. James, Jr. 115
Chickamauga Creek 78, 79, 80, 81, 89, 92, 133, 137; south 119, 122, 123, 127
Chickamauga, Georgia 73, 85, 114, 115, 117, 119, 120, 136; battle of 97; mentioned in journal 113; mentioned in letter 178
Chickamauga Station 120, 122, 123, 137
Chickasaw Bayou, Mississippi 54, 56; battle of 55
Childers, Pvt. R. W. 311
Choat, Pvt. William Franklin 302
Christopher, Pvt. J. 311
Church, Capt. Benjamin B. 34
Churchill, Brig.-Gen. Thomas James 57
Cincinnati, Ohio 229
Citico Creek 122
Citronelle, Alabama 239
Clark, Pvt. John 291
Clark, Pvt. Robert 280
Clay, Capt. A. B. 85
Clay, Pvt. John C. 319
Clayton, Maj.-Gen. Henry DeLamar 176, 183, 186, 187; brigadier general 86, 89, 176; brigade of 128, 135, 136, 161, 168, 169, 170, 171; division of 180, 182, 186; biography of 265

Cleburne, Maj.-Gen. Patrick Ronayne 91, 93, 115, 120, 122, 127, 128, 133, 137, 138, 180, 186, 187; division of 78, 89, 92, 161, 165, 172, 191, 230
Clements, Cpl. James 317
Cleveland Road 165
Cleveland, Tennessee 118
Clinton, Mississippi 62, 63, 65, 69, 70, 71
Clinton-Jackson Road 62, 63, 64, 65, 70
Cloman, Sgt. J. W. 309
Cobb County, Georgia 114
Cobham, Col. George A., brigade of 126
Coburn, Col. John, brigade of 168
Cockrell, Brig.-Gen. Francis Marion 230, 237; division of 236
Cockrell, Pvt. T. J. 319
Cockrell, Pvt. William S. 319
Coffee Bluff, mentioned in journal 52, 55, 56, 58
Coldwater River 57
Cole Island, South Carolina 28
Coleman, Capt. Edward L. 308
Coleman, Cpl. Robert 179
Collins, Pvt. J. B. 311
Collins, Lt. R. M. 89
Collins, Lt. Samuel W. 287
Colquitt, Col. Peyton H. 61, 62, 63, 65, 67, 92
Colt Revolving Rifle 96
Colton, Pvt. J. R. 331
Columbia Pike 230
Columbia, Tennessee 230
Columbus, Kentucky 53, 54
Committee of Fifteen 11
Committee on Confederation 12
Compton, Cpl. Charles S. 278
Conasauga River 163, 166, 167
Condren, Pvt. John 331
Confederate Defense Fleet 45
Confederate Roll of Honor 97
Confederate States of America: constitution 13; provisional congress 14; capitol 16
Connell, Col. John M., brigade of 85
Connelly, Pvt. Thomas 291
Conner, Capt. Thomas N. 327
Connor, Pvt. M. 302
Conrad, Charles Magill, delegate 12
Considine, Pvt. T. 311
Cook, Pvt. A. J. 311
Cookern, Pvt. O. P. 311
Cooney, Pvt. John C. 319
Cooper, James 96
Cooper, Gen. Samuel 176
Coosa River Valley 162
Coosawattee River 163
Corbert, Pvt. John 319
Corinth, Mississippi 231; mentioned in journal 27, 28, 29, 40
Corrin, Cpl. Thomas 317
Corse, Brig.-Gen. Montgomery Dent 127; brigade of 117; division of 186, 187
Cosh, Pvt. M. 311

Cosh, Pvt. R. 311
Costley, Pvt. Benjamin L. 302
Cotton Hill, Virginia 18; mentioned in journal 21; occupation of 22
Couch, F. M.: election to second-lieutenant 15; mentioned in journal 51; biography of 276
Couch's House 185
Coulston, Pvt. Elijah 331
Course, Pvt. Charles F. 319
Cox, Brig.-Gen. Jacob Dolson, division of 165, 166
Cox, Pvt. Stephen St. Louis 291
Craig, Capt. David A. 67
Crandell, Pvt. S. W. 280
Crane, Pvt. Patrick Huston 302
Crane, Pvt. William H. A. 302
Cravens, Robert, house of 124, 125
Crittenden, Maj.-Gen. Thomas Leonidas 77, 78, 79, 80, 81, 82, 87, 88, 95
Crocker, Brig.-Gen. Marcellus Monroe 65; division of 63, 67
Crouth, Cpl. D. Hardeman 278
Crow, Pvt. James W. H. 311
Crow Valley 165
Croxton, Col. John Thomas 83, 84, 85; brigade of 82
Cruft, Brig.-Gen. Charles R. 136, 166; division of 123, 135
Crutchfield Road 133, 137
Cumberland Gap 117
Cumberland Mountains 77
Cumberland Plateau 77
Cumming, Brig.-Gen. Alfred 187
Cunningham, Lt.-Col. Edward H. 168, 174, 182
Cunningham, Pvt. T. L. 311
Curren, Sgt. Robert N. 277
Cushing, Caleb 8

Dallas, Georgia 169, 170, 172, 173, 174, 175
Dallas Road 172
Dalton, Georgia 137, 156, 158, 162, 163, 165, 169, 229; mentioned in letter 159, 178
Dalton-Resaca Road 167
Dalton's Ford 80
Dana, Charles A. 138
Dancy, Cpl. William Stodard 278
Daniels, Pvt. 302
Daniels, Cpl. Robert F. 289
Daniels, Pvt. Thomas 280
Daugherty, Pvt. John D. 280
Daugherty, Pvt. John M. 280
Dauphin Island, Alabama 232
Davidson, Brig.-Gen. Henry Brevard, brigade of 82, 83, 84
Davidson, Thomas Green, congressman 11
Davidson, Pvt. William 302
Davis, Capt. Alfred Vidal 16, 315
Davis, Flag-Officer 46, 47, 48
Davis, President Jefferson 14, 16, 48, 59, 60, 71, 76, 114, 115, 118, 137, 156, 176, 180, 228, 231; administration of 138
Davis, Brig.-Gen. Jefferson Columbus 88, 94, 120; division of 87, 172, 173, 182
Davis, Pvt. John D. 291
Davis, Pvt. M. 302
Davis, Col. Newton N. 121
Dawson, Georgia 227
Dawson, Pvt. Joseph S. 280
Dawson's Georgia Battery 129
Deal, Pvt. Andrew Jackson 302
Dean, Pvt. E. P. 291
Deas, Brig.-Gen. Zachariah Cantey, brigade of 128, 132, 133, 187
Decatur Road 180, 229
Declouet, Alexander, delegate 12
Delaney, Pvt. J. 312
Delaney, Pvt. Thomas 280
Delhi, Louisiana, mentioned in letter 17, 179
Democratic Convention, meeting at Baton Rouge 6;
Democratic Party 6, 8
Demopolis, Alabama 157
DeMoss, Sgt. David H. 277
Denning, Pvt. William G. 312
Dennis, Brig.-Gen. Elias Smith, brigade of 65
Department of Alabama, Mississippi and East Louisiana 228
Department of Mississippi and East Louisiana 48
Department of South Carolina and Georgia 28
Department of the Gulf 231
Department of the Tennessee 113
DeShazo, Pvt. C. J. 280
DeSoto Peninsula 46
Dew, Pvt. John 291
Dey, Pvt. M. M. 319
Deyo, Cpl. A. C. 310
Dibrell, Col. George Gibbs 85; brigade of 83, 84
Dicks, Pvt. James G. 319
Dicks, Lt. John A. 315
Dicks, Pvt. Thomas G. 319
Dickson, Pvt. Rodger H. 312
Dillard, Pvt. L. K. 291
Dillon, Pvt. J. H. 291
District of the Gulf (C.S.) 231
Dixon, Pvt. John 319
Dixon, Ord.-Sgt. John S. 273, 280
Dixon, Pvt. William Henry 281
Dodge, Brig.-Gen. Grenville Mellen 162, 165, 182; corps of 163, 172, 179
D'Olive's Creek 232
Donaldsonville, Louisiana 8
Dorman, Pvt. William L. 303
Dougherty, Pvt. O. R. 319
Doughty, Pvt. John 292
Douglas, Stephen Arnold 6, 7, 8, 9
Douglas, Sgt. Thomas J. 288
Douglas's Battery 127
Dowdy, Pvt. James G. 331
Doyal, Lt. Isaac 298
Doyal, Cpl. John W. 300
Doyle, Lt., mentioned in journal 49
Doyle, Capt. Richard N. 34
Drayton, Capt. Percival 31
Drew, Pvt. Michael 303

Dry Valley Road 82, 89, 95, 96
Dublin Depot, Virginia 23; mentioned in letter 158
Duck River 230
Duckport, Louisiana 57
Dufour, Pvt. Charles 319
Dug Gap 78, 158
Dunham, Sgt. J. Thomas 288
Dunlavey, Pvt. James 292
Dyer, John: field of 89, 95; home of 94
Dyer, Pvt. William 331

East Baton Rouge Parish, Louisiana 9
East Point, Georgia 180, 185
Eckells, Capt., mentioned in journal 72
Ector, Brig.-Gen. Matthew Duncan 85; brigade of 67, 84, 92
Eden, Pvt. Anderson 281
Eden, Comm.-Sgt. John P. 273, 281
Edisto, South Carolina 41
Edwards, Pvt. Jonathan M. 281
Edwards Station, Mississippi 69
Eighteenth Alabama Infantry 86, 136
Eighteenth U.S. Infantry 85
Eighth Georgia Battalion Infantry 61, 92
Eighth Iowa Infantry 235
Eighth Kansas Infantry 87
Eighth Michigan Infantry 32, 33, 34, 37
Eighth Wisconsin Infantry 54
Eightieth Ohio Infantry 63
Eighty-Ninth Illinois Infantry 173
Eighty-Seventh Indiana Infantry 84
Eldridge's Artillery Battalion 171
Eleventh Corps (U.S.) 123
Eleventh Tennessee Infantry 133
Elkwater, Virginia 18
Elliott, Pvt. D. Wansley, letter to sister 17, 18, 303
Elliott, Pvt. Tavnor H. 303
Elliott's Cut 30
Ellis, Pvt. Henry 320
England, mentioned in journal 40
English, Pvt. William 312
Enterprise, Alabama 238
Episcopal Church 79
U.S.S. *Essex* 47
Essig, Pvt. Daniel John 292
Etier, Pvt. John 303
Etowah River 170, 173
Eutaw Battalion 30, 31
Evans, Brig.-Gen. Nathan George "Shank" 30, 31, 32; biography of 255
Ewing, Brig.-Gen. Hugh 127
Ezra Church 180, 182, 187; battle of 183

Fankenbridge, Pvt. William W. V. 281
Fanning, Sgt. M. 316
Farquharson, Col. Robert 63, 65
Farragut, Rear-Adm. David Glas-

gow 157; captain 44, 45, 46, 47, 48, 57
Farrand, Flag-Off. Ebenezer 238
Farrar, Pvt. Thornton H. 320
Farrar, Pvt. W. H. H. 312
Faust, Pvt. M. M. 292
Fay, Pvt. John 331
Fayette, Virginia 18, 21; courthouse 20, 22
Fayetteville Road 185
Feltonburg, Sgt. H. 309
Fenner's Louisiana Battery 169, 171
Fenton, Col. William Matthew 32, 33, 34
Ferguson, Capt. Thomas B. 61
Ferguson's South Carolina Battery 61
Ferrand, Pvt. Horace 281
Fetters, Cpl. John N. 289
Fetters, Pvt. Thomas P. 274, 292
Fife, Pvt. B. P. 303
Fife, John, mentioned in letter 160
Fife, Pvt. John Mayfield 303
Fife, Pvt. R. C. 303
Fife, Pvt. Saxton Shaw 303
Fife, Pvt. W. 303
Fifteenth Alabama Infantry 119
Fifteenth Corps (U.S.) 63, 70, 163, 186
Fifteenth Indiana Infantry 129
Fifteenth Ohio Infantry 173
Fifteenth Tennessee Infantry 89
Fifteenth Texas Cavalry (Dismounted) 89
Fifteenth Wisconsin Infantry 87, 88
Fifth Confederate Infantry 179
Fifth Indiana Battery 166, 167, 176
Fifth Kentucky Infantry 121
Fifth Minnesota Infantry 64
Fifty-Eighth Alabama Infantry 89, 136
Fifty-Fourth Virginia Infantry 88
Fifty-Ninth Indiana Infantry 67
C.S.S. *Fingal*, mentioned in journal 58, 59
Finley, Brig.-Gen. Jesse Johnson, brigade of 128, 161, 187
First Connecticut Light Artillery 31, 33, 34
First Florida Cavalry (Dismounted) 88
First Florida Infantry 88
First Georgia Cavalry 82
First Georgia Sharpshooters Battalion 61, 63, 64, 67, 69, 79, 85
First Illinois Light Artillery 64
First Iowa Battery 174
First Louisiana Cavalry (C.S.) 8
First Manassas, battle of 16, 17, 28
First Michigan Engineers and Mechanics 118
First Mississippi Light Artillery 236, 237
First Missouri Engineers 186
First Missouri Light Artillery (U.S.) 63, 67
First New York Engineers 32, 33
First South Carolina Artillery 31, 37

First South Carolina Battalion 33
First South Carolina Infantry 30, 32
First Tennessee Legion 83
Fish River 232
Fleming, Pvt. John 312
Flint River 185, 186, 187
Florence, Alabama 229
Florida, state of 7, 43, 228; troops of 161
Flowers, Pvt. Jesse 292
Floyd, Brig.-Gen. John Buchanan 18, 23; mentioned in journal 19, 21; abandonment of mountain 22; biography of 266
Flynn, Pvt. F. M. 292
Flynn, Pvt. George L. 303
Flynn, Pvt. James F. 312
Flynn, Pvt. Michael 292, 303
Folly River 30
Folmer, Pvt. B. F. 292
Fondren, Pvt. Meek M. 320
Ford's Theatre 239
Foreman, Cpl. George 310
Forest, Mississippi 67
Forrest, Lt.-Gen. Nathan Bedford 228, 229, 230, 231; major general 54, 158; brigadier-general 82, 83, 84, 85; quote from 112
Fort Blakely 232, 233, 236, 237, 239
Fort Boggs, Georgia 41
Fort Donelson 53; mentioned in journal 25
Fort Doyle, mentioned in journal 49, 50
Fort Jackson 10, 28, 41, 44, 45, 47, 52, 72
Fort Johnson 29, 30
Fort Johnston, mentioned in journal 72
Fort Lamar 33
Fort McAllister, mentioned in journal 56, 58
Fort McDermott 235
Fort Negley 130
Fort Pemberton: South Carolina 29, 30; Mississippi 57
Fort Pike 10
Fort Pillow 46; mentioned in journal 29
Fort Pulaski, mentioned in journal 25, 26, 27, 52
Fort St. Philip 10, 44, 45, 47
Fort Sumter 14, 29, 41; mentioned in journal 40, 73
Fort Wagner, mentioned in journal 72
Fort Wood 120, 121, 122, 130
Fortieth Alabama Infantry 125
Fortieth Ohio Infantry 125
Forty-First Ohio Infantry 121, 134, 173
Forty-Ninth Ohio Infantry 173
Forty-Seventh Georgia Infantry 30, 32; mentioned in journal 50
Forty-Seventh New York Infantry 37
Forty-Sixth Georgia Infantry 61, 62, 92; mentioned in journal 48

Forty-Sixth Mississippi Infantry 236
Forty-Sixth New York Infantry 32
Foster, Sgt. Jonathan H. 328
Fourteenth Corps (U.S.) 77, 185, 191, 192
Fourteenth Louisiana Battalion Sharpshooters 171
Fourteenth Mississippi Infantry 62
Fourteenth Ohio Infantry 82
Fourth Corps (U.S.) 120, 165, 166, 172, 180, 183, 185, 191, 192, 229, 230
Fourth Georgia Battalion Sharpshooters 89
Fourth Iowa Cavalry 63
Fourth Kentucky Infantry (U.S.) 82, 83
Fourth Louisiana Battalion Infantry 15, 16, 17, 18, 23, 28, 29, 30, 35, 37, 39, 41, 43, 61, 63, 67, 70, 73, 76, 79, 81, 84, 85, 97, 113, 115, 122, 128, 133, 138, 158, 159, 162, 168, 169, 175, 176, 179, 183, 230, 231, 238, 239, 240
Fourth Military District (C.S.) 63
Fourth U.S. Artillery 84
Fox, Lt. Benjamin D. 315
Fox, Sgt. George D. 309
Fox, Asst. Sec. Gustavus Vasa 46
Fox, Pvt. William H. H. 320
Foy, Lt.-Col. James C. 119
France, mentioned in journal 40
Frank, N. 240
Franklin Life Guard 15, 16; mentioned in journal 49
Franklin Parish, Louisiana 15, 17, 159, 176
Franklin Pike 231
Franklin, Tennessee 230, 231
Frazer, Brig.-Gen. John Wesley 117
Fredericksburg, Virginia, mentioned in journal 56, 61
French, Brig.-Gen. Samuel Gibbs 157, 236; division of 70, 180, 229, 231
French Quarter, New Orleans 12, 14
Friend, Pvt. Benjamin F. 331
Friend, Cpl. G. A. 289
Frisbey, Pvt. Daniel W. 97, 281
Front Royal, mentioned in letter 159, 240
Fugitive Slave Law 5, 9
Fuller, Sgt. John N. 288
Fulton, Col. John S. 87

Gahan, Pvt. William C. 320
Gaillard, Lt.-Col. Peter Charles 32, 37
Gaines Mill 87
Gainesville, Alabama, mentioned in letter 17
Gallman, Pvt. J. T. 312
Garrard, Brig.-Gen. Kenner 172
Garrett, Isaac, board member 10
Garrett, Pvt. Isaiah L. 292
Garrity's Battery 132
Gauley Bridge 18
Gauley River 21

Gay, Pvt. James 281
Geary, Brig.-Gen. John White 124, 126; division of 119, 125, 135, 167, 168, 170, 171, 174
Geety, Pvt. James G. 281
Genesis Point, mentioned in journal 55, 56
Gentry, Pvt. Thomas S. 282
George, Pvt. R. B. 292
Georgetown, South Carolina 28
Georgia, state of 7, 61, 64, 73, 76, 97, 138, 162, 176, 228, 229; coast of 23; mentioned in journal 49; northwest 77; battery from 133; mentioned in letter 179; brigade from 168, 170
German Battery 167
Gettysburg, Pennsylvania 69, 71, 76, 230
Gibson, Pvt. Preston J. 282
Gibson, Brig.-Gen. Randall Lee 168, 169, 174, 182, 232, 233, 235, 236, 238; colonel, brigade of 128, 129, 133, 136, 161, 162, 170, 171, 175, 183, 187, 231; mentioned in letter 160; farewell address of 239; biography of 267
Gibson, Col. William H., brigade of 173
Gilbert, Cpl. W. F. 310
Gilchrist, Capt. Charles A. 63
Giles, Pvt. W. B. 312
Gillem's Bridge 170
Gist, Brig.-Gen. States Rights 30, 61, 79, 230; brigade of 62, 67, 92, 180
Gladden, Pvt. Charles S. 331
Gleason, Pvt. David 292
Gleason, Pvt. John 293
Glenn, Eliza 87, 94; field of 88; home of 89, 95
Glenn Hill 93
Goldsboro, North Carolina, mentioned in journal 55
Goode, Col. C. T. 83
Gordon, Maj.-Gen. John Brown 76
Govan, Col. Daniel 173; brigade of 81, 127, 161, 172
C.S.S. *Governor Moore* 45
Gracey, Lt. Frank P., battery of 133
Gradine, Alfred 28
Grafton, Virginia 18
Granbury, Brig.-Gen. Hiram Bronson 230; brigade of 173, 187
Grand Gulf, Mississippi 59, 60, 67
Grand Junction, Tennessee 53, 54
Granger, Maj.-Gen. Gordon 96, 120, 121, 129, 130, 131, 238
Granny White Pike 231
Grant, Pvt. Franklin J. 331
Grant, Frederick 67, 160
Grant, Lt.-Gen. Ulysses Simpson 161, 229, 231, 232, 239; promotion of 160; major-general 28, 53, 54, 55, 57, 58, 59, 60, 62, 63, 64, 67, 69, 70, 71, 77, 97, 112, 113, 116, 117, 119, 120, 122, 123, 124, 126, 127, 128, 130, 131, 137, 138; mentioned in letter 178

Graves, Cpl. James L. 329
Graves, Pvt. James Q. 282
Graves, Pvt. Robert 331
Green, Pvt. Elias 320
Green, Adjt. John W. 17; biography of 271, 277
Green, Brig.-Gen. Martin Edwin 60
Green, Pvt. Michael J. 320
Green, Pvt. Thomas 320
Greenbrier River, Virginia 18
Greeneville, Tennessee 117
Greensboro, North Carolina 239
Greenwood, Mississippi 47
Gregg, Brig.-Gen. John 62, 63, 64, 65, 67; brigade of 81; mentioned in journal 113
Grenada, Mississippi 53, 54, 70, 157
Griest, Pvt. Alva 90
Griffith, Sgt. John T. 316
Grigsby, Col. J. Warren, cavalry brigade of 123, 163
Grimball, South Carolina 29, 30, 31
Griswold, Pvt. Edward 34
Guice, Pvt. Thomas Reed 320
Guilfoil, Pvt. Michael S. 282
Guirot, Antoine Joseph 13
Gulf of Mexico 43, 44
Guss, Col. Henry R. 35
Gustine, Pvt. Samuel 282
Guy, Pvt. Henry 34
Guynn, Pvt. Edward Wade 293

Haddox, Pvt. Henry 282
Haddox, Pvt. Robert 274, 282
Hagood, Col. Johnson 30, 31, 35
Haibrook, Pvt. Allen M. 304
Hale, Senator John Parker 9
Hall, Pvt. William F. 274, 304
Halleck, Gen. Henry Wager 39, 53, 57, 116, 160, 179, 183, 192, 227, 231
Hamilton, Lt. S. W.: election to first-lieutenant 15; mentioned in journal 20, 22; biography of 276
Hammond, Pvt. W. D. 293
Hammond, Lt. Wiley F. 299
Hampton, Pvt. Wade 304
Hanson, Pvt. Elbert M. 304
Harbison, Pvt. M. P. 274, 312
Hard Times, Louisiana 60
Hardee, Lt.-Gen. William Joseph 122, 123, 124, 127, 130, 133, 138, 156, 170, 173, 176, 185, 187, 189, 191, 192, 228; mentioned in letter 158; corps of 165, 168, 169, 172, 179, 180, 186, 192; biography of 261
Hardy, Capt. Alanso B. 287
Hardy, Pvt. Covington 293
Hardy, Lt. Thomas J. 288
Harker, Col. Charles Garrison, brigade of 95, 135, 165
Harley, Surg. H. H. 271, 273, 299
Harpers Ferry, Virginia 5, 6
Harpeth River 230
Harris, Pvt. Daniel G. 320
Harris, Pvt. Green S. 320

Harris, Mr., mentioned in letter 159
Harris, Pvt. Richard 293
Harrison, Col. George Paul, brigade of 41, 61; mentioned in journal 55; biography of 268
Harrow, Brig.-Gen. William, division of 180, 182
Hart, Pvt. C. 320
Hart, Col. 83
Hart, Capt. J. B. 236
Hart, Pvt. W. W. 312
U.S.S. *Hartford* 45
Harvey, Pvt. William H. 282
Haskin, Brevet Major Joseph Able 10
Hatch, F. H. 7
Hathaway, Pvt. John C. 283
Hawkins, Brig.-Gen. John Parker 236; troops of 237
Haynes Bluff, Mississippi 58
Hazelhurst, Mississippi 67
Hazelton, Sgt. William A. 328
Hazen, Brig.-Gen. William Babcock 89; brigade of 86, 118, 119, 121, 130, 132, 133, 134, 135, 167, 173
Heartsill, Pvt. William 89
Hebert, Paul Octave, board member 10
Heckford, Pvt. John 331
Heg, Col. Hans Christian 87, 88; brigade of 94
Helena, Arkansas 48, 54
Helm, Brig.-Gen. Benjamin Hardin 91; brigade of 92
Helm, Pvt. L. R. 312
Henderson, Comm.-Sgt. Thomas 273, 274, 283
Henrico County, Virginia 16
Herlong, Pvt. George W. 304
Heroine, former blockade runner 238
Herrin, Pvt. David J. 304
Herring, Cpl. Robert Charles 289
Herron, Lt. Daniel B. 327
Herron, Pvt. John E. 331
Herron, Pvt. Stephen J. 332
Herron, Sgt. Thomas C. 328
Hickman, Virginia 18
Hickman, Pvt. William F. T. 283
Hicks, Pvt. Elias A. 304
Hicks, Pvt. John 332
Hill, Pvt. Benjamin 304
Hill, Maj.-Gen. Daniel Harvey 78, 80, 91, 92, 114; corps of 90
Hill, Pvt. Joseph T. 176, 274
Hillis, Col. David B. 63, 67
Hillsburgh, Mississippi 157
Hilton Head, South Carolina 28, 30, 41
Hindman, Pvt. Charles M. 304
Hindman, Maj.-Gen. Thomas Carmichael 78, 93, 168, 170; division of 90, 128, 165, 167, 169, 172, 176, 180; suspension from command 114; biography of 262
Hines, Hosp.-Stew. Curtis T. 273
Hinman, Sgt. Curtis P. 276, 277
Hitchings, Pvt. Joseph 283

Hober, Pvt. John 274, 332
Holley, Pvt. G. James 293
Holley, Sgt. George J. 288
Holley, Pvt. Thomas D. 274, 293
Holloway, Pvt. John 332
Holly Springs, Mississippi 53, 54
Holmes, Col. Samuel A. 63, 67
Holmes Brigade 63
Holston River Valley 117
Holston Valley Railroad 22
Holt, Judge Adv. Gen. Joseph 39
Holtzclaw, Col. J. T. 128, 235; brigade of 183, 231, 233, 236
Honeycutt, Pvt. Ebenezer 332
Honeycutt, Cpl. John B. 289
Hood, Lt. General John Bell 174, 179, 180, 182, 183, 185, 186, 187, 191, 192, 227, 228, 229, 230, 231; major-general 81, 83, 87, 88, 95, 114, 166, 167, 168, 171, 172; column of 94; corps of 86, 90, 93, 165, 170, 175, 176; biography of 258
Hooker, Maj.-Gen. Joseph "Fighting Joe" 112, 116, 117, 118, 119, 123, 124, 126, 127, 135, 136, 137, 138, 166, 167, 168, 171, 172, 173, 175, 180; corps of 170, 174
Hooter, Lt. John W. 299
Hopper, Pvt. J. H. 332
Hopper, Pvt. Thomas 332
Horne, Pvt. Pierce 283
Horney, Lt.-Col. Leonidas 63, 67
Hornsby, Pvt. Benjamin Franklin 320
Hornsby, Hosp.-Stew. O. W. 273, 321
Hornsby, Pvt. W. W. 320
Horseshoe Ridge 95, 96, 97
House, Pvt. Alfred Henry 321
House Committee on Federal Relations, Louisiana 6
Howard, Pvt. John 332
Howard, Maj.-Gen. Oliver Otis 119, 120, 127, 166, 167, 173, 176, 179, 182, 185, 186, 187, 191, 192; corps of 112, 122, 123, 165, 171, 172, 180
Howard's Grove 17
Howe, Pvt. Charles M. 321
Howe, Pvt. John 293
Howe, Pvt. William 321
Howell, Lt. Evan P. 85
Howell, Cpl. Lewis M. 310
Hubbard, Pvt. Alonzo R. 321
Huber, Pvt. Lewis 293
Hudson, Cpl. William B. 329
Hughes, Pvt. A. 312
Hughes, Cpl. George 33
Humphreys, Brig.-Gen. Benjamin Grubb, brigade of 95
Hunter, Maj.-Gen. David 28, 29, 30, 39; at Chattanooga 119, 120
Hunter, Robert Alexander 7
C.S.S. *Huntsville* 237, 238
Huntsville, Alabama 162
Hurt, Augustus, home of 179
Huwald, Capt. Gustave, battery of 82, 84
Hyams, Lt.-Governor Henry Michael 13

Illinois, state of 9, 43, 53, 54; troops from 54, 126
Inzer, Col. John W. 136
Iowa, state of 43
Ireland, Col. David, brigade of 125, 168
Ireland, Pvt. George A. 321
Ireland, Pvt. Thomas 321
Isle of Hope 23; mentioned in journal 25, 26

Jacks, Pvt. James H. 304
Jackson, Abraham 28
Jackson, Capt., artillery 21
Jackson, Brig.-Gen. John King 125, 126; division of 118, brigade of 128
Jackson, Mississippi 41, 48, 53, 61, 62, 63, 64, 65, 67, 69, 70, 71, 73; mentioned in journal 113; mentioned in letter 178
Jackson, Pvt. Silas J. 293
Jackson, Color-Cpl. Sydney M. 275, 283
Jackson, Tennessee 54
Jackson, Maj.-Gen. Thomas J. "Stonewall," mentioned in journal 29, 40, 51, 58, 61, 67
Jackson, Brig.-Gen. William Hicks "Red," cavalry of 70, 172, 185, 186, 187, 229
Jackson Ferry, Virginia 19
Jackson River, Virginia 18
James, Pvt. Mark W. 283
James, Pvt. R. 312
James Island Creek 29
James Island, South Carolina 28, 29, 30, 38, 41; mentioned in journal 39, 49, 50, 72
James River 47; mentioned in journal, 27
Jamison, Capt. Joshua 32
Jarrett, Sgt. Henry T. 328
Jay's Mill 82, 84
Jay's Mill Road 82, 83
Jefferson Parish, Louisiana 9
Jenkins, Brig.-Gen. Micah 119; mentioned in journal 115
Johns, Sgt. David 309
Johnson, Vice-President Andrew: ascension to presidency 239; Johnson Administration 28
Johnson, Brig.-Gen. Bushrod Rust 81, 88, 95; division of 87, 93, 94, 96
Johnson, Maj.-Gen. Edward, division of 230
Johnson, Pvt. John R. 332
Johnson, Brig.-Gen. Richard 86, 89, 90, 130; division of 128, 136, 137, 165, 172, 173
Johnson, Pvt. Robert W. 293
Johnston, Gen. Albert Sidney, mentioned in journal 26
Johnston, Gen. Joseph Eggleston 41, 43, 61, 62, 63, 67, 69, 70, 71, 115, 138, 156, 157, 158, 162, 163, 165, 166, 167, 168, 169, 170, 171, 172, 173, 174, 175, 176, 228, 231, 238; mentioned in journal 27, 28, 72; mentioned in letter 179; surrender of 239; biography of 251
Johnston Plantation, Mississippi 54
Jones, Charles 7
Jones, David 28
Jones, Maj.-Gen. Samuel 117, 118
Jonesboro, Georgia 185, 186, 189, 191, 192; battle of 187
Jordan, Pvt. W. H. 304
Judah, Brig.-Gen. Henry Moses, division of 165, 166
Justice, Pvt. Thomas W. 293

Kammerling, Col. August Gustave 93
Kanawha River 18, 21
Kanawha Valley, Virginia 18, 23
Kansas, state of 5
Kansas/Nebraska Bill 5
Kearney, Cpl. Michael 290
Keep, Pvt. T. F. 321
Keitt, Capt. George Daniel 31, 32
Kelley's Ferry 116, 119
Kellogg, Capt. Sanford C. 94
Kelly, Elijah: field of 82, 90, 91, 93, 95, 96; farm of 84
Kelly, Brig.-Gen. John Herbert, division of 173
Kelly, Pvt. L. H. 312
Kelly's Ford 119
Kenner, Duncan Farrar, delegate 12
Kennesaw Mountain 175; battle of 176
Kennon, Lt. Beverly 45
Kenton, Sgt. Phillip C. 299
Kentucky Campaign, mentioned in journal 52
Kentucky, state of 43, 77, 228, 229; mentioned in journal 48, 49; battery from 133
U.S.S. *Keokuk*, mentioned in journal 59
Kershaw, Brig.-Gen. Joseph Brevard, division of 93, 95
Ketteringham, Pvt. Frank K. 321
Kilpatrick, Brig.-Gen. Judson H., cavalry of 186, 187
Kimberly, Lt.-Col. Robert L. 130
King, Brig.-Gen. John Haskell 85, 92
King, Surgeon 271
King's Highway 30, 35
Kingsport, Tennessee 118
Kingston, Georgia 169
Kittrell, Pvt. G. 321
Knefler, Col. Frederick, brigade of 173
Knoxville, Tennessee 77, 117, 162
Kolb's Farm 175, 176

La Fayette, Georgia 78, 80, 163
La Fayette Road 79, 82, 83, 86, 87, 88, 89, 90, 91, 92, 93, 96
Lafayette Square, New Orleans 8, 13
Lafourche Parish, Louisiana 7, 9
Laiboldt, Col. Bernard, brigade of 94

Lake Concordia, Louisiana 16
Lake Providence, Louisiana 57
Lake Station, Mississippi 62
Lamar, Col. Thomas Gresham 31, 32, 33, 37
Lambert's Ford 80, 81
Lammonds, Pvt. John A. 332
Lammons, Pvt. D. R. 332
Lammons, Pvt. J. M. 332
Land, Lt. James B. 327
Landrum, John Morgan, congressman 11
Langdon, Lt.-Col. E. Bassett 119
Lanier, Pvt. Joseph H. 322
Lanier, Pvt. R. J. 322
Lard, Pvt. William 283
Lark, Pvt. James R. 332
La Sere, Emile 7
Lasley, Pvt. William 283
Lassiter, Pvt. Irvin 304
Lauman, Brig.-Gen. Jacob Gartner 71
Law, Brig.-Gen. Evander McIvor, division of 87, 93, 95
Lawrence, Effingham 7
Lawrence, Pvt. G. W. 293
Lawrence, Pvt. M. F. 294
Lawrence, Sgt. S. C. 316
Lay's Ferry 167
Lea, Pvt. Henry J. 29, 30, 35, 231
Lea, Cpl. Henry J., Sr. 329
Leakey, Maj. 34
Lear, Pvt. Charles 312
Leasure, Col. David 34, 35
Leavell, Sgt. Jonathan Quincy Adams 299
Lee, Capt., mentioned in letter 178
Lee, Pvt. R. A. 304
Lee, Gen. Robert Edward 18, 78, 114, 115, 117, 160, 229, 230, 231, 239; mentioned in journal 51, 55, 61, 72
Lee, Cmdr. Samuel Phillips 46
Lee, Lt.-Gen. Stephen Dill 180, 182, 186, 189, 228, 229, 231; corps of 185, 187, 192, 230; biography of 262
Lee and Gordon's Mill 78, 79, 80, 81, 82, 87, 88, 90
Lee-Gordon Mansion 80
Lemunyan, Sgt. H. D. 316
Lenard, Pvt. Henry 304
Leturno, Pvt. Louis 332
Levins, Pvt. R. 332
Lewell, Pvt. John Quincy Adams 322
Lewis, Pvt. C. W. 175, 294
Lewis, Capt. DeWitt Clinton 37
Lewis, Brig.-Gen. Joseph Horace, brigade of 128, 161, 185, 186
Lewisburg, Virginia 19
Lexington, Tennessee 54
Leyon, Pvt. Andrew 283
Libby Hill, Richmond 16, 17
Libby Prison 16
Lick Skillet Road 180, 182, 183
Liddell, Brig.-Gen. St. John Richardson 79, 85, 232, 236, 237; division of 81

Lightburn, Brig.-Gen. Joseph Andrew Jackson, brigade of 182
Lighthouse Creek 35
Lightning Brigade 81
Lincoln, President Abraham 29, 39, 43, 44, 46, 53, 57, 58, 61, 76, 91, 92, 97, 112, 160, 179; election of 6, 9; administration 18; mentioned in journal 48; assassination of 239
Linder, Pvt. Samuel H. 283
Lindsay, Mayor Lazarus 46
Lindsay, Lt.-Col. Robert H. 232, 238
Logan, Maj.-Gen. John Alexander 180; brigadier-general 63; division of 65; corps of 163, 172, 179, 186
Lolley, Pvt. Arwell Harvey 332
Long, Pvt. A. J. 283
Long, Pvt. Thomas 283
Longstreet, Lt.-Gen. James "Pete," 78, 80, 90, 93, 94, 96, 114, 115, 117, 118, 119, 120, 122, 123, 137; wing of 92, 95; corps of, mentioned in letter 178
Lookout Creek 124, 125, 126
Lookout Mountain 77, 78, 119, 123, 124, 126, 136; flank of 122
Lookout Point 124, 126
Lookout Valley 116, 117, 118, 119, 123
Loop Creek, Virginia 22
Loop Mountain, Virginia 22
Loring, Brig.-Gen. William Wing 18, 57, 176; division of 70, 163, 166, 180, 182, 183
Lost Mountain 175
Lott, Lt. Arthur J. 308
Loudon, Tennessee 118
C.S.S. *Louisiana* 45
Louisiana, state of 5, 6, 7, 9, 10, 11, 12, 14, 15, 35, 43, 44, 57, 58, 60, 79, 159, 162, 231, 238; delegates 8; ordinance of secession 11, 12; people of 12; flag of 13; confederate congressional districts 14; levee fund 15; brigade from 128, 161, 168, 169, 174, 182, 187, 232, 239; bishop of 176
Louisiana Legislature 5, 10, 13, 15
Louisville, Kentucky 116
Love, Cpl. T. R. 317
Lovejoy's Station 186, 189, 192, 227, 228
Lowrey, Brig.-Gen. Mark Perrin 186, 187; brigade of 127, 173
Lusk, Capt. William Thompson 38
Lyles, Pvt. James M. 332
Lynch Creek 64
Lynch Creek Bridge 64
Lynchburg, Virginia, mentioned in letter and journal 17
Lyons, Lt. Benjamin 33
Lytle, Brig.-Gen. William Haynes: brigade of 94; death of 95

MacArthur, Lt. Arthur, Jr. 135
MacArthur, Gen. Douglas 135
Mackall, Brig.-Gen. William W. 180

Macon and Western Railroad 185, 189
Macon, Georgia 176, 189, 192, 227, 228; mentioned in journal 113
Madison Infantry 15, 16, 17
Madison Parish, Louisiana 9, 15, 17
Magee, Pvt. H. L. 294
Magee, Pvt. Zaborn D. 284
Main Street, richmond 17
Major, Pvt. W. T., Jr. 284
C.S.S. *Manassas* 45
Maney, Brig.-Gen. George Earl 180, 185, 186; brigade of 168, 187
Manigault, Brig.-Gen. Arthur Middleton 121, 132, 133, 230; brigade of 128, 182, 186
Mann, W. T., home of 63
Manning, John Laurence, former South Carolina governor 11
Manning, Lt.-Col. P. T. 90
Mansfield, Pvt. Lawrence 294
Marietta, Georgia 169, 175, 228, 229
Marine Hospital 238
Marks, Maj. Washington 237
Marsh, Pvt. Fred 332
Marshall, Hospital-Steward Charles L. 273, 284
Marshall, Henry, delegate 12
Martin, Capt. Robert 64
Martin, Cpl. W. H. 310
Martin's Georgia Battery 61, 63, 64, 67, 85
Mary, former blockade runner 238
Mary E. Keene, steamer 16
Maryland, state of 7; mentioned in journal 29, 51, 52; mentioned in letter 240
Mason, Pvt. John Thomas 274, 284
Massachusetts, state of 8
Mathews, Pvt. Thompson B. 284
Matthews, Cpl. John E. 329
Matthies, Brig.-Gen. Charles "Karl" Leopold, brigade of 64, 65
Marks, Capt. Frank N. 287
Marsh, Pvt. Fred 332
Marsh, Pvt. Thomas A. 294
Martin, Pvt. Thomas 313
Massey, Pvt. J. H. 295
Masters, Pvt. James 305
Mathews, Pvt. Lazarus 305
Maulding, Pvt. E. W. 322
Maury, Maj.-Gen. Dabney Herndon 231, 232, 233, 235, 236, 237, 238; biography of 256
Maus, Pvt. Henry 284
Maxey, Brig.-Gen. Samuel Bell 62, 63, 67
McAlister, Pvt. Charles L. 322
McArthur, Brig.-Gen. John, division of 71
McCarty, Pvt. W. 312
McClellan, Maj.-Gen. George Brinton 18, 28; 44; mentioned in journal 27, 29
McClendon, Sgt. Davis J. 288
McClendon, Lt. J. W. 309

McClendon, Pvt. James 294
McClendon, Pvt. P. H. 294
McClendon, Pvt. Travis J. 294
McClernand, Maj.-Gen. John Alexander 53, 54, 55, 56, 57, 59, 63, 69; corps of 60, 62
McCook, Maj.-Gen. Alexander McDowell 77, 79, 80, 94, 95
McCook, Col. Daniel, Jr. 82
McCown, Col. James 236
McCrary, Pvt. William 294
McCue, Pvt. Luke 294
McCullough, Col. James 61
McDonald, Pvt. A. 312
McDonald, Pvt. John 322
McDonald, John, farm of 83
McDonald, Pvt. William B. 304
McDonough, Georgia 191
McDonough Road 189
McDougal, Pvt. Anguish 304
McDuffie, Cpl. James 329
McEachern, Cpl. Daniel H. 278
McEnery, Surg. H. O. 271, 283
McEnery, Lt.-Col. John 23, 35, 37, 168; mentioned in journal 24, 26, 50, 52; sword presentation 41; biography of 270; 287
McGehee, Pvt., J. P. 322
McGehee, Pvt. M. M. 322
McGiniss, Pvt. Patrick 304
McGuire, Pvt. Thomas 294
McGuirk, Col. John 186
McHatton, James A. 7
McInalty, Pvt. Patrick 294
McKisick, Asst.-Surg. J. W. 272
McLaws, Maj.-Gen. LaFayette, mentioned in journal 115
McLean Brig.-Gen. Nathaniel Collins, brigade of 173
McLemore's Cove 78, 80, 82, 90
McLeod, John, mentioned in letter 159
McLeod, William, mentioned in letter 159
McMillen, Col. William L. 64, 65
McNair, Brig.-Gen. Evander, brigade of 67
McNeil, Pvt. John W. 17, 18, 22, 23, 29, 39, 48, 55, 58, 61, 67, 71, 113, 115; biography of 283
McPherson, Pvt. James 284
McPherson, Maj.-Gen. James Birdseye 57, 63, 65, 67, 69, 160, 162, 163, 165, 167, 170, 171, 172, 173, 174, 179; corps of 60, 62; promotion of 161
McRae, Lt.-Col. George R. 79
Meade, Maj.-Gen. George Gordon 160
Meadow Bluff, Virginia 19
Mealy, Cpl. J. L. 310
Meehan, Pvt. Thomas 313
Meharg, Pvt. John P. 305
Memphis, Tennessee 16, 44, 45, 53, 54, 55, 157, 158; mentioned in journal 29
Meng, Surg. James S. 272, 322
Mercer, Brig.-Gen. Hugh Wheedon 23; mentioned in journal 26, 49, 52; biography of 269

Meridian, Mississippi 61, 67, 157, 238, 239
Metairie Cemetery 14
Metairie Race Course 14
Metcalf, Lt.-Col. Edwin 35, 37
Mexican War 29, 163
Mexico 44
Meyer, Pvt. John 305
Middle Ground Battery 28
Middleton, Lt. John C. 272
Middleton, Lt. Jonathan C. 309, 315
Middleton, Pvt. W. Clark 322
Milam's Bridge 170
Military Division of the Mississippi (U.S.) 157, 160, 161; creation of 112
Military Division of the West (C.S.) 228
Mill Creek 165
Mill Creek Gap 162, 169
Millen, Georgia, mentioned in journal 113
Miller, Pvt. Collins 305
Miller, Pvt. H. 332
Miller, Pvt. John 284, 322
Miller, Pvt. Perkins Poole 313
Miller, Pvt. William H. 332
Milliken's Bend, Louisiana 15, 57, 59
Mills, Pvt. George W. 295
Mills, Pvt. Irvin 305
Mills, Pvt. J. W. 305
Mills, Sgt. Sebron W. 309
Minnesota, state of 43
Minty, Col. Robert H. G., brigade of 81
Missionary Ridge 96, 120, 121, 122, 123, 124, 126, 127, 128, 130, 132, 133, 135, 137, 161; battle of, mentioned in letter 178
Mississippi Central Railroad 53, 70
Mississippi River 10, 16, 43, 44, 46, 53, 54, 57, 59, 60, 157; mentioned in journal 27, 29
Mississippi Sound 44
Mississippi Springs, Mississippi 63, 64
Mississippi, state of 7, 8, 11, 43, 47, 54, 58, 61, 69, 70, 71, 73, 76, 78, 112, 113, 157, 161, 165, 231, 236; brigade from 132; mentioned in letter 159, 178
Mississippi State Troops–First Battalion 63, 64
Mississippi Valley 116
Missouri Brigade 60, 236
Missouri, state of 17, 43
Mitchell Street, Atlanta 227
Mobile, Alabama 61, 157, 186, 230, 231, 232, 233, 236, 237, 238
Mobile and Ohio Railroad 61
Mobile Bay 238
Mobile City Hospital 238
Mobile River 238
Moccasin Point 116, 122, 124
Mock, Pvt. Alonzo M. 305
Mock, Lt. William T. 299
Mondey, Pvt. C. 313

Monongahela River 18
Monroe, Louisiana 15, 23; mentioned in letter 179
Montgomery, Alabama 12, 16, 61, 232; convention delegates 13
Montgomery, Pvt. J. D. 305
Montgomery and West Point Railroad 228
Montrose, Pvt. E. A. 295
Moon, Sgt. Samuel A. 309
Mooney, Pvt. P. 313
Moore, Brig.-Gen. John Creed 125, 126; brigade of 124, 128
Moore, Cpl. Joseph H. 300
Moore, Pvt. Joseph Lawson 274, 322
Moore, Governor Thomas Overton 6, 9, 10, 11, 13, 14
Moreland, Color-Sgt. William Willis 275, 313
C.S.S. *Morgan* 233, 237, 238
Morgan, Sgt. Ephraim 299
Morgan, Brig.-Gen. George Washington 54, 57
Morgan, Pvt. Reuben C. 332
Morris, Pvt. G. E. 305
Morris, Pvt. Josiah 333
Morris, Pvt. Thomas J. 333
Morris, Sgt. William Everett 288
Morris Island, mentioned in journal 72
Morrison, Lt.-Col. David 34
Morrow's Mill 185
Morton, Mississippi 73; mentioned in letter 178
Mosby, Pvt. W. B. 322
Moultry, Cpl. Y. 310
Mounger, Pvt. John A. 305
Mount Zion Church 175
Mouton, Alexander, delegate 7, 8, 11, 13
Mower, Brig.-Gen. Joseph Anthony, brigade of 64, 65
Mulkey, Pvt. John W. 322
Mullins, Pvt. George W. 333
Mullins, Pvt. T. S. 333
Munford, Pvt. John H. 284
Murfreesboro, Tennessee 116
Murphy, Col. Robert C. 54
Murrays, Pvt. George C. 305

Nance, Lt. Thomas R. 277
Nash, Cpl. Julius E. 290
Nash, Pvt. W. A. 333
C.S.S. *Nashville* 233, 237, 238; mentioned in journal 58
Nashville and Chattanooga Railroad 118
Nashville and Decatur Railroad 229
Nashville, Tennessee 116, 160, 162, 228, 230, 231; mentioned in journal 25, 48
Natchez, Mississippi 16, 41, 45, 158, 240; mentioned in letter 159
Natchez Rifles 16
Neal, Lt. Andrew J. 227
Neal, Pvt. Robert 284
Negley, Maj.-Gen. James Scott 78, 79, 80, 91; division of 89

Nelson, Pvt. M. R. 333
Nelson, Pvt. William 305
Nelson's Georgia Cavalry Company 67
New Carthage, Louisiana 59, 60
New Hope Church 170, 171, 172, 173, 174; battle of 175
New Jersey, state of 8
New Liners 6, 7
New Madrid, mentioned in journal 26
New Orleans Bee 9
New Orleans Country Club 14
New Orleans Daily-Crescent 7, 8
New Orleans Daily-Delta 8
New Orleans Daily-Picayune 6, 8, 10, 11, 13
New Orleans, Jackson, and Great Northern Railroad 14, 64, 67
New Orleans, Louisiana 5, 10, 11, 14, 15, 35, 43, 44, 45, 46, 48, 133; convention at 12, 13; city hall 13; mentioned in journal 27, 28; injury of grant at 116
New Orleans Price-Current 14
New River, Virginia 18
New York, state of 17, 125, 227
Newburn, Virginia, mentioned in journal 23
Newton, Lt. Algera Emmett 315
Newton, Maj.-Gen., division of 165
Nickels, Pvt. Henry A. 323
Ninety-Fifth Ohio Infantry 64, 65, 67
Ninety-Seventh Pennsylvania Infantry 35, 37
Ninety-Sixth Illinois Infantry 125, 126
Ninety-Third Ohio Infantry 121
Ninth Corps (U.S.) 70, 117, 118
Ninth Indiana Infantry 136
Ninth Ohio Infantry 85, 93
Ninth South Carolina Battalion 33, 34, 37
Nixon, James Oscar 8
Noland, Cpl. James P. 278
Norfolk, Virginia 47; mentioned in journal 27
Norris, Pvt. Samuel J. 305
Norris, Lt. Samuel R. 299
North Carolina, state of 7; mentioned in journal 26; mentioned in letter 177, 178
Norton, Color-Sgt. Ambrose D. 173
Nunnery, Pvt. Jacob 284
Nunnery, Pvt. John M. 284
Nunnery, Cpl. Nathaniel 278

O'Brien, Pvt. John 323
Odom, Pvt. Robert J. W. 295
O'Donell, Pvt. Patrick 295
Ogechee River, mentioned in journal 55, 56, 58
Oglethorpe Hospital, mentioned in journal 39, 40
Ohio, state of 18; troops from 173
Ohio River 44, 231
Old Capitol Prison 240
Old Liners 6, 7
One Hundred Eleventh Pennsylvania Infantry 191
One Hundred Forty Ninth New York Infantry 125
One Hundred Thirty Seventh New York Infantry 125
One Hundred Twenty Fifth Ohio Infantry 230
One Hundredth Pennsylvania Infantry 32, 33, 34
O'Neal, Col. Edward A., brigade of 182
Oostanaula River 158, 162, 163, 165, 166, 167, 168, 169
Opdycke, Col. Emerson 230
Orange County, Georgia, mentioned in letter 159
Orchard Knob 120, 121, 123, 129, 130, 133
Ord, Maj.-Gen. Edward Otho Cresap 71; corps of 70
O'Riley, Pvt. Charles 284
O'Riley, Cpl. John 278
Orleans Parish, Louisiana 9, 12
Orphan Brigade 91
Orr, Pvt. Peter 97, 305
Osbanks, Cpl. Charles 310
Osburn, Pvt. Noble R. 333
Osterhaus, Brig.-Gen. Peter Joseph, division of 123, 135, 136
Osterhaut, Pvt. A. 313
O'Sullivan, Pvt. Pat 284
Ouachita Blues 16; mentioned in journal 51, 52
Ouachita Parish, Louisiana 9, 23
Ouachita Rebels 23
Overton Hills 231
Owen, Pvt. Jennings J. 284
Owen, Pvt. John J. 313
Owen's Mill 170

Packer, Pvt. Alexander N. 295
Paint Rock, steamer 119
Palmer, Maj.-Gen. John McCauley 86, 90, 183; corps of 167, 171
Palmetto, Georgia 228
Parke, Maj.-Gen. John Grubb, corps of 70
Parker, Pvt. Henry A. 333
Parker, Pvt. K. 306
Parkersburg, Virginia 18
Parris Island 28
Parsin, W. S.: election to captain 17; declined appointment 19
Patton, Col. Isaac W. 238
Peachtree Creek, battle of 179
Peachtree Road 180, 185
Pearce, Benjamin Wiley 7
Pearl River 70, 71
Pee Dee Battalion 32
Peebles, Pvt. Shelton 333
Pegram, Brig.-Gen. John 82, 83, 84; division of 85
Pelican Regiment 238, 239
Pemberton, Lt.-Gen. John Clifford 48, 53, 54, 57, 60, 61, 62, 67, 69, 70, 77; major-general 28, 29, 30; biography of 253
Pennsylvania, state of 18, 28, 69, 230

Penny, Sgt. J. K. 41, 316
Pensacola, Florida 15, 232
Perkins, John J., delegate 12
Perkins, John, Jr., delegate 12
Perryman, Sgt. William J. 316
Peterson, Cpl. George 317
Peterson, Pvt. Peter A. 284
Peterstown, Virginia, mentioned in journal 23
Pettus, Brig.-Gen. Edmund Winston, brigade of 126
Pettus, Governor John Jones 11
Peyton, John B., residence of 63
Pheir, Sgt. William 316
Phelps, Col. Edward H., brigade of 133
Phillips, Color-Cpl. Francis M. 275
Phillips, Pvt. Richard J. 323
Phillips, Pvt. William E. 285
Pickens, Pvt. A. H. 323
Pickett, Maj.-Gen. George Edward: division of 117; charge of 230
Pickett's Mill 172, 173
Pickins, Pvt. David A. 323
Pigeon Mountain 78, 80
Pinch Gut Creek, Virginia, mentioned in journal 20
Pinch Gut Mountain, Virginia, mentioned in journal 20
Pine Mountain 176
Pinet Creek, Virginia 22
Pinner, Pvt. Adam N. 333
Pistole, Pvt. Edward 333
Pitzman, Capt. Julius 64
Planter, steamer 28, 29
Plantz, Pvt. Charles L. F. 323
Plattsmier, Capt. Ambrose A. 237
Poe Field 89, 93
Poindexter, Pvt. W. S. 295
Polk, Lt.-Gen. Leonidas 79, 80, 83, 90, 91, 92, 114, 115, 157, 163, 167, 170, 172; wing of 96; army of 165; corps of 168, 169; death of 176; biography of 263
Polk, Brig.-Gen. Lucius, brigade of 127, 161
Polk's Spur 132
Pollard, Alabama 232
Pollard, Edward Alfred 44
Poor House 182
Port Gibson, Mississippi 60
Port Hudson, Louisiana 62; mentioned in journal, 72
Port Royal 28, 29
Porter, Adm. David Dixon: commander 44, 45, 46, 47; admiral 53, 57, 58, 59, 60, 71
Porter, Pvt. Rodney 306
Post of Arkansas 56
Potomac River, mentioned in journal 51, 52
Powell, Dr. Balitha: mentioned in journal 25; biography of 272
Powell, Capt. William Jack 15; election to captain 20; mentioned in journal 51, 52; biography of 276
Powers, Pvt. James 285
Powers, Pvt. Patrick Michael 323

Pratt, Pvt. Leander, J. 295
Preston, Brig.-Gen. William 115; division of 88
Prewitt, Pvt. J. J. 159; signs letter 160
Puckett, Pvt. A. P. 295
Puckett, Pvt. P. B. 313
Pugh, Pvt. Columbus 285
Pugh, Bvt. Brig.-Gen. Isaac C., brigade of 71
Pugh, Pvt. Joseph S. 285
Pugh, Sgt. William T. S. 275, 277
Pulaski House, mentioned in journal 52
Pulliam, Pvt. C. M. 295
Pumpkinvine Creek 170, 172, 174
Putcher, Pvt. Adam 313

Quarles, Brig.-Gen. William Andrew 230; brigade of 182
U.S.S. *Queen of the West* 47

Raccoon Mountain 118
Ragan, Pvt. John W. 306
Ragan, Pvt. Thomas C. 306
Raleigh Court House, Virginia, mentioned in journal 20, 23
Ramey, Pvt. H. M. 295
Rampey, Sgt. Thomas F. 328
Randolph, Pvt. Benjamin A. 306
Rankin's Ferry 116
Rapides Parish, Louisiana 6, 10
Rasberry, Pvt. Richard J. 306
Rawlins, Asst. Adj.-Gen. John Aaron 71, 160
Ray, Sgt. John B. 289
Ray, Pvt. L. C. 295
Rayford, Pvt. Harrison C. 295
Raymond, Mississippi 62, 63
Raymond-Jackson Road 67, 70
Rearden, Pvt. M. 97
Reardon, Pvt. M. 313
Reconstruction Era 28
Red Gauntlet, former blockade runner 238
Red River 57
Redoubt Fisk 169
Redoubt Winans 169
Reed, Pvt. Ira 306
Reed's Bridge 81; road, 82, 83, 84, 91, 93
Rehwinkel, Pvt. R. 323
Reid, Capt. Samuel J. 32
Relyea, Capt. Charles J. 28
Renfroe Place 185
Republican Party 5, 7, 9
Resaca, Georgia 158, 162, 163, 165, 166, 167, 169, 229
Reynolds, Brig.-Gen. Alexander Welch, brigade of 133, 182
Reynolds, Brig.-Gen. Daniel Harris, brigade of 182, 185, 186
Reynolds, Pvt. J. W. 323
Reynolds, Maj.-Gen. Joseph Jones 87, 89; brigadier general 18; division of 86, 94, 96
Rhodes, Pvt A F 324
Rials, Pvt. Samuel L. 333
Rice, Pvt. E. P. 333
Rice, Cpl. Reuben H. 311

Richmond Daily-Examiner 44
Richmond, Louisiana 15; mentioned in journal 25
Richmond Press 119
Richmond, Virginia 15, 16, 28, 62, 78, 97, 114, 115, 117, 137, 138, 160, 161, 228, 229, 231; democratic convention 8, letter dated 17; mentioned in journal 23, 24, 27, 28, 29, 39, 40, 41, 48, 49, 50
Rife, Pvt. J. W. 324
Riggs, Pvt. G. A. A. 324
the Rigolets 10
Riley, Pvt. John Hampton 306
Riley, Pvt. Sion 333
Ringgold Gap 137, 138
Ringgold, Georgia 90, 137
Rio Grande 43
Roach, Pvt. Anthony 306
Roach, Lt. Eugene 315
Roanoke Island, mentioned in journal 25
Robb, Pvt. B. F. 313
Roberts, Pvt. Luke 295
Roberts, Pvt. Robert 306
Robertson, Brig.-Gen. Jerome Bonaparte 87, 88
Robinson, Lt. Dick M. 277
Robinson, Pvt. J. L. B. 296
Robinson, Col. James S., brigade of 171
Robinson, Pvt. John L. 295
Robinson, Pvt. S. W. 296
Robinson, Pvt. Wiley 313
Robinson, Pvt. William 285
Rockwell, Capt. Alfred P. 31, 32
Rocky Face Ridge 158, 162, 165, 169
Rodney Road 60
Rollins, Sgt. M. B. 309
Rome, Georgia 138, 162, 163, 228
Romney Point, mentioned in journal 24
Rosecrans, Maj.-Gen. William Starke 76, 77, 78, 80, 81, 82, 86, 87, 88, 89, 90, 91, 93, 94, 95, 96, 97, 112, 117, 136; brigadier-general 18, 21, 22, 29; mentioned in letter 178
Rosedew Island, mentioned in journal 55
Rosson, Pvt. James M. 285
Rossville 96, 97, 126, 162
Rossville Gap 126, 127, 129, 135, 136
Rossville Road 135
Roswell, Georgia 114
Roswell Manufacturing Company 114
Rough and Ready, Georgia 185, 189, 192, 227
Rounsavall, Pvt. Isaac E. 333
Ruger, Brig.-Gen. Thomas, brigade of 171
Rule, Pvt. Nathaniel 285
Rushbrook, Pvt. Samuel B. 275, 313
Russell, Col. Daniel, mentioned in journal 19, 20
Ryan, Pvt. Edward D. 296

Saint Cloud Hotel 116
Saint James Parish, Louisiana 9

Saint John the Baptist Parish, Louisiana 9
Saint Louis, Missouri 44
Saint Tammany Parish, Louisiana 9
Sanborn, Capt. Lucien B 67
Sand Mountain 77
Sanford, Lt. William D. Sr. 328
Saul, Pvt. Charles 324
Savage, Pvt. Moses 307
Savannah, Georgia 23, 28, 41, 61, 67, 71, 113; mentioned in journal 24, 26, 27, 29, 39, 40, 48, 49, 52, 55, 58, 73; brigade 61; mentioned in letter 177, 178
Savannah-Republican 41, 69, 113
Savannah River 28; mentioned in journal, 25
Sawyer, Pvt. C. M. 324
Saxon, Pvt. B. F. 313
Scannton, Cpl. 34
Scarborough, Pvt. W. J. 313
Schenk, Brig.-Gen. Robert Cumming 22
Scheuber, Pvt. Charles 324
Scheuber, Pvt. William H. 324
Schofield, Maj.-Gen. John McAllister 160, 162, 165, 167, 172, 174, 175, 185, 189, 192, 229, 230
Scothorn, Pvt. Henry L. 324
Scott, Pvt. Charles B. 285
Scott, Pvt. John W. 307
Scott, Pvt. R. D. 314
Scott, Sgt. Robert T. 277
Scott, Pvt. Thomas J. 324
Scott, Brig.-Gen. Thomas Moore 230
Scott, Gen. Winfield 43, 44
Scott, Chaplain Winfrey Bond 275
Scribner, Col. Benjamin Franklin, brigade of 85
Seaborn, Pvt. O. 314
Seaman, Pvt. Henry 285
Sears, Brig.-Gen. Claudius Wistar, brigade of 236
Secessionville Causeway 35
Secessionville, South Carolina 29, 30, 31, 32, 41, 48; mentioned in journal 40, 49, 51
Second Alabama Reserves 237
Second Iowa Battery 64
Second Kentucky Infantry (U.S.) 21
Second Minnesota Infantry 84, 93
Seddon, Sec. of War James Alexander 60, 61, 70, 115
Selma, Alabama 61, 157, 232, 238
Seltzer, Pvt. Charles B. 324
Semler, Pvt. Augustus T. 285
Sessions, Pvt. Rufus D. 333
Seventeenth Corps (U.S.) 186
Seventeenth Iowa Infantry 63, 67
Seventh Connecticut Infantry 32, 33
Seventh Florida Infantry 88
Seventh Michigan Battery 60
Seventh-Third Illinois Infantry 135
Seventy-Fourth Indiana Infantry 82, 84

Seventy-Ninth New York Infantry 32, 33, 34, 35, 38
Seventy-Second Indiana Infantry 90
Seward, Sec. of State William Henry Seward 44; senator 9
Shaaff, Maj. Arthur 79
Shackleford, Pvt. Andrew J. 307
Shady Springs, Virginia, mentioned in journal 20
Shafer, Pvt. Joseph T. 285
Shaffer, Pvt. J. T., mentioned in journal 73
Shallow Ford Road 133
Sharp's Spur 132, 133
Shay, Pvt. Dennis W. 286
Shell Road 48, 51
Shepherd, Pvt. William Albert 324
Sheppard, Pvt. Andrew C. 296
Sheppard, Pvt. B. F 296
Sheppard, Pvt. Richard M. 296
Sheridan, Maj.-Gen. Phillip Henry 130; division of 88, 93, 94, 95, 120, 122, 128, 129, 134, 135, 136, 137
Sherman, Col. Francis Trowbridge 135
Sherman, Maj.-Gen. William Tecumseh 54, 55, 56, 57, 58, 63, 64, 65, 67, 69, 70, 71, 73, 113, 116, 119, 120, 122, 123, 124, 126, 127, 128, 138, 157, 158, 160, 161, 162, 163, 165, 166, 167, 168, 169, 170, 171, 172, 173, 174, 175, 176, 179, 180, 182, 183, 185, 191, 192, 227, 228, 229, 231, 239; Louisiana seminary superintendent 5, 10; corps of 60, 62; quote of 156
Sherring, Pvt. Edward 296
Sherrouse, Pvt. Charles M. 307
Shiloh, Tennessee 53; mentioned in journal 26
Ship Island, Mississippi 44
Ship's Gap 163
Shively, Pvt. William 97, 296
Shoal Creek Church 185
Shores, Cpl. William H. 329
Shoup, Brig.-Gen. Francis Asbury 180, 182, 183
Shreveport-Southwestern 12
Sidway, Pvt. G. D. 273, 325
Sikes, Pvt. Joseph L. 296
Simmons, Cpl. John H. 329
Simms, Pvt. Benjamin 286
Simonson, Capt. Peter 176
Simonton, Lt.-Col. Charles Henry 31
Simpson, Mary, mentioned in letter 158
Sisters of Charity 238
Sixteenth Corps (U.S.) 162, 163, 185, 186
Sixteenth South Carolina Infantry 61
Sixth Georgia Cavalry 82, 83
Sixth Indiana Infantry 119
Sixth Kentucky Infantry 121
Sixth Ohio Infantry 132
Sixth Wisconsin Battery 65, 67
Sixtieth New York Infantry 125, 191

Sixtieth North Carolina Infantry 135
Skidway Island 23; mentioned in journal 24, 25, 26, 27
Skidway River, mentioned in journal 25
Slaughter, Cpl. Hudson H. 300
Slidell, John, senator 6, 7, 10, 11, 12
Slocomb, Capt. Cuthbert H. 133, 134, 137; captured guns of 135
Slocum, Maj.-Gen. Henry Warner 180, 192; corps of 112
Small, Jacob 28
Small, Robert 28
Smith, Lt.-Col. Alexander D. 32
Smith, Pvt. Alfred W. 325
Smith, Brig.-Gen. Andrew Jackson 54
Smith, Ensign Austin Williams 239, 275, 325
Smith, Pvt. Frank 276, 325
Smith, Capt. George 85
Smith, Brig.-Gen. Giles, brigade of 123, 167
Smith, Cpl. J. Davidson 317
Smith, Pvt. J. L. 314
Smith, Pvt. James 296
Smith, Brig.-Gen. James Argyle, brigade of 127
Smith, Brig.-Gen. John Eugene 123, 127; brigade of 65
Smith, Maj.-Gen. Martin Luther 54, 180; brigadier-general 46
Smith, Brig.-Gen. Morgan Lewis 54, 123, 127; division of 180, 182
Smith, Pvt. R. T. 325
Smith, Pvt. Samuel 325
Smith, Col. Thomas 89
Smith, Pvt. Thomas 334
Smith, Cpl. W. J. 317
Smith, Pvt. William A. 296
Smith, Brig.-Gen. William Duncan 30; biography of 269
Smith, Brig.-Gen. William Farrar "Baldy," 116, 117, 118, 119, 122, 130
Smith, Pvt. William J. 307
Smith, Pvt. William R. 307
Smith, Brig.-Gen. William Sooy 157, 158
Smith, Pvt. Zachariah H. 286
Snake Creek Gap 158, 162, 163, 165, 166, 167
Snodgrass, George Washington, home of 95
Snodgrass Field 96
Snodgrass Hill 95, 96, 97
Snyder's Bluff, Mississippi 53, 54
Sorrel, Lt.-Col. Moxley 90
South Carolina, state of 6, 7, 23, 29, 228; secession of 10
Southern Constitutional Democratic Convention 8
Southern Railroad 63, 67, 69; mentioned in letter 178
Southern Republic, steamer 238
Southern Rights Association 10
Southwest Pass 44
Spangler, Pvt. Adam H. 325
Spanish Fort, Alabama 231, 232, 233, 235, 236, 237, 238

Sparrow, Edward, delegate 12
Spoor, Capt. Nelson T. 64
Spring Hill, Alabama 231
Spring Hill, Tennessee 230
Spurlock, Pvt. Allen 307
Spurlock, Pvt. W. J. 325
Stanley, Maj.-Gen. David Sloane 180, 230; division of 166
Stanton, Sec. of War Edwin 57, 112, 160, 192
Stead, Pvt. James J. 325
Steedman, Brig.-Gen. James Blair, division of 96
Steele, Maj.-Gen. Frederick Steele 54, 65, 232, 236, 237; division of 69; corps of 70
Steele's Bayou 58
Stephenson, Cpl. George W. 278
Stevens, Brig.-Gen. Clement Hoffman, brigade of 180; colonel 31, 32, 61, 92
Stevens, Brig.-Gen. Isaac Ingalls 31, 32, 33, 34, 37, 39
Stevens Gap 77
Stevenson, Alabama 116, 117
Stevenson, Maj.-Gen. Carter Littlepage 118, 123, 124, 125, 126, 127, 167, 170; division of 117, 165, 166, 168, 169, 171, 185, 186
Stevenson, Brig.-Gen. John Dunlap, brigade of 65
Stewart, Lt.-Gen. Alexander Peter 176, 180, 182, 183, 189, 228, 230; major general 87, 88, 89, 168; division of 86, 91, 92, 93, 115, 122, 127, 128, 133, 135, 136, 137, 161, 165, 166, 167, 169, 170, 171, 175; artillery of 129; corps of 185, 191, 192; biography of 265
Stewart, Cpl. Charles A. 317
Stewart, Cpl. James T. 329
Stewart, Pvt. Joseph M. 286
Stewart, Pvt. W. W. 273, 314
Sthreshley, Adjt. William H. 35; mentioned in journal 26; biography of 271, 316
Stinson, Pvt. R. James 296
Stockman, Pvt. John Roane 325
Stockton Road 236
Stoker, Sgt. William H. P. 299
Stokes, Cpl. C. Lester 300
Stokes, Sgt. Isaiah C. 289
Stokes, Pvt. James Thomas 296
Stone, Col. William M. 60
Stone Hill, Virginia, mentioned in journal 40
Stono River 29, 30
Stoughton, Col. William L., brigade of 136
Stovall, Brig.-Gen. Marcellus Augustus, brigade of 91, 128, 136, 161, 168, 169, 170, 171, 186
Stowers, Capt. Louis Edward 308
Strachan, Pvt. William 325
Strahan Battery 32
Strahl, Brig.-Gen. Otho French 230; brigade of 128, 133, 136, 185, 186
Strickland, Pvt. Drary H. 325
Stroud, Pvt. F. 314

Stroud, Pvt. J. 314
Stuart, Maj.-Gen. J.E.B., mentioned in journal 40
Sullivan, Pvt. Michael 297
Sullivan, Pvt. Timothy 334
Suman, Col. Isaac C. B. 136
Summertown Road 125, 126
Sumter County, Alabama 179
Sunderland, Pvt. James O. 297
Swett's Battery 127
Swofford, Sgt. William R. 328
Swords, Editor James M. 43
Sydner, Pvt. John George 286

Talbot, Augustus G. 7
Taliaferro, Gen., mentioned in journal 58, 59
Tallahatchie River 53, 57
Tangipahoa Parish, Louisiana 14
Tangipahoa Station 14
Tarleton, John 7
Tarleton, Susan 230
Taylor, Pvt. Fred C. 325
Taylor, Pvt. John C. 307
Taylor, Lt.-Gen. Richard 228, 231, 232, 236, 239; delegate 7, 9; quote of 227; biography of 254
Taylor, Pvt. Richard H. 325
Taylor, Col. Thomas H. 232
Tecona Plantation 16
Tennessee River 77, 118, 119, 120, 122, 123, 162, 228, 229, 231
Tennessee, state of 43, 54, 86, 87, 88, 116, 228, 229, 232; mentioned in journal 25, 49; mentioned in letter 178; east 76, 77, 78, 114, 117, 118, 119, 122, 123, 137; west 157; southeastern 77; brigade from 128, 133; troops from 167, 168, 230
Tensas River 232, 237
Tenth Confederate Cavalry 82, 83
Tenth Indiana Infantry 82
Tenth Kentucky Infantry (U.S.) 82, 83, 84
Tenth Missouri Infantry (U.S.) 63, 65
Texas Brigade 87
Texas, state of 7, 43, 44, 62, 88; brigade from 127, 187, 235
Thedford's Ford 80, 81
Third Kentucky Mounted Infantry (C.S.) 63, 64, 67
Third New Hampshire Infantry 35, 37
Third Rhode Island Heavy Artillery 35, 37
Third Texas Cavalry, mentioned in letter 178
Thirteenth Corps (U.S.) 70
Thirteenth Illinois Infantry 136
Thirtieth Georgia Infantry 61, 63, 78, 81, 85; mentioned in newspaper, 70
Thirtieth Mississippi Infantry 81
Thirty-Eighth Alabama Infantry 86, 136
Thirty-Fifth Illinois Infantry 87, 130
Thirty-Fifth Ohio Infantry 84

Thirty-First Ohio Infantry 85
Thirty-Fourth Mississippi Infantry 81
Thirty-Ninth Indiana Mounted Infantry 158
Thirty-Second Georgia Infantry 30
Thirty-Second Indiana Infantry 132
Thirty-Seventh Georgia Infantry 89
Thirty-Seventh Mississippi Infantry 163
Thirty-Seventh Tennessee Infantry 89
Thirty-Sixth Alabama Infantry 86, 136
Thomas, Sgt. Benjamin F. 289
Thomas, Brig.-Gen. Bryan Morel 237
Thomas, Maj.-Gen. Henry 77, 78, 82, 84, 90, 91, 92, 93, 94, 95, 96, 97, 112, 116, 119, 120, 121, 122, 123, 124, 126, 128, 129, 130, 132, 136, 137, 157, 158, 162, 165, 166, 170, 171, 173, 174, 179, 180, 185, 189, 191, 192, 229, 230, 231
Thomas, Pvt. J. C. C. 297
Thomas, Cpl. Oreon E. 317
Thomas, Pvt. William C. 297
Thomason, Pvt. Hamilton 307
Thompkin, Pvt. L. T. 297
Thompkins, Pvt. B. F. 297
Thompson, Col. Albert P. 65, 67
Thompson, Pvt. Alfred G. 272, 297
Thompson, Pvt. George W. 297
Thompson, Pvt. J. N. 297
Thompson, Pvt. John M. 297
Thunderbolt River, mentioned in journal 58
Thurman Home 133
Tilton, Georgia 163
Tilton-Resaca Road 166
Tombigbee River 238
Tower Battery 31, 32, 33, 34, 35, 37, 39
Town Creek 65
Tracy, Brig.-Gen. Elisha Leffingwell 14
Trenton, Georgia 119
Trigg, Col. Robert C., brigade of 88
Tucker, Sgt. Jesse B. 299
Tucker, Col. William F. 128, 132, 133
Tullahoma 60, 67; mentioned in journal 61
Tunnel Hill 127, 229
Tupelo, Mississippi 231
Turchin, Brig.-Gen. John B., brigade of 118, 132
Turner, Pvt. Edward Bowman 314
Turner, Pvt. Franklin 297
Turner, Pvt. L. A. 298
Turner, Cpl. William D. 317
C.S.S. *Tuscaloosa* 238
Tuttle, Brig.-Gen. James Madison, division of 64, 65, 69
Twelfth Corps (U.S.) 123, 185

Twelfth Mississippi Cavalry 238
Twentieth Corps (U.S.) 77, 183, 192, 229
Twentieth Street, Richmond 16
Twentieth Tennessee Infantry 89, 96
Twenty-Eighth Alabama Infantry 121
Twenty-Eighth Massachusetts Infantry 32, 33
Twenty-Fifth Georgia Infantry 61, 79, 85; mentioned in newspaper 70
Twenty-Fifth Illinois Infantry 87
Twenty-Fifth Louisiana Infantry 231
Twenty-First Corps (U.S.) 77
Twenty-First Ohio Infantry 96, 97
Twenty-Fourth Alabama Infantry 121
Twenty-Fourth Mississippi Infantry 81
Twenty-Fourth South Carolina Infantry 30, 31, 32, 61, 62, 65, 92
Twenty-Fourth Wisconsin Infantry 135
Twenty-Ninth Georgia Infantry 61, 79, 85; mentioned in newspaper 70
Twenty-Ninth Mississippi Infantry 81
Twenty-Second Louisiana Infantry 237, 238
Twenty-Second South Carolina Infantry 32
Twenty-Seventh Mississippi Infantry 81
Twenty-Seventh Missouri Infantry (U.S.) 135
Twenty-Third Corps (U.S.) 118, 191, 229, 230
Twenty-Third Kentucky Infantry (U.S.) 118, 119
Tyler, Brig.-Gen. Robert Charles, colonel 128; brigade of 161, 187
Tyree, Pvt. Jesse James 326

Underwood, Pvt. J. H. 326
U.S. Army Engineers Corps 29
U.S. Army Paymaster Department 29
U.S. Arsenal & Barracks 10
U.S. Colored Troops-First Division 236
U.S. Congress 160
U.S. Constitution 12
U.S. Marine Corps 28
U.S. Medal of Honor 37, 135
U.S. Mint, New Orleans 12
U.S. Regular Brigade 85
U.S. Senate 12
Upshaw, Pvt. Jonathan W. 314
Upshaw, Sgt. William Elisha 309
Utoy Post Office 185

Vallandingham, Pvt. John 286
Van Cleve, Maj.-Gen. Horatio Phillips 89; division of 86, 87, 88
Van Den Corput, Capt. Max, battery of 167

Vanderburg, Sgt. Joshua S. 299
Van Derveer, Col. Ferdinand 83, 84, 85, 132, 133; brigade of 93
Van Dorn, Maj.-Gen. Earl 54; mentioned in journal 61
Varner, Pvt. Eli F. 334
Vaughan, Brig.-Gen. Alfred Jefferson, Jr., brigade of 128, 133, 167
Vaughan, Mrs., mentioned in letter 159, 240
Vaughn, Pvt. R., mentioned in journal 39
Vaughn, Pvt. Rufus L. 286
Vaught, Lt. W. C. D. 133
Veatch, Brig.-Gen. James Clifford, division of 163, 165
Vernon, Mississippi, mentioned in newspaper 69
Vicksburg Campaign 41, 67, 76
Vicksburg Daily-Citizen 43
Vicksburg, Mississippi 28, 43, 44, 45, 46, 47, 48, 53, 54, 55, 57, 58, 59, 60, 67, 69, 70, 71, 73, 76, 77, 97, 112, 117, 138, 157, 158; mentioned in journal 72; mentioned in letter 178; military district of 180
Villanow and Ship's Gap 162
Villanow and Snake Creek Gap 165
Vines, Pvt. Jackson David 314
Vines, Pvt. John 314
Viniard Farm 87, 88
Viniard Field 88
Virgin, former blockade runner 238
C.S.S *Virginia*, mentioned in journal 27
Virginia, state of 6, 7, 15, 16, 17, 18, 60, 77, 80, 229, 240; mentioned in journal 72; mines in 117, 118
Vollman, Pvt. F., mentioned in journal 58, 61
Vollman, Pvt. Ferdinand 286
Voorhees, Lt. John V. C. 328

Waddill, Major George C.: election to captain 15; major 16, 17; mentioned in journal 19, 22, 24; resignation of 23; biography of 271, 276
Waddill, Pvt. John M. 326
Wade, Senator Benjamin Franklin 9
Wagner, Brig.-Gen. George Day 129; brigade of 135
Wagner, Lt.-Col. Thomas M. 37
Walden's Ridge 116
Walker, Capt. James H. 23, 38, 327
Walker, Secretary of War Leroy Pope 14
Walker, Pvt. Robert L. 97, 334
Walker, Sgt. S. G. 310
Walker, Maj.-Gen. William Henry Talbot 76, 80, 83, 84, 85, 91, 92, 161, 168; brigadier-general 61, 62, 63, 65, 67; brigade of 69; division of 70, 73, 115, 165, 166, 167, 172, 180; reserve corps of 79, 81, 86, 90; biography of 264

Waller, Pvt. Archibald P. 307
Waller, Pvt. George 286
Wall's Cut, mentioned in journal 25
Walters, Pvt. J. Louis 326
Walters, Pvt. Thomas 326
Walthall, Maj.-Gen. Edward Cary 176, 183, 185; brigadier general 81, 125; brigade of 124, 126, 128; division of 180, 182
Walton, Cpl. Albert W. 317
War Department (C.S.) 117
War Department (U.S.) 138, 160
Ward, Pvt. Charles R. 326
Ward, Pvt. Felix 334
Ward, Sgt. Hyram 310
Ward, Pvt. Isaac M. 307
Ward, Capt. J. Lawrence 298
Ward, Brig.-Gen. William Thomas, brigade of 167, 168
Wardlow, Pvt. G. B. 326
Warren, Pvt. James 298
Warren, Pvt. John 334
Warrenton, Mississippi 53; batteries of 59
Warsaw Island, mentioned in journal 24, 25
Warsaw, Louisiana 17
Warsaw Sound, mentioned in journal 58
Washington, George 160
Washington Artillery 13, 133
Washington, D.C. 10, 15, 18, 29, 44, 53, 112, 160, 229, 239, 240; mentioned in journal 51
Washington Street, Atlanta 227
Waters' Alabama Battery 133
Watters, Capt. Z. L. 61
Wauhatchie 125
Wauhatchie Station 118, 119
Weidle, Pvt. William 286
Weir, Pvt. Joseph T. 326
Welch, Pvt. James J. 326
Welles, Navy Sec. Gideon 44, 46, 47, 48
Wells, Sgt.-Maj. Robert W. 158, 240; biography of 272, 327
Wells, Pvt. Thomas 286
West, Pvt. John H. 286
West, Pvt. William J. 299
West Baton Rouge Parish, Louisiana 6, 9
West Point 29, 180
West Point Railroad 185
West Virginia, state of 18
Westcott, Pvt. O. F. 314
Western and Atlantic Railroad 158, 162, 163, 165, 175, 229
Western Flotilla 46
Whatley, Sgt. Elisha 300
Wheat, Hospital-Steward Moses 273, 307
Wheatley, Pvt. William 286
Wheat's Battalion, mentioned in journal 49
Wheeler, Maj.-Gen. Joseph 165, 167, 170, 172; cavalry of 80, 118, 174, 179
Wheeling, Virginia 18
Whitaker, Gen., troops of 125, 166

White, Pvt. Alexander 307
White, Col., mentioned in newspaper 70
White, Pvt. John P. 327
White, Pvt. Milton 287
White, Pvt. Patrick 287
White, Pvt. Thomas J. 298
White, Sgt. Virginius F. 328
White Bluff, Georgia 48
White House 44, 160
White Sulphur Springs, Virginia 19
Whitehead, Pvt. D. O. 327
Whitehead, Pvt. J. A. 327
Whitney, Pvt. John M. 308
Wickliffe, Governor Robert Charles 5
Wilder, Col. John T. 88; brigade of 81, 87, 93
Wiley, Col. Aquila 121
Williams, Lt.-Col. A. J. 79
Williams, Brig.-Gen. Alpheus Starkey 171; division of 166, 167, 168
Williams, Pvt. Archie 298
Williams, Pvt. B. F. 298
Williams, Pvt. Bryant 287
Williams, Pvt. Ezra F. 308
Williams, Pvt. J., mentioned in journal 39
Williams, Pvt. J. B. 298
Williams, Pvt. J. N. 298
Williams, Sgt. J. T. 317
Williams, Pvt. James 287
Williams, Pvt. Matthew 308
Williams, Pvt. Maurice 287
Williams, Col. Robert 31, 35, 37
Williams, Brig.-Gen. Thomas 45, 46, 47, 57
Williams, Pvt. Thomas G. 298
Williamson, Col. James A. 135
Willich, Brig.-Gen. August von 121, 132; brigade of 86, 130
Willis, Pvt. John Y. 298
Wilmington Island, mentioned in journal 58
Wilmington, North Carolina 41; mentioned in journal 56, 73; mentioned in letter 177
Wilson, Pvt. A. J. 308
Wilson, Col. Claudius Charles 76, 83, 85; mentioned in newspaper 69; brigade of 73, 79, 84, 92, 115; biography of 270
Wilson, Pvt. Jacob R. 287
Wilson, Pvt. John C. 34
Wilson, Pvt. O. 334
Winchester, Virginia, mentioned in letter 240
Winfrey Cornfield 84
Winstead Hill 230
Winston, John Anthony, former Alabama governor 11
Winston Gap 77
Wirz, Capt. Hartmann Heinrich "Henry," 15, 239, 240; biography of 277
Wisconsin, state of 43; troops from 54, 174
Witcher, Pvt. William J. 298

Withers, D. D. 7
Witt, Sgt. William H. 277
Womack, Pvt. John P. 334
Womack, Pvt. W. H. 308
Wood, Col. Gustavus A. 129
Wood, Brig.-Gen. Thomas John 128, 129; division of 88, 94, 95, 120, 122, 124, 130, 172, 173, 180, 182
Woods, Brig.-Gen Charles R., brigade of 135, 167
Woodson, Pvt. J. M. 334
Words, Mrs. 177
World War II 135
Wright, Brig.-Gen. Horatio Gouverneur 31, 37
Wright, Brig.-Gen. Marcus J. 123
Wright, O. P., farm of 62
Wright Home 65
Wylly, Lt. Charles Spaulding 277

Yalobusha River 53
Yancey, William Lowndes 7
Yazoo City, Mississippi, mentioned in newspaper 70
Yazoo Pass 57
Yazoo River 44, 47, 53, 54, 55, 57, 58, 157
Yorktown, Virginia, mentioned in journal 27
Young, Pvt. Frank W. 287
Young, Pvt. James R. 308
Young, Pvt. L. M., mentioned in journal 50
Youngblood Family: field of 84; farm of 85
Young's Point, Mississippi 57

Zacharie, Col. Francis C. 271
Ziegler, A.C.M. William H. 273
Ziegler, Pvt. William H. 287
Zinken, Col. Leon von 183
Zurich, Switzerland 15

www.ingramcontent.com/pod-product-compliance
Lightning Source LLC
Chambersburg PA
CBHW081536300426
44116CB00015B/2647